The Blackwell Guide to

Philosophical Logic

Blackwell Philosophy Guides

Series Editor: Steven M. Cahn, City University of New York Graduate School

Written by an international assembly of distinguished philosophers, the *Blackwell Philosophy Guides* create a groundbreaking student resource – a complete critical survey of the central themes and issues of philosophy today. Focusing and advancing key arguments throughout, each essay incorporates essential background material serving to clarify the history and logic of the relevant topic. Accordingly, these volumes will be a valuable resource for a broad range of students and readers, including professional philosophers.

The Blackwell Guide to
Philosophical Logic

Edited by

Lou Goble

Blackwell
Publishing

© 2001 by Blackwell Publishers Ltd
a Blackwell Publishing company
except for editorial material and organization © 2001 by Lou Goble

350 Main Street, Malden, MA 02148-5018, USA
108 Cowley Road, Oxford OX4 1JF, UK
550 Swanston Street, Carlton, Victoria 3053, Australia
Kurfürstendamm 57, 10707 Berlin, Germany

First published 2001 by Blackwell Publishers Ltd
Reprinted 2002

Library of Congress Cataloging-in-Publication Data

The Blackwell guide to philosophical logic / edited by Lou Goble.
    p. cm. — (Blackwell philosophy guides)
   Includes bibliographical references and index.
   ISBN 0-631-20692-2 (alk. paper) — ISBN 0-631-20693-0 (pb. : alk. paper)
   1. Logic. I. Title: Guide to philosophical logic. II. Goble, Lou. III. Series.

   BC71 B565 2001
   160—dc21   00-069788

A catalogue record for this title is available from the British Library.

Set in 10 on 12.5pt Galliard
by Graphicraft Ltd., Hong Kong

For further information on
Blackwell Publishing, visit our website:
http://www.blackwellpublishing.com

Contents

Contents

List of Contributors

Patricia A. Blanchette
Associate Professor of Philosophy, University of Notre Dame

John P. Burgess
Professor of Philosophy, Princeton University

M. J. Cresswell
Professor of Philosophy, Massey University

Dirk van Dalen
Philosophy Department, Utrecht University

Dorothy Edgington
Professor of Philosophy, University of Oxford

Lou Goble
Professor of Philosophy, Willamette University

Anil Gupta
Distinguished Professor of Philosophy, University of Pittsburgh

Alan Hájek
Associate Professor of Philosophy, California Institute of Technology

Risto Hilpinen
Professor of Philosophy, University of Miami (Coral Gables)

Wilfrid Hodges
Professor of Mathematics, Queen Mary and Westfield College, University of London

John F. Horty
Professor, Philosophy Department and Institute for Advanced Computer Studies, University of Maryland

Karel Lambert
Research Professor of Logic and Philosophy of Science, University of California at Irvine and the University of Salzburg

Grzegorz Malinowski
Professor, University of Łódź

Edwin D. Mares
Senior Lecturer in Philosophy, Victoria University of Wellington

Alice ter Meulen
Professor of Linguistics and Cognitive Science, University of Groningen

J.-J. Ch. Meyer
Professor of Computer Science, Utrecht University

Robert K. Meyer
Emeritus Professor, Australian National University

Stewart Shapiro
Professor of Philosophy, The Ohio State University at Newark; Professorial Fellow, Department of Logic and Metaphysics, University of St. Andrews

Raymond Smullyan
Oscar Ewing Professor of Philosophy, Emeritus, Indiana University

Yde Venema
Assistant Professor, Institute for Logic, Language and Information, University of Amsterdam

Heinrich Wansing
Professor of Philosophy of Science and Logic, Dresden University of Technology

Dag Westerståhl
Professor of Theoretical Philosophy, Göteborg University

Preface

This *Guide* introduces the many worlds of philosophical logic. Or perhaps I should say, many of the worlds of philosophical logic, for it cannot pretend completeness. That would be impossible. Nevertheless, these 20 chapters present a central core of what constitutes philosophical logic today, and they provide a solid foundation for further study. I will say more in the Introduction about what philosophical logic is, and about the selection and arrangement of the chapters.

Each of these chapters is newly written for this volume by a distinguished scholar in its subject area. Their purpose is to provide the reader with basic knowledge of the current state of that aspect of philosophical logic, including its concepts, motivations, methods, major results, and even applications. Each chapter is independent of the others, so they can be read in any order or selected to suit different interests. I have, however, included cross-references among the chapters since their subjects often overlap. (Each chapter was also written independently of the others, and so their authors might have different views about common subjects.)

This volume should be accessible and useful to anyone interested in philosophical logic, expert and non-expert alike. It could form the basis for a general course on philosophical logic, or it could serve as a supplementary resource and reference work for the study of its specialized topics. Experienced logicians will discover sufficient substance here to occupy their attention, while the general reader who merely wants to know what a subject is about will find a definitive introduction to that field. Philosophical logic is recommended not only for philosophers and logicians. These days, it is also of great importance for research in computer science, cognitive science, artificial intelligence (AI), and theoretical linguistics; and, like all logic, it belongs hand in hand with mathematics.

Logic is a technical discipline, with its specialized language, notation, and methods. As a result, a reader would benefit from having had a first course in formal logic, or from having studied any of countless elementary texts, and to have some familiarity with the logician's language and techniques. Even so, the chapters here presume little and explain much, so that even the uninitiated reader should profit from them.

A logician's language uses a lot of special symbols. But different logicians often use different symbols for the same purposes, and sometimes different logicians use

the same symbols for different purposes. I have not tried to impose a uniform notation or style of expressing formal concepts on these chapters, for I believe it is better
for students of logic to become familiar with a variety of styles since that is what they
will meet in the literature beyond this book. The authors of these chapters do,
however, explain their symbols and notations as they introduce them, and readers
should be able to understand new patterns without difficulty and learn to move
among them effortlessly.

I have profited much from working with the authors of these chapters; I learned
a lot from every one of them – as, I'm sure, readers will too – and our collaboration
was always a pleasure for me. My heartfelt gratitude goes to them all. This is their
volume more than it is mine. Throughout the development and completion of this
project, I have also been very gratified by how encouraging, generous and helpful
everyone was with whom I discussed it. In addition to the authors of the chapters,
I would especially like to thank Nuel Belnap, Johan van Benthem, Mark Brown,
Brian Chellas, Mike Dunn, John Etchemendy, Dov Gabbay, Ernie Lepore, Penelope
Maddy, Don Nute, Alasdair Urquhart, Bas van Fraassen, and many others. Thanks
too to Steve Smith and Beth Remmes of Blackwell Publishers, to Steve for launch-
ing the project, to Beth for piloting it into port, with wise advice and wonderful
patience. Thanks also to Jenny Lawson and her First-Class crew for manning the
rigging.

Perhaps my greatest debt in this area, though, is to Alan Ross Anderson and Nuel
D. Belnap, Jr. for introducing the many worlds of philosophical logic to me a long
time ago.

Introduction

Lou Goble

What is philosophical logic? Philosophical logic is philosophy that is logic, and logic that is philosophy. It is where philosophy and logic come together and become one. Philosophical logic is not a special kind of logic, some species distinct from mathematical logic, symbolic logic, formal logic, informal logic, modern logic, ancient logic, or logic with any other familiar modifier. There is only logic. Logic is the theory of consequence relations, of valid inferences. As such, it can be investigated and presented in many ways, although the mathematical methods of modern formal or symbolic logic have proved extraordinarily fruitful.

Within logic so construed, there are still, of course, many different sorts – as witnessed by the variety of chapters of this volume. Philosophical logic comprises the sorts of logic that hold greatest interest for philosophers. Philosophical logic develops formal systems and structures to be applied to the analysis of concepts and arguments that are central to philosophical inquiry. So, for example, such traditional philosophical concepts as necessity, knowledge, obligation, time and existence, not to mention reasoning itself, are usefully investigated through modal logic, epistemic logic, deontic logic, temporal logic, free logic, probability logic, nonmonotonic logic, etc. Similarly, logical investigation has contributed immeasurably to our understanding of the structure of language, including the languages of our normal use as well as the formal languages of logic itself, and this resounds throughout philosophy. By the same token, many of the developments within philosophical logic have been motivated by broad philosophical concerns. Intuitionistic logic reflects a particular perspective on the nature of judgment and truth. Many-valued logic grew out of Łukasiewicz's effort to construct a logic that could avoid the conclusions of fatalism or determinism. Other developments within philosophical logic were driven by philosophical concern regarding logic itself. Relevant logic sprang from a critique of the classical consequence relation; so did free logic.

Thus, logic supports philosophy, and philosophy feeds logic. They join. The result is philosophical logic. The chapters that follow present the basic formal methods, models and systems that have been developed in this area. Their emphasis, however, is on the presentation of the fundamental logical structures as such, as well as their motivations, rather than their application to specific philosophical questions.

Nevertheless, that these structures do have philosophical application is a common theme running through all the chapters.

I would distinguish philosophical logic, as it is presented in this volume, from other, related enterprises that also sometimes go under the name of 'philosophical logic'. I would distinguish it from the philosophy of language, with its pursuit of the concepts of meaning and reference, naming and predication, of the structure of propositions, questions of analyticity, the nature of speech acts, etc. I would also distinguish it from the philosophy of logic, with its investigation of the epistemological and ontological positions of the propositions of logic, of a priority, of conventionality, of questions about what, if anything, is a logical constant, about the nature of logical truth and logical consequence (though see chapter 6), and even the question 'What is Logic?' itself. Inevitably, of course, the questions and concerns of all these areas – philosophical logic, philosophy of language, philosophy of logic – intertwine, and it would be a mistake to try to establish real boundaries between them.

Philosophical logic is easily seen as logic for philosophy. It is important, however, also to recognize that it has other applications in other disciplines as well. Today, much of the most flourishing research in philosophical logic is being done by computer scientists, working, for example, on aspects of knowledge representation, system verification, or AI. Several of the chapters here are written by computer scientists. The results of philosophical logic are also useful in cognitive science and theoretical linguistics. This volume ends with chapters linking logical investigation to inquiry into the structure of language, including natural language. And, we must not forget, logic is a part of mathematics, and so properly of interest to mathematicians.

The term 'logic', as Wilfrid Hodges observes at the start of chapter 1, is ambiguous. It can refer to collections of languages that possess particular structures, or to the study of the rules of sound arguments, which occur in ordinary, natural language. The latter is how many might think of logic first. In the chapters here, however, the primary focus will be on logic in the first sense; this provides the entryway to the other. Logic begins with language, and so the chapters that follow typically include the specification of the languages of their investigation (or else they will explicitly presuppose that the language is given, taking for granted that its grammar is well enough known, perhaps, for example, from earlier chapters). The results determined for such constructed languages, and their consequence relations, will then extend to natural languages insofar as our natural languages, or portions of them, share the structures of the logicians' constructed languages. Then we come to logic in the second sense, to the analysis and evaluation of propositions and arguments in the languages we use.

The expressions of a language, especially its *well-formed formulas* (wff), can stand in many relations, and these relations can be described in different ways, which reflect different ways of looking at logic and logical consequence. Some relations can be characterized syntactically, in terms of the grammatical structures of the expressions themselves. Then we often speak of 'logical syntax'. Of central importance are relations of *derivability* or *deducibility*, of when an expression can be (syntactically) drawn from others; here one would typically speak of a *proof* A formula, C, is derivable from a set of formulas, Γ, if there is a proof of C from Γ where a proof is a structure of formulas of the language that meets specific conditions. Here 'proof', and hence 'derivability', must be understood as relative to a particular deductive system or calculus that determines those conditions. Such systems might be defined axiomatically, or as systems of natural deduction rules (familiar from many logic courses), or in other ways. These distinction are somewhat artificial, though. Axiomatic systems usually have several axioms and very few rules of inference, while natural deduction systems have many rules of inference and few, or no, axioms. Typically, axiomatic systems are difficult to work with but easier to prove things about, while natural deduction systems are easy to work with, but harder to prove things about. One would like to have both, and, for many of the sorts of logic presented here, we do.

Relations between expressions in a language can also, however, be determined in terms of properties that reach beyond language, through the expressions' evaluation. Then we often speak of 'logical semantics'. To speak of the validity of an inference in terms of the relation of possible truth-values of the premises and the conclusion – An argument is valid if it is not possible for all of its premises to be true and its conclusion false – is to describe validity semantically. Similarly for the specification of the (semantical) consequence relation of a constructed language. To define relations among expressions in this way, the logician will usually describe a *model*, which is a structure in terms of which formulas are evaluated, and rules for their evaluation in a model. Then one might say that a formula, C, is a consequence of others, Γ, or that the inference from Γ to C is semantically valid, just in case every model that verifies every formula in Γ verifies C. Truth-tables are a familiar elementary form of logical semantics.

The chapters that follow develop both approaches to their logics, the proof-theoretic and the model-theoretic or semantical, though, in keeping with contemporary practice, semantics may be emphasized over proof theory. Given these two approaches, it is natural to ask about the relation between them. Suppose one has a syntactically defined derivability relation and a semantically defined relation of validity for a common language, then one relation might include the other, or they might coincide, i.e., apply to exactly the same inferences. Given a semantical specification of validity, we say that a syntactically defined logic **L** is *sound* or *consistent* or *correct* with respect to that semantics if whenever a formula C is derivable from a set of formulas Γ in **L**, C is a semantical consequence of Γ. This means that the rules of the logic never yield invalid inferences, that they do not prove too much. (Alternatively, given the prior deductive system **L**, we might say the semantic theory is *adequate* or does not undergenerate with respect to the derivable inferences of **L**.) If, conversely, whenever the inference from Γ to C is semantically valid, C can be derived from Γ in **L**, then we say that **L** is *complete* with respect to that semantics. This means that **L** has captured all that is contained in the structures of the models, that it does not prove too little (or, alternatively, that the semantic theory does not generate too much).

Often it is helpful, and desirable, to know that a certain deductive system is sound and complete with respect to a certain pattern of interpretation. Then results established for one consequence relation can be readily extended to the other. But more than that, when one can establish soundness and completeness for a logic, then one has a sense that one has got things right. The syntactical system is likely to be transparent; one can see at a glance its commitments. It codifies the properties of the inference relation. The semantics keeps it from being entirely arbitrary. The relations defined by the logic are, after all, supposed to do philosophical work. Thus, many of the chapters here discuss and demonstrate the soundness and completeness, and related properties, of their systems. There are limits, though. Not all syntactically defined systems of logic are complete with respect to any appropriate semantics. Not all semantical interpretations can be axiomatized. Even among philosophically interesting and important systems, incompleteness can arise, the most famous, and significant, being the incompleteness of formalized arithmetic, discussed in chapter 4. This too is important to recognize, for it reveals that there are limits to what formal (deductive) systems can do. There are also limits to model-theoretic semantics. What to make of those limits is a paramount question for the philosophy of logic and mathematics, and philosophy generally.

The chapters of this volume are arranged into four rough groups. Chapters 1–6 present *classical logic*, or logic from a classical perspective. 'Classical logic' here does not mean the logic of antiquity; it is not Aristotle's logic. Historically, the roots of classical logic are seen in the nineteenth century, in the work of Boole and DeMorgan, and, on another front, Peirce, among others. It reached its mature growth, however, following the groundbreaking work of Frege and of Whitehead and Russell. This, or at least its elementary part, is the sort of logic one is most likely to learn in a basic logic course. I will not try to define precisely what classical logic is, but leave that to the first two chapters. Briefly, though, classical logic is logic that makes the simplest, and hence the strongest, assumptions about language, truth and consequence. It is logic in a narrowly circumscribed language that is *two-valued*, in the sense that every sentence in that language is presumed to be either true or false, but not both, and that is furthermore *extensional*, in the sense that expressions can be replaced by others with the same denotation or truth-value in any context and the result will have the same denotation or truth-value as the original. In addition, logical consequence is usually assumed to mean formal truth preservation; an argument is valid just in case it has a valid form, and a form is valid just in case it has no instance or interpretation that would make all the premises true and the conclusion false. (These are rough characterizations; if they prompt questions, the reader should welcome the chapters that follow.)

Chapters 1 and 2 present classical logic itself, first *First-Order Classical Logic* and then *Higher-Order Classical Logic*. Set Theory, the topic of chapter 3, could be regarded as a part of mathematics more than logic. Whether that is so, whether it matters, the concepts and results of set theory are so central to contemporary logical inquiry, it seems valuable to include this chapter here. Also, set theory can, in a sense, be seen as a complement, or an alternative, to higher-order logic, and so chapter 3 is a natural successor to chapter 2.

Gödel's Incompleteness Theorems are among the premier results concerning classical logic, including both higher-order logic and set theory. They establish the ineluctable separation of the concepts of truth and provability within formal systems for languages of a certain power. These results are widely known; how to prove them less so. Chapter 4 leads the reader through a number of different ways to establish these and other closely related results in a very transparent way, so that one can easily appreciate the concepts employed in the proofs, and understand the significance of the theorems themselves.

At the heart of philosophical and logical inquiry is the concept of *Truth*. Most of the chapters here use this concept freely; in chapter 5, it is the object of study itself. Here it is paramount to cope with the famous 'Liar' paradox and related problems. This chapter presents methods for defining truth that have been developed in recent years as alternatives to Tarksi's own, now classic, account of truth that seems so commonplace to many.

Logic, we say, is the theory of the consequence relation. What this might mean, and what the results of formal systems of logic indicate about this relation, is the topic of chapter 6 on *Logical Consequence*. This chapter directs attention to the connection between logic in the first sense mentioned above and logic in the second sense, how deductive and model-theoretic consequence for a formal system **S** may (or may not) be reliable indicators of our pretheoretical relation of logical consequence. This chapter is a natural transition between the first group of chapters and the groups to follow.

The chapters of the second group, chapters 7–10, present *extensions* of classical logic, where the expressive power of the classical language is augmented by the addition of new, non-extensional operators. Although there are other ways to extend classical logic, these chapters all present types of *modal logic*. They add non-truth-functional operators to express modalities of necessity and possibility (*Modal Logic*, chapter 7), obligation, permission and prohibition (*Deontic Logic*, chapter 8), knowledge and belief (*Epistemic Logic*, chapter 9), and temporality (*Temporal Logic*, chapter 10). These are clearly motivated by philosophical purposes and applications, and they also have important applications that go beyond philosophy, e.g., in computer science.

The chapters of the third group, chapters 11–16, describe a number of different *alternatives* to classical logic. Each one challenges one or more of the classical assumptions about truth or consequence, such as the law of bivalence (that every sentence of the language is either true or false), or that validity can be defined solely in terms of relations of truth-value, and develops the logic that results from an alternative or more general point of view. (Sometimes classical logic can be seen as a special case of the alternative.) Thus, *Intuitionistic Logic*, chapter 11, works from quite a different understanding of truth and the meanings of the logical connectives and operations; here the idea of *constructions*, including *proofs*, is of central importance. *Free Logics*, chapter 12, are free of the assumption that singular (also general) terms must have existential import, while they still regard quantifiers in the ordinary ways as ranging only over what exists. *Relevant Logics* (often called relevance logics), chapter 13, require that for an inference to be valid there must be a connection of meaning, or use, i.e., some *relevance*, between premises and conclusion; among other things, these logics are particularly designed to avoid the various paradoxes of implication. *Many-Valued Logics*, chapter 14, reject the classical law of bivalence and, as the name suggests, allow that there be more than the two truth-values, true and false; there are many ways this can be done, and these logics have a wide range of applications. *Nonmonotonic Logic*, chapter 15, as its name too suggests, is concerned with consequence relations that are not monotonic, i.e., that allow for inferences where a conclusion follows validly from a set of premises, but when additional premises are added to the argument, the resulting inference is no longer valid. Such logics are particularly important for the fields of AI and cognitive science. In *Probability Logic*, chapter 16, statements are evaluated not only in terms of truth-value, but also probability, and validity is defined not just in terms of the preservation of truth, but also the transmission of probabilities. This too proves important for analyzing ordinary reasoning.

The fourth group of chapters examines more closely some of the concepts that seem particularly fundamental to logic and all of the sorts of logic presented in the earlier chapters. Chapter 17 addresses *Conditionals*, especially the indicative 'if . . . then _' as it occurs in natural languages. Many regard the conditional as *the* central connective of logical inquiry. Chapter 18 examines *Negation*, a concept that has vexed philosophers since the most ancient times, and looks at a variety of forms it can take. Chapter 19 reveals how, even at the level of first-order languages, *Quantifiers* can be very much richer than one might suppose from a typical first course in logic. These three concepts are central not only to formal logic, but also to the logic of our natural languages, and so, in these chapters, we see increasing attention to the connection between the two. The relation between *Logic*, that is, formal logic, and *Natural Language* is the subject of our final chapter, chapter 20, which focuses especially on varieties of formal semantics for natural languages; this is a thriving area of research, especially in theoretical linguistics today.

Although the divisions between these four groups are convenient, they are also somewhat artificial, and so I have not divided the volume into discrete 'Parts.' For example, modal logic, here presented as an extension of classical logic, was originally introduced by C. I. Lewis as a theory of 'strict implication' that was meant to be an alternative to classical 'material implication' with the aim of avoiding what were seen as paradoxical consequences if the classical connection were truly taken to be implication. Similarly, although relevant logic is described here as an alternative to classical logic, based on concerns similar to Lewis's, in an important sense it also contains classical logic, and so might be considered an extension of that logic. Gödel's Incompleteness Theorems are not limited to strictly classical languages. Likewise, the issues of truth and of logical consequence discussed in chapters 5 and 6 span the full range of logical perspectives.

The 20 chapters of this volume present a central core of philosophical logic today. But for the limits of a volume like this, however, there could have been many more subjects treated. There could easily have been separate chapters on Proof Theory, on Combinatory Logic, the λ-calculus, and Type Theory, or on Algebraic Logic, which are touched on in various chapters here. There could have been a chapter on Correspondence Theory, which concerns relations between modal logics and first-order logic. Relevant Logic (chapter 13) is a kind of Paraconsistent Logic, and it is a kind of Substructural Logic. Both of those could have provided separate chapters of their own. Dynamic Logic is a sort of modal logic that can be important for the analysis of action; it also has particular application within computer science. There could have been chapters on the Logic of Questions, and of Imperatives. There could have been chapters on other logical connectives and operators, like conjunction and disjunction. There could have been a chapter on alternative interpretations of quantifiers, such as substitutional or truth-functional interpretations that contrast with the domain-of-discourse interpretation primarily employed here. There are further topics on the relation between the formal languages of logic and natural language. There could have been chapters on names, and predicates, on definite descriptions, on indexicals. And so it goes. This, however, is an introductory volume, and from this introduction, the reader should have the grounding to pursue those other topics, and more.

Furthermore, the 20 chapters that are here are only introductions to their subjects. Each could easily say far, far more about those subjects, and it is only due to the limitations of a volume like this that they do not. There are more variations within these logics, more properties, more results and more methods of proof that ultimately are essential for fully understanding the subjects than could be discussed here. Since each chapter is only an introduction, each one includes a list of Suggested Further Reading to guide the reader to additional sources. The forthcoming *Blackwell Companion to Philosophical Logic*, edited by Dale Jacquette, will also offer further discussion of these topics, and many others, and so provides a natural companion to this volume. Another very valuable resource is the *Handbook of Philosophical Logic*, edited by Dov Gabbay and Franz Guenthner. The first edition (D. Reidel, Dordrecht; 1984–89) is in four volumes, with monograph-length articles on many of the same subjects as the chapters here, as well as many others. The second edition, edited by Gabbay and now in production, is projected to comprise over 14 volumes! The present *Guide* might be considered a stepping stone to that monumental work. Beyond these sources, one should look to the books, monographs and journal articles, of the authors here, and of countless others. That is where the great ongoing work of philosophical logic occurs.

A glance at the chapters here will reveal a wide array of different logical systems. What is one to make of such profusion? Logicians all profess to be interested in the same thing, logical consequence. Why then are there so many logics? Questions like these come to the fore when one considers the relations between the two senses of 'logic' mentioned above. In the first sense, there are so many logics because there are so many languages that logicians devise. But when one is interested in logic in the second sense, in logic as a theory of valid reasoning in a sense that will do philosophical work, then one might naturally wonder which, if any, of all these logics, in the first sense, is correct and which is best to rely on.

To some extent, of course, the different kinds of logics complement each other. For example, one could well combine alethic modal logic with deontic logic or epistemic logic, etc., and ultimately one would want to, in order to be able to express and analyze arguments and claims of mixed modes (e.g., that 'ought' implies 'can'). And one can develop relevant or intuitionistic modal logics, to bring those perspectives on the consequence relation to the study of the modalities, just as there are also relevant and intuitionistic set theories and higher-order logics. Yet, within each specialized category, one is still confronted with a wide variety of different systems. There are infinitely many modal logics. Many, indeed most, might have merely mathematical interest, if even that, but still there will be several that have serious claim to philosophical significance. Are they all correct, or should one select just one as the real logic of necessity? (Some years ago, a distinguished logician is reported to have remarked that, although there are many modal logics, **S4** is the true one. One rarely hears such sentiments today.) Or consider the law of the excluded middle, *p* or not-*p*. Classical logic and relevant logic, for example, are committed to this principle, while intuitionistic logic and many-valued logics deny it. Is the law true or not? How one answers would seem to force one toward one sort of logic and away from another. (With wit, though, one might answer 'neither'; with more wit one might answer 'both'. Where does one go then?) In a similar vein, classical logic and intuitionistic logic both embrace the validity of the inference scheme *ex falso quodlibet*, that a contradiction implies anything – *p* and not-*p*, so *q* – which relevant logic rejects. Again, it would seem that one cannot have it both ways, and thus that, at least with respect to this, one sort of logic gets it right, while another does not.

Considerations like these might naturally lead one to think there must, after all, be one true logic that accurately captures the consequence relation, and that the various systems are competitors to that claim. But perhaps it is not so simple. The questions themselves might be complex, and require complex and multiple answers. For example, consider modal logic again and the number of interesting systems there. One might maintain that each captures a different sense of necessity, and hence they are not really rivals at all. Similarly, with respect to the law of the excluded middle, one might say that the classical logician and the intuitionist are simply working with different concepts of disjunction and negation, and so, again, there is no real disagreement. Perhaps all the logics can be combined into a great potpourri and all are correct (like the complementation strategy above). On the other hand, while such an ecumenical spirit could seem congenial to some, I suspect it distorts the way the different logics regard their own work, and what they each have to say. There are other responses, however, that might allow one to accept multiple sorts of logic as equally correct, complements more than rivals, yet still not susceptible to being combined. For it might be that, while there are not multiple concepts of necessity, for example, or more importantly, of logical consequence itself, as they are ordinarily understood, nevertheless, these pretheoretical concepts are protean enough not to be captured by a single formal system. It might be that, in certain settings, certain criteria of necessity or validity are paramount while, in others, others are. Instead of asking which is the one true correct logic, perhaps one should ask first, True to what?, Correct for what?

These are substantial questions that deserve philosophical attention. The place to begin is with a thorough understanding of the structures of the logics themselves, and their motivations. That is the purpose of the chapters of this volume.

—————— Chapter 1 ——————

Classical Logic I:
First-Order Logic

Wilfrid Hodges

1.1. First-Order Languages

The word 'logic' in the title of this chapter is ambiguous.

In its first meaning, a *logic* is a collection of closely related artificial languages. There are certain languages called *first-order languages*, and together they form first-order logic. In the same spirit, there are several closely related languages called modal languages, and together they form modal logic. Likewise second-order logic, deontic logic and so forth.

In its second but older meaning, *logic* is the study of the rules of sound argument. First-order languages can be used as a framework for studying rules of argument; logic done this way is called *first-order logic*. The contents of many undergraduate logic courses are first-order logic in this second sense.

This chapter will be about first-order logic in the first sense: a certain collection of artificial languages. In Hodges (1983), I gave a description of first-order languages that covers the ground of this chapter in more detail. That other chapter was meant to serve as an introduction to first-order logic, and so I started from arguments in English, gradually introducing the various features of first-order logic. This may be the best way in for beginners, but I doubt if it is the best approach for people seriously interested in the philosophy of first-order logic; by going gradually, one blurs the hard lines and softens the contrasts. So, in this chapter, I take the opposite route and go straight to the first-order sentences. Later chapters have more to say about the links with plain English.

The chief pioneers in the creation of first-order languages were Boole, Frege and C. S. Peirce in the nineteenth century; but the languages became public knowledge only quite recently, with the textbook of Hilbert and Ackermann (1950), first published in 1928 but based on lectures of Hilbert in 1917–22. (So first-order logic has been around for about 70 years, but Aristotle's syllogisms for well over 2000 years. Will first-order logic survive so long?)

From their beginnings, first-order languages have been used for the study of deductive arguments, but not only for this – both Hilbert and Russell used first-order formulas as an aid to definition and conceptual analysis. Today, computer science has still more uses for first-order languages, e.g., in knowledge representation and in specifying the behavior of systems.

You might expect at this point to start learning what various sentences in first-order languages *mean*. However, first-order sentences were never intended to mean anything; rather they were designed to express *conditions which things can satisfy or fail to satisfy*. They do this in two steps.

First, each first-order language has a number of symbols called *nonlogical constants*; older writers called them *primitives*. For brevity, I shall call them simply *constants*. To use a first-order sentence ϕ, something in the world – a person, a number, a colour, whatever – is attached (or in the usual jargon, *assigned*) to each of the constants of ϕ. There are some restrictions on what kind of thing can be assigned to what constant; more on that later. The notional glue that does the attaching is called an *interpretation* or a *structure* or a *valuation*. These three words have precise technical uses, but for the moment 'interpretation' is used as the least technical term.

Second, given a first-order sentence ϕ and an interpretation I of ϕ, the *semantics* of the first-order language determine either that I makes ϕ true, or that I makes ϕ false. If I makes ϕ true, this is expressed by saying that I *satisfies* ϕ, or that I is a *model* of ϕ, or that ϕ is *true in I* or *under I*. (The most natural English usage seems to be 'true in a structure' but 'true under an interpretation.' Nothing of any importance hangs on the difference between 'under' and 'in,' and I will not be entirely consistent with them.) The *truth-value* of a sentence under an interpretation is Truth if the interpretation makes it true, and Falsehood if the interpretation makes it false.

The main difference between one first-order language and any other lies in its set of constants; this set is called the *signature* of the language. (First-order languages can also differ in other points of notation, but this shall be ignored here.) If σ is a signature of some first-order language, then an interpretation is said to be *of signature σ* if it attaches objects to exactly those constants that are in σ. So an interpretation of signature σ contains exactly the kinds of assignment that are needed to make a sentence of signature σ true or false.

Examples of first-order languages must wait until some general notions are introduced in the next section, but as a foretaste, many first-order languages have a sentence that is a single symbol

$$\perp$$

pronounced 'absurdity' or 'bottom.' Nobody knows or cares what this symbol *means*, but the semantic rules decree that it is false. So, it has no models. It is not a nonlogical constant; its truth-value does not depend on any assignment.

1.2. Some Fundamental Notions

In the definitions below, it is assumed that some fixed signature σ has been chosen; the sentences are those of the first-order language of signature σ and the interpretations are of signature σ. So each interpretation makes each sentence either true or false:

true? false?
interpretations $I \leftrightarrow$ sentences ϕ

This picture can be looked at from either end. Starting from an interpretation I, it can be used as a knife to cut the class of sentences into two groups: the sentences which it satisfies and the sentences which it does not satisfy. The sentences satisfied by I are together known as the (first-order) *theory of I*. More generally, any set of sentences is called a *theory*, and I is a *model* of a theory T if it is a model of every sentence in T. By a standard mathematical convention, every interpretation is a model of the empty theory, because the empty theory contains no sentence that is false in the interpretation.

Alternatively, the picture can be read from right to left, starting with a sentence ϕ. The sentence ϕ separates the class of interpretations into two collections: those which satisfy it and those which do not. Those which satisfy ϕ are together known as the *model class* of ϕ. In fact, a similar definition can be given for any theory T: the *model class* of T is the class of all interpretations that satisfy T. If a particular class **K** of interpretations is the model class of a theory T, then T is a *set of axioms* for **K**. This notion is important in mathematical applications of first-order logic, because many natural classes of structures – e.g., the class of groups – are the model classes of first-order axioms.

Two theories are said to be *logically equivalent*, or more briefly *equivalent*, if they have the same model class. As a special case, two sentences are said to be *equivalent* if they are true in exactly the same interpretations. A theory is said to be (semantically) *consistent* if it has at least one model; otherwise, it is (semantically) *inconsistent*. There are many semantically inconsistent theories, for example the one consisting of the single sentence '$\perp$'. The word 'semantically' is a warning of another kind of inconsistency, discussed at the end of section 1.8.

Suppose T is a theory and ψ is a sentence. Then T *entails* ψ if there is no interpretation that satisfies T but not ψ. Likewise, ψ is *valid* if every interpretation makes ψ true. One can think of validity as a special case of entailment: a sentence is valid if and only if it is entailed by the empty theory.

The symbol '$\vdash$' is pronounced 'turnstile.' A *sequent* is an expression

$$T \vdash \psi$$

where T on the left is a theory and ψ on the right is a sentence. The sentences in T are called the *premises* of the sequent and ψ is called its *conclusion*. The sequent is *valid* if T entails ψ, and *invalid* otherwise. If T is a finite set of sentences, the sequent '$T \vdash \psi$' can be written as a *finite sequent*

$$\phi_1, \ldots, \phi_n \vdash \psi$$

listing the contents of T on the left. The language under discussion (i.e. the first-order language of signature σ) is said to be *decidable* if there is an algorithm (i.e. a mechanical method which always works) for telling whether any given finite sequent is valid.

A *proof calculus* C consists of

(i) a set of rules for producing patterns of symbols called *formal proofs* or *derivations*, and
(ii) a rule which determines, given a formal proof and a sequent, whether the formal proof is a *proof* of the sequent.

Here 'proof of' is just a set of words; but one of the purposes of proof calculi is that they should give 'proofs of' all and only the valid sequents. The following definitions make this more precise:

1   A sequent

$$T \vdash \psi$$

is *derivable in* C, or in symbols

$$T \vdash_C \psi$$

if some formal proof in the calculus C is a proof of the sequent.

2   A proof calculus C is *correct* (or *sound*) if no invalid sequent is derivable in C.
3   C is *complete* if every valid sequent is derivable in C.

So a correct and complete proof calculus is one for which the derivable sequents are exactly the valid ones. One of the best features of first-order logic, from almost anybody's point of view, is that it has several excellent correct and complete proof calculi. Some are mentioned in section 1.8.

1.3. Grammar and Semantics

As in any language, the sentences of first-order languages have a grammatical structure. The details vary from language to language, but one feature that all first-order languages share is that *the grammatical structure of any given sentence is uniquely determined*. There are no grammatically ambiguous sentences like Chomsky's

They are flying planes.

This property of first-order languages is called the *unique parsing property*.

To guarantee unique parsing, first-order formulas generally have a large number of brackets. There are conventions for leaving out some of these brackets without introducing any ambiguity in the parsing. For example, if the first and last symbols of a sentence are brackets, they can be omitted. Any elementary textbook gives further details.

For historical reasons, there is a hitch in the terminology. With a first-order language, the objects that a linguist would call 'sentences' are called *formulas* (or in some older writers *well-formed formulas* or wff), and the word 'sentence' is reserved for a particular kind of formula, as follows.

Every first-order language has an infinite collection of symbols called *variables*:

$$x_0, x_1, x_2, \ldots$$

To avoid writing subscripts all the time, it is often assumed that

$$x, y, z, u, v$$

and a few similar symbols are variables too. Variables are not in the signature. From a semantic point of view, variables can occur in two ways: when a variable at some point in a formula needs to have an object assigned to it to give the formula a truth-value, this occurrence of the variable is called *free*; when no such assignment is needed, it is called *bound*. A *sentence* is a formula with no free occurrences of variables. To avoid confusing variables with constants, an assignment of objects to the variables is called a *valuation*. So, in general, a first-order formula needs an interpretation I of its constants *and* a valuation v of its variables to have a truth-value. (It will always be clear whether 'v' means a variable or a valuation.)

The definitions of the previous section all make sense if 'sentence' is read as 'first-order sentence'; they also make sense if 'sentence' is read as 'first-order formula' and 'interpretation' as 'interpretation plus valuation'. Fortunately, the two readings do not clash; for example, a sequent of first-order sentences is valid or invalid, regardless of whether the first-order sentences are regarded as sentences or as formulas. That needs a proof – one that can be left to the mathematicians. Likewise, according to the mathematicians, a first-order language is decidable in terms of sentences if and only if it is decidable in terms of formulas. (Be warned though that 'first-order theory' normally means 'set of first-order sentences' in the narrow sense. To refer to a set of first-order formulas it is safest to say 'set of first-order formulas.')

The next few sections present the semantic rules in what is commonly known as the *Tarski style* (in view of Tarski (1983) and Tarski and Vaught (1957). In this style, to find out what interpretations-plus-valuations make a complex formula ϕ true, the question is reduced to the same question for certain formulas that are simpler than ϕ. The Tarski style is not the only way to present the semantics. A suggestive alternative is the Henkin–Hintikka description in terms of games; see Hintikka (1973, ch. V), or its computer implementation by Barwise and Etchemendy (1999). Although the Tarski-style semantics and the game semantics look very different, they always give the same answer to the question: 'What is the truth-value of the sentence ϕ under the interpretation I?'

Throughout this chapter, symbols such as 'ϕ', 'α' are used to range over the formulas or terms of a first-order language. They are *metavariables*; in other words, they are not in the first-order languages but are used for talking about these languages. On the other hand, so as not to saddle the reader with still more metavariables for the other expressions of a first-order language, for example, when making a general statement about variables, a typical variable may be used as if it was a meta-variable. Thus 'Consider a variable x' is common practice. More generally, quotation marks are dropped when they are more of a nuisance than a help.

1.4. The First-Order Language with Empty Signature

The simplest first-order language is the one whose signature is empty. In this section, this language is referred to as L.

An interpretation I with empty signature does not interpret any constants, but – for reasons that will appear very soon – it does have an associated class of objects, called its *universe* or *domain*. (The name 'domain' is perhaps more usual; but it has other meanings in logic so, to avoid confusion, 'universe' is used instead.) Most logicians require that the universe shall have at least one object in it; but, apart from this, it can be any class of objects. The members of the domain are called the *elements* of the interpretation; some older writers call them the *individuals*. A *valuation in I* is a rule v for assigning to each variable x_i an element $v(x_i)$ in the universe of I.

For the grammatical constructions given here, an interpretation I and a valuation v in I are assumed. The truth-values of formulas will depend partly on I and partly on v. A formula is said to be *true in I under v*.

Some expressions of L are called *atomic formulas*. There are two kinds:

- Every expression of the form '$(x = y)$', where x and y are variables, is an atomic formula of L.
- '$\perp$' is an atomic formula of L.

It has already been noted that '$\perp$' is false in I. The truth-value of $(x_1 = x_3)$, to take a typical example of the other sort of atomic formula, is

Truth   if $v(x_1)$ is the same element as $v(x_3)$

Falsehood   if not

So, given I and v, truth-values are assigned to the atomic formulas.

Next, a class of expressions called the *formulas* of L is defined. The atomic formulas are formulas, but many formulas of L are not atomic. Take the five symbols

$$\sim \quad \& \quad \vee \quad \supset \quad \equiv$$

which are used to build up complex formulas from simpler ones. There is a grammatical rule for all of them.

If ϕ and ψ are formulas, then so are each of these expressions:

$$(\sim \phi) \quad (\phi \& \psi) \quad (\phi \vee \psi) \quad (\phi \supset \psi) \quad (\phi \equiv \psi)$$

This chart, called a *truth-table*, shows which of these formulas are true, depending on whether ϕ and ψ are true:

ϕ	ψ	$(\sim \phi)$	$(\phi \,\&\, \psi)$	$(\phi \vee \psi)$	$(\phi \supset \psi)$	$(\phi \equiv \psi)$
T	T	F	T	T	T	T
T	F		F	T	F	F
F	T	T	F	T	T	F
F	F		F	F	T	T

(Here T = Truth and F = Falsehood.) Because of this table, the five symbols '$\sim$', '&', '$\vee$', '$\supset$', and '$\equiv$' are known as the *truth-functional symbols*.

For example, the formula

$$(((x_2 = x_3) \,\&\, (x_5 = x_2)) \supset (x_5 = x_3))$$

is false in just one case, namely where $v(x_2)$ and $v(x_3)$ are the same element, and $v(x_5)$ and $v(x_2)$ are the same element, but $v(x_5)$ and $v(x_3)$ are not the same element. Since this case can never arise, the formula is true regardless of what I and v are.

There remain just two grammatical constructions. The grammatical rule for them both is:

If ϕ is any formula and x is any variable, then the expressions

$$(\forall x)\phi \qquad (\exists x)\phi$$

are both formulas.

The expressions '$(\forall x)$' and '$(\exists x)$' are called respectively a *universal quantifier* and an *existential quantifier*, and read respectively as 'for all x' and 'there is x'. In the two formulas given by the rule, the occurrence of x inside the quantifier is said to *bind* itself and any occurrences of the *same* variable in the formula ϕ. These occurrences stay bound as still more complex formulas are built. In any formula, an occurrence of a variable which is not bound by a quantifier in the formula is said to be *free*. A formula with no free variables is called a *sentence*. (And this is what was meant earlier by 'sentences' of first-order languages. The syntactic definitions just given are equivalent to the semantic explanation in the previous section.) For example, this is not a sentence:

$$(\exists y)(\sim (x = y))$$

because it has a free occurrence of x (though both occurrences of y are bound by the existential quantifier). But this is a sentence:

$$(\forall x)(\exists y)(\sim (x = y))$$

because its universal quantifier binds the variable x.

The semantic rules for the quantifiers are one of the harder concepts of first-order logic. For more than two millennia, some of the best minds of Europe struggled to formulate semantic rules that capture the essence of the natural language expressions 'all' and 'there is.'

- '$(\forall x)\phi$' is true in I under v if: for every element a in the universe of I, if w is taken to be the valuation exactly like v except that $w(x)$ is a, then ϕ is true in I under w.
- '$(\exists x)\phi$' is true in I under v if: there is an element a in the universe of I, such that if w is taken to be the valuation exactly like v except that $w(x)$ is a, then ϕ is true in I under w.

For example, the formula

$$(\exists y)(\sim (x = y))$$

is true in I under v, iff (if and only if) there is an element a such that $v(x)$ is not the same element as a. So the sentence

$$(\forall x)(\exists y)(\sim (x = y))$$

is true in I under v iff for every element b there is an element a such that b is not the same element as a. In other words, it is true iff the universe of I contains at least two different elements.

Note that this last condition depends only on I and not at all on v. One can prove that the truth-value of a formula ϕ in I and v never depends on $v(x)$ for any variable x that does not occur free in ϕ. Since sentences have no free variables, their truth-value depends only on I and the valuation slips silently away.

These rules capture the essence of the expressions 'all' and 'there is' by stating precise conditions under which a sentence starting with one of these phrases counts as true. The same applies to the truth-functional symbols, which are meant, in some sense, to capture at least the mathematical use of the words 'not', 'and', 'or', 'if . . . then', and 'if and only if'.

1.5. Some Notation

The notation in this section applies to all first-order languages, not just the language with empty signature.

Writing a formula as $\phi(x_1, \ldots, x_n)$, where $x_1, \ldots, x_n$ are different variables means that the formula is ϕ and it has no occurrences of free variables except perhaps for $x_1, \ldots, x_n$. Then

$$I \vDash \phi[a_1, \ldots, a_n]$$

means that ϕ is true in the interpretation I and under some valuation v for which $v(x_1), \ldots, v(x_n)$ are $a_1, \ldots, a_n$ respectively (or under any such valuation v – it makes no difference). When ϕ is a sentence, the $a_1, \ldots, a_n$ are redundant and

$$I \vDash \phi$$

simply means that ϕ is true in I.

Here is another useful piece of notation:

$$\phi(y/x)$$

means the formula obtained by replacing each free occurrence of x in ϕ by an occurrence of y. Actually, this is not quite right, but the correction in the next paragraph is rather technical. What is intended is that the formula $\phi(y/x)$ 'says about y' the same thing that ϕ 'said about x.'

Suppose, for example, that ϕ is the formula

$$(\forall y)(x = y)$$

which expresses that x is identical with everything. Simply putting y in place of each free occurrence of x in ϕ, gives

$$(\forall y)(y = y)$$

This says that each thing is identical to itself; whereas the intention was to make the more interesting statement that y is identical with everything. The problem is that y is put into a place where it immediately becomes bound by the quantifier $(\forall y)$. So $\phi(y/x)$ must be defined more carefully, as follows. First, choose another variable, say z, that does not occur in ϕ, and adjust ϕ by replacing all bound occurrences of y in ϕ by bound occurrences of z. After this, substitute y for free occurrences of x. (So $\phi(y/x)$ in our example now works out as

$$(\forall z)(y = z)$$

which says the right thing.) This more careful method of substitution is called *substitution avoiding clash of variables.*

The language L of the previous section is a very arid first-order language. The conditions that it can express on an interpretation I are very few. It can be used to say that I has at least one element, at least two elements, at least seven elements, either exactly a hundred or at least three billion elements, and similar things; but nothing else. (Is there a single sentence of L which expresses the condition that I has infinitely many elements? No. This is a consequence of the compactness theorem in section 1.10.)

Nevertheless L already shows some very characteristic features of first-order languages. For example, to work out the truth-value of a sentence ϕ under an interpretation I, one must generally consider the truth-values of subformulas of ϕ

under various valuations. As explained in section 1.3, the notion of a valid sequent applies to formulas as well as sentences; but for formulas it means that every interpretation-plus-valuation making the formulas on the left true makes the formula on the right true too.

Here are two important examples of valid sequents of the language L. The sequent

$$\vdash (x = x)$$

is valid because $v(x)$ is always the same element as $v(x)$. The sequent

$$(x = y) \vdash (\phi \supset \phi(y/x))$$

is valid because if two given elements are the same element, then they satisfy all the same conditions.

1.6. Nonlogical Constants: Monadic First-Order Logic

Section 1.5 ignored the main organ by which first-order formulas reach out to the world: the signature, the family of nonlogical constants.

The various constants can be classified by the kinds of feature to which they have to be attached in the world. For example, some constants are called *class symbols* because their job is to stand for classes. (Their more technical name is 1-*ary relation symbols*.) Some other constants are called *individual constants* because their job is to stand for individuals, i.e. elements. This section concentrates on languages whose signature contains only constants of these two kinds. Languages of this type are said to be *monadic*. Let L be a monadic language.

Usually, individual constants are lower-case letters 'a', 'b', 'c' etc. from the first half of the alphabet, with or without subscripts. Usually class symbols are capital letters 'P', 'Q', 'R' etc. from the second half of the alphabet, with or without number subscripts.

Grammatically these constants provide some new kinds of atomic formula. It is helpful first to define the *terms* of L. There are two kinds:

- Every variable is a term.
- Every individual constant is a term.

The definition of *atomic formula* needs revising:

- Every expression of the form '$(\alpha = \beta)$', where α and β are terms, is an atomic formula of L.
- If P is any class symbol and α any term, then '$P(\alpha)$' is an atomic formula.
- '$\perp$' is an atomic formula of L.

Apart from these new clauses, the grammatical rules remain the same as in section 1.4.

What should count as an interpretation for a monadic language? Every interpretation I needs a universe, just as before. But now it also needs to give the truth-value of $P(x)$ under a valuation that ties x to an element $v(x)$, which might be any element of the universe. In other words, the interpretation needs to give the class, written P^I, of all those elements a such that $P(x)$ is true under any valuation v with $v(x)$ equal to a. (Intuitively P^I is the class of all elements that satisfy $P(x)$ in I.) Here P^I might be any subclass of the universe.

In the branch of logic called model theory, the previous paragraph turns into a definition. A *structure* is an interpretation I of the following form:

- I has a universe, which is a set (generally taken to be non-empty).
- For each class symbol P in the signature, I picks out a corresponding class P^I, called the *interpretation of P under I*, all of whose members are in the universe.
- For each individual constant a in the signature, I picks out a corresponding element a^I in the universe, and this element is called the *interpretation of a under I*.

Writing σ for the signature in question, this interpretation I is called a σ-*structure*. So a σ-structure contains exactly the information needed to give a truth-value to a sentence of signature σ. Note that the interpretations a^I are needed to deal with sentences such as $P(a)$. (The requirement that the universe should be a set rather than a class is no accident: a set is a mathematically well-behaved class. The precise difference is studied in texts of set theory. [See chapter 3.])

However, this model-theoretic definition is not as old as first-order logic. In the early days, logicians would give an interpretation for a by writing down a name or a description of a thing or person. They would give an interpretation for P by writing down a sentence of English or their own native language with x in place of one or more pronouns. Or sometimes they would write a sentence with 'He' or 'It' left off the front; or more drastically, a sentence with 'He is a' left off. For example an interpretation might contain the items:

P : x is kind to people who are kind to x.

Q : is mortal

R : taxpayer

The third style here is the least flexible, but anyway it is not needed; it can easily be converted to the second style by writing 'is a taxpayer.' The second style in turn is less flexible than the first, and again is not needed. Q and R could be written 'x is mortal', 'x is a taxpayer'. A sentence with variables in place of some pronouns is sometimes called a *predicate*.

Can every interpretation by predicates be converted into a structure? Yes, provided that each of the predicates has a certain property: *the question whether an element of the universe satisfies the predicate always has a definite answer (Yes or No) which depends only on the element and not on how it is described.* Predicates with this property are said to be *extensional*. The following predicates seem not to be extensional

– though this is an area where people have presented strong arguments for some quite surprising conclusions:

x is necessarily equal to 7.

I recognized x.

The prevailing view is that to handle predicates like these, a logic with a subtler semantics than first-order logic is needed. Modal logic takes on board the first example, epistemic logic the second. [See chapters 7 and 9.]

The predicate

x is bald.

also fails the test, not because it is possible to be bald under one name and bushy-haired under another, but because there are borderline cases – people who aren't definitely bald or definitely not bald. So this predicate does not succeed in defining a class of people. Truth to tell, most natural language predicates are at least slightly vague; even logicians have to live with the roughnesses of the real world.

Given an interpretation I that uses predicates, a first-order sentence ϕ can often be translated into an English sentence which is guaranteed to be true if and only if ϕ is true in I. The translation will generally need to mention the universe of the interpretation, unless a predicate is used to describe that too. Here are some examples, using the interpretation a couple of paragraphs above, together with the universe described by 'x is a person':

$(\forall x)(R(x) \rightarrow Q(x))$
Every person who is a taxpayer is mortal.

$(\exists x)P(x)$
At least one person is kind to people who are kind to him or her.

$(\exists x)(R(x)\ \&\ (\forall y)(R(y) \equiv (y = x)))$
Exactly one person is a taxpayer.

The reader may well agree with the following comment: If these first-order sentences are being used to express the English sentences in question, then it is artificial to ask for a universe at all. In ordinary speech, no one asks people to state their universes.

This comment needs answers on several levels. First, mathematical objects – such as groups, rings, boolean algebras and the like – consist of a set of objects with certain features picked out by nonlogical constants. So it was natural for the mathematical creators of first-order logic to think of this set of objects as a universe.

Second, there is a mathematical result that takes some of the sting out of the requirement that a universe has to be chosen. An occurrence of a universal quantifier is *restricted* if it occurs as follows:

$$(\forall x)(P(x) \supset \cdots)$$

i.e. followed immediately by a left bracket, a class symbol with the same variable, and then '$\supset$'. Likewise an occurrence of an existential quantifier is *restricted* if it looks like this:

$$(\exists x)(P(x) \,\&\, \cdots)$$

The mathematical result states:

> **Theorem 1.1** Let ϕ be a sentence of the first-order language L of signature σ, and suppose that all occurrences of quantifiers in ϕ are restricted. Let I be a σ-structure and J be another σ-structure which comes from I by removing some elements which are not inside P^I for any class symbol P. Then ϕ has the same truth-value in I and in J.

First-order sentences that serve as straightforward translations of English sentences usually have all their quantifiers restricted, as in the first and third examples above. (The second example can be rewritten harmlessly as

$$(\exists x)(P(x) \,\&\, P(x))$$

and then its quantifier is restricted too.) So the choice of universe may be largely *ad hoc*, but it is also largely irrelevant. (This theorem remains true for first-order languages that are not monadic.)

Third, if the class symbols are interpreted by predicates rather than by classes, the choice of universe certainly can make a difference to truth-values, even for sentences covered by the theorem just stated. Suppose, for example, that an interpretation is being used, with

P : x is a person.

Q : x will be dead before the year 2200.

With such an interpretation, the sentence

$$(\forall x)(P(x) \rightarrow Q(x))$$

expresses that every person will be dead before the year 2200. This is probably true of people alive now, but probably false if 'person' includes people yet to be born. So different universes give different truth-values. Why does this not contradict Theorem 1.1? Because the predicate 'x is a person' picks out different classes according as future people are excluded or included, so that the corresponding σ-structures differ in their assignments to P and Q, not just in their universes.

If a universe can contain future people, can it contain possible people, or fictional people, or even impossible people (like the man I met who wasn't there, in the children's jingle)? Or to be more metaphysical, can a universe contain as separate elements myself-now and myself-ten-years-ago? First-order logic is very robust about questions like these: it doesn't give a damn. If you think that there are fictional people and that they have or fail to have this property or that, and can meaningfully be said to be the same individuals or not the same individuals as one another, then fine, put them in your universes. Likewise, if you think there are time-slices of people. If you don't, then leave them out.

All these remarks about universes apply equally well to the more general first-order languages of section 1.7. Here is a theorem that does not.

Theorem 1.2 If L is a monadic first-order language with a finite signature, then L is decidable.

See, for example, Boolos and Jeffrey (1974, ch. 25, 'Monadic versus dyadic logic') for a proof of this theorem.

1.7. Some More Nonlogical Constants

Most logicians before about 1850, if they had been set to work designing a first-order language, would probably have been happy to stick with the kinds of constant already introduced here. Apart from some subtleties and confusions about empty classes, the traditional syllogistic forms correspond to the four sentence-types

$$(\forall x)(P(x) \supset Q(x)) \qquad (\forall x)(P(x) \supset {\sim} Q(x))$$
$$(\exists x)(P(x) \mathrel{\&} Q(x)) \qquad (\exists x)(P(x) \mathrel{\&} {\sim} Q(x))$$

The main pressure for more elaborate forms came from mathematics, where geometers wanted symbols to represent predicates such as:

x is a point lying on the line y.

x is between y and z.

Even these two examples show that there is no point in restricting ourselves in advance to some fixed number of variables. So, class symbols are generalized to *n-ary relation symbols*, where the *arity*, n, is the number of distinct variables needed in a predicate that interprets the relation symbol.

Like class symbols, relation symbols are usually 'P', 'Q', etc., i.e. capital letters from near the end of the alphabet. An *ordered n-tuple* is a list

$$\langle a_1, \ldots, a_n \rangle$$

where a_i is the ith item in the list; the same object may appear as more than one item in the list. The interpretation R^I of a relation symbol R of arity n in an interpretation I is a set of ordered n-tuples of elements in the universe of I. If R^I is specified by giving a particular predicate for R, then which variables of the predicate belong with which places in the lists must also be specified. An example shows how:

$R(x, y, w)$: w is between x and y.

Class symbols are included as the relation symbols of arity 1, by taking a list

$\langle a \rangle$

of length 1 to be the same thing as its unique item a.

There can also be relation symbols of arity 0 if it is decided that there is exactly one list $\langle \rangle$ of length 0. So the interpretation p^I of a 0-ary relation symbol p is either the empty set (call it Falsehood) or else the set whose one element is $\langle \rangle$ (call this set Truth). All this makes good sense set-theoretically. What matters here, however, is the outcome: relation symbols of arity 0 are called *propositional symbols*, and they are always interpreted as Truth or as Falsehood. A sentence which contains neither '=', quantifiers nor any nonlogical constants except propositional symbols is called a *propositional sentence*. Propositional logic is about propositional sentences.

The language can be extended in another way by introducing nonlogical symbols called *n-ary function symbols*, where n is a positive integer. The interpretation F^I of such a symbol F is a function which assigns an element of I to each ordered n-tuple of elements of I. (Again, there is a way of regarding individual constants as 0-ary function symbols, but the details can be skipped here.)

The new symbols require some more adjustments to the grammar. The clause for *terms* becomes:

- Every variable is a term.
- Every individual constant is a term.
- If F is a function symbol of arity n, and $\alpha_1, \ldots, \alpha_n$ are terms, then '$F(\alpha_1, \ldots, \alpha_n)$' is a term.

The definition of *atomic formula* becomes:

- Every expression of the form '$(\alpha = \beta)$', where α and β are terms, is an atomic formula of L.
- Every propositional symbol is an atomic formula.
- If R is any relation symbol of positive arity n and $\alpha_1, \ldots, \alpha_n$ are terms, then '$R(\alpha_1, \ldots, \alpha_n)$' is an atomic formula.
- '$\perp$' is an atomic formula.

The semantic rules are the obvious adjustments of those in the previous section.

Some notation from section 1.5 can be usefully extended. If ϕ is a formula and α is a term,

$\phi(\alpha/x)$

represents the formula obtained from ϕ by replacing all free occurrences of x by α. As in section 1.5, to avoid clash of variables, the bound variables in ϕ may need to be changed first, so that they do not bind any variables in α.

1.8. Proof Calculi

First-order logic has a range of proof calculi. With a very few exceptions, all these proof calculi apply to all first-order languages. So, for the rest of this section assume that L is a particular first-order language of signature σ.

The first proof calculi to be discovered were the *Hilbert-style* calculi, where one reaches a conclusion by applying deduction rules to axioms. An example is described later in this section. These calculi tend to be very *ad hoc* in their axioms, and maddeningly wayward if one is looking for proofs in them. However, they have their supporters, e.g., modal logicians who need a first-order base to which further axioms can be added.

In 1934, Gentzen (1969) invented two other styles of calculus. One was the *natural deduction calculus* (independently proposed by Jaśkowski slightly earlier). An intuitionistic natural deduction calculus is given in chapter 11, which, as noted there, can be extended to make a calculus for classical first-order logic by the addition of a rule for double-negation elimination. Gentzen's second invention was the *sequent calculus*, which could be regarded as a Hilbert-style calculus for deriving finite sequents instead of formulas. With this subtle adjustment, nearly all of the arbitrariness of Hilbert-style systems falls away, and it is even possible to convert each sequent calculus proof into a sequent calculus proof in a very simple form called a *cut-free proof*. The popular *tableau* or *truth-tree* proofs are really cut-free sequent proofs turned upside down. A proof of a sequent in any of the four kinds of calculi – Hilbert-style, natural deduction, sequent calculus, tableaux – can be mechanically converted to a proof of the same sequent in any of the other calculi; see Sundholm (1983) for a survey.

The *resolution calculus* also deserves a mention. This calculus works very fast on computers, but its proofs are almost impossible for a normal human being to make any sense of, and it requires the sentences to be converted to a normal form (not quite the one in section 1.10 below) before the calculation starts; see, for example, Gallier (1986).

To sketch a Hilbert-style calculus, called $\mathcal{H}$, first define the class of *axioms* of $\mathcal{H}$. This is the set of all formulas of the language L which have any of the following forms:

H1 $\phi \supset (\psi \supset \phi)$

H2 $(\phi \supset \psi) \supset ((\phi \supset (\psi \supset \chi)) \supset (\psi \supset \chi))$

H3 $(\sim \phi \supset \psi) \supset ((\sim \phi \supset \sim \psi) \supset \phi)$

H4 $((\phi \supset \perp) \supset \perp) \supset \phi$

H5 $\phi \supset (\psi \supset (\phi \,\&\, \psi))$

H6 $(\phi \,\&\, \psi) \supset \phi, \ (\phi \,\&\, \psi) \supset \psi$

H7 $\phi \supset (\phi \vee \psi), \ \psi \supset (\phi \vee \psi)$

H8 $(\phi \supset \chi) \supset ((\psi \supset \chi) \supset ((\phi \vee \psi) \supset \chi))$

H9 $(\phi \supset \psi) \supset ((\psi \supset \phi) \supset (\phi \equiv \psi))$

H10 $(\phi \equiv \psi) \supset (\phi \supset \psi), \ (\phi \equiv \psi) \supset (\psi \supset \phi)$

H11 $\phi(\alpha/x) \supset \exists x \phi \ (\alpha \text{ any term})$

H12 $\forall x \phi \supset \phi(\alpha/x) \ (\alpha \text{ any term})$

H13 $x = x$

H14 $x = y \supset (\phi \supset \phi(y/x))$

A *derivation* (or *formal proof*) in $\mathcal{H}$ is defined to be a finite sequence

$$(\langle \phi_1, m_1 \rangle, \ldots, \langle \phi_n, m_n \rangle)$$

such that $n \geq 1$, and for each i $(1 \leq i \leq n)$ one of the five following conditions holds. (Clauses (c)–(e) are known as the *derivation rules* of $\mathcal{H}$.)

(a) $m_i = 1$ and ϕ_i is an axiom.
(b) $m_i = 2$ and ϕ_i is any formula of L.
(c) $m_i = 3$ and there are j and k in $\{1, \ldots, i-1\}$ such that ϕ_k is $\phi_j \to \phi_i$.
(d) $m_i = 4$ and there is j $(1 \leq j < i)$ such that ϕ_j has the form $\psi \to \chi$, x is a variable not occurring free in ψ, and ϕ_i is $\psi \to \forall x \chi$.
(e) $m_i = 5$ and there is j $(1 \leq j < i)$ such that ϕ_j has the form $\psi \to \chi$, x is a variable not occurring free in χ, and ϕ_i is $\exists x \psi \to \chi$.

The *premises* of this derivation are the formulas ϕ_i for which $m_i = 2$. Its *conclusion* is ϕ_n. We say that ψ is *derivable in* $\mathcal{H}$ from a set T of formulas, in symbols

$$T \vdash_{\mathcal{H}} \psi$$

if there exists a derivation whose conclusion is ψ and all of whose premises are in T.

Proofs are usually written vertically rather than horizontally. For example here is a proof of $(\phi \supset \phi)$, where ϕ is any formula:

(1) $(\phi \supset (\phi \supset \phi)) \supset ((\phi \supset ((\phi \supset \phi) \supset \phi)) \supset (\phi \supset \phi))$ [Axiom H2]

(2) $\phi \supset (\phi \supset \phi)$ [Axiom H1]

(3) $(\phi \supset ((\phi \supset \phi) \supset \phi)) \supset (\phi \supset \phi)$ [Rule (c) from (1), (2)]

(4) $\phi \supset ((\phi \supset \phi) \supset \phi)$ [Axiom H1]

(5) $\phi \supset \phi$ [Rule (c) from (3), (4)]

To save the labor of writing this argument every time a result of the form $\phi \supset \phi$ is needed, this result can be quoted as a lemma in further proofs. Thus $\sim\!\perp$ can be proved as follows:

(1) $\sim\!\perp \supset \sim\!\perp$ [Lemma]

(2) $(\sim\!\perp \supset \sim\!\perp) \supset ((\sim\!\perp \supset \perp) \supset (\sim\!\perp \supset \sim\!\perp))$ [Axiom H1]

(3) $(\sim\!\perp \supset \perp) \supset (\sim\!\perp \supset \sim\!\perp)$ [Rule (c) from (1), (2)]

(4) $((\sim\!\perp \supset \perp) \supset (\sim\!\perp \supset \sim\!\perp)) \supset (((\sim\!\perp \supset \perp) \supset ((\sim\!\perp \supset \sim\!\perp) \supset \perp)) \supset ((\sim\!\perp \supset \perp) \supset \perp))$

                                                                            [Axiom H2]

(5) $((\sim\!\perp \supset \perp) \supset ((\sim\!\perp \supset \sim\!\perp) \supset \perp)) \supset ((\sim\!\perp \supset \perp) \supset \perp)$

                                                                            [Rule (c) from (3), (4)]

(6) $(\sim\!\perp \supset \perp) \supset ((\sim\!\perp \supset \sim\!\perp) \supset \perp)$ [Axiom H3]

(7) $(\sim\!\perp \supset \perp) \supset \perp$ [Rule (c) from (5), (6)]

(8) $((\sim\!\perp \supset \perp) \supset \perp) \supset \sim\!\perp$ [Axiom H4]

(9) $\sim\!\perp$ [Rule (c) from (7), (8)]

Then this result can be quoted in turn as a lemma in a proof of $(\phi \supset \perp) \supset \sim \phi$, and so on.

A theory T is $\mathcal{H}$-*inconsistent* if there is some formula ϕ such that $(\phi \ \& \sim \phi)$ is derivable from T in $\mathcal{H}$. If the language L contains $\perp$, then it can be shown that this is equivalent to saying that $\perp$ is derivable from T in $\mathcal{H}$. T is $\mathcal{H}$-*consistent* if it is not $\mathcal{H}$-inconsistent. $\mathcal{H}$-inconsistency is one example of *syntactic inconsistency*; other proof calculi give other examples.

1.9. Correctness and Completeness

Theorem 1.3 (*Correctness Theorem for $\mathcal{H}$*) Suppose $\phi_1, \ldots, \phi_n$ and ψ are sentences. If ϕ is derivable in $\mathcal{H}$ from $\phi_1, \ldots, \phi_n$, then the sequent

$$\phi_1, \ldots, \phi_n \vdash \psi$$

is valid.

Proof sketch This is proved by induction on the length of the shortest derivation of ψ from $\phi_1, \ldots, \phi_n$. Unfortunately, the formulas in the derivation need not be sentences. So for the induction hypothesis something a little more general needs to be proved:

Suppose $\phi_1, \ldots, \phi_n$ are sentences and ψ is a formula whose free variables are all among $x_1, \ldots, x_m$. If ψ is derivable in $\mathcal{H}$ from $\phi_1, \ldots, \phi_n$, then the sequent

$$\phi_1, \ldots, \phi_n \vdash \forall x_1 \cdots \forall x_m \psi$$

is valid.

The argument splits into cases according to the last derivation rule used in the proof. Suppose, for example, that this was the rule numbered (5) above, and ψ is the formula $\exists y \theta \supset \chi$ where y is not free in χ. Then, from the induction hypothesis, the sequent

$$\phi_1, \ldots, \phi_n \vdash \forall x_1 \cdots \forall x_n \forall y (\theta \supset \chi)$$

is valid. Using the fact that y is not free in χ, it can be checked that the sequent

$$\forall x_1 \cdots \forall x_n \forall y (\theta \supset \chi) \vdash \forall x_1 \cdots \forall x_n (\exists y \theta \supset \chi)$$

is valid. By this and the induction hypothesis, the sequent

$$\phi_1, \ldots, \phi_n \vdash \forall x_1 \cdots \forall x_n (\exists y \theta \supset \chi)$$

is valid as required.   QED

Now, the completeness question:

Theorem 1.4 (*Completeness Theorem for* $\mathcal{H}$)   Suppose that T is a theory and ψ is a sentence such that the sequent

$$T \vdash \psi$$

is valid. Then ψ is derivable from T in $\mathcal{H}$.

In fact one proves the special case of the Completeness Theorem where ψ is $\bot$; in other words

If T is a theory with no models, then $T \vdash_{\mathcal{H}} \bot$.

This is as good as proving the whole theorem, since the sequent

$$T \cup \{\sim \psi\} \vdash \bot$$

is equivalent to '$T \vdash \psi$' both semantically and in terms of derivability in $\mathcal{H}$.

Here, the Completeness Theorem is proved by showing that if T is any $\mathcal{H}$-consistent theory then T has a model. A technical lemma about $\mathcal{H}$ is needed along the way:

Lemma 1.5   Suppose c is a constant which occurs nowhere in the formula ϕ, the theory T or the sentence ψ. If

$$T \vdash_{\mathcal{H}} \phi(c/x) \supset \psi$$

then

$$T \vdash_{\mathcal{H}} \exists x \phi \supset \psi$$

Proof sketch of the Completeness Theorem   This is known as a *Henkin-style* proof because of three features: the constants added as witnesses, the construction of a maximal consistent theory, and the way that a model is built using sets of terms as elements. The proof uses a small amount of set theory, chiefly infinite cardinals and ordinals. [See chapter 3.]

Assume a $\mathcal{H}$-consistent theory T in the language L. Let κ be the number of formulas of L; κ is always infinite. Expand the language L to a first-order language L^+ by adding to the signature a set of κ new individual constants; these new constants are called *witnesses*. List the sentences of L^+ as $(\phi_i : i < \kappa)$. Now define for each $i < \kappa$ a theory T_i, so that

$$T = T_0 \subseteq T_1 \subseteq \cdots$$

and each T_i is $\mathcal{H}$-consistent. To start the process, put $T_0 = T$. When i is a limit ordinal, take T_i to be the union of the T_j with $j < i$; this theory is $\mathcal{H}$-consistent since any inconsistency would have a proof using finitely many sentences, all of which would lie in some T_j with $j < i$.

The important choice is where i is a successor ordinal, say $i = j + 1$. If $T_j \cup \{\phi_j\}$ is not $\mathcal{H}$-consistent, take T_{j+1} to be T_j. Otherwise, put $T_j' = T_j \cup \{\phi_j\}$. Then if ϕ_j is of the form $\exists x \psi$, choose a witness c that appears nowhere in any sentence of T_j', and put $T_{j+1} = T_j' \cup \{\psi(c/x)\}$; otherwise put $T_{j+1} = T_j'$. By Lemma 1.5, T_{j+1} is $\mathcal{H}$-consistent in all these cases.

Write T^+ for the union of all the theories T_i. It has the property that if ϕ_j is any sentence of L^+ for which $T^+ \cup \{\phi_j\}$ is $\mathcal{H}$-consistent, then $T_j \cup \{\phi_j\}$ was already $\mathcal{H}$-consistent and so ϕ_j is in T^+ by construction. (As noted, T^+ is *maximal consistent*.) Moreover if T^+ contains a sentence ϕ_j of the form $\exists x \psi$, then by construction it also contains $\psi(c/x)$ for some witness c.

Two witnesses c and d are *equivalent* if the sentence '$c = d$' is in T^+. Now if '$c = d$' and '$d = e$' are both in T^+, then (appealing to the axioms and rules of $\mathcal{H}$) the theory $T^+ \cup \{c = e\}$ is $\mathcal{H}$-consistent, and so '$c = e$' is also in T^+. This and similar arguments show that 'equivalence' is an equivalence relation on the set of witnesses. Now build a structure A^+ whose universe is the set of equivalence classes $c^{\sim}$ of witnesses c. For example, if P is a 2-ary relation symbol in the signature, then take P^{A+} to be the set of all ordered pairs $\langle c^{\sim}, d^{\sim} \rangle$ such that the sentence '$P(c, d)$' is in T^+. There are a number of details to be checked, but the outcome is that A^+ is a model of T^+. Now, stripping the witnesses out of the signature gives a structure A whose signature is that of L, and A is a model of all the sentences of L that are in T^+. In particular, A is a model of T, as required. (Note that A has at most κ elements, since there were only κ witnesses.)   QED

1.10. Metatheory of First-Order Logic

The *metatheory* of a logic consists of those things that one can say *about* the logic, rather than in it. All the numbered theorems of this chapter are examples. The metatheory of first-order logic is vast. Here are a few high points, beginning with some consequences of the Completeness Theorem for $\mathcal{H}$.

Theorem 1.6 (*Compactness Theorem*) Suppose T is a first-order theory, ψ is a first-order sentence and T entails ψ. Then there is a finite subset U of T such that U entails ψ.

Proof If T entails ψ then the sequent

$$T \vdash \psi$$

is valid, and so by the completeness of the proof calculus $\mathcal{H}$, the sequent has a formal proof. Let U be the set of sentences in T which are used in this proof. Since the proof is a finite object, U is a finite set. But the proof is also a proof of the sequent

$$U \vdash \psi$$

So by the correctness of $\mathcal{H}$, U entails ψ.   QED

Corollary 1.7 Suppose T is a first-order theory and every finite subset of T has a model. Then T has a model.

Proof Working backwards, it is enough to prove that if T has no model then some finite subset of T has no model. If T has no model then T entails $\bot$, since $\bot$ has no models. So by the Compactness Theorem, some finite subset U of T entails $\bot$. But this implies that U has no model.   QED

The next result is the weakest of a family of theorems known as the *Downward Löwenheim–Skolem Theorem*.

Theorem 1.8 Suppose L is a first-order language with at most countably many formulas, and let T be a consistent theory in L. Then T has a model with at most countably many elements.

Proof Assuming T is semantically consistent, it is $\mathcal{H}$-consistent by the correctness of $\mathcal{H}$. So the sketch proof of the Completeness Theorem in section 1.9 constructs a model A of T. By the last sentence of section 1.9, A has at most countably many elements.   QED

There is also an *Upward Löwenheim–Skolem Theorem*, which says that every first-order theory with infinite models has arbitrarily large models.

A *basic conjunction* is a formula of the form

$(\phi_1 \& \cdots \& \phi_m)$

where each ϕ_i is either an atomic formula or an atomic formula preceded by $\sim$. (Note that $m = 1$ is allowed, so that a single atomic formula, with or without $\sim$, counts as a basic conjunction.) A formula is in *disjunctive normal form* if it has the form

$(\psi_1 \vee \cdots \vee \psi_n)$

where each ψ_j is a basic conjunction. (Again, $n = 1$ is allowed, so that a basic conjunction counts as being in disjunctive normal form.)

A first-order formula is said to be *prenex* if it consists of a string of quantifiers followed by a formula with no quantifiers in it. (The string of quantifiers may be empty, so that a formula with no quantifiers counts as being prenex.)

A formula is in *normal form* if it is prenex and the part after the quantifiers is in disjunctive normal form.

Theorem 1.9 (*Normal Form Theorem*) Every first-order formula ϕ is equivalent to a first-order formula ψ of the same signature as ϕ, which has the same free variables as ϕ and is in normal form.

The next theorem, Lyndon's Interpolation Theorem, deserves to be better known. Among other things, it is the first-order form of some laws which were widely known to logicians of earlier centuries as the Laws of Distribution (Hodges, 1998). It is stated here for sentences in normal form; by Theorem 1.9, this implies a theorem about all first-order sentences.

Suppose ϕ is a first-order sentence in normal form. An occurrence of a relation symbol in ϕ is called *positive* if it has no '$\sim$' immediately in front of it, and *negative* if it has.

Theorem 1.10 (*Lyndon's Interpolation Theorem*) Suppose ϕ and ψ are first-order sentences in normal form, and ϕ entails ψ. Then there is a first-order sentence θ in normal form, such that

- ϕ entails θ and θ entails ψ
- every relation symbol which has a positive occurrence in θ has positive occurrences in both ϕ and ψ, and
- every relation symbol which has a negative occurrence in θ has negative occurrences in both ϕ and ψ.

Lyndon's theorem can be proved either by analyzing proofs of the sequent '$\phi \vdash \psi$', or by a set-theoretic argument using models of ϕ and ψ. Both arguments are too complicated to give here.

An important corollary of Lyndon's Interpolation Theorem is Craig's Interpolation Theorem, which was proved a few years before Lyndon's.

Corollary 1.11 (*Craig's Interpolation Theorem*)   Suppose ϕ and ψ are first-order sentences, and ϕ entails ψ. Then there is a first-order sentence θ such that

- ϕ entails θ and θ entails ψ
- every relation symbol that occurs in θ occurs both in ϕ and in ψ.

Craig's Interpolation Theorem in turn implies Beth's Definability Theorem, which was proved earlier still. But all these theorems are from the 1950s, perhaps the last great age of elementary metatheory.

Corollary 1.12 (*Beth's Definability Theorem*)   Suppose ϕ is a first-order sentence in which a relation symbol R of arity n occurs, and suppose also that there are not two models I and J of ϕ which are identical except that R^I is different from R^J. Then ϕ entails some first-order sentence of the form

$$(\forall x_1) \cdots (\forall x_n) \, (\psi \equiv R(x_1, \ldots, x_n))$$

where ψ is a formula in which R never occurs.

Finally, note a metatheorem of a different kind, to contrast with Theorem 1.2 above: a form of *Church's Theorem on the Undecidability of First-Order Logic*.

Theorem 1.13   Suppose L is a first-order language whose signature contains at least one n-ary relation symbol with $n > 1$. Then L is not decidable.

A reference for all the metatheorems in this section except Theorems 1.9 and 1.13 is Hodges (1997). Theorem 1.9 is proved in both Kleene (1952, pp. 134f, 167) and Ebbinghaus et al. (1984, p. 126), together with a wealth of other mathematical information about first-order languages. Boolos and Jeffrey (1974) contains a proof of the undecidability of first-order logic (though to reach Theorem 1.13 above from its results, some coding devices are needed).

Suggested further reading

There are many places where the subjects of this chapter can be pursued to a deeper level. Of those mentioned already in this chapter, Boolos and Jeffrey (1974) is a clear introductory text aimed at philosophers, while Hodges (1983) is a survey with an eye on philosophical issues. Ebbinghaus et al. (1984) is highly recommended for those prepared to face some nontrivial mathematics. Of older books, Church (1956) is still valuable for its philosophical and historical remarks, and Tarski (1983) is outstanding for its clear treatment of fundamental questions.

References

Barwise, J. and Etchemendy, J. 1999: *Tarski's World 5.1*, available with *Language, Proof and Logic*, (Seven Bridges Press, New York and London).

Boolos, G. S. and Jeffrey, R. C. 1974: *Computability and Logic*, (Cambridge University Press, Cambridge).

Church, A. 1956: *Introduction to Mathematical Logic*, (Princeton University Press, Princeton, NJ).

Ebbinghaus, H.-D., Flum, J. and Thomas, W. 1984: *Mathematical Logic*, (Springer, New York).

Gallier, J. H. 1986: *Logic for Computer Science: Foundations of Automated Theorem Proving*, (Harper and Row, New York).

Gentzen, G. 1969: "Untersuchungen über das Logische Schliessen," translated in *The Collected Papers of Gerhard Gentzen*, M. Szabo, ed., (North-Holland, Amsterdam), 68–131.

Hilbert, D. and Ackermann, W. 1950: *Grundzuge der Theoretische Logik* (1928); English translation *Principles of Mathematical Logic*, R. E. Luce, ed., (Chelsea Publishing Company, New York).

Hintikka, J. 1973: *Logic, Language-Games and Information*, (Oxford University Press, Oxford).

Hodges, W. 1983: "Elementary Predicate Logic," in *Handbook of Philosophical Logic – Vol. I: Elements of Classical Logic*, D. M. Gabbay and F. Guenthner, eds., (D. Reidel, Dordrecht), 1–131.

Hodges, W. 1997: *A Shorter Model Theory*, (Cambridge University Press, Cambridge).

Hodges, W. 1998: "The Laws of Distribution for Syllogism," *Notre Dame Journal of Formal Logic*, 39, 221–30.

Kleene, S. C. 1952: *Introduction to Metamathematics*, (North-Holland, Amsterdam).

Sundholm, G. 1983: "Systems of Deduction," in *Handbook of Philosophical Logic – Vol. I: Elements of Classical Logic*, D. M. Gabbay and F. Guenthner, eds., (D. Reidel, Dordrecht), 133–88.

Tarski, A. 1983: "The Concept of Truth in Formalized Languages," in *Logic, Semantics, Metamathematics, Papers from 1923 to 1938*, J. H. Woodger, tr., and J. Corcoran, ed., (Hackett Publishing Co., Indianapolis), 152–278.

Tarski, A. and Vaught, R. 1957: "Arithmetical Extensions of Relational Systems," *Compositio Math.*, 13, 81–102.

Chapter 2

Classical Logic II: Higher-Order Logic

Stewart Shapiro

2.1. Introduction and Overview

A typical interpreted formal language has (first-order) variables that range over a collection of objects, sometimes called a *domain-of-discourse*. The domain is what the formal language is about. A language may also contain *second-order variables* that range over properties, sets, or relations on the items in the domain-of-discourse, or over functions from the domain to itself. For example, the sentence 'Alexander has all the qualities of a great leader' would naturally be rendered with a second-order variable ranging over qualities. Similarly, the sentence 'there is a property that holds of all and only the prime numbers' has a variable ranging over properties of natural numbers. *Third-order variables* range over properties of properties, sets of sets, functions from properties to sets, etc. For example, according to some logicist accounts, the number 4 is the property shared by all properties that apply to exactly four objects in the domain. Accordingly, the number 4 is a third-order item. Fourth-order variables, and beyond, are characterized similarly. The phrase 'higher-order variable' refers to the variables beyond first-order.

A language is first-order if it has first-order variables and no others. A language is second-order if it has first-order and second-order variables and no others, etc. A language is *higher-order* if it is at least second-order.

The study of first-order formal languages is sometimes called *first-order* logic, or elementary logic. It occupies the bulk of contemporary logical theory. Most textbooks either ignore higher-order languages or else give them passing mention or brief treatment as an afterthought. However, virtually all of the founders of modern mathematical logic, such as Frege (1879), Peano (1889), and Whitehead and Russell (1910), presented higher-order languages. First-order logic appeared as a separate study when some authors separated out first-order languages as *subsystems* for special treatment. Hilbert and Ackermann (1950 [1928]) dub first-order logic the '*restricted* functional calculus.' (For more on the historical emergence of first-order logic, see Moore (1996 [1980]), Moore (1988) and Shapiro (1991, ch. 7).)

The early study of first-order logic revealed a number of important features [see chapter 1, esp. sections 1.9, 1.10]. *Gödel's completeness theorem*, first published in 1931, is that there is a complete, sound, and effective deductive system D for first-order logic: if Γ is a set of formulas in a first-order language and Φ is a single formula in that language, then Φ is deducible from Γ in D iff (if and only if) Φ is satisfied by every model of Γ. It follows that first-order logic is *compact*: for every set Γ of first-order formulas, if every finite subset of Γ is satisfiable, then Γ itself is satisfiable. The *downward Löwenheim–Skolem theorem* is that if Γ is a finite or denumerable set of first-order formulas that is satisfied by a model whose domain is infinite, then Γ is satisfied in a model whose domain is the natural numbers. The *upward Löwenheim–Skolem theorem* is that if Γ is a set of first-order formulas such that for each natural number n, Γ is satisfied in a model whose domain has at least n elements, then for every infinite cardinal κ, Γ is satisfied in a model whose domain has cardinality at least κ.

These results are sometimes called 'limitative theorems,' since they indicate restrictions on the expressive resources of first-order languages. Many central mathematical notions, such as finitude, countability, and well-foundedness cannot be characterized in any first-order language, nor can there be an adequate description of structures like the natural numbers, the real numbers, and Euclidean space. None of these limitative theorems apply to higher-order languages, and there are second-order characterizations of the aforementioned concepts and structures. Second- and higher-order languages thus have strong expressive resources, almost as strong as the informal languages of mathematics. As a result, they are difficult to study, perhaps intractable. Cowles (1979, p. 129) put the situation well:

> It is well-known that first-order logic has a limited ability to express many of the concepts studied by mathematicians . . . [and] first-order logic . . . [has] an extensively developed and well-understood model theory. On the other hand, full second-order logic has all the expressive power needed to do mathematics, but has an unworkable model theory.

Barwise (1985, p. 5), wrote, "As logicians, we do our subject a disservice by convincing others that logic is first-order and then convincing them that almost none of the concepts of modern mathematics can really be captured in first-order logic." He concluded that "one thing is certain. There is no going back to the view that logic is first-order logic."

Section 2.2 presents a brief account of the languages, deductive system, and semantics of second-order logic, with brief mention of higher-order logic along the way. Section 2.3 provides sketches of the basic meta-theory, focusing on the fate of the limitative theorems and the expressive resources of second-order languages. The final section concerns general issues of logic-choice that underlie the trade-off between higher-order logic, with its 'semantics complex enough to say something,' and first-order logic with a semantics 'simple enough to say something *about*' (Cowles, 1979, p. 129).

2.2. What Higher-Order Logic is

Here we present the basics of a higher-order logical system, including a sketch of several formal languages, a deductive system, and several different model-theoretic semantics. For a fuller treatment, see Shapiro (1991, ch. 3).

2.2.1. Languages and deductive systems

A *formal language* is, in part, a set of strings on a fixed alphabet. The strings are called *well-formed-formulas* (wff), or simply *formulas*. For each language, a set K consisting of the *non-logical* terminology is designated. In arithmetic, for example, K would be $\{0, s, +, \cdot\}$, the symbols for zero, successor, addition, and multiplication.

The reader is assumed to have some exposure to first-order logic; see [chapter 1], Boolos and Jeffrey (1989) or Mendelson (1987), for example. Our first group of languages, called L1K, is first-order without identity. Variables are lower-case Roman letters toward the end of the alphabet, with or without numerical subscripts. As noted above, these are the *first-order variables*. The connectives are negation $\neg$, conjunction &, disjunction $\vee$, material implication $\rightarrow$, and the material biconditional $\equiv$. The language has a universal quantifier $\forall$ and an existential quantifier $\exists$. A *sentence* is a formula without free variables, and a *theory* is a set of formulas.

A *first-order language* with *identity* L1K= is obtained from L1K by adding a binary relation symbol =. The identity symbol is regarded as logical and is not in K. If t and u are terms, then we abbreviate $\neg t = u$ as $t \neq u$.

The language L2K is obtained from L1K (not L1K=) by adding a stock of *relation variables* and *function variables*. These are called *second-order variables*. Relation variables are upper-case Roman letters toward the end of the alphabet, and function variables letters like f, g, and h. Sometimes a superscript is used to indicate the *degree*, or number of places, of each second-order variable: X^1 is a monadic predicate variable; X^2 is a binary relation variable; f^1 is a unary function variable; f^2 is a binary function variable, etc. In most cases, the context determines the degree of a variable, and so we omit the superscript.

Let $\langle t \rangle_n$ represent a finite sequence of terms $t_1, \ldots, t_n$, and let $\langle v \rangle_n$ represent a finite sequence of *distinct* first-order variables $v_1, \ldots, v_n$. The form $\forall \langle v \rangle_n$ is an abbreviation of $\forall v_1 \cdots \forall v_n$. There are four new formation rules:[1]

If f^n is an n place *function variable* and $\langle t \rangle_n$ a sequence of n terms, then $f^n \langle t \rangle_n$ is a term.

If R^n is an n place *relation variable* and $\langle t \rangle_n$ a sequence of n terms, then $R^n \langle t \rangle_n$ is an atomic formula.

If Φ is a formula and V^n a relation variable, then $(\forall V^n \Phi)$ is a formula.

If Φ is a formula and f^n a function variable, then $(\forall f^n \Phi)$ is a formula.

The existential quantifiers are introduced as abbreviations:

$$\exists V^n \Phi: \neg \forall V^n \neg \Phi$$

$$\exists f^n \Phi: \neg \forall f^n \neg \Phi$$

Thus, for example, $\exists X \forall x \neg Xx$ asserts the existence of an 'empty' property, one which applies to nothing, and $\exists X \forall x Xx$ asserts the existence of a 'universal' property.

The symbol for identity between (first-order) objects is also introduced as an abbreviation. The relevant principle is the *identity of indiscernibles*:

$$t = u: \forall X(Xt \equiv Xu)$$

in which t and u are terms. This definition/abbreviation is not meant as a deep philosophical thesis about Identity.

Consider the sentences:

$$\exists f[\forall x \forall y(fx = fy \rightarrow x = y) \; \& \; \exists x \forall y fy \neq x]$$

$$\exists f \exists x \forall P[(Px \; \& \; \forall w(Pw \rightarrow Pfw)) \rightarrow \forall x Px]$$

Notice that these sentences have no non-logical terms. The first 'asserts' that the domain is (Dedekind) infinite, while the second asserts that the domain is at most countable.

At this stage, a symbol for identity between second-order items like relations and functions is not included. This avoids, or at least postpones, a sticky philosophical issue concerning the nature of the items in the range of the second-order variables. Among contemporary authors, Quine is a longstanding and persistent critic of second-order logic. One of his early attacks (Quine, 1941) targets traditional systems in which the second-order variables range over *intensional* entities like properties, propositional functions, or attributes. Quine is skeptical of the existence of such entities, since there is no consensus on *which* properties, say, exist, nor on conditions under which two properties are identical or distinct. Is the property of being an equilateral triangle the same property as that of being an equiangular triangle? Quine's slogan "no entity without identity" indicates that one is not entitled to speak of entities unless there is a clear and determinate criterion of identity on them. Quine argues that these intractable metaphysical matters should not soil our pristine work in logic and the foundations of mathematics. Trying to be helpful, he suggests that variables ranging over properties be replaced with variables ranging over respectable *extensional* entities like sets, so it is possible to 'identify' the property which applies to m and m alone with the singleton set $\{m\}$.

For the present study, one can think of relations and functions as extensional, or as intensional, or one can leave it open. Little turns on this here and so words like 'property', 'class', and 'set' are used interchangeably.[2]

Some advocates of intensional entities, like properties or attributes, argue that they must be defined or constructed in *levels*, so that properties defined at a given level become available for use in definitions at later levels; see, for example, Whitehead and Russell (1910) or for a readable and sympathetic development, see Hazen (1983). The relevant thesis is sometimes called the *vicious circle principle*. Accordingly, a relation is *predicative*, or of level 0, if it can be defined without referring to relations. A relation is of level 1 if it is not predicative, but can be defined with reference to predicative relations only. A relation is of level 2 if it is not of level 1 but can be defined with reference to level 1 and predicative relations. To develop this, it might be stipulated that each higher-order variable have a numerical subscript to indicate its level. For example, the sentence $\forall P_3 \exists Q_1 \forall x (Q_1 x \equiv P_3 x)$ asserts that for each level 3 predicate there is a level 1 predicate with the same extension. Call the resulting language L2pK, with the 'p' standing for 'predicative'. I do not have much to say about ramified, or predicative, languages, except by way of comparison.

There are two directions for further expansion of our languages. One concerns the set K of non-logical terminology. Second-order variables, as well as non-logical predicate, relation, and function names, may be called *higher-order terms*, since they denote relations and functions. By way of analogy, this opens the possibility of non-logical symbols (in K) for functions on relations, etc. An example would be a property TWO of properties such that TWO(P) 'asserts' that P applies to exactly two things.

A second expansion is to introduce *variables* for relations on relations, functions of predicates, functions of functions, etc. These would be *third-order* variables. Then one could add non-logical constants (to K) for relations on functions of predicates, and the like, and one could add *fourth-order* variables ranging over such things, thus producing a fourth-order language, and so on.

These higher-order languages can also be ramified. Each variable would be annotated somehow to indicate both its *type*, the kinds of objects, relations, etc. it applies to, and its *level*, the place in the hierarchy at which it is defined. A type 3 level 0 predicate would be a predicate of type 2 predicates defined by reference to type 2 relations. A type 3 level 1 predicate would be a predicate of type 2 predicates defined by reference to type 3 level 0 relations, etc. This ramified type theory is a notational nightmare.

2.2.2. Deductive system

Assuming that the reader is familiar with a standard first-order deductive system, this section presents an extension to the second-order languages L2K. First the quantifier axioms and rules to the second-order quantifiers are adapted. For a Frege–Church type system, these would be:

$\forall X^n \Phi(X^n) \to \Phi(T)$, where T is either an n place relation variable free for X^n in Φ, or an n place relation letter in the set K of non-logical terminology.

$\forall f^n \Phi(f^n) \to \Phi(p)$, where p is either an n place function variable free for f^n in Φ, or a non-logical n place function letter.

From $\Phi \to \Psi(X)$ infer $\Phi \to \forall X \Psi(X)$, provided that X does not occur free in Φ, or in any premise of the deduction.

From $\Phi \to \Psi(f)$ infer $\Phi \to \forall f \Psi(f)$, provided that f does not occur free in Φ, or in any premise of the deduction.

Next there is the axiom scheme of *comprehension*:

$$\exists X^n \forall \langle x \rangle_n (X^n \langle x \rangle_n \equiv \Phi \langle x \rangle_n)$$

one instance for each formula Φ in L2K and each relation variable X^n, provided that X^n does not occur free in Φ. The scheme registers the thesis that every formula determines a relation or, more precisely, for every formula there is a relation with the same extension.

The final item is a form of the axiom of choice:[3]

$$\forall X^{n+1}(\forall \langle x \rangle_n \exists y X^{n+1} \langle x \rangle_n y \to \exists f^n \forall \langle x \rangle_n X^{n+1} \langle x \rangle_n f \langle x \rangle_n)$$

The antecedent of this conditional asserts that for each sequence $\langle x \rangle_n$ there is at least one y such that the sequence $\langle x \rangle_n y$ satisfies X^{n+1}. The consequent asserts the existence of a function that 'picks out' one such y for each $\langle x \rangle_n$.

Call this deductive system D2. Recall that the language L2K does not contain a primitive symbol for (first-order) identity. Rather, $x = y$ is taken to be an abbreviation of

$$\forall X(Xx \equiv Xy)$$

To justify this, one should derive the counterparts of the identity-axioms of L1K=:

$\forall x(x = x)$, which comes to $\forall x \forall X(Xx \equiv Xx)$

For each formula Φ, $\forall x \forall y(x = y \to (\Phi(x) \to \Phi(y)))$, which comes to $\forall x \forall y[\forall X(Xx \equiv Xy) \to (\Phi(x) \to \Phi(y))]$ (with the proviso that y be free for x in $\Phi(x)$).

These are tedious exercises in Frege–Church type systems, and they are virtually immediate in their natural deduction counterparts.

It is straightforward, but perhaps tedious, to establish an indiscernibility principle for relation variables:

$$\vdash_{D2} \forall \langle x \rangle_n (P \langle x \rangle_n \equiv Q \langle x \rangle_n) \to (\Phi(P) \to \Phi(Q))$$

for each formula Φ such that Q is free for P in $\Phi(P)$. The (meta-theoretic) proof of this principle proceeds by induction on the complexity of the formula Φ. This partly justifies an extensional orientation toward the higher-order terminology.

The deductive system needs to be modified for the ramified languages L2pK. Recall that each relation variable of L2pK is to contain a subscript to indicate its level in the hierarchy of definition. Each relation must be definable in terms of variables ranging over lower-level relations. The distinctive feature of the ramified system is its comprehension scheme. Recall the unramified version:

$$\exists X^n \forall \langle x \rangle_n (X^n \langle x \rangle_n \equiv \Phi \langle x \rangle_n)$$

If the formula Φ itself contains bound higher-order variables, then the corresponding instance of the comprehension scheme is called *impredicative*, and it represents a violation of the 'vicious circle principle' that motivates the ramification. Thus, one can replace the unrestricted comprehension scheme with an axiom scheme of *ramified comprehension*:

$\exists X_i \forall \langle x \rangle_n (X_i \langle x \rangle_n \equiv \Phi(\langle x \rangle_n))$, provided that X_i has degree n and the level of each relation variable (free or bound) that occurs in Φ is *less than i*.

It is straightforward to extend the other quantifier rules to the ramified system. First, if $j \le i$ and X_j has the same degree as X_i and is free for X_i in Φ, then $\forall X_i \Phi(X_i) \to \Phi(X_j)$ is an axiom. That is, if Φ holds for all relations of a certain degree and level, then Φ holds of any relation of the same degree and the same or lower level. The other rule, from $\Phi \to \Psi$ infer $\Phi \to \forall X_i \Psi$ (provided that X_i does not occur free in Φ or in any premise of the deduction) carries over without change. Call this deductive system D2p. The axiom of choice is *not* included, since the philosophical tendency underlying ramified systems is to restrict the variables to *definable* relations.

The aforementioned derivations in D2 of the first-order identity axioms cannot be carried out in D2p, since they involve the full comprehension principle. In fact, it is not clear that a satisfactory characterization of identity can be given in L2pK.

Whitehead and Russell (1910) include an *axiom of reducibility*:

$$\forall X_i \exists Y_0 \forall x (Y_0 x \equiv X_i x)$$

asserting that for every level i relation, there is a predicative relation with the same extension. This has the effect of collapsing the levels and making the system equivalent to D2 (minus the axiom of choice).

Deductive systems for the further extensions of L2K and L2pK, to third- and higher-order languages, are straightforward extensions of those just considered, and so will not be given here.

2.2.3. Semantics

This sub-section presents three model-theoretic semantics for the unramified second-order languages L2K. Familiarity with standard model-theoretic semantics for first-order languages is assumed [see chapter 1], with just this pause to establish notation. Each *model* or interpretation of the first-order L1K or L1K= is a structure $M = \langle d, I \rangle$, in which d is a non-empty set, the *domain* of the model, and I is an *interpretation function* that assigns appropriate items constructed from d to the non-logical terminology. For example, if b is an individual constant in K, then $I(b)$ is a member of d, and if B is a binary relation symbol in K, then $I(B)$ is a subset of $d \times d$. A *variable-assignment s* is a function from the variables of L1K to d.

For each model and assignment, there is a *denotation function* that assigns a member of the domain to each term of the language. The relation of *satisfaction* between models, assignments, and formulas is then defined in the usual manner. If a model M and an assignment s on M satisfy Φ, then we write $M, s \vDash \Phi$. If $M, s \vDash \Phi$ for every assignment s and every formula Φ in a set Γ, then M is said to be a *model of* Γ. A formula Φ is a *semantic consequence* of Γ if for every model M and assignment s on M, if $M, s \vDash \Psi$ for every Ψ in Γ, then $M, s \vDash \Phi$. This is sometimes written $\Gamma \vDash \Phi$.

Our first two semantics for the second-order L2K build on the semantics for its first-order counterpart L1K. Each model has $\langle d, I \rangle$ as a substructure where, as above, d is the domain and I an interpretation of the items in K. What is added in each case is a range for the relation and function variables. For the second-order languages, a *variable assignment* is a function that assigns a member of d to each first-order variable and an appropriate item to each relation and function variable. The denotation function for the terms of L2K is a straightforward extension of the denotation function for L1K. The new clause is:

Let M be a model and s an assignment on M. Let f^n be an n place function variable and $\langle t \rangle_n$ a sequence of n terms. The denotation of $f^n \langle t \rangle_n$ under M, s is the value of the function $s(f^n)$ at the sequence of members of the domain denoted by the members of $\langle t \rangle_n$.

There are three new clauses in the definition of *satisfaction*:

If X^n is a relation variable and $\langle t \rangle_n$ a sequence of n terms, then $M, s \vDash X^n \langle t \rangle_n$ if the sequence of members of the domain denoted by the members of $\langle t \rangle_n$ is an element of $s(X^n)$.

$M, s \vDash \forall X \Phi$ if $M, s' \vDash \Phi$, for every assignment s' that agrees with s at every variable except possibly X.

$M, s \vDash \forall f \Phi$ if $M, s' \vDash \Phi$, for every assignment s' that agrees with s at every variable except possibly f.

All that remains is to specify the range of the second-order variables.

Our first specimen is *standard semantics*, which makes the logic properly second-order. A *standard model* of L2K is the same as a model of the first-order L1K, namely a structure $\langle d, I \rangle$. A *variable-assignment* is a function that assigns a member of d to each first-order variable, a subset of d^n to each n place relation variable, and a function from d^n to d to each n place function variable. Thus, under standard semantics, the monadic relation variables range over the entire powerset of the domain – every subset of the domain is in the range of these variables. Similarly, the binary predicate variables range over the entire powerset of $d \times d$, one place function variables range over the collection of all functions from the domain to itself, etc.

The notions of validity and satisfiability are defined in the usual manner: a formula Φ is *standardly valid* or is a *standard logical truth*, if $M, s \vDash \Phi$ for every model M and assignment s on M; a set Γ of formulas is *standardly satisfiable* if there is an M, s such that $M, s \vDash \Phi$ for every Φ in Γ; and Φ is a *standard consequence* of Γ if the union of

Γ with $\{\neg\Phi\}$ is not standardly satisfiable. In the following, 'valid' is sometimes used for 'standardly valid,' 'satisfiable' for 'standardly satisfiable,' etc. This reflects my own preferences, but it is also more or less the received practice.

Notice that a standard model for L2K is the same as a model of its first-order counterpart L1K. That is, in standard semantics, by fixing a domain one thereby fixes the range of both the first-order variables and the second-order variables. There is no further 'interpreting' to be done. This is not the case with the next semantics, where one must separately determine a range for the first-order variables and a range for the second-order variables.

The central feature of *Henkin semantics* is that in a given model, the relation variables range over a *fixed collection* of relations on the domain, which may not include all of the relations. Similarly, the function variables range over a fixed collection of functions on the domain. A *Henkin model* of L2K is a structure $M^H = \langle d, D, F, I \rangle$, in which d is a domain and I an interpretation function, as above. For each n, $D(n)$ is a non-empty subset of the powerset of d^n and $F(n)$ is a non-empty collection of functions from d^n to d. The idea is that $D(n)$ is the range of the n place relation variables and $F(n)$ is the range of the n place function variables. A *variable-assignment* is thus a function s such that s assigns a member of d to each first-order variable (as usual), s assigns a member of $D(n)$ to each n place relation variable, and s assigns a member of $F(n)$ to each n place function variable. In Henkin semantics, then, variable assignments are restricted to those that assign members of the various $D(n)$ and $F(n)$ to the higher-order variables. The notions of *Henkin-validity*, *Henkin-satisfaction*, and *Henkin-consequence* are defined in the straightforward manner.

It is immediate that a standard model of L2K is equivalent to the Henkin model in which for each n, $D(n)$ is the powerset of d^n, and $F(n)$ is the collection of all n place functions from d^n to d. Such Henkin models are sometimes called *full-models*. Let M be a standard model and M^F the corresponding full-model. Then for each assignment s and each formula Φ, $M, s \vDash \Phi$ under standard semantics iff $M^F, s \vDash \Phi$ under Henkin semantics. Thus, if a formula Φ is a Henkin-consequence of a set Γ, then Φ is a standard consequence of Γ. Section 2.3 shows that the converse fails.

On both of these semantical systems, the items in the range of higher-order variables are extensional entities – either sets or functions. However, since there is no symbol for 'higher-order identity' in the language, one is free to maintain an intensional understanding of the higher-order entities. For the purposes of model-theoretic semantics, sets can serve as surrogates for the relevant attributes, properties, or propositional functions. Henkin semantics might be attractive to an advocate of intensional items. Such a philosopher might suggest that in a given Henkin model, the specified range of the monadic relation variables, for example, would be the collection of sets that are the extensions of the relevant attributes, properties, or propositional functions (Cocchiarella, 1996 [1988]). If our advocate of intensional items believes that for every arbitrary collection S of n-tuples on the domain, there is an attribute whose extension is S (and similarly for functions-in-intension), then she will favor standard semantics.

Boolos (1996a [1984], 1996b [1985]) has proposed an alternate way to understand at least the monadic second-order relation variables. According to both standard and Henkin semantics, a monadic, second-order existential quantifier $\exists X$ can be read

There is a set X.

or

There is a property X.

in which case, of course, the locution invokes classes or properties. Against this, Boolos suggests that the quantifier be considered a counterpart of a *plural quantifier*,

There are (objects)

in natural language. Consider this sentence:

Some critics admire only one another.

It has a (more or less) straightforward second-order rendering, taking the class of critics to be the domain of discourse:

$\exists X(\exists x Xx \,\&\, \forall x \forall y((Xx \,\&\, Axy) \to (x \neq y \,\&\, Xy)))$

According to standard or Henkin semantics, the formula would correspond to

There is a non-empty *class* (or property) X of critics such that for any x in X and any y, if x admires y, then $x \neq y$ and y is in X.

But this implies the existence of a class (or property), while the original 'some critics admire only one another' does not, at least *prima facie*.

Natural languages, like English, allow the plural construction and, in particular, English contains plural quantifiers like

There are some dogs that like each other and hate most cats.

Boolos argues that the plural construction be employed in the meta-language used in developing formal semantics. The relevant locution is

There are objects X, such that . . . .

As in the first-order case, the variable serves as a place-holder, for purposes of cross reference, much like a pronoun. Construed this way, a monadic second-order language has *no* ontology beyond that of its first-order counterpart. In set theory, for example, the Russell sentence, $\exists X \forall x(Xx \equiv x \notin x)$, is a consequence of the comprehension scheme. According to standard semantics, it entails that there is a *class* that is not coextensive with any set in the domain. Admittedly, this takes some getting used to. On Boolos's interpretation, however, the Russell sentence reads

There are some sets such that any set is one of them just in case it is not a member of itself.

which is a harmless truism. Omitting the details of Boolos's (1996b [1985]) rigorous, model-theoretic semantics for second-order languages with monadic relation variables, it is worth noting that the end result has similar meta-theoretic properties to standard semantics, as presented here.

2.3. Meta-Theory and Expressive Resources

This section presents some of the main results concerning the ability of second-order languages to capture central mathematical structures and notions. For more detail, see Shapiro (1991, ch. 4, 5).

2.3.1. Henkin semantics

As presented, Henkin semantics is *not* sound for the deductive system D2. Although it is routine to verify that every Henkin model satisfies the axioms and rules of a first-order deductive system and the instances of the second-order quantifier axioms and rules, some Henkin models do not satisfy the comprehension scheme. Consider, for example, a structure $M = \langle d, D, F, I \rangle$ in which d is a set with two members $a \neq b$; $D(2)$ has a single member, the relation $\{\langle a, a \rangle, \langle b, a \rangle\}$; and $F(1)$ has a single member, the identity function. Then M does not satisfy the following instance of the comprehension scheme:

$$\exists X \forall x \forall y (Xxy \equiv x \neq x)$$

In effect, this axiom asserts the existence of an empty binary relation, but M does not have one. Similarly, M, s does not satisfy the axiom of choice.

Define a Henkin model to be *faithful to D2*, or simply *faithful*, if it satisfies the axiom of choice and every instance of the comprehension scheme. That is, a Henkin model is faithful if it contains every relation definable via the comprehension scheme and the functions promised by the axiom of choice. All subsequent discussion is restricted to faithful models.

Soundness is now immediate:

Theorem 2.1 *Soundness* If $\Gamma \vdash_{D2} \Phi$, then Φ is satisfied by every faithful Henkin model that satisfies every member of Γ.

In most respects, languages like L2K under Henkin semantics are like first-order languages. In particular, Henkin semantics is complete, compact, and satisfies both Löwenheim–Skolem theorems.

Theorem 2.2 *Completeness* (Henkin, 1950)   Let Γ be a set of formulas of L2K. If Γ is consistent in D2, then there is a faithful Henkin model that satisfies Γ. Equivalently, for every formula Φ and set Γ, $\Gamma \vdash_{D2} \Phi$ if $M, s \vDash \Phi$ for every faithful Henkin model M and assignment s that satisfies every member of Γ.

The proof is a straightforward adaption of the Henkin construction establishing Gödel's theorem for the completeness of first-order logic (Shapiro (1991, pp. 89–91)).[4]

If the set K of non-logical terminology is countable, then the constructed Henkin model might be called *doubly countable* in that the domain *and* each $D(n)$, $F(n)$ is either finite or denumerably infinite. That is, the constructed model has only countably many relations and functions. Since each infinite domain has uncountably many relations, some (indeed, most) are not in range of the higher-order quantifiers of the indicated Henkin model. Thus, if the constructed Henkin model has an infinite domain, it is not a full model.

As in the first-order case, compactness is a corollary of completeness:

Theorem 2.3 *Compactness*   Let Γ be a set of formulas of L2K. If every finite subset of Γ is satisfiable in a faithful Henkin model, then Γ itself is satisfiable in a faithful Henkin model.

Let $M = \langle d, D, F, I \rangle$ be a Henkin model. Define $M' = \langle d', D', F', I' \rangle$ to be a *Henkin-submodel* of M if

1   $d' \subseteq d$
2   for each natural number n, each relation in $D'(n)$ is the restriction to d' of a relation in $D(n)$
3   each function in $F'(n)$ is the restriction to d' of a function in $F(n)$
4   I' and I assign the same elements to each individual constant, and
5   the interpretation of each predicate, relation, and function symbol under I' is the restriction to d' of its interpretation under I.

Theorem 2.4 *Downward Löwenheim–Skolem theorem*   Let $M = \langle d, D, F, I \rangle$ be a Henkin-model of L2K. Then there is a Henkin-submodel $M' = \langle d', D', F', I' \rangle$ of M such that

1   d' and each $D'(n)$, $F'(n)$ are all at most denumerably infinite (or the cardinality of the set K, if K is uncountable), and
2   if Φ is any formula and s' any variable assignment on M', then there is a corresponding variable assignment s on M such that $M', s' \vDash \Phi$ iff $M, s \vDash \Phi$.

In other words, for every Henkin model M there is a countable Henkin-submodel M' such that M is equivalent to M'.

The proof is a more or less straightforward adaptation of a proof of the corresponding first-order theorem; see Shapiro (1991, pp. 93–4); [see also chapter 1]. It makes essential use of the axiom of choice (in the meta-theory).

As with the first-order case, the next theorem is a corollary of compactness:

Theorem 2.5 *Upward Löwenheim–Skolem theorem*   Let Γ be a set of sentences of L2*K*. If, for each natural number *m*, there is a faithful Henkin model of Γ whose domain has at least *m* elements, then for every infinite cardinal κ there is a faithful Henkin model of Γ whose domain has at least κ-many elements.

A set Γ of sentences is *categorical* if any two models of Γ are isomorphic. As in the first-order case, theorems 2.4 and 2.5 indicate that no theory with an infinite Henkin-model is what may be called 'Henkin-categorical.' Thus, second-order languages with Henkin semantics are not adequate to characterize infinite structures up to isomorphism.

In this regard, the results reported in this sub-section indicate that second-order languages with Henkin semantics are much like first-order languages. One can think of a language like L2*K* as a multi-sorted first-order language, with the predication (or membership) relation between objects and relations (or sets) as non-logical – like the members of *K*. Shapiro (1991, ch. 3, 4) develops a semantics along these lines and shows it to be equivalent to Henkin semantics. In particular, each multi-sorted first-order model is equivalent to a corresponding Henkin model, and vice versa.

When it comes to first-order languages, variables can range over any type of entity, so long as there are coherent things to say about them. Unless a philosopher has qualms about the existence of relations or sets on a domain *d*, there can be no objection to a language like L2*K*. However, with Henkin semantics (restricted to faithful models), the only relations/sets that are assumed to exist are some choice functions and those relations/sets *definable* in the language. The distinctive expressive resources of higher-order logic come when one assumes that the second-order variables range over *every* function and relation/set on *d*. Thus the next subsection turns to standard semantics.

2.3.2.   Standard semantics

One important meta-theorem does carry over from first-order logic to second-order logic with standard semantics. As noted above, D2 is not sound for Henkin semantics. However, since full Henkin models are faithful, D2 is sound for standard semantics:

Theorem 2.6 *Soundness*   Let Γ be a set of formulas and Φ a single formula of L2*K*. If Φ can be deduced from Γ in D2, then Φ is a standard consequence of Γ.

Like the first-order case, the proof is a straightforward check of each axiom and rule of inference. Most of the axioms and rules require no substantial assumptions about the set-theoretic universe underlying the model theory. The clause involving the comprehension scheme uses a principle of separation in the background set theory, and the clause for the axiom of choice uses a principle of choice in the meta-theory. The apparent circularity is the same as in the first-order case. One uses principles in the meta-theory to show that certain axioms and rules are sound. Readers who are uncomfortable with separation or choice can remove those principles from D2.

The primary item here is the *refutation* of completeness, compactness, and the Löwenheim–Skolem theorems for standard semantics. The key items are the existence of categorical axiomatizations of the natural numbers and the real numbers, and Gödel's theorem on the *incompleteness* of arithmetic.

The *language of arithmetic* has $A = \{0, s, +, \cdot\}$ as its set of non-logical terminology. The following axioms are first-order.

Successor axiom: $\quad \forall x(sx \neq 0) \,\&\, \forall x \forall y(sx = sy \rightarrow x = y)$

Addition axiom: $\quad \forall x(x + 0 = x) \,\&\, \forall x \forall y(x + sy = s(x + y))$

Multiplication axiom: $\forall x(x \cdot 0 = 0) \,\&\, \forall x \forall y(x \cdot sy = x \cdot y + x)$

Then there is the *induction axiom*, a proper second-order statement:

Induction axiom: $\quad \forall X[(X0 \,\&\, \forall x(Xx \rightarrow Xsx)) \rightarrow \forall x Xx]$

Let AR (for 'arithmetic') be the conjunction of these four axioms.

Let N be the model of L2A whose domain is the set of natural numbers and which assigns zero to 0, and assigns the successor function, the addition function, and the multiplication function to s, $+$, and $\cdot$, respectively. This, of course, is the intended interpretation. Then $N \vDash AR$. The next theorem is that, in an important sense, N is the *only* (standard) model of AR:

Theorem 2.7 *Categoricity of arithmetic* (Dedekind) Let $M1 = \langle d_1, I_1 \rangle$ and $M2 = \langle d_2, I_2 \rangle$ be two (standard) models in the language L2A. If $M1 \vDash AR$ and $M2 \vDash AR$, then $M1$ and $M2$ are *isomorphic*: there is a one-to-one function f from d_1 onto d_2 that preserves the structure of the models.

(See Shapiro (1991, pp. 82–3) for details of the proof, although Dedekind (1963 [1888]) remains a readable source.) It follows from theorem 2.7 and the fact that $N \vDash AR$ that if M is a model of AR, then the domain of M is denumerably infinite.

Corollary 2.8 Let Φ be a sentence of L2A. Then Φ is true of the natural numbers (i.e., $N \vDash \Phi$) iff $AR \rightarrow \Phi$ is a (standard) logical truth.

In *real analysis*, the non-logical terminology is $B = \{0, 1, +, \cdot, \leq\}$. The first axioms are those of an ordered field, all of which are first-order.[5] The sole second-order statement is the *axiom of completeness*, asserting that every bounded property (or set) has a least upper bound:

$$\forall X\{(\exists y Xy \,\&\, \exists x \forall y(Xy \rightarrow y \leq x)) \rightarrow \exists x[\forall y(Xy \rightarrow y \leq x) \,\&\, \forall z(\forall y(Xy \rightarrow y \leq z) \rightarrow x \leq z)]\}$$

Let AN (for 'analysis') be the conjunction of the axioms of real analysis. The real number structure constitutes the intended model, and AN is categorical:

Theorem 2.9 *Categoricity of analysis* Let $M1$ and $M2$ be two models in the language L2B. If $M1 \vDash AN$ and $M2 \vDash AN$, then $M1$ and $M2$ are isomorphic.

See Barwise and Feferman (1985, p. 84) for a sketch of the proof.

We now refute the analogues of theorems 2.2–5 for L2K with standard semantics. The Löwenheim–Skolem theorems are easiest. Second-order arithmetic, AR, is categorical (theorem 2.7). It has denumerably infinite models and no uncountable models. Second-order analysis, AN, is also categorical (theorem 2.9). It has uncountable models and no countable models. Thus,

Theorem 2.10 Both of the Löwenheim–Skolem theorems fail for second-order languages with standard semantics.

The following purely logical sentence

(FIN) $\quad \forall f \neg (\forall x \forall y (fx = fy \rightarrow x = y) \ \& \ \exists x \forall y (fy \neq x))$

asserts that there is no one-to-one function from the domain to a proper subset of the domain. Thus, FIN is satisfied by all and only those models whose domains are (Dedekind) finite. The compactness of first-order logic and Henkin semantics for L2K indicates that there is no characterization of finitude in those systems. The upward Löwenheim–Skolem theorem entails that any formula that is satisfied in every finite model also has (arbitrarily large) infinite models.

Let Γ be the set of sentences consisting of FIN and

$$\{\exists x_1 \exists x_2 (x_1 \neq x_2), \ \exists x_1 \exists x_2 \exists x_3 (x_1 \neq x_2 \ \& \ x_1 \neq x_3 \ \& \ x_2 \neq x_3), \ldots \}$$

In other words, the set Γ contains a formula asserting that the domain is finite and, for each natural number n, Γ contains a formula asserting that the domain has at least n elements. Thus, Γ is not satisfiable. Let Γ' be any finite subset of Γ, and let m be the maximum number of occurrences of the existential quantifier in any one member of Γ'. Then any structure whose domain has at least m elements satisfies every member of Γ'. Thus, Γ' is satisfiable and we have:

Theorem 2.11 Standard semantics for L2K is not compact.

Our last item is the refutation of completeness. Let D be any effective deductive system that is sound for the language L2A (under standard semantics). Consider the set

$$\Gamma = \{\Phi \mid \vdash_D (AR \rightarrow \Phi)\}.$$

Since D is effective, the set Γ is recursively enumerable and, from corollary 2.8, every member of Γ is true of the natural numbers. Gödel's *in*completeness theorem – see, for example, Gödel (1965 [1934]); [see chapter 4] – is that the collection of true first-order sentences of arithmetic is not recursively enumerable. So let Ψ be a true sentence of first-order arithmetic that is not in Γ. Then, by corollary 2.8 (AR $\rightarrow \Psi$)

is a (standard) logical truth, but $(AR \rightarrow \Psi)$ is not derivable in D. Thus, there is no effective, sound deductive system that is complete for standard semantics:

Theorem 2.12 Let D be any effective deductive system that is sound for L2A. Then D is not weakly complete: there is a logical truth that is not a theorem of D. In short, standard semantics is *inherently incomplete*.

A *fortiori*, D2 is incomplete.

2.3.3. First-order and (standard) second-order theories

In first-order arithmetic, the (second-order) induction principle is replaced by a scheme. If Φ is a formula in the *language* L1$A=$ *of first-order arithmetic*, then

$$(\Phi(0) \ \& \ \forall x(\Phi(x) \rightarrow \Phi(sx))) \rightarrow \forall x \Phi(x)$$

is an axiom scheme of first-order arithmetic. The theory thus has infinitely many axioms.

Similarly, in the characterization AN of real analysis, the second-order item is the principle of completeness, stating that every bounded non-empty set of real numbers has a least upper bound. First-order real analysis is obtained by replacing the single completeness axiom with the *completeness scheme*,

$$(\exists x \Phi(x) \ \& \ \exists x \forall y(\Phi(y) \rightarrow y \leq x)) \rightarrow \exists x [\forall y(\Phi(y) \rightarrow y \leq x) \ \& \ \forall z(\forall y(\Phi(y) \rightarrow y \leq z) \rightarrow x \leq z)]$$

one instance for each formula Φ of the language L1$B=$ of real analysis that contains neither x nor z free.

The difference between, say, second-order real analysis and its first-order counterpart is that, in the latter, one cannot directly state that every non-empty bounded set has a least upper bound. The closest one can come is a separate principle for each such set which is definable by a formula in the language of first-order analysis. The mathematician who uses first-order analysis thus cannot apply the completeness principle to a set until she is assured the set is definable in the relevant language. Since there are sets which are not definable, the first-order theory has models which are not isomorphic to the real numbers. These are sometimes called *non-standard models*. Indeed, the Löwenheim–Skolem theorems indicate that for every infinite cardinal κ, there are models of first-order arithmetic and models of first-order analysis whose domain has cardinality κ. The study of non-standard models has proven fruitful in illuminating the original informal theories.

As noted above, there is a second-order characterization of finitude, but no first-order characterization. There are also second-order characterizations of countability, well-foundedness, minimal closure, and many other central mathematical notions. It follows from the compactness of first-order logic that there are no first-order (or Henkin-second-order) characterizations of these notions. Any consistent attempt to formulate such a characterization of these notions in a first-order (or Henkin-second-order) theory will have unintended models that miss the mark.

Lindström (1969) showed that, in a sense, the limitative properties *characterize* first-order logic. Let L be any model-theoretic type of logic and assume that L has the property of the downward Löwenheim–Skolem theorem. If L is also compact, then there is a sense in which L is equivalent to first-order logic: L cannot make any distinction among models that cannot be made with the corresponding first-order language. For better or worse, then, standard semantics is what makes second-order logic distinctive. The categoricity results and the concomitant failure of the limitative properties are the source of both the expressive strength and the main shortcoming of second-order logic.

2.4. Philosophical Issues: How to Pick a Logic

It is widely agreed – at least implicitly – that mathematicians succeed in describing various notions and structures up to isomorphism and they succeed in communicating information about these structures to each other. Most agree that when mathematicians refer to the 'natural numbers,' the 'real numbers,' etc., they are talking about the same structures. Similarly, there is little doubt among mathematicians and most philosophers that notions like finitude and well-foundedness are clear and unequivocal. In other words, there is a near (but not universal) consensus that the *informal* language of mathematics has expressive resources sufficient for the ordinary description and communication of these basic structures and notions.

Advocates of higher-order logic argue that to capture the semantics of the informal languages of mathematics, a logical system should register the successful description and communication of mathematical structures and concepts. The desideratum is that the expressive resources of the formal languages should match those of the mathematical discourse it models. Wang (1974, p. 154) takes a similar line:

> When we are interested in set theory or classical analysis, the Löwenheim–Skolem theorem is usually taken as a sort of defect (often thought to be inevitable) of the first-order logic . . . [W]hat is established (by Lindström's theorems) is not that first-order logic is the only possible logic but rather that it is the only possible logic when we in a sense deny reality to the concept of uncountable . . .

See also Montague (1965), Corcoran (1996 [1980]), Isaacson (1987), and Shapiro (1991, ch. 5).

Kreisel (1967) delimited some epistemological features of the second-order axiomatizations of mathematical theories. He argued that relying on infinitely many axioms presented via an axiom scheme is unnatural. Suppose, for example, that someone is asked why he believes that each instance of the completeness scheme of first-order real analysis is true of the real numbers. The theorist cannot give a separate justification for each of the infinitely many axioms. Nor can he claim that the scheme characterizes the real numbers since, as already seen, no first-order axiomatization can characterize this structure. Kreisel argued that the reason mathematicians believe the instances of the axiom scheme is that each instance follows from the single second-order completeness *axiom*. It is not clear that the informal generalization over the instances of a scheme is any less problematic than the explicit generalization over properties or sets in the second-order axiom.

A related problem is that each first-order scheme is tied to the ingredients of the particular first-order language in use at the time. Mathematicians, however, are quick to apply the induction or completeness principles to sets regardless of whether they are definable in the given first-order language. Indeed, they usually do not check for definability in this or that language. This is manifest in the practice of embedding structures in each other. For example, when one sees that there is a structure isomorphic to the real numbers in the set-theoretic hierarchy, one can use set theory to shed light on the real numbers. This works by applying the completeness principle of analysis to sets of real numbers definable in set theory, whether or not such sets can be defined in the language of analysis. One cannot tell in advance what resources are needed to shed light on a mathematical structure – even after the structure has been adequately characterized.

In the section on second-order logic of his (otherwise) influential textbook, Church (1956, p. 326n) remarked:

> our definition of the [standard second-order] consequences of a system of postulates ... can be seen to be not essentially different from [that] required for the ... treatment of classical mathematics ... It is true that the non-effective notion of consequence, as we have introduced it ... presupposes a certain absolute notion of ALL propositional functions of individuals. But this is presupposed also in classical mathematics, especially classical analysis.

On the other hand, the expressive power of second-order languages under standard semantics carries a cost. For example, there is a single second-order sentence χ that is a categorical characterization of the first inaccessible rank of the set-theoretic hierarchy. Virtually any truth of any branch of mathematics short of set theory is a logical consequence of χ, and corresponds to a logical truth in the form $\chi \to \Phi$. So mathematical truth for just about any branch of mathematics (short of set theory) can be reduced to second-order *logical truth*. Moreover, there is a second-order sentence, with no non-logical terminology, that is equivalent to the generalized continuum hypothesis. The sentence is logically true if and only if the generalized continuum hypothesis holds; see Shapiro (1991, ch. 5). We have already encountered a second-order sentence equivalent to the axiom of choice. It is perhaps counterintuitive to hold that these mathematical statements are principles *of logic*.

For these reasons, some authors argue that second-order logic (with standard semantics) is not logic at all, but is rather an obscure form of mathematics. A first-order theory, with an intended interpretation, has variables ranging over a domain-of-discourse. A second-order theory has variables ranging over the entire powerset of the domain, a larger collection. Quine (1986, ch. 5), for example, argues that with the presence of set-theoretic notions in the language, one crosses the border out of logic, into mathematics. He calls second-order logic "set theory in disguise," a wolf "in sheep's clothing." The idea, presumably, is that proper mathematics is powerful and awe-inspiring; logic is, or ought to be, a mere 'sheep': "Set theory's staggering existential assumptions are . . . hidden . . . in the tacit shift from schematic predicate letter to quantifiable set variable" (p. 68).[6]

Come right back. A popular theme in contemporary philosophy, at least in North America, is that there are no sharp borders between disciplines. Quine himself is a champion of this idea, arguing that in the seamless 'web of belief' there is no sharp distinction – no difference in kind – between mathematics and, say, zoology. Mathematics occurs throughout the 'web.' Why should logic, especially the logic of *mathematics*, be different? Why expect logic to be free of substantial expressive resources?

In short, most parties to this debate agree that the *informal* language of mathematics is adequate to describe and communicate the various structures and notions. The second-order camp follows Church and accepts a mathematically rich language, while the first-order camp, led by Quine, argues that logic must fail where informal mathematics succeeds.[7] Perhaps the boundary dispute is not of much interest. As long as no deceit is intended, one can apply the honorific label 'logic' at will. The deeper issues concern the purposes of logical study. Historically, one goal of logical study was to present a canon of inference. The plan would be to present a *calculus* which codifies correct inference patterns. From this perspective, second-order logic is a non-starter. It follows from Gödel's completeness theorem that the consequence relation of first-order logic is effective, but as we have seen, second-order logic (with standard semantics) is inherently incomplete. Indeed, the set of second-order logical truths is not even definable in (second-order) arithmetic.

The presentation of calculi as canons of inference do not exhaust the traditional scope of logic. It is widely (but not universally) held that deductive systems must themselves adhere to a prior notion of *logical consequence*. Must this prior notion be effective? Informally, logical consequence is sometimes defined in terms of the *meanings* of a certain collection of terms, the so-called 'logical terminology.' This is consonant with the slogan that logical consequence is a matter of 'form.' Most theorists agree that the truth functional connectives ('¬,' '&,' '∨,' '→,' '≡') and the first-order quantifiers are logical. From this perspective, the issue of second-order logic is whether the membership (or predication) relation and bound variables ranging over relations or classes are logical. We have here another border dispute, but perhaps one can be eclectic. In correspondence, Tarski once wrote (1987, p. 29):

> sometimes it seems . . . convenient to include mathematical terms, like the [membership] relation, in the class of logical ones, and sometimes I prefer to restrict myself to terms of 'elementary [i.e., first-order] logic.' Is any problem involved here?

Let a thousand flowers bloom.

Suggested further reading

The technical development of higher-order logic can be found in some textbooks on mathematical logic. Hilbert and Ackerman (1950 [1928]) remains a readable source, while Church (1956) and Boolos and Jeffrey (1989) provide a more contemporary perspective.

Van Heijenoort (1967) collects together many of the seminal historical works on the subject (in English translation). My own Shapiro (1991) consists of a detailed development of second-order logic, and a defense of its use in foundational studies, as well as an extensive bibliography. Quine (1986, ch. 5), Jané (1993), Tharp (1996 [1975]), and Weston (1996 [1976]) constitute a sample of the opposition to second-order logic. The Shapiro (1996) anthology contains reprints of journal articles both defending and attacking higher-order logic, and articles on the Skolem paradox. Shapiro (1999) is a reply to some of the critics of Shapiro (1991), and includes references to some of the literature. Lewis (1991) includes an informative treatment of the philosophical issues concerning plural quantification. The contrasting shortcomings of first-order logic and higher-order logic has led to the development and study of systems that are, in a sense, intermediate between them. See Shapiro (2001) for a broad overview and Barwise and Feferman (1985) for some highly technical samples.

Notes

1 For the sake of readability, I do not always note the distinction between object language variables (like x_1) and meta-variables (like v_1) that range over object language variables. Context will indicate which is meant. Incidentally, no generality would be lost if we left out function variables, since an $n+1$ place relation variable can serve as a surrogate for an n place function variable.

2 If pressed, I would follow Quine and adopt an extensional interpretation. One option would be to take the identity sign as an abbreviation, using the *principle of extensionality*.

$$P = Q \equiv \forall \langle x \rangle_n (P \langle x \rangle_n \equiv Q \langle x \rangle_n) \qquad \text{and} \qquad f = g \equiv \forall \langle x \rangle_n (f \langle x \rangle_n = g \langle x \rangle_n)$$

3 The axiom of choice has a troubled history, but it now is essential to most branches of mathematics, including mathematical logic. If the axiom of choice is dropped from the deductive system, it should be replaced with a principle of comprehension for functions (or one could just omit the variables ranging over functions).

4 In a presentation to a conference honoring Alonzo Church (Buffalo, May 1990), Henkin remarked he first discovered the completeness of higher-order logic under (what is here called) Henkin semantics, and only later adapted the proof to the first-order case.

5 The axioms for an ordered field are that addition and multiplication are associative and commutative, multiplication is distributive over addition, 0 is the additive identity, 1 is the multiplicative identity, every element has an additive inverse, every element but 0 has a multiplicative inverse, $\leq$ is a linear order, and the elements greater than or equal to 0 are closed under addition and multiplication. See any treatment of abstract algebra, for example MacLane and Birkhoff (1967, ch. IV, V).

6 Historically the 'shift' went in the other direction, from the 'quantifiable variable' of higher-order logic to the non-logical schemes of first-order logic.

7 There is another, currently less popular line that rejects the presupposition that the mathematical structures and notions in question are unequivocal. The Löwenheim–Skolem theorems indicate that there are no unambiguous notions of 'finite', 'countable', 'natural number', etc. This skeptical view is sometimes called 'Skolemite relativism'. The underlying thesis is that the model theory of first-order logic (or Henkin semantics) accurately reflects the ontological/epistemic/semantic situation. There is nothing unequivocal to capture or describe with either formal or informal languages of mathematics. So advocates of this relativism favor first-order logic.

References

Barwise, J. 1985: "Model-Theoretic Logics: Background and Aims," in Barwise and Feferman (1985, 3–23).

Barwise, J. and Feferman, S. 1985: *Model-Theoretic Logics*, (Springer-Verlag, New York).

Boolos, G. 1996a: "To Be is to Be a Value of a Variable (or to Be Some Values of Some Variables)," *Journal of Philosophy*, 81 (1984), 430–49; reprinted in Shapiro (1996, 331–50).

Boolos, G. 1996b: "Nominalist Platonism," *Philosophical Review*, 94 (1985), 327–44; reprinted in Shapiro (1996, 351–68).

Boolos, G. and Jeffrey, R. 1989: *Computability and Logic*, 3rd edn., (Cambridge University Press, Cambridge).

Church, A. 1956: *Introduction to Mathematical Logic*, (Princeton University Press, Princeton, NJ).

Cocchiarella, N. 1996: "Predication versus Membership in the Distinction between Logic as Language and Logic as Calculus," *Synthese*, 77 (1988), 37–72; reprinted in Shapiro (1996, 473–508).

Corcoran, J. 1996: "Categoricity," *History and Philosophy of Logic*, 1 (1980), 187–207; reprinted in Shapiro (1996, 241–61).

Cowles, J. 1979: "The Relative Expressive Power of Some Logics Extending First-Order Logic," *Journal of Symbolic Logic*, 44, 129–46.

Dedekind, R. 1963: *Was sind und was sollen die Zahlen?*, (Vieweg, Brunswick), 1888; tr. as "The Nature and Meaning of Numbers," in *Essays on the Theory of Numbers*, W. W. Beman, ed., (Dover, New York), 31–115.

Frege, G. 1967: *Begriffschrift, eine der arithmetischen nachgebildete Formelsprache des reinen Denkens*, (Louis Nebert, Halle), 1879; tr. in van Heijenoort (1967, 1–82).

Gödel, K. 1965: "On Undecidable Propositions of Formal Mathematical Systems," (1934), in *The Undecidable*, M. Davis, ed., (The Raven Press, Hewlett, NY), 39–74.

Hazen, A. 1983: "Predicative Logics," in *Handbook of Philosophical Logic*, Vol. 1, D. Gabbay and F. Guenthner, eds., (D. Reidel, Dordrecht), 331–407.

Henkin, L. 1950: "Completeness in the Theory of Types," *Journal of Symbolic Logic*, 15, 81–91.

Hilbert, D. and Ackermann, W. 1950: *Grundzüge der theoritischen Logik*, (Springer-Verlag, Berlin), 1928; *Principles of Mathematical Logic*, tr. by L. Hammond, G. Leckie and F. Steinhardt, (Chelsea Publishing Company, New York).

Isaacson, D. 1987: "Arithmetical Truth and Hidden Higher-Order Concepts," in *Logic Colloquium 85*, ed. by The Paris Logic Group, (North Holland, Amsterdam), 147–69.

Jané, I. 1993: "A Critical Appraisal of Second-Order Logic," *History and Philosophy of Logic*, 14, 67–86; reprinted in Shapiro (1996, 177–96).

Kreisel, G. 1967: "Informal Rigour and Completeness Proofs," in *Problems in the Philosophy of Mathematics*, I. Lakatos, ed., (North Holland, Amsterdam), 138–86.

Lewis, D. 1991: *Parts of Classes*, (Blackwell, Oxford).

Lindström, P. 1969: "On Extensions of Elementary Logic," *Theoria*, 35, 1–11.

MacLane, S. and Birkhoff, G. 1967: *Algebra*, (MacMillan, New York).

Mendelson, E. 1987: *Introduction to Mathematical Logic*, 3rd edn., (van Nostrand, Princeton, NJ).

Montague, R. M. 1965: "Set Theory and Higher-Order Logic," in *Formal Systems and Recursive Functions*, J. Crossley and M. Dummett, eds., (North Holland, Amsterdam), 131–48.

Moore, G. H. 1988: "The Emergence of First-Order Logic," in *History and Philosophy of Modern Mathematics*, Minnesota Studies in the Philosophy of Science, Vol. 11, W. Aspray and P. Kitcher, eds., (University of Minnesota Press, Minneapolis), 95–135.

Moore, G. H. 1996: "Beyond First-Order Logic: The Historical Interplay between Logic and Set Theory," *History and Philosophy of Logic*, 1 (1980), 95–137; reprinted in Shapiro (1996, 3–45).

Peano, G. 1967: *Arithmetices principia, nova methodo exposita*, (Bocca, Turin), 1889; trans. in van Heijenoort (1967, 85–97).

Quine, W. V. O. 1941: "Whitehead and the Rise of Modern Logic," in *The Philosophy of Alfred North Whitehead*, P. A. Schilpp, ed., (Tudor Publishing Company, New York), 127–63.

Quine, W. V. O. 1986: *Philosophy of Logic*, 2nd edn., (Prentice-Hall, Englewood Cliffs, NJ).

Shapiro, S. 1991: *Foundations without Foundationalism: A Case for Second-Order Logic*, (Oxford University Press, Oxford).

Shapiro, S. (ed.) 1996: *The Limits of Logic: Higher-Order Logic and the Löwenheim–Skolem Theorem*, (Dartmouth Publishing Company, Aldershot).

Shapiro, S. 1999: "Do not Claim Too Much: Second-Order Logic and First-Order Logic," *Philosophia Mathematica*, 7, 42–64.

Shapiro, S. 2001: "Systems between First-Order Logic and Second-Order Logics," in *Handbook of Philosophical Logic*, Vol. I, 2nd edn., D. Gabbay, ed., (Kluwer Academic Publisher, Dordrecht, 131–84.)

Tarski, A. 1987: "A Philosophical Letter of Alfred Tarski," (ed. by Morton White), *Journal of Philosophy*, 84, 28–32.

Tharp, L. 1996: "Which Logic is the Right Logic?," *Synthese*, 31 (1975), 1–31; reprinted in Shapiro (1996, 47–67).

van Heijenoort, J. (ed.) 1967: *From Frege to Gödel: A Sourcebook in Mathematical Logic*, (Harvard University Press, Cambridge, MA).

Wang, H. 1974: *From Mathematics to Philosophy*, (Routledge & Kegan Paul, London).

Weston, T. 1996: "Kreisel, the Continuum Hypothesis and Second-Order Set Theory," *Journal of Philosophical Logic*, 5 (1976), 281–98; reprinted in Shapiro (1996, 385–402).

Whitehead, A. N. and Russell, B. 1910: *Principia Mathematica 1*, (Cambridge University Press, Cambridge).

Chapter 3

Set Theory

John P. Burgess

Set theory is the branch of mathematics concerned with the general properties of aggregates of points, numbers, or arbitrary elements. It was created in the late nineteenth century, mainly by Georg Cantor. After the discovery of certain contradictions euphemistically called paradoxes, it was reduced to axiomatic form in the early twentieth century, mainly by Ernst Zermelo and Abraham Fraenkel. Thereafter it became widely accepted as a framework – or 'foundation' – for the development of the other branches of modern, abstract mathematics. Today, its basic notions and notations are widely used even outside mathematics proper.

Set theory impinges on philosophy in several ways. First, the more formal areas of philosophy are among the areas outside mathematics proper where set-theoretic notions and notations are used. Further, the main topic of set theory (considered as a branch of mathematics in its own right rather than a framework for developing other branches of mathematics) is infinity, traditionally a topic of philosophical speculation. Finally, the fact that mathematics is in some sense reducible to set theory – though the specification of just what sense this is remains itself a philosophical problem – means that many problems of philosophy of mathematics reduce to problems of philosophy of set theory.

3.1. Basic Notions and the Algebra of Sets

A *set* is one thing composed of many things, its *elements*, the relation of element a to set A being written $a \in A$, with the negation abbreviated $a \notin A$. When every element of the set A is also an element of the set B, A is said to be *a subset* of B, written $A \subseteq B$. The mathematical notion of set is distinguished from the metaphysical notion of property by the axiom of *extensionality*, according to which two sets having exactly the same elements are identical.

It follows that for any condition $\Phi(x)$ there can be at most one set whose elements are all and only the x for which the condition holds. This set is denoted $\{x \mid \Phi(x)\}$, and several variations on this notation are also used. Thus if u is a set and

$\Phi(x)$ a condition, then the result of separating out from the given set just those of its elements for which the given condition holds, that is, $\{x \mid x \in u$ and $\Phi(x)\}$, is written $\{x \in u \mid \Phi(x)\}$. Thus also, if u is a set and $\Psi(x, y)$ a condition such that for every x there is a unique $y = \psi(x)$ for which $\Psi(x, y)$ holds, then the result of replacing the elements of the given set by the elements associated with them by the given condition, that is, $\{y \mid \Psi(x, y)$ for some $x \in u\}$, is written $\{\psi(x) \mid x \in u\}$. Also, if $a_1, a_2, \ldots, a_n$ are any given finitely many elements, the set $\{x \mid x = a_1$ or $x = a_2$ or $\ldots$ or $x = a_n\}$ is written $\{a_1, a_2, \ldots, a_n\}$. In particular, the *empty* set $\{x \mid x \neq x\}$, the *singleton* set $\{x \mid x = a\}$, and the (*unordered*) *pair* $\{x \mid x = a$ or $x = b\}$ are written $\{\}$, $\{a\}$, and $\{a, b\}$.

Widely used basic notions of set theory include the following.

- The *intersection* $A \cap B$ of two sets A and B is the set whose elements are all and only those x that are elements both of A and of B.
- Two sets are called *disjoint* if their intersection is empty.
- The *union* $A \cup B$ of two sets A and B is the set whose elements are all and only those x that are elements either of A or of B or of both. More generally, the union $\cup X$ of a set X of sets is the set whose elements are all and only those x such that $x \in A$ for some $A \in X$.
- The *difference* $A - B$ of two sets A and B is the set of all x that are elements of A but are not elements of B.
- The *power set* $\wp(U)$ of a given set U is the set of all its subsets.

In a context where one is concerned only with subsets of U, the difference $U - A$ may be written simply $-A$ and called the *complement* of A.

Various basic 'algebraic' laws of intersection, union, and complement, follow immediately from the foregoing definitions and the logical properties of conjunction 'and,' disjunction 'or,' and negation 'not.' (For example, $-(A \cap B) = -A \cup -B$.) The derivation of such laws of the algebra of sets constitutes the first chapter in the development of set theory.

3.2. Further Basic Notions: Relations and Functions

The derivation of the basic laws of relations forms the second chapter in the development of set theory. But prior to the notion of relation comes the notion of the *ordered pair* (a, b) with first component a and second component b, which is subject to the following basic law:

$(a, b) = (c, d)$ if and only if $a = c$ and $b = d$.

A (*binary*) *relation* on a set A (respectively: between elements of one set A and those of another set B) is then any set of ordered pairs whose two components are both elements of A (respectively: whose first component is an element of A and whose second component is an element of B). One often writes aRb for $(a, b) \in R$.

One may also consider ordered triples and trinary relations, ordered quadruples and quaternary relations, and so on.

- If R is a relation, the *converse* (also called *inverse*) relation R^{-1} is the relation $\{(a, b) \mid bRa\}$. Thus if R is the relation of parent to child, R^{-1} would be the relation of child to parent.
- If R and S are relations, the *composition* $S \circ R$ is the relation $\{(a, c) \mid$ for some b, aRb and $bSc\}$. Thus if S is the relation of parent to child, and R the relation of sibling to sibling, then $S \circ R$ would be the relation of aunt or uncle to niece or nephew.
- The *domain* of a relation R is $\{a \mid aRb$ for some $b\}$ and the *range* is $\{b \mid aRb$ for some $a\}$.

Various basic 'algebraic' laws follow immediately from the foregoing definitions and logic. (For example, $(S \circ R)^{-1} = R^{-1} \circ S^{-1}$.)

Notions and results pertaining to several special kinds of relations are also widely used outside mathematics proper, and throughout in set theory itself; and some of these may be collected here for future reference. One important special kind of relation is an *equivalence* relation E on a set A, by which is meant any relation for which the following three properties hold for all a, b, $c \in A$:

1   *Reflexivity* aRa.
2   *Symmetry*   If aRb then bRa.
3   *Transitivity*   If aRb and bRc then aRc.

The set $\{b \mid aEb\}$ is then called the *equivalence class* of a.

- A *selector* for an equivalence E on A is a subset S of A having exactly one element from each equivalence class.
- A *partition* of a set A is a set X of subsets of A such that any two distinct sets in X are disjoint and the union of all the sets in X is all of A.

The notions of equivalence and partition are linked by the fact that if E is an equivalence on A, then the set of E-equivalence classes is a partition of A, while if X is a partition of A, then the relation aEb defined to hold if any only if a and b belong to the same set in X is an equivalence on A.

Other special kinds of relations are ordering relations:

- A *partial order* R on a set A is any relation with the three properties of reflexivity, transitivity, and *anti-symmetry*, where the last requires that for all a, $b \in A$, if aRb and bRa, then $a = b$.
- A (*total*) *order* is a partial order with the additional property of *connectedness*, requiring that for all a, $b \in A$, either aRb or bRa.
- Associated with any partial or total order R is the *strict* partial or total order R' given by: $aR'b$ iff (if and only if) aRb but not $a = b$.

When the order R is written $\leq$, the associated strict order R' is written $<$. Terminology such as 'least' and 'greatest' is used in connection with orders in the obvious senses.

- A *well-order* R on a set A is an order with the property that every non-empty subset of A has an R-least element. (For example, the usual order on the natural numbers $\mathbb{N}$ is a well-order in this sense.)

Perhaps the most important special kind of relations are functions. Here a *function* from a set A to a set B is a relation f between elements of A and elements of B such that for every $a \in A$ there exists a unique $b \in B$ such that afb. This unique b is written $f(a)$.

- If $U \subseteq A$, then the *image* $f[U]$ of U under f is defined to be $\{f(a) \mid a \in U\}$, and if $V \subseteq B$, then the *pre-image* $f^{-1}[V]$ of V under f is defined to be $\{a \mid f(a) \in V\}$.
- If for every $b \in B$ there exists at most one $a \in A$ with $f(a) = b$, then the function is said to be *one-to-one* or an *injection*.
- If for every $b \in B$ there exists at least one $a \in A$ with $f(a) = b$, then the function is said to be *onto* or a *surjection*.
- A function that is both an injection and a surjection is called a *bijection*.
- A bijection from a set to itself is called a *permutation*.
- A (*binary*) *operation* on A is a function from the set of ordered pairs of elements of A to A itself, and if $\S$ is such an operation, one often writes $a_1 \S a_2$ for $\S(a_1, a_2)$. (For example, addition and multiplication on any of the usual number systems of algebra are operations in this sense.)

3.3. Transfinite Cardinals

The greatest novelty introduced by Cantor was his theory of transfinite numbers. He defined two sets A and B to have the same *cardinal number* $\|A\| = \|B\|$ iff there exists a bijection from A to B. He also defined $\alpha \leq \beta$ to mean that there are sets A and B with $\|A\| = \alpha$ and $\|B\| = \beta$ having $A \subseteq B$. This notion $\leq$ has the properties of a partial order. (The anti-symmetry property, that if $\alpha \leq \beta$ and $\beta \leq \alpha$ then $\alpha = \beta$, is a substantial result, called the *Cantor–Bernstein Theorem*.) The natural numbers are also called the *finite cardinals*, the cardinal number of the set $\{0, 1, \ldots, n-1\}$ of natural numbers less than a given natural number n being identified with n itself. Cantor called the cardinal of the set $\mathbb{N}$ of all natural numbers $\aleph_0$, and the cardinal of the set $\mathbb{R}$ of all real numbers $\mathbf{c}$. Sets of cardinal $\aleph_0$ are called *denumerable*, and sets that are either finite or denumerable are called *countable*.

Cantor also introduced an arithmetic of cardinal numbers. First, auxiliary notions of addition, multiplication, and exponentiation on sets may be defined as follows:

- *Addition* $\quad A + B = \{(0, a) \mid a \in A\} \cup \{(1, b) \mid b \in B\}$
- *Multiplication* $\quad A \cdot B = \{(a, b) \mid a \in A \text{ and } b \in B\}$
- *Exponentiation* $\quad A^B$ or $A \uparrow B = \{f \mid f \text{ is a function from } B \text{ to } A\}$.

Then notions of addition, multiplication, and exponentiation for cardinals may be defined in terms of these auxiliary notions:

- *Addition* $\|A\| + \|B\| = \|A + B\|$
- *Multiplication* $\|A\| \cdot \|B\| = \|A \cdot B\|$
- *Exponentiation* $\|A\|^{\|B\|}$ or $\|A\| \uparrow \|B\| = \|A \uparrow B\|$.

(For these latter definitions to make sense, it is first shown that if $\|A\| = \|C\|$ and $\|B\| = \|D\|$, then $\|A + B\| = \|C + D\|$, $\|A \cdot B\| = \|C \cdot D\|$, and $\|A \uparrow B\| = \|C \uparrow D\|$.) The notions thus defined agree with the usual notions for finite cardinals or natural numbers. Many of the basic laws that hold for finite cardinals can be shown to hold for all cardinals.

Other such laws fail strikingly for transfinite cardinals. One of Cantor's more striking results was that $\aleph_0 \cdot \aleph_0 = \aleph_0$ (from which it follows also that $\aleph_0 + \aleph_0 = \aleph_0$). To establish this, a bijection between pairs of natural numbers and single natural numbers is set up, whose pattern may be guessed from the following:

(0,0)	(1,0)	(0,1)	(1,1)	(2,0)	(2,1)	(0,2)	(1,2)	(2,2)	. . .
0	1	2	3	4	5	6	7	8	. . .

Cantor also established that $2 \uparrow \aleph_0 = c$, and in general $2 \uparrow \|A\| = \|\wp(A)\|$. It then follows that $\aleph_0 < c$ as a consequence of the celebrated result, known simply as *Cantor's Theorem*, that in general $\|A\| < \|\wp(A)\|$. This last was established by Cantor's celebrated *diagonal argument*: Supposing there is a bijection f between A and $\wp(A)$, consider the set $D = \{a \in A \mid a \notin f(a)\}$. Since f is a surjection, there is some $d \in D$ such that $f(d) = D$. But then we have the contradiction that $d \in D$ if and only if $d \notin f(d) = D$. As special cases or easy applications of some of the kinds of theorems just cited, Cantor showed that there are no more rational than natural numbers, more real than rational numbers, but again no more complex than real numbers.

3.4. Transfinite Ordinals

Let now R and S be orders on sets A and B respectively. An *isomorphism* between R and S (or between 'the set A equipped with the order R' and 'the set B equipped with the order S') is a bijection f from A to B with the further property that it is *order preserving*, meaning that if a_1 and a_2 are elements of A and $b_1 = f(a_1)$ and $b_2 = f(a_2)$ the associated elements of B, then we have $a_1 R a_2$ iff $b_1 S b_2$. An isomorphism shows that R and S 'have the same structure,' differing only by the substitution of elements of B for elements of A. A notion of isomorphism for operations is similarly defined. Isomorphism is indeed a central concept in modern, abstract mathematics.

Cantor defined well-orders R and S on sets A and B to have the same *ordinal number* $|R| = |S|$ iff there exists an isomorphism between R and S. He defined $\rho \leq \sigma$

to mean there are well-orders R and S on sets A and B with $|R| = \rho$ and $|S| = \sigma$ having R an *initial segment* of S. This last condition means intuitively that S looks like R with some additional elements added at the end, or more formally that the following hold:

1   $A \subseteq B$.
2   If $a_1, a_2 \in A$, then $a_1 S a_2$ iff $a_1 R a_2$.
3   If $a \in A$ and $b \in B - A$, then $a S b$.

The notion $\leq$ has the properties of a well-order. (This is not obvious: the anti-symmetry property, that if $\rho \leq \sigma$ and $\sigma \leq \rho$ then $\rho = \sigma$, and the connectedness property, that either $\rho \leq \sigma$ or $\sigma \leq \rho$, are fairly substantial results.) The natural numbers are also the *finite ordinals*, the ordinal of the usual order on the set $\{0, 1, \ldots, n-1\}$ of the set of natural numbers less than a given natural number n (to which every other order on this set is isomorphic) being identified with n itself. Cantor called the ordinal of the natural numbers in their usual order ω.

The least ordinal is 0. For every ordinal ρ, there is a least ordinal greater than it, the (*immediate*) *successor* ρ' of ρ. It may be given an explicit description as follows:

If $\rho = |R|$ where R is a well-order on a set A, and B consists of A with one additional element b, and S is the well-order on B that is like the well-order R on A but with the additional element b placed after every element of a, then $\rho' = |S|$.

For every set T of ordinals, there is a least ordinal τ at least as great as all elements of T, called the *supremum* of T, written sup T. It may also be given an explicit description, though it is a rather complicated one. An ordinal that is neither zero nor a successor is called a *limit*. The least limit ordinal is ω.

Cantor also introduced an arithmetic of ordinal numbers. The notions of addition, multiplication, and exponentiation may be defined by the following *recursion equations* (though it is a substantial theorem that such equations do suffice to determine the values of sums, products, and powers, uniquely).

$$\rho + 0 = 0 \qquad \rho + (\sigma') = (\rho + \sigma)' \qquad \text{at limits } \rho + \tau = \sup\{\rho + \sigma \mid \sigma < \tau\}$$

$$\rho \cdot 0 = 0 \qquad \rho \cdot (\sigma') = (\rho \cdot \sigma) + \rho \qquad \text{at limits } \rho \cdot \tau = \sup\{\rho \cdot \sigma \mid \sigma < \tau\}$$

$$\rho \uparrow 0 = 1 \qquad \rho \uparrow \sigma' = (\rho \uparrow \sigma) \cdot \rho \qquad \text{at limits } \rho \uparrow \tau = \sup\{\rho \uparrow \sigma \mid \sigma < \tau\}$$

Thus after the finite ordinals comes the ordinal ω, after which come

$$\omega' = \omega + 1, \ \omega + 2, \ \omega + 3, \ldots, \ \omega + \omega = \omega \cdot 2, \ \omega \cdot 2 + 1, \ \omega \cdot 2 + 2, \ldots, \ \omega \cdot 3, \ldots,$$
$$\omega \cdot 4, \ldots, \ \omega \cdot \omega = \omega \uparrow 2, \ \omega \uparrow 2 + 1, \ldots, \ \omega \uparrow 2 + \omega, \ldots, \ \omega \uparrow 2 \cdot \omega = \omega \uparrow 3, \ldots,$$
$$\omega \uparrow 4, \ldots, \ \omega \uparrow \omega, \ldots$$

and so on. The notions thus defined agree with the usual notions for finite ordinals or natural numbers. Many of the basic laws that hold for natural numbers can be shown to hold for all ordinals. Other such laws fail for transfinite ordinals. Notably the commutative law fails, since for instance $1 + \omega = \omega \neq \omega + 1$.

The cardinal associated with an ordinal $\rho = |R|$, where R is a well-order on A, is the cardinal of the underlying set, $\|A\|$. Thus the cardinal associated with the ordinal ω is $\aleph_0$. In the infinite case, there are many ordinals associated with the same cardinal. In particular (as a consequence of the fact that $\aleph_0 \cdot \aleph_0 = \aleph_0 + \aleph_0 = \aleph_0$), all the ordinals mentioned in the preceding paragraph are associated with the same cardinal $\aleph_0$. In fact, Cantor showed that given a cardinal α having ordinals associated with it, the cardinal number of the set of such ordinals is greater than α itself. It may be denoted α^+, and then $\aleph_0^+$ is denoted $\aleph_1$, and $\aleph_1^+$ is denoted $\aleph_2$, and so on, with $\sup\{\aleph_n \mid n = 0, 1, 2, \ldots\}$ being denoted $\aleph_\omega$. There is, in fact, a whole series of larger and larger cardinals $\aleph_\rho$, one for each ordinal ρ, and a number of theorems established for $\aleph_0$ can be generalized to all these $\aleph_\rho$, one such generalization being that $\aleph_\rho \cdot \aleph_\rho = \aleph_\rho + \aleph_\rho = \aleph_\rho$.

3.5. The Axiom of Choice (AC)

The arithmetic of cardinal numbers would be simplified if it could be assumed that every cardinal α comes somewhere in the series of alephs, so that $\alpha = \aleph_\rho$ for some ordinal ρ. In particular, this would imply that the partial order $\leq$ on cardinals is in fact a (total) order, and that all infinite cardinals satisfy $\alpha \cdot \alpha = \alpha + \alpha = \alpha$. The assumption that every cardinal is an aleph amounts to the assumption that for every set A there exists some well-order R of A. Cantor, however, found himself unable to establish this *Well-Ordering Principle* (WO), or even to establish that there exists some well-order of the set of real numbers.

The first proof of WO was published by Zermelo, who based his argument on the *Axiom of Choice* (AC), according to which, for every equivalence, there exists a selector. This axiom had been implicitly used by Cantor and others, but was made explicit in Zermelo's work. While the derivation of WO from AC is a substantial result, the converse fact, that WO implies AC, is much easier to establish. For let A be a set and E an equivalence on it. WO supplies a well-order R of A, from which we easily obtain the selector $S = \{a \mid a$ is the R-least element of its E-equivalence class$\}$. WO is only one of several principles known to be equivalent to AC. Another is the assertion that for any two cardinals α and β, either $\alpha \leq \beta$ or $\beta \leq \alpha$. Yet another is *Zorn's Lemma*, widely used in mathematics, whose statement is too technical to be given here.

A distinctive feature of AC is that it asserts the existence of a certain set, a selector S for a given equivalence E on a given set A, without giving any condition specifying the set, such as would allow it to be written as $S = \{x \in A \mid \Phi(x)\}$. Largely owing to this feature, AC remained controversial for at least a couple of decades after its introduction, and, even today, mathematical textbooks sometimes flag those theorems whose proofs depend on AC.

Among many striking consequences of AC perhaps the best known is the *Banach–Tarski theorem*. This asserts that there exist two spheres S and T of unequal radius in three-dimensional Euclidean space, and a decomposition of each into a small number of disjoint pieces, $S = A_1 \cup \cdots \cup A_n$ and $T = B_1 \cup \cdots \cup B_n$ with $A_i \cap A_j$ and $B_i \cap B_j$ empty for distinct i and j, such that corresponding pieces A_i and B_i are geometrically congruent, meaning they can be made to coincide by rotating and translating one of them.

For present purposes, a *measure* on subsets of n-dimensional Euclidean space may be defined as a function assigning such sets non-negative real numbers, and having the following three properties:

1 *Normality* The measure of a simple set of the kind considered in elementary geometry is simply its volume (if $n = 3$) or area (if $n = 2$) or length (if $n = 1$) as defined in elementary geometry.
2 *Invariance* The measures of geometrically congruent sets are equal.
3 *Countable additivity* The measure of the union of countably many disjoint sets is the sum of the measures of those sets.

The Banach–Tarski theorem shows that in dimension $n = 3$, there is no measure defined on all sets, even if one weakens the requirement of countable additivity to finite additivity. Actually, the axiom of choice implies that, in no dimension, is there a measure defined on all sets. Thus some of the consequences of the axiom are 'negative' results.

3.6. The 'Reduction' of Mathematics to Set Theory

The exposition of set theory to this point has made mention of several sorts of entities over and above sets: ordered pairs, natural and rational and real and complex numbers, transfinite cardinals and ordinals. If pure set theory, in which the only entities considered are sets, is to serve as a framework for the development of mathematics, set-theoretic surrogates must be found for these other sorts of entities, and ordered pairs and numbers of various kinds 'identified' with these set-theoretic surrogates. The case of ordered pairs provides a paradigm of what goes on in such identifications. The ordered pair (a, b) is defined to be $\{\{a\}, \{a, b\}\}$, and from this definition the basic law of ordered pairs, that $(a, b) = (c, d)$ iff $a = c$ and $b = d$, is deduced. It is not pretended that this definition reveals what ordered pairs 'really were all along.' What the definition and derivation of the basic law do show is that the positing of ordered pairs subject to this basic law as entities over and above sets is, in a sense, superfluous.

As for Cantor's transfinite numbers, on the identification generally adopted today, each ordinal is identical with the set of its predecessors. Thus zero, which has no predecessors, is the empty set, and: $0 = \{\}$, $1 = \{0\}$, $2 = \{0,1\}$, $\ldots$, $\omega = \{0, 1, 2, \ldots\}$, $\omega + 1 = \{0, 1, 2, \ldots, \omega\}$, and so on. Also, each cardinal is identified with the least ordinal associated with it, so that for instance $\aleph_0 = \omega = \mathbb{N}$, the set of natural numbers. As for other kinds of numbers, in the late nineteenth century these were already, in a process distinct from but related to the development of set theory, being identified with certain (set-theoretic) constructions from natural numbers, and set theory merely takes over these identifications.

Consider, to begin with, the non-negative rationals $\mathbb{Q}^+$. Intuitively, any pair of natural numbers (m, n) with $n \neq 0$ represents a rational number m/n, with two such pairs (m_1, n_1) and (m_2, n_2) representing the same rational number if and only if $m_1 \cdot n_2 = m_2 \cdot n_1$. Formally, one considers the set of pairs of naturals (m, n) with $n \neq 0$, shows that the condition $m_1 \cdot n_2 = m_2 \cdot n_1$ defines an equivalence relation on such pairs, and defines m/n to be the equivalence class of (m, n), and $\mathbb{Q}^+$ to be the set of all such equivalence classes. One then defines operations on non-negative rationals in terms of operations on natural numbers, so that $m/n + p/q = (m \cdot q + p \cdot n)/n \cdot p$ and $(m/n) \cdot (p/q) = (m \cdot p/n \cdot q)$, and derives the basic laws of arithmetic for non-negative rationals from those for natural numbers. Order on non-negative rationals may also be defined in terms of order on natural numbers, so that $m/n \leq p/q$ if and only if $m \cdot q \leq p \cdot n$.

(Note that, in principle, if the symbols $+$ and $\cdot$ and $\leq$ are used for addition and multiplication and order on natural numbers, they should not also be used to denote addition and multiplication on the non-negative rationals; and if the symbols $0, 1, 2, \ldots$ are used for the natural numbers, they should not also be used to denote the non-negative rational numbers $0/1, 1/1, 2/1, \ldots$. In practice, mathematicians ignore such distinctions, and no real confusion results from this 'abuse of language.')

A particularly important construction, deriving from Dedekind's modern adaptation of Eudoxus' ancient theory of proportion, is that of the non-negative reals $\mathbb{R}^+$ from the non-negative rationals $\mathbb{Q}^+$. Intuitively, a non-negative real number a is completely determined by the set A of non-negative rational numbers less than it. (In case $a = \sqrt{2}$, for instance, $A = \{r \in \mathbb{Q}^+ \mid r^2 < 2\}$.) Such a set is non-empty, its complement is non-empty, it has no largest element, and it is closed downwards in the sense that $r \in A$ whenever $r \leq s$ and $s \in A$. If a set with these properties is called a *cut*, then, intuitively, not only does every non-negative real number determine a cut, but every cut determines a non-negative real number. Formally, one defines non-negative real numbers simply to be these cuts. One can then define sums and products by

$$A + B = \{r + s \mid r \in A \text{ and } s \in B\}$$

and

$$A \cdot B = \{t \mid t \leq r \cdot s \text{ for some } r \in A \text{ and } s \in B\}$$

and order by

$$A \leq B \text{ iff } A \subseteq B$$

and the basic laws of addition and multiplication and order for non-negative reals will follow from those for non-negative rationals.

Negative numbers can then be introduced by another simple construction. (Alternatively, they could have been introduced earlier, proceeding directly from the natural numbers $\mathbb{N}$ to the signed integers $\mathbb{Z}$ and thence to the rationals $\mathbb{Q}$ and reals $\mathbb{R}$.) So can the complex numbers $\mathbb{C}$ and the numerous and varied other structures considered in modern mathematics. In particular, the points of the n-dimensional Euclidean space $\mathbb{E}_n$ are simply n-tuples of real numbers $(x_1, \ldots, x_n)$.

3.7. Axiomatic Set Theory and the Iterative Conception of Set

It cannot be assumed that every condition $\Phi(x)$ determines a set, and, in particular, this cannot be assumed for the condition $x \notin x$, since if $A = \{x \mid x \notin x\}$ there is the contradiction that $A \in A$ iff $A \notin A$. This contradiction, known as the *Russell paradox*, is only the most easily stated of several related set-theoretic paradoxes that became widely known in the years immediately after 1900. (Another is the *Burali–Forti paradox*, which results if it is assumed that there is a set of all ordinals. The order $\le$ on ordinals would then be a well-order of this set, and its order type would be the largest ordinal. But as has already been mentioned, there is no largest ordinal.) Cantor himself had been aware of some of these paradoxes, and in his correspondence had stated informal principles as to when a condition may be assumed to determine a set, but he never published this material. In the wake of the paradoxes, Zermelo published an axiom system for set theory, including rigorously stated assumptions about when a condition $\Phi(x)$ does determine a set. Fraenkel and others proposed amendments, and the axiom system as amended is known as ZF. Adding AC to ZF produces ZFC, today the most widely accepted axiomatic system for set theory.

The axioms of ZF are as follows. First, there is *extensionality*, already stated at the beginning of this chapter, according to which sets with the same elements are identical. Then there are the principles of *separation*, guaranteeing the existence of $\{x \in u \mid \Phi(x)\}$ for any set u and any condition Φ, and of *replacement*, guaranteeing the existence of $\{\psi(x) \mid x \in u\}$ for any set u and any condition Ψ such that for each x there exists a unique $y = \psi(x)$ for which $\Psi(x, y)$ holds. (In a fully rigorous treatment, the vague notion of 'condition' would be replaced by a precise notion of 'formula,' and separation and replacement would not be single axioms but rather *axiom schemes*, or infinite lists of axioms, one for each relevant formula Φ or Ψ.)

In addition, there are existence axioms of *pairing, union, powers,* and *infinity*, asserting the existence of $\{a, b\}$ for any a and b, of $\cup X$ for any X, of $\wp(U)$ for any U, and of the set of natural numbers. These axioms are sufficient to establish the existence of all the other sets introduced in the developments outlined so far, though occasionally (as in the case of the product $A \cdot B$) the existence proofs are not trivial. These axioms are also more than sufficient for the development of modern, abstract mathematics, except for the uses in certain areas of higher mathematics of the axiom of choice AC, already mentioned.

There is an intuitive picture, often called the *iterative conception* of set, associated with the axioms, according to which sets lie in a hierarchy of levels, where the elements of a set at one level must come from levels below it. (Thus no set is an element of itself, there are no two-element loops with $x_2 \in x_1$ and $x_1 \in x_2$, there are no three-element loops with $x_2 \in x_1$ and $x_3 \in x_2$ and $x_1 \in x_3$, and so on; and, moreover, there are no infinite descending chains with $x_1 \in x_0$, $x_2 \in x_1$, $x_3 \in x_2$, and so on.) Since, in pure set theory, the only objects considered are sets, at the bottom of the hierarchy, there is just the empty set $0 = \{\}$. If x is a set, then $\{x\}$ always lies at a level immediately above that of x. Thus $1 = \{0\}$ lies at the next-to-bottom level, $2 = \{0, 1\}$ lies at the next-to-next-to-bottom level, and $\mathbb{N} = \{0, 1, 2, \dots\}$ lies at an infinite level immediately above all finite levels, $\{\mathbb{N}\}$ lies above that, and so on; and there is no top level. The hierarchy is supposed to be as tall (to have as many levels) and to be as wide (to have as many sets at each level) as possible, an intuition partly expressed by the various existence axioms.

In more formal terms $V(\rho)$, the ρth level of the *cumulative hierarchy* of sets, is defined for all ordinals ρ by these recursion equations:

$$V(0) = \{\}$$

$$V(\rho') = V(\rho) \cup \wp(V(\rho)) \qquad \text{at limits } V(\tau) = \cup \{V(\sigma) \mid \sigma < \tau\}$$

The *rank* of a set x is the least ρ such $x \in V(\rho + 1)$. The assumption of the iterative conception that all sets belong to the cumulative hierarchy is equivalent to several other assumptions, of which the most simply stated is the axiom of *foundation* or *regularity*, according to which if a set x has any elements at all, then it has an element y that has no elements in common with it. (The equivalence of the different formulations of the assumption is non-trivial.) This is the last axiom of ZF.

A variant ZFU (or ZF *mit Urelementen*) allows a bottom level of 'individuals' (or *Urelemente*), which have no elements but may be elements of sets of any level. A different variant NBG (deriving from von Neumann, Bernays, and Gödel) allows a top level of 'classes,' which may have sets of any level as elements but are not themselves sets or elements of anything. Yet other variants drop foundation or regularity and allow loops and chains, or depart from ZFC and its underlying intuitive picture in more radical ways. Detailed consideration of such variants is beyond the scope of this chapter.

3.8. Descriptive Set Theory

Considered as a subject in its own right, set theory has several branches. Cantor's earliest work was concerned specifically with sets of points in Euclidean spaces, and there is a substantial branch of mathematics, called *descriptive set theory*, concerned even more specifically with those sets of points in Euclidean spaces that can be generated by comparatively simple processes.

The *basic* sets in n-dimensional Euclidean space are those of the form $\{(x_1, \dots, x_n) \mid a_1 < x_1 < b_1 \text{ and } \dots \text{ and } a_n < x_n < b_n\}$ for some real numbers a_i and b_i. (If $n = 1$, these are open intervals; if $n = 2$, open rectangles; and if $n = 3$, open rectangular parallelepipeds.)

- An *open* set is one that is a union of countably many basic sets.
- A *closed* set is one that is the complement of an open set.
- An F_σ set is one that is a union of countably many closed sets.
- A G_δ set is one that is the complement of an F_σ set.

The famous 'fractal' sets depicted in so many computer drawings are sets of this level of complexity.

- The *projection* of an $(n + 1)$-dimensional set A to dimension n is the set $\pi A = \{(x_1, \ldots, x_n) \mid \text{for some } y, (x_1, \ldots, x_n, y) \in A\}$.
- An *analytic* set is one that is a projection of a G_δ set.
- A *co-analytic* set is one that is the complement of an analytic set.
- A PCA set is one that is a projection of a co-analytic set.

Repeatedly taking projections and complements in this way one obtains the *projective* sets. Though this is, in many senses, a large family of sets, it can be shown that the number of projective sets is only c, whereas the number of arbitrary subsets of Euclidean space is $2 \uparrow c$. Descriptive set theory, or the theory of projective sets, is perhaps the branch of set theory closest to other branches of mathematics (such as real analysis and probability theory). To give at least one example of the kind of question considered in this branch of set theory, recall that it is impossible to define a notion of measure for all subsets of Euclidean space. Nonetheless, Henri Lebesgue succeeded in defining a notion of measure applicable to a very large family of sets, which descriptive set theorists have shown to include all analytic and co-analytic sets. Whether all PCA sets, or even perhaps all projective sets, are Lebesgue measurable are open questions of descriptive set theory. The hypothesis that PCA (respectively: projective) sets are all Lebesgue measurable may be called PCAM (respectively: PM).

3.9. The Topology of the Real Line

Another branch of set theory, closely connected with the branch of mathematics known as general topology, is concerned with arbitrary (rather than just projective) sets of real numbers, or what comes to the same thing, of points on the line. Here there are some positive results going back to Cantor himself.

One such result (proved by a celebrated method called the *back-and-forth* argument) states that if R is an order on a set A, then it will be isomorphic to the usual order on the rational numbers if and only if it has these three properties:

1 *Absence of extrema* There is no least and no greatest element in the R-order.
2 *Density* Whenever aRc there exists $a\ b \in A$ with aRb and bRc.
3 *Countability* The underlying set A is denumerable.

Another such result states that if R is an order on a set A, then it will be isomorphic to the usual order on the real numbers iff it has the following four properties:

1 Absence of extrema.
2 Density.
3 *Completeness* Whenever a non-empty subset $B \subseteq A$ has an *upper bound*, an element $a \in A$ such that bRa for all $b \in B$, then it has a *least upper bound*, an upper bound c such that for any other upper bound d we have cRd.
4 *Separability* There is a countable subset $B \subseteq A$ such that whenever $a, c \in A$ and aRc there is a $b \in B$ such that aRb and bRc.

The *Suslin hypothesis* SH is the conjecture that in the last-stated theorem the last assumption (4) can be weakened to the following:

4′ *Countable chain condition* There is no uncountable set of disjoint, non-empty open intervals.

The status of SH is an open question of the topology of the real line.

However, the most important open question about arbitrary sets of real numbers or points of the line is whether such a set can have a cardinal number intermediate between $\aleph_0$ and $\mathbf{c}$. The conjecture, made by Cantor himself, that there are no such intermediate cardinals, which amounts to the conjecture that $2 \uparrow \aleph_0 = \aleph_1$, is known as the *continuum hypothesis* CH. Rival possibilities that have been considered are the proposition CH* that there is just one intermediate cardinal, so that $2 \uparrow \aleph_0 = \aleph_2$, and the proposition CH† that the number of intermediate cardinals is $\mathbf{c}$ itself. (A few alternatives can be ruled out. For instance, it can be proved that $2 \uparrow \aleph_0 \neq \aleph_\omega$.)

3.10. Infinitary Combinatorics

Just as, associated with the ordinary arithmetic of the natural numbers, there is a sophisticated theory of finite combinatorics, concerned with counting permutations, combinations, and the like, so also with transfinite arithmetic there is associated an *infinitary combinatorics*. To give one example of a positive result in this branch of set theory, there is *Ramsey's theorem*, which in its simplest form says that if I is a set of cardinal $\aleph_0$ and the set $I^{[2]}$ of unordered pairs of distinct elements of I is partitioned into two disjoint pieces, $I^{[2]} = A \cup B$, then there is a subset $J \subseteq I$ also of cardinal $\aleph_0$ such that all the pairs from J belong to the same piece, that is, either $J^{[2]} \subseteq A$ or $J^{[2]} \subseteq B$.

There are many open questions in this branch of set theory, and again the most important such question is the most basic one, the question of the status of the *generalized continuum hypothesis* GCH, according to which $2 \uparrow \aleph_\rho = \aleph_{\rho+1}$ for all ordinals ρ. (CH is thus the special case $\rho = 0$ of GCH.)

3.11. Independence Results: Constructible Sets and Forcing

According to Gödel's first incompleteness theorem [see chapter 4], for any formal theory or axiom system that is consistent and strong enough to develop a modicum of mathematics, there will be statements that can be formulated in the language of the theory that cannot be decided one way or the other within the system. So, in particular, assuming ZFC is consistent, there must be a statement A in the language of ZFC such that is *independent* of ZFC in the sense that neither A nor its negation $\sim A$ can be proved in ZFC, or to put the matter another way, such that both the result ZFC + $\sim A$ of adding $\sim A$ to ZFC and the result ZFC + A of adding A to ZFC are consistent. Indeed, by Gödel's second incompleteness theorem, the statement Con(ZFC) expressing formally the assertion that ZFC is consistent is such an independent statement A. Note that, by this last result, if ZFC is consistent, we cannot hope to prove absolutely or unconditionally in ZFC itself that ZFC + A or ZFC + $\sim A$ is consistent. The most one can hope to prove is relative consistency, the conditional assertion that if ZFC is consistent, then so are ZFC + A and ZFC + $\sim A$. These general results of Gödel's, however, leave entirely open whether there are any specific set-theoretic questions *actually raised in the mathematical literature* that are thus independent of ZFC.

In fact, there are many such statements. Gödel himself, in the 1930s, showed that GCH (and hence CH) is consistent relative to ZFC (and at the same time that AC is consistent relative to ZF). His method of *inner models* was to define a special class of sets, the *constructible* sets, containing all ordinals and just enough other sets to make it provable in ZF for each of the axioms of ZF that it comes out true when 'set' is interpreted to mean 'constructible set.' He also proved in ZF that the *axiom of constructibility* (V = L), according to which the constructible sets are in fact all the sets there are, itself comes out true when 'set' is interpreted to mean 'constructible set,' and in this way showed V = L to be consistent relative to ZF. He also proved V = L implies (AC and) GCH (and hence CH). It is now known that V = L also implies ~PCAM (a result foreseen by Gödel and worked out in detail by J. W. Addison) and ~SH (a result of Ronald Jensen, who has derived innumerable other unexpected consequences from V = L), which is sufficient to establish the relative consistency of these statements as well.

Cohen, in the 1960s, showed that ~CH (and hence ~GCH) is consistent relative to ZFC (and at the same time that ~AC is consistent relative to ZF), introducing for this purpose his celebrated method of *forcing* (which he combined with the method of inner models for the proof about ~AC). Soon elaborate refinements of that method were developed by other set theorists, notably Solovay and Martin. Together the two last-named workers applied these methods to prove the relative consistency of a technical statement now known as *Martin's axiom* (MA), or rather, of the conjunction of MA and ~CH. This conjunction implies, among many other things, SH (whose relative consistency had been proved by Solovay and Tennenbaum) and PCAM (whose relative consistency also admits of other proofs). But the examples mentioned are but a tiny fraction of the statements whose independence has been established in the wake of the work of Gödel, Cohen, and their immediate successors.

3.12. Large Cardinals and Determinacy

The fact that the currently accepted axioms do not suffice to settle many basic questions of set theory has motivated the consideration of new axioms. One large class of candidates is constituted by the *large cardinal axioms*, each of which asserts the existence of some cardinal $\aleph_\rho$ that, so to speak, towers over all smaller cardinals $\aleph_\sigma$ for $\sigma < \rho$ in some of the ways in which $\aleph_0$ towers over the finite cardinals, with different axioms of this class focusing on different such ways.

One way in which $\aleph_0$ exceeds all smaller cardinals is by having the following two properties:

1   *Regularity*   Any union of fewer than $\aleph_0$ sets each of cardinal less than $\aleph_0$ itself has cardinal less than $\aleph_0$.
2   *Strong limit*   If κ is a cardinal less than $\aleph_0$, then $2 \uparrow \kappa$ is still less than $\aleph_0$.

A cardinal $\aleph_\rho$ with $\rho > 0$ having the analogous properties would be called *inaccessible*. The hypothesis of the existence of such a cardinal may be called IC. The least such cardinal would be far larger than the cardinal of any set considered in mainstream mathematics.

As to the status of the hypothesis IC, the following may be said. In ZFC each of the axioms of ZFC can be proved to come out true if 'set' is interpreted to mean 'set in $V(\alpha)$' or 'set of rank $< \alpha$,' where α is an inaccessible cardinal. It follows that in ZFC + IC one can prove Con(ZFC), from which it follows by Gödel's second incompleteness theorem that if ZFC + IC is consistent, then in ZFC + IC one can*not* prove the conditional 'if Con(ZFC) then Con(ZFC + IC).' In other words, one cannot hope to prove even the *relative* consistency of IC (though the relative consistency of ~IC is comparatively easily proved). In jargon, ZFC + IC is said to have greater *consistency strength* than ZF.

Another way in which $\aleph_0$ exceeds all smaller cardinals is expressed in Ramsey's theorem as stated earlier. A cardinal $\aleph_\rho$ with $\rho > 0$ having the analogous property would be called *weakly compact*. The hypothesis of the existence of such a cardinal may be called WCC. The least such cardinal would be far larger than the least inaccessible cardinal: indeed, if α is weakly compact, the number of inaccessible cardinals less than α is itself α; and the hypothesis WCC is of much greater consistency strength than the hypothesis IC.

Many large cardinal axioms of still greater consistency strength have been considered in the literature under various exotic names, such as the hypothesis of the existence of *supercompact* cardinals, or SCC. In general, their definitions are too technical to be given here. It has often been argued that large cardinal axioms may be thought of as further expressions of the intuitive idea, included in the iterative conception of set, that the cumulative hierarchy is as 'tall' as possible; though admittedly the argument becomes less compelling as the large cardinals grow larger.

A completely different class of axioms, involving the notion of infinite games, has been considered by descriptive set theorists. Given a set A of real numbers, say between zero and one, a game for two players may be as follows.

- Player I picks the first digit in the decimal expansion of a real number.
- Player II then picks the second digit.
- Player I then picks the third digit.
- Player II then picks the fourth digit, and so on.

In this way (though infinitely many moves are required), a real number a is generated. Player I wins if $a \in A$, and else player II wins.

- A *strategy* for a player is a rule telling that player what digit to choose at each step, as a function of the opposing player's choices at previous steps.
- A *winning* strategy for player I is one such that if player I follows it, then player I will win regardless of what player II does; and the notion of a winning strategy for player II is similarly defined. Obviously, there cannot exist winning strategies for both players.
- The set A is called *determinate* if there exists a winning strategy for one or the other of the players.

The *axiom of determinacy* AD asserts that every set of real numbers is determinate. AD itself can be disproved in ZFC, though the disproof does make use of AC. More restricted axioms in the same direction have therefore been considered, notably the axiom PD of *projective determinacy*, according to which all projective sets are determinate. This axiom has many, many 'positive' consequences in descriptive set theory, notably PM (and hence PCAM), and, indeed, these consequences are the main motive for interest with the axiom, whose bare statement no one pretends to find especially compelling.

During the 1970s and 1980s, PM was intensively investigated by a group of logicians including Moschovakis, Kechris, Martin (already mentioned above), Steel, and Woodin. Their work culminated in proofs by the three last-named of this group that the assumption of sufficiently large large cardinals – inaccessible or weakly compact cardinals are not nearly large enough, but cardinals in the neighborhood of supercompact suffice – implies much determinacy, including PD; and conversely, though such determinacy hypotheses do not literally imply the existence of large large cardinals, they at least imply their consistency. Thus a connection is established between two classes of axioms having entirely different motivations, arguably considerably increasing the strength of the motivation for each.

To date, however, no axiom such as would settle CH (let alone GCH) has garnered nearly as much support as large cardinal or determinacy axioms, and it can perhaps hardly be said of any the three rival hypothesis CH, CH*, and CH† that it is substantially more widely accepted than the others. In response to this situation, various philosophical positions have been taken. Thus *platonism* (usually written with a small 'p' to acknowledge the tenuousness of its connection with Plato) maintains that there is a fact of the matter as to the size of c, whether or not set theorists are able to discover that fact, and that if they wish to do so, set theorists will simply have to work harder. But *formalism* maintains that the acceptance of one rather than another of the various equally consistent rival hypotheses about c would be a matter of pure convention or stipulation. (Thus platonism and formalism are roughly speaking the analogues in philosophy of mathematics of legal realism and legal positivism in philosophy of law.) There are (as in the analogous case of philosophy of law) both substantial reasons for dissatisfaction with each of the two extreme positions, but also substantial difficulties involved in any attempt to articulate a clear intermediate position.

Suggested further reading

For an elementary introduction to set theory, especially in its role as a framework for the rest of mathematics, see the perennially popular textbook Halmos (1960). For a more detailed exposition, see Barwise (1977), a standard reference containing surveys on a generous scale, mostly by distinguished contemporary set theorists, of the different branches of the subject, with attribution of results to their original authors and references to the original technical literature. While in mathematics, as in other sciences, historical sources tend to be superseded quickly by later treatments, the original writings of the pioneers made available in English translation (and with substantial introductory essays by present-day scholars) in van Heijenoort (1967) remain of considerable interest. Philosophical problems about the nature of the 'reduction' of mathematics to set theory are raised in the classic paper Benacerraf (1965). The search for new axioms for set theory is surveyed from a sympathetic philosophical perspective in Maddy (1988), with special attention to the advances of the 1980s.

References

Barwise, J. (ed.) 1977: *Handbook of Mathematical Logic*, (North-Holland, Amsterdam), 317–522.

Benacerraf, P. 1965: "What Numbers Could Not Be," *Philosophical Review*, 74, 47–73.

Halmos, P. 1960: *Naïve Set Theory*, (van Nostrand, New York).

Maddy, P. 1988: "Believing the Axioms," *Journal of Symbolic Logic*, 53, 481–511, 736–64.

van Heijenoort, J. (ed.) 1967: *From Frege to Gödel: A Sourcebook in Mathematical Logic*, (Harvard University Press, Cambridge, MA).

Chapter 4

Gödel's Incompleteness Theorems

Raymond Smullyan

4.1. Introduction

At the turn of the century, there appeared two comprehensive mathematical systems, which were indeed so vast that it was taken for granted that all mathematics could be decided on the basis of them. However, in 1931, Kurt Gödel (1992 [1964]) surprised the entire mathematical world with his epoch-making paper which begins with the following startling words:

> The development of mathematics in the direction of greater precision has led to large areas of it being formalized, so that proofs can be carried out according to a few mechanical rules. The most comprehensive formal systems to date are, on the one hand, the Principia Mathematica of Whitehead and Russell, and, on the other hand the Zermelo–Fraenkel system of axiomatic set theory. Both systems are so extensive that all methods of proof used in mathematics today can be formalized in them – i.e., can be reduced to a few axioms and rules of inference. It would seem reasonable, therefore, to surmise that these axioms and rules of inference are sufficient to decide *all* mathematical questions which can be formulated in the system concerned. In what follows it will be shown that this is not the case, but rather that, in both of the cited systems, there exist relatively simple problems of the theory of ordinary whole numbers which cannot be decided on the basis of the axioms.

Gödel then went on to explain that the situation did not depend on the special nature of the two systems under consideration but held for an extensive class of mathematical systems. (More on this 'extensive' class is explained later on.)

How did Gödel manage to find a sentence which, though true, is not provable in the system under consideration? Roughly speaking, what Gödel did was to assign to each sentence of the system a positive whole number, subsequently known as the *Gödel number* of the sentence, and then he very ingeniously constructed a sentence *G* that asserted that a certain number *n* was the Gödel number of a sentence that was *not* provable in the system, but the number *n* was the Gödel number of the very sentence *G*! Thus *G* asserted that its own Gödel number was the Gödel number of an unprovable sentence (unprovable in the system, that is), which is tantamount to saying that *G* asserts that *G* is not provable in the system. Thus if *G* is true, then, as it asserts, it is not provable in the system; whereas if *G* is false, then what it asserts is *not* the case, which would mean that it *is* provable in the system. Thus, one of two alternatives holds:

1   *G* is true but not provable in the system.
2   *G* is false but provable in the system.

Alternative (2) was really out of the question, since the system was obviously set up so that only *true* sentences were provable, hence it must be alternative (1) that holds, and hence *G* is true, but not provable in the system.

I once gave the following somewhat humorous illustration of this. Consider the following sentence:

This sentence can never be proved.

Is there a paradox here? Well, it seems so, because if the sentence is false – if it is false that it can never be proved – then it *can* be proved, which means it must be true. So if it is false, it must also be true, which is impossible. Therefore, it cannot be false; it must be true. Now, I have just proved that the sentence is true. Since it is true, then what it says is really the case, which means that it can never be proved. So, how come I have just proved it?

What is the fallacy in the above reasoning? The fallacy is that the notion of *provable* is not well defined. One important purpose of the field known as 'Mathematical Logic' is to make the notion of *proof* a precise one. However, there has not been given a fully rigorous notion of proof in any absolute sense; one speaks rather of *provability within a given system*. Now, suppose there is a system – call it system *S* – in which the notion of provability within the system *S* is clearly defined. Suppose also that the system *S* is correct in the sense that everything provable in the system is really true. Now consider the following sentence:

This sentence is not provable in system *S*.

The paradox disappears! Instead of a paradox, there is now an interesting truth – namely, that the above sentence must be a true sentence which is not provable in system *S*, because if it were false, then unlike what it says, it *would* be provable in system *S*, contrary to the given fact that *S* is a *correct* system which never proves any false sentences. Thus, the sentence is true and hence also not provable in system *S*. This sentence is a crude formulation of Gödel's famous sentence *G* discussed earlier. Some more refined formulations are discussed later on.

Now consider another heuristic illustration: In a certain land, every inhabitant is classified as either Type T or Type F. All statements made by those of Type T are *true*, whereas all statements made by those of Type F are *false* (hence the letters 'T' and 'F'). One day, a logician visited this land. Now, this logician was completely accurate in all his proofs; he never proved anything that was not true. He came across an inhabitant of this land called 'Jal.' Well, Jal made a certain statement, from which it logically follows that Jal must be of Type T, but the logician could never possibly prove that he is of Type T! What statement could accomplish this? (Can the reader solve this before reading further?)

One solution is that Jal said: "You can never prove that I am of Type T." Could Jal be of Type F? Well, if he were, then his statement would be false, which would mean that the logician *could* prove that Jal is of Type T, contrary to the given condition that the logician never proves anything false. Thus Jal cannot be of Type F; he must be of Type T. Since he is of Type T, his statement was true which means that the logician can never prove that he is of Type T. Thus Jal really is of Type T, but the logician can never prove that he is.

Now, to carry the matter a bit further, suppose that, in addition, the logician knows logic as well as you and I. Well, having just proved that Jal must be of Type T, what is to prevent the logician from going through the same reasoning and hence coming up with the conclusion that Jal is of Type T? He would thus *prove* that Jal is of Type T, which would falsify Jal's statement, thus making Jal in reality to be of Type F! Thus the logician would prove that Jal is of Type T, whereas Jal would really be of Type F, contrary to the given condition that the logician never proved anything false. Is this not therefore a paradox? No, not really. (Can the reader see why without reading further?)

The only way for there not to be a paradox is if the logician does not know everything that you and I know. We are told that the logician knows logic as well as you and I, but could there be something else that we know but which he does not? Yes, there is! I told you that the logician was always accurate in his proofs, but I never told you that he *knew* or could *prove* that he was accurate! Indeed, if we retract the assumption that he is always accurate, then if he could prove that he is always accurate, he would lapse into an inaccuracy as follows: He would reason:

> Suppose Jal is of Type F, then his statement is false, which means that I *could* prove he is of Type T, and hence I would be inaccurate. Now, I am never inacccurate (*sic!*); hence he cannot be of Type F, he must be of Type T.

Thus, the logician has proved that Jal is of Type T, thus falsifying Jal's statement, and so, Jal must really be of Type F. Thus, by assuming his own accuracy, the logician has lapsed into an inaccuracy (and was punished for his own conceit!).

This is closely related to the result known as Gödel's *Second* Incompleteness Theorem, which is that for any of the mathematical systems under consideration, if it could prove its own consistency, it would be inconsistent, and hence if the system is consistent (which it certainly seemed to be), then it could never prove its own consistency. I will say more about Gödel's second theorem later on, but for now, here is an inkling as to how Gödel managed to construct a sentence that was 'self-referential' in that it asserted its own non-provability.

4.1.1. A Gödelian machine

Here is a computing machine that illustrates Gödelian self-reference in a very in-structive way. It prints out various sentences built from five symbols:

$$N \quad P \quad D \quad (\quad)$$

Informally the symbol N stands for *not*; the symbol P stands for *printability* (by the machine); and the parentheses are used for *naming* expressions. For any combination X of the five symbols, by its *name* is meant the expression (X) – i.e., X enclosed in parentheses. For example, the name of *PNDP* is *(PNDP)*. By the *diagonalization* of an expression X is meant $X(X)$ i.e., the expression followed by its own name (X). For example the diagonalization of *PDNP* is *PDNP(PNDP)*. The symbol D stands for *diagonalization*.

By a *sentence* is meant any combination of the five symbols that is of one of four forms (where X is any combination of those symbols whatsoever):

$P(X)$ for example, $P(NDNP)$

$NP(X)$ for example, $NP(DDN)$

$PD(X)$ for example, $PD(NDP)$

$NPD(X)$ for example, $NPD(PNN)$

I will explain what the sentences mean in a moment. An expression is called *printable* if the machine can print it. The machine is so programmed that anything it *can* print, it *will* print sooner or later.

Now here is what the sentences mean:

$P(X)$ means that X is printable and is, accordingly, called *true* iff (if and only if) X is printable. (For example, $P(NDNP)$ is true if *NDNP* is printable and false if *NDNP* is not printable.)

$NP(X)$ is called true iff it is *not* the case that X is printable – in other words that X is not printable.

$PD(X)$ means that the *diagonalization* of X is printable. Thus, $PD(X)$ is *true* iff $X(X)$ is printable.

$NPD(X)$ means the opposite of $PD(X)$ – in other words that $X(X)$ is *not* printable.

This constitutes a perfectly precise definition of what it means for a sentence to be *true*. We have here an interesting loop: The machine is self-referential in that it prints out various sentences that assert what the machine can and cannot print. (Such machines are of interest to the field known as *artificial intelligence*.) Now, the machine is totally accurate, in that every sentence it prints is true; it *never* prints anything false! This has several ramifications: For any expression X, if the machine can print $P(X)$, then $P(X)$ must be true, hence X will be printed sooner or later. If $PD(X)$ is printable, then $X(X)$ will be printed sooner or later. If $NP(X)$ is printable, then X itself will never be printed.

Now, suppose X is printable, does it necessarily follow that $P(X)$ is printable? Well, X being printable makes $P(X)$ *true*; however, we are not given that all true sentences are printable, but only that no false sentences are printable, and so we have no reason to believe that $P(X)$ is printable on the mere basis that $P(X)$ is true. As a matter of fact, there *is* a true sentence that is definitely *not* printable, and the reader is invited to try to construct such a sentence before reading the solution. (Hint: Construct a sentence that asserts its own non-printability – just like the inhabitant of Type T who said that the logician could never prove him to be of Type T.)

Here is the solution: A sentence that works is *NPD*(*NPD*) Why? Well, for any expression X, the sentence *NPD*(X) asserts that the diagonalization $X(X)$ of X is *not* printable. In particular, taking *NPD* for X, the sentence *NPD*(*NPD*) asserts that the diagonalization of *NPD* is not printable. But the diagonalization of *NPD* is the very sentence *NPD*(*NPD*)! Thus, *NPD*(*NPD*) asserts its own non-printability. If the sentence were false, then what it asserts would *not* be the case, which would mean that the sentence *is* printable, contrary to the given condition that the machine is accurate and never prints any false sentences! Therefore, the sentence cannot be false; it must be true, and hence must be non-printable, as it asserts. Thus, *NPD*(*NPD*) is true but the machine cannot print it.

Remarks The above is a Gödel-type argument reduced to about a bare minimum. Obviously, no accurate machine can possibly print a sentence that says that the machine cannot print it! (The situation is reminiscent of the scene in *Romeo and Juliet* in which the nurse comes running to Juliet and says, "Do you not see that I am out of breath?" Juliet replies, "How art thou out of breath, when thou has breath to say to me that thou art out of breath?")

An interesting thing about the above machine language is that if S is any of the mathematical systems subject to Gödel's argument, it is possible to translate any sentence X of the machine language to a sentence such that X is true iff its translation is a true sentence of the system S, and also X is printable by the machine iff its translation is *provable* in S. It then follows that the translation of the sentence *NPD*(*NPD*) must be a true sentence of S which is not provable in S.

4.2. Incompleteness in a General Setting

Now to the heart of the matter: What are the features of those mathematical systems subject to Gödel's (and also later) incompleteness arguments? Well, the systems in question have the following features: First, there is a well-defined infinite set of expressions, some of which are called *sentences*, some of which are called *predicates*. Informally, sentences express *propositions*, which are either true or false, whereas *predicates* act as names of properties or sets of (whole) numbers. (There may be expressions that have other functions as well, but these are not of concern here.) To every expression X and every number n, is associated an expression denoted by $X[n]$ and that for every predicate H, the expression $H[n]$ is a *sentence*. Informally, $H[n]$ expresses the proposition that n belongs to the set named by H. Let every expression be assigned a number called its *Gödel number*, and for any expressions X and Y, define $X(Y)$ to mean $X[y]$ where y is the *Gödel number* of Y. (In this manner, the necessity of constantly referring to Gödel numbers is circumvented and thus the expressions themselves can be dealt with more directly.) In particular, for any predicate H and any expression X, the expression $H(X)$ is a *sentence* that informally asserts that the set named by H contains the *Gödel number* of X.

To each pair of numbers x and y is associated a number denoted by $x * y$ such that if x is the Gödel number of an expression X and y is the Gödel number of an expression Y, then $x * y$ is the Gödel number of the expression $X(Y)$.

Now, to the important notion of *diagonalizers*. For each predicate H is associated a predicate $H^\#$ called the *diagonalizer* of H. Informally, for any number n, the sentence $H^\#[n]$ expresses the proposition that $n * n$ lies in the set named by H. Thus $H^\#[n]$ expresses the same proposition as the sentence $H[n * n]$. Also, therefore, for any expression X, the sentence $H^\#(X)$ expresses the same proposition as $H(X(X))$.

To each expression X is associated an expression $\overline{X}$ (more often written $\sim X$) called the *negation* of X, such that if X is a sentence, so is $\overline{X}$ (which informally asserts that X is not true) and also, if H is a predicate, so is $\overline{H}$; and for any number n, the sentence $\overline{H}[n]$ is the negation of $H[n]$ (thus $\overline{H}[n] = \overline{H[n]}$) and so also for any expression X, the sentence $\overline{H}(X)$ is the negation of $H(X)$. Informally, $H[n]$ asserts that n belongs to the set named by H, hence $\overline{H}[n]$ asserts that n does *not* belong to the set named by H.

In each of the systems under consideration, there is a well-defined notion of *provability* (within the system). A sentence S is called *refutable* (in the system) if its negation $\overline{S}$ is provable in the system. The systems under consideration use what is known as *classical* logic, one aspect of which is that for any sentence S, its double negation $\overline{\overline{S}}$ is provable iff S itself is provable (reminiscent of the adage, 'Two negatives make a positive'). Therefore, $\overline{S}$ is refutable iff S is provable. Thus there is the symmetry: S is refutable iff $\overline{S}$ is provable, and also, S is provable iff $\overline{S}$ is refutable.

The system is called *consistent* if no sentence is both provable and refutable; otherwise, it is called *inconsistent*. The underlying logic of the system is such that if so much as *one* sentence is both provable and refutable, then *every* sentence becomes provable, and thus the whole system collapses!

The system is called *complete* if every sentence is either provable or refutable, otherwise, *incomplete*. As indicated earlier, before Gödel's discovery, it was erroneously taken for granted that the two main mathematical systems of the time were complete. Gödel showed (under a certain very reasonable assumption, which is explained later) that these systems – as well as an important variety of others – were incomplete.

Now, turning to some general incompleteness arguments: The first incompleteness argument to be considered is a slightly later variant of Gödel's original argument, but it is given here first, since it is the simplest. It employs the notion of *truth*, which was not formalized until 1936 by Tarski (1956).

Each sentence of the system is classified as either *true* or *false* and in the systems under consideration, the following three conditions hold:

T_1:   For each sentence S, either S is true and $\overline{S}$ is false, or S is false and $\overline{S}$ is true.

T_2:   For each predicate H and every number n, the sentence $H^\#[n]$ is true iff $H[n * n]$ is true (and thus for every expression X, the sentence $H^\#(X)$ is true iff $H(X(X))$ is true).

T$_3$: There is a predicate P such that for every expression X, the sentence $P(X)$ is true iff X is a provable sentence of the system.

Under the assumption that the system is *correct*, in that no false sentences are provable, it logically follows from conditions T$_1$, T$_2$ and T$_3$, that there must be a true sentence which is not provable in the system, and hence also that the system must be incomplete. Here is why:

Let Q be the predicate $\bar{P}^{\#}$ (the diagonalization of the negation of the predicate P). Then, for any expression X, the sentence $Q(X)$ must be true iff $X(X)$ is *not* a provable sentence (because by T$_2$, $\bar{P}^{\#}(X)$ is true iff $\bar{P}(X(X))$ is true, which by T$_1$ is, in turn, the case iff $P(X(X))$ is not true (since $\bar{P}(X(X))$ is the negation of $P(X(X))$), which by T$_3$ is, in turn, the case iff $X(X)$ is not provable in the system). Thus, either $Q(Q)$ is true but not provable in the system, or $Q(Q)$ is false but provable. The latter alternative is ruled out by the assumption that the system is *correct*. Thus, $Q(Q)$ is true but not provable in the system. It further follows that the *negation* of $Q(Q)$ is false hence also not provable (by the assumption of correctness), thus $Q(Q)$ is neither provable nor refutable in the system, and so the system is incomplete.

Note In each of the systems studied by Gödel, there is also a predicate R such that for any expression X, the sentence $R(X)$ is true iff X is a *refutable* sentence of the system. As pointed out in Smullyan (1961), this leads to a variant of the above argument which is a bit simpler: Let K be the predicate $R^{\#}$. Then for any expression X, the sentence $K(X)$ is true iff $X(X)$ is a *refutable* sentence of the system (because $R^{\#}(X)$ is true iff $R(X(X))$ is true, which in turn is the case iff $X(X)$ is a refutable sentence). In particular, the sentence $K(K)$ is true iff it is refutable. Thus, it is either true and refutable, or false but not refutable. If it were true and refutable, then its negation would be false and provable, contrary to the assumption that the system is correct. Hence, it must be that the sentence is false but not refutable, and therefore its negation is true but not provable, and so again there is a sentence that is true but not provable in the system.

Informally, the sentence $Q(Q)$ described earlier can be thought of as saying, 'I am not provable,' whereas the sentence $K(K)$ says, 'I *am* refutable.'

Going back to the conditions T$_1$, T$_2$ and T$_3$, notice that, in proving that these conditions *do* hold for the systems studied by Gödel, the proofs of the first two are relatively simple, but the proof of T$_3$ is extremely elaborate!

4.2.1. Tarski's Theorem

Assuming conditions T$_1$ and T$_2$, can there exist a predicate H such that for every sentence X, the sentence $H(X)$ is true iff X is true? Such a predicate, if there is one, would be called a *truth predicate*. Well, Tarski's celebrated result (1956 [1936]) is that there cannot be such a predicate (assuming conditions T$_1$ and T$_2$), because if there were such a predicate H, then for any predicate K, the sentence $\bar{H}^{\#}(K)$ would be true iff $\bar{H}(K(K))$ were true, which, in turn, would be so iff $H(K(K))$ were false, which, in turn, would be the case iff $K(K)$ were false (since H is a truth predicate). In particular, taking $H^{\#}$ for K, gives the absurdity that $\overline{H}^{\#}(\overline{H}^{\#})$ is true iff $\overline{H}^{\#}(\overline{H}^{\#})$ is false! Therefore, assuming T_1 and T_2, there cannot be a truth predicate.

Notice that, from Tarski's theorem and condition T_3, it is immediate that the system must be incomplete (assuming correctness), because if truth and provability coincided, then by T_3, the predicate P *would* be a truth predicate, which it is not, by Tarski's theorem. Since they do not coincide, then either some true sentence is not provable or, contrary to correctness, some provable sentence is not true, and so it must be that some true sentence is not provable. (However, this proof does not establish the more specific fact that $\overline{P}^{\#}(\overline{P}^{\#})$ is a true sentence that is not provable.)

4.2.2. *Gödel's original proof*

As noted, the above proof came later than Gödel's original proof, since Tarski's definition of *truth* came five years later (1936). Now, to the method actually used by Gödel:

Each formal *proof* of the system consists of a finite sequence of sentences constructed according to purely mechanical rules. Gödel assigned numbers not only to expressions, but also to *proofs*. And now, for any positive integer n and any sentence X, X is said to be *provable at stage n* iff there is a proof of X whose Gödel number is n. As before, there is a predicate P such that for any sentence X, the sentence $P(X)$ informally expresses the proposition that X is provable. But also, for each positive integer n, there is a predicate P_n such that for any expression X, the sentence $P_n(X)$ informally expresses the proposition that X is a sentence *provable at stage n*. In the systems subject to Gödel's argument, these three conditions hold:

G_1: For any positive integer n and any sentence X, if X is provable at stage n, then $P_n(X)$ is provable, and if X is not provable at stage n, then $P_n(X)$ is refutable.

G_2: If for at least one n, the sentence $P_n(X)$ is provable, then $P(X)$ is provable.

G_3: For any predicate H and any expression X, if either of the two sentences $H^{\#}(X)$ and $H(X(X))$ is provable, so is the other, and if either one is refutable so is the other.

Informally, the idea behind G_1 is that, at any stage, the system has memory, so to speak, of what has and what has not already been proved. And so, if X is proved at stage n, then (perhaps at a later stage) $P_n(X)$ will be proved, and if X is not proved at stage n, then $P_n(X)$ is false and will sooner or later be refuted. As for G_2, it is obvious that if X is provable at stage n, then it is certainly provable at some stage or other, and so if $P_n(X)$ is true, so is $P(X)$. The point now is that the system is strong enough so that if $P_n(X)$ is *provable*, then $P(X)$ is not only true, but actually provable in the system.

As already indicated, under the intended interpretation, $P(X)$ asserts that X is provable (at some stage or other) whereas $P_n(X)$ asserts that X is provable at stage n. Now, suppose that there is a sentence X such that $P(X)$ is provable, yet each of the infinitely many sentences $P_1(X), P_2(X), \ldots, P_n(X), \ldots$ are refutable. Now if $P(X)$ is true, then X must be provable at some stage or other, hence it cannot be that all the sentences $P_1(X), P_2(X), \ldots, P_n(X), \ldots$ are false. In other words, if X is provable at some stage or other, then it cannot be that for *every* number n, the sentence X is not provable at stage n! Therefore, if $P(X)$ is provable, but if also for each n, $P_n(X)$ is refutable, then the system is certainly not correct (with respect to the intended interpretation), but this does not mean that the system is necessarily inconsistent (which means that some sentence and its negation are both provable). Well, if there is some sentence X such that $P(X)$ is provable and also all the sentences $P_1(X), P_2(X), \ldots, P_n(X), \ldots$ are refutable, then the system is called *un-stable*, otherwise the system is called *stable*. As noted, instability does not necessarily imply inconsistency (it is known that there are unstable systems which are neverthe-less consistent), but stability certainly implies consistency, because if a system of the type considered is inconsistent, *all* sentences are provable, which, of course, implies instability. Also, if the system is *correct*, it must also be stable. Thus correctness implies stability which, in turn, implies consistency, and so stability is a property midway in strength between correctness and consistency.

Notice that *stability* is a special case of the condition known as *ω-consistency* (omega-consistency): A system is called *ω-inconsistent* if there is some property of (whole) numbers such that, on the one hand, it can be proved that there exists some number or other that has the property, but, on the other hand, for any *particular* number n, it is provable that n does *not* have the property.

Now, Gödel's incompleteness proof did not require the assumption that the system was *correct* (which was required in the last proof) but only that the system was ω-consistent – or at least, stable. In fact, Gödel constructed a sentence G from which it can be shown that if the system is consistent, then G is not provable, and if the system is stable, then G is also not refutable. Well, as shall be seen, such a sentence can be constructed from just the conditions G_1, G_2 and G_3. In fact, it turns out that $\overline{P^{\#}(P^{\#})}$ is such a sentence.

To begin with, note that the systems under discussion are such that, for any predicate H and any expression X, the sentence $\overline{H}(X)$ is refutable iff $H(X)$ is provable (because $\overline{H}(X)$ is the negation of $H(X)$). In particular, taking $P^{\#}$ for H, the sentence $\overline{P^{\#}}(X)$ is refutable iff $P^{\#}(X)$ is provable, which, in turn, is the case iff $P(X(X))$ is provable (by G_3). Thus, for any expression X, the sentence $\overline{P^{\#}}(X)$ is refutable iff $P(X(X))$ is provable. In particular, taking $\overline{P^{\#}}$ for X, $\overline{P^{\#}(P^{\#})}$ is refutable iff $P(\overline{P^{\#}}(\overline{P^{\#}}))$ is provable. And so taking G to be the sentence $\overline{P^{\#}(P^{\#})}$ gives the following key fact:

G is refutable iff $P(G)$ is provable.

Now, suppose G is provable. Then it is provable at some stage n, hence $P_n(G)$ is provable (by condition G_1) and therefore $P(G)$ is provable (by condition G_2). And so, if G is provable, so is $P(G)$. But by the above key condition, if $P(G)$ is provable, then G is refutable, and so if G were provable, it would also be refutable, which means the system would be inconsistent! Therefore, if G is consistent, then G is not provable.

Now, suppose that the system is stable. Then it is also consistent, and hence G is not provable, as seen above, and so G is not provable at any stage n. Therefore, by condition G_1, for every n, the sentence $P_n(G)$ is refutable. Hence, assuming stability, $P(G)$ is not provable, and so again by the above key fact, G is not refutable. This proves the following result:

Proposition G *A Generalization of Gödel's Theorem* Any stable system satisfying conditions G_1, G_2 and G_3 must be incomplete.

More specifically, under conditions G_1, G_2 and G_3, there is a sentence G (namely, $\overline{P^{\#}(P^{\#})}$) with the following two properties:

1 If the system is consistent, then G is not provable;
2 If the system is stable, then G is neither provable nor refutable.

4.2.3.   The Rosser Incompleteness Theorem

Rosser (1964 [1936]) showed the surprising result that for the systems proved incomplete by Gödel, it was not necessary to assume stability (or more generally, ω-consistency), but the assumption of (simple) consistency sufficed. Now, he did not show that under the assumption of consistency, Gödel's sentence G was neither provable nor refutable, but rather that some other (more complex) sentence Z was.

Continue to assume conditions G_1 and G_3, but G_2 is now irrelevant. In fact, Rosser did not use Gödel's predicate P at all, but rather a more complex predicate H which informally has the following meaning:

For any sentence X, the sentence $H(X)$ informally means that for every number n, if X is provable at stage n, then for some number m less than or equal to n, the sentence X is provable at stage m.

Now, Rosser showed for the systems studied by Gödel, that not only conditions G_1 and G_3 hold, but also that for any sentence X and any number n, these two conditions hold:

R$_1$:   If $P_n(X)$ is provable and $P_m(X)$ is refutable for every m less than or equal to n, then $H(X)$ is refutable.

R$_2$:   If $P_n(\overline{X})$ is provable and $P_m(X)$ is refutable for every m less than or equal to n, then $H(X)$ is provable.

It will soon be shown that from conditions G_1, G_3, R$_1$ and R$_2$, it follows that if the system is consistent, then some sentence is neither provable nor refutable in it. But first, it should be pointed out that conditions R$_1$ and R$_2$ are *correct* under the intended meanings of the predicates P_n and H, in that these two conditions hold if 'provable' is replaced by 'true,' and 'refutable' is replaced by 'false.' To see this, consider R_1: $H(X)$ says that for every number n such that X is provable at stage n, there is some m less than or equal to n such that X is provable at stage m. Thus, to say that $H(X)$ is *false* is to say that there is at least one n such that X is provable at stage n, but there is no m less than or equal to n such that $\overline{X}$ is provable at stage m. Well, this is precisely the case if $P_n(X)$ is provable and if $P_m(\overline{X})$ is refutable for each m less than or equal to n (because X is then provable at stage n and $\overline{X}$ is *not* provable at any stage m where m is less than or equal to n), and so $H(X)$ is then false. Thus, R_1 is correct (under the intended interpretation of the predicates). As for R_2, the argument is a bit more subtle: Suppose that $P_n(\overline{X})$ is true and that for every m less than or equal to n, the sentence $P_m(X)$ is false. Then, $\overline{X}$ is provable at stage n and for every m less than or equal to n, X is not provable at stage m. Thus, for every number m, if X is provable at stage m, then m must be greater than n, and so there *is* a number x less than or equal to m – namely n – such that X is provable at stage x, and so $H(X)$ is therefore true. Thus R_2 is also correct (under the intended interpretation of the predicates).

Now for Rosser's argument: Assume conditions G_1, G_3, R_1 and R_2 and aim to show that, if the system is consistent, then there is a sentence that is neither provable nor refutable in the system – in fact, it will be shown that $H^\#(H^\#)$ is such a sentence.

Step 1 If X is provable, then $H(X)$ is refutable, and if X is refutable, then $H(X)$ is provable. Reason: Suppose X is provable. If the system is not consistent, then of course $H(X)$ is refutable (every sentence is), so suppose that the system is consistent. Then, since X is provable, $\overline{X}$ is not provable. Then X is provable at some stage n, hence $P_n(X)$ is provable (by condition G_1). Since $\overline{X}$ is not provable, then for every m less than or equal to n (in fact, for every m whatsoever) $\overline{X}$ is not provable at stage m, hence $P_m(\overline{X})$ is refutable. Then, by condition R_1, the sentence $H(X)$ is refutable. Thus, if X is provable, $H(X)$ is refutable.

Now suppose X is refutable. This means that $\overline{X}$ is provable. If the system is inconsistent, then certainly $H(X)$ is provable, so suppose that the system is consistent. Then X is not provable, hence there is some n such that $\overline{X}$ is provable at stage n, but there is no m less than or equal to n (in fact, no m at all) such that X is provable at stage m. Thus, $P_n(\overline{X})$ is provable but for every m less than or equal to n, $P_m(X)$ is refutable (again by G_1). Then by condition R_2, the sentence $H(X)$ is provable.

Step 2 By condition G_3, for any expression X, the sentence $H^\#(X)$ is provable (refutable) iff $H(X(X))$ is provable (respectively, refutable). In particular, taking $H^\#$ for X, note that $H^\#(H^\#)$ is provable (refutable) iff $H(H^\#(H^\#))$ is provable (refutable). Take Z to be the sentence $H^\#(H^\#)$ and note that Z is provable iff $H(Z)$ is provable, and is refutable iff $H(Z)$ is refutable.

Step 3 Suppose Z is provable, then $H(Z)$ is also provable (by step 2), but also $H(Z)$ is then refutable (by step 1): an inconsistency. Therefore, if the system is consistent, the sentence Z is not provable.

Suppose Z is refutable. Then $H(Z)$ is on the one hand refutable (by step 2), but also provable (by step 1): another inconsistency. Thus, if the system is consistent, then Z is not refutable either.

Discussion Gödel's sentence G might be thought of as saying,

I am not provable.

and (assuming consistency) is therefore true (under the intended interpretation of the predicate P) by virtue of the very fact that it is not provable in the system! Rosser's sentence Z, on the other hand, is a more complex one which might be thought of as saying,

At any stage that I am provable, there is an earlier stage at which I am refutable.

Since Z is not provable at all (assuming consistency), then what it says is really so, hence Z is true (under the intended interpretation of the predicate H).

4.2.4. Parikh sentences

Suppose that a sentence X is provable *by* stage n (as distinct from *at* stage n) if X is provable at stage m, for some m less than or equal to n. Now, given predicates P_1, $P_2, \ldots, P_n$ satisfying conditions G_1, it is easy to obtain, for each n, a predicate S_n such that for any sentence X, two conditions hold:

B_1:   If X is provable *by* stage n, then $S_n(X)$ is provable.

B_2:   If X is not provable *by* stage n, then $S_n(X)$ is refutable.

Note that if the system is consistent, then the converse of conditions B_2 must also hold, because suppose that $S_n(X)$ is refutable. If X were provable by stage n, then by B_1, $S_n(X)$ would be provable and the system would be inconsistent. Thus:

B_3: $S_n(X)$ is refutable iff X is not provable by stage n.

Now, Parikh (1971) made a very interesting observation: For each n, let Y_n be the sentence $S_n^\#(S_n^\#)$. By G_3, the sentence Y_n is provable iff $S_n(Y_n)$ is provable. Thus, Y_n is provable iff $S_n(Y_n)$ is refutable. But also, assuming consistency, $S_n(Y_n)$ is refutable iff Y_n is not provable by stage n (by B_3), and therefore, Y_n is provable iff Y_n is not provable by stage n. Thus, either Y_n is not provable and also provable by stage n, which is absurd, or provable but not by stage n. And so, Y_n is provable, but not by stage n. There is thus a uniform method for obtaining, for each number n, a sentence Y_n that is provable but not by stage n! More interesting yet, the *proof* that Y_n is provable is relatively short and provable at a relatively earlier stage. That is, for n sufficiently large, the sentence $P(Y_n)$ (where P is Gödel's provability predicate), which asserts that Y_n is provable – this sentence $P(Y_n)$ is provable at a stage m, where *m* is less than *n* (considerably less than *n*, for *n* sufficiently large). This might be paraphrased by saying that, for sufficiently large *n*, the sentence Y_n is *provably provable* long before it is provable!

4.2.5. Gödel's second incompleteness theorem

Let *f* be any refutable sentence of the system (Gödel chose for *f* the sentence $1 = 0$). If *f* were provable, then every sentence would be provable and the system would be inconsistent. Conversely, if the system were inconsistent, then *f* would be provable. Thus, the system is consistent iff *f* is not provable, and so, the sentence $P(f)$ is true iff the system is consistent, and so this sentence can be thought of as expressing the consistency of the system. This sentence has an important role and has been dubbed '*Consis.*' This sentence *Consis* is an arithmetic one that expresses the consistency of the system. Now, an interesting question arises: Is the sentence *Consis* itself provable in the system? This is tantamount to asking whether the consistency of the system is provable within the system.

Before answering this, it should be pointed out that the technical symbol for *implication* is '⊃'. For any sentences *X* and *Y*, the sentence $X \supset Y$ is read 'If *X*, then *Y*'. Obviously, anything implied by a true proposition must be true, and so if *X* and $X \supset Y$ are both true, so is *Y*. Well, in any of the systems under consideration, if *X* and $X \supset Y$ are both *provable* in the system, so is *Y*. Now, *G* expresses the non-provability of *G* itself and *Consis* expresses the consistency of the system, and so the sentence $Consis \supset G$ expresses the proposition that if the system is consistent, then *G* is not provable. Well, this is the first half of Gödel's (first) incompleteness theorem, and so the sentence $Consis \supset G$ is indeed true. Moreover, the sentence $Consis \supset G$ is not only true, but is even provable in the system! (The demonstration of this is *extremely* elaborate!) Therefore, if *Consis* were also provable, then from the two sentences *Consis* and $Consis \supset G$, one could infer *G*, and hence *G* would be provable, which would mean that the system was inconsistent (by Gödel's First Incompleteness Theorem). And so, if the system is consistent, then the sentence *Consis* is *not* provable in the system! Thus, the system, if consistent, cannot prove its own consistency. This is the result known as *Gödel's Second Incompleteness Theorem*.

Unfortunately, Gödel's second theorem has sometimes been misinterpreted to mean that one can never know that mathematics is consistent! To see how wrong that is, suppose it had turned out that *Consis was* provable in the system – or to be more realistic, imagine considering a system that could prove its own consistency. Would that be any reasonable grounds for trusting the consistency of the system? Of course not! If the system were inconsistent, then it could prove every sentence – including the statement of its own consistency! To trust the consistency of a system on the grounds that it can prove its own consistency is as foolish as trusting a person's veracity on the grounds that he claims that he never lies. And it is likewise irrational to have doubts about the consistency of a system just because it cannot prove its own consistency. The fact that a system, if consistent, cannot prove its own consistency sheds not the faintest light on whether the system is consistent. Whether a given system is consistent must be judged on other grounds.

4.3. The Unsolvable

The philosopher Leibniz envisioned the possibility that one day a universal calculator would be found that would mechanically solve *all* mathematical problems (as well as all philosophical ones). Is this dream of Leibniz realizable? To answer this, some background is necessary.

There is a type of computing machine whose function is to *generate* a set of (positive whole) numbers. (From now on, 'number' will mean *positive integer*.) For example, a machine might be programmed to do two things:

1   Print the number 2.
2   Whenever you print a number x, follow it by printing $x + 2$.

These are the only two instructions the machine has. Then, obviously, the machine will successively print the numbers 2, 4, 6, 8 – that is, it will generate the set of *even* numbers. If, on the other hand, the machine's first instruction had been to print 1, instead of 2, then it would have generated the set of odd numbers. For any set A of (positive whole) numbers, say that a machine M *enumerates* or *generates* A if M prints out all numbers in A but no number outside A. And a set A is called *recursively enumerable* (an alternative term might be *mechanically generatable*) if there is a machine M that generates it. Examples of recursively enumerable sets abound in mathematics (as examples, the set of even numbers, the set of odd numbers, the set of prime numbers, the set of all numbers divisible by 3 – virtually all the sets that are dealt with in number theory).

For any set A, let A' be the set of all numbers that are *not* in A. The set A' is called the *complement* of A. For example, the complement of the set of even numbers is the set of odd numbers. Now, a set A of numbers is called *solvable* or *recursive* if both A and its complement A' are recursively enumerable. The reason for the word 'solvable' is this: Suppose one machine M generates A and another machine N generates the complement A' of A. Thus, for any number n, there is an effective test to see whether n belongs to A: Set both machines going simultaneously and wait for the numbers. If n is in A, then sooner or later, it will become clear, since M will eventually print n. If n is not in A, this will also become clear, since N will sooner or later print n. Thus, there is a mechanical 'solution' to the problem of which numbers are in A and which ones are not.

Now suppose a set A is recursively enumerable but not solvable. Then there is a machine M that generates A but no machine to generate the complement A' of A. Suppose again that one would like to know whether a given number n is or is not in A. The best that can be done is to set the machine going and hope for the best: If n is in A, sooner or later this will become known, since M will sooner or later print it, but if n is not in A, then M will never print n. But no matter how long is waited, there is no assurance that M might not print n at some later time. Thus, if n is in A, sooner or later this will be known, but if n is not in A, then at no time can one definitely know that it isn't (at least by observing only the machine M). Such a set A is aptly called *semi-solvable*.

There are infinitely many of these possible generating machines – as many as there are positive integers. Each of these machines has a program which is not given in English, but is coded into a positive integer, and matters can be arranged so that every positive integer is the code of some generating machine (but it may be that a machine may have several different code numbers). For each number n, let M_n be the machine whose code is n, and imagine all the machines listed in the infinite sequence $M_1, M_2, \ldots, M_n, \ldots$

Also code every pair (x, y) of numbers to a single number $x * y$ (a simple coding device that works is to take $x * y$ to be a string of 1s of length x followed by a string of 0s of length y – for example, $3 * 4$ would be the number 1110000).

The first important feature of this battery of generating machines is that one of them U is a so-called *universal* machine which is programmed to systematically observe the behavior of all the machines $M_1, M_2, M_3, \ldots, M_n, \ldots$ and whenever a machine M_x prints out a number y, the universal machine U reports this fact by printing the number $x * y$, and these are the only numbers that U ever prints. Thus, for any numbers x and y, the machine U prints $x * y$ iff M_x prints y.

For example, suppose M_7 is programmed to generate the set of even numbers and M_9 is programmed to generate the set of odd numbers. Then U will print the numbers $7 * 2, 7 * 4, 7 * 6$, etc. and also the numbers $9 * 1, 9 * 3, 9 * 5$, etc. but U will never print $7 * 3$, or $9 * 4$.

This universal machine is a wonderful thing, in that access to this one machine U is as good as having access to the entire infinite battery of the generating machines, since whenever machine M_x prints y, one will know it by just observing the behavior of U, which will then print $x * y$.

A second important feature of these machines is that to each machine M_a there is associated a machine M_b which is said to *diagonalize* M_a, such that M_b prints those and only those numbers x such that M_a prints $x * x$. M_b, 'keeps watch,' so to speak, on M_a and is instructed to print out x whenever M_a prints $x * x$.

Let us record these two vital facts.

Fact 4.1 The universal machine U prints those and only those numbers $x * y$ such that M_x prints y.

Fact 4.2 For each machine M_a its diagonalizer M_b prints those and only those numbers x such that M_a prints $x * x$.

Let K be the set generated by the universal machine U. This set K (which has been dubbed the *complete* set) will be seen to contain *all* the information about *all* mathematical systems: If one could solve this one set K, then one could solve *all* questions about all mathematical systems, so the vital question is this: Is the set K solvable? Since U generates K, the question is thus whether there is a generating machine that generates the *complement* K' of K. In other words, is there a generating machine that prints all and only those numbers that the universal machine U does not print?

Well, let M be any one of the generating machines. By fact 2, there is a number h such that M_h *diagonalizes* M. Now, for any number h, the universal machine U

prints $h * x$ iff M_h prints x, which, in turn, is the case iff M prints $x * x$. Since this holds for *every* number x, then, in particular, it holds when x is the number h, and so U prints $h * h$ iff M prints $h * h$. Thus, if we let k be the number $h * h$, we see that either U and M both print k, or neither one prints k. Thus, it is *not* the case that M prints k iff U does not print k, and so it is not the case that for *all* numbers x, the machine M prints x iff U does not print x. Thus, there is no generating machine that prints those and only those numbers that U does not print!

Letting K be the set generated by U, it has just be shown that there is no generating machine M that generated the complement K' of K. This leads to the following basic result:

Proposition 4.1. The set K generated by U, though recursively enumerable, is not solvable (not recursive).

Now, let us see some of the important ramifications of Proposition 4.1: First of all, it yields yet another method of proving the incompleteness of the type of system under consideration: A predicate H is said to *represent* (in the system) the set of all numbers n such that $H[n]$ is provable in the system. Thus, for any set A of numbers, to say that H *represents* A is to say that for every number n, the sentence $H[n]$ is provable in the system iff n is a member of A. And a set A is said to be *representable* in the system if some predicate H represents it. Now, there is a variety of systems called *formal* systems having the property that every set representable in the system is recursively enumerable. Thus, for every predicate H of such a system, there is a machine M that prints those and only those numbers n such that $H[n]$ is provable in the system. All of the systems investigated by Gödel are indeed formal systems. Moreover, *all* recursively enumerable sets are representable in each of these systems (assuming consistency). A system is called *Gödelian* if it is formal and if all recursively enumerable sets are representable in it. Thus, the sets representable in a Gödelian system are precisely the recursively enumerable sets – a set is representable in the system iff it is recursively enumerable. Note that a Gödelian system is automatically consistent, since if a system is inconsistent, then the *only* representable set is the set N of *all positive* integers, and moreover *every* predicate H represents N, since $H[n]$ is provable for *every* number n (all sentences are provable). Thus, a Gödelian system is consistent.

Well, Proposition 4.1 has a very important consequence for Gödelian systems: Consider any Gödelian system. Since all recursively enumerable sets are representable in it, then, in particular, the set K generated by the universal machine U is representable in it. Let H be a predicate of the system that represents K. By Proposition 4.1, the complement K' of K is not recursively enumerable, hence not representable in the system (since only recursively enumerable sets are representable in a Gödelian system). In particular, the negation $\bar{H}$ of H fails to represent the set K'. This means that either $\bar{H}[n]$ fails to be provable for some n in K', or there is some n not in K' (and hence in K) for which $\bar{H}[n]$ is provable. But if $\bar{H}[n]$ were provable for some n in K, the system would be inconsistent, because $H[n]$ is provable for every n in K, and $\bar{H}[n]$ and $H[n]$ cannot both be provable in a consistent system. Since the system is assumed consistent (being Gödelian) it cannot be that $\bar{H}[n]$ is provable for some n outside K', and, therefore, it must be that $\overline{H}[n]$ fails to be provable for some n in K'. The sentence $H[n]$ is not provable for such an n either, since n is not in the set represented by H. And so, neither $H[n]$ nor its negation $\overline{H}[n]$ is provable in the system.

Thus Proposition 4.1 yields:

Proposition 4.2 Every Gödelian system is incomplete. More specifically, in a Gödelian system, there is a predicate H that represents the set K generated by U, and there is a number n in K' such that neither $H[n]$ nor its negation $\overline{H}[n]$ is provable in the system.

Having now seen how Proposition 4.1 is related to Gödel's theorem, how is it related to Leibniz's vision?

Any formal mathematical problem can be translated into a question of whether a machine M_n does or does not print out a number m. That is, given any formal system, one can assign Gödel numbers to all the sentences of the system and find a number n such that the machine M_n prints out the Gödel numbers of the provable sentences of the system and no others. And so, to find out whether a given sentence is or is not provable in the system, for its Gödel number m one can ask whether machine M_n does or does not print m, or equivalently, whether the universal machine does or does not print the number $n * m$. Therefore, a complete knowledge of U would entail a complete knowledge of all formal systems. Conversely, any question of whether a given machine prints out a given number can be reduced to a question of whether a certain sentence is provable in a certain system, because one can take a formal system in which the set K is represented by a predicate H, and so for any number n, the machine U prints n iff $H[n]$ is provable in the system. Thus, a complete knowledge of the set K is tantamount to a complete knowledge of *all* formal mathematical systems.

Now, what does all this mean with respect to Leibniz's vision? Strictly speaking, one cannot prove or disprove the feasability of Leibniz's hope, because it was not stated in an exact form. Indeed, no precise notion of a 'calculating machine' or 'generating machine' existed in Leibniz's day; these notions have been rigorously defined only in this century. They have been defined in many different ways by various mathematical logicians (including Gödel), but all these definitions have been shown to be equivalent. If by 'solvable' is meant solvable according to any of these equivalent definitions, then Leibniz's hope is not realizable, because the fact simply is that there is a universal machine U and each machine has a diagonalizer, hence Proposition 4.1 does hold and thus the set K generated by U is not solvable; it is only semi-solvable (recursively enumerable). Therefore, there is no purely 'mechanical' procedure for finding out which sentences are provable in which formal systems. Thus, any attempt to invent a clever 'mechanism' that will solve all mathematical problems is simply doomed to failure.

In the prophetic words of the logician Post (1964 [1944]), this means that mathematical thinking is, and must remain, essentially creative. Or, as commented by the mathematician Rosenbloom (1950), it means that man can never eliminate the necessity of using his own intelligence, regardless of how cleverly he tries.

Suggested further reading

A systematic approach to Gödel's theorems presupposes some first-order logic, for which (Smullyan, 1995) is an introduction (emphasizing the relatively modern method of tableaux). The first eight chapters constitute sufficient preparation for Smullyan (1992). [See also chapter 1 of the present volume.] The author's (1992), though completely rigorous, contains what is probably the simplest available proof of Gödel's Theorem. The usual machinery of primitive recursive functions and the Chinese Remainder Theorem are completely avoided. Smullyan (1994) is a very comprehensive treatment of many topics bearing on Self-Reference, including abstract self-reference, elementary formal systems, incompleteness theorems, recursion theory and combinatory logic. It combines an introduction with a presentation of new results in these fields. Only one chapter, not even necessary for any of the others, presupposes any knowledge of first-order logic; all the other chapters are self-contained. Quine (1940, ch. 7; 1946) was the original inspiration for the modern approach to Gödel's theorems used in Smullyan (1992). It introduces the interesting subject of *Protosyntax Self-Applied*. Quine (1946) offers a very clever and influential idea subsequently used in the simplification of Gödel's proof.

References

Davis, M. (ed.) 1964: *The Undecidable*, (Raven Press, New York).

Gödel, K. 1992: *On Formally Undecidable Propositions of Principia Mathematica and Related Systems*, (trans. by E. Mendelson from the original German paper of 1931 in Davis (1964, 4–38)). Also available as its own book, trans. by B. Meltzer (Dover Publications, New York).

Parikh, R. 1971: "Existence and Feasibility in Arithmetic," *Journal of Symbolic Logic*, 36, 494–508.

Post, E. L. 1964: "Recursively Enumerable Sets of Positive Integers and their Decision Problems," *Bulletin of the American Mathematical Society*, (1944). Reprinted in Davis (1964, 304–39).

Quine, W. V. O. 1940: *Mathematical Logic*, (W. W. Norton & Co., New York).

Quine, W. V. O. 1946: "Concatenation as a Basis for Arithmetic," *Journal of Symbolic Logic*, 11, 105–14.

Rosenbloom, P. C. 1950: *The Elements of Mathematical Logic*, (Dover Publications, New York).

Rosser, J. B. 1964: "Extensions of Some Theorems of Gödel and Church," *Journal of Symbolic Logic*, 1 (1936), 87–91. Reprinted in Davis (1964, 230–35).

Smullyan, R. 1961: "Theory of Formal Systems," *Annals of Mathematics Studies 47*, (Princeton University Press, Princeton, NJ).

Smullyan, R. 1992: *Gödel's Incompleteness Theorems*, (Oxford University Press, Oxford).

Smullyan, R. 1994: *Diagonalization and Self-Reference*, (Clarendon Press, Oxford).

Smullyan, R. 1995: *First Order Logic*, Dover Edition (Dover Publications, New York).

Tarski, A. 1956: "Der Wahrheitsbegriff in den formalisierten Sprachen," *Studia Philosophie*, 1 (1936), 261–405. (English trans. "The Concept of Truth in Formalized Languages," in A. Tarski, *Logic, Semantics, Metamathematics*, translations by J. H. Woodger, (Clarendon Press, Oxford), 152–278.)

Chapter 5

Truth

Anil Gupta

5.1. Introduction

The concept of truth serves in logic not only as an instrument but also as an object of study. Eubulides of Miletus (fl. fourth century BCE), a Megarian logician, discovered the paradox known as 'the Liar,' and, ever since his discovery, logicians down the ages – Aristotle and Chrysippus, John Buridan and William Heytesbury, and Alfred Tarski and Saul Kripke, to mention just a few – have tried to understand the puzzling behavior of the concept of truth.[1]

In Eubulides' paradox, it is supposed that a person X says

What I am now saying is false.

and he says nothing more. The supposition is plainly coherent, but it leads via highly plausible arguments to absurd conclusions. If what X says is true, then X's statement must be assessed to be false (because X claims to have said something false). But if what X says is false, then X's statement must be assessed to be true (because, again, X claims to have said something false). The truth of X's statement implies, therefore, its falsity, and the falsity of X's statement implies, in turn, its truth. The original supposition seems thus to imply a contradiction.

The very simplicity of Eubulides' paradox has provoked numerous simple 'solutions' of it. There is, for instance, the idea (put forward by Bar-Hillel and others) that the paradox is removed, and the entire problem solved, simply by noting that truth is a property of propositions (not of sentences) and that X's words do not express a proposition.[2] But the solution fails. First, the paradox reappears if X's statement is reformulated a little:

I am not now expressing a true proposition.

If X's words do not express a proposition, they do not express a true proposition. Hence what X says should be assessed to be true, and one is again on the path to a contradiction. Second, paradoxical behavior is sometimes exhibited by contingent statements, and it is not plausible to maintain that these do not express propositions. St. Paul attributes, in his *Epistle to Titus*, the following remark to the Cretan Epimenides:

The Cretans are always liars.

Let us assume that 'liar' applies to people who have never uttered a truth (even unintentionally). Then, as has often been noted, the Epimenides remark is paradoxical if all other Cretan utterances happen to be untrue, and the remark is not paradoxical (but simply false) otherwise. Suppose that no other Cretan utterance is true. Then the Epimenides remark is contingently paradoxical, but it expresses a proposition. For the remark can be embedded in a true belief attribution – for example,

St. Paul believed that the Cretans were always liars.

a belief attribution that can explain some of St. Paul's behavior (Gupta and Belnap, 1993, pp. 7–12).

The central problem posed by the Liar paradox remains whether one takes propositions or sentences to be the bearers of truth. In fact, the major current theories of truth and paradox can be formulated for either type of truth bearer. So, for simplicity, assume sentences to be the bearers of truth; this allows one to bypass the theory of propositions. If context-sensitive elements are present, truth can be treated as a relational property: a sentence will count as true *relative* to the relevant contextual elements. The complexities of paradox appear even in languages without context-sensitive elements, and, for the most part, attention is restricted here to such languages.

The paradox brings to the surface a problem with the basic principles governing truth, the principle that a sentence A follows from its truth attribution "'A' is true' (*Truth Elimination*) and the converse principle that "'A' is true' follows from A (*Truth Introduction*). The principles can be combined, following Tarski, into the T-schema:

(T)   'A' is true if and only if A.

Instances of the T-schema will be called '*T-biconditionals*'. The paradox shows that, in the presence of certain kinds of self-reference, the T-biconditionals imply a contradiction. Suppose that l denotes 'l is not true', so l says of itself that it is not true.[3] Then,

$$l = \text{'}l \text{ is not true'} \tag{5.1}$$

Now the T-biconditional for l,

'l is not true' is true if and only if l is not true

and (5.1) together imply a contradiction within classical logic.

Gödel showed that self-referential statements can always be formulated in a language that contains certain syntactic resources (such as concatenation and names for symbols). [See chapter 4.] The problem the paradox presents can therefore be formulated as follows: the combination

T-biconditionals + Syntactic richness + Classical Logic

leads to contradictions. None of these elements is easily abandoned – not the T-biconditionals, not the syntactic resources, and not classical logic. The paradox thus creates a difficult problem. It has led some (e.g., Chihara and Priest) to espouse the *inconsistency view* of truth, the view that the rules governing truth are inconsistent. But this move only deepens the mystery created by the paradox. The concept of truth is used in ordinary, everyday situations without falling into incoherence. How is this achieved, working with an inconsistent concept? How can an inconsistent concept do useful work?[4] Notwithstanding the paradoxes, it is possible to make clear and unproblematic truth-attributions, for example, to the sentences 'Snow is white', ''Snow is white' is true', and 'Some of Aristotle's claims are not true'. How can this be done? The primary challenge that the paradox poses is to provide a better logical understanding of the concept of truth, one that explains the ordinary and the extraordinary behavior of the concept in a rich setting (rich syntax and, for example, full classical logic). The argument of the paradox can be blocked in numerous ways. It is possible, for instance, to weaken syntactic resources or eliminate negation from the language. But such moves do not meet the challenge.

The argument of the paradox not only raises a good problem; it serves a constructive purpose as well. It figures in Tarski's proof of his indefinability theorem: the set of Gödel numbers of the truths of arithmetic is not the extension of any arithmetical formula; more briefly, arithmetical truth is not definable within the arithmetical language [see chapter 4]. The arithmetical language L can be extended to a new language L' by adding to it a predicate that expresses arithmetical truth (i.e., 'true in L,' or more explicitly, 'Gödel number of a true sentence of L'). But the set of Gödel numbers of the truths of L' will not be definable in L'. One can move to a richer language, L'', by adding to L' a new predicate that expresses 'true in L'.' But, again, truth for L'' will not be definable in L''. The move of adding new truth predicates can be repeated indefinitely and generates a Tarskian hierarchy of increasingly richer languages, L, L', L'', ...

The Tarskian hierarchy of languages and truth predicates can be constructed by beginning with any interpreted base language that is free of truth and related notions. Let L_0 be such a language and let the expressions 'snow', 'is white', 'grass', and 'is green' belong to it. Then the next language in the hierarchy, L_1, contains a truth predicate, 'true$_1$', that applies to all the true sentences of L_0. For example, 'true$_1$' applies to sentences such as

Snow is white.

and

Grass is green.

and not to sentences such as

Snow is green.

and

'Snow is white' is $true_1$.

L_2, the next higher language, contains a truth predicate, '$true_2$', that has a wider application than '$true_1$'. '$True_2$' applies also to sentences of L_1 such as

'Snow is white' is $true_1$.

that do not belong to L_0. In general, a truth predicate of level n, '$true_n$', applies only to lower-level sentences, i.e. to sentences that belong to $L_m (m < n)$; it does not apply to sentences of level $\geq n$. The T_n-schema for '$true_n$'

(T_n)   'A' is $true_n$ if and only if A

holds only for sentences A of levels $< n$. The restriction means that '$true_n$' is bound to be free from paradox. Suppose l_n denotes 'l_n is not $true_n$'. Then l_n does not belong to the extension of '$true_n$', for its level is too high. So l_n is not $true_n$. But no contradiction follows, because the T_n-schema cannot be instantiated with 'l_n is not $true_n$'.

The hierarchy provides, then, an effective way of constructing paradox-free concepts of truth. Until about the late 1960s, it was the predominant view in philosophical logic that the hierarchy provides the only way of making sense of the ordinary concept of truth: meaningful uses of 'true' must be seen as representing one of the truth predicates in a Tarskian hierarchy. This conception was regarded not so much as a *view*, but as something that was *forced* by the paradoxes – or by some related mathematical theorems (e.g., Tarski's theorem) or some related principles of philosophical logic (e.g., Russell's vicious circle principle). Truth attributions, it was held, *had* to be expressed in a 'higher metalanguage.' In 1967, Prior wrote (p. 230):

> Further, Tarski argues, a sentence asserting that some sentence S is a true sentence of some language L cannot itself be a sentence of the language L, but must belong to a metalanguage in which the sentences of L are not used, but are mentioned and discussed. He is led to this view by the paradox of the "liar".

Prior endorses the point he attributes to Tarski, as did many others when Prior wrote his article.

It was in this environment that the groundbreaking and seminal work of Martin and Woodruff (1984 [1975]) and Kripke (1984 [1975]) appeared on the philosophical scene. These authors established, contrary to the prevalent dogma, that attributions of truth do not always force a move to a metalanguage. They proved via a fixed-point argument that certain three-valued languages contain their own truth predicates. Kripke's essay, in particular, introduced mathematical tools (e.g., his definition of 'groundedness') that were, and remain, fruitful.[5] The 'fixed-point' theories of Martin, Woodruff, and Kripke are presented in section 5.2.

Fixed-point constructions work, as shall be seen, only when languages are expressively weak – i.e., only when certain logical or syntactic notions are not expressible in them. The fundamental problem raised by the paradoxes – the problem of interpreting truth in rich languages – thus remains. The theories developed by Herzberger, Belnap, and me – the *revision* theories – offer a solution to this problem. These theories are presented in section 5.3.

Theories of the third group, the *contextual* theories, have been advocated by Parsons, Burge, Gaifman, and others. These theories make the interpretation of the truth predicate dependent on context. The motivating intuitions for this idea are explained in section 5.4.

Before I turn to an exposition of these three types of theories – the fixed-point, revision, and contextual theories – let me stress the limitations of this essay. First, the literature on truth is vast and I have not even attempted to summarize it. In particular, the three main types discussed here encompass many different theories, and I have provided an exposition only of some representative members. Visser's (1989) and Chapuis's (1998) articles are valuable surveys for further information. Second, I have restricted myself to semantical topics and issues. There is also a rich proof-theoretical side of the subject. A useful guide to this is provided by Sheard (1994). Third, I have not attempted to explain the applications of the theories discussed here to the paradoxes of class, property, belief, rationality, and other concepts.[6]

Preliminary matters. We shall identify interpreted languages L with ordered-triples $\langle L, M, \rho \rangle$, where L carries syntactic information about L, M provides interpretations for the non-logical constants of L (M is called variously 'model,' 'structure,' and 'interpretation'), and ρ is the semantic scheme for determining the interpretations of compound expressions. Of particular interest are *classical* languages. In these languages, the model M can be identified with an ordered pair $\langle D, I \rangle$, where D, the *domain*, is a non-empty set and I, the *interpretation* function, assigns to each name a member of D, to each n-ary function symbol a member of $D^n \rightarrow D$, and to each n-ary predicate a member of $D^n \rightarrow \{t, f\}$. The *extension* of an n-ary predicate G is the set of n-tuples that are assigned the value t by $I(G)$. We shall sometimes specify the interpretation of a predicate G in a classical language L by providing the extension of G in L. We shall call the classical scheme 'τ' and we shall assume Tarskian definitions of notions such as 'object d satisfies a formula $A(x)$ in L' and 'sentence A is true in L'. [See chapter 1.]

5.2. Fixed-Point Theories

Martin, Woodruff, and Kripke showed via a fixed-point argument that certain three-valued languages can contain their own truth predicates. This section begins with a brief account of one of the three-valued languages – one based on Kleene's strong valuation scheme (henceforth Strong Kleene) – and then turns to fixed points and their significance.

In a three-valued language, sentences can be true, false, or neither-true-nor-false. The semantic values of sentences include, therefore, not only the classical **t** ('the true') and **f** ('the false') but also the value **n** ('the neither-true-nor-false'). The interpretation of an *n*-place predicate G in a three-valued model M $(= \langle D, I \rangle)$ is a member of the set $D^n \to \{\mathbf{t}, \mathbf{f}, \mathbf{n}\}$. (In other respects, three-valued models are exactly like the classical ones.) The *extension* of G in M is the set of *n*-tuples that are assigned the value **t** by $I(G)$, and the *antiextension* is the set of *n*-tuples that are assigned the value **f**. If the extension and the antiextension of G exhaust the set D^n – that is, if **n** does not belong to the range of $I(G)$ – then the interpretation of G is said to be *classical*. If all predicates receive classical interpretations in M, then M is a classical model. By these definitions, all classical models count as three-valued but, of course, not all three-valued models are classical.

The Strong Kleene valuation scheme, κ, evaluates sentences for truth and falsity as follows. If, in a model M, the terms $t_1, \ldots, t_n$ denote the objects $d_1, \ldots, d_n$, respectively, then the semantic value of $G(t_1, \ldots, t_n)$ in M is $I(G)(d_1, \ldots, d_n)$. So $G(t_1, \ldots, t_n)$ is true in M iff (if and only if) the sequence $\langle d_1, \ldots, d_n \rangle$ belongs to the extension of G; the sentence is false iff $\langle d_1, \ldots, d_n \rangle$ belongs to the antiextension; and it is neither true nor false, otherwise. The connectives $\sim$ and & express the following functions:

$$\sim\mathbf{f} = \mathbf{t} \qquad \sim\mathbf{n} = \mathbf{n} \qquad \sim\mathbf{t} = \mathbf{f}$$

and

$$(\mathbf{t} \ \& \ \mathbf{t}) = \mathbf{t}$$
$$(\mathbf{n} \ \& \ \mathbf{t}) = (\mathbf{t} \ \& \ \mathbf{n}) = (\mathbf{n} \ \& \ \mathbf{n}) = \mathbf{n}$$
$$(\mathbf{v} \ \& \ \mathbf{f}) = (\mathbf{f} \ \& \ \mathbf{v}) = \mathbf{f} \qquad \text{for all } \mathbf{v} \in \{\mathbf{t}, \mathbf{f}, \mathbf{n}\}.$$

Finally, the universal quantifier $\forall$ expresses a generalized conjunction. The other connectives ($\vee$, $\to$, $\leftrightarrow$) and the quantifier ($\exists$) receive their standard definitions. It follows therefore that a disjunction, for example, is true iff one of its disjuncts is true; the disjunction is false iff both the disjuncts are false; and the disjunction is neither true nor false, otherwise. For another example, $\exists x Fx$ is true iff F is true of at least one object in the domain; it is false iff F is false of all the objects in the domain; and it is neither true nor false, otherwise. (See Gupta and Belnap (1993, section 2A), for a more leisurely exposition of the Strong Kleene and other schemes. [See also chapter 14.])

Two properties of the Strong Kleene scheme κ deserve notice. First, κ respects classical semantics: if the components of a compound receive classical values, then κ's assessment of the compound coincides with that of the classical scheme. Hence, the two schemes display perfect agreement on classical models. Second, the scheme has the following *monotonicity* property. Impose on the set of values $\{\mathbf{t}, \mathbf{f}, \mathbf{n}\}$ the following *information* ordering $\leq$: $\mathbf{n} \leq \mathbf{t}$, $\mathbf{n} \leq \mathbf{f}$, and **t** and **f** are incomparable. (See

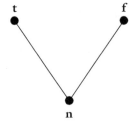

Figure 5.1

figure 5.1.) This ordering yields pointwise an information ordering ≤ on the inter-pretations of predicates:[7] Let $M = \langle D, I \rangle$ and let h, h' ∈ $D^n \to$ {**t**, **f**, **n**}. Then h ≤ h' iff, for all $d_1, \ldots, d_n \in D^n$, $h(d_1, \ldots, d_n) \le h'(d_1, \ldots, d_n)$. A model M' $(= \langle D', I' \rangle)$ is said to be *at least as informative* as M (M ≤ M') iff D = D', and I and I' assign the same interpretations to names and function symbols, and for all predicates G, $I(G) \le I'(G)$. Now the monotonicity property is this: if M ≤ M' then the sentences that are true (false) in M are also true (false) in M'. That is, as one moves to more informative models, there is never a reversal of earlier classical values.

Let $L (= \langle L, M, \kappa \rangle; M = \langle D, I \rangle)$ be a Strong Kleene language and T be a one-place predicate not in L. (Our aim is to interpret T as 'true'.) Let L^+ be L extended with T. Further, let the domain D of L contain all the sentences of L^+ (or the codes, e.g., the Gödel numbers, of the sentences of L^+).[8] For h ∈ D → {**t**, **f**, **n**}, let M + h be the model just like M except that T is assigned the interpretation h. Call M a *ground* model, and M + h a *standard* model, of L^+. Finally, let $L_h = \langle L^+, M + h, \kappa \rangle$ and say that G is a *T-predicate* of L_h iff the extension of G in L_h contains all and only the truths of L_h and the antiextension of G contains all and only the falsehoods of L_h. (Adopt here the usual – and, in the present context, unimportant – assumption that nonsentences fall among the falsehoods.) It is a remarkable property of the Strong Kleene scheme that an interpretation h can invariably be found under which T is a T-predicate of L_h – i.e., one under which the interpretation of T coincides with that of 'true sentences of L_h'.

A reformulation of this property will prove useful. Set H = D → {**t**, **f**, **n**}. For U, V ⊆ D and U ∩ V = Ø, let (U, V) be the unique member h of H such that U = {d ∈ D: h(d) = **t**} and V = {d ∈ D: h(d) = **f**}. Define the operation κ_M ('the Strong Kleene jump for M') on H as

$$\kappa_M(h) = (U', V')$$

where U' is the set that contains the true sentences of L_h, and V' is the set that contains the false sentences of L_h as well as the nonsentences. Observe that h is a *fixed point* of κ_M – i.e., $\kappa_M(h) = h$ – iff T is a T-predicate of L_h. The remarkable property of the Strong Kleene scheme can now be stated thus: κ_M invariably has fixed points.

Two proofs of the existence of fixed points are sketched here: one is algebraic and gives significant information about the structure of the fixed points of κ_M; the other relies on an iterative construction and reveals much about one particularly important fixed point.

The first proof rests on the properties of the structure $\langle H, \leq \rangle$ of the possible interpretations of T under the information ordering. This structure is a particular kind of poset (i.e., a partially ordered set: $\leq$ is reflexive, antisymmetric, and transitive). To specify the kind of poset it is, first recall that

- y is an *upper bound* of a subset Z of a poset $\langle X, \leq \rangle$ iff $y \in X$ and, for all $z \in Z$, $z \leq y$;
- y is the *least* element of Z iff $y \in Z$ and, for all $z \in Z$, $y \leq z$; and
- y is a *maximal* element of Z iff $y \in Z$ and there is no $z \in Z$ such that $z \neq y$ and $y \leq z$.

The notions of *lower bound*, *greatest* element, and *minimal* element receive dual definitions (i.e., definitions obtained by replacing '$\leq$' by '$\geq$'). Recall also that

- y is the *supremum*, $\bigvee Z$, of Z iff y is an upper bound of Z and y is the least of the upper bounds of Z, and
- y is the *infimum* of Z iff y is a lower bound of Z and y is the greatest of the lower bounds of Z.

Let us say, following Visser (1989, p. 656), that

- Z is *consistent* iff every $\{u, v\} \subseteq Z$ has an upper bound, and
- $\langle X, \leq \rangle$ is a *coherent complete partial order* (*ccpo*) iff every consistent subset of X has a supremum.

Examples: The values $\{t, f, n\}$ under the informational ordering constitute a ccpo (see figure 5.1). The dual of this structure – one obtained by flipping figure 5.1 about the horizontal – is not a ccpo. Finally, the structure $\langle H, \leq \rangle$ is a ccpo – indeed it is a general fact that if $\langle X, \leq \rangle$ is a ccpo then the function space X^D under the pointwise ordering induced by $\leq$ is also a ccpo. Here are some further properties of ccpos to note.

- First, every ccpo has a least element – for $\emptyset$ is invariably consistent and so has a supremum, which is also the least element of the ccpo.
- Second, every nonempty subset Z has an infimum – for the lower bounds of Z are consistent and hence have a supremum, which is also the infimum of Z.
- Third, every ccpo has maximal elements. (This follows by Zorn's lemma; see Visser (1989) or Gupta and Belnap (1993, section 2C).)

Observe that κ_M is a *monotone* operation on $\langle H, \leq \rangle$ in the sense that, for all h, $h' \in H$, if $h \leq h'$ then $\kappa_M(h) \leq \kappa_M(h')$. This follows immediately from the monotonicity of the Strong Kleene scheme: If $h \leq h'$, then $M + h'$ is at least as informative as $M + h$. Hence the sentences true (false) in $M + h$ must also be true (false) in $M + h'$. Consequently, $\kappa_M(h) \leq \kappa_M(h')$. Now the following theorem implies the existence of the fixed points of κ_M.

Visser's Fixed-Point Theorem (Visser, 1989, p. 659). Suppose that f: $X \to X$ is a monotone operation on a ccpo $\langle X, \leq \rangle$. Let F $(= \{x \in X: f(x) = x\})$ be the set of fixed points of f, and let $\leq\!\upharpoonright\!F$ be the relation $\leq$ restricted to F. Then $\langle F, \leq\!\upharpoonright\!F \rangle$ is a ccpo.

A compressed proof. Let us say that $x \in X$ is *sound* iff $x \leq f(x)$. Further, for $Y \subseteq X$, let us identify the structure $\langle Y, \leq\!\upharpoonright\!Y \rangle$ with the set Y. Now consider an arbitrary $U \subseteq F$ such that U is consistent in the poset F. We need to show that U has a supremum in F. Observe that if a set $Y \subseteq X$ is consistent, and if Y contains only sound points, then the supremum $\bigvee Y$ of Y is sound. (Argument: For arbitrary $y \in Y$, $y \leq \bigvee Y$. So, by the monotonicity of f, $f(y) \leq f(\bigvee Y)$. Since y is sound, $y \leq f(y) \leq f(\bigvee Y)$. So $f(\bigvee Y)$ is an upper bound of Y. Hence $\bigvee Y \leq f(\bigvee Y)$.) It follows that if x is sound, then the set of sound points $z \geq x$ is a ccpo. Now U is a set that contains only sound points. So $\bigvee U$ is sound and the set $V = \{x \in X: x \leq f(x)$ and $\bigvee U \leq x\}$ is a ccpo. Therefore V must have a maximal element v. We know that $\bigvee U \leq v \leq f(v)$. By monotonicity and the soundness of $\bigvee U$, $\bigvee U \leq f(\bigvee U) \leq f(v) \leq f(f(v))$. So $f(v) \in V$. Since v is a maximal element of V, $f(v) = v$. This implies that the set $W = \{x \in X: f(x) \leq x$ and $\bigvee U \leq x\}$ is nonempty. Hence W must have an infimum z in the ccpo X. This element z is a fixed point and is also the supremum of U in the ccpo F. (Argument: For arbitrary $w \in W$, $z \leq w$. By monotonicity, $f(z) \leq f(w) \leq w$. So $f(z)$ is a lower bound of W, and thus $f(z) \leq z$. It is easily verified that $\bigvee U \leq f(z)$. So $f(z) \in W$. But z is a lower bound of W and $f(z) \leq z$. So $f(z) = z$. Every fixed point that is an upper bound of U belongs to W. So z must be the supremum of U in F.) QED

The number of fixed points of κ_M can range from 1 to the cardinality of the continuum – the number depends upon the sorts of vicious reference exemplified in M. The theorem above shows that the fixed points of κ_M, irrespective of their number, always constitute a ccpo. This tells us, among other things, that κ_M has maximal fixed points, that every nonempty set of its fixed points has an infimum, and that κ_M has a least fixed point.

The second proof of the existence of the fixed points of κ_M proceeds via Kripke's iterative construction of the least fixed point. (Incidentally, Martin and Woodruff proved the existence of maximal fixed points for Kleene's weak valuation scheme [see chapter 14].) Let us see how the construction works by way of an example. Suppose that the nonlogical symbols of L are the one-place predicates G and H, the names a, b, and c, and the quotational names 'A' for all $A \in S$, the set of sentences of L^+. Fix M' $(= \langle D', I' \rangle)$ to be the following classical model of L.

> $D' = S \cup \{0\}$. I' assigns to the quotational names their intended interpretation; it assigns to the names a, b, and c the denotations 0, $\sim Tb$, and Tc, respectively; and it assigns to G and H the extensions $\{0\}$ and $\{T`T`Ga''\}$, respectively.

The iterative construction builds up an interpretation of T as follows. At the initial stage, stage 0, the interpretation of T is set as $(\emptyset, \emptyset)$.[9] This stage may be pictured as representing our initial ignorance of the extension and the antiextension of T. Now, despite this ignorance, the scheme κ can be used to determine the truths U_1

and the falsehoods V_1 of the model $M' + (\emptyset, \emptyset)$. It is easy to see that Ga, $\sim Ha$, and $\sim \forall x Hx$, for example, belong to U_1 and the negations of these sentences belong to V_1. Note that Ta and all other truth attributions are neither true nor false, for both the extension and the antiextension of T are $\emptyset$. At the next stage, stage 1, T is assigned the richer interpretation (U_1, V_1) $[= \kappa_{M'}((\emptyset, \emptyset))]$. And the truths U_2 and the falsehoods V_2 of the model $M' + (U_1, V_1)$ are determined as before. By monotonicity, $U_1 \subseteq U_2$ and $V_1 \subseteq V_2$. But some of the sentences that were earlier assessed as neither true nor false now receive a classical value. For example, Ta and $T'Ga'$ were earlier assessed as neither true nor false, but now the former is assessed as false and the latter as true. At stage 2, T is assigned the richer interpretation (U_2, V_2) $[= \kappa_{M'}((U_1, V_1))]$. The process can then be repeated to construct yet richer interpretations of T at higher stages. The process can be continued into the transfinite by taking the interpretation at a limit stage α to be the supremum – $(\cup_{\beta<\alpha}U_\alpha, \cup_{\beta<\alpha}V_\alpha)$ – of the earlier interpretations. (Since the earlier interpretations constitute a consistent set, the supremum is bound to exist.) The sentences of L^+ constitute a set, so the iterative process must reach 'closure' at some stage α: the interpretation of T at α must coincide with that at $\alpha + 1$. This interpretation is a fixed point – in fact, the least fixed point – of the Strong Kleene jump. In the example above, the *closure* ordinal – the least ordinal at which closure occurs – is ω, the first infinite ordinal. The closure ordinal depends on the type of vicious reference in the ground model and can, in general, be much higher. Beginning with the standard model of arithmetic (and with the standard Gödel numbering of sentences), the fixed point is reached at ω_1^{CK}, the first nonrecursive ordinal.

Kripke (1984 [1975]) calls a sentence *grounded* in M iff it belongs to the extension or to the antiextension of T in the least fixed point of κ_M. The sentences $T'Ga'$ and $\forall x (Hx \rightarrow Tx)$ are examples of the grounded truths of M' and $T'\sim T'Ga''$ and $\forall x (Tx \rightarrow Hx)$ of the grounded falsehoods of M'. The sentences $\sim Tb$ (the Liar) and Tc (the Truth Teller, which says of itself that it is true) are not grounded in M'. The truth and falsity of grounded sentences can be traced to some 'nonsemantic' facts in the ground model. This tracing fails for the Liar and the Truth Teller; hence they are ungrounded. The Liar and the Truth Teller are intuitively different – the Truth Teller, unlike the Liar, can coherently be said to be true or to be false – and this difference is reflected in the fixed points. Kripke defines a sentence to be *paradoxical* iff it does not have a classical value in any fixed point. By this definition, the Liar $\sim Tb$ is paradoxical but the Truth Teller Tc is not. In fact, there is a fixed point in which Tc is true and another in which it is false. Note that $\kappa_{M'}$ has exactly three fixed points – in one Tc is n; in the second, f; and in the third, t – and these constitute a ccpo isomorphic to the one pictured in figure 5.1.[10]

The entire theory sketched above goes through for *any* three-valued scheme that has the monotonicity property. (In fact, it goes through for any scheme, *n*-valued or another, for which an analog of monotonicity holds.)[11] One such scheme is the supervaluations of Bas van Fraassen (1966) [see also chapter 12]:

A sentence is true (false) in a three-valued model M by the supervaluation scheme iff the sentence is true (false) in every classical model M_0 such that $M \leq M_0$.

Observe that Kripke's definition of paradoxicality implies that the sentence $\forall x \sim (Tx \ \& \sim Tx)$ is paradoxical. If the supervaluation scheme is used in place of the Strong Kleene, then this sentence is assessed not as paradoxical but as grounded.

It is important to be clear about the intuitive meaning of fixed points. In a fixed-point language L_h $(= \langle L^+, M + h, \kappa \rangle)$, T is a T-predicate. What this means is that *if T* has the interpretation h *then* it is a T-predicate of L_h: T is true (false) precisely of the truths (falsehoods) of L_h and so is coextensive with the concept 'true sentence of L_h'. This does not mean that if T had *meant* truth – that if it had *expressed* the concept of truth – then its interpretation would have been h. (Sometimes a fixed point can be the interpretation of T only if T does not express the concept of truth.) Fixed points do not reveal the interpretation of truth absolutely. They reveal what the interpretation of truth would be only under an antecedent hypothesis about the interpretation of T. The fact that κ has fixed points does not establish therefore that any of the fixed points are the proper interpretation of a predicate that expresses the concept of truth (Gupta and Belnap, 1993, section 3A).

The Strong Kleene and the other schemes that allow for the existence of fixed points are expressively incomplete. For example, consider the Łukasiewicz biconditional $\equiv$, which expresses the following function.

> For all $\mathbf{v}, \mathbf{v}' \in \{\mathbf{t}, \mathbf{f}, \mathbf{n}\}$:
> $(\mathbf{v} \equiv \mathbf{v}') = \mathbf{t}$ if $\mathbf{v} = \mathbf{v}'$
> $(\mathbf{v} \equiv \mathbf{v}') = \mathbf{n}$ if exactly one of $\mathbf{v}$ and $\mathbf{v}'$ is $\mathbf{n}$, and
> $(\mathbf{v} \equiv \mathbf{v}') = \mathbf{f}$, otherwise

[See chapter 14.] The Łukasiewicz biconditional is true, then, iff both its components have the same value; it is false iff the components have different classical values; and it is neither true nor false, otherwise. Any scheme ρ in which the Łukasiewicz biconditional is expressible fails, in general, to allow for the existence of fixed points. Consider a ground model M with the following features:

(i)   there is a sentence A that is false in M;
(ii) there is a name b that denotes $(A \equiv Tb)$ in M; and
(iii) there is a name c that denotes $(Tb \equiv Tc)$ in M.

Suppose, for reductio, that there is a fixed point h for M and ρ. Then $h(Tb) = \mathbf{n}$, for Tb is Liar-like. Now if $h(Tc)$ is classical then $(Tb \equiv Tc)$ is neither true nor false and hence contradicts our initial hypothesis that h is a fixed point. So $h(Tc) = \mathbf{n}$. But this implies that $(Tb \equiv Tc)$ is true and therefore also contradicts the initial hypothesis. The reductio is complete: there cannot be a fixed point for ρ in M.

In fixed-point languages, the semantic value of a sentence A is identical with the semantic value of the truth attribution $T\text{'}A\text{'}$. The argument above shows, however, that the equivalence of A and $T\text{'}A\text{'}$ cannot be expressed in the fixed-point languages, for the relevant biconditional is inexpressible in them.[12] Another example of inexpressibility is provided by exclusion negation $\neg$:

$$\neg \mathbf{t} = \mathbf{f} \qquad \neg \mathbf{n} = \mathbf{f} \qquad \text{and} \qquad \neg \mathbf{f} = \mathbf{t}$$

The Liar is assessed as neither true nor false in the fixed-point languages. So it is assessed to be untrue but, because of the absence of exclusion negation, this assessment is not expressible within the languages themselves. The fixed-point languages are weak, then, in their logical resources. They are also bound to be weak in the semantic predicates they contain. A Strong Kleene fixed-point language, for example, cannot in general contain its own 'neither-true-nor-false' predicate.[13] The situation with three-valued languages is similar, therefore, to the one that obtains for classical languages. If a classical language is expressively weakened – for example, by dispensing with negation – then it too can contain its own truth predicate. On the other hand, an expressively rich three-valued language, like an expressively rich classical language, cannot contain its own truth predicate.

The problem of gaining a semantical understanding of the concept of truth thus remains. As was observed above, the concept is used – successfully for the most part – in expressively rich languages. But for such languages fixed points do not exist. How then is one to make semantic sense of the concept of truth?

5.3. Revision Theories

Revision theories make two principal claims:

(i)   Logical and semantic sense can be made of circular definitions and concepts.[14]
(ii)   Truth is a circular concept.

These claims are motivated by a striking parallel that obtains between the behavior of the concept of truth and the behavior of concepts with circular definitions. The concept of truth is plainly unproblematic over a large range of sentences. It applies unproblematically to

Snow is white.

and

All theorems of Peano Arithmetic are true.

and numerous other similar sentences, and it fails to apply to their negations. But there are sentences – for example, the Liar and the Truth Teller – over which the concept behaves in a problematic and perplexing way. Now compare this behavior of the concept of truth with the behavior of a predicate G that is given a circular definition:

$$Gx =_{df} [x = \text{Socrates}] \lor [x = \text{Plato} \ \& \ Gx] \lor [x = \text{Aristotle} \ \& \ {\sim}Gx] \qquad (5.2)$$

Notice that definition (5.2), though circular, renders the definiendum G unproblematic over a large range of objects. In fact, the definition renders G unproblematic over all objects except Plato and Aristotle: it implies that Socrates is G and the rest are not G. Over Plato and Aristotle, G behaves in a problematic and perplexing way. But observe that the pathology G exhibits parallels exactly the one that truth exhibits over the Truth Teller and the Liar. First, all attempts to determine whether Plato and Aristotle are G end up cycling in a loop, mimicking what happens with the Truth Teller and the Liar. Second, just as an arbitrary stipulation about the truth of the Truth Teller can be sustained, similarly one can sustain an arbitrary stipulation about the G-ness of Plato. One can coherently assert that Plato is G and also that Plato is not G. Finally, an uncritical use of the rules governing definitions (Definiendum Introduction and Definiendum Elimination) allows one to go back and forth between the claim that Aristotle is G and the claim that Aristotle is not G – just as an uncritical use of the rules governing truth (Truth Introduction and Truth Elimination) allows one to go back and forth between the claim that the Liar is true and the claim that the Liar is not true.

More generally, several different kinds of pathologies are exhibited by the concept of truth and these, it turns out, coincide with the pathologies exhibited by concepts with circular definitions. This suggests, contrary to traditional ideas, that semantic sense can perhaps be made of circular concepts and definitions, and that the perplexing behavior of the concept of truth may be rooted in a circularity in the concept.

How can one make semantic sense of predicates with circular definitions? A definition – say, $Gx =_{df} A(x)$ – may be viewed as providing a rule for determining the extension of its definiendum (i.e., G) in terms of its definiens (i.e., A): to determine whether an object d falls in the extension of G one determines whether d satisfies the definiens $A(x)$. The problem is that, with circular definitions, this procedure breaks down. For, in circular definitions, the definiendum occurs in the definiens. Consequently, information is needed about the extension of G so as to determine whether the object satisfies the definiens. Observe though, that despite this difficulty, the procedure is not entirely useless. The procedure can be applied provided one supplies it with a hypothesis about the extension of G. For example, hypothesize the extension of G in definition (5.2) to be $\emptyset$. It is now easily verified that Socrates and Aristotle satisfy the definiens. Hence, under the stated hypothesis, the procedure yields {Socrates, Aristotle} as the extension of G.

A circular definition does not provide a categorical rule for determining the extension of its definiendum. It provides instead a hypothetical rule, a rule that yields an extension of the definiendum *relative* to a hypothesis about the extension. The central idea of revision theories is that this rule should be viewed as a *rule of revision*: an application of the rule yields a hypothesis that is a better candidate – or, at least, it is as good a candidate – for the extension of the definiendum as the initial hypothesis.

The revision rule has a hypothetical character, but it provides a basis for categorical judgments. The intuitive idea for making the transition to the categorical is this. One considers *all* possible hypotheses for the extension of the definiendum, and one tries to improve them through repeated applications of the revision rule. Hypotheses that survive this process – those that are found to occur over and over again in the course of revision – are the ones that are deemed best by the revision rule. If a claim holds under all the best hypotheses, then it is true categorically. If a claim fails under all these hypotheses, then it is false categorically. And if neither of these alternatives holds – that is, if the revision rule yields no categorical verdict – then the claim is pathological.

This intuitive idea can be made precise as follows. Let M ($= \langle D, I \rangle$) be a classical model for L and let L be extended to L^+ by the addition of a new one-place predicate G. Further, let G be governed by the (possibly) circular definition $\mathcal{D}$,

$$(\mathcal{D}) \qquad Gx =_{\mathrm{df}} A(x, G)$$

where $A(x, G)$ is a formula that contains no free occurrences of variables other than x. Let us call members of the set $D \to \{\mathbf{t}, \mathbf{f}\}$ *hypotheses*. And, for h a hypothesis, let M + h be the model of L^+ that is just like M except that it assigns to G the interpretation h. The rule of revision $\delta_{\mathcal{D},M}$ for $\mathcal{D}$ in M is an operation on the set $D \to \{\mathbf{t}, \mathbf{f}\}$ that satisfies the condition

$$\delta_{\mathcal{D},M}(h)(d) = \mathbf{t} \leftrightarrow d \text{ satisfies } A(x, G) \text{ in } M + h$$

Note that, in general, the revision rule $\delta_{\mathcal{D},M}$ is not monotone in any interesting sense. It cannot be used to iteratively build up an interpretation of G. (In fact, $\delta_{\mathcal{D},M}$ may lack fixed points altogether.) To extract categorical information from the revision rule, the notion of 'revision sequence' is defined. Suppose S is a sequence of hypotheses and suppose that the length, $\mathrm{lh}(S)$, of S is either a limit ordinal or the class On of all ordinals. For $\alpha < \mathrm{lh}(S)$, let S_α be the αth member of S and let $S{\restriction}\alpha$ be S restricted to α.

- An object d is *stably* $\mathbf{t}(\mathbf{f})$ in S iff there is an ordinal $\alpha < \mathrm{lh}(S)$ such that for all ordinals β if $\alpha \leq \beta < \mathrm{lh}(S)$ then $S_\beta(d) = \mathbf{t}(\mathbf{f})$.
- S is a *revision sequence* for $\delta_{\mathcal{D},M}$ iff, for all $\alpha < \mathrm{lh}(S)$, S satisfies two conditions:
  (i)   if $\alpha = \beta + 1$ then $S_\alpha = \delta_{\mathcal{D},M}(S_\beta)$;
  (ii) if α is a limit ordinal then, for all $d \in D$, if d is stably $\mathbf{t}(\mathbf{f})$ in $S{\restriction}\alpha$ then $S_\alpha(d) = \mathbf{t}(\mathbf{f})$.

In a revision sequence S, then, one begins with an arbitrary initial hypothesis S_0. At stage 1 – and at successor stages generally – one revises the hypothesis at the previous stage by an application of the revision rule. At a limit stage α, the results of earlier revision are summed up:

- If an object is stably $\mathbf{t}(\mathbf{f})$ up to α then it is declared $\mathbf{t}(\mathbf{f})$ at α.
- Otherwise, it is arbitrarily assigned one of the truth values.

(This treatment of limit stages is due to Belnap.)

It can now be seen how the system **S*** of Gupta and Belnap (1993) makes semantic sense of circular definitions. A hypothesis h is α-*reflexive for* $\delta_{\mathcal{D},M}$ iff there is a revision sequence S for $\delta_{\mathcal{D},M}$ such that $\alpha < \mathrm{lh}(S)$ and $S_0 = S_\alpha = h$; and h is *reflexive for* $\delta_{\mathcal{D},M}$ iff h is α-reflexive for some ordinal $\alpha > 0$. It is easy to show that reflexive hypotheses are precisely the ones that occur over and over again in On-long revision sequences – they are the ones that survive the revision process. Now a sentence A is *valid on* $\mathcal{D}$ *in* M *in* the system $\mathbf{S}^*$ iff, for all hypotheses h that are reflexive for $\delta_{\mathcal{D},M}$, A is true in $M + h$; and $\mathcal{D}$ *implies* A *in* $\mathbf{S}^*$ iff, for all classical models M of L, A is valid on $\mathcal{D}$ in M in $\mathbf{S}^*$.[15] An argument $A_1, \ldots, A_n \therefore B$ is *valid on* $\mathcal{D}$ *in* $\mathbf{S}^*$ iff $\mathcal{D}$ implies $((A_1 \& \cdots \& A_n) \rightarrow B)$ in $\mathbf{S}^*$.

Example: Consider definition (5.2) and suppose M represents the actual state of affairs – so that Socrates, Plato, and Aristotle are distinct individuals. Then the revision rule has four reflexive hypotheses: {Socrates}, {Socrates, Plato}, {Socrates, Aristotle}, and {Socrates, Plato, Aristotle}.[16] Of the following sentences,

$G(\text{Plato})$

$G(\text{Aristotle})$

$G(\text{Socrates})$

$\forall x(Gx \rightarrow x = \text{Socrates} \vee x = \text{Plato} \vee x = \text{Aristotle})$

the last two are valid – they are true under all reflexive hypotheses – but the first two are not. They are *pathological*: true under some reflexive hypotheses and false under others. Different kinds of pathologicality can be distinguished; the details are omitted here, so refer to Gupta and Belnap (1993, section 5D.15).

The traditional theory imposes two requirements on definitions: noncreativity and eliminability. Noncreativity requires that the addition of a definition should not create essentially new validities. Under the $\mathbf{S}^*$ semantics, all definitions, ordinary as well as circular, meet this requirement: if a sentence A of L is deemed valid in M by the $\mathbf{S}^*$ semantics then A must be true in M. Eliminability, on the other hand, requires that occurrences of the definiendum must be eliminable: for every sentence A, the definition should imply the equivalence of A with a sentence B that contains no occurrences of the definiendum.[17] The $\mathbf{S}^*$ semantics does not meet this requirement. Indeed the requirement cannot be met by any theory that aims to accommodate all circular definitions. One important intuition underlying eliminability is, however, respected in $\mathbf{S}^*$: a definition fixes completely the meaning of its definiendum. Note also that $\mathbf{S}^*$ respects eliminability for noncircular definitions. More generally, with noncircular definitions, $\mathbf{S}^*$ leaves intact our ordinary preconceptions about definitions and also our ordinary ways of working with them. Only on the domain of the circular does $\mathbf{S}^*$ dictate some modification of our ideas and practices.

A remark about the expressive power of circular definitions under $\mathbf{S}^*$: A construction due to Kremer (1993) establishes that inductive and co-inductive sets are definable using first-order circular definitions. Expressive power goes hand in hand with complexity. Kremer (1993) and Antonelli (1994) have shown that there are finite sets of definitions whose implications in $\mathbf{S}^*$ constitute a Π_2^1 set.

Tarski wrote of the T-biconditional that it "may be considered a partial definition of truth, which explains wherein the truth of . . . one individual sentence consists" (1944, section 4). Notice that Tarski's suggestion can be accepted only if one is prepared to countenance *circular* partial definitions. For the definiens supplied by some T-biconditionals contain the term 'true.' *Example*:

'Everything Jones says is true' is true $=_{df}$ everything Jones says is true.

With the theory of definitions **S*** one can now implement Tarski's suggestion. Suppose, as before, that the one-place predicate **T** is added to L ($= \langle L, M, \tau \rangle$; $M = \langle D, I \rangle$), that the sentences of L^+ are in the domain D, and that L has quotational names of all the sentences of L^+. Suppose further that **T** is governed by the Tarski biconditionals – **T**'A' $=_{df}$ A – and the principle that only sentences are true. Suppose, that is, that **T** is governed by the following infinitistic circular definition:[18]

$$Tx =_{df} (x = \text{'}A_1\text{'} \ \& \ A_1) \lor (x = \text{'}A_2\text{'} \ \& \ A_2) \lor \cdots \lor (x = \text{'}A_n\text{'} \ \& \ A_n) \lor \cdots$$

This definition yields a rule of revision τ_M for **T** in M. The rule can be characterized thus: for all hypotheses h and all $d \in D$,

$$\tau_M(h)(d) = \mathbf{t} \leftrightarrow d \text{ is a sentence that is true in } M + h$$

Example: Consider the model M' from the previous section. Let h be the hypothesis under which the extension of **T** is $\varnothing$ – so, $h(d) = \mathbf{f}$, for all $d \in D$. The first three applications of the revision rule $\tau_{M'}$ to h yield three interpretations.

(i) $\{Ga, \sim T\text{'}Ga\text{'}, \sim T\text{'}\sim Ga\text{'}, \forall x \sim Tx, \sim Tc, \sim Tb, \dots\}$ $= \tau_{M'}(h)$
(ii) $\{Ga, T\text{'}Ga\text{'}, T\text{'}\sim T\text{'}Ga\text{''}, \sim \forall x \sim Tx, \sim Tc, Tb, \dots\}$ $= \tau_{M'}(\tau_{M'}(h))$
(iii) $\{Ga, T\text{'}Ga\text{'}, T\text{'}T\text{'}Ga\text{''}, T\text{'}T\text{'}\sim T\text{'}Ga\text{'''}, \sim Tc, \sim Tb, \dots\} = \tau_{M'}(\tau_{M'}(\tau_{M'}(h)))$

Note that, in the course of revision, sentences move both in and out of the extension of **T**.

The revision rule τ_M has the following remarkable property. In a large class of models – models that can roughly be characterized as those without vicious reference – repeated applications of the revision rule to a hypothesis culminate in a fixed point, and furthermore, no matter where one begins the process of revision, it leads to the same fixed point. In these models, the **S*** semantics dictates that truth has a classical interpretation and that the usual preconceptions about it hold.[19]

The presence of vicious reference destroys the ideal of convergence to a unique fixed point. A Truth Teller destroys convergence: it makes the outcome of revision dependent on the initial hypothesis. In the example above the Truth Teller **Tc** stays out of the extension of **T** at successive stages of revision, reflecting the initial hypothesis that it is untrue. If the initial hypothesis were that it is true, then the Truth Teller would have stayed in the extension of **T** at all successive stages. A Liar sentence, on the other hand, destroys the stability of revision. Note that the Liar $\sim Tb$ flips in and out throughout the revision process. Consequently, the process does not settle down; at every stage of revision, the outcome is revised to a different one.

Even in the presence of vicious reference, many sentences receive a categorical assessment in the revision process. These sentences eventually settle either in the extension or in the antiextension of truth. Furthermore, they settle the same way irrespective of the initial hypothesis of revision. Note that the grounded truths of the

Strong Kleene scheme, and of the supervaluation scheme, are valid – they invariably settle in the extension. (There are valid sentences, however, that are not grounded on either scheme.) The theorems of classical logic are also valid. Furthermore, the material biconditionals, $T'A' \leftrightarrow A$ are valid for nonpathological sentences A, but they may fail to be valid for pathological sentences.

There is thus a fundamental distinction between the definitional equivalences $T'A' =_{df} A$ and the material equivalences $T'A' \leftrightarrow A$. The former are acceptable, but the latter are not. The distinction provides a natural diagnosis of the fallacy in the Liar argument: equivocation. When the T-biconditionals are read definitionally, they are acceptable but they fail to imply any contradictions. (No definition implies contradictions in $\mathbf{S^*}$.) When they are read materially, the T-biconditionals imply contradictions but they are unacceptable.

The foregoing gives a sketch of some of the shared features of revision theories. Now, turning to differences: The main difference centers on how revision theories extract categorical information from the revision rule and, in particular, how they treat limit stages. Belnap's limit rule, on which the theory $\mathbf{S^*}$ is based, is the simplest and the most liberal. It allows arbitrary choice with respect to unstable elements. The other limit rules impose constraints on how choices are made. Herzberger's (1984 [1982]) limit rule is the strictest: it requires the unstable elements to be removed from the extension. Yaqūb (1993) has argued against Belnap's and Herzberger's rules (and also against another that I had suggested) and has proposed an intricate one of his own. Chapuis (1996) has studied a treatment of limit stages that results in 'fully-varied' revision sequences. This treatment seems to me to be especially promising.

The choices made at limit stages can contaminate the revision process, though the effects of contamination are reduced by subsequent applications of the revision rule. It is natural, therefore, to ignore a finite number of stages near limits when assessing stability. If this is done, one obtains the system $\mathbf{S^\#}$ of Gupta and Belnap (1993); for a more precise account, see Gupta and Belnap (1993, section 5D). It is important to draw attention to one substantial and important difference between $\mathbf{S^*}$ and $\mathbf{S^\#}$. The theory of truth based on $\mathbf{S^*}$ does not imply the semantical laws – laws such as

$\sim A$ is true iff A is not true.

A conjunction is true iff its conjuncts are true.

and

If every object has a name, then a universal quantification is true iff all its instances are true.

The semantic law of negation, for instance, fails to be valid in $\mathbf{S^*}$ because it is false at all limit stages at which both the Liar and its negation are declared to have the value $\mathbf{t}$. The theory of truth based on $\mathbf{S^\#}$, on the other hand, does validate the semantic laws. For the failure of the laws occurs only at limit stages, which can be neglected in $\mathbf{S^\#}$ in assessments of validity. This advantage of $\mathbf{S^\#}$ is intimately connected, however, to a feature that some critics regard as a grave flaw: on the $\mathbf{S^\#}$ theory some definitions imply ω-inconsistencies. ($S^\#$ respects the requirement of noncreativity, so no definition implies outright contradictions. However, there are definitions that, for each object d, validate the sentence $\sim A\bar{d}$ – $\bar{d}$ a name of d – and validate also the sentence $\exists x Ax$.) McGee (1991, pp. 29–31) has shown that, under minimal conditions, the semantic laws imply ω-inconsistencies. So one cannot gain the semantic laws without countenancing ω-inconsistent definitions. I myself am attracted to the system $S^\#$ and am willing to entertain seriously the idea that there are ω-inconsistent definitions and that the Tarskian definition of truth is one such.[20]

5.4.   Contextual Theories

According to contextual theories, the interpretation of 'true' depends on context. The precise account of the dependence varies considerably from theory to theory, however. Parsons (1984 [1974]) was the first in the contemporary debate to argue for contextual theories. He suggested that the relevant contextual contribution is a 'scheme of interpretation,' a scheme that specifies the ranges of quantifiers, the interpretation of indirect-discourse terms such as 'say', etc. Burge (1984 [1979]) defined hierarchies of truth predicates. The contribution of context in his theory is the *level* at which 'true' is interpreted. Barwise and Etchemendy (1987) proposed what they called an *Austinian theory* in which the relevant contextual contribution is the portion of the world that a proposition is about. (They also presented an interesting modeling of circular propositions within Aczel's non-well-founded set theory.) The theories of Koons (1992) and Simmons (1993) are closely related to those of Parsons and Burge. Relevant contextual factors in their theories include intentions of speakers; these help to determine something like a scheme of interpretation. A distinguishing mark of Simmons's theory is its avoidance of hierarchies. The theories of Skyrms (1984) and Gaifman (1992) can also be seen as falling in the contextual category. These authors look at the network generated by the process of semantic evaluation, and the interpretation of 'true' in an utterance depends on the place of the utterance in this network. (See the discussion of the Chrysippus intuition below for a simple example.)

Three ideas – *Universality, the Strengthened Liar*, and *the Chrysippus intuition* (though these are not always clearly distinguished) – have played a dominant role in the motivation of the modern contextual theories. These theories are *not* motivated, it should be stressed, by the ordinary unproblematic uses of 'true'. Before the work of Kripke and others, there was the idea that contextual elements are also needed for the interpretation of 'true' in unproblematic sentences. For example, if 'true' in

Nothing X said at t is true.

is interpreted as 'true$_n$' in a Tarskian hierarchy, then the level n has to depend on such contextual factors as what X actually said at t. If X did not use the truth predicate (and other similar devices), then n can be 1; otherwise, n has to be higher. But the modern theories avoid contextual shifts in the interpretation of unproblematic sentences. (They do so by piggybacking on a type-free theory, e.g., a fixed-point theory.) Context comes into play in the modern theories only to account for certain ideas and intuitions connected with the paradoxes. The next subsections examine the more important of these ideas and intuitions.

5.4.1.   Universality

Tarski expressed the view that the source of the paradoxes is the universality of natural languages. He wrote (Tarski, 1969, p. 67)

> [W]e have to analyze those features of the common language that are the real source of the antinomy of the liar. When carrying through this analysis, we notice at once an outstanding feature of this language – its all-comprehensive, universal character. The common language . . . is supposed to provide adequate facilities for expressing everything that can be expressed at all, in any language whatsoever.

Several authors have accepted Tarski's diagnosis that the real source of the paradoxes is the universality of natural languages,[21] and they have treated universality as a desideratum for any adequate theory of truth. In practice, the desideratum is weakened to the following: the theory must show how *semantic self-sufficiency* is possible. That is, the theory must show how there can be languages L such that a complete semantic theory for L is expressible in L itself. This desideratum plays a large role in, for example, Simmons's work. Simmons (1993) uses it to argue against fixed-point and revision theories, and he aims to satisfy it through his own contextual theory.

The ideas of universality and semantic self-sufficiency need philosophical clarification and justification before they can be accepted as providing desiderata for a theory of truth. Ordinary English – to take the most immediate example of a natural language – is plainly not universal: it does not have the resources to express everything. It is true that English is highly flexible – its expressive power can be extended indefinitely (e.g., through the addition of new vocabulary). And it may be that, for everything that can be expressed in any language, there is an extension of English that expresses it.[22] But this provides no reason to believe that English has extensions that are semantically self-sufficient. The large literature on the subject has yet to provide a good argument for the claim that semantically self-sufficient languages are possible.[23]

There is a related, but much weaker, thesis that is a plausible desideratum for theories of truth: a natural language can express – either as it is or through an extension – any semantic concept whatsoever. This thesis (call it '*weak universality*') implies that the status of pathological sentences such as the Liar can be expressed in natural languages (or their extensions). So, if a theory declares the Liar to be neither true nor false (or not categorical or not true in a context c), then weak universality requires that the theory show how a language can express not only its own concept of truth but also its own concept of neither-true-nor-false (or 'not categorical' or 'not true in a context c').

5.4.2. The strengthened Liar

An example of the strengthened Liar is the following statement *SL*.

(*SL*)   Either *SL* is neither-true-nor-false or it is not true.

If *SL* is either true or false, then *SL* reduces to the Liar and is paradoxical. Further, *SL* cannot be assessed to be neither true nor false, for that implies that *SL* is true (because the first disjunct of *SL* is true). *SL* thus raises a serious problem for any theory that assesses the paradoxes to be neither true nor false.

The strengthened Liar plays a significant role in Parsons's (1984 [1974]) and Burge's (1984 [1979]) contextual theories. They rely on it in their objections against the truth-value-gap theories; and they use it to lend plausibility to the idea that the Liar statement (and also *SL*) is in one sense untrue. This point is closely connected with the Chrysippus intuition and is discussed below.

The strengthened Liar is a problem for any theory that attempts to meet weak universality. Let a theory declare the Liar to be *K* (where *K* is an arbitrary semantic concept). A new strengthened version of the Liar can be formed by mimicking the earlier one:

(*KL*)   'This very statement is *K* or else it is not true'.

As before, one cannot assess *KL* as *K*, for this implies that *KL* is true; furthermore, one cannot assess *KL* as not *K*, for then *KL* reduces to the Liar and is paradoxical. So the semantic character of *KL* lies beyond the reach of the concept *K*. More generally, the addition of semantic concepts to a language can result in new paradoxes that cannot be adequately described using those very semantic concepts. To meet weak universality, a theory of truth must give an account of the paradoxes that arise not only from the concepts that are the *object* of investigation but also those that arise from the concepts that the theory *invokes*; see Gupta and Belnap (1993, 6E and pp. 253–9).

5.4.3. The Chrysippus intuition

Suppose Zeno says at time *t*,

(Z)   What Zeno says at *t* is not true.

Chrysippus overhears Zeno, reflects on his remark, and finds that it has 'no meaning at all' and therefore rejects is (Bocheński, 1961, p. 133). Chrysippus reports his assessment by saying

(C)   What Zeno says at *t* is not true.

Zeno and Chrysippus use the same sentence in making their claims. But, according to the Chrysippus intuition, Zeno's statement is to be assessed as pathological and

Chrysippus's statement is to be assessed as true. This intuition is shared, as far as I know, by all advocates of contextual theories. If the intuition is correct, then the argument for the contextual theories is straightforward: Zeno and Chrysippus use the same sentence to make different statements. Context must therefore make a contribution to what they say, and this contribution can plausibly be located at only one place, namely, the interpretation of 'true'.[24]

According to Skyrms (1984) and Gaifman (1992), the important difference between the statements of Zeno and Chrysippus is their location in the network of semantic evaluation. To evaluate Zeno's statement Z, one has to find the denotation of 'what Zeno says at t' and evaluate it for truth. But the denotation is Z itself. So one is forced to repeat the process, and is caught in an unending loop. Evaluating Chrysippus's statement C, leads to evaluating not C but Z, which then results in a loop. There is an important difference between Z and C, according to Skyrms and Gaifman: Z is caught up in a pathological loop, but C stands outside this loop and can therefore semantically assess Z. (See figure 5.2.) In general, complex networks of semantic evaluation may contain pathological loops with many interdependent statements. Statements that stand outside these loops can give, according to Skyrms and Gaifman, true semantic assessments of one or more members in the loop. See Gaifman (1992) for a particularly clear and elegant development of the idea.

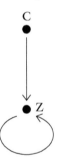

Figure 5.2

The contextual theories are primarily motivated, as noted above, by ideas and intuitions about the paradoxes. Nevertheless, they have important consequences for ordinary practices. Suppose that a trusted friend and a political insider informs you:

Everything Senator X will say tonight is untrue.

You may have all the good reasons to believe him, but on the contextual theories your reiteration of the friend's claim may be logically illegitimate: the interpretation of 'true' in your reiteration might be different from that in your friend's utterance. For example, it is possible that your reiteration lies in a pathological loop, whereas your friend's utterance lies outside this loop. So, it is possible that your friend's utterance is true but your reiteration is nonetheless pathological and hence untrue.

The Chrysippus intuition is often closely associated with the thesis of weak universality, but the two are quite different. The Chrysippus intuition embodies a descriptive claim about the uses of 'true' – namely, that the pathological sentences can correctly be described as 'untrue'. The thesis of weak universality, on the other hand, makes no particular claims about the proper vocabulary for the assessment of pathological sentences. This thesis is immune, therefore, from an entirely natural doubt to which the Chrysippus intuition is subject: if our final assessment is that the Liar is untrue, then should that not lead one to say that the Liar is true after all (because the Liar says of itself that it is not true)?

The Chrysippus intuition is a theoretical intuition. It arises from theoretical reflection on the paradoxes and is tied to one specific type of theoretical response. If the response is, for example, that the Liar statement is meaningless or that it is neither true nor false, then one is led to say that the Liar statement is untrue. Weak universality now dictates that this assessment should be expressible in natural languages, and one arrives at the Chrysippus intuition. The theoretical response is not forced, however. An alternative response is to judge the Liar to be pathological and to judge the truth-attributions to the Liar – that the Liar is true and that the Liar is neither true nor false – to be pathological also. Weak universality now requires the theory to show how the assessment that the Liar is pathological can itself be expressed in a natural language. This is a significant demand, but it is different from the one imposed by the Chrysippus intuition.

Suggested further reading

Tarski's essay (1944) and the essays in Martin (1984) are a good place to begin one's study of paradox. After that the reader should turn to Gupta and Belnap (1993), McGee (1991), and Barwise and Etchemendy (1987).

Acknowledgments

I completed this essay during my fellowship at the Center for Advanced Study in the Behavioral Sciences, Stanford, California. I wish to thank the Center, the Andrew W. Mellon Foundation, and Indiana University for their generous support. I also wish to thank Nuel Belnap for many years of encouragement and illumination on the topics discussed here. Finally, thanks to André Chapuis and Lou Goble for their comments on this essay.

Notes

1 See Bocheński (1961) and Spade (1988). The paradox was also discussed in Indian logic and semantics, notably by Bhartṛhari (seventh century CE); see Houben (1995).
  Note: A more detailed treatment of many topics discussed in this essay can be found in Belnap's and my book *The Revision Theory of Truth* (1993).
2 Bar-Hillel calls propositions 'statements.' See the bibliography of (Gupta and Belnap, 1993) for references to Bar-Hillel's work. The reader should consult this bibliography for references to works alluded to below that, for reasons of space, are not included in the list of References.
3 I will often suppress the relativity of truth to language.
4 Priest (1987) tries to deal with the problem by weakening classical logic.

5 Historical note: There was substantial work on three-valued approaches to the Liar in the late 1960s and the early 1970s. But much of this work was concerned with questions different from the one Martin, Woodruff, and Kripke settled. One concern in this work was to provide a rationale for the idea that paradoxical statements suffer from truth-value gaps. Another concern was with certain simple but powerful objections (e.g., the strengthened Liar) to the truth-value gap idea. Three-valued approaches were also defended in the medieval literature on the Liar. And Bochvar's work on the subject dates from 1937. – The true anticipations of Martin, Woodruff, and Kripke occurred in partial set theory, in the work of Fitch and Gilmore. Gilmore proves and applies a fixed-point theorem to a problem that parallels the Liar; see Feferman (1984, section 14), for more historical information. Kripke's essay stands out, however, for its philosophical clarity and force.

6 Chapuis and Gupta (1999) contains some recent essays on truth theories and their applications.

7 Here and below, the symbol '≤' is used to designate several different orderings. The context will always make the intended reference of '≤' clear.

8 I shall often omit the parenthetical clause.

9 Recall that, by our earlier definition, (∅, ∅) is the function that assigns **n** to each member of the domain.

10 For more information about the fixed points of κ_M, see Burgess (1986) and Visser (1989). As Kripke briefly notes, the least fixed point has important connections with the theory of inductive definitions (see Kripke (1984 [1975]) and McGee (1991)).

11 See Visser (1984) and Woodruff (1984) for an application to a four-valued semantics and McGee (1991) for an application to what he calls 'partially interpreted languages'. It can be shown that fixed points exist in certain nonmonotonic schemes also; see Gupta and Belnap (1993, section 2E).

12 Note that the equivalence cannot be expressed using the biconditional ↔, because (**n** ↔ **n**) = **n**.

13 This observation was first made by John Hawthorn (1983). Note that a Weak Kleene language can contain both its truth and its 'neither-true-nor-false' predicate (Gupta and Martin, 1984). Like other three-valued languages, however, it cannot contain a predicate that expresses 'untrue'.

14 There is a more general version of this thesis: logical and semantic sense can be made of systems of mutually interdependent definitions and of mutually interdependent concepts. For the sake of notational simplicity, I discuss only the narrower thesis, and here too I restrict myself to definitions of one-place predicates.

15 Gupta and Belnap (1993) uses '*A* is valid on $\mathcal{D}$ in **S***' in place of the present '$\mathcal{D}$ implies *A* in **S***'.

16 Recall that extensions fix classical interpretations. It will sometimes prove useful to identify an interpretation with the corresponding extension.

17 See Belnap (1993) for an illuminating discussion of the two requirements.

18 By accepting this definition we are not forced to view the T-biconditionals as fixing the meaning or the sense of 'true'. One may view them as fixing only the intension of 'true' (Gupta and Belnap, 1993, pp. 20–29).

19 See Gupta and Belnap (1993, sections 6A and 6B). Kremer (2001, forthcoming) has recently contributed a valuable study of the phenomenon. Kremer's paper contains negative solutions for problems 6B.12 and 6B.15 of Gupta and Belnap (1993).

20 Koons argues against **S**# in his critical essay (Koons, 1994). Further criticisms of revision theories may be found in Simmons (1993), McGee (1997), and Martin (1997).

21 The diagnosis is questionable, however, because the paradoxes occur in languages that are far from universal.

22 Note well the order of the quantifiers here. Sometimes Tarski means universality in this weaker sense. The above quote from Tarski continues, "[the common language] is continually expanding to satisfy this requirement [i.e., universality]" (1969, p. 67).
23 The construction of a semantically self-sufficient language ℒ is more likely, I believe, if the syntactic resources of ℒ are judiciously restricted; see Gupta (1984 [1982], section II). For further discussion of universality and semantic self-sufficiency, see McGee's, D. A. Martin's, and my papers in Villanueva (1997).
24 The argument is straightforward but not indubitable. Perhaps the contextual contribution is to shift the interpretation of 'not.' Perhaps it is to invoke a new sense of 'true'.

References

Antonelli, A. 1994: "The Complexity of Revision," *Notre Dame Journal of Formal Logic*, 35, 67–72. [A correction appears in Antonelli's ms. "The Complexity of Revision, revised."]

Barwise, J. and Etchemendy, J. 1987: *The Liar: An Essay on Truth and Circularity*, (Oxford University Press, New York).

Belnap, N. D. Jr. 1993: "On Rigorous Definitions," *Philosophical Studies*, 72, 115–46.

Bocheński, I. M. 1961: *A History of Formal Logic*, (Chelsea, New York).

Burge, T. 1984: "Semantical Paradox," *Journal of Philosophy*, 76 (1979), 169–98; reprinted in Martin (1984, 83–117).

Burgess, J. P. 1986: "The Truth is Never Simple," *Journal of Symbolic Logic*, 51, 663–81.

Chapuis, A. 1996: "Alternative Revision Theories of Truth," *Journal of Philosophical Logic*, 25, 399–423.

Chapuis, A. 1998: "Recent Theories of Truth," *Journal of Indian Council of Philosophical Research*, 15, 89–123.

Chapuis, A. and Gupta, A. 1999: *Circularity, Definition, and Truth*, (Indian Council of Philosophical Research, New Delhi).

Feferman, S. 1984: "Toward Useful Type-Free Theories I," *Journal of Symbolic Logic*, 49 (1984), 75–111; reprinted in Martin (1984, 237–87).

Gaifman, H. 1992: "Pointers to Truth," *Journal of Philosophy*, 89, 223–61.

Gupta, A. 1984: "Truth and Paradox," *Journal of Philosophical Logic*, 11 (1982), 1–60; reprinted in Martin (1984, 175–235).

Gupta, A. and Belnap, N. 1993: *The Revision Theory of Truth*, (MIT Press, Cambridge, MA), 1993.

Gupta, A. and Martin, R. L. 1984: "A Fixed Point Theorem for the Weak Kleene Valuation Scheme," *Journal of Philosophical Logic*, 13, 131–5.

Hawthorn, J. 1983: The Liar and Theories of Truth, Doctoral dissertation, McGill University.

Herzberger, H. 1984: "Notes on Naive Semantics," *Journal of Philosophical Logic*, 11 (1982), 61–102; reprinted in Martin (1984, 133–74).

Houben, J. E. M. 1995: "Bhartṛhari's Solution to the Liar and Some Other Paradoxes," *Journal of Indian Philosophy*, 23, 381–401.

Koons, R. C. 1992: *Paradoxes of Belief and Strategic Rationality*, (Cambridge University Press, Cambridge).

Koons, R. C. 1994: "Review of *Revision Theory of Truth*," *Notre Dame Journal of Formal Logic*, 35, 600–31.

Kremer, P. 1993: "The Gupta–Belnap Systems **S**# and **S*** are not Axiomatisable," *Notre Dame Journal of Formal Logic*, 34, 583–96.

Kremer, P. 2001: "Does Truth Behave like a Classical Concept When There is No Vicious Reference?", *forthcoming*.

Kripke, S. 1984: "Outline of a Theory of Truth," *Journal of Philosophy*, 72 (1975), 690–716; reprinted in Martin (1984, 53–81).

Martin, D. A. 1997: "Revision and Its Rivals," in Villanueva (1997, 407–18).

Martin, R. L. (ed.) 1984: *Recent Essays on Truth and the Liar Paradox*, (Clarendon Press, Oxford).

Martin, R. L. and Woodruff, P. W. 1984: "On Representing 'True-in-L' in L," *Philosophia*, 5 (1975), 217–21; reprinted in Martin (1984, 47–51).

McGee, V. 1991: *Truth, Vagueness, and Paradox: An Essay on the Logic of Truth*, (Hackett, Indianapolis IN).

McGee, V. 1997: "Revision," in Villanueva (1997, 387–406).

Parsons, C. 1984: "The Liar Paradox," *Journal of Philosophical Logic*, 3 (1974), 381–412; reprinted in Martin (1984, 9–45).

Priest, G. 1987: *In Contradiction: A Study of the Transconsistent*, (M. Nijhoff, Dordrecht).

Prior, A. N. 1967: "Correspondence Theory of Truth," in *The Encyclopedia of Philosophy*, Vol. 2, P. Edwards, ed., (Macmillan, New York), 223–32.

Sheard, M. 1994: "A Guide to Truth Predicates in the Modern Era," *Journal of Symbolic Logic*, 59, 1032–54.

Simmons, K. 1993: *Universality and the Liar: An Essay on Truth and the Diagonal Argument*, (Cambridge University Press, Cambridge).

Skyrms, B. 1984: "Intensional Aspects of Semantical Self-Reference," in Martin (1984, 119–31).

Spade, P. V. 1988: *Lies, Language, and Logic in the Late Middle Ages*, (Variorum Reprints, London).

Tarski, A. 1944: "The Semantic Conception of Truth," *Philosophy and Phenomenological Research*, 4, 341–76.

Tarski, A. 1969: "Truth and Proof," *Scientific American*, 220, 63–77.

van Fraassen, B. 1966: "The Completeness of Free Logic," *Zeitschrift für Mathematische Logik und Grundlagen der Mathematik*, 12, 219–34.

Villanueva, E. (ed.) 1997: *Truth (Philosophical Issues 8)*, (Ridgeview Publishing Company, Atascadero, CA).

Visser, A. 1984: "Four Valued Semantics and the Liar Paradox," *Journal of Philosophical Logic*, 13, 181–212.

Visser, A. 1989: "Semantics and the Liar Paradox," in *Handbook of Philosophical Logic*, Vol. 4, D. Gabbay and F. Guenthner, eds., (D. Reidel, Dordrecht), 617–706.

Woodruff, P. W. 1984: "Paradox, Truth and Logic – I," *Journal of Philosophical Logic*, 13, 213–32.

Yaqūb, A. M. 1993: *The Liar Speaks the Truth: A Defense of the Revision Theory of Truth*, (Oxford University Press, New York).

Chapter 6

Logical Consequence

Patricia A. Blanchette

6.1. Introduction

Whenever one asserts a claim of any kind, one engages in a commitment not just to that claim itself, but to a variety of other claims that follow in its wake, claims that, as we tend to say, *follow logically* from the original claim. To say that Smith and Jones are both great basketball players is to say something from which it follows that Smith is a great basketball player, that someone is a great basketball player, that there is something at which Smith is great, and so on.

This general fact, that certain claims follow logically from others, is the central concern of a theory of logical consequence. Logical consequence is just the relation that connects a given claim or set of claims with those things that follow logically from it; to say that B is a logical consequence of A is simply to say that B follows logically from A. All of ordinary reasoning turns on the recognition of this relation. When one notices, for example, that a certain prediction follows from a given theory, that a particular view is a consequence of some initial commitments, that a collection of premises entails a given conclusion, and so on, one is engaged in reasoning about logical consequence.

The other logical properties and relations whose recognition is central to ordinary reasoning are closely related to, and can be defined in terms of, logical consequence:

- An argument is *valid* iff (if and only if) its conclusion is a logical consequence of its premises.
- A set of claims Γ *entails* a claim α iff α is a logical consequence of Γ.
- A set of claims Γ is *consistent* iff no contradiction is a logical consequence of it.
- A claim α is *independent* of a set of claims Γ iff α is not a logical consequence of Γ.
- A claim α is a *logical truth* iff it is a logical consequence of the empty set of claims.

The investigation of logical consequence and related notions consists largely in the attempt

---

115

(a)   to give a systematic treatment of the *extension* of this relation, i.e., of the issue of *which* claims do in fact follow logically from which others; and

(b)   to give an informative account of the *nature* of the relation.

There is much room for debate about both of these issues. Though there is no doubt about the fact that some claims do in fact follow logically from others, and (perhaps more obviously) that some sets of beliefs are inconsistent, that some arguments are definitely not valid, and so on, there is room for disagreement about cases. Philosophers have disagreed, for example, about whether certain purely mathematical claims are logical consequences of apparently non-mathematical claims. They have disagreed about whether existential claims about properties follow logically from ordinary predications. And so on.

To give a determinate answer to each and every question of the form 'Does this follow logically from that?' will require, among other things, a decision about the precise boundaries separating logical consequence from set-theoretic or mathematical fact, and a decision about the metaphysical commitments of various kinds of claims. The project of clarifying the extension of the logical consequence relation thus turns, to some extent, on issues outside the scope of the philosophy of logic proper, on issues, for example, that fall within the camp of pure metaphysics, philosophy of mathematics, and related fields. But some of the central questions about the extent of the relation depend for their answers on the second of the two topics noted above, namely on the issue of the *nature* of logical consequence. Reflection on some clear, easily recognized cases of logical consequence, such as that

Socrates is mortal.

follows logically from the pair of claims

All humans are mortal.

and

Socrates is human.

easily reveals some straightforward necessary conditions for logical consequence. It is uncontroversial, for example, that the relation of logical consequence is *truth-preserving*, i.e., that the logical consequences of true claims must themselves be true. But things become more difficult, and more contentious, when one tries to fill in more details. Some of the disagreements here turn, for example, on questions about whether the conclusion of a valid argument must, in some sense, be 'about' the same subject-matter as are its premises, and about whether there is a clear sense in which the fundamental principles of logic must hold independently of any particular subject-matter, to be, as it is often put, *topic-neutral*. Further disagreements arise about whether, and in what sense, logical truths must always be *necessary* truths, and so on. Different answers to these questions will deliver different views about the precise extension of the logical consequence relation, and will consequently give rise to different systematic treatments of consequence in the form of formal systems of logic.

The purpose of this chapter is to provide a brief introduction to the central issues surrounding the nature and the extension of logical consequence, and to the role of formal systems in the investigation of consequence.

6.2. Early Formal Systems and Accuracy

A *formal system* of logic consists of a rigorously specified *formal language* (i.e., a collection of formulas defined solely in terms of their syntax) together with a *deductive system* (i.e., a specification of those series of formulas that will count as *deductions* of particular formulas from collections of formulas). Since the end of the nineteenth century, formal systems have been widely used as means of codifying and analyzing the relation of logical consequence and its associated notions.

The earliest formal systems, e.g., Frege's, were intended to give a way of rigorously demonstrating relations of logical consequence – i.e., of demonstrating of particular claims that they were indeed logical consequences of particular sets of claims. The intention in designing the system was, to put it somewhat loosely, that the system would include a *deduction* of a formula φ from a set Σ of formulas only if φ was indeed a logical consequence of Σ. Deducibility within the system was to have been a reliable indicator of logical consequence.

The 'somewhat loose' character of the above description is due to the fact that the formulas themselves – i.e., strings of marks on paper – are not, in fact, the items that bear the logical consequence relation to one another. Thus one cannot, strictly speaking, describe the goal of system-design as one of making sure the deducibility relation is included in the logical consequence relation. As Frege saw it, the items that bear logical relations to one another are nonlinguistic propositions, the kinds of things that are expressed by fully interpreted sentences, and that are the objects of the propositional attitudes. And, as Frege saw it, his formulas as they appeared in deductions always expressed determinate propositions. Thus the Fregean goal for an adequate formal system can be described, now accurately, as

a formula φ is to be deducible from a set Σ of formulas only if the proposition expressed by φ is a logical consequence of the propositions expressed by the members of Σ.

See Frege (1964 [1893], Vol. I), esp. the Introduction and sections 14, 15, 18, 20.

It is, in principle at least, a straightforward matter to check whether a system satisfies this requirement. Since the *deducibility* relation is typically defined in the familiar way in terms of axioms and rules of inference, the quality-control check is (in principle, at least) simple: one checks to see that every proposition expressible by an axiom is a truth of logic, and that each rule of inference countenances the deduction of a formula α from a n-tuple of formulas $\beta_1 \ldots \beta_n$ only if the proposition expressed by α is a logical consequence of those expressed by $\beta_1 \ldots \beta_n$.

Frege himself did not offer any uniform method for carrying out this 'checking,' i.e., for demonstrating that a given proposition is, in fact, a truth of logic, or that a given proposition does, in fact, follow logically from a particular collection of propositions. He seems to presume that the very simplest cases of logical truth and of logically valid inference are obvious when encountered. The accuracy of the formal system was to have been established by simply pointing out that the propositions expressed by axioms were indeed obvious truths of logic, and that the rules of inference obviously generated only logical consequences from premises. The importance of the formal system was, in large part, that once an audience had granted the handful of (ostensibly) immediately obvious logical principles required for axioms and rules of inference, it was a straightforward matter to demonstrate the validity of considerably more complicated and non-obvious arguments. The accuracy of the system as a whole rested simply on the logical status of the axioms and rules of inference, and the validity of extremely complicated arguments was guaranteed by the accuracy of the system.

As it turned out, Frege's favored formal system (1964 [1893]) was not, in fact, accurate. His deducibility relation contained a subtle but important flaw, with the result that the system contains deductions of both a formula φ and its negation $\sim\varphi$ from the empty set of premises. And since the propositions expressed by such pairs of formulas cannot both be logical truths, Frege's deducibility relation cannot be considered a reliable indicator of logical consequence. Some of the fundamental claims that Frege took to be 'obvious' logical truths were in fact falsehoods.[1]

Successors to Frege's system, of course, avoid this particular error, and a number of them offer presumably accurate indications of logical consequence. Before turning to a discussion of contemporary formal systems, two features of Frege's approach to formal systems are worth nothing.

The first is the Fregean view of the *bearers* of the logical relations. Of central concern in the philosophy of logic, the question is this: what kinds of things, exactly, are the logical truths, the relata of the logical consequence relation, the components of valid arguments, and so on? Frege's answer is, as noted above, that these bearers of logical relations are a particular kind of abstract object, namely, nonlinguistic *propositions*. The attraction of this view stems from the fact that these propositions are also, as Frege and most proposition-theorists see it, both the semantic values of our utterances and the objects of our propositional attitudes. The combination of these views gives an easy explanation of the fact that not only our assertions, but also our beliefs, the contents of our hopes and fears, and so on, can have logical implications. The view also helps to make sense of the apparent logical connections between these different kinds of entities; the very thing that forms the content of one person's desire can logically contradict the content of another's assertion and of yet a third person's belief; and the straightforward explanation of this, on the propositional view, is that the desire, the assertion, and the belief all have propositions as their contents. But the view is not without problems. The central difficulty with the view of nonlinguistic propositions as the bearers of the logical relations is that, arguably, it is doubtful that there are such things as nonlinguistic propositions. Reasons for doubting the existence of propositions stem primarily from the difficulty of giving clear criteria of individuation for propositions, from general worries about abstract objects, and from considerations of ontological parsimony. See Quine (1953b [1948], 1970, ch. 1) and Cartwright (1987c [1962]).

Skepticism about nonlinguistic propositions leads to the alternative view that *sentences* are the bearers of the logical relations. Some caution is required here, however, about precisely what is meant by the claim that sentences are logical truths, are logical consequences of one another, and so on. Taking a sentence to be simply a series of marks or sounds, the view that the logical relations are borne by sentences is untenable. The string of symbols

All men are mortal.

does not, by itself, have any logical implications, any more than does the string

Axz%f

Though it is tempting to view the first string as having a rich collection of logical implications, it is important to note that this temptation is felt only when we take the sentence to be not merely a string of shapes on paper, but rather to be something with a determinate *meaning*. A bare series of symbols does not have any logical properties at all, though a string of symbols together with the right kind of semantic value certainly does. The view that the logical relations obtain between *sentences*, then, is only a reasonable view if by 'sentence' one means something like 'series of symbols together with a determinate meaning.' The view, in short, is that the bearers of the logical relations are meaningful sentences.

The two views in question (that nonlinguistic propositions are the primary bearers of the logical relations, and that sentences together with their meanings are the primary bearers of the logical relations) are not importantly different if, as is sometimes done, one takes the meanings of sentences just to be nonlinguistic propositions. But if one takes the meaning of a sentence to be something non-propositional, for example, a pattern of use in a given population, then the two views are importantly different, with the first but not the second committed to the existence of something like Fregean propositions. The latter understanding of 'meaning' is of course required by those whose view is motivated by skepticism about the existence of nonlinguistic propositions.

Despite the intrinsic interest of this issue, the difference between the two views (propositional and sentential) of the bearers of the logical properties and relations will not be terribly important in what follows, and it is not necessary here to adjudicate between them. The important point about both views is that they are fundamentally 'semantic' in the sense that they construe the logical relations as obtaining either between meanings themselves (propositions), or between pairs of syntactic items and meanings. And this is as it should be; as noted above, the logical relations do not obtain between bare syntactic items, but only between items which make some determinate claim on the world; which are, in brief, meaningful. In what follows, the relata of the logical relations will simply be referred to as *claims*, taking the word to be ambiguous between nonlinguistic propositions and meaningful sentences. Except where noted, everything said below applies on either reading.

The second feature worth noting here about the conception of logic underlying Frege's and similar formal work concerns the distinction between the pretheoretic relation of logical consequence and the various relations of formal deducibility given by particular formal systems. The relation of logical consequence is *pretheoretic* in the sense that neither the relation itself, nor our recognition of the relation, depends upon the existence or the deliverances of formal systems. Similarly for the related notions of logical truth, consequence, consistency, and so on. When one infers

Katy is wise.

from the pair of claims

All of John's children are wise

and

Katy is a child of John's

one recognizes a connection between these claims that would have held whether or not anyone had ever invented formal systems, and whether or not any of those systems had pronounced the inference valid. Similarly for the ordinary notions of inconsistency, validity, entailment, and so on that are recognized in everyday reasoning. These logical properties and relations link assertions, beliefs, and theories one to another in ways that do not depend upon the results of work in formal logic. The dependence is, rather, the other ways round; standard systems of formal logic will count the argument just noted (or a formalized version of it) as valid because those systems are designed to reflect the pretheoretic logical properties and relations accurately. It is only with respect to this sense of a system-independent notion of logical consequence that one can make sense of the idea of a formal system's being accurate or inaccurate, since the accuracy of the system is a matter of the extent to which its relation of formal deducibility reliably indicates the pretheoretic relation of logical consequence. And, of course, it is only against the background of such a system-independent notion of logical consequence that one can agree with Frege's later assessment of his own formal system as inaccurate in the way noted above.

6.3. Contemporary Formal Systems

Contemporary formal systems differ from Frege's in two ways that are relevant to the issue of their accurate reflection of the logical properties and relations. First of all, one does not, these days, typically view the formulas that occur in deductions as each expressing unique claims. Each formula is typically thought, rather, to be capable of expressing a broad range of claims. The guidelines governing precisely *which* claims each formula can appropriately express are seldom made explicit; they are simply the rules of thumb passed on when teaching students how to do 'translations' between formal and natural languages. They are, in the typical case, rules about the fixed meanings to be assigned to the logical constants, the kinds of meanings assignable to the members of each syntactic category, rules of compositionality, and so on. These are the rules borne in mind when one notes that, for example, '$\exists x Fx$' can be used to formalize the claims

> There's at least one prime number.

or

> Someone is French.

but not

> All cows are mammals.

The second relevant difference between Fregean and standard contemporary systems is that the latter typically incorporate a *model-theoretic* apparatus. A *model* for a formal language is a function which, while meeting a variety of requirements specific to that language, assigns a truth-value to each closed formula of the language. The standard requirements include, for example, the requirement that a model assigns *true* to a formula of the form (α & β) only if it assigns *true* to both α and β. For a quantified language, the assignment of truth-values proceeds via an assignment of individuals and sets to the atomic parts of formulas. [See chapter 1.]

Instead of assessing the adequacy of formal systems in the Fregean way, by directly examining the relationship between deducible formulas and the claims they express, typical practice with contemporary systems is to assess the adequacy of a system by examining the relationship between deducible formulas and the truth-values assigned those formulas by various models. Where Σ is a set of formulas of a formal system **S** and φ is a formula of **S**,

- φ is a *model-theoretic consequence* in **S** of Σ if every one of **S**'s models that assigns *true* to each member of Σ also assigns *true* to φ. This is abbreviated

$$\Sigma \vDash_S \varphi$$

- A formula φ is a *model-theoretic* truth of **S** if every one of **S**'s models assigns *true* to φ.

A central question that arises for a formal system with a model-theoretic apparatus is that of the coincidence between the relation of model-theoretic consequence and the relation of deducibility. Abbreviating 'φ is deducible in **S** from Σ' as '$\Sigma \vdash_S \varphi$', the two halves of the coincidence claim form the *soundness* and *completeness* theorems for **S**, as follows:

Soundness of **S**:   For every set Σ of formulas of **S**, and every formula φ of **S**, if $\Sigma \vdash_S \varphi$, then $\Sigma \vDash_S \varphi$.

Completeness of **S**:   For every set Σ of formulas of **S**, and every formula φ of **S**, if $\Sigma \vDash_S \varphi$, then $\Sigma \vdash_S \varphi$.

If one's primary interest is in devising a formal system whose deductive and model-theoretic consequence relations coincide, then the soundness and completeness theorems are of interest in their own right. When, on the other hand, the purpose is the design of a formal system that will be a reliable indicator of logical consequence, these theorems are of interest largely because they allow one to infer the adequacy of each of these consequence-like relations (deducibility or model-theoretic consequence) from the other. If one knows that model-theoretic consequence within a system **S** is a reliable indicator of logical consequence, then the soundness theorem for **S** will give a reliability result for **S**'s deducibility relation. If, on the other hand, one has an independent guarantee of the reliability of **S**'s deducibility relation with respect to logical consequence, then the completeness theorem for **S** will establish the reliability in this regard of **S**'s model-theoretic apparatus.

Because unlike their Fregean antecedents, standard contemporary systems take each formula to be capable of formalizing a wide range of claims, somewhat more complexity is needed in formulating the questions of the reliability of the model-theoretic and the deductive consequence relations of formal systems. One cannot simply ask whether φ's being a model-theoretic consequence in **S** of Σ entails that *the claim* expressed by φ is a logical consequence of *the set of claims* expressed by Σ, since there are no unique claim and set of claims expressed by φ and by Σ, respectively. One wants, rather, to ask whether this implication holds for *all* of the claims and sets of claims expressible by φ and Σ respectively. Similarly for the relation $\Sigma \vdash_S \varphi$.

Consider, for example, the set of formulas $\{\forall x(Fx \rightarrow Gx), Fa\}$ and the formula Ga of standard first-order logic. These formulas could be taken to express, respectively, the claims

All prime numbers are odd.

Seven is a prime number.

Seven is odd.

On another occasion, these formulas might represent the trio

All sheep are mammals.

Dolly is a sheep.

Dolly is a mammal.

Each such assignment of claims to the formulas of a formal language is what are called a *reading* of that language. That is to say, a *reading* of a language is an assignment of claims to its closed formulas in a way that satisfies the usual 'rules of thumb,' as mentioned above, for that language. When one asks whether deducibility in a given formal system **S** is a reliable indicator of logical consequence, the interest is in whether this reliability holds for *each* of the readings of the language. Similarly for the question of the reliability of the model-theoretic consequence relation for **S**.

Where Σ and φ are a set of formulas and a formula, respectively, of the language of a formal system **S**, and R is a reading of that language, '$R(\Sigma)$' shall mean the set of claims assigned by R to Σ, and '$R(\varphi)$' the claim assigned by R to φ. For example, where R_1 is the first reading given in the above example, $R_1(\{\forall x(Fx \rightarrow Gx), Fa\})$ is the set of claims

{All primes are odd. Seven is prime}

and $R_1(Ga)$ is the claim

Seven is odd.

Questions about the reliability of the deductive and model-theoretic consequence relations of a formal system **S**, then, can be expressed as the questions of whether it is generally true that:

(i)   If $\Sigma \vdash_S \varphi$, then $R(\varphi)$ is a logical consequence of $R(\Sigma)$
(ii) If $\Sigma \vDash_S \varphi$, then $R(\varphi)$ is a logical consequence of $R(\Sigma)$.

If (i) holds for all Σ, φ, and R for a formal system **S**, then **S**'s deducibility relation is reliable. If (ii) holds for all Σ, φ, and R for a system **S**, then **S**'s model-theoretic consequence relation is reliable.

It is sometimes assumed that, at least for those formal systems standardly in use, the model-theoretic consequence relation is 'automatically' a reliable indicator of logical consequence, which is to say that (ii) is obviously satisfied by such systems. This assumption tends to rest on the view that the relation of model-theoretic consequence is merely a tidied up version of, or a successful re-description of, the pretheoretic relation of logical consequence itself. If this is the case, then the question of the reliability of the deducibility relation is immediately reducible to the question of its satisfaction of the soundness theorem. This assumption of the coincidence between model-theoretic consequence and logical consequence has, however, been challenged, and the grounds for inferring deductive reliability from soundness are by no means obvious; see Blanchette (2000), Etchemendy (1999 [1990]), McGee (1992), Shapiro (1998), and Sher (1991).

Satisfaction of (i) and (ii) are two of the central issues to be treated in establishing the accuracy of a formal system that has both a deductive and a model-theoretic apparatus. If one is interested in the use of the system not only to give positive judgments of logical consequence, but also negative such judgments, one will be interested in the stronger biconditional versions of (i) and (ii).

The central difficulty in establishing either (i) or (ii) (or their strengthened biconditional versions) is that there is no independent test for satisfaction of the consequent of each. After all, if there already was a reliable test of logical consequence, one would not be in the position of devising formal systems to provide such a test. Nevertheless, it is possible, in fact, to formulate some relatively straight-forward necessary conditions on logical consequence, some of which can be used to give at least partial evaluations of formal systems. The idea, roughly, is that if **C** is some condition that must be met by the logical consequence relation, then no formal system whose deductive/model-theoretic consequence relation fails to meet **C** can be said to satisfy (i)/(ii). The next section looks at a small sample of such conditions.

6.4. Conditions on Consequence

The logical consequence relation is evidently truth-preserving, i.e., if each of a set of claims is true, then so too are all of its logical consequences. This provides a very minimal condition on formal systems: given a reading R of the language, it must never be the case that $\Sigma \vdash_S \varphi$ if each member of $R(\Sigma)$ is true while $R(\varphi)$ is false. Similarly for $\vDash_S$. It is a relatively straightforward matter to check for satisfaction of this condition, and it is indeed satisfied by all of the standard propositional and first-order formal systems [see chapter 1]. (For issues about second-order systems' satis-faction of this criterion, see below.)

Presumably, however, the intention is for a much stronger connection between premises and conclusion than mere truth-preservation when one says that the latter is a logical consequence of the former. One assumes, for example, that agents are committed to the logical consequences of the claims they explicitly avow, though of course without presuming them to be committed to all of the truths in virtue of a commitment to one of them. Hence one assumes that unanticipated commitments can be discovered simply by following out the consequences of the explicit claims. Similarly for theories; the consequences of a theory's assertions are entirely within the realm of claims on the basis of which the theory is to be found adequate or wanting, whether or not one takes theories themselves to be closed under logical consequence. In short, an important feature of logical consequence is that it *trans-mits* epistemic and theoretical commitment.

In addition to transmitting commitment, logical consequence would appear to be epistemically inert, in the sense that the logical consequences of things knowable *a priori*, or knowable non-empirically or without the aid of intuition, are themselves, respectively, knowable *a priori*, non-empirically, without the aid of intuition. For any kind K of objects, things knowable without access to objects of kind K pass on this property to their logical consequences. There is a rough sense, then, in which the logical consequences of a claim have no 'new content' over and above that had by the original claim. Whether this conception of content can be characterized sufficiently clearly, independently of the relation of consequence, to provide much elucidation here is unclear; for now, it will suffice to note that the consequence relation preserves the epistemic categories just noted.

Finally, there is, it is usually agreed, a certain *modal* characteristic of logical consequence. The fundamental idea here is that there is a necessary connection between a claim and its logical consequences: if a claim α is a logical consequence of a set of claims Γ, then it is *not possible* for α to be false while the members of Γ are true. Similarly, if an argument is valid, then it is *impossible* for its premises to be true while its conclusion is false.

All of these features of the logical consequence relation provide conditions that must be met by any reliable deductive or model-theoretic account of consequence. Some of them are more easily formulable and systematically tested than others. This section looks briefly at the criterion given by the last mentioned condition, namely the modal character of logical consequence.

The relevant criteria of adequacy for the deductive and model-theoretic consequence relations for a system **S** are that:

(i')   If $\Sigma \vdash_S \varphi$, then it is impossible for each member of $R(\Sigma)$ to be true while $R(\varphi)$ is false

(ii') If $\Sigma \vDash_S \varphi$, then it is impossible for each member of $R(\Sigma)$ to be true while $R(\varphi)$ is false.

As usual, R is an assignment of claims (meeting the usual 'rules of thumb') to **S**'s formulas. Only if a formal system **S** satisfies both (i') and (ii') for every Σ, φ, and R will that system's model-theoretic and deductive consequence relations prove reliable indicators of logical consequence. Satisfaction of (i') is relatively easily established (or refuted); one simply checks each axiom to see that it expresses only necessary truths, and checks each rule of inference to see that it preserves this property. In the case of propositional logic, for example, one simply notes that the axioms – instances of a small handful of forms, like

$$((A \& B) \to A)$$

express only necessary truths, and that the rule(s) of inference (e.g., *modus ponens*) generate only necessary consequences.

A similar argument *almost* suffices for the usual first-order deductive systems. The only difficult point here concerns the 'non-empty universe' assumption built into standard first-order systems [see chapter 1]. Such formulas as

$$(\exists x)x = x$$

and

$$(\exists x)(Fx \to Fx)$$

are deductive theorems of standard first-order systems. But the claims expressible by these formulas are not uncontroversially necessary truths, and hence not uncontroversially logical consequences of the empty set.[2] If indeed these formulas do express non-necessary truths, then standard first-order systems fail to satisfy (i'), and hence fail to satisfy (i). Aside from these existential formulas, however, it is relatively uncontroversial that standard first-order systems do satisfy the modal requirement (i').

In both the propositional and first-order cases, the completeness theorem can be used to show satisfaction of (ii′) via satisfaction of (i′). So standard propositional systems do, and standard first-order systems either do satisfy, or almost satisfy (ii′) as well.

It is also possible to establish satisfaction of (ii′) directly in certain cases, and it is instructive to see how non-trivial this can be, even in the case of propositional logic. Here, for example, is an argument adapted from one by Cartwright (1987a) that establishes satisfaction of (ii′) by standard systems of classical propositional logic:

Let the language L be a set of formulas freely generated from a non-empty set of formulas by the binary operation & and the unary operation N. Let a *valuation* be a function from L into $\{T, F\}$. Where $\vDash$ is any relation that takes sets of wffs to wffs, and V is a set of valuations, say that V *induces* $\vDash$ iff, for every set X of wffs and every wff α, $X \vDash \alpha$ iff, for every $v \in V$, if $v(x) = T$ for every $x \in X$, then $v(\alpha) = T$. Roughly speaking, the more valuations V contains, the smaller will be the relation induced by V; where V is empty, the induced relation is universal, and where V contains every valuation, the induced relation will be minimal, amounting merely to membership of the conclusion in the set of premises, i.e., $X \vDash \alpha$ iff $\alpha \in X$. Say that a valuation v is *Boolean* iff, for all α and β, $v(\alpha) \neq v(N\alpha)$, and $v(\&\alpha\beta) = T$ iff $v(\alpha) = v(\beta) = T$. Let $\vDash_B$ be the relation induced by the set of Boolean valuations. Notice that $\vDash_B$ is the relation of truth-table implication; to say that $\Sigma \vDash_B \varphi$ is to say, essentially, that any row of a standard truth-table (treating '&' as conjunction and 'N' as negation) that assigns T to every member of Σ will assign T to φ.

The question of the satisfaction of (ii′) by a standard propositional system is the question of whether, for every set Γ of wffs and every wff φ, if $\Gamma \vDash_B \varphi$, then the appropriate necessary connection obtains between the claims made by the members of Γ and that made by φ. Here, something must be known about the claims expressible by L's formulas. Let these be governed by the usual constraint:

(C) For all formulas α and β, Nα expresses the negation of what α expresses, and &$\alpha\beta$ expresses the conjunction of what α and β express.

Say that a valuation is *admissible* if it represents a possible distribution of truth-values to the formulas, given the constraint (C) on readings. Thus e.g., a valuation assigning T to some wff (well-formed formula) α and to Nα is not admissible, since no claim and its negation can both be true. $\vDash_B$ satisfies (ii′) just in case every admissible valuation is Boolean. So suppose v is not Boolean. Then either:

(a) for some wff α, $v(\alpha) = v(N\alpha)$, in which case v is not admissible (since it is not possible for a claim and its negation to be both true or both false); or
(b) for some wffs α and β, either $v(\&\alpha\beta) = F$ and $v(\alpha) = v(\beta) = T$, in which case v is not admissible (since it is not possible for two claims to be true while their conjunction is false), or $v(\&\alpha\beta) = T$ and either $v(\alpha) = F$ or $v(\beta) = F$, in which case v is not admissible (since it is not possible for a conjunction of claims to be true while one conjunct is false).

So every admissible valuation is Boolean.   QED

For systems lacking a completeness theorem, e.g., typical systems of second-order logic [see chapter 2], establishment of (ii′), if indeed (ii′) holds, must be by some such direct method. The question of the modal adequacy of second-order systems is too large to treat in detail here, but some of the relevant concerns are as follows.

First of all, a complication is that the question of precisely *which* claims a given formula can be taken to express is considerably less clearly answered for second-order systems than it is for first-order and propositional systems. For example, the formula

$$\exists X \forall y (Xy \leftrightarrow y = y)$$

might, or might not, be taken as an appropriate formalization of the claim that there exists a set of all the self-identical things. If it is taken to be capable of formalizing such a claim, then the system in question will fail (ii′), since the formula is a model-theoretic truth, but the claim is not a necessary truth, and is indeed a falsehood. If, on the other hand, this reading of the formula is ruled illegitimate, then this particular counterexample to (ii′) is not available. Similarly for a large number of potentially problematic model-theoretic truths of second-order logic; on some construals of the expressive power of the language, a variety of such formulas express false claims. Though on such understandings of the language, the model-theoretic consequence relation clearly fails to reliably indicate logical consequence, this does not indict the deductive consequence relation, since again such formal systems lack a completeness theorem. The reliability of the deductive system, i.e., the satisfaction of (i) and of (i′), is of course to be established by looking at the details of particular second-order deductive systems; see Shapiro (1991); [see also chapter 2].

For any of the criteria outlined (truth-preservation, topic-neutrality, necessity, etc.), the task of checking the reliability of a particular deductive system is relatively straightforward, since satisfaction of the criteria by the deductive system as a whole can be traced to the satisfaction of these very criteria by the relatively manageable collection of axioms and rules of inference. Checking the reliability of model-theoretic systems, particularly in the absence of a completeness theorem, is often a considerably more difficult matter. Arguments here will sometimes turn on *ad hoc* features of the model-theoretic output of a given system. A nice example of such a feature arises in the case of second-order logic with respect to the continuum hypothesis. This example is discussed by Etchemendy in (1999 [1990], ch. 8.)

The continuum hypothesis is the hypothesis that there are no sets whose cardinality is larger than that of the natural numbers ($\mathbb{N}$) and smaller than that of the real numbers ($\mathbb{R}$). It is generally agreed (following the work of Gödel and Cohen) that the continuum hypothesis (CH) is *independent of* the axioms of ZFC (Zermelo-Fraenkel set theory with the axiom of choice). [See chapter 3.]

The status of the continuum hypothesis makes a difference to model theory. When asking whether a given formula is true on every model (i.e., is a model-theoretic truth), one is asking whether there *exist* models which falsify that formula. Thus which formulas turn out to be true on every model will depend to a certain extent on what kinds of models – i.e., on what kinds of sets – there are. Because, in second-order logic, the properties *being of smaller/larger cardinality than* $\mathbb{N}$ and *being of smaller/larger cardinality than* $\mathbb{R}$ can be defined, there are sentences of second-order logic whose status as model-theoretic truths will depend on the disposition of the continuum hypothesis. Specifically, if the continuum hypothesis is true, then this sentence will be true on every model:

$$(\forall X)(X > \mathbb{N} \to \mathbb{R} \leq X) \tag{6.1}$$

where '... $> \mathbb{N}$' and '$\mathbb{R} \leq$ ...' are abbreviations for the definable properties just noted.

If the continuum hypothesis is false, then there will be models the powerset of whose domain contains sets larger than $\mathbb{N}$ but smaller than $\mathbb{R}$, and hence models which falsify (6.1) In this case, however, the sentence

$$(\exists X)X > \mathbb{N} \to (\exists X)(X > \mathbb{N} \ \& \ X < \mathbb{R}) \tag{6.2}$$

will be true on every model.

This would seem to pose a problem for the view that the model-theoretic truths of such a language are always logical truths – and hence for the view that model-theoretic consequence in such a system reliably indicates logical consequence. For assuming that the continuum hypothesis really is, as above, independent of the axioms of ZFC, one knows that neither the continuum hypothesis nor its negation is a truth of logic. For no truths of logic are independent of ZFC. And if the continuum hypothesis is not a truth of logic, then it is not a truth of logic that every set larger than $\mathbb{N}$ is at least as large as $\mathbb{R}$. And since (6.1) simply says that every set larger than $\mathbb{N}$ is at least as large as $\mathbb{R}$, one must conclude that (6.1) is not a truth of logic. Similarly, if the negation of the continuum hypothesis is not a truth of logic, then it is not a truth of logic that if there are sets larger than $\mathbb{N}$, then there are sets larger than $\mathbb{N}$ and smaller than $\mathbb{R}$.[3] So, from the fact that the negation of the continuum hypothesis is not a truth of logic, one must conclude that (6.2) is not a truth of logic either. Hence the problem: Either (6.1) or (6.2) is a model-theoretic truth, but neither (6.1) nor (6.2) is a truth of logic. So, at least one model-theoretic truth is not a truth of logic.

A potential response to this problem is that it simply shows that there is no firm boundary between set theory and logic, hence no firm boundary between set-theoretic truth and logical truth. This may well be so. But it is not of much help for the view that model-theoretic consequence and truth in this system reliably indicate logical consequence and truth. For, to defend the reliability of the model-theoretic account, one must hold that either (6.1) or (6.2) *is* in fact a logical truth, and hence that either the continuum hypothesis or its negation is a logical truth. But this conflicts with the uncontroversial independence results which prompt the problem in the first place. If logical truth and set-theoretic truth come to the same thing, then the independence results demonstrate that neither the continuum hypothesis nor its negation is a set-theoretic truth, in which case there is no support for the view that either (6.1) or (6.2) is a logical truth. If there are set-theoretic truths which are not logical truths, then the fact (if it is one) that either the continuum hypothesis or its negation is a set-theoretic truth does not support the view that either (6.1) or (6.2) is a logical truth. In either case, this example would seem to provide a reason for deeming the usual second-order model-theoretic consequence relation unreliable as an indicator of logical consequence. This does not, of course, provide anything like an indictment of second-order logic in general, and, in particular, says nothing about the reliability of various second-order deductive systems as indicators of logical consequence.

6.5. Different Formal Systems

Not every formal system is designed to reflect the full extent of the logical consequence relation. Systems of propositional logic, for example, are intended to reflect only a small part of the consequence relation as it applies to the claims expressible in the languages of those systems. Thus, one way in which two formal systems can differ over their assessments of logical consequence is that one of the systems can reflect logical consequences not reflected, and not intended to be reflected, by the other. Such differences need not indicate any underlying disagreement about the extension (or nature) of the logical consequence relation; they can simply be viewed as more or less partial treatments of an agreed upon relation.

However, more robust disagreements are possible as well, disagreements that stem from fundamental disagreements about the nature of the logical consequence relation itself. As noted above, there are those who hold that the logical consequences of a given claim must have a subject matter that is, in some sense, *relevant* to that of the claim itself. On this view, for example, one cannot validly argue from the premises

Jones is wise.

and

Jones is not wise.

to

Smith is athletic.

Standard propositional and quantified systems of logic count the formalized version of this argument as both deductively and model-theoretically valid, with the result that the relevance theorist must take those systems to be unreliable indicators of logical consequence. These theorists argue that more reliable indications of consequence and its related logical notions are given by alternative systems of logic, called systems of *relevance* logic [see chapter 13].

Similarly, systems of *intuitionist* logic are prompted by the perceived unreliability of classical systems. For the intuitionist, it is simply not the case in all domains (for example, when dealing with mathematical existence assertions) that for each claim φ, the corresponding disjunction *either* φ *or not-*φ is always true. On this view, classical logic is wildly unreliable in its assessments of logical consequence. Intuitionist logics are those systems of logic designed to provide reliable indications of logical consequence and related notions as these are understood by the intuitionist [see chapter 11].

Other disagreements with the classical conception of logical consequence have given rise to yet more alternative systems [see, for example, also chapters 12, 14, 15, and 16]. In all cases, the same principle is at work: a given conception of the pretheoretic relation of logical consequence prompts the construction of a particular kind of formal system, one that will give an accurate, systematic treatment of logical consequence and its related notions.

6.6. Analysis of the Relation

Finally and briefly, this section turns to the intensional question: What is it that *makes* one claim a logical consequence of others? A response to this question can take one of two forms. The first, dismissive, response is that the relation of logical consequence is primitive and unanalyzable, and hence that one cannot reduce the fact of *A*'s following logically from *B* to any more basic facts about *A* and *B*, or to any more basic relationship between them. The second form of response is to explain logical consequence in terms of more fundamental facts about *A* and *B* and their relationship to one another.

Looking at the claims expressible by formulas of a particular formal system, one might be tempted to provide an analysis of logical consequence in terms of deducibility in that system, or in terms of truth-preservation across the models of that system. But a moment's reflection will make it clear that no such system-specific analysis of logical consequence can succeed in clarifying what logical consequence consists in, i.e., of what makes it the case that certain claims are logical consequences of others. Deducibility within just *any* system will not do, since there are countless systems, easily definable, which count exactly the wrong things as logical consequences of others. Similarly for model-theoretic consequence. So the attempt to analyze logical consequence via deducibility or model-theoretic consequence must take the analysans here to be deducibility or model-theoretic consequence within a *particular* well-chosen system or kind of system. And the question then arises of what recommends that system or kind of system as an acceptable standard of logical consequence. The attempt to answer *this* question, however, threatens to return us to our original question, that of what makes one claim a logical consequence of others.

An alternative approach is motivated by the fact that logically valid arguments come in patterns, patterns like Aristotle's syllogistic forms, or the argument schemes validated by formal systems, or even the natural language patterns emphasized in teaching critical thinking. Noticing this, it is tempting to define the logical properties and relations in terms of these patterns. Thus, for example, one might define the logical truths as the instances of patterns each instance of which is true, and the logically valid arguments as the instances of patterns each instance of which is truth-preserving (i.e., no instance of which has true premises and a false conclusion).

Whether such a characterization will be extensionally accurate will turn on what counts as a 'pattern.' The first difficulty here is that patterns themselves are definable only for a given language, and facts about which claims and arguments instantiate the same pattern will vary with the language in question. Consider the argument

> Jones and Smith are of the same height.
> Jones is 6′ tall.
> ─────────────────────────
> Therefore, Smith is 6′ tall.

Let $L1$ be a language in which this argument can be formalized as

$$h(j) = h(s)$$
$$h(j) = a$$
$$\overline{}$$
$$h(s) = a$$

while $L2$ formalizes it as

$$H(j, s)$$
$$T(j)$$
$$\overline{}$$
$$T(s)$$

Making the obvious parallel assumptions about the other kinds of claims formalizable by these series of formulas in $L1$ and $L2$, one can see that, although each argument formalizable by the $L1$ series is truth-preserving, this is not the case with the $L2$ series. So the question of whether our original argument exhibits a pattern each instance of which is truth-preserving, and hence (on the current proposal) the question of whether that argument is valid, will depend on which language one has in mind when characterizing the 'pattern.' The first problem, then, with the pattern analysis of the logical relations is that its deliverances will depend in unwanted ways on the chosen language.[4]

There will indeed be languages for which such a pattern characterization of the logical relations is extensionally accurate, languages in which the sentence patterns, e.g.,

$$((\alpha \,\&\, \beta) \to \alpha)$$

each of whose instances is true, will turn out to be patterns each of whose instances expresses a logical truth. The clear candidates here are the formal languages of modern logic. Things are less tidy for languages not intentionally designed to have such a result. It is important for the extensional adequacy of the pattern characterization of logical truth that, e.g.

> Smith did it for Jones' uncle.

and

Smith did it for Jones' sake.

do not count as instantiating the same pattern. And it is important for the attempt to (non-circularly) analyze the logical relations in terms of patterns that the different logical implications had by such pairs of sentences not be appealed to in distinguishing their patterns. In brief, the second difficulty of the pattern analysis of the logical properties and relations is this: Though one can, for certain specified formal languages, give an extensionally accurate characterization of the logical properties in terms of truth-preservation across patterns, this is no reason to suppose that the logical properties are *due* to, or explicable in terms of, characteristics of these sentence patterns. For the formulas of these languages are expressly designed so that they will instantiate the same syntactic patterns when and only when the claims they express have relevantly similar logical properties. The two English sentences just displayed are formalized very differently *because* they express claims with very different logical implications; the logical properties are not recognized on the basis of the patterns. And when turning attention to natural languages, it is difficult to find a characterization of *patterns* that is plausible, extensionally speaking, without making covert appeal to the very logical properties and relations at issue (Etchemendy, 1983).

A perhaps more promising approach is the analysis of logical truth as a kind of *analytic* truth. The difficulties of characterizing analyticity itself are legion, but these are left aside here. The question is whether, granting for the moment the coherence of the notion of analytic truth, an account of logical truth can be given in terms of it. Where analytic truths are, roughly, sentences whose truth is due entirely to matters of meaning (as opposed to matters of 'fact'), the logical truths will be those whose truth is due entirely to the meanings of a certain small, select group of terms. These terms, the 'logical constants', include the usual 'and', 'or', 'not', 'for all', 'exists', perhaps '=', and terms definable in terms of these. Thus while

All professors are academics.

is arguably an analytic truth in the broad sense,

If all professors are arrogant then all professors are arrogant.

falls into the narrower camp of logical truth, since its truth is guaranteed simply by the meanings of its logical constants.

There are at least two difficulties with this approach. The first is, as noted, that it is not entirely clear that sense can be made of the notion of analytic truth. The second is that this characterization of the logical properties and relations seems to appeal, once again, to the very things it is trying to characterize. To say that the meanings of a collection of terms 'suffices for' or 'guarantees' the truth of a sentence seems to mean little more than that the sentence's truth *follows logically from* facts about those meanings, or that its falsehood would be *logically inconsistent with* those facts, etc. And if this is right, then one cannot, without vicious circularity, give a characterization of the logical properties and relations in terms of meanings.

This last problem, the circularity of the proposed analysis, would seem likely to pose difficulties for virtually any attempted analysis of the tight circle of inter-defined logical properties and relations. For to give an analysis of logical truth is to say what it is about a given truth that *makes it* a logical truth. Similarly for the notions of validity, logical consequence, inconsistency, and so on. But to say that certain features *F* of a sentence or claim *make* that claim a logical truth is to say something dangerously close to saying that the sentence's having *F entails* that the sentence is a logical truth. And in saying this, then one has proceeded in a very small circle. Similarly when the analysis is given as a 'reduction.' One can try to informatively reduce the property of logical truth to a collection of non-logical features *F* of sentences or claims, holding that to *say* that a claim α is a logical truth is just to *say* that α has features *F*. And this brief discussion has certainly not exhausted all of the possible ways of fleshing out such an attempted reduction. But the potential difficulty faced by all such attempts is that of saying precisely how *F* and the logical relationships in question are related, without making recourse to anything like *entailment* between the two.

Analysis and reduction are typically intimately connected with the logical properties and relationships; complex notions are analyzed in terms of simpler ones, or some are reduced to others, in part by noting logical connections between the analysans and analysandum. Facts about *inconsistencies* between affirmations of analysans and denial of analysandum, of *entailments* between claims about one and claims about the other, and so on are noted. If this general pattern is, in fact, a necessary feature of analysis and reduction, then the logical properties and relations will be analyzable in terms of, and reducible to, only other members of the circle of logical properties and relations, and not to any outside it. If so, then we will have to be content with explanations of these notions that consist of making explicit their role in our overall semantic and other cognitive activities, but that do not give simple, informative answers to questions of the form, What *makes* this a logical consequence of that?

Suggested further reading

Perhaps the most provocative book written in recent years on the topic of logical consequence is Etchemendy's (1999 [1990]), which provides a sustained criticism of the assumption that model-theoretic consequence relations generally provide adequate analyses of logical consequence. Reactions to this criticism can be found in McGee's (1992) and Shapiro's (1991). The question of whether model-theoretic consequence relations can guarantee the required modal connection between premises and conclusion is treated in Shapiro's (1991) and in the author's paper (Blanchette, 2000). For discussion of the bearers of the logical relations, and particularly of the difficulties involved in supposing the existence of nonlinguistic propositions, see Quine (1953b [1948], 1970, esp. ch. 1). Also see Cartwright (1987c) and Strawson (1952, esp. ch. 1). For the classic criticism of the notion of analytic truth and related notions, together with an influential treatment of logical truth, see Quine (1953c [1951]), while Strawson (1971 [1957]) gives a response. A number of useful papers on related topics can be found in Hughes (1993). Haack (1978) presents a very readable discussion of many of these issues.

Notes

1 The problem arises from Frege's assumption that, to every predicate or open sentence, there corresponds a set-like entity called an *extension*. As Russell's Paradox [see chapter 3] shows, this assumption is false. See Russell's letter to Frege of 16 June 1902 and Frege's response of 22 June 1902, both translated and printed in Frege (1980, pp. 130–3). See also Frege (1964, Vol. II, Appendix, pp. 127–41).
2 Some free logics, so-called *universally* free logics, reject the 'non-empty universe' assumption, and thus deny that these formulas and, e.g., '$\forall xFx \rightarrow \exists xFx$,' express necessary truths [see chapter 12].
3 Assuming, of course, that it is not a truth of logic that there are no sets larger than $\mathbb{N}$. If it is, then both (6.1) and (6.2) will be truths of logic, but so too will be the continuum hypothesis.
4 This difficulty remains even when the *claims* are, as above, interpreted sentences. For we presumably want a sentence S to count as a logical truth iff all sentences synonymous with it are as well, and this will not generally be the case on the proposed account.

References

Blanchette, P. 2000: "Models and Modality," *Synthese*, 124, 45–72.
Cartwright, R. 1987a: "Implications and Entailments," in Cartwright (1987b, 237–56).
Cartwright, R. 1987b: *Philosophical Essays*, (MIT Press, Cambridge and London).
Cartwright, R. 1987c: "Propositions," in *Analytical Philosophy*, 1st Series; R. J. Butler, ed., (Blackwell, Oxford), 1962, 81–103; reprinted in Cartwright (1987b, 33–53).
Etchemendy, J. 1983: "The Doctrine of Logic as Form," *Linguistics and Philosophy*, 6, 319–34.
Etchemendy, J. 1999: *The Concept of Logical Consequence*, (Harvard University Press, Cambridge, MA), 1990; reprinted by CSLI Publications, Stanford.
Frege, G. 1964: *Grundgesetze der Arithmetik*, Vol. I: 1893; Vol. II: 1903, (Verlag Hermann Pohle, Jena); partially translated by M. Furth as *The Basic Laws of Arithmetic*, (University of California Press, Berkeley and Los Angeles). (Page references are to this translation.)
Frege, G. 1980: *Philosophical and Mathematical Correspondence*, G. Gabriel, H. Hermes, F. Kambartel, C. Thiel, A. Veraart, B. McGuinness, eds., (University of Chicago Press, Chicago).
Haack, S. 1978: *Philosophy of Logics*, (Cambridge University Press, Cambridge, UK).
Hughes, R. I. G. 1993: *A Philosophical Companion to First-Order Logic*, (Hackett Publishing Co., Indianapolis and Cambridge, UK).
McGee, V. 1992: "Two Problems with Tarski's Theory of Consequence," *Proceedings of the Aristotelian Society*, 92, 273–92.
Quine, W. V. O. 1953a: *From a Logical Point of View*, (Harvard University Press, Cambridge, MA).
Quine, W. V. O. 1953b: "On What There Is," *Review of Metaphysics*, 2 (1948), 21–38; reprinted in Quine, (1953a, 1–19).
Quine, W. V. O. 1953c: "Two Dogmas of Empiricism," *Philosophical Review*, 60 (1951), 20–43; reprinted in Quine (1953a, 20–46).
Quine, W. V. O. 1970: *Philosophy of Logic*, (Prentice Hall, Englewood, NJ).
Shapiro, S. 1991: *Foundations without Foundationalism: A Case for Second-Order Logic*, (Oxford University Press, Oxford).

Shapiro, S. 1998: "Logical Consequence: Models and Modality," in *The Philosophy of Mathematics Today*, M. Schirn, ed., (Clarendon Press, Oxford), 131–56.

Sher, G. 1991: *The Bounds of Logic*, (MIT Press, Cambridge, MA).

Strawson, P. F. 1952: *Introduction to Logical Theory*, (Methuen & Co., London).

Strawson, P. F. 1971: "Propositions, Concepts, and Logical Truths," *Philosophical Quarterly*, 7 (1957); reprinted in P. F. Strawson, *Logico-Linguistic Papers*, (Methuen & Co., London), 116–29.

Chapter 7

Modal Logic

M. J. Cresswell

Modal logic is the logic of necessity and possibility, of 'must be' and 'may be'. These may be interpreted in various ways. If necessity is necessary truth, there is *alethic modal logic*; if it is moral or normative necessity, there is *deontic logic* [see chapter 8]. It may refer to what is known or believed to be true, in which case, there is an *epistemic logic* [chapter 9], or to what always has been or to what henceforth always will be true, which gives an aspect of *temporal logic* [chapter 10]. Another interpretation is to read 'Necessarily *p*' as 'it is provable that *p*'. This chapter will present the general framework of modal logic applicable to all of these, though with emphasis on alethic modal logics.

In this chapter, the symbol '*L*' represents the necessity operator, with '*Lp*' to be read 'Necessarily *p*'. Correlative to this is the possibility operator, '*M*', with '*Mp*' being read 'Possibly *p*'. ('□' is often used instead of '*L*' and '◇' instead of '*M*'; '*N*' is also sometimes used instead of '*L*'.) Either operator may be defined in terms of the other. Thus, if the modal language contains '*L*' as a primitive operator, then '*Mα*' may be defined as '~*L*~*α*', for any formula *α*. Impossibility may similarly be expressed by '~*M*' (or '*L*~'); contingent propositions are those that are neither necessary nor impossible.

7.1. Propositional Modal Logic

This section offers a study of propositional modal logics, after which section 7.2 examines the place of modal operators in first-order predicate logic. This section is confined to modal logics that are extensions of classical logic [see chapter 1], although it is also possible to form non-classical modal logics, e.g., by extending intuitionistic logic [chapter 11] or relevant logic [chapter 13]. For the language of propositional modal logic, assume the language of the classical propositional calculus, PC, based on propositional variables, *p*, *q*, *r*, . . . etc., and ~ (for negation) and ∨ (for disjunction), with other truth-functional operators being defined in the usual ways. To this, add the new monadic operator *L* with the understanding that the formation rules for PC formulas apply to all the formulas of the extended language and with the additional rule:

If α is a well-formed formula (wff), then so is *Lα*.

A *system of* (propositional) *modal logic* may be defined as a class **S** of wff. A formula α is a *theorem* of **S** – or ⊢ₛ α – iff (if and only if) α ∈ **S**. The logics studied here will all be *normal modal logics*, which are extensions of a minimal system called **K**.

K is defined axiomatically as the class of all wff that may be obtained from these five axioms and transformation rules:

PC If α is a valid wff of PC, then α is an axiom of **K**

K $L(p \supset q) \supset (Lp \supset Lq)$

US *Uniform substitution* The result of uniformly replacing any variable or variables $p_1, \ldots, p_n$ in a theorem by any wff $\beta_1, \ldots, \beta_n$ respectively is a theorem.

MP *Modus ponens*, or *Detachment* If α and α ⊃ β are theorems, so is β.

N (*Necessitation*) If α is a theorem, so is *Lα*.

Other systems of modal logic will be formed by adding additional axioms to this base, with the result being closed under the three rules.

7.1.1. Validity

Modal logic, as the logic of necessity and possibility, takes into account not only the truth and falsity of the way things actually are, but also what would be true or false if things were different. If one thinks of the way things are as the actual world, one may then think of how things might have been different as how they are in alternative, non-actual but possible worlds. As logic is concerned with truth and falsity, modal logic is concerned with truth and falsity in other possible worlds as well as the real one. A proposition is then necessary in a world just in case it is true in all the worlds that are possible alternatives to that world, and possible just in case it is true in some alternative possible world.

This provides the basis of our formal definition of validity for modal logic.[1] A *frame* is an ordered pair ⟨W, R⟩, where W is a non-empty set of objects (worlds), and R is a binary relation defined over the members of W. R is often called a relation of 'alternativeness' or 'accessibility'; when wRw' is sometimes expressed by saying w 'can see' w'. A *model* is an ordered triple ⟨W, R, V⟩ where ⟨W, R⟩ is a frame and V is a function assigning values to wffs at worlds w ∈ W, according to the following conditions:

[Vpv] For any propositional variable, p, and any w ∈ W, either V(p, w) = 1 or V(p, w) = 0, but not both.

[V~] For any wff, α, and any $w \in W$, $V(\sim\alpha, w) = 1$ if $V(\alpha, w) = 0$; otherwise $V(\sim\alpha, w) = 0$.

[V∨] For any wff α and β, and any $w \in W$, $V((\alpha \vee \beta), w) = 1$ if either $V(\alpha, w) = 1$ or $V(\beta, w) = 1$; otherwise $V((\alpha \vee \beta), w) = 0$.

and, of special interest for modal logic, and following the informal interpretation of necessity as truth in all alternative possible worlds,

[VL] For any wff α and for any $w \in W$, $V(L\alpha, w) = 1$ if $V(\alpha, w') = 1$ for every $w' \in W$ such that wRw'; otherwise $V(L\alpha, w) = 0$.

Evaluation conditions for other, defined operators are just what one would expect [see chapter 1], though it is convenient to note:

[VM] For any wff α and for any $w \in W$, $V(M\alpha, w) = 1$ if $V(\alpha, w') = 1$ for some $w' \in W$ such that wRw'; otherwise $V(M\alpha, w) = 0$.

A model $\langle W, R, V \rangle$ is said to be *based on* the frame $\langle W, R \rangle$.

Validity is defined by saying first that a wff α is *valid in* a model $\langle W, R, V \rangle$ iff for every $w \in W$, $V(\alpha, w) = 1$. Then a wff α is said to be *valid on* a frame $\langle W, R \rangle$ iff α is valid in every model based on that frame. Specific sorts of validity are defined by specifying relevant classes of frames on which formulas are valid. Thus, a wff is said to be valid with respect to a class of frames *F* (*F*-valid) iff it is valid on every frame in *F*, and a system **S** is *sound* with respect to *F* iff every theorem in **S** is *F*-valid. **S** is *complete* with respect to *F* iff every wff that is *F*-valid is a theorem of **S**. When **S** is both sound and complete with respect to *F*, *F* is said to *characterize* **S**. For a particular frame $F = \langle W, R \rangle$, if every theorem of **S** is valid on *F*, *F* is said to be a *frame for* **S**.

A wff is *K-valid* iff it is valid on *every* frame.

Theorem 7.1 Every theorem of **K** is *K*-valid.

To prove this, it suffices to prove that

1 every axiom of **K** is valid on every frame, and
2 the rules US, MP and N preserve validity on a frame – i.e. that if they are applied to formulas which are valid on a frame, the resulting formulas are also valid on that frame.

It is more useful, however, to prove a more general theorem, from which theorem 7.1 follows immediately:

Theorem 7.2 If Λ is a set of modal wff and *F* is a class of frames such that every member of Λ is valid on every member of *F*, then **K** + Λ is sound with respect to *F*

where $K + \Lambda$ is the system obtained by adding all the formulas of Λ as extra axioms to K with the result closed under the rules US, MP and N. Like theorem 7.1, theorem 7.2 is proved by induction on proofs in $K + \Lambda$; this amounts to showing that every axiom of K is valid on any frame in F and that the rules preserve validity on a frame, since it is given that all the axioms in Λ are valid on all the frames in F. Theorem 7.1 follows from theorem 7.2 by taking F to be the class of all frames.

Theorem 7.2 is important for the following reason. K is the weakest modal system discussed here; each of the other systems is a proper extension of it. Usually, these other systems are defined axiomatically by adding one or more extra axioms to the basis of K; these are the wff in Λ. For each such system $K + \Lambda$, there is also (or at least one tries to find) a definition of validity which matches it in the way that K-validity matches the system K; i.e., which is such that the theorems of the system are precisely the wff which are valid by that definition. Theorem 7.2 establishes that to prove that $K + \Lambda$ is sound with respect to a class of frames F, it suffices to show that every member of Λ is valid on every frame in F.

The system **T** If necessity is thought of as necessary truth, it is natural to expect the formula

T $Lp \supset p$

to be valid, for it says merely that if p is necessarily true, then it is true. Nevertheless, T is not K-valid. (Consider a frame $\langle \{w, w'\}, R \rangle$ where wRw', and $w'Rw'$, but not wRw; if p is false at w but true at w', then T is false at w.) By theorem 7.1, this means that T is not a theorem of K. Let **T** be the result of adding T to K; i.e., in the notation above $T = K + \{T\}$, or, more simply, $K + T$, or KT. By theorem 7.2, since T is valid on every *reflexive frame* $\langle W, R \rangle$, i.e., every frame in which R is reflexive, the system **T** is sound with respect to the class of all reflexive frames. (Notice that the frame just described to falsify T is not reflexive.)

The system **D** If, however, L has a deontic interpretation, if, that is, it expresses obligatoriness ('normative necessity'), $Lp \supset p$ would not be regarded as valid, since it would mean that whatever ought to be the case actually is the case. More plausible is

D $Lp \supset Mp$

which says that whatever is obligatory is permissible, which sounds reasonable enough. [See chapter 8 for further discussion of deontic intepretations.]

Adding D as an axiom to K produces the system known as **D**. D is clearly a theorem of **T**, so **D** is included in **T**, just as **K** is included in **D**. It is worth noting that since $L(p \supset p)$ is in **D**, then because of D, so is $M(p \supset p)$. $M(p \supset p)$ is not, however, a theorem of **K**, for **K** has no theorems of the form $M\alpha$. Any extension of **K** that does have theorems of the form $M\alpha$ will contain D, and so be at least as strong as **D**.

To define validity for **D**, notice that some frames may have so-called 'dead end' or 'blind' worlds, worlds which have no accessible alternatives or which cannot see any world in that frame at all. For such worlds w [VL] entails that $L\alpha$ is (trivially) true in w, no matter what α is (even $p \wedge \sim p$), and [VM] entails that $M\alpha$ is (trivially) false in w. Hence, if a frame contains any dead end or blind world w, then D is not valid on that frame. Since there are such frames D is not **K**-valid and therefore not a theorem of **K**. Consider, however, the class of frames containing no dead ends, i.e., for every $w \in W$, there is a $w' \in W$ such that wRw'. Such a relation R is called *serial*, and such frames *serial frames*. D is valid on every serial frame. Hence, by theorem 7.2, **D** is sound with respect to the class of all serial frames. (The model above that showed that T is not **K**-valid is based on a serial frame; hence T is not **D**-valid either, and so not in **D**. Hence, T is a proper extension of **D**. Any reflexive frame will, of course, be serial.)

7.1.2. *Iterated modalities*

Some formulas in the language of modal logic contain sequences of the modal operators L and M, e.g., the formulas LLp, $LMLp$, etc. Such sequences are called *iterated modalities*. Under some interpretations, it is difficult to know how to understand such formulas intuitively. In some systems, however, certain iterations may be replaced by shorter ones, which helps to simplify the problem. A theorem of equivalence which allows such replacement is called a *reduction law* of any system of which it is a member. Here are the four most important of these:

R1 $Mp \equiv LMp$

R2 $Lp \equiv MLp$

R3 $Mp \equiv MMp$

R4 $Lp \equiv LLp$

None of these is a theorem of **T**; indeed, **T** contains no reduction laws at all. **T** does, of course, contain $LLp \supset Lp$ and $LMp \supset Mp$, and their equivalents, under the definition of M, $Lp \supset MLp$ and $Mp \supset MMp$. Hence, to extend **T** to contain reduction laws, it is enough to add the converses of these formulas. Moreover, from $Lp \supset LLp$, one can derive $MMp \supset Mp$ (substituting $\sim p/p$), and from $Mp \supset LMp$ one can derive $MLp \supset Lp$ similarly. In addition, $Lp \supset LLp$ is derivable from $Mp \supset LMp$, though $Mp \supset LMp$ is not derivable from $Lp \supset LLp$. This suggests two extensions of **T**, one that results by the addition of $Lp \supset LLp$ as an axiom and one the results by the addition of $Mp \supset LMp$. (The latter will, of course, contain the former.) These are the systems known as **S4** and **S5**.

The system S4   **S4** is **T** with addition of the axiom

4      $Lp \supset LLp$

or **K + T + 4**. If a *modality* is defined as any unbroken sequence of zero or more monadic operators ($\sim$, L, M), then in **S4** every modality is equivalent to those

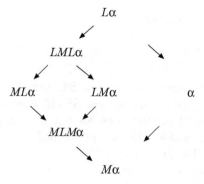

Figure 7.1

shown in figure 7.1 or their negations, where the arrows indicate implication relations. For negative cases, a corresponding diagram results by negating all the formulas and reversing the direction of the arrows. Thus, in **S4**, there are exactly 14
distinct modalities, and any modality may be reduced to one containing no more
than three modal operators in sequence.

The **S4** axiom 4, $Lp \supset LLp$, will be valid on any *transitive frame*, i.e., any frame in
which the relation R is transitive. Since **S4** also contains T, **S4** is sound with respect
to the class of all frames that are both reflexive and transitive. (To show that axiom
4 is not a theorem of **T**, it suffices to give a reflexive frame that is not transitive.)

The system S5 **S5** is **T** plus the additional axiom

E $Mp \supset LMp$

or **K** + T + E. Since the **S4** axiom 4 is provable in **S5**, **S5** is an extension of **S4**, and
it is a proper extension since E is not a theorem of **S4**. **S5** contains all the reduction
laws R1–R4, which means that in any pair of adjacent modal operators one may
delete the first. This procedure may be repeated indefinitely, giving the more general
rule that, in **S5**, one may delete all but the last modal operator in any sequence.
Hence, **S5** has just six non-equivalent modalities: p, Mp, and Lp, and their negations.

Axiom E is valid on every frame in which R is *Euclidean*, i.e., if wRw' and wRw'',
then $w'Rw''$. Notice that if such an R is also reflexive, then it is *symmetric* and
transitive as well. Relations that are reflexive, symmetric and transitive are called
equivalence relations. Since **S5** contains T, it is sound with respect to the class of all
frames that are reflexive and Euclidean; hence, it is sound with respect to class of
all frames whose relations R are equivalence relations. (This is how **S5** is usually
described. Sometimes, however, it is useful to separate axiom E from axiom T, to
form systems weaker than **S5**, like **K45** [see chapter 9], and then it is important to
characterize the relation R as merely Euclidean, or Euclidean and transitive, rather
than a full equivalence relation.)

*The system **B*** This theorem of **S5**:

B $p \supset LMp$

has a special interest. B is not a theorem of **S4**, and if it were added as an extra axiom to **S4**, it would produce the system **S5**. If, however, B were added to **T** instead of to **S4**, it would produce not **S5** but a weaker system which neither contains nor is contained in **S4**. This system is called the *Brouwerian system*, and B the *Brouwerian axiom*. The system **B** is **T** + B, or **K** + **T** + B. B is valid on every frame in which R is symmetric. Since T is valid on every reflexive frame, and **B** = **K** + **T** + B, theorem 7.2 entails that **B** is sound with respect to the class of all frames which are both reflexive and symmetric.

Adding B to **S4** gives **S5**; since **S4** is weaker than **S5**, it follows that B is not in **S4**, and hence that **S4** does not contain the system **B**. Nor does **B** contain **S4** since there are reflexive and symmetric frames that are not transitive. So **B** and **S4** are independent systems, in the sense that neither contains the other, though each lies between **T** and **S5**.

Other systems   There are infinitely many modal systems that may obtained by adding extra axioms to **K**. Already some others can easily be defined. For example, instead of adding 4 to **T** to produce **S4**, one could add it merely to **K** or to **D**. The resulting systems are often called *K4* and *KD4* respectively. If *K4*-frames are defined as those which are transitive (whether or not they are reflexive), and *KD4*-frames as those which are both serial and transitive, then the results proved so far suffice to show that all the theorems of **K4** are valid on all *K4*-frames and all the theorems of **KD4** are valid on all *KD4*-frames. Similarly, one could add B to **K** or to **D** instead of **T**, to obtain the systems **KB** and **KDB**, which are sound with respect to the classes of symmetrical frames and serial and symmetrical frames respectively. **K45**, mentioned above, is sound with respect to the class of frames that are transitive and Euclidean, and **KD45** sound with respect to the class of serial, transitive and Euclidean frames.

7.1.3.   Completeness

The *canonical* model for a system **S** is a special model with the property that a wff α is valid in it iff $\vdash_S \alpha$. This section shows that every (consistent) normal modal system **S** has such a model. This fact makes it easy to establish completeness results, at least for the systems being discussed, by the following strategy. Suppose there is a class *F* of frames, and suppose one can establish that the frame of the canonical model of **S** is in *F*, then if α is *F*-valid, α will be valid on the frame of the canonical model for **S**, and so *a fortiori* valid in the canonical model itself. But that entails that $\vdash_S \alpha$. So if α is *F*-valid then $\vdash_S \alpha$, which is what the completeness of **S** with respect to *F* means. Thus, for each specific system, it suffices to show that the frame of its canonical model is indeed in *F*. For **K**, this is immediate since the relevant class *F* is the class of all frames. For **D**, *F* is the class of serial frames and so it must be shown that the frame of the canonical model for **D** is serial; for **T** it must be shown that it is reflexive; for **S4**, **B**, **S5** that it is reflexive and, respectively, transitive, symmetrical, and Euclidean, and similarly for other systems.

Following procedures familiar from non-modal logic [see chapter 1, section 1.9], a set of wff, Λ, is said to be **S**-*consistent* if there is no finite collection $\alpha_1, \ldots, \alpha_n \in \Lambda$, such that $\vdash_S \sim(\alpha_1 \wedge \cdots \wedge \alpha_n)$, where **S** is any normal modal logic. Γ is *maximal* iff for every wff α either $\alpha \in \Gamma$ or $\sim\alpha \in \Gamma$. Γ is *maximal consistent with respect to* **S** iff it is both maximal and **S**-consistent. Then lemma 7.3 holds simply because **S** contains the classical propositional calculus (PC).

Lemma 7.3 If Λ is an **S**-consistent set of wff, then there is a maximal **S**-consistent set of wff Γ such that $\Lambda \subseteq \Gamma$.

The next lemma is appropriate to modal logics. Where Λ is any set of wff of modal logic, let $L^-(\Lambda)$ be the set consisting precisely of every wff β for which $L\beta$ is in Λ; i.e., $L^-(\Lambda) = \{\beta: L\beta \in \Lambda\}$.

Lemma 7.4 If **S** is any normal propositional modal logic, and Λ is an **S**-consistent set of wff containing $\sim L\alpha$, then $L^-(\Lambda) \cup \{\sim\alpha\}$ is **S**-consistent.

Proof Suppose $L^-(\Lambda) \cup \{\sim\alpha\}$ is not **S**-consistent. Then there are $\beta_1, \ldots, \beta_n$ of $L^-(\Lambda)$, such that $\vdash_S \sim(\beta_1 \wedge \cdots \wedge \beta_n \wedge \sim\alpha)$, and so, by PC, $\vdash_S (\beta_1 \wedge \cdots \wedge \beta_n) \supset \alpha$. By principles of **K**, $\vdash_S (L\beta_1 \wedge \cdots \wedge L\beta_n) \supset L\alpha$, and so $\vdash_S \sim(L\beta_1 \wedge \cdots \wedge L\beta_n \wedge \sim L\alpha)$. Thus the set $\{L\beta_1, \ldots, L\beta_n, \sim L\alpha\}$ is not **S**-consistent. Since each $\beta_i \in L^-(\Lambda)$, each $L\beta_i \in \Lambda$; it is given that $\sim L\alpha \in \Lambda$, so $\{L\beta_1, \ldots, L\beta_n, \sim L\alpha\} \subseteq \Lambda$. Hence, under the hypothesis, Λ is not **S**-consistent. Therefore, if Λ, containing $\sim L\alpha$, is **S**-consistent, $L^-(\Lambda) \cup \{\sim\alpha\}$ is **S**-consistent. QED

Now, define the canonical model for **S** as the triple $\langle W, R, V \rangle$ in which: W is the set of all maximal **S**-consistent sets of wff; if w and w' are both in W then wRw' iff for every wff β if $L\beta \in w$ then $\beta \in w'$, or, using the L^- notation, wRw' iff $L^-(w) \subseteq w'$; and $V(p, w) = 1$ iff $p \in w$.

Lemma 7.5 If $\langle W, R, V \rangle$ is the canonical model so defined for a normal propositional model system **S**, then for any wff α and any $w \in W$, $V(\alpha, w) = 1$ iff $\alpha \in w$.

Proof The result is defined to hold for the propositional variables; for complex wff, it may be proved by induction on the construction of wff. The only complicated case is the induction for L.

(a) Suppose that $L\alpha \in w$. By definition of R, $\alpha \in w'$ for every w' such that wRw'. Since the lemma is assumed to hold for α, $V(\alpha, w') = 1$ for every w' such that wRw'. Hence by [VL], $V(L\alpha, w) = 1$.
(b) Suppose now that $L\alpha \notin w$. Then by the maximality of sets w, $\sim L\alpha \in w$. Hence, by lemma 7.4, $L^-(w) \cup \{\sim\alpha\}$ is **S**-consistent. So by lemma 7.3 and the definition

of W, there is some $w' \in W$ such that $L^-(w) \cup \{\sim\alpha\} \subseteq w'$, and therefore such that

(i) $L^-(w) \subseteq w'$ and
(ii) $\sim\alpha \in w'$.

By the definition of R, (i) gives wRw', and since w' is maximal **S**-consistent, (ii) gives $\alpha \notin w'$. Hence, since this lemma is assumed to hold for α, $V(\alpha, w') = 0$. So [VL] gives $V(L\alpha, w) = 0$.   Q.E.D.

Theorem 7.6 Any wff α is valid in the canonical model of **S** iff $\vdash_S \alpha$.

Proof Let $\langle W, R, V \rangle$ be the canonical model of **S**. First suppose $\vdash_S \alpha$. Then α is in every maximal **S**-consistent set of wff (from the definitions). Hence, α is in every $w \in W$, and so, by lemma 7.5, $V(\alpha, w) = 1$ for every $w \in W$; i.e. α is valid in $\langle W, R, V \rangle$. Suppose now that not-$\vdash_S \alpha$. Then $\{\sim\alpha\}$ is **S**-consistent and so, by lemma 7.3, there is some maximal **S**-consistent set, i.e. some $w \in W$, such that $\sim\alpha \in w$ and hence $\alpha \notin w$. So by lemma 7.5, $V(\alpha, w) = 0$. Hence, if not-$\vdash_S \alpha$, then α is not valid in $\langle W, R, V \rangle$.   Q.E.D.

Theorem 7.6 yields the completeness of many modal logics according to the strategy described above. For **K**, the result is immediate, since for **K** one takes *F* to be the class of all frames, which, trivially, includes the frame of the canonical model. For extensions of **K**, it is easy to prove:

Lemma 7.7 If **S** contains the formula T, then the frame of its canonical model is reflexive; likewise if it contains D, the frame is serial; if 4, then it is transitive; if B then it is symmetric; and if 5 then it is Euclidean.

From this, the completeness of all the systems so far discussed follows directly:

Theorem 7.8 The system **K** is complete with respect to the class of all frames, and the systems **K4, KB, K5, K45, T, D, KD4, KDB, KD45, S4, B**, and **S5** are complete with respect to the class of all frames that are respectively: transitive; symmetric; Euclidean; transitive and Euclidean; reflexive; serial; serial and transitive; serial and symmetric; serial, transitive and Euclidean; reflexive and transitive; reflexive and symmetric; reflexive, transitive and symmetric.

These results may be considerably generalized. Notice that each of the axioms characteristic of the systems so far discussed is equivalent to one of the form

$G^{k,l,m,n}$ $M^k L^l p \supset L^m M^n p$

for $k, l, m, n \geq 0$, where $L^n \alpha$ is α preceded by n Ls, and similarly for $M^n \alpha$. It is known that $G^{k,l,m,n}$ is valid on a frame $\langle W, R \rangle$ iff the frame meets this condition: $(g^{k,l,m,n})$ for all $w, w', w'' \in W$, if $wR^k w'$ and $wR^m w''$, then there is a w''' such that $w'R^l w'''$ and $w''R^n w'''$, where R^n is the nth relative product of R, i.e., $wR^0 w'$ iff

$w = w'$, and if $n > 0$, $wR^n w'$ iff there is a w'' such that wRw'' and $w''R^{n-1}w'$. Further-more, if **S** contains $G^{k,l,m,n}$ then the frame of its canonical model does meet $(g^{k,l,m,n})$. Hence, theorem 7.9:

Theorem 7.9 Systems $\mathbf{KG}^{k,l,m,n}$ are sound and complete with respect to the class of frames that satisfy conditions $g^{k,l,m,n}$.

Here $\mathbf{KG}^{k,l,m,n}$ is the result of adding any number of formulas $G^{k,l,m,n}$ as axioms to **K**. Theorem 7.8 gives special cases of this. See Chagrov and Zakharyaschev (1997, p. 79) and Chellas (1980, pp. 85–90, 182–4).)

7.1.4. *The Finite Model Property*

Canonical models provide a very convenient way to demonstrate the completeness of modal logics, although, as shall be seen, this method does not work for all systems. The frames of these models are very large, however, and for many systems most of this size is wasted. A logic **S** has the *finite model property* iff it is character-ized by a class of finite models, or, equivalently, by a class of finite frames. Any system with this property is complete, and so demonstrating this property is some-times an alternative way of establishing completeness when the original method fails. Moreover, the finite model property is important because if a logic **S** (whether modal or not) has the finite model property and it is finitely axiomatizable, then it is *decidable*, i.e., there is an effective procedure that will determine in a finite number of steps whether a given wff is a theorem of the system.

It can be shown that a system **S** has the finite model property by constructing, as it were, mini-canonical models; for each non-theorem its falsifying model will be constructed out of its own well-formed parts. Given a wff α, let Φ_α be the set of sub-formulas of α. Let W be the set of all Φ_α-maximal **S**-consistent sets of wff, where a set is Φ_α-maximal iff for every $\beta \in \Phi_\alpha$, either β or $\sim\beta$ is in the set. For $\mathbf{S} = \mathbf{K}, \mathbf{D}$, or $\mathbf{T}$, let R be defined as for canonical models above, and for each $w \in W$, let $V(p, w) = 1$ iff $p \in w$. It is straightforward then to prove the analogues of lemmas 7.3, 7.4, and 7.5 for the models $\langle W, R, V \rangle$ so defined. For these three systems, lemma 7.7 remains true, and so there is another proof of their completeness, but this time based on frames of finite size.

The preceding does not apply to systems **S4**, **B**, or **S5**, however, because relation R so defined might not be transitive or symmetric or Euclidean. In regular canonical models for **S4**, for example, transitivity is guaranteed by $Lp \supset LLp$, so that if $L\beta \in w$, $LL\beta \in w$, but now there is no assurance that $LL\beta \in \Phi_\alpha$ just because $L\beta$ is. The easiest way around this problem is to redefine R, so that now, for **S4**, wRw' iff $L\beta \in w'$ whenever $L\beta \in w$, for all wff β. This relation is transitive and reflexive. For **K4**, define R so that wRw' iff both $L\beta \in w'$ and $\beta \in w'$ whenever $L\beta \in w$. For **B**, define R so that wRw' iff $\beta \in w'$ if $L\beta \in w$ and $\beta \in w$ if $L\beta \in w'$. For **S5**, wRw' iff $L\beta \in w'$ if $L\beta \in w$ and $L\beta \in w$ if $L\beta \in w'$, and so on for the other systems discussed. For each system, it is necessary to define a relation R that has the requisite proper-ties for frames for that system. This must be done system by system. Furthermore, because R has been redefined from the regular canonical models, it is necessary to return to the proof of lemma 7.5 to verify that it continues to hold under the new definition. This may, however, be done for these systems, and for many others, with the result that they are thereby shown to have the finite model property.[2]

7.1.5. *Beyond K, D, T, S4, B, and S5*

The systems **K, D, T, S4, B,** and **S5** and their characteristic axioms have been introduced because they are historically and philosophically important, and because they are easily shown to possess a number of desirable properties. It has been shown that they are sound and complete with respect to their appropriate classes of frames, and that they have the finite model property, and, because they are finitely axiomatizable, they are decidable. They are also *compact*, in that every **S**-consistent set of wff is satisfiable in a frame for **S**, for **S** being one of these systems, and they are *canonical* in that the frames of their canonical models are frames for these systems.

Not all normal modal logics are so well-behaved, however, and the methods described above do not always apply. For example, the system **KW** = **K** +

W $\quad L(Lp \supset p) \supset Lp$

is neither compact nor canonical. (Although, trivially, every theorem is valid *in* its canonical model, not every theorem is valid *on* the frame of that model.) As a result, the original proof of completeness will not work for this system. Nevertheless, using the method of mini-canonical models, **KW** may still be proved sound and complete with respect to the class of frames that are finite, irreflexive and transitive. For this, define R so that wRw' iff

(i) both $L\beta \in w'$ and $\beta \in w'$ whenever $L\beta \in w$, and
(ii) there is some $L\beta \in w'$ such that $L\beta \notin w$.

This also shows that **KW** has the finite model property.[3]

Not all normal modal logics do possess the finite model property, however. One that does not is **Mk** = **T** +

Mk $\quad L(LLp \supset Lq) \supset (Lp \supset q)$

Nevertheless, **Mk** is complete with respect to a fairly easily specifiable class of frames.

Completeness too is not universal. There exist countless systems that can be proved to be *incomplete* in the sense that there is *no* class F of frames such that their theorems are precisely the F-valid wff. One simple example is the system **KH** = **K** +

H $\quad L(Lp \equiv p) \supset Lp$

(Interestingly, the class of frames for **KH** characterizes **KW**.)

Much current research in modal logic is devoted to the systematic study of large families of logics to examine the conditions under which they have, or lack, properties like these.[4]

7.2. First-Order Modal Logic

First-order modal logic, or modal predicate logic, is an extension – grammatically, axiomatically and semantically – of the propositional modal logic discussed above; it is also an extension of non-modal first-order logic, or the lower predicate calculus, LPC [see chapter 1]. The language of modal predicate logic simply adds the modal operator L to the language of LPC, but the interpretation of this language introduces some interesting questions and complications.

First: an obvious generalization of the interpretation of the non-modal language. A model now consists of a quadruple $\langle W, R, D, V \rangle$ in which $\langle W, R \rangle$ is a frame, as previously discussed, and D is a domain of individuals. To interpret the predicates of the language, each n-place predicate is assigned a set of n-tuples from D *in each world*. Intuitively, these are the (sequences of) individuals that satisfy that predicate in that world. Alternatively, one may think of V as assigning to each n-place predicate a set of $n+1$-tuples, in each one of which the first n terms are from D and the final term is from W. To say that $\langle u_1, \ldots, u_n, w \rangle \in V(\phi)$ is to say that ϕ is true of $u_1, \ldots, u_n$ (in that order) in world w.

More precisely, a model is a quadruple $\langle W, R, D, V \rangle$ in which W is a non-empty set (worlds), R a binary relation on W, D another non-empty set (individuals) and V a function such that, where ϕ is an n-place predicate, $V(\phi)$ is a set of $n+1$-tuples each of the form $\langle u_1, \ldots, u_n, w \rangle$ for $u_1, \ldots, u_n \in D$ and $w \in W$. In such a model an assignment μ to the variables is a function such that, for each variable x, $\mu(x) \in D$. Where ρ is also an assignment to the variables, μ and ρ are *x-alternatives* iff for every variable y except possibly x, $\rho(y) = \mu(y)$. Every wff has a truth-value at a world relative to an assignment μ determined as follows:

[Vϕ] $V_\mu(\phi x_1 \ldots x_n, w) = 1$ if $\langle \mu(x_1), \ldots, \mu(x_n), w \rangle \in V(\phi)$, and 0 otherwise.

[V~] $V_\mu(\sim\alpha, w) = 1$ if $V_\mu(\alpha, w) = 0$, and 0 otherwise.

[V∨] $V_\mu(\alpha \vee \beta, w) = 1$ if $V_\mu(\alpha, w) = 1$ or $V_\mu(\beta, w) = 1$, and 0 otherwise.

[V∀] $V_\mu(\forall x\alpha, w) = 1$ if $V_\rho(\alpha, w) = 1$ for every x-alternative ρ of μ, and 0 otherwise.

[VL] $V_\mu(L\alpha, w) = 1$ if $V_\mu(\alpha, w') = 1$ for every w' such that wRw', and 0 otherwise.

Our definitions of validity can be extended now to say that a wff α is valid in $\langle W, R, D, V \rangle$ iff $V_\mu(\alpha, w) = 1$ for every $w \in W$ and every assignment μ, and α is valid on a frame $F = \langle W, R \rangle$ iff α is valid in every model based on F.

Given a system of normal propositional modal logic, **S**, system LPC + **S** is defined as follows:

S'   If α is an LPC substitution-instance of a theorem of **S** then α is an axiom of LPC + **S**.

MP   If α and α ⊃ β are theorems of LPC + **S** then so is β.

∀1   If α is any wff and *x* and *y* any variables and α[*y*/*x*] is α with free *y* replacing every free *x*, then ∀*x*α ⊃ α[*y*/*x*] is an axiom of LPC + **S**.

∀2   If α ⊃ β is a theorem of LPC + **S** and *x* is not free in α then α ⊃ ∀*x*β is a theorem of LPC + **S**.

N   If α is a theorem of LPC + **S** then so is *L*α.

An additional principle of considerable interest is the *Barcan formula*

BF   ∀*xL*α ⊃ *L*∀*x*α

named after Ruth Barcan (now Ruth Barcan Marcus) who first introduced it (Barcan, 1946). Systems **S** + BF are systems LPC + **S** with the addition of BF. It turns out that for some propositional systems **S**, e.g. **B** and **S5**, BF is already a theorem schema of LPC + **S**, while for others, e.g. **K**, **D**, **T** or **S4**, it is not. This section only considers systems which contain this formula, whether as a derived theorem or as a postulated axiom.

Many theorems of modal LPC are obvious instances of theorems of propositional modal logic, e.g. $L(\forall x\phi x \supset \exists x\psi x) \supset (L\forall x\phi x \supset L\exists x\psi x)$, which is an instance of **K**, while others are instances of theorems of non-modal LPC, e.g. $\forall xL\phi x \supset L\phi y$. Modal predicate logic, however, also offers various mixed principles, like the Barcan formula, BF, and its converse

CBF   *L*∀*x*α ⊃ ∀*xL*α

that exhibit interrelations among modal operators and quantifiers that cannot be stated in modal propositional logic or in non-modal LPC alone. (CBF is provable in LPC + **K** as it stands, and so does not need to be postulated separately.)

Another mixed principle, easily proved without the Barcan formula, is

(i)   ∃*xL*α ⊃ *L*∃*x*α

Its converse is not provable, however, and, in fact, is not valid. Consider a case,

(ii)   *L*∃*x*φ*x* ⊃ ∃*xL*φ*x*

To see that (ii) is not valid under the intended interpretation, let φ*x* be '*x* is the number of the planets'. Then the antecedent is true, for there must be some number which is the number of the planets (even if only 0), but the consequent is false, for there is no number which must be the number of the planets since it is contingent how many planets there are.

Each of the following systems is sound and complete with respect to the class of frames listed beside it:

K + BF: all frames

D + BF: serial frames

T + BF: reflexive frames

K4 + BF: transitive frames

KB + BF: symmetrical frames

S4 + BF: reflexive transitive frames

B + BF: reflexive symmetrical frames

S5 + BF: equivalence frames

(These results may be proved by adapting the method of maximal consistent sets previously described. In general, the completeness of **S** + BF follows when the frame of its canonical model is a frame for **S**.)[5]

7.2.1. De re *and* de dicto

As seen in the components of the mixed principles that are proper to modal predicate logic, and not merely generalizations of propositional modal logic or of non-modal predicate logic, some formulas in modal predicate logic have a variable x free inside the scope of the modal operator L and some formulas have no free variables inside the scope of L. The former are called *de re*, and the latter *de dicto*. To see the nature of this distinction, consider the parts of (ii) above. Its consequent, $\exists x L \phi x$, says that there is a thing (in Latin, a *res*) and concerning this thing (*de re*), *it*, i.e., that very same thing, is ϕ in every accessible world. By contrast, (ii)'s antecedent, $L\exists x \phi x$, does not carry this implication. It says, concerning the proposition (*dictum*) that something is ϕ, that this proposition is a necessary truth, i.e., that in every accessible world *something* (but not necessarily the same thing in each world) is ϕ. (Don't worry whether the Latin descriptions are really accurate; what matters is the distinction itself.)

De re formulas, containing quantification into the scope of modal operators, are often thought to be philosophically more problematic than *de dicto* expressions (Quine, 1953). Hence, it would be convenient if they could be eliminated, or rather, shown always to be equivalent to *de dicto* wff. This, however, is not the case. In particular, $\exists x L \phi x$ is not equivalent to any *de dicto* wff even in **S5** + BF, and so not in any weaker system (Tichy, 1973).

7.2.2. *Validity without the Barcan formula*

The Barcan formula is valid on the definition of validity given above for modal predicate logics. As noted, this formula is a theorem of some systems LPC + **S**, e.g., those containing system **B**, but not of others. How, then, shall one give an account of validity for those systems lacking the Barcan formula?

This question becomes all the more important as a number of philosophical objections have been raised against this formula.[6] The basic Barcan formula is the wff

$$\forall x L \phi x \supset L \forall x \phi x$$

Under the standard interpretation this means that if everything necessarily possesses a certain property ϕ, then it is necessarily the case that everything possesses that property. But now, it is sometimes argued, even if everything that actually exists is necessarily ϕ, this does not preclude the possibility that there might have existed some other things which were not ϕ, and in that case it would not be a necessary truth that everything is ϕ.

This objection depends on the assumption that in various possible worlds, not merely might objects have different properties from those they have in the actual world, but there might even be objects which do not exist in the actual world at all. It looks as though the semantics given above for modal predicate logic implicitly denies this assumption since each model has only a single domain of individuals, the same for each world. That is what yields the validity of the Barcan formula. This suggests that one might obtain a semantics which does not validate this formula by admitting models in which different domains are associated with different worlds.

Accordingly, for systems LPC + **S**, which may lack the Barcan formula, define a model as a quintuple $\langle W, R, D, Q, V \rangle$ in which W, R, and D are as before, and Q is a function from members of W to subsets of D. Intuitively, $Q(w)$ – often written D_w – is the set of individuals which exist in w. For now, suppose that these models satisfy the *inclusion requirement*, that if wRw' then $D_w \subseteq D_{w'}$. To evaluate atomic formulae ϕx in a world w, it is not a requirement that the value assigned to free x be a member of D_w, but rather each model may determine whether such formulas are true or false in w (Kripke, 1963b). That is, leave intact the specification that $V(\phi)$ is a set of $n+1$-tuples each of the form $\langle u_1, \ldots, u_n, w \rangle$ for $u_1, \ldots, u_n \in D$ and $w \in W$ without constraints that each $u_i \in D_w$. Then $[V\phi]$, $[V{\sim}]$, $[V\vee]$, and $[VL]$ remain as before, but $[V\forall]$ now becomes

[V∀′] $V_\mu(\forall x \alpha, w) = 1$ if $V_\rho(\alpha, w) = 1$ for every x-alternative ρ of μ such that $\rho(x) \in D_w$, and 0 otherwise.

This has the effect of making the quantifiers range over just the individuals that exist in the world w. Furthermore, importantly, the definition of validity is modified to say that a wff is valid in a model $\langle W, R, D, Q, V \rangle$ iff $V_\mu(\alpha, w) = 1$ for every $w \in W$ and every assignment μ such that $\mu(x) \in D_w$ for every variable x.

Under this specification every theorem of LPC + **S** is valid, but the Barcan formula, BF, is not always. (Given the inclusion requirement, if relation R is symmetric, then if wRw' then $D_w = D_{w'}$, and then BF will be valid. This reflects the provability of BF in the systems LPC + **B** and LPC + **S5**.) The systems LPC + **S**, where **S** = **K**, **D**, **T**, or **S4** (and a number of others) lacking the Barcan formula may also be proved complete using the methods described earlier.

Models for systems that do contain the Barcan formula are obviously a special case of models for systems without it since a model will satisfy BF if $Q(w) = D$ for every $w \in W$. So if one wants the quantifiers in each world to range only over the things that exist in that world, and one doesn't believe that the same things exist in every world, one would probably not want the Barcan formula. But one would probably not want its converse, CBF, either. For consider

$$L\forall x\phi x \supset \forall x L\phi x \tag{7.1}$$

which is an instance of CBF. It could happen that in every world everything which exists *in that world* is ϕ, but that something in our world fails to be ϕ in some other world. That other world will, of course, be a world in which the object in question does not exist.

CBF is, however, valid on the account given so far; it is valid because of the inclusion requirement. But since the reason for rejecting CBF requires violating that condition, one might consider abandoning it so as to avoid both the Barcan formula and its converse. This will raise problems of its own, however (as one should expect since CBF is provable in LPC + **S** without extra assumptions). In particular, the rule of necessitation will no longer preserve validity. Although

$$\forall x\phi x \supset \phi y \tag{7.2}$$

is valid,

$$L(\forall x\phi x \supset \phi y) \tag{7.3}$$

is not.

One way to preserve necessitation is to return to the original definition of validity in a model, placing no restrictions on μ. This, however, makes (7.2) itself no longer valid, for if everything in every world is ϕ except for some $u \notin D_w$ then $V_\mu(\forall x\phi x \supset \phi y, w) = 0$ if $\mu(y) = u$. The problem with (7.2) is that y might be assigned something which does not exist (in the world), while the quantifiers are restricted to things that do. The restriction on μ was designed to exclude such cases. This suggests that one might make the restriction explicit by adding a predicate, E, for existence (in a world). This has the semantics:

[VE] $\langle u, w \rangle \in V(E)$ iff $u \in D_w$

Then although (7.2) fails to be valid, its counterpart

$(\forall x \phi x \land Ey) \supset \phi y$ $(7.2')$

is valid. And more generally, although the postulate $\forall 1$ (given on page 148) will not be valid, it may be replaced by

$\forall 1E$ $(\forall x \alpha \land Ey) \supset \alpha[y/x]$

($\forall 1E$ is the standard replacement for $\forall 1$ in what is called *free logic* [see chapter 12]).[7]

7.2.3. Axiomatization of systems with an existence predicate

Replacing $\forall 1$ with $\forall 1E$ requires some other changes to the LPC basis of these systems. In particular, one cannot easily use $\forall 2$ as it stands, and so it will be helpful to state the basis for these systems explicitly. Where **S** is any normal propositional modal logic, LPCE + **S** is defined as follows:

S′   Any LPC substitution-instance of a theorem of **S** is an axiom of LPCE + **S**.

$\forall 1E$ Where x and y are any individual variables, and α is any wff then $(\forall x \alpha \land Ey) \supset \alpha[y/x]$ is an axiom of LPCE + **S**.

$\forall^\supset$ $\forall x(\alpha \supset \beta) \supset (\forall x \alpha \supset \forall x \beta)$ is an axiom of LPCE + **S**, where α and β are any wff and x is any variable.

VQ $\alpha \equiv \forall x \alpha$ is an axiom of LPCE + **S**, provided x is not free in α.

UE $\forall x Ex$ is an axiom of LPCE + **S**.

UG   If α is a theorem of LPCE + **S**, then $\forall x \alpha$ is a theorem of LPCE + **S**.

UGL$\forall^n$ If $\alpha_1 \supset L(\alpha_2 \supset \cdots \supset L(\alpha_n \supset L\beta) \cdots)$ is a theorem of LPCE + **S**, and x is not free in $\alpha_1, \ldots, \alpha_n$, then $\alpha_1 \supset L(\alpha_2 \supset \cdots \supset L(\alpha_n \supset L\forall x \beta) \ldots)$ is a theorem of LPCE + **S**.

Such systems LPCE + **S**, lacking both the Barcan formula and its converse, may then be shown to be sound and complete by the methods previously described.[8]

7.2.4. Kripke-style systems

Kripke (1963b) advocated a different way of axiomatizing systems containing neither BF nor CBF. Instead of introducing an existence predicate, he restricted the theorems of the systems to their universal closures, since even though (7.2) is not valid, its closure, $\forall y(\forall x \phi x \supset \phi y)$, is. This version of LPC is called 'LPCK,' for 'Kripke-style,' although the axiomatization here is not exactly the same as Kripke's. Where **S** is any normal system of propositional modal logic LPCK + **S** is just like LPCE + **S** but without UE and without UGL$\forall^n$, and with $\forall 1E$ replaced by

∀1K   Where x, y and z are any individual variables, and α is any wff then $\forall y \forall z (\forall x \alpha \supset \alpha[y/x])$ is an axiom of LPCK + S.

(The presence of $\forall z$ in ∀1K is needed to prove $\forall x \forall y \alpha \supset \forall y \forall x \alpha$.) The semantics is as for LPCE + S except that V(E) is no longer required. Completeness may then be proved for many of the Kripke-style systems, though there are some limitations since it is not obvious how to deal with systems containing B.

7.2.5. Identity in modal predicate logic

Now, suppose one adds a predicate $\phi_=$, or more familiarly '=', for identity to the language for modal predicate logic. In keeping with its intended interpretation, stipulate that in all models $V(\phi_=)$ is the set of triples $\langle u, u, w \rangle$ for $u \in D$, and $w \in W$. With this interpretation an axiomatic basis for systems S + I may be provided by adding to LPC + S the axiom schemes

I1 $x = x$

I2 $x = y \supset (\alpha \supset \beta)$

where α and β differ only in that α has free x in 0 or more places where β has free y.

These postulates yield the theorem

LI $x = y \supset Lx = y$

by taking α as $Lx = x$ and β as $Lx = y$. Further, some systems, e.g., all extensions of B, also contain the analogous principle for non-identities.

LNI $x \neq y \supset Lx \neq y$

Intuitively LI and LNI seem to stand or fall together, and so if a modal system contains LI it should also contain LNI. Both, after all, are valid under the interpretation given above for $\phi_=$. Systems S + LNI add LNI to S + I, which, of course, already contains LI. (As noted, LNI may already be a theorem in some S + I systems.) These systems may be proved sound and complete. More generally, when S is consistent, S + LNI is sound, and completeness holds for all systems S + LNI whose canonical model is based on a frame for S. These results also apply to systems without BF and to systems with an existence predicate.

    LI is a matter of some controversy, however. It seems to say that all identity statements are necessary, i.e., whenever x and y are the same object, then it is a necessary truth that they are. Now it seems easy to think of counterexamples to this. E.g., the sentence:

The person who lives next door is the mayor.   (7.4) seems to assert an identity between the person who lives next door and the mayor; if so, one could rewrite (7.4), semi-formally, as:

The person who lives next door = the mayor.

Yet surely, one would think, this is contingent, for it is logically possible that the person who lives next door is not the mayor.[9] Notice, though, that (7.4) is not stated using variables; rather, it uses the definite descriptions 'the person next door' and 'the mayor'. This suggests applying Russell's (1905) theory of descriptions to cases like (7.4). Let ϕ be the predicate 'lives next door' and let ψ be 'is the mayor.' On Russell's account, (7.4) becomes

$$\exists^1 x\phi x \wedge \exists^1 x\psi x \wedge \forall x\forall y((\phi x \wedge \psi y) \supset x=y) \tag{7.5}$$

($\exists^1 x\phi x$ means 'exactly one x is ϕ', which may be defined as $\exists y\forall x(\phi x \equiv x=y)$.) Now (7.5) is true but not necessarily true, so putting L in front of the whole conjunction gives a false sentence. But LI does not license that move from (7.5); it only allows the move to

$$\exists^1 x\phi x \wedge \exists^1 x\psi x \wedge \forall x\forall y((\phi x \wedge \psi y) \supset Lx=y) \tag{7.6}$$

and this results in no problems of interpretation.

7.2.6. Contingent identity

Russell's theory gives one way in which the classical view of identity in modal predicate logic, with both LI and LNI, can accommodate such apparent counterexamples as (7.4). Nevertheless, LI and LNI might still be thought unintuitive, and so one should see whether one can adapt the semantics to avoid having them as valid. Consider the status of LI with respect to an assignment μ to individual variables. One can falsify LI only if μ is allowed to give variables different values in different worlds. In (7.5), for example, letting x stand for 'the person next door' and y stand for 'the mayor,' would mean requiring μ to assign to x in a world w whoever it is who in w lives next door and assign to y whoever it is who in w is the mayor. Thinking in this way, then, of course, $\mu(x)$ and $\mu(y)$ may coincide in w but not in w'. More generally, now suppose that an assignment μ determines a value in D for x at w, $\mu(x, w) \in D$, and modify [Vϕ] to

[Vϕ'] $V_\mu(\phi x_1, \ldots, x_n, w) = 1$ if $\langle \mu(x_1, w), \ldots, \mu(x_n, w), w \rangle \in V(\phi)$, and 0 otherwise.

LI is not valid on such a semantics, as desired, and hence neither is I2, although all instances of I2 in which α and β contain no modal operators remain valid.

Systems with I2 weakened in this way are called *contingent identity systems*, or systems $S + CI$; in them I2 is replaced by

12' $x = y \supset (\phi x_1 \cdots x_n \equiv \phi y_1 \cdots y_n)$

where each x_i, for $1 \leq i \leq n$ either is the very same variable as y_i, or else x_i is x and y_i is y. Nevertheless, such systems do not correspond to the semantics just described, for this semantics validates the schema:

$$L \exists x \alpha \supset \exists x L \alpha \tag{7.7}$$

which is not derivable in any of the contingent identity systems (since these are weaker than the LNI systems and (7.7) is not derivable in any of those).

This formula (7.7) has been encountered before, and it was noted then that it does not seem valid. To adapt an example given by Quine (1953, p. 148), in certain games, it is necessary that some player will win, but there is no individual player who is bound to win. One might, however, make (7.7) sound plausible by taking an expression such as 'the winner' as, in a sense, standing for a single object, though it would be one which, in a more usual sense of 'object,' would be one object in one situation but a different one in another. In that case, if it is necessary that someone will win, then there is someone who is bound to win, namely, the winner. Such so-called objects are often called *intensional objects* or *individual concepts*, and the interpretation now being considered would thus seem to provide a semantics for a logic in which the individual-variables range over intensional objects.

On this view of object as intensional object, the semantics seems to allow one to make an object out of any string of members of D whatever. For example, suppose there are two worlds, w_1 and w_2, then where u_1 and u_2 are members of D it seems one is entitled to make up the object which is u_1 in w_1 and u_2 in w_2. Viewed in this way, the LNI systems might be considered as requiring that the only strings of members of D which count as objects are strings consisting of the same member of D in each world (i.e., the only objects recognized in these systems are the straight-forward members of D themselves). This suggests that an adequate semantics for contingent identity systems, $S + CI$, which lack schema (7.7), would neither require that only strings consisting of a single member of D count as objects, nor allow that any string whatsoever of members of D should count. This may be done by having each model stipulate a set of 'allowable' intensional objects (Parks, 1974). This will yield soundness and completeness for systems of contingent identity.

If the quantifiers range over *all* intensional objects, then, as noted, (7.7) $L \exists x \phi x \supset \exists x L \phi x$ becomes valid. This raises the question of what axiomatic systems are correct for this full logic of intensional objects based on an underlying propositional system S. The answer is that for most choices of S, including all the systems discussed here, except for $S5$, the logic of intensional objects based on S is unaxiomatizable (Garson, 1984, section 3; Thomason, 1970b).

Suggested further reading

See Hughes and Cresswell (1996) for a comprehensive introduction to the topics discussed here, and other topics in modal logic, presented in much the same style as this chapter. For propositional modal logic, Bull and Segerberg (1984) is a rich source, while Chagrov and Zakharyaschev (1997) presents a very thorough, but more advanced mathematical treatment. All three of these have extensive bibliographies of primary work in the field. Chellas (1980) presents another convenient introduction to propositional modal logic. For the properties of first-order modal logics, Garson (1984) presents a helpful overview. And for a discussion of some of the philosophical issues concerning quantification and modality, see Cocchiarella (1984) and the references cited there.

Notes

1   This kind of account of validity appeared in the late 1950s and early 1960s. It is associated especially with the work of Kripke, e.g., (1959), (1963a), and so our frames are often called 'Kripke-frames', but similar ideas appear in the work of others around that time, e.g., Kanger (1957), Bayart (1958), Montague (1960) and Hintikka (1961). Earlier, related accounts may be seen in Wajsberg (1933), McKinsey (1945), Carnap (1946), among others. Jónsson and Tarski (1951) presents an algebraic description of this notion of validity, though the connection with modal logic was not made in that article.

2   Another related method commonly used to demonstrate the finite model property is the method of *filtrations*; see Hughes and Cresswell (1984, pp. 136–45), Bull and Segerberg (1984, pp. 43f.), or Chagrov and Zakharyaschev (1997, pp. 140f.).

3   This system is called **W** by Segerberg (1971, p. 84), though it is also widely called **G** after Gödel since it has been studied as the modal logic of 'provability', e.g., by Boolos (1979). For a more recent survey of the history of provability logic, see Boolos and Sambin (1990). The system dates at least from Löb (1966).

4   For demonstration of these and other results, see, for example, Hughes and Cresswell (1996, pt 2), and the references cited there. See also Bull and Segerberg (1984) and Chagrov and Zakharyaschev (1997).

5   It is noteworthy that completeness in modal LPC is sometimes more difficult to achieve than in modal propositional logic. For instance, although **S4.2** ($= $**S4**$ + MLp \supset LMp$) is characterized by frames which are reflexive, transitive and convergent, and all its frames have these properties, its first-order counterpart, **S4.2** $+$ BF, is not characterized by any class of frames. (The incompleteness of **S4.2** $+$ BF is stated, without proof, in Shehtman and Skvorcov (1991); Cresswell (1995) presents a proof based on the fact that

$$M(\exists x \phi x \wedge \forall x(\phi x \supset L\psi x) \wedge L{\sim}\forall x\psi x) \wedge M\forall x(\phi x \vee L\psi x) \wedge \forall x(M\phi x \supset L(\exists x \phi x \supset \phi x))$$

is not satisfiable on any convergent frame but is consistent in **S4.2**.)

6   See Prior (1957, pp. 26–8 *passim*), also Hintikka (1961), and Myhill (1958, p. 80). For a defence of the formula, see Barcan (1962, pp. 88–90) and Cresswell (1991).

7   See Garson (1984, p. 261). An existence predicate is introduced by Rescher (1959), and also assumed by Fine (1978).

8   See Thomason (1970a) though, who uses an existence predicate defined in terms of identity (p. 57). The rules UGL∀" first appear in that paper.

9   Examples like this date at least from Frege (1952). Quine (1947), however, first called attention to the problems they raise for modal predicate logic, and the literature since then has flourished. We shall not enter that philosophical discussion here, but only describe briefly some different options one might take for interpreting modal systems. LI is derived as a theorem in Barcan (1947).

References

Barcan Marcus, R. C. 1946: "A Functional Calculus of First Order Based on Strict Implication," *Journal of Symbolic Logic*, 11, 1–16.

Barcan Marcus, R. C. 1947: "The Identity of Individuals in a Strict Functional Calculus of Second Order," *Journal of Symbolic Logic*, 12, 12–15.

Barcan Marcus, R. C. 1962: "Interpreting Quantification," *Inquiry*, 5, 252–9.

Bayart, A. 1958: "La Correction de la Logique Modale du Premier et Second Ordre S5," *Logique et Analyse*, 1, 28–44.

Boolos, G. 1979: *The Unprovability of Consistency*, (Cambridge University Press, Cambridge).

Boolos, G. and Sambin, G. 1990: "Provability: The Emergence of a Mathematical Modality," *Studia Logica*, 50, 1–23.

Bull, R. A. and Segerberg, K. 1984: "Basic Modal Logic," in Gabbay and Guenthner (1984, 1–88).

Carnap, R. 1946: "Modalities and Quantification," *Journal of Symbolic Logic*, 11, 33–64.

Chagrov, A. and Zakharyaschev, M. 1997: *Modal Logic*, (Clarendon Press, Oxford).

Chellas, B. F. 1980: *Modal Logic: An Introduction*, (Cambridge University Press, Cambridge).

Cocchiarella, N. 1984: "Philosophical Perspectives on Quantification in Tense and Modal Logic," in Gabbay and Guenthner (1984, 309–53).

Cresswell, M. J. 1991: "In Defence of the Barcan Formula," *Logique et Analyse*, 135–6, 271–82.

Cresswell, M. J. 1995: "Incompleteness and the Barcan Formula," *Journal of Philosophical Logic*, 24, 379–403.

Fine, K. 1978: "Model Theory for Modal Logic, Part I, the *de re/de dicto* Distinction," *Journal of Philosophical Logic*, 7, 125–56. (Part II 277–306.)

Frege, G. 1952: "On Sense and Reference", *Translations from the Writings of Gottlob Frege*, P. T. Geach and M. Black, eds., (Blackwell, Oxford).

Gabbay, D. M. and Guenthner, F. 1984: *Handbook of Philosophical Logic, Vol. II.*, (D. Reidel, Dordrecht).

Garson, J. W. 1984: "Quantification in Modal Logic," in Gabbay and Guenthner (1984, 249–307).

Hintikka, J. 1961: "Modality and Quantification," *Theoria*, 27, 110–28.

Hughes, G. E. and Cresswell, M. J. 1984: *A Companion to Modal Logic*, (Methuen, London).

Hughes, G. E. and Cresswell, M. J. 1996: *A New Introduction to Modal Logic*, (Routledge, London and New York).

Jónsson, B. and Tarski, A. 1951: "Boolean Algebras with Operators," *American Journal of Mathematics*, 73, 891–939.

Kanger, S. 1957: *Provability in Logic*, (Almqvist & Wiksell, Stockholm).

Kripke, S. A. 1959: "A Completeness Theorem in Modal Logic," *Journal of Symbolic Logic*, 24, 1–14.

Kripke, S. A. 1963a: "Semantical Analysis of Modal Logic I: Normal Propositional Calculi," *Zeitschrift für Mathematische Logik und Grundlagen der Mathematik*, 9, 67–96.

Kripke, S. A. 1963b: "Semantical Considerations on Modal Logics," *Acta Philosophica Fennica – Modal and Many-valued Logics*, 16, 83–94.

Löb, M. H. 1966: "Extensional Interpretations of Modal Logics," *Journal of Symbolic Logic*, 31, 23–45.

McKinsey, J. C. C. 1945: "On the Syntactical Construction of Systems of Modal Logic," *Journal of Symbolic Logic*, 10, 83–96.

Montague, R. M. 1960: "Logical Necessity, Physical Necessity, Ethics and Quantifiers," *Inquiry*, 4, 259–69.

Myhill, J. R. 1958: "Problems Arising in the Formalization of Intensional Logic," *Logique et Analyse*, 1, 74–83.

Parks, Z. 1974: "Semantics for Contingent Identity Systems," *Notre Dame Journal of Formal Logic*, 15, 333–4.

Prior, A. N. 1957: *Time and Modality*, (Oxford University Press, Oxford).

Quine, W. V. O. 1947: "The Problem of Interpreting Modal Logic," *Journal of Symbolic Logic*, 12, 43–8.

Quine, W. V. O. 1953: "Reference and Modality," in *From a Logical Point of View*, (Harvard University Press, Cambridge, MA), 139–59.

Rescher, N. 1959: "On the Logic of Existence and Denotation," *Philosophical Review*, 58, 157–80.

Russell, B. 1905: "On Denoting," *Mind*, 14, 479–93.

Segerberg, K. 1971: *An Essay in Classical Modal Logic*, (3 vols.), (Filosofiska Studier, Uppsala).

Shehtman, V. B. and Skvorcov, D. P. 1991: "Semantics of Non-classical First-Order Predicate Logics," in *Mathematical Logic, Proceedings of Heyting 88 at Chajka (Bulgaria) 1988*, P. P. Petkov, ed., (Plenum Press, New York), 105–16.

Thomason, R. H. 1970a: "Some Completeness Results for Modal Predicate Calculi," in *Philosophical Problems in Logic*, K. Lambert, ed., (D. Reidel, Dordrecht), 56–76.

Thomason, R. H. 1970b: "Modality and Metaphysics," in *The Logical Way of Doing Things*, K. Lambert, ed., (Yale University Press, New Haven), 119–146.

Tichy, P. 1973: "On *de dicto* Modalities in Quantified S5," *Journal of Philosophical Logic*, 2, 687–92.

Wajsberg, M. 1933: "Ein erweiteter Klassenkalkül," *Monatshefte für Mathematik und Physik*, 40, 113–26.

Chapter 8

Deontic Logic

Risto Hilpinen

8.1. Introduction

Deontic logic is an area of logic which investigates normative concepts, systems of norms, and normative reasoning. The word 'deontic' is derived from the Greek expression 'déon', which means 'what is binding' or 'proper'. Thus, Jeremy Bentham (1983) used the word 'deontology' for "the science of morality," and the Austrian philosopher Ernst Mally (1926), who developed in the 1920s a system of the "fundamental principles the logic of ought," called his theory 'Deontik'. Normative concepts include the concepts of obligation (*ought*), permission (*may*), prohibition (*may not*), and related notions, such as the concept of right. Systems of deontic logic contain, in addition to the usual sentential connectives and quantifiers, logical constants which represent some of these normative concepts.

Much of the recent work on deontic logic has been based on the view that deontic logic is a branch of modal logic [see chapter 7], and that the concepts of obligation, permission, and prohibition are related to each other in the same way as the alethic modalities *necessity, possibility* and *impossibility*. This view goes back to medieval philosophy; some fourteenth-century philosophers observed the analogies between deontic and alethic modalities, and studied the deontic (normative) interpretations of various laws of modal logic. In the same way, Leibniz (1930) called the deontic categories of the obligatory, the permitted and the prohibited 'legal modalities' (*Iuris modalia*), and observed that the basic principles of modal logic hold for the legal modalities. In fact, Leibniz suggested that deontic modalities can be defined in terms of the alethic modalities; according to him, the permitted (*licitum*) is

what is possible for a good man to do

and the obligatory (*debitum*) is

what is necessary for a good man to do

The contemporary development of deontic logic since the publication of von Wright's (1957 [1951]) pioneering paper "Deontic Logic" has been based on the study of the analogies between normative and alethic modalities.

8.2. The Standard System of Deontic Logic (SDL)

A simple system of deontic logic can be obtained by reading Leibniz's definition of the concept of obligation (ought) as

(O.Leibniz$_1$) p is obligatory for a iff (if and only if) p is necessary for a's being a good person

that is,

(O.Leibniz$_2$) $O_a p$ iff $N(G(a) \supset p)$

where 'N' is the alethic necessity operator and '$G(a)$' means that a is 'good' (in the sense intended by Leibniz). Deleting the explicit reference to an agent gives the following definition of the concept of ought:

(O.Leibniz$_3$) $Op \equiv N(G \supset p)$

The corresponding Leibnizian concept of permission (or the concept of may) is expressed by

(P.Leibniz$_3$) $Pp \equiv M(G \& p)$

(where 'M' is the operator for alethic possibility). These schemata can be regarded as partial reductions of deontic logic to 'ordinary' (alethic) modal logic. The Leibnizian analysis of the concepts of obligation and permission was rediscovered by the Swedish philosopher Kanger in 1950, who interpreted the constant G as 'what morality prescribes' (Kanger, 1981 [1957]). According to this interpretation, Op (it ought to be the case that p) means that p follows from the requirements of morality. Anderson (1967 [1956]) put forward a reduction schema equivalent to Kanger's,

(O.S) $Op \equiv N(\neg p \supset S)$

where S may be taken to mean the threat of a sanction or simply the proposition that the requirements of law or morality have been violated.

If the alethic N-operator satisfies the axioms of the modal logic **T** (Chellas, 1980, p. 131) [or see chapter 7], viz.

(K) $N(p \supset q) \supset (Np \supset Nq)$

(T) $Np \supset p$

and the modal 'rule of necessitation'

(RN)   If p is provable, Np is provable, or briefly, p/Np

it is easy to see that the ought-operator defined by $(O.\text{Leibniz}_3)$ satisfies the deontic K-principle

(K_D) $O(p \supset q) \supset (Op \supset Oq)$

and the rule of 'deontic necessitation'

(RN_D) p/Op

The additional assumption that being good is possible,

(D_G) MG

yields the principle of deontic consistency

(D_D) $Op \supset Pp$

where 'P' represents the concept of permission, definable in terms of 'O' by

(P) $Pp \equiv \neg O\neg p$

Similarly, the concept of prohibition, F, is defined by

(F) $Fp \equiv O\neg p$

where a state of affairs p is prohibited iff not-p is obligatory. The system of (propositional) deontic logic obtained by adding to propositional logic the axioms (or axiom schemata) K_D and D_D and the rule RN_D is usually called the 'standard system of deontic logic' (SDL). Among its theorems are:

$O(p \& q) \supset (Op \& Oq)$	(Conjunctive distributivity of O)	(8.1)
$Op \& Oq \supset O(p \& q)$	(Aggregation principle for O)	(8.2)
$Op \supset O(p \vee q)$		(8.3)
$O(p \supset q) \supset (Pp \supset Pq)$		(8.4)
$Pp \supset P(p \vee q)$		(8.5)
$P(p \vee q) \supset (Pp \vee Pq)$	(Disjunctive distributivity of P)	(8.6)
$P(p \& q) \supset Pp$		(8.7)

while the rules of inference

(RM_D) $p \supset q / Op \supset Oq$

(RE_D) $p \equiv q / Op \equiv Oq$

are derivable. On the basis of the axioms K_D and D_D, this system may be called the system **KD**, or simply **D**; it is a member of the family of *normal* modal logics, all of which contain (a counterpart of) the rule RN; [see chapter 7] (Chellas, 1980, p. 114).

8.3. The Semantics of the Standard Deontic Logic

The sentences of SDL can be interpreted in terms of possible worlds (or world states) in the same way as other normal modalities. A possible worlds' interpretation of SDL is a triple $M = \langle W, I, R \rangle$, where W is a universe of possible worlds, I is an interpretation function which assigns to each sentence a subset of W, i.e., the worlds $u \in W$ where the sentence is true; the truth of p at u under M is expressed 'M, $u \vDash p$,' or briefly '$u \vDash p$.' If p is not true at u, it is false at u. R is a 2-place relation on W, called the relation of deontic alternativeness. The interpretation function assigns each sentence a truth value at each possible world. A sentence is called *valid* (logically true) iff it is true at every world $u \in W$ for any interpretation M, and q is a logical consequence of p iff there is no interpretation M and world u such that M, $u \vDash p$ and not M, $u \vDash q$. The interpretation function is subject to the usual Boolean conditions which ensure that the truth-functional compounds of simple sentences receive appropriate truth-values at each possible world. The alternativeness relation R is needed for the interpretation of sentences involving the deontic operators. In the semantics of modal logic, necessary truth at a given world u is understood as truth at all worlds which are possible relative to u or *alternatives* to u, and possibility at u means truth at some alternative to u. For the concepts of obligation (or ought) and permission (may), these conditions can be formulated as follows:

(CO) $u \vDash Op$ iff $v \vDash p$ for every $v \in W$ such that $R(u, v)$

(CP) $u \vDash Pp$ iff $v \vDash p$ for some $v \in W$ such that $R(u, v)$

For the axiom D_D to be valid, it is necessary to regard R as a serial relation, in other words,

(CD)   For every $u \in W$, there is a $v \in W$ such that $R(u, v)$

Different further assumptions about the structural properties of the R-relation validate different deontic principles, and lead to different systems of deontic logic. For example, it is clear that

$Op \supset p$ (8.8)

is not a logical truth, and therefore R cannot be assumed to be a reflexive relation, but the principle

$$O(Op \supset p) \tag{8.9}$$

seems a valid principle of deontic logic: It ought to be the case that whatever ought to be the case is the case. The validity of (8.9) follows from the assumption that R is secondarily reflexive, in other words,

(C.OO)   If $R(u, v)$ for some u, then $R(v, v)$.

((8.9) is not derivable in SDL, but it can be added as an additional axiom. It is derivable from the Kanger–Anderson reduction in alethic modal logic if that logic contains T.)

The semantics sketched above, due initially to Hintikka (1957, 1981) and Kanger (1981 [1957]), may be termed the 'standard semantics' of deontic logic. It gives an intuitively plausible account of the meanings of simple deontic sentences when the deontic alternatives to a given world u are taken to be worlds (or situations) in which everything that is obligatory at u is the case; they are worlds in which all obligations are fulfilled. Hence, the worlds related to a given world u by R may be termed *deontically perfect* or *ideal* worlds (relative to u). If possible worlds are regarded as possible courses of events or histories which are partly constituted by an agent's actions, the semantics of SDL simply divides such histories into deontically acceptable and deontically unacceptable histories. An action is permitted iff it is part of some deontically acceptable course of events or if there is some deontically acceptable way of performing the action, and an action is obligatory iff no course of events is acceptable unless it exemplifies the action in question. The set of acceptable courses of action (relative to a given action situation) may be termed the *field of permissibility* (Lewis, 1979). According to the deontic consistency principle (CD), the field of permissibility is never empty; some action is permissible in any situation.

8.4. Problems and Paradoxes

SDL, like any logical system designed for certain applications, faces two kinds of problems:

(a) Problems of interpretation and application:
     How should the deontic operators O, P, and F and the non-logical (propositional) symbols p, q, $r, \ldots,$ of the system be interpreted, and how should the metalogical and semantic concepts *truth*, *validity*, and *logical consequence* be understood in this context?
(b) Problems about the adequacy of the formalization of normative reasoning provided by the standard system:
     Does SDL give an adequate and correct account of the logical relationships among norms or normative propositions?

These questions (or classes of questions) are obviously interrelated; the adequacy of a system of deontic logic depends on its interpretation. Both questions have been discussed extensively in the recent literature.

Deontic logic is usually defined as the logic of the basic normative concepts or, more generally, as the logic of normative or prescriptive discourse. This characterization gives rise to an interesting question about the metalogical concepts of validity and logical consequence in deontic logic. These concepts were defined above in the standard way in terms of the concept of truth, but norms and directives cannot be said to be true or false in the same sense as statements and assertions, and therefore the standard concepts of validity and logical consequence, familiar from the logic of descriptive or assertoric discourse, seem inapplicable to the logic of normative discourse. The Danish philosopher Jørgensen presented this observation in the 1930s as an objection to the very possibility of the logic of imperatives (commands). Since imperatives are not true or false, it does not, strictly speaking, make sense to speak about the logic of imperatives. Norms are, in this respect, analogous to imperatives. On the other hand, as Jørgensen (1937/8) observed, it seems clear that directives or imperatives can be inferred from other directives or that two directives can be logically inconsistent. This difficulty is called *Jørgensen's dilemma*; Makinson (1999) describes it as "the fundamental problem of deontic logic."

Many philosophers have proposed to solve this problem by making a distinction between two uses of norm sentences; they can be used for expressing norms or directives and for making normative statements (statements about norms). The latter are descriptive statements which state that something is obligatory, permitted or prohibited according to a given system of norms (Bulygin, 1982). For example, the deontic sentence

Motor vehicles ought to use the right-hand side of a road.

can be regarded as a directive addressed to drivers, or as a statement which gives information about the traffic code of some (unspecified) country. If it is regarded as a statement about the U.S. traffic regulations, it is a true statement; understood as a statement about the U.K. regulations, it is false. Normative statements, unlike the norms themselves, are true or false, and the logical relationships among normative statements can therefore be understood in the usual way. If deontic logic is regarded as the logic of normative statements, Jørgensen's problem does not arise.

This way out of Jørgensen's difficulty does not mean that the prescriptive or genuinely normative use of deontic sentences is not subject to logical laws, because the distinction between the normative and the descriptive use of deontic sentences can be understood as two ways of using normative *statements* (which are true or false). As Kamp (1973/4, 1979) has pointed out, a normative sentence, like the above

Motor vehicles ought to use the right-hand side of the road.

(which is true or false), can be used or uttered *performatively*, to create or sustain a norm, or *assertorically*, to describe an independently existing norm system. In the former case, the utterance of the statement in the appropriate circumstances (by a proper norm authority) has normative force, and is sufficient to make the statement true; in the latter case, the truth of the statement depends on whether it fits a norm system whose content is independent of the utterance in question. Thus the pre-scriptive–descriptive distinction coincides with the distinction between two uses of deontic statements, the performative use and the assertoric use; and, in both cases, the statements in question can be regarded as true or false. Consequently, the concepts of validity and logical consequence can be defined in deontic logic in terms of the concept of truth in the same way as in other areas of logic. According to Kamp, the assertoric use of deontic sentences should depend on their performative use. In their performative use, the function of O- and F-sentences (obligation and prohibition sentences) is to restrict the range of normatively acceptable options available to an agent (the addressee), whereas permission-sentences have the opposite effect; they enlarge the set of deontically acceptable action possibilities. For example, Kamp has put forward the following principle concerning the performative and assertoric uses of permission sentences:

(PP)　　An assertoric utterance of a permission sentence Ps in a context c is true iff all those worlds already belong to the options of the agent that a performative use of Ps would have added to the set of the agent's options if they had not already belonged to it.

Kamp has also observed that it is not always clear whether a deontic sentence is used performatively or assertorically. However, if the assertoric use of deontic sentences is governed by (PP) (and by analogous principles for ought-sentences and prohibition-sentences), assertoric utterances of deontic sentences can guide and direct the agent's actions in the same way as their performative utterances. For example, in the case of a permission sentence, "either the utterance is a performative and creates a number of new options, or else it is an assertion; but then if it really is appropriate it must be true; and its truth then guarantees that these very same options already exist" (Kamp, 1979, p. 264). The practical consequences of the utterance for the addressee are the same in both cases.

According to SDL, deontic logic is a branch of modal logic, and many principles of deontic logic are special cases of more general modal principles. This approach to deontic logic has sometimes been criticized on the ground that it ignores or misrep-resents many significant features of normative discourse which distinguish it from other varieties of modal discourse. It has been argued that some principles of SDL, including some of the principles (8.1)–(8.7) listed above, lead to paradoxes and are therefore unacceptable. For example, some philosophers have felt that there is some-thing paradoxical about the formula (8.3), which says that if it ought to be the case that p, then it ought to be the case that $p \lor q$. (8.3) authorizes, e.g., the inference from the directive (8.10) to (8.11):

Peter ought to mail a letter. (8.10)

Peter ought to mail a letter or burn it. (8.11)

which seems to some an unacceptable inference. This is known as Ross's paradox, originally due to the Danish philosopher Alf Ross (1941). A somewhat similar (putative) paradox depends on principle (8.5), according to which the permissibility of p entails the permissibility of $p \vee q$ (for any q); for example, according to (8.5), (8.12) entails (8.13):

Peter may drink water. (8.12)

Peter may drink water or drink whisky. (8.13)

which also seems counter-intuitive. These inferences are of course valid if sentences (8.10)–(8.13) are understood in terms of the possible worlds semantics outlined above. If Peter mails a letter in all deontically perfect situations, then he mails a letter or burns it in all such situations, and if Peter drinks water in some deontically satisfactory situation, then he drinks water or whisky in some such situation. But this may be taken as evidence that the semantics of SDL fails to do justice to significant features of normative discourse.

The inferences in question may seem especially paradoxical if the sentences (8.10)–(8.13) are thought of as being used performatively or normatively, i.e., if they are used for issuing a norm or a permission and not merely for describing the content of a system of norms. It is obvious that the effects of a normative utterance of (8.11) are not the same as the effects of (8.10); unlike (8.10), (8.11) does not suffice to make the action of posting the letter obligatory or required (for Peter). (8.10) excludes more possibilities (restricts the field of permissibility more) than (8.11). In the same way, the normative effects of a performative utterance of (8.13) are not the same as those of (8.12). If (8.12) is used performatively, it opens (makes permitted) some possibilities in which Peter drinks water, but (8.13) opens a more vaguely defined set of possibilities, namely, some possibilities where Peter drinks water or whisky. The claim that the inference of (8.11) and (8.13) from (8.10) and (8.12) is paradoxical or unacceptable seems to be tacitly based on the following principle:

(IntP) If a norm (permission) N_1 entails N_2, then the normative (performative) effects of N_1 entail the effects of N_2.

But this principle is obviously false; logical deduction should not be expected to preserve the effects of a norm on a norm system any more than logical deduction preserves the effects of the acceptance of a declarative statement on a person's belief system (or corpus of knowledge). The effects of the acceptance of a disjunctive proposition on a person's belief system are quite different, and usually less significant, than the effects of the acceptance of one of the disjuncts; a disjunctive belief adds less content to a belief system than either of the disjuncts.

The apparent paradox related to disjunctive permissions seems more interesting than Ross's paradox. According to the SDL, the normative use of (8.13) should make acceptable some worlds (or situations) in which Peter drinks water or whisky. This can be accomplished by allowing some situations in which Peter drinks water. However, a normative utterance of (8.13) is normally taken to permit some situations in which Peter drinks whisky as well as some situations in which Peter drinks water; in other words, (8.13) usually seems to have the same effect as the utterance of the conjunction

Peter may drink water and Peter may drink whisky. $\qquad$ (8.14)

A disjunctive permission seems to offer a choice between the two disjuncts and thus entail a conjunction of two permissions. This feature of disjunctive permissions cannot be explained on the basis of SDL alone, but depends on some pragmatic features of disjunctive permissions. However, a disjunctive permission does not necessarily permit both disjuncts, but may leave the determination of the field of permissibility partly open, as in the case of the statement (Kamp, 1979, p. 271)

Yes, you may drink water or whisky, but you have to consult your doctor before you drink whisky. $\qquad$ (8.15)

(8.15) may be an instance of a normative (performative) use of a permission sentence; a norm authority makes a disjunctive action permitted, but refers to another authority for the determination of the permissibility of one of the disjuncts. This suggests that the principle

$$P(p \vee q) \supset Pp \ \& \ Pq \qquad (8.16)$$

should not be regarded as a general principle for the concept of permission.

Another much discussed paradox is related to rule (RM_D). If q is a logical consequence of p, then, according to (RM_D), Op entails Oq. Since knowing that p entails the truth of p,

$$OK_a p \supset Op \qquad (8.17)$$

is a valid formula, where '$K_a p$' means that a knows that p. For example, if Gladys, who is a firefighter, ought to know that there is a fire, then, according to (8.17), there ought to be a fire, which is quite counter-intuitive (Åqvist, 1967). In other words, according to (8.17), the following statements cannot be all true:

$$p \supset OK_a p \qquad (8.18)$$

$$p \qquad (8.19)$$

$$O \neg p \qquad (8.20)$$

But a situation in which there is a fire, (8.18)–(8.20) seem all true; if there is a fire, Gladys ought to know it, but there ought not to be a fire. Some philosophers have regarded this paradox (the ought-to-know paradox or the paradox of epistemic obligation) and other similar paradoxes as evidence that (RM_D) is not a valid principle of deontic logic (Goble, 1991).

8.5. Conditional Norms

In the example above, (8.18) expresses a conditional obligation: Gladys ought to know that there is a fire if there is one, not otherwise. As was observed above, in the semantics of SDL, the interpretation of deontic sentences is based a division of possible worlds or situations into 'deontically perfect' or normatively faultless worlds and normatively unacceptable or imperfect worlds. Systems of conditional norms (conditional obligations) are often semantically more complex, and an attempt to formalize them in SDL is apt to lead to paradoxes. Chisholm (1963) has given an example of such a set: The following sentences seem jointly consistent and pairwise logically independent:

(Ch1)   Jones ought to go to help his neighbors.

(Ch2)   Jones ought to tell his neighbors he is coming if he is going to help them.

(Ch3)   If Jones does not go to help his neighbors, he ought not to tell them he is coming.

(Ch4)   Jones does not go to help his neighbors.

In the language of SDL, these sentences might be expressed as follows:

$$Oh \tag{8.21}$$

$$O(h \supset t) \tag{8.22}$$

$$\neg h \supset O\neg t \tag{8.23}$$

$$\neg h \tag{8.24}$$

where h says that Jones goes to help his neighbors, and t says that Jones tells his neighbors that he is coming. According to SDL, (8.21) and (8.22) entail

$$Ot \tag{8.25}$$

and (8.23) and (8.24) entail

$$O\neg t \tag{8.26}$$

by propositional logic, in other words, (8.21)–(8.24) entail

$$Ot \ \& \ O\neg t \tag{8.27}$$

and according to the consistency principle (D_D), (8.27) entails

$$Ot \ \& \ \neg Ot \tag{8.28}$$

Thus the suggested interpretation of (Ch1)–(Ch4) makes them jointly inconsistent. This seems intuitively unsatisfactory; (Ch1)–(Ch3) seem a reasonable and consistent set of requirements, and the fact that Jones does not go to help his neighbors should not make them jointly inconsistent.

It may be suggested that there is an unjustified logical asymmetry between (8.22) and (8.23); in (8.22), the O-operator precedes $\supset$, but, in (8.23), their order is reversed. The corresponding asymmetry between (Ch2) and (Ch3) does not seem to be semantically significant. If (Ch2) is represented by

$$h \supset Ot \tag{8.29}$$

or (Ch3) is formalized as

$$O(\neg h \supset \neg t) \tag{8.30}$$

the contradiction is avoided; (8.21) and (8.29) do not entail (8.25), and (8.24) and (8.30) do not entail (8.26). However, according to SDL, (8.29) is a logical consequence of (8.24), and, on the other hand, (8.30) is a logical consequence of (8.21). Both results are intuitively unacceptable; as was noted above, the sentences (Ch1)–(Ch4) seem to be pairwise logically independent of each other.

Sentence (Ch3) tells what Jones ought to do in a situation where he has failed to fulfill his duty to help his neighbors; it expresses a *contrary-to-duty* (CTD) obligation. For this reason, Chisholm's paradox may also be called the paradox of CTD obligation. Chisholm's example shows that systems of norms which contain both primary obligations and CTD obligations cannot be formalized in SDL in a satisfactory way. Some authors have proposed to avoid the inconsistency of between (8.25) and (8.26) by relativizing the concept of obligation (or the concept of ought) to time since, it has been suggested, e.g., by Åqvist and Hoepelman (1981), (8.25) and (8.26) hold at different points of time. However, this does not seem to be an essential feature of Chisholm's paradox. There are many non-temporal versions of the CTD-paradox, such as the following situation: Assume that dogs are not permitted in a certain village, but if anyone happens to have a dog, there ought to be a warning sign about it in front of the owner's house. Moreover, warning signs ought not to be posted without sufficient reason. Thus the following normative statements seem to be true:

(Ds1)   There ought to be no dog.

(Ds2)   There ought to be no warning sign if there is no dog.

(Ds3)   If there is a dog, there ought to be a warning sign.

(Ds4)   There is a dog.

(Ds1)–(Ds4) are formally analogous to Chisholm's example, and an attempt to formalize them in SDL leads to a similar inconsistency (Carmo and Jones, 2001; Prakken and Sergot, 1997).

The deduction of the contradiction (8.27) from (8.25) and (8.26) depends on the principle of normative consistency (D_D), $Op \supset \neg O \neg p$. This principle has been criticized independently of Chisholm's example. (D_D) excludes the possibility of normative conflicts, but such conflicts are not unusual in morality and law, and it may be argued that they do not amount to paradoxes (Chellas, 1974, p. 24; Goble, 1999, p. 332). If the consistency principle is rejected, the aggregation principle (8.2), $Op \& Oq \supset O(p \& q)$, should be rejected as well, because the latter principle undermines the distinction between a conflict between obligations and the existence of a self-contradictory obligation; the recognition of the possibility of normative conflicts does not mean that one should also admit the possibility of self-contradictory obligations. Thus logicians have developed systems of deontic logic in which (D_D) and the aggregation principle do not hold (Chellas, 1980, pp. 201–2). Nevertheless, such systems do not help to give a satisfactory solution to the puzzles about the CTD-obligations. They enable one to conclude only that CTD-situations involve conflicting obligations without offering any analysis of CTD-obligations and their relationship to the 'primary' obligations.

It is not difficult to see why Chisholm's example cannot be represented in a satisfactory way in SDL. As observed above, the semantics of SDL is based on a division of worlds or situations into acceptable (deontically perfect) and unacceptable worlds, and the O-sentences describe how things are in the deontically perfect worlds. But sentence (Ch3) in Chisholm's example does not tell how things are in a deontically faultless world; it tells what the agent (Jones) ought to do under deontically imperfect conditions, i.e., in situations in which Jones does not act in accordance with his duties. (Ch3) is a *contrary-to-duty* obligation. The situation could be described by saying that among the (less than perfect) worlds where Jones does not fulfill his duty to help his neighbors, those in which he does not tell them he is coming are preferable to the circumstances where he makes a false promise Thus the interpretation of Chisholm's example seems to require a distinction between different degrees of deontic perfection.

According to this interpretation, (Ch2) can be taken to mean that, in deontically perfect circumstances, where Jones is going to help his neighbors, he tells them that he is coming, and (Ch3) says that in the best worlds where he is not going to help his neighbors, he does not tell them he is coming (Hansson, 1981, p. 143). Express these conditional obligations of by

$$O(t/h) \tag{8.31}$$

$$O(\neg t/\neg h) \tag{8.32}$$

respectively. Call worlds where p is true simply 'p-worlds'; in other words, u is a p-world iff $u \in I(p)$. Let the p-worlds that are normatively least objectionable relative to a given situation u be called deontically optimal p-worlds relative to u, briefly, $\mathrm{Opt}(p, u)$. The concept of deontically optimal p-world is a generalization of the concept of a deontically perfect world of SDL; the (absolute) deontic perfection of w relative to u, i.e., $R(u, w)$, can be taken to mean that w is $\top$-optimal relative to u, where $\top$ is a logical truth:

(COT) $Op =_{df} O(p/\top)$

The assumption that for any consistent proposition p, there is a nonempty set of deontically optimal p-worlds, is a generalization of the principle (CD) of SDL, i.e., the principle that any world has a nonempty set of deontic alternatives. The truth of the conditional ought-statement $O(q/p)$ at u can be taken to mean that q is true in all deontically optimal p-worlds (relative to u), i.e.,

(CO.cond) $u \models O(q/p)$ iff q is true in every world $w \in \mathrm{Opt}(p, u)$

If p entails r and p is true in some r-optimal world (relative to u), the p-optimal worlds (relative to u) are obviously the r-optimal worlds where p is true; in other words, the concept of optimality (or relative deontic perfection) is subject to the following condition:

(C.Opt)   If $I(p) \subseteq I(r)$ and $I(p) \cap \mathrm{Opt}(r, u)$ is non-empty, then
$\mathrm{Opt}(p, u) = I(p) \cap \mathrm{Opt}(r, u)$.

Thus, according to (C.Opt), the truth of

Op (8.33)

means that $\mathrm{Opt}(p, u) = \mathrm{Opt}(\top, u)$, and

$O(q/p)$ (8.34)

means that all optimal p-worlds are q-worlds; hence, according to (C.Opt), (8.33) and (8.34) entail

Oq (8.35)

Hence, according to this semantics, the principle of 'deontic detachment'

(DDet) $O(q/p) \supset (Op \supset Oq)$

is a valid principle for conditional obligations. On the other hand, the principle of 'factual detachment'

(FDet) $O(q/p) \supset (p \supset Oq)$

does not hold. If (Ch2) and (Ch3) are interpreted in this way, (Ch1)–(Ch4) do not lead to a contradiction; (Ch1) and (Ch2) entail the obligation Ot (8.25), but (Ch3) and (Ch4) do not entail $O\neg t$ (8.26).

Another possible response to Chisholm's paradox is the replacement of the truth-functional conditional in (8.22) and (8.23) by an intensional or subjunctive conditional (Mott, 1973) or even a relevant conditional (Goble, 1999) without introducing a special concept of conditional obligation. It has been known since the beginning of the twentieth century, indeed, from antiquity, that conditional statements are usually not truth-functional. Philosophers have attempted to represent if-then-sentences as truth-functional (or 'material') conditionals for want of a better theory, but the situation changed in the early 1970s when David Lewis (1973) and others developed intensional theories of conditionals. In the representation of Chisholm's example in SDL, the logical asymmetry between (8.22) and (8.23) is required by the assumption of the logical independence of (Ch1)–(Ch4), and this makes it possible to derive the inconsistency (8.25)–(8.26). If the two conditionals are expressed as intensional conditionals with a Lewis-type semantics, this problem does not arise. An intensional conditional, e.g., a subjunctive conditional, 'q if p' can be regarded as true in a situation u iff q is true in all possible worlds (situations) in which p is true but which resemble u in other respects as much as possible. The truth of such a conditional is not a consequence of the falsity of p (or of the truth of q) at u.

If the conditional 'q if p' is symbolized '$p > q$', and (Ch2) and (Ch3) are represented by

$$h > Ot \qquad\qquad (8.36)$$

$$\neg h > O\neg t \qquad\qquad (8.37)$$

respectively, no contradiction will arise. If the counterpart of the *modus ponens* principle holds for the conditional connective, i.e., if

$$(\text{FDet}>) \qquad (p > q) \supset (p \supset q)$$

is logically true, (Ch3) and (Ch4) entail (8.26), but (Ch1) and (Ch2) do not entail (8.25). The former analysis of conditional obligations, as $O(q/p)$, leads in Chisholm's example to the result that Jones ought to tell his neighbors that he is coming to help them, but the second analysis, $p > Oq$, gives the result that Jones ought not to tell his neighbors that he is coming. Thus the two analyses seem to involve two different senses of 'ought' (or 'obligation'). The first interpretation of (Ch1)–(Ch4) seems to take the statements as expressions of 'ideal' or *prima facie* obligations; (Ch1)–(Ch2) can be regarded as saying that insofar as Jones ought to help his neighbors, he ought to tell them that he is coming – but if he is in fact not going to help his neighbors, he has an 'actual' or practical obligation not to tell them he is coming. There seems to be no logical or deductive connection between the two kinds of ought, but the existence of an ideal (or prima facie) obligation serves as evidence for the corresponding practical obligation. The inference of actual obligations from ideal obligations is an abduction rather than a deduction.

Both forms of conditional obligation, $O(q/p)$ and $p > Oq$, are defeasible in the sense that they do not satisfy the principle of strengthening the condition of the obligation or strengthening the antecedent of the conditional; in other words, the principles

$$O(q/p) \supset O(q/p \,\&\, r) \qquad\qquad (8.38)$$

$$(p > Oq) \supset ((p \,\&\, r) > Oq) \qquad\qquad (8.39)$$

are not valid. However, according to Lewis's (1973) semantics for subjunctive conditionals, the counterpart of *modus ponens* holds for the >-connective, making the detachment of actual obligations from factual premises possible; the Lewis-type conditionals are 'strict,' albeit only 'variably strict.' In the recent literature, however, many authors have analyzed conditional obligations (including CTD-obligations) by means of defeasible conditionals for which *modus ponens* does not hold, for example, when the conditional $p > q$ is read 'Normally, q holds in circumstances p' (Alchourrón, 1993, p. 75; Makinson, 1993, pp. 363–5). According to this interpretation, (8.24) and (8.37) do not entail (8.26) in the standard sense of logical consequence, but provide only evidence for it. Different variants of Chisholm's example and the attempts to represent various CTD-obligations and other conditional obligations in formal systems of deontic logic have generated an extensive literature on the subject; see Carmo and Jones (2001) and the articles in Nute (1997).

8.6. On the Representation of Actions in Deontic Logic

Above, the schematic letters p, q, r, etc., are propositional symbols; they represent propositions. However, in informal normative discourse deontic concepts are usually applied to actions rather than propositions. Philosophers have made a distinction between two kinds of ought, the ought-to-be (*Seinsollen*) and the ought-to-do (*Tunsollen*) – see, for example, Castañeda (1972 [1970]) – and it has been suggested that since the deontic operators of SDL are propositional operators, the standard deontic logic and the extensions and revisions discussed above should be regarded as theories of the ought-to-be rather than theories of the ought-to-do. It has been argued that in a satisfactory theory of the ought-to-do, deontic operators should be construed as action modalities rather than propositional modalities. Deontic concepts were understood in this way by Leibniz and by other authors of the seventeenth and the eighteenth centuries (Hilpinen, 1993a, pp. 85–6). Von Wright's first system of deontic logic (1957 [1951]) can be regarded as an attempt to articulate and formalize this view. In this system, the deontic operators O, P and F are prefixed, not to propositional expressions (statements), but to expressions for action-types or, in von Wright's terminology, 'act-qualifying properties.' Castañeda (1972 [1970], 1981) adopted a similar approach; he stressed the importance of distinguishing action-descriptions, or *practitions*, from propositional expressions. According to Castañeda, deontic reasoning is reasoning about practitions (as opposed to propositions which describe the conditions or circumstances of action), and deontic operators can be applied only to practitions, not to propositions.

Von Wright's and Castañeda's distinction between propositions and action terms (or practitions) has been formalized and developed further in dynamic deontic logic; see Czelakowski (1997), Meyer (1988) and Segerberg (1982). In dynamic logic, the interpretation of action terms reflects the common philosophical view that an action can often be described as the bringing about of a change in the world. According to this interpretation, an action transforms a given situation or a world-state into a new state (or keeps it unchanged). For example, in his 'action-state semantics' for imperatives, Hamblin (1987) has analyzed actions or deeds in terms of successive world-states. Thus the distinction between propositions and action terms is interpreted in the semantics of (dynamic) deontic logic as the distinction between sets of world-states (propositions) and relations between world-states. Let A, B, C, ... be action terms or action descriptions. Action terms can be simple or complex; the latter are formed from simple action terms by act-connectives, some of which are analogous to propositional connectives. For example, if A and B are action terms, the following expressions are also action terms:

(ActT1) $A + B$: doing A or B

(ActT2) $A \bullet B$: doing A and B together

It is also convenient to have an expression for the omission of an act,

(ActT3) OmA: omitting A

OmA is applicable to all actions (world state transitions) which fail to exemplify A. Systems of dynamic logic usually also contain act-connectives which have no counterparts in propositional logic, for example,

(ActT4) $A;B$: A followed by B

(ActT5) A^*: doing A a finite number of times

For the sake of simplicity, this chapter considers only complex actions of types (ActT1–3).

Actions change the world, thus an action in a space W of possible worlds or situations may be interpreted as a binary relation, i.e., as a set of ordered pairs (u, w) such that the action in question can transform the first situation into the second. The ordered pairs assigned to an action-term A may be called the possible *performances* of the action A. A world-state w is said to be possible relative to u or accessible from u iff it is possible for some action or sequence of actions to lead from u to w. Denote the accessibility relation by Poss, and let Poss_u be the set of transitions which originate from u. The semantics of SDL can be applied to action terms in a relatively straightforward way. In SDL, possible worlds are divided into acceptable (deontically correct) and unacceptable worlds; and, in the deontic logic of action, world state transitions can be divided in an analogous way into deontically acceptable (legal) and deontically unacceptable (illegal) transitions. Let Leg_u be the set of legal transitions which originate from u, and let Ill_u be the set of illegal transitions from u. It is assumed that any possible transition from u is either legal or illegal (there is no deontic indeterminacy), and no transition is both legal and illegal; in other words

(Ddet) $\text{Leg}_u \cup \text{Ill}_u = \text{Poss}_u$

(Dcons) $\text{Leg}_u \cap \text{Ill}_u = \varnothing$

The assumption that there is some legal way out of every situation, in other words,

(DactD)   For every $u \in W$, Leg_u is nonempty

corresponds to principle (D) of SDL, i.e., the postulate that every world (situation) has some deontic alternative. Let I be an interpretation function which assigns to each action A its possible performances (a subset of $W \times W$), and let $I_u(A)$ be the performances of A which originate from u; thus $I_u(A) \subseteq \text{Poss}_u$.

The basic normative concepts (deontic action modalities) can be defined by these truth-conditions:

(CF.act) $u \vDash FA$ iff $I_u(A) \subseteq \text{Ill}_u$

(CP.act) $u \vDash PA$ iff $I_u(A) \cap \text{Leg}_u \neq \varnothing$

(CO.act) $u \vDash OA$ iff $I_u(OmA) \subseteq \text{Ill}_u$

These definitions are simple generalizations of the truth-conditions of normative propositions in SDL. According to (CF.act), an act A is prohibited in a given situation if every possible performance of A at that situation is illegal, and A is permitted iff it can be performed in a legal way. According to (CO.act), A is obligatory at u iff its omission at u would be illegal.

According to (CP.act), the permissibility of an action A means that some possible performances of A (in a given situation u) are deontically acceptable. For example, A may be permitted in this sense if it can be performed together with some other acts. This is a 'weak' concept of permission which corresponds to that defined in SDL. In the present framework, it is possible to define another concept of permission which may be termed a strong permission. When one says that an act A is permitted in a given situation, one often means that A itself is not illegal, i.e., that no sanction is attached to A, and not only that some (possible) performances of A would be deontically acceptable in the situation. This sense of permission can also be expressed in the form of a conditional; if the agent a were to do A, a would not do anything illegal. The truth-conditions of such a conditional can be formulated by means of a selection function f which selects from $I_u(A)$ the transitions which exemplify A but change the original situation u in other respects in a 'minimal' way. Such transitions may often be described by saying that the agent does *only* A. The concept of strong permission may be defined as

(CP^s.act) $u \vDash P^sA$ iff $f(I_u(A), u) \subseteq \text{Leg}_u$.

One might say that the f-function selects from $I_u(A)$ the *minimal* performances of A. For example, if Oscar's mother gives him permission to take one cookie, it means that the action of taking one cookie is acceptable; in other words, the mother would not punish Oscar if he were to take one cookie and do nothing else. On the other hand, it is permitted for a driver to flash her right turn signal – but only if she is going to make a right turn as well. The latter action is an example of weakly permitted action, whereas the former action (taking a cookie) is strongly permitted.

The formulation (CP^s.act) is analogous to one of the standard ways of expressing the truth-conditions of conditionals by means of a selection function $f(I(p), u)$ which selects, for each proposition $I(p)$ and a situation u, the p-worlds closest (most similar) to u; a conditional $p > q$ is true at u iff the consequent q is true at all selected p-worlds. Thus (CP^s.act) fits the most natural reading of a strong permission to do A; if you were to do A, you would not be doing anything illegal. The selection function f used in (CP^s.act) selects the 'minimal' performances of A from the set of all possible performances of A, just as the truth of a conditional $p > q$ is determined by the selection of the p-worlds minimally different from the actual situation (or the situation where the conditional is being evaluated) (Hilpinen, 1993b, p. 309).

If the disjunctive permission 'You may do A or B' is interpreted as a strong permission in the sense defined by (CP^s.act), the truth of

$$P^s(A + B) \supset P^s A \ \& \ P^s B \tag{8.40}$$

depends on whether

$$f(I_u(A), u) \cup f(I_u(B), u) \subseteq f(I_u(A + B), u) \tag{8.41}$$

In other words, it depends on whether the minimal performances of a disjunctive act include the minimal performances of both disjuncts. The example (8.15) (on page 167) suggests that this need not always be the case; therefore (8.40) is not a logical truth, but it may hold in many cases; and, for pragmatic reasons, it may normally be expected to hold in situations in which permission sentences are used performatively, because otherwise it would not be clear what has been permitted, i.e., which performances of $A + B$ have been made deontically acceptable. In the example (8.15), the disjunctive permission is given together with the information that the permissibility of one of the disjuncts will be determined by another norm authority, and, consequently, there is no reason to assume that (8.40) should hold in the example.

8.7. Deontic Logic and the Logic of Agency

In most recent systems of the logic of the ought-to-do, simple action descriptions are not regarded as primitive terms, as outlined above, but are obtained from propositional expressions by means of an action operator which is usually read 'a sees to it that' or 'a brings it about that.' Thus simple action descriptions have the form $Do(a, p)$, where Do is a modal operator for action or agency, a names an agent, and p is a propositional expression. This analysis of action sentences goes back to the eleventh-century philosopher St. Anselm, who investigated the formal properties of the Latin verb *facere*, 'to do' (Segerberg, 1992).

Kanger (1972) presented an interesting analysis of the concept of seeing to it that p. He regarded a statement of the form 'a sees to it that p', $Do(a, p)$, as a conjunction

(CDO) $Do(a, p) \equiv Ds(a, p) \ \& \ Dn(a, p)$

where Ds may be said to represent the *sufficient condition aspect* of agency and Dn stands for the *necessary condition aspect* of agency. Kanger read $Ds(a, p)$ as p is necessary for something a does, and $Dn(a, p)$ as p is sufficient for something a does. These readings are equivalent to

$Ds(a, p)$:   Something a does is sufficient for p (8.42)

$Dn(a, p)$:   Something a does is necessary for p (8.43)

Kanger interpreted the agency operators Ds and Dn in terms of two alternativeness relations on possible worlds:

(CDS) $u \vDash Ds(a, p)$ iff $w \vDash p$ for every w such that $S_{DS}(u, w)$

(CDN) $u \vDash Dn(a, p)$ iff $w \vDash \neg p$ for every w such that $S_{DN}(u, w)$

The worlds w such that $S_{DS}(u, w)$ can be regarded as worlds in which the agent a performs the same actions as in u. Kanger (1981 [1957]) took $S_{DN}(v, w)$ to mean that 'the opposite' of everything a does in u is the case in w. One possible interpretation of this expression is that a does not do any of the things she does in u, but (for example) is completely passive (insofar as this is possible), or, for any action B that a performs at u, she does something else (i.e., some alternative to B) at w.

This analysis of the concept of agency has a form which has become widely accepted in the recent work on the logic of action. The first condition, the Ds-condition, may be termed the *positive* condition, and the second condition, the Dn-condition, may be termed the *negative* condition of agency. The latter condition is a *counterfactual* condition of agency; it states that if the agent had not acted the way she did, p would not have been the case. An analysis of this kind was put forward by von Wright (1963, 1968); other versions of the analysis of agency by means of a positive and a negative condition have been formulated by Åqvist (1974), Åqvist and Mullock (1989), Lindahl (1977), Pörn (1977), and more recently by Belnap, Horty, Perloff, and others; see Horty (2000) and the references given in it.

Philosophers have disagreed about the formulation of the negative condition. Pörn (1977) has argued that, instead of Kanger's Dn-condition (CDN), one should accept only a weaker negative requirement: $\neg Dn(a, \neg p)$, abbreviated here $Cn(a, p)$.

(ACN) $u \vDash Cn(a, p)$ iff $w \vDash \neg p$ for some w such that $S_{DN}(u, w)$

This condition can be read: but for a's action it might not have been the case that p (Pörn, 1977, p. 7); in other words, it was not unavoidable for a that p. Åqvist (1974, p. 81) has accepted a similar weak form of the counterfactual condition. According to Pörn and Åqvist, the negative condition should be formulated as a might-statement or a might-conditional, not as a would-conditional. (For a discussion of different forms of the positive and the negative condition of agency, see Hilpinen (1997).)

The *Do*-operator makes it possible to distinguish four modes of action with respect to a result (state of affairs or event) p:

$Do(a, p)$: a sees to it that p

$\neg Do(a, p)$: a does not see to it that p

$Do(a, \neg p)$: a sees to it that $\neg p$

$\neg Do(a, \neg p)$: a does not see to it that $\neg p$

The combination of different modes of action with deontic concepts makes it possible to represent several types of obligation and permission and different legal or deontic relations between individuals. For example, consider a state of affairs involving two persons, $F(a, b)$. According to Kanger (1981) and Kanger and Kanger (1966), the *Do*-operator can be combined with deontic operators to distinguish four basic types of right (or different sense of the expression 'right'):

(R1) $ODo(b, F(a, b))$

(R2) $\neg ODo(a, \neg F(a, b)) \equiv P \neg Do(a, \neg F(a, b))$

(R3) $\neg O \neg Do(a, F(a, b)) \equiv PDo(a, F(a, b))$

(R4) $O \neg Do(b, F(a, b))$

(R1)–(R4) define four basic normative relations between a and b which from a's perspective can be regarded as different relational concepts of right. In (R1), b has a duty to see to it that $F(a, b)$; this is equivalent to a's *claim* in relation to b that $F(a, b)$. (R2) can be described as a's freedom (or *privilege*) in relation to b that $F(a, b)$; this means that a has no obligation to see to it that $\neg F(a, b)$. Kanger called (R3) a's *power* in relation to b that $F(a, b)$, and (R4) a's *immunity* in relation to b that $F(a, b)$. The replacement of the state of affairs $F(a, b)$ by its opposite $\neg F(a, b)$ yields four additional concepts of right which Kanger and Kanger (1966) called counter-claim (R1'), counter-freedom (R2'), counter-power (R3'), and counter-immunity (R4'). Kanger and Kanger called the eight relations defined in this way *simple* types of right. The normative relationship between any two individuals with respect to a state of affairs p can be characterized completely by means of the conjunctions of the eight simple types of right or their negations. There are $2^8 = 256$ such conjunctions, but the simple types of right are not logically independent of each other; according to the logic of the deontic *O*-operator and the agency operator *Do*, only 26 combinations of the simple types of right or their negations are logically consistent. Kanger and Kanger (1966) called these 26 relations the 'atomic types of right.' The atomic types provide a complete characterization of the possible legal relationships between two persons with respect to a single state of affairs. It is perhaps misleading to call these 26 relations 'types of right,' because they include as their constituents duties as well as claims and freedoms. Thus Kanger's theory of normative relations can be regarded as a theory of duties as well as rights (Lindahl, 1994).

Kanger's concepts (R1)–(R4) correspond to the four ways using the word 'right' (or four concepts of a right) distinguished by Hohfeld (1919), from which he adopted the expressions 'privilege', 'power', and 'immunity'. Although Kanger apparently intended (R1)–(R4) as approximate explications of Hohfeld's notions, his concepts of power and immunity differ from Hohfeld's. According to Kanger, both power and freedom are permissions; a power consists in the permissibility of actively seeing to it that something is the case, whereas freedom means that there is no obligation to see to it that the opposite state of affairs should be the case. Lindahl (1977) and others have argued that Hohfeld's concept of power should be analyzed as a legal *ability* rather than a permission (a *can* rather than a *may*); see Bulygin (1992), Lindahl (1994) and Makinson (1986).

An agency operator such as the *Do*-operator considered above can be iterated, and it is possible to form sentences which contain several nested occurrences of deontic operators, agency operators (or action operators), and epistemic operators, relativized to possibly different agents. This feature has facilitated the applications deontic logic and the logic of agency to the analysis of complex social and normative phenomena, for example, the analysis of different kinds of rights relations and other normative relations (H. Kanger, 1984; Lindahl, 1994; Makinson, 1986), governmental structures and the concept of parliamentarism (Kanger and Kanger, 1966), normative positions and normative change (Jones and Sergot, 1993; Lindahl, 1977; Sergot, 1999), the analysis of normative control, influence, and responsibility (Pörn, 1989; Santos and Carmo, 1996), and the analysis of trade procedures and the concept of fraud (Firozabadi et al., 1999).

Suggested further reading

Deontic Logic: Introductory and Systematic Readings (Hilpinen, 1981a [1971]) contains some pioneering contributions to deontic logic, including those by Kanger and Hintikka. *New Studies in Deontic Logic: Norms, Actions and the Foundations of Ethics* (Hilpinen, 1981b) contains papers on the ontology of norms, deontic paradoxes, temporal deontic logic, and the interpretation of quantifiers in deontic logic. Horty's *Agency and Deontic Logic* (2000) analyzes the concepts of action and agency in deontic logic and discusses the relevance of deontic logic to ethical theories, for example, utilitarianism. *Norms, Logics, and Information Systems*, edited by McNamara and Prakken (1999), contains recent papers on the philosophical foundations of deontic logic, norm conflicts, and computer systems applications of deontic logic. The papers in Nute's *Defeasible Deontic Logic* (1997) analyze defeasible reasoning in normative discourse, and Carmo and Jones' essay "Deontic Logic and Contrary-to-Duties" (2001) is a good survey of the problems about CTD obligations.

Acknowledgment

I wish to thank Professor Lou Goble for advice and suggestions concerning this paper.

References

Alchourrón, C. 1993: "Philosophical Foundations of Deontic Logic and the Logic of Defeasible Conditionals," in Meyer and Wieringa (eds.) (1993, 43–84).

Anderson, A. R. 1967: "The Formal Analysis of Normative Systems," in *The Logic of Decision and Action*, N. Rescher, ed., (University of Pittsburgh Press, Pittsburgh), 147–213. (First published as Technical Report No. 2, Contract No. SAR/Nonr-609 (16)) New Haven: Office of Naval Research, Group Psychology Branch, 1956.)

Åqvist, L. 1967: "Good Samaritans, Contrary-to-Duty Imperatives, and Epistemic Obligations," *Noûs*, 2, 361–79.

Åqvist, L. 1974: "A New Approach to the Logical Theory of Actions and Causality," in *Logical Theory and Semantic Analysis*, S. Stenlund, ed., (D. Reidel, Dordrecht), 73–91.

Åqvist, L. and Hoepelman, J. 1981: "Some Theorems about a 'Tree' System of Deontic Tense Logic," in Hilpinen (ed.) (1981b, 187–221).

Åqvist, L. and Mullock, P. 1989: *Causing Harm*, (Walter de Gruyter, Berlin-New York).

Bentham, J. 1983: *Deontology; together with A Table of the Springs of Action; and the Article on Utilitarianism*, A. Goldworth, ed., (Clarendon Press, Oxford).

Bulygin, E. 1982: "Norms, Normative Propositions, and Legal Statements," in *Contemporary Philosophy. A New Survey. Vol. 3: Philosophy of Action*, G. Fløistad, ed., (Martinus Nijhoff, The Hague), 127–52.

Bulygin, E. 1992: "On Norms of Competence," *Law and Philosophy*, 11, 201–16.

Carmo, J. and Jones, A. J. I. 2001: "Deontic Logic and Contrary-to-Duties," in *Handbook of Philosophical Logic*, 2nd edn., Vol. 4, D. Gabbay, ed., (Kluwer Academic Publishers, Dordrecht), 287–366.

Castañeda, H.-N. 1972: "On the Semantics of the Ought-to-Do," *Synthese*, 21 (1970), 449–68; reprinted in *Semantics of Natural Language*, D. Davidson and G. Harman, eds., (D. Reidel, Dordrecht), 675–94.

Castañeda, H.-N. 1981: "The Paradoxes of Deontic Logic: The Simplest Solution to All of Them in One Fell Swoop," in Hilpinen (ed.) (1981b, 37–85).

Chellas, B. F. 1974: "Conditional Obligation," in *Logical Theory and Semantic Analysis*, S. Stenlund, ed., (D. Reidel, Dordrecht), 23–33.

Chellas, B. F. 1980: *Modal Logic – An Introduction*, (Cambridge University Press, Cambridge).

Chisholm, R. M. 1963: "Contrary-to-Duty Imperatives and Deontic Logic," *Analysis*, 24, 33–6.

Czelakowski, J. 1997: "Action and Deontology," in *Logic, Action and Cognition*, S. Lindström and E. Ejerhed, eds., (Kluwer Academic Publishers, Dordrecht and Boston), 47–88.

Firozabadi, B. S., Tan, Y.-H. and Lee, R. M. 1999: "Formal Definitions of Fraud," in McNamara and Prakken (eds.) (1999, 275–87).

Goble, L. 1991: "Murder Most Gentle: The Paradox Deepens," *Philosophical Studies*, 64, 217–27.

Goble, L. 1999: "Deontic Logic with Relevance," in McNamara and Prakken (eds.) (1999, 331–45).

Hamblin, C. L. 1987: *Imperatives*, (Basil Blackwell, Oxford).

Hansson, B. 1981: "An Analysis of Some Deontic Logics," in Hilpinen (ed.) (1981a, 121–47); reprinted from *Noûs*, 3 (1969), 373–98.

Hilpinen, R. (ed.) 1981a: *Deontic Logic: Introductory and Systematic Readings*, (D. Reidel, Dordrecht), 1971. (2nd printing with a new Introduction, 1981.)

Hilpinen, R. (ed.) 1981b: *New Studies in Deontic Logic: Norms, Actions and the Foundations of Ethics*, (D. Reidel, Dordrecht).

Hilpinen, R. 1993a: "Actions in Deontic Logic," in Meyer and Wieringa (eds.) (1993, 85–100).

Hilpinen, R. 1993b: "On Deontic Logic, Pragmatics, and Modality," in *Pragmatik: Handbuch Pragmatischen Denkens*, Band IV: *Sprachphilosophie, Sprachpragmatik und formative Pragmatik*, H. Stachowiak, ed., (Felix Meiner Verlag, Hamburg), 295–319.

Hilpinen, R. 1997: "On States, Actions, Omissions, and Norms," in *Contemporary Action Theory*, Vol. I: *Individual Action*, G. Holmström-Hintikka and J. Tuomela, eds., (Kluwer Academic Publishers, Dordrecht), 83–108.

Hintikka, J. 1957: "Quantifiers in Deontic Logic," *Societas Scientiarum Fennica, Commentationes Humanarum Litterarum*, 23:4, 1–23, Helsinki.

Hintikka, J. 1981: "Some Main Problems of Deontic Logic," in Hilpinen (ed.) (1981a, 59–104).

Hohfeld, W. N. 1919: *Fundamental Legal Conceptions as Applied in Judicial Reasoning*, W. W. Cook, ed., (Yale University Press, New Haven).

Horty, J. 2000: *Agency and Deontic Logic*, (Oxford University Press, New York).

Jones, A. J. I. and Sergot, M. 1993: "On the Characterization of Law and Computer Systems: The Normative Systems Perspective," in Meyer and Wieringa (eds.) (1993, 275–307).

Jørgensen, J. 1937/1938: "Imperatives and Logic," *Erkenntnis*, 7, 288–96.

Kamp, H. 1973/1974: "Free Choice Permission," *Aristotelian Society Proceedings* N.S. 74, 57–74.

Kamp, H. 1979: "Semantics versus Pragmatics," in *Formal Semantics and Pragmatics for Natural Languages*, F. Guenther and S. J. Schmidt, eds., (D. Reidel, Dordrecht), 255–87.

Kanger, H. 1984: *Human Rights in the U.N. Declaration, Acta Universitatis Uppsaliensis*, (University of Uppsala, Uppsala).

Kanger, S. 1972: "Law and Logic," *Theoria*, 38, 105–132.

Kanger, S. 1981: "New Foundations for Ethical Theory," in Hilpinen (ed.) (1981a, 36–58). (Originally published in 1957.)

Kanger, S. and Kanger, H. 1966: "Rights and Parliamentarism," *Theoria*, 32 (1966), 85–115; reprinted in 1972, with changes, in *Contemporary Philosophy in Scandinavia*, R. E. Olson and A. Paul, eds., (The Johns Hopkins Press, Baltimore and London), 213–36.

Leibniz, G. W. 1930: "Elementa iuris naturalis," in G. W. Leibniz, *Sämtliche Schriften und Briefe. Sechste Reihe: Philosophische Schriften*. Bd. 1. Darmstadt: Otto Reichl Verlag, 431–85.

Lewis, D. K. 1973: *Counterfactuals*, (Basil Blackwell, Oxford).

Lewis, D. K. 1979: "A Problem about Permission," in *Essays in Honour of Jaakko Hintikka on the Occasion of His Fiftieth Birthday*, E. Saarinen, R. Hilpinen, I. Niiniluoto and M. P. Hintikka, eds., (D. Reidel, Dordrecht), 163–175.

Lindahl, L. 1977: *Position and Change*, (D. Reidel, Dordrecht and Boston).

Lindahl, L. 1994: "Stig Kanger's Theory of Rights," in *Logic, Methodology and Philosophy of Science IX*, D. Prawitz, B. Skyrms and D. Westerståhl, eds., (Elsevier Science B. V., Amsterdam), 889–911.

Makinson, D. 1986: "On the Formal Representation of Rights Relations. Remarks on the Work of Stig Kanger and Lars Lindahl," *Journal of Philosophical Logic*, 15, 403–25.

Makinson, D. 1993: "Five Faces of Minimality," *Studia Logica*, 52, 339–79.

Makinson, D. 1999: "On a Fundamental Problem of Deontic Logic," in McNamara and Prakken (eds.) (1999, 29–54).

Mally, E. 1926: *Elemente des Sollens. Grundgesetze der Logik des Willens*, (Leuschner & Lubensky, Graz).

McNamara, P. and Prakken, H. (eds.) 1999: *Norms, Logics, and Information Systems*, (IOS Press, Amsterdam).

Meyer, J.-J. Ch. 1988: "A Different Approach to Deontic Logic: Deontic Logic Viewed as a Variant of Dynamic Logic," *Notre Dame Journal of Formal Logic*, 29, 109–36.

Meyer, J.-J. Ch. and Wieringa, R. J. (eds.) 1993: *Deontic Logic in Computer Science: Normative System Specification*, (John Wiley & Sons, Chichester-New York).

Mott, P. L. 1973: "On Chisholm's Paradox," *Journal of Philosophical Logic*, 2, 197–211.

Nute, D. (ed.) 1997: *Defeasible Deontic Logic*, (Kluwer Academic Publishers, Dordrecht).

Pörn, I. 1977: *Action Theory and Social Science*, (D. Reidel, Dordrecht).

Pörn, I. 1989: "On the Nature of a Social Order," in *Logic, Methodology and Philosophy of Science VIII*, J. E. Fenstad, T. Frolov and R. Hilpinen, eds., (North-Holland, Amsterdam), 553–67.

Prakken, H. and Sergot, M. 1997: "Deontic Logic and Contrary-to-Duty Obligations," in Nute (ed.) (1997, 223–62).

Ross, A. 1941: "Imperatives and Logic," *Theoria*, 7, 53–71.

Santos, F. and Carmo, J. 1996: "Indirect Action, Influence, and Responsibility," in *Deontic Logic, Agency, and Normative Systems*, M. A. Brown and J. Carmo, eds., (Springer, Berlin-Heidelberg-New York), 194–215.

Segerberg, K. 1982: "A Deontic Logic of Action," *Studia Logica*, 41, 269–82.

Segerberg, K. 1992: "Getting Started: Beginnings in the Logic of Action," *Studia Logica*, 51, 347–78.

Sergot, M. 1999: "Normative Positions," in McNamara and Prakken (eds.) (1999, 289–308).

von Wright, G. H. 1957: "Deontic Logic," *Mind*, 60 (1951), 1–15; reprinted in G. H. von Wright, *Logical Studies*, (Routledge & Kegan Paul, London), 58–74.

von Wright, G. H. 1963: *Norm and Action*, (Routledge & Kegan Paul, London).

von Wright, G. H. 1968: "An Essay in Deontic Logic and the General Theory of Action," *Acta Philosophica Fennica*, 21, (North-Holland Publ. Co., Amsterdam).

Chapter 9

Epistemic Logic

J.-J. Ch. Meyer

9.1. Introduction: A Brief History of Knowledge

Knowledge has been a subject of philosophical study since ancient times. This is not surprising since knowledge is crucial for humans to control their actions and the appetite for acquiring it seems innate to the human race. Philosophy, therefore, has always occupied itself with the question as to the nature of knowledge. This area of philosophy is generally referred to as epistemology from the Greek word for knowledge: *episteme*. Plato defined knowledge as *"justified true belief*,*"* and this definition has influenced philosophers ever since; cf. Gettier (1963) and Pollock (1986). Although sensible, this definition does not yet explain the nature of knowledge, since all of the three notions of 'justification', 'truth', and 'belief' are not yet clear and still subject to discussion. It would go beyond the scope of our purposes here to go into this at this moment, but it is touched on later in this chapter.

Further issues concerning knowledge include the question of how it comes to us. There is the controversy between rationalists, such as Plato and Descartes, who argued that knowledge only comes via reason(ing), and empiricists, such as Locke and Hume, who maintained that knowledge derives from sense experience. Kant considered categories of *analytical* knowledge ('derivable by purely logical argument') versus *synthetic* knowledge (where this is not the case) and of *a posteriori* knowledge (based on experience) versus *a priori* knowledge (where this is not the case), which led to a big debate whether *synthetic a priori* knowledge is possible.

As is the case with so many things, in the twentieth century, the notion of knowledge became amenable to formal-logical analysis. With the development of formal mathematical logic in the second half of the nineteenth century, the formal approach also became available to the study of philosophical notions such as time, necessity, obligation, and also knowledge itself. Most of these logics are collected under the heading of modal logics, namely logics of certain modalities such as necessity and possibility. [See chapter 7.] While (formal) modal logics had been around since the publication of C. I. Lewis' (1912) paper on an axiomatic approach of strict implication, the inception of formal modal *epistemic* logic is often taken to be Hintikka's (1962). The period 1912 up to the 1950s are referred to by Bull and Segerberg (1984) as the 'First Wave' of (formal) modal logic, where syntactic and algebraic approaches were prevailing, while the period of roughly 1950–80, where the focus shifted towards model-theoretic semantic approaches, is referred to as the 'Second Wave'. Hintikka's work marks the beginning of this Second Wave. In this chapter, however, epistemic logic is treated as a particular modal logic and models are considered that have become standard for modal logics in general, namely so-called Kripke models, based on the work by Kripke (1963), another leading figure in the Second Wave of formal modal logic. These models employ the notion of a *possible world* dating back to the philosopher and mathematician Leibniz. Carnap, Prior and Kanger also contributed to coining the notion of a possible world model (Bull and Segerberg, 1984).

In the 1980s, computer scientists and researchers in the area of artificial intelligence (AI) picked up the subject of epistemic logic as a means to reason about the knowledge ascribed to processors in processes of computation and that of knowledge-based systems, such as advanced databases, expert systems and so-called agent-oriented systems, respectively. (In an important sense, this work belongs to a kind of 'Third Wave' of modal logic: the use of modal logics in application areas such as computer science, linguistics and AI.) This chapter reviews briefly their contributions to epistemic logic and its application, since these concentrate on slightly different but also quite interesting aspects of knowledge, and their work also, in its turn, has influenced philosophers again. (Moreover, links were established with another interesting area of AI – nonmonotonic reasoning – which has some definite relations with philosophy as well [see chapter 15].)

9.2. The Modal Logic Approach to Knowledge

This section looks at the basic idea behind modal epistemic logic: modeling knowledge or rather ignorance (as shall be seen) by means of accessibility relations as they are present in Kripke models.

To prepare for the formal treatment, first consider the following situation. Imagine a person in Amsterdam wondering what the weather is like in New York (possibly since a friend of his is there on holiday), in particular whether it is raining in New York. Since he has no information pertaining to this (and clearly cannot obtain this information by direct observation – unless he is clairvoyant or has access to an internet site with this information, which is assumed not to be the case), this person will consider two possible situations, one in which it rains in New York, and one in which this is not the case. Note that the lack of knowledge of an agent can be represented as the agent's considering a number of situations as possible. In this example, there are only two such possible situations, resulting from being ignorant about one propositional item, but clearly, if one lacks knowledge about more items, the number of possible situations that are held possible will increase. Generally, if one has ignorance about the truth of n propositional atoms, one has to consider 2^n situations. For example, if one totally lacks knowledge about whether it rains in New

York (p) and whether it rains in Los Angeles (q), one has to reckon with four situations: one in which both p and q are true, one in which p is true and q is false, one in which p is false and q is true, and one in which both p and q are false. Since the situations to be considered stem from (lack of) knowledge, they are called *epistemically* alternative worlds or shortly *epistemic alternatives*.

The idea of considering several epistemic alternatives in case one has not complete knowledge about the situation at hand can be molded perfectly into the framework of Kripke-style possible world semantics. Assume a set $\mathcal{P}$ of propositional atoms. Use the symbols T and F for the truth values (true and false, respectively). Formally a Kripke model is a structure of the form:

Definition 9.1   A Kripke model is a structure $\mathcal{M}$ of the form $\langle S, \pi, R \rangle$, where

- S is a non-empty set (the set of possible worlds);
- $\pi : S \rightarrow \mathcal{P} \rightarrow \{T, F\}$ is a truth assignment function to the atoms per possible world;
- $R \subseteq S \times S$ is the knowledge accessibility relation.

By means of a Kripke model, one can represent exactly what an agent considers as the epistemic alternatives in a certain situation: given a situation (represented again by a possible world $s \in S$), the epistemic alternatives for the agent are given by the set $\{t \in S \mid R(s, t)\}$, i.e. all possible worlds t that are accessible from s by means of the relation R.

Thus the example above can be represented in a Kripke model as follows; see figure 9.1. Suppose that the actual situation at hand (which the agent does not have complete knowledge about) is that it rains in New York but not in LA, represented by a state $s_1 \in S$ for which it holds that $\pi(s_1)(p) = T$ and $\pi(s_1)(q) = F$. Now the model can be represented by taking $S = \{s_0, s_1, s_2, s_3\}$, where s_0 is such that $\pi(s_0)(p) = \pi(s_0)(q) = T$, s_1 is as above, s_2 is such that $\pi(s_2)(p) = F$ and $\pi(s_2)(q) = T$, and s_3 is such that $\pi(s_3)(p) = \pi(s_3)(q) = F$. The relation R of the model is given by $R(s_1, t)$ for every $t \in S$. To represent that the agent has more information in situation s_2, e.g., that the agent knows that it is raining in LA (perhaps because the situation is so unusual that it has been on the news), the relation R in the model can be extended by stipulating $R(s_2, t)$ for $t = s_0, s_2$. Now the agent has no doubt anymore about the truth of proposition q, but is still ignorant about the truth value of proposition p.

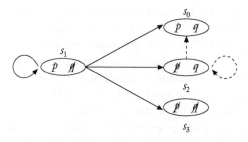

Figure 9.1

On the basis of the Kripke models a modal logic of knowledge can be devised. To this end, introduce a modal operator K, to be interpreted as 'it is known that,' and give it a formal semantic by a clause: for Kripke model $M = \langle S, \pi, R \rangle$ and $s \in S$,

$M, s \vDash K\varphi$ iff (if and only if) for all t with $R(s, t)$ it holds that $M, s \vDash \varphi$

This clause states that, in a possible world s, it is known (by the agent) that the formula φ is true iff φ is true in all the worlds t that the agent deems epistemic alternatives. In other words, although one may have doubts about the true nature of the world (if one considers more than one epistemic alternative as possible), one has no doubts about the truth of φ: this formula holds in all epistemic alternatives. Thus, it can really be said that, in this case, one *knows* the formula φ.

To complete the logic, assume that, besides propositional atoms from P, formulas can also be composed by means of the usual propositional connectives $\neg$ (not), $\wedge$ (and), $\vee$ (or), $\rightarrow$ (implication) and $\leftrightarrow$ (bi-implication), with their usual semantics, such as, e.g.,

$M, s \vDash \neg\varphi$ iff not $M, s \vDash \varphi$

$M, s \vDash \varphi \wedge \psi$ iff $M, s \vDash \varphi$ and $M, s \vDash \psi$

Propositional atoms $p \in P$ are, of course, interpreted by using the truth assignment function π:

$M, s \vDash p$ iff $\pi(s)(p) = T$

Finally, a formula φ in this logic is said to be valid, notation $\vDash \varphi$, if $M, s \vDash \varphi$ for all Kripke models $M = \langle S, \pi, R \rangle$ and all $s \in S$.

By interpreting the operator K in the above way, one directly obtains a number of validities:

Proposition 9.1

1    $\vDash K(\varphi \rightarrow \psi) \rightarrow (K\varphi \rightarrow K\psi)$

2   If $\vDash \varphi$ then $\vDash K\varphi$

This proposition says that by modeling knowledge in this way, it is closed under logical consequence. Furthermore, validities are always known. With respect to an idealized notion of knowledge, these properties are certainly defensible. For more practical purposes (when using the notion of knowledge in certain applications, e.g., describing the knowledge of human or artificial beings such as robots) they may be undesirable. In this case, one may speak of the so-called problem of *logical omniscience*, discussed in section 9.5 below. For the time being, one accepts these properties of knowledge, and wonders what other properties knowledge should satisfy.

Finally in this section, note that the valid formulas with respect to the class of Kripke models that have been introduced here can be axiomatized by the following

Hilbert-style system (called system **K** in the literature of modal logic), consisting of the axioms:

(P)   any axiomatization of propositional logic

(K) $K(\varphi \to \psi) \to (K\varphi \to K\psi)$

and rules *modus ponens* (MP) and

(N_K) $\varphi / K\varphi$

The validity (K) is generally referred to as the *K-axiom*, while rule N_K is called the *necessitation rule*.

Technically, one can show that this system **K** is *sound* and *complete* with respect to the class of all Kripke models, which states that the set of theorems in this system is exactly the set of validities (with respect to the class of all Kripke models). Since the proof of this is rather technical, it is omitted here, but it can be found in many textbooks on modal logic; see, for example, Chellas (1980), Hughes and Cresswell (1984) and Meyer and van der Hoek (1995), [and chapter 7].

9.3.   The Systems T, S4, and S5

As seen in section 9.2, the notion of knowledge, as captured by a modal logic based on Kripke models of the form introduced there, satisfies certain properties. However, some properties that intuitively hold of knowledge are not validities in this setting. For instance, one of the defining properties of knowledge is that it is *true*! That is, in a formula: $K\varphi \to \varphi$, if it is known that φ then φ must be true. This formula, however, is not a validity in the framework given thus far [see chapter 7].

This can be remedied, however, by putting constraints on the class of Kripke models being considered. By stipulating that the accessibility relation R is *reflexive*, i.e., satisfies the constraint $R(s, s)$ for all $s \in S$, then the formula $K\varphi \to \varphi$ becomes valid with respect to this new class of models.

Proposition 9.2   Any Kripke model $\mathcal{M} = \langle S, \pi, R \rangle$ where R is reflexive, satisfies $\mathcal{M} \models K\varphi \to \varphi$.

Extending system **K** of the previous section with axiom $K\varphi \to \varphi$ gives the system referred to as system **T**. This system can be shown to be *sound* and *complete* with respect to the new class of models, i.e. the class of all Kripke models in which the accessibility relation is reflexive ([see chapter 7]; see also Chellas (1980), Hughes and Cresswell (1984), and Meyer and van der Hoek (1995).)

Furthermore, it would also be reasonable to have a property stating that knowledge is known itself, expressed by the formula $K\varphi \to KK\varphi$: if one knows φ, then one also knows that one knows φ. This formula is not a validity in the setting presented thus far either. But, again, constraints on the class of Kripke models can be introduced to overcome this difficulty. If the accessibility relation R in a model $M = \langle S, \pi, R \rangle$ is required to be transitive, i.e., satisfies the constraint that

$$R(s, t) \wedge R(t, u) \Rightarrow R(s, u)$$

for all $s, t, u \in S$, then the formula $K\varphi \rightarrow KK\varphi$ becomes a validity with respect to this class of models.

Proposition 9.3 Any Kripke model $M = \langle S, \pi, R \rangle$ where R is transitive, satisfies $M \vDash K\varphi \rightarrow KK\varphi$.

Extending the system **T** with axiom $K\varphi \rightarrow KK\varphi$ gives a system called **S4**, which is a well-known axiom system for knowledge (at least in philosophy). The axiom is called the *positive introspection* axiom, since it states something about the agent's own knowledge about knowledge. Again, it can be shown that **S4** is *sound* and *complete* with respect to models with accessibility relations that are reflexive and transitive ([see chapter 7]; see also Chellas (1980), Hughes and Cresswell (1984) and Meyer and van der Hoek (1995).)

Now one can ask the question whether there is more to knowledge? Can further properties of knowledge be identified? This issue will be discussed later, but first it is relevant to mention here that in computer science and AI, where epistemic logic is employed to describe the 'knowledge' of artificial systems like (distributed) computer systems, information systems and 'intelligent' systems such as 'agent systems' and robots (Meyer and van der Hoek, 1995), it is customary to also add another axiom, which says something about knowledge of ignorance.

This axiom is called the *negative introspection* axiom:

$$\neg K\varphi \rightarrow K\neg K\varphi$$

It states that if the agent does *not* know formula φ, then it *knows* that it does not know φ. Of course, for human agents this axiom is highly unlikely to hold in general, since one may not even be aware of one's not knowing φ. However, for some artficial agents, dealing with *finite* information, like only a finite set P of propositional atoms and a finite set of formulas that it knows, the truth of this axiom may be argued (informally) like this: if the artificial agent does not know a formula, then this formula does not follow from the agent's finite information, and the agent is able to detect this, so that it knows that it does not know the formula. Also, in some cases, the validity of the axiom follows directly from the special kind of models that is used in applications – as in the case of using epistemic logic in distributed systems, cf. Halpern and Moses (1990) and Meyer and van der Hoek (1995).

To cater to the validity of the negative introspection axiom, one has to constrain the (accessibility relations of the) Kripke models even further. One can show that by requiring the relation R to be an *equivalence* relation, namely a relation that satisfies the three properties:

- *Reflexivity:* $R(s, s)$ for all $s \in S$
- *Transitivity:* $R(s, t) \wedge R(t, u) \Rightarrow R(s, u)$ for all $s, t, u \in S$
- *Symmetry:* $R(s, t) \Rightarrow R(t, s)$ for all $s, t \in S$

one obtains that the negative introspection axiom as well as all axioms of system **S4** are valid with respect to this new class of Kripke models. (And, of course, also the rules of *modus ponens* and necessitation remain sound.)

The new system is known as **S5**, and, as noted above, is very popular among computer scientists who use epistemic logic.[1] One of the reasons is the very intuitive interpretation of the models with equivalence relations as accessibility relations that are briefly discussed below. For the reason given before, philosophers do not regard **S5** as a correct logic for knowledge. They usually stick to **S4**, and possibly some logics in between **S4** and **S5**. The system **S5** can be shown *sound* and *complete* with respect to the class of Kripke models in which the accessibility relations are equivalence relations ([see chapter 7]; see also Chellas (1980), Hughes and Cresswell (1984), and Meyer and van der Hoek (1995).)

Equivalence relations divide the set of possible worlds into equivalence classes, the members of which are all mutually accessible. An equivalence class is, so to speak, a bunch of worlds that are epistemic alternatives of each other. One can show that in the case that one has only one knowledge operator as here, one can restrict oneself to equivalence relations with only *one* equivalence class without losing soundness and completeness of the logic. Such a model is particularly simple: it just consists of a set of states which are *all* mutually accessible, or speaking in epistemic terms: are all each other's epistemic alternative. So, in such a case, it does not matter what is the actual world where one is considering alternatives: for each world there is exactly the same set of alternatives: the *whole* set S of possible worlds (Meyer and van der Hoek, 1995).

A final note: as can be verified – see, for example Meyer and van der Hoek (1995) – the system **S5** contains a redundancy: the positive introspection axiom can be deleted since it can be derived from the other axioms together with the rules. Nevertheless, in the sequel when speaking about the system **S5**, it is convenient to include the positive introspection axiom as well.

9.4. Belief: The Systems K45 and KD45

Belief is mostly regarded as a weaker form of knowledge (but see later in section 9.6.2). The crucial difference between knowledge and belief is that the former must be true whereas the latter need not. When considering properties (axioms) of belief rather than knowledge, those of knowledge can be copied except for the one stating that knowledge is true. Mostly, the modal operator for belief is denoted B: $B\varphi$ is read as 'it is believed that φ' or 'the agent believes that φ.' Copying the system **S5** without the 'truth axiom' for belief gives the system known as **K45**:

- any axiomatization of propositional logic
- $B(\varphi \rightarrow \psi) \rightarrow (B\varphi \rightarrow B\psi)$

- $B\varphi \to BB\varphi$
- $\neg B\varphi \to B\neg B\varphi$

and rules *modus ponens* (MP) and

(N_B) $\varphi/B\varphi$

The class of Kripke models with respect to which system **K45** is *sound* and *complete* consists of those models in which the accessibility relation R (now used to interpret the operator B, of course) is *transitive* and *Euclidean*, the latter meaning that R satisfies:

$$R(s,\ t) \wedge R(s,\ u) \Rightarrow R(t,\ u)$$

for all $s,\ t,\ u,\ \in S$; ([see chapter 7], also Meyer and van der Hoek (1995).)

Mostly, also it is stipulated that beliefs should be consistent, in a formula: $\neg B(p \wedge \neg p)$, for some $p \in P$. Adding this formula to the system **K45** as an axiom (often called the D-axiom, since it was held a typical axiom of *deontic* logic [see chapter 8]) yields the system **KD45**, or **weak S5**. This system can be proven *sound* and *complete* with respect to Kripke models in which the accessibility relation is *transitive, Euclidean*, and *serial*, where seriality of a relation R means that for all $s \in S$ there exists $t \in S$ such that $R(s,\ t)$. This property expresses that, in any possible world, the agent considers at least one epistemic alternative.

As with **S5**, it can be shown (Meyer and van der Hoek, 1995) that **K(D)45** is (sound and) complete with respect to a class of simpler models, in this case models consisting of an 'actual' world s_0, and a set S of worlds not including s_0 such that the accessibility relation R satisfies $R(s_0,\ s)$ for each $s \in S$ and $R(s,\ t)$ for any $s,\ t \in S$. In case one considers **KD45**, the set S is non-empty, whereas, in the case of **K45**, it may be empty. This provides a neat picture which can be interpreted philosophically in a very intuitive way: these simple models for **K(D)45**-belief consist of an actual world (representing the current state of the external world) together with a set of epistemic alternatives, or put differently, an actual world and an (S5-)epistemic model, which in the case of **K45** may be empty (representing inconsistent belief). In general, the actual world may have nothing to do with the epistemic model, reflecting the fact that beliefs may be 'counterfactual' in the sense that they may be false in reality.

Note: contrary to the case of **S5** the positive introspection axiom for belief is *not* redundant in the systems **K45** and **KD45**!

9.5. Logical Omniscience: The Problem and Some Solutions

As seen in a previous section, a modal approach to knowledge (and belief) based on Kripke models of the kind as defined thus far yields that knowledge (belief) is closed under logical consequence and that validities are known (believed) (proposition 9.1).

In fact, there are a number of further properties, collectively called properties of *logical omniscience*, since they have to do with some idealizations on the part of the knowing (believing) agent (here $\square$ stands for either the knowledge operator K or the belief operator B):

Proposition 9.4

LO1: $\models \square\varphi \wedge \square(\varphi \to \psi) \to \square\psi$

LO2: $\models \varphi \Rightarrow \models \square\varphi$

LO3: $\models \varphi \to \psi \Rightarrow \models \square\varphi \to \square\psi$

LO4: $\models \varphi \leftrightarrow \psi \Rightarrow \models \square\varphi \leftrightarrow \square\psi$

LO5: $\models (\square\varphi \vee \square\psi) \to \square(\varphi \vee \psi)$

LO6: $\models \square\varphi \to \square(\varphi \vee \psi)$

LO7: $\models \neg(\square\varphi \wedge \square\neg\varphi)$

Properties LO1 and LO2 were already mentioned in proposition 9.1 for K. More precisely, LO1 says that if both φ and the implication $\varphi \to \psi$ is known (believed) then also ψ is known (believed). LO3 is a similar property but slightly different: if some formula ϕ is known (believed) then also everything (ψ) that is a logical consequence is known (believed). LO4 says that logically equivalent formulas are either both known (believed) or both not known (believed). LO5 says that if both φ is known (believed) and ψ is known (believed) then also the conjunction of φ and ψ is known. LO6 says that if ϕ is known (believed) then it is also known (believed) that φ or ψ. (In fact, this is a direct consequence of property LO3.) LO7 says that it cannot be the case that both a formula and its negation is known (believed).

Sometimes, it is very convenient to consider these properties as true, but in some more practical situations these formulas might be deemed unrealistic. For instance, it is very unlikely that human agents will know (believe) all logical consequences of their knowledge (beliefs) including all validities. Although at first sight a reasonable property, even LO4 is unlikely to hold for human agents: imagine two logically equivalent formulas both of length greater than 10 million characters. These formulas are not even parsable for the unfortunate agent, let alone known to be equivalent! So, sometimes it is argued that on the grounds of the *resource boundedness* of an agent one has to deny or at least weaken the properties LO1–LO7. However, this is not as simple as it sounds. Recall that these validities are the very properties of Kripke-style modal logic as expounded thus far. The formulas LO1–LO6 are true of all Kripke models. (LO7 can be denied by taking accessibility relations that are not serial, as seen before. However, in the case of knowledge one is still stuck with this property: the models that are associated with the systems **S4** and **S5** have reflexive, and thus serial, accessibility relations.)

Therefore, to deny the above properties something 'non-standard' is needed. In the literature (Thijsse, 1992; Meyer and van der Hoek, 1995) there appear quite a number of approaches varying in 'drasticality.' Three such approaches are presented here, starting with a rather radical method considering 'non-standard' Kripke models in which nonstandard ('impossible') worlds are present. Here, the focus will be on solving the logical omniscience problem for *belief* rather than knowledge, since, in the context of belief, the problem seems to be more pregnant.

9.5.1. *Rantala models*

Rantala models are a non-standard type of Kripke models in which, besides the possible worlds, also so-called *'impossible worlds'* are incorporated (Rantala, 1982). The idea behind these 'impossible' worlds is that, as the name suggests, strange things may hold there: in these impossible worlds, anything may be the case, even contradictions may be true there! Thus these worlds are impossible in the true sense of the word. However, they can nevertheless be regarded as epistemic alternatives by agents which are not ideal reasoners (are less rational). And this is exactly what is needed to avoid the agent's logical omniscience.

Formally, (epistemic) Rantala models are structures of the following kind (here $\mathcal{L}$ stands for the whole logical language):

Definition 9.2 A(n epistemic) Rantala model is a structure $\mathcal{M}$ of the form $\langle S, \sigma, T, S^* \rangle$, where

- S is a non-empty set, the set of (possible *and* impossible) worlds;
- $S^* \subseteq S$ is the set of *impossible* worlds;
- $\sigma : (S \backslash S^* \rightarrow (\mathcal{P} \rightarrow \{T, F\})) \cup (S^* \rightarrow (\mathcal{L} \rightarrow \{T, F\}))$, a function assigning truth to atoms on possible worlds, and truth to *arbitrary formulas* on impossible worlds, is a truth assignment function to the atoms per state;
- $T \subseteq S \times S$ is the belief accessibility relation, for which seriality and *Rantala-model versions of transitivity and Euclidicity* are required:[2]

  1   for all $s, t, u \in S \backslash S^*$: $R(s, t)$ & $R(t, u)$ implies $R(s, u)$, and for all $s \in S \backslash S^*$, $t^* \in S^*$: $R(s, t^*)$ & $\sigma(t^*)(\neg B \neg \varphi) = T$ implies $\mathcal{M}, t' \vDash \varphi$ for some $t' \in S$ with $R(s, t')$.

  2   for all $s, t, u \in S \backslash S^*$: $R(s, t)$ & $R(s, u)$ implies $R(t, u)$, and for all $s \in S \backslash S^*$, $t^* \in S^*$: $R(s, t^*)$ & $\sigma(t^*)(B\varphi) = T$ implies $\mathcal{M}, t' \vDash \varphi$ for all $t' \in S$ with $R(s, t')$.

Formulas in *possible* worlds $s \in S \backslash S^*$ are interpreted in exactly the same way as in Kripke models including the clause for the modal operator $\square$:

$\mathcal{M}, s \vDash \square\varphi$ iff $\mathcal{M}, t \vDash \varphi$ for every $t \in S$ such that $T(s, t)$.

However, in *impossible* worlds $s^* \in S^*$ every formula is regarded as atomic, and given its truth value by means of the truth assignment function σ:

$\mathcal{M}, s^* \vDash \varphi$ iff $\sigma(s^*)(\varphi) = T$

Thus, it may happen that for example, the formula $p \land \neg p$ is assigned the value T by the function σ in an impossible world $s^* \in S^*$. Formulas are valid if they are true in every *possible world* $s \in S \backslash S^*$ in any Rantala model $M = \langle S, \sigma, T, S^* \rangle$. This is very understandable: the worlds in which one evaluates are the worlds from which one takes up a stance and considers epistemic alternatives. Although these alternatives may be 'impossible,' the worlds of evaluation represent the actual world and thus must be 'possible'!

The feature of allowing for these impossible worlds gives one the possibility to deny all of the formulas LO1–LO7, so that none of them are validities with respect to Rantala models. For instance, consider the possibility of denying LO7 in Rantala models. This is very easy: just by taking a model $M = \langle S, \sigma, T, S^* \rangle$ with $S = \{s, s^*\}$, $S^* = \{s^*\}$, $T = \{(s, s^*), (s^*, s^*)\}$, and $\sigma(s^*)(\varphi) = \sigma(s^*)(\neg\varphi) = T$. Then $M, s \vDash \Box\varphi \land \Box\neg\varphi$, i.e., $M, s \vDash \neg LO7$. Moreover by stipulating that $\sigma(s^*)(\varphi \lor \neg\varphi) = F$ one can deny the validity of LO2, since now $M, s \nvDash \Box(\varphi \lor \neg\varphi)$. In the same way, the other logical omniscience properties can be denied. Finally, note too that, due to the condition of 'Rantala-transitivity' on the model, the positive introspection axiom is a validity again, as can be easily verified.

9.5.2. Sieve models

The second approach to avoiding logical omniscience of the agent is quite different. Again a variation of a standard Kripke model is employed, but now instead of introducing nonstandard worlds, the model is endowed with a function A that acts as a kind of sieve: it determines whether some formula is allowed to be known (believed) (Fagin and Halpern, 1988). Intuitively, the function A expresses some kind of awareness on the agent's part: it indicates whether the agent is *aware* of the formula at hand in a particular situation (world), and thus is amenable to be known (believed) by the agent in that world.

Formally these models have the following form (again, use L for the whole logical language):

Definition 9.3 A(n epistemic) sieve model is a structure M of the form $\langle S, \pi, T, A \rangle$, where

- S is a non-empty set (the set of *states* or *possible worlds*);
- $\pi : S \rightarrow (\mathcal{P} \rightarrow \{T, F\})$ is a truth assignment function to the atoms per state;
- $T \subseteq S \times S$ is the belief accessibility relation, which is assumed to be serial, transitive and Euclidean again;
- $A : S \rightarrow \wp(L)$ is the awareness function, assigning per state the set of formulas that the agent is aware of; for any $s \in S$, $A(s)$ is assumed to contain all instances of the D-axiom and the introspection axioms.

Let the language contain an 'awareness' operator A as well as the epistemic operator $\Box$. These are interpreted on a sieve model $M = \langle S, \pi, T, A \rangle$ and a state $s \in S$ as follows:

$M, s \vDash A\varphi$ iff $\varphi \in A(s)$

and

$$M, s \vDash \Box\varphi \text{ iff } \varphi \in \mathcal{A}(s) \ \& \ M, t \vDash \varphi \text{ for all } t \text{ such that } T(s, t)$$

So from the definition, one can see how indeed the function $\mathcal{A}$ acts as a sieve: only those formulas are considered as knowledge (beliefs) that are indicated as being aware of by it. By the condition put on this function (which states something like that the agent is aware of the D-axiom and both introspection axioms), and the fact that the rest of the model is a standard **KD45** model, it is easy to see that these axioms are validities again.

Since the sieve model approach can only filter out formulas to be known (believed), by this approach only the validities LO1–LO6 can be avoided. This is obvious by taking a model that contains a possible world s where the formula to be denied, say ψ, is not being aware of, namely take $\mathcal{A}$ such that $\psi \notin \mathcal{A}(s)$. Then immediately $M, s \nvDash A\psi$, and hence $M, s \nvDash \Box\psi$. This can be used to show that LO1–LO6 are not valid.

9.5.3. Cluster models

Finally, here is a method with which one can avoid LO7 while still keeping the axiom D (or, in semantical terms, keeping serial accessibility relations). This method is strongly related to the use of what Chellas (1980) calls *minimal models* for so-called non-normal modal logic, and goes back to so-called neighborhood semantics by Scott (1970) and Montague (1974 [1968]). Chellas was mainly interested in applying it to deontic logic, but something very similar was re-invented by Fagin and Halpern (1988) in the context of epistemic logic and dubbed *local reasoning* by means of *cluster models*.

Cluster models are variants of standard Kripke models in the sense that instead of a set of epistemic alternatives a set of *sets of* epistemic alternatives is incorporated in the models. The intuition behind this is that what is normally the set of epistemic alternatives (as viewed from an actual world) is partitioned in subsets ('clusters'), where these clusters correspond to coherent bodies of knowledge while two clusters can be mutually incoherent. The typical example of such a partition of knowledge (represented by a set of epistemic alternatives) is the theory of mechanics in physics which can be partitioned into classical mechanics and quantum mechanics, where these two subtheories of mechanics are mutually inconsistent. Nevertheless, and this is very important, it is perfectly rational for a physicist to consider both theories and apply them when appropriate. [See also chapter 13, section 13.4.]

Formally, cluster models are defined as follows:

Definition 9.4 A cluster model is a structure M of the form $\langle S, \pi, C \rangle$, where

- S is a non-empty set (the set of *possible worlds*);
- $\pi : S \to (\mathcal{P} \to \{T, F\})$ is a truth assignment function to the atoms per state;
- $C : S \to \wp(\wp(S))$, such that, for every s, $C(s)$ is a non-empty collection of non-empty subsets (clusters) of S.

The belief operator may now be interpreted as follows:

$$\mathcal{M}, s \vDash B\varphi \text{ iff } \exists T \in \mathcal{C}(s)\forall t \in T \ \mathcal{M}, t \vDash \varphi$$

Validity is defined as usual again.

With this interpretation of belief, one may now indeed deny LO7: take a model $\mathcal{M} = \langle S, \pi, C\rangle$, with $S = \{s, t\}$, $C(s) = \{\{s\}, \{t\}\}$, and $\pi(s)(p) = \text{T}$, $\pi(t)(p) = \text{F}$. Then $\mathcal{M}$, $s \vDash Bp \wedge B\neg p$, thus falsifying LO7. Note that, on the other hand, it is still the case that $\mathcal{M}, s \nvDash B(p \wedge \neg p)$!

Cluster models as defined above are not yet models of epistemic logic: they do not yet satisfy the D-axiom and the two introspection axioms. Thijsse (1992) gives necessary and sufficient conditions for turning cluster models into 'epistemic cluster models.' Since these are rather technical (they follow from a correspondence to neighborhood semantics in the style of Scott–Montague, and have a topological meaning), they are mentioned here without further comments.

Let $c^{\uparrow}(s)$ be defined as the set $\{X \mid T \subseteq X \text{ for some } T \in C(s)\}$. Then to cater for the positive introspection axiom, impose the condition that

$$X \in c^{\uparrow}(s) \Rightarrow \{v \mid X \in c^{\uparrow}(v)\} \in c^{\uparrow}(s)$$

and for the negative introspection axiom impose the condition

$$X \notin c^{\uparrow}(s) \Rightarrow \{v \mid X \notin c^{\uparrow}(v)\} \in c^{\uparrow}(s)$$

9.6. Further Refinements and Extensions

Having looked at the 'standard' treatment of knowledge by means of the systems **S4** and **S5**, this section discusses some of the more advanced systems that have been proposed to deal with knowledge more adequately.

9.6.1. Other systems for knowledge

Philosophers, who do not judge the system **S5** as an adequate formalization of knowledge, have asked whether it is possible to find a suitable system for capturing the properties of knowledge that goes beyond **S4**, but stays 'below' **S5**, so to speak. Indeed, such systems between **S4** and **S5** have been proposed (Lenzen, 1980; Voorbraak, 1991, 1993). For instance, Lenzen (1980) observed that if one takes knowledge to be *true belief*, i.e., defining

$$K'\varphi = B\varphi \wedge \varphi$$

where B satisfies the logic **KD45**, one obtains a logic for K' that is known under the name **S4.4**, which is the logic **S4** together with the axiom

$$\varphi \rightarrow (\neg K'\neg K'\varphi \rightarrow K'\varphi)$$

It is not directly obvious whether this property is intuitively a suitable one for knowledge. Other candidate logics of knowledge include that of *rationally believed objective knowledge K‴*, defined as

$$K''\varphi = K\varphi \wedge B\varphi$$

where K is the usual **S5**-style type of knowledge and B is a **KD45**-type of belief. This operator K'' appears to be axiomatized by the logic **S4F**, which consists of the system **S4** extended with the axiom (using M'' as the dual of K'')

$$(M''\varphi \wedge M''K''\psi) \rightarrow K''(M''\varphi \vee \psi)$$

See Voorbraak (1993). Finally; the concept of *justified knowledge* (K^j) that is considered by Voorbraak (1993). By giving a careful and rather ingenious semantic analysis of this notion by means of a generalized form of Kripke models, he argues that the logic for this type of knowledge should be the system **S4.2**, which consists of **S4** together with the axiom

$$M^j K^j \varphi \rightarrow K^j M^j \varphi$$

(using M^j as the dual of K^j).

9.6.2. Systems for combining knowledge and belief

After having looked at the notions of knowledge and belief separately, it is natural to question what the relations between these two notions are, and whether these relations may be formalized in a logical system. Such a system might then be used in cases where it is important to distinguish between an agent's knowledge and beliefs, and reason about both these notions. A starting point of such a combined logical system would be to take the logic **S5** for knowledge (K) and add to it the logic **KD45** for belief (B). Of course, to make this a little more exciting, one should also add some connecting axioms. Kraus and Lehmann (1986) have done so by adding the axioms[3]

$$K\varphi \rightarrow B\varphi$$

$$B\varphi \rightarrow KB\varphi$$

The former expresses that knowledge is stronger than belief, whereas the latter expresses that if one believes something then one knows that one believes this (a kind of generalized form of introspection). In itself, these two axioms are rather intuitive and seem innocuous. However, as Kraus and Lehmann (1986) themselves observe, they would have also liked to include another intuitive axiom – $B\varphi \rightarrow BK\varphi$, stating that one believes to know what one believes – but this would cause the notions of knowledge and belief to collapse, since then $K\varphi \leftrightarrow B\varphi$ would become derivable! This indicates that something is wrong with the intuitions. Voorbraak (1993) blames it on having the axiom $K\varphi \rightarrow B\varphi$, in line with his views on **S5** being a weak form of objective knowledge that cannot be stronger than rational belief (as represented by the logic **KD45**). Van der Hoek (1993) offers a different solution to the problem; he sacrifices the negative introspection axiom for knowledge – thus essentially adopting an **S4**-type of knowledge – which allows him to add the above mentioned formula $B\varphi \to BK\varphi$ as an axiom as well as the two KB-connecting axioms of Kraus and Lehmann above. (In fact, Van der Hoek shows that by thus dropping the negative introspection axiom for knowledge, some room is created for an unproblematic (simultaneous) addition of some more axioms like $\neg B\varphi \to K\neg B\varphi$ and $\neg K\varphi \to B\neg K\varphi$, expressing a kind of cross-over negative introspection.)

9.6.3. Knowledge in a group of agents

So far, only the notion of knowledge (and belief) of a single agent has been discussed. When considering a group of agents, one can, of course, consider the knowledge (K_i) of every individual agent i, so that a Kripke model of the form to describe the knowledge of the various agents may be used:

Definition 9.5 An (n agents) Kripke model is a structure $\mathcal{M}$ of the form $\langle S, \pi, R_1, \ldots, R_n \rangle$, where

- S is a non-empty set (the set of *possible worlds*);
- $\pi : S \to (\mathcal{P} \to \{T, F\})$ is a truth assignment function to the atoms per possible world;
- for $1 \le i \le n$, $R_i \subseteq S \times S$ is the knowledge accessibility relation for agent i, assumed to be an equivalence relation.

The validities with respect to these (multi-modal) models are simply axiomatized by a multi-modal version of **S5**: for each K_i one takes an **S5**-axiomatization.

However, it is also worthwhile examining notions of knowledge that have to do with the group as a whole. This has been done by Halpern and Moses (1985). At least two such notions come to mind immediately. The first is knowledge that is shared by everyone: the facts that *every* agent in the group knows, denoted by E ('everybody knows'). The axiomatization of E-knowledge is trivial: just take as an axiom (assuming there are n agents in the group):

$$E\varphi \leftrightarrow K_1\varphi \wedge \cdots \wedge K_n\varphi$$

Semantically E can be associated with an accessibility relation $R_E = \cup_{i=1}^{n} R_i$ (intuitively this means that all agents put their sets of epistemic alternatives together in one big set), and define

$$\mathcal{M}, s \models E\varphi \text{ iff } \mathcal{M}, t \models \varphi \text{ for every } t \text{ with } R_E(s, t)$$

Now the above axiom becomes a validity. Intuitively, this is because since the agents have collected their epistemic alternatives, the only things they can be sure of as a group are those formulas that are true in *all* of these alternatives.

Moreover, E satisfies the basic properties of a modal (necessity-type) operator, namely the K-axiom and necessitation rule:

$$E(\varphi \rightarrow \psi) \rightarrow (E\varphi \rightarrow E\psi)$$

$$\varphi / E\varphi$$

It also satisfies the T-axiom

$$E\varphi \rightarrow \varphi$$

E does *not*, however, satisfy the introspection axioms. The technical reason is that the union of reflexive, transitive, Euclidean relations is again reflexive, but not in general transitive or Euclidean. That E fails to satisfy introspection should not come as a surprise: It might very well be that every agent of a group (consisting, say, of agents 1 and 2) knows some fact p, while, for example, agent 2 does not know that 1 knows p. This situation is described by the formula

$$K_1 p \wedge K_2 p \wedge \neg K_2 K_1 p$$

As one might verify easily, this formula implies $Ep \wedge \neg EEp$.

The second kind of group knowledge that comes to mind is perhaps the knowledge of *some* agent in the group, write F for this notion, axiomatized by the axiom

$$F\varphi \leftrightarrow K_1 \varphi \vee \cdots \vee K_n \varphi$$

However, this is not such an interesting notion. It does not even satisfy the K-axiom. A better idea is to look at knowledge that is implicit in the group in the sense that if everyone shares his knowledge with everyone, it becomes knowledge in the group. Semantically, this can be obtained as follows. Consider the sets of the epistemic alternatives regarded by the agents separately. If there is communication between the agents, they can help each other to rule out epistemic alternatives. In fact, what remains after such a group communication, is the intersection of the sets of epistemic alternatives. Thus, one can directly define an accessibility relation $R_G = \cap_{i=1}^n R_i$, and associate a modal operator G with it by means of

$$\mathcal{M}, s \models G\varphi \text{ iff } \mathcal{M}, t \models \varphi \text{ for every } t \text{ with } R_G(s, t)$$

Of course, one may wonder as to the properties/axiomatization of such an operator. It is directly clear that apart from K-axiom and necessitation it also satisfies

$$K_i \varphi \rightarrow G\varphi$$

However, somewhat surprisingly, since this axiom appears to express only that $R_G \subseteq \cap_{i=1}^n R_i$, this is already sound and complete, as shown by, for example, van der

Hoek and Meyer (1992). The rather technical details are omitted here, but the secret is that this type of modal logic is too coarse to distinguish between models where $R_G = \cap_{i=1}^n R_i$ and those where $R_G \subseteq \cap_{i=1}^n R_i$, so that due to this 'deficiency' one can still obtain completeness!

Although the above notion of group knowledge seems intuitively clear at first sight, it is not completely evident what it amounts to exactly. This is also reflected somewhat in the history of the naming of the operator: the operator was first called 'implicit' knowledge by, for example, Halpern and Moses (1985), then renamed 'distributed' knowledge by Halpern and Moses (1992). However, as it is shown in van der Hoek et al. (1999 [1995]), both the properties of implicitness and of 'distributedness' are debatable for the notion of group knowledge as defined above. In particular, it is shown that, without further restrictions on the models, it may happen that group knowledge is really stronger than what can be derived from the agents' individual knowledge, when pooled together by means of communication, which is rather counter-intuitive!

Another very interesting notion that has been introduced and studied in the literature is that of *common knowledge*. Something is common knowledge within a group of agents if not only everybody in the group knows it but also the fact that it is known by everyone is known by everyone, and the same for this fact, *ad infinitum*. Thus, intuitively one would define common knowledge of φ, denoted $C\varphi$, as $E\varphi \wedge EE\varphi \wedge \cdots$. However, infinite formulas are not part of our logical language.

Formally, given an n agent Kripke model $M = \langle S, \pi, R_1, \ldots, R_n \rangle$, the accessibility relation R_C associated with the modal operator C is given as the (reflexive) transitive closure of the relation R_E: $R_C = R_E^*$. This means that $R_C(s, t)$ iff there is a sequence $s = s_0, s_1, \ldots, s_m = t$ such that $R_E(s_i, s_{i+1})$ for all $0 \le i \le m-1$. This means that the relation R_C connects all those possible worlds that are in 0 or more steps accessible via the relation R_E, or in other words, via some relation R_i, where at each step a different R_i may be chosen.

If the relations R_i are assumed to be equivalence relations (**S5**), this definition amounts to the following validities, which are taken as axioms for the modality C:

(K_C) $C(\varphi \to \psi) \to (C\varphi \to C\psi)$

(T_C) $C\varphi \to \varphi$

(K_G) $G(\varphi \to \psi) \to (G\varphi \to G\psi)$

(T_G) $G\varphi \to \varphi$

(4_G) $G\varphi \to GG\varphi$

(5_G) $\neg G\varphi \to G\neg G\varphi$

(KE) $E\varphi \leftrightarrow (K_i\varphi \wedge \cdots \wedge K_m\varphi)$

(EC) $C\varphi \to EC\varphi$

$(C\text{-ind})$ $C(\varphi \to E\varphi) \to (\varphi \to C\varphi)$

and to complete the system one takes rules *modus ponens* (MP) and

(N_i) $\varphi / K_i \varphi$

(N_C) $\varphi / C\varphi$

In addition to a multi-agent version of the system **S5** (with the axioms and rules for each operator K_i) the resulting system can again be proven to be sound and complete, which due to the rather complex notion of C is not exactly obtained *sine cura* (Meyer and van der Hoek, 1995). Note that the modality C satisfies the same basic **S5**-like axioms and rules. Furthermore, note the axiom C-ind, which, as its name suggests, is a kind of induction axiom to capture the infinite behaviour of the C-modality in a finite axiom! In semantical terms, it really is about induction along the R_C relation. It states that if anywhere along a chain of R_E-related worlds it holds that if φ holds somewhere, it also holds one R_E-related world further, then if φ holds at the beginning of such a chain then it holds also at every world along the chain (which is exactly the same as saying that in the intial world it is common knowledge that φ).

9.7. Conclusion

This chapter has taken a peek into epistemic (and doxastic) logic, the logic of knowledge and belief. More accurately, it has looked at epistemic logic as a special branch of *modal* logic. This has led to consideration of possible world models as a suitable semantics for epistemic logic, and the modal systems **S4** and **S5** for knowledge, and **K(D)45** for belief. As seen, this sometimes gave too idealized properties of knowledge and belief, giving rise to the problem(s) of logical omniscience. This, in turn, gave rise to approaches in the literature where the possible world semantics was modified (or 'polluted' if one prefers this term) to cope with that problem. The more properties one wants to avoid, the more one has to deviate (pollute) from Kripke-style possible world semantics with non-standard elements. Finally some more sophisticated notions and issues have been discussed, such as other systems for knowledge that have been proposed in the literature, systems in which knowledge and belief can be reasoned with at the same time, and epistemic notions that are related to a group of agents.

Suggested further reading

First of all, Lenzen (1980) is a 'classic' comprehensive textbook on epistemic logic in German; it is written from a philosophical perspective and also covers the notion of probability. A number of issues touched on in this chapter are elaborated much more extensively by Meyer and van der Hoek (1995). For example, much more attention is paid to the formal aspects of the logics of knowledge and belief, such as the issue of completeness, while the logical omniscience problem and various ways of dealing with it are also treated in more depth. Here too one may find material on the relation of knowledge (and epistemic logic more in particular) with defeasible (or 'nonmonotonic') reasoning in AI. Some of the more technical material on that will also appear in a compact form in the author's forthcoming chapter (Meyer,

2001), of the new edition of the *Handbook of Philosophical Logic*. Fagin et al. (1995) is an influential book, which emphasizes employing epistemic logic for reasoning about dynamic (computer-based) systems. Many fundamental results are presented on how knowledge may evolve (e.g., be obtained) within computer networks where the communication links are not completely secure, in the sense that information may be lost or mutilated in the communication process. The successful series of proceedings of the TARK (Theoretical Aspects of Reasoning about Knowledge, and later Theoretical Aspects of Rationality and Knowledge) and LOFT (LOgic and the Foundations of game and decision Theory) conferences on the multi-disciplinary use of epistemic logic (especially in computer science and economic theory) are also worth mentioning; see, for example, Bacharach et al. (1997), Gilboa (1998), and Halpern (1986). Finally, Laux and Wansing (1995) offers a recent collection of papers on modern topics in epistemic logic.

Acknowledgments

The author wishes to thank Rogier van Eijk and Wiebe van der Hoek for discussions on the topics treated in this chapter. Rogier is also greatly thanked for his help with the figure that appears in it.

Notes

1   Voorbraak (1991, 1993) generalizes the argument to defend **S5** as the logic of distributed systems to refer to **S5** as the logic of *objective knowledge*, a weak kind of knowledge that may be ascribed to artificial systems, like computer-based systems or even a thermometer. In this case, the so-called introspective axioms have little to do with true introspection by an agent, but rather are a way of expressing that nested forms of knowledge (like KK, or $K\neg K$) can always be eliminated by reducing it to non-nested forms of knowledge (like K and $\neg K$, respectively).

2   Admittedly, these conditions lack the elegance and beauty of those for standard Kripke models in order to deal with impossible worlds where truth is defined rather syntactically by means of the function σ. However, it is rather natural to still demand the validity of the introspection axioms, and therefore these conditions are added for the sake of completeness.

3   Actually, Kraus and Lehmann (1986) propose a much richer system involving notions like common knowledge, which we will encounter later on. Here we consider the part of the system involving only the modal operators K and B.

References

Bacharach, M. O. L., Gérard-Varet, L.-A., Mongin, P. and Shin, H. S. (eds.) 1997: *Epistemic Logic and the Theory of Games and Decisions*, (Kluwer, Dordrecht).

Bull, R. A. and Segerberg, K. 1984: "Basic Modal Logic," in *Handbook of Philosophical Logic*, Vol. II, D. Gabbay and F. Guenthner, eds., (D. Reidel, Dordrecht), 1–88.

Chellas, B. F. 1980: *Modal Logic: An Introduction*, (Cambridge University Press, Cambridge).

Fagin, R. and Halpern, J. Y. 1988: "Belief, Awareness and Limited Reasoning," *Artificial Intelligence*, 34, 39–76.

Fagin, R., Halpern, J. Y., Moses, Y. and Vardi, M. Y. 1995: *Reasoning about Knowledge*, (The MIT Press, Cambridge, Massachusetts).

Gettier, E. 1963: "Is Justified True Belief Knowledge?," *Analysis*, 23, 121–3.

Gilboa, I. (ed.) 1998: *Theoretical Aspects of Rationality and Knowledge, Proceedings of the 7th Conference*, (Morgan Kaufmann, San Francisco).

Halpern, J. Y. (ed.) 1986: *Theoretical Aspects of Reasoning about Knowledge, Proceedings of the 1986 Conference*, (Morgan Kaufmann, Los Altos, CA).

Halpern, J. Y. and Moses, Y. O. 1985: "A Guide to the Modal Logics of Knowledge and Belief," in *Proceedings of the 9th International Joint Conference on Artificial Intelligence*, A. Joshi, (ed.), (Morgan Kaufmann, Los Altos, CA), 480–90.

Halpern, J. Y. and Moses, Y. O. 1990: "Knowledge and Common Knowledge in a Distributed Environment," *J. ACM*, 37, 549–87.

Halpern, J. Y. and Moses, Y. O. 1992: "A Guide to Completeness and Complexity for Modal Logics of Knowledge and Belief," *Artificial Intelligence*, 54, 319–79.

Hintikka, J. 1962: *Knowledge and Belief*, (Cornell University Press, Ithaca, NY).

van der Hoek, W. 1993: "Systems for Knowledge and Belief" *J. of Logic and Comp.*, 3, 173–95.

van der Hoek, W. and Meyer, J.-J. Ch. 1992: "Making Some Issues of Implicit Knowledge Explicit," *Int. J. of Foundations of Computer Science*, 3, 193–223.

van der Hoek, W., van Linder, B. and Meyer, J.-J. Ch. 1999: "Group Knowledge Isn't Always Distributed (Neither Is It Always Implicit)," *Mathematical Social Sciences*, 38, 215–40.

Hughes, G. E. and Cresswell, M. J. 1984: *A Companion to Modal Logic*, (Methuen, London).

Kraus, S. and Lehmann, D. 1986: "Knowledge, Belief and Time," in *Proceedings of the 13th Int. Colloquium on Automata, Languages and Programming*, Rennes, LNCS 226, L. Kott, ed., (Springer-Verlag, Berlin), 186–95.

Kripke, S. 1963: "Semantic Analysis of Modal Logic," *Zeitschrift für Mathematische Logik und Grundlagen der Mathematik*, 9, 67–96.

Laux, A. and Wansing, H. (eds.) 1995: *Knowledge and Belief in Philosophy and Artificial Intelligence*, (Akademie Verlag, Berlin).

Lenzen, W. 1980: *Glauben, Wissen und Wahrscheinlichkeit, Systeme der epistemische Logik*, (Springer-Verlag, Vienna).

Lewis, C. I. 1912: "Implication and the Algebra of Logic," *Mind* (N.S.), 21, 522–31.

Meyer, J.-J. Ch. 2001: "Modal Epistemic and Doxastic Logic," in *Handbook of Philosophical Logic*, 2nd edn., Vol. 10, D. Gabbay, ed. (Kluwer Academic Publishers, Dordrecht).

Meyer, J.-J. Ch. and van der Hoek, W. 1995: *Epistemic Logic for AI and Computer Science*, (Cambridge University Press, Cambridge).

Montague, R. M. 1974: "Pragmatics," in *Contemporary Philosophy: A Survey*, R. Klibansky, ed., (La Nuovo Italia Editrice, Florence), 1968, 102–122; reprinted in R. Montague, *Formal Philosophy*, R. Thomason, ed., (Yale University Press, New Haven), 95–118.

Pollock, J. L. 1986: *Contemporary Theories of Knowledge*, (Hutchinson, London).

Rantala, V. 1982: "Impossible World Semantics and Logical Omniscience," *Acta Philosophica Fennica*, 35, 106–15.

Scott, S. D. 1970: "Advice on Modal Logic," in *Philosophical Problems in Logic*, K. Lambert, ed., (D. Reidel, Dordrecht), 143–73.

Thijsse, E. 1992: "Partial Logic and Knowledge Representation," PhD Thesis, Tilburg University, 1992.

Voorbraak, F. 1991: "The Logic of Objective Knowledge and Rational Belief," in *Logics in AI (Proceedings of JELIA '90)*, LNCS 478, J. van Eijck, ed., (Springer-Verlag, Berlin), 499–516.

Voorbraak, F. 1993: "As Far as I Know: Epistemic Logic and Uncertainty," PhD Thesis, Utrecht University, Utrecht.

—————— Chapter 10 ——————

Temporal Logic

Yde Venema

10.1. Introduction

Time must be the most paradoxical concept our minds have to deal with. To quote from the *Confessions* of St. Augustine:

> What then, is time? If no one asks me, I know; but if I wish to explain it to someone who should ask me, I do not know.

One of time's most puzzling aspects concerns its ontological status: on the one hand, it is a subjective and relative notion, based on our conscious experience of successive events; yet, on the other hand, our civilization and technology are based on the understanding that something like objective, absolute Time exists. Some philosophers have taken this paradox so far as to conclude that time is unreal; others, accepting the existence of absolute time, have engaged in heated debates regarding its structure, be it linear or circular, bounded or unbounded, dense or discrete.

Even leaving such metaphysical issues aside, time obviously plays such a fundamental role in our thinking that there is a clear need for *precise reasoning* about it, such as is seen in physics, formal linguistics, computer science, and artificial intelligence (AI). While these enterprises are not necessarily concerned with the *same* concept of time, they all could go under the heading of temporal logic. Often, however, a more restricted, technical definition is used in which temporal logic – or tense logic – is a branch of *modal* logic, an approach that began about forty years ago with the work of Arthur Prior. This chapter is largely confined to this modal perspective, though, as shall be seen, this still includes a great variety of systems.

Section 10.2 discusses some of the most well-known mathematical modelings of time. These are the structures the formal languages of temporal logic are designed to talk about. The main part of this chapter, section 10.3, is devoted to a fairly detailed exposition of Prior's basic tense logic; the aim of this is not only to present this particular system, but perhaps even more to introduce the kinds of questions that temporal logicians tend to ask. Sections 10.4 and 10.5 describe some extensions

—————— 203 ——————

and alternatives to this base system. Section 10.6 sketches some developments that have taken place over the last ten years or so. Finally, the Epilogue attempts to answer the question: what *is* temporal logic?

10.2. Flows of Time

Before starting a discussion of various logics of time, it helps to look at some standard mathematical models of time. When asked to think of time in an abstract way, many people will form a picture of a line – only the simplest of the many spatial metaphors that people use for temporal concepts! The mathematics of this picture is given by a set of time points, together with an ordering relation and perhaps a metric measuring the distance between two points. Section 10.5 discusses some objections and alternatives to this point-based paradigm. For now, consider formally representing time as a *frame*; that is, a structure $\mathcal{T} = (T, <)$ such that $<$ is a binary relation on T, called the *precedence relation*. Elements of T are called *time points*; if a pair (s, t) belongs to $<$, s is said to be *earlier than t*. The remainder of this section discusses a number of more or less intuitive conditions that have been imposed on such structures to make them useful as models of time. (This section frequently uses first- and second-order logic for describing these properties; the *first order frame language* used here has only one dyadic predicate symbol, which is denoted by R and interpreted as $<$.)

Obviously, many frames will not qualify as intuitively acceptable representations of time. At a minimum, one should require that $<$ be irreflexive and transitive. Call a frame satisfying these conditions a *flow of time*. Flows of time are known from mathematics as strict partial orders, and, in accordance with this, familiar notation like $s > t$ will be used for 's is later than t' and $s \le t$ for 'either $s = t$ or $s < t$'. For a point t, the set $\{s \in T \mid t < s\}$ will be called the *future of t*; the *past of t* is defined likewise. (In the sequel, definitions pertaining to the past are omitted if they mirror an obvious counterpart for the future.)

Standard candidates are given by the familiar orderings of well-known number sets: $\mathcal{N} = (\mathbb{N}, <)$ (the natural numbers), $\mathcal{Z} = (\mathbb{Z}, <)$ (the integer numbers), $\mathcal{Q} = (\mathbb{Q}, <)$ (the rational numbers) and $\mathcal{R} = (\mathbb{R}, <)$ (the real numbers). Less familiar examples are the *binary tree* $\mathcal{B} = (\mathbb{B}, <)$ (where $\mathbb{B}$ is the set of sequences of 0s and 1s, while $s < t$ holds if s is an initial segment of t), and four-dimensional *Minkowski spacetime* $\mathcal{S} = (\mathbb{R}^4, \lhd)$; here, $(x_0, x_1, x_2, t) \lhd (x'_0, x'_1, x'_2, t')$ if not only the temporal component of the first point is smaller than that of the second one ($t < t'$), but also the spatial distance between the two points should enable one to *reach* the one point from the other without having to travel faster than the speed of light.

Observe that this definition excludes circular time: if there were a series of time points $s_1 < s_2 < \cdots s_n < s_1$ then by transitivity $s_1 < s_1$ which is not possible since the flow of time is assumed to be irreflexive. Since it is not the *logician*'s task to choose between different ontologies, why not allow circular time? After all, many civilizations have regarded time as being essentially cyclic in nature. Also, practical applications of circular time are easily conceivable, such as the construction of rotas. The only reason is simply that circular time has received very little attention in the logical literature.

On the other hand, the reader may have missed one condition in the definition of a flow of time, namely linearity. A strict partial ordering is called *linear* if any two distinct points are related; expressed in first-order logic, the structure is to satisfy the sentence $\forall xy(Rxy \lor x = y \lor Ryx)$. This perspective on time is dominant in science and, probably for that reason, has become the standard in most people's minds; in particular, all of the given number examples are linear flows of time. Nevertheless, so-called *branching-time* structures such as $\mathcal{B}$ and $\mathcal{S}$ have received a lot of attention in the literature on temporal logic. A structure is called *branching to the future* if there is some point having two unrelated points in its future, and *not branching to the future*, if, on the contrary, the future of each point is linearly ordered. A flow of time is *not branching* if it is neither branching to the future nor branching to the past; note that this condition differs from linearity in that it does not exclude 'parallel' time lines. In the literature, one often encounters the condition that flows of time are allowed to branch to the future, but not to the past; this condition reflects the idea that at any moment, the past is determined while the future is not. As shall be seen later, the logic of branching time ties up with the logic of necessity and possibility, i.e., with alethic modal logic [see chapter 7]. The sequel of this section is confined to linear time, but this is not to say that the concepts to be defined would not make sense outside of this context.

Questions concerning the boundedness of time have occupied philosophers, theologians and physicists for centuries, but for the logician this is generally not the most interesting issue. It suffices just to mention the definitions pertaining to the future: $\mathcal{T}$ has a first point if it satisfies $\exists x \forall y(Rxy \lor x = y)$, while it is called *right-serial* if each point has a non-empty future.

A more fundamental choice, it seems, is that between *denseness* and *discreteness* of a flow of time. A linear ordering $\mathcal{T}$ is dense if between any two distinct points there is a third point; formally: $\forall xy(Rxy \to \exists z(Rxz \land Rzy))$. Because this way of representing time is very convenient for modeling the notion of movement, dense flows of time such as the orderings of the rational or the real numbers are common. However, for computer scientists and economists, time has a very different flavor in that it is supposed to proceed in discrete *steps*: with each non-final point is associated a *next* point or *immediate successor*, i.e., $\forall xy(Rxy \to \exists z(Rxz \land \neg \exists u(Rxu \land Ruz)))$. Standard examples of discrete flows of time are given by the natural or the integer numbers.

Density is often confused with *continuity*. Suppose that the set of rational numbers is cut into a left and a right half, of numbers smaller and bigger than $\sqrt{2}$, respectively. Such a cut, without a proper point on either edge, is called a *gap*, and a flow of time is called *continuous* if it has no gaps. $\mathcal{Q}$ thus forms the standard counterexample, whereas $\mathcal{R}$ and $\mathcal{Z}$ are continuous.

Unlike the properties discussed before, continuity is essentially a second-order notion, its definition necessarily involving a quantification over *sets* of time points. There are many other interesting second-order conditions that one may impose on temporal structures. For example, one might argue that abstract time exists independently of the events 'filling it,' and that therefore, the structure of time should be 'the same everywhere.' One way of making this precise is to demand that a flow of time is *homogeneous*: for any two points s and t of T, there should be an automorphism of T (that is, a bijection f from T onto T satisfying $x < y$ iff (if and only if) $f(x) < f(y)$ for all x and y in T) mapping s to t. Another second-order property that is met further on is that of having finite intervals; this means that there can be at most finitely many points between any two points. Observe that this condition implies discreteness of both $<$ and $>$.

10.3. Basic Temporal Logic

This section shows temporal logic at work. That is, it presents Prior's basic system of temporal logic, and discusses some of the fundamental logical questions pertaining to it.

10.3.1. *Syntax and semantics*

To define the syntax and semantics of temporal logic, one should first note that temporal logic is an extension of classical propositional logic. Recall that classically, propositional formulas are interpreted as truth values (either 1 for 'true' or 0 for 'false'); this truth value is inductively determined by a *valuation*: a function mapping propositional variables to truth values. Once the valuation is known, the truth value of any formula is fixed. Now what to do with the fact that the truth value of statements like

It is raining.

or

I am carrying an open umbrella.

will *change* from time to time? For instance, it may be raining today but sunny tomorrow; or, I may be carrying my umbrella up now but fold it some time after the rain stops.

The first basic idea underlying temporal logic is to make valuations time-dependent; more precisely, one associates a separate valuation with each point of a given flow of time. Formally, let $T = (T, <)$ be a flow of time; a *valuation* on T is a map $\pi: (T \to (\Phi \to \{0, 1\}))$. ($\Phi$ denotes the set of propositional variables.) A *model* is a pair $M = (T, \pi)$ consisting of a flow of time and a valuation.

Observe that, with this definition, one can already interpret classical formulas in each point of a model in a standard way. For instance, the formula $p \wedge \neg q$ is said to be true at a time point t precisely if $\pi(t)(p) = 1$ and $\pi(t)(q) = 0$. The spice of temporal logic, however, lies in its second basic idea, namely to use *new*, non-classical connectives to relate the truth of formulas in possibly *distinct* time points. This section discusses two such operators: *F* and *P*. These names are mnemonics for 'future' and 'past' respectively: the intended meaning of the formula '$F\varphi$' is 'at some time in the future, φ is the case,' while '$P\varphi$' is to be read as 'at some time in the past, φ holds.'

Formally, define the set L_t of *Priorean formulas* as the smallest set containing the propositional variables that is closed under constructing new formulas using the Boolean connectives $\neg$ and $\wedge$, and the temporal operators *G* and *H*. For technical reasons, take *F* and *P* to be *defined* operators in this set-up; $F\varphi$ abbreviates $\neg G \neg \varphi$ and $P\varphi$ abbreviates $\neg H \neg \varphi$. $G\varphi$ and $H\varphi$ are read as 'henceforth, φ' and 'hitherto, φ,' respectively. As further abbreviations, use $\bot, \top, \wedge, \rightarrow$ and $\leftrightarrow$ in their usual meaning. Note also that the *mirror image* of a formula is simply the formula one obtains by simultaneously replacing all *H*s with *G*s and vice versa.

Bringing the previous observations together, gives the following inductive definition of the notion of *truth* of a formula φ at a time point t in a model $M = (T, <, \pi)$:

$$M, t \Vdash q \qquad \text{if } \pi(t)(q) = 1$$

$$M, t \Vdash \neg\varphi \qquad \text{if not } M, t \Vdash \varphi$$

$$M, t \Vdash \varphi \wedge \psi \qquad \text{if } M, t \Vdash \varphi \text{ and } M, t \Vdash \psi$$

$$M, t \Vdash G\varphi \qquad \text{if } M, s \Vdash \varphi \text{ for all } s \text{ with } t < s$$

$$M, t \Vdash H\varphi \qquad \text{if } M, s \Vdash \varphi \text{ for all } s \text{ with } t > s \qquad (10.1)$$

If $M, t \Vdash \varphi$ then φ is said to *hold* or *be true at t*.

As an example, consider the ordering $\mathcal{N}$ of the natural numbers; let τ be the valuation making q true at all numbers bigger than 1000, and r at all even numbers. With this valuation, it is easy to see that the formula FGq holds at the point 0. For, the formula Gq holds at those points of which the future is a subset of the set of 'q-points,' and this is the case for any number bigger than 999. But from $M, 1000 \Vdash Gq$ and $0 < 1000$ it follows that $M, 0 \Vdash FGq$. It is likewise easy to see that the formula FGr does *not* hold at 0, or indeed, at any point in this model; the formula GFr on the other hand holds throughout M.

Finally, observe that from the *technical* point of view, this system is very similar to systems of alethic modal logic [see chapter 7] since *G* and *H* are very much like the necessity operator *L*. The difference is that in Priorean temporal logic there are *two* modal operators instead of one. One might then expect that one would interpret this language in structures with *two* accessibility relations, say, R_F and R_P. And, in fact, it is possible to adopt a perspective in which one sees $<$ and $>$ as these two distinct accessibility relations; however, it is a crucial aspect of temporal logic that these two accessibility relations are each other's converse. The main distinction between alethic modal logic and temporal logic is thus one of aim: temporal logic starts with structures (flows of time), for which one is trying to find good modal description languages; whereas, in alethic modal logic, it has more often been the other way around.

10.3.2. *Validity and definability*

Temporal logicians are generally not so much interested in the truth or falsity of formulas in specific models, but rather in those formulas that remain true throughout the flow of time even if the valuation is changed. It is felt that such formulas provide essential information concerning the structure of the underlying flow of time. Formally, a formula φ is said to be *valid* on a flow of time T (notation: $T \Vdash \varphi$) if for every valuation π on T, and every point of T, (T, π), $t \Vdash \varphi$. A formula is valid in a class of flows of time if it is valid on each member of the class. The notion of satisfiability is defined dually: a formula φ is said to be *satisfiable* in a flow of time (a class of flows of time) if its negation is not valid on the flow of time (in the class of flows of time, respectively).

As an example, it can be shown that the formula $Fq \rightarrow FFq$ is valid on the class of dense linear orderings. Assume that T is a dense linear flow of time; to show that $Fq \rightarrow FFq$ holds on it, consider an arbitrary valuation π on T, and an arbitrary point t in T such that (T, π), $t \Vdash Fq$. By the truth definition, there is a later point s where q holds. But by density, there must be some point u between t and s; from $u < s$, Fq holds at u; but then $t < u$ implies that FFq holds at t; since t and π were arbitrary, this suffices to show that $T \Vdash Fq \rightarrow FFq$.

On the other hand, it is easy to see that the formula $Fq \rightarrow FFq$ is not valid on the ordering of the integers. For, take the points 0 and 1 and consider the valuation π that makes q true *only* at 1; then obviously, Fq is true at 0; but since there is no integer number between 0 and 1, the formula FFq cannot be true at 0. This shows that indeed $Z \nVdash Fq \rightarrow FFq$. It is possible, in fact, to generalize this argument to show that the formula $Fq \rightarrow FFq$ can be falsified on *every* non-dense frame. For, any non-dense frame must contain two points $s < t$ without intermediate points; so the valuation making q true only at t will make the formula $Fq \rightarrow FFq$ false at s. Hence, the formula $Fq \rightarrow FFq$ is very informative; it is a reliable witness of the density of a flow of time.

In general, a Priorean formula φ is said to *define* a class C of flows of time within a class K if for every flow of time T in K, $T \Vdash \varphi$ iff T belongs to C. If C is given as the class of frames satisfying some first-order property α, φ is also said to correspond to α (within K). For instance, as has just been seen, the formula $Fq \rightarrow FFq$ corresponds to density.

Not every property of flows of time is definable; for instance, one can prove that there is no Priorean formula that defines the class of branching flows of time. On the other hand, there is a formula defining the flows of time that are *not* branching; for, the formula $PFq \rightarrow (Pq \vee q \vee Fq)$ corresponds to non-branchingness to the future. Hence, the conjunction of this formula and its mirror image defines the flows of time that are not branching.

Especially if flows of time confined to linear orderings, many interesting properties *can* be defined in the Priorean language. In this list, a number of such correspondences holding for linear flows of time are given, together with the names of the modal formulas. Here, $\Diamond\varphi$ abbreviates $P\varphi \vee \varphi \vee F\varphi$, and $\Box\varphi \equiv H\varphi \wedge \varphi \wedge G\varphi$.

Having a first point	$H\bot \lor PH\bot$	(A1)
Left-seriality	$P\top$	(A2)
Having a final point	$G\bot \lor FG\bot$	(A3)
Right-seriality	$F\top$	(A4)
Discreteness	$(F\top \land q \land Hq) \to FHq$	(A5)
Density	$Fq \to FFq$	(A6)
Continuity	$(Fq \land \Diamond\neg q \land \Box(q \to Hq)) \to$ $\Diamond((q \land G\neg q) \lor (\neg q \land Hq))$	(A7)
Having finite intervals	$(G(Gq \to q) \to (FGq \to Gq)) \land$ $(H(Hq \to q) \to (PHq \to Hq))$	(A8)

Finally, since Priorean formulas may be interpreted on *all* frames (also ones that are not strictly partial orders), the question naturally arises whether the class of flows of time itself is definable. Since, analogous to the case of ordinary modal logic, transitivity may be defined by the formula $Gp \to GGp$, this reduces to the problem of finding a correspondent for irreflexivity (within the class of transitive frames). Unfortunately, there is *no* such formula.

10.3.3. *Axiomatics*

As mentioned already, temporal logic starts with flows of time; but obviously, this does not diminish the interest in finding complete calculi for various classes of flows of time. Obviously, there are close connections with the axiomatics of alethic modal logic [see chapter 7]. In particular, analogous to **K**, there is a *minimal temporal* logic for the Priorean language as well; it is called **K**$_t$ and defined as the smallest class of Priorean formulas that is closed under the following axioms and derivation rules:

(CT)	all classical propositional tautologies	
(DB)	$G(q \to r) \to (Gq \to Gr)$	
	$H(q \to r) \to (Hq \to Hr)$	(*Distribution*)
(CV)	$q \to GPq$	
	$q \to HFq$	(*Converse*)
(4)	$Gq \to GGq$	(*Transitivity*)
(US)	if φ is a theorem, then so is $\varphi[\psi/q]$	(*Uniform substitution*)
(MP)	if φ and $\varphi \to \psi$ are theorems, then so is ψ	(*Modus ponens*)
(TG)	if φ is a theorem, then so are $G\varphi$ and $H\varphi$	(*Temporal generalization*)

Here $\varphi[\psi/q]$ denotes the result of substituting the formula ψ for the propositional variable q, uniformly throughout φ.

Most of these axioms and all of these rules are, perhaps under different names, familiar from ordinary modal logic. The exception is the Converse axiom (CV); as will be seen, this axiom is needed to ensure that the accessibility relations for the operators G and H are each other's converse. The formula (4) reflects the transitivity of the intended accessibility relation of a modal operator [see chapter 7]; thus, our constraints on flows of time explain its presence as an axiom. Recall from the previous subsection that the property of being irreflexive is not definable in the Priorean language; now notice that irreflexivity does not even yield any extra validities. (This is not the rule in modal logics: frame conditions that are not definable in the modal language may nevertheless *imply* the validity of modal formulas.)

> **Theorem 10.1** The logic K_t is sound and complete with respect to the class of all flows of time.

For lack of space, the proof of Theorem 10.1 is omitted. Instead, this section concentrates on completeness for the class of linear flows of time. Let **Lin** be the extension of K_t with the axiom (NB), which is the conjunction of the axiom $PFq \to (Pq \vee q \vee Fq)$ (defining non-branching to the future) and its mirror image $FPq \to (Fq \vee q \vee Pq)$.

> **Theorem 10.2** The logic **Lin** is sound and complete with respect to the class of linear flows of time.

Proof This proof method makes use of familiar canonical models [see chapter 7]. Let W^c be the set of maximal **Lin**-consistent sets of formulas, and define the relation R^c on W^c by $R^c wv$ iff $\varphi \in v$ for all $G\varphi \in w$. The structure $\mathcal{F} = (W^c, R^c)$ is called the *canonical frame*; on it, define the *canonical valuation* π^c so that $\pi^c(q)(w) = 1$ iff $p \in w$.

The first aim is to prove a Truth Lemma for this model, stating that for all Priorean formulas and every point w of the *canonical* model $\mathcal{M}^c = (\mathcal{F}^c, \pi^c)$ 'truth coincides with membership':

$$\mathcal{M}^c, w \Vdash \varphi \text{ iff } \varphi \in w \qquad (10.2)$$

As usual, (10.2) is proved by formula induction. There is only one minor problem, caused by the fact that now there are two modal operators, and only the one accessibility relation. This is precisely where the Converse axioms come in: they make it possible to show that the canonical accessibility relation not only works well for G but also for H. For, it can be proved (details are left to the reader) that $R^c wv$ iff $\varphi \in w$ for all $H\varphi \in v$.

Now it follows easily from (10.2) that every **Lin**-consistent set of formulas is satisfiable in the canonical model, but unlike the case of modal logics like **S4** it does not finish here. It is important to satisfy the **Lin**-consistent set of formulas in a linear flow of time. Now it is easy to verify that the canonical accessibility relation is transitive (use the axiom (4), as in modal completeness proofs); it is not very difficult to show that R^e is not branching (the details of this proof are left to the reader – use the axiom (NB)); but it is impossible to prove that R^e is a linear ordering, because in general this will not be true! The main problem is that nothing guarantees irreflexivity of canonical accessibility relation. The difficult part of the proof consists in showing that it is possible to *transform* the canonical frame into a strict linear order, while truth of formulas is preserved.

A frame $\mathcal{F} = (W, R)$ is called a *pseudo-line* if R is transitive and strongly connected, i.e., satisfying $\forall xy(Rxy \vee x = y \vee Ryx)$. Now given any maximal **Lin**-consistent set Σ, it is possible to restrict consideration to the part of the canonical frame that is connected (via R^e) to Σ and still prove the analogue of the Truth Lemma (10.2). It thus follows that every consistent formula is satisfiable in a pseudo-line. But then the missing link in the proof of the completeness theorem for **Lin** is the following claim.

If φ is satisfiable on a pseudo-line, then also on a linear flow of time. (10.3)

To prove claims like (10.3), several methods of 'frame surgery' have been developed; to give the reader an idea of such techniques, a brief sketch of the *bulldozing* method is given here. Assume that φ is satisfiable in the model $\mathcal{M} = (\mathcal{F}, \pi)$ based on the pseudo-line $\mathcal{F} = (W, R)$. The first observation is that $\mathcal{F}$ may be represented as a linear ordering $<$ of so-called *clusters* which are special subsets of W. Each point s of W belongs to a unique cluster C_s which is either *degenerate* (consisting of a single irreflexive point) or *proper* (if R is universal on it). The relation $<$ is defined such that $C_s < C_t$ iff $C_s \neq C_t$ and Rst.

The key idea is now to 'bulldoze' each proper cluster into a special linear ordering L_C and to replace each C with L_C. Obviously, replacing each proper cluster with a linearly ordered model yields a linear order; but is φ still satisfiable in the new model? To understand the positive answer to this question, note that any proper cluster introduces an infinity of information recurrence in both the forward and backward directions: one can follow paths within C, moving either forwards and backwards along R, for as long as one pleases. Thus, when a cluster C is replaced with a linear ordering, it is important to ensure that the linear ordering duplicates all the information in C infinitely often, and in both directions. Bulldozing does precisely this, in the most straightforward way possible. For instance, suppose that the cluster C has three elements only: s_0, s_1 and s_2, with associated classical valuations σ_0, σ_1 and σ_2. Then L_C is given as the model $(\mathbb{Z}, \pi_C)$; here π_C is given by $\pi_C(z) = \sigma_{z \bmod 3}$; that is, L_C consists of an unbounded (in both directions) series of points with associated classical valuations σ_0, σ_1 and σ_2, as in $\ldots \sigma_1 \sigma_2 \sigma_0 \sigma_1 \sigma_2 \sigma_0 \ldots$.

There is thus an obvious relation linking points in the new, transformed model to points in the old one; using this one may prove that φ is indeed satisfiable in the new model. This finishes the proof sketch of (10.3). QED

Turning to the axiomatics of specific structures, let us define the following logics:

Lin.N:	Lin +A1 +A4 +A8
Lin.Z:	Lin +A2 +A4 +A8
Lin.Q:	Lin +A2 +A4 +A6
Lin.R:	Lin +A2 +A4 +A6 +A7

For these logics, the following result applies.

Theorem 10.3 The logics **Lin.N, Lin.Z, Lin.Q** and **Lin.R** are sound and complete axiomatizations of the set of validities of the flows of time $\mathcal{N}$, $\mathcal{Z}$, $\mathcal{Q}$ and $\mathcal{R}$, respectively.

One may conclude that temporal logicians have been rather successful in axiomatizing the standard flows of times and the most natural classes of flows of time. Nevertheless, it would be wrong to conclude that conversely, (axiomatically defined) tense logics are always characterized by a class of flows of time. As in modal logic, incompleteness is the rule; in fact, the very first example of an incomplete (poly-)modal logic was found in tense logic.

10.3.4. *Decidability and complexity*

The completeness theorems mentioned in the previous subsection are important, of course, but if one wants to do actual reasoning in one of these logics, further properties are required. Minimally, one wants the logic to be decidable; i.e., the existence is required of a terminating algorithm separating the logic's theorems from its non-theorems. Fortunately, all the complete logics defined in the previous subsection have this property. More explicitly:

Theorem 10.4 The Priorean tense logics of the classes of all flows of time, and of all linear flows of time, are decidable.

This follows from the fact that these logics are finitely axiomatizable and have the *finite model property*. The latter may be proved through the method of *filtrations* or the method of mini-canonical models [see chapter 7], with allowance for complexities analogous to the proof of completeness for **Lin**.

For practical purposes, decidability is not enough, however; one would like to have an efficient calculus. A more fine-grained analysis is needed to reveal the *computational complexity* of temporal logics. There is not enough space to go into details here, but only mention the result that the satisfiability problem for linear time is in NP. To be more precise, one can devise a non-deterministic Turing machine algorithm that correctly tells whether a Priorean formula φ is satisfiable in a linear frame or not, while arriving at this answer within $f(\varphi)$ computation steps. Here f is a linear function that grows at the same rate as the length of the formula φ.

10.4. Extending the Language

The discussion in section 10.3 was based on the basic temporal language having G and H as its only primitive operators. For many applications, however, this language is too poor in expressivity, and several extensions with new operators have been suggested. This section examines some of the most important of these, especially the terms 'since' and 'until,' and also operators for branching time structures.

10.4.1. Since and until

Hans Kamp introduced two dyadic operators, S and U, with the intended meaning of 'since' and 'until', as in the sentences

Ever since the roof caved in, it's been wet in the house.

and

Until we get the roof fixed, it will be damp in the house.

Let $\mathcal{L}_{su}$ denote the extension of the Priorean language with these two new connectives, the formal truth definition of which is given as follows.

$\mathcal{M}, t \Vdash U\varphi\psi$ if $\mathcal{M}, s \Vdash \varphi$ for some s such that $t < s$
and $\mathcal{M}, u \Vdash \psi$ for all u with $t < u < s$

$\mathcal{M}, t \Vdash S\varphi\psi$ if $\mathcal{M}, s \Vdash \varphi$ for some s such that $s < t$
and $\mathcal{M}, u \Vdash \psi$ for all u with $s < u < t$

It is interesting to observe that the 'old' operators can be expressed in this new language, for instance $F\varphi$ may be seen to abbreviate $U\varphi\top$. But conversely, the new operators really add expressive power to the language; it can be proved that they cannot be defined in terms of the old.

Another interesting temporal operator is the so-called *nexttime* or *tomorrow* operator X; the formula $X\varphi$ holds at a time point t if φ holds at the next moment in time (if there is such a next moment). Obviously, such an operator only makes sense in a discrete flow of time, as, for instance, in computer science, where one wants to talk about the next state of a process. However, adding this new connective to $\mathcal{L}_{su}$ would not add any expressive power, since $X\varphi$ can already be defined as an abbreviation for $U\varphi\bot$.

This raises the question whether perhaps *every* temporal operator can be defined in this apparently expressive language $\mathcal{L}_{su}$. The answer to this question is positive; i.e., it is possible to prove some sort of *functional completeness* result for $\mathcal{L}_{su}$.

Theorem 10.5 (Kamp) Over the class of linear, continuous orderings, every temporal operator can be defined in $\mathcal{L}_{su}$.

Note: By 'temporal operator' is meant any operator whose truth definition is expressible in first-order logic. The restriction in the theorem to certain flows of time is essential. In particular, once the condition of linearity is dropped, the results tend to be negative; for instance, over the class of all flows of time it is not possible to find a *finite* expressively complete set of operators.

Finally, for the language $\mathcal{L}_{su}$ one can ask the same kind of questions as for $\mathcal{L}_t$; and indeed, several results have been proved concerning definability, axiomatizability and decidability. In general, these results are positive, but there is not enough space to give details here.

10.4.2. Branching time languages

As mentioned above, allowing flows of time that branch to the future means that one can no longer assume that the past determines everything that is going to happen. But if the formalism has to take into account that there are many *different* courses of events possible, it seems appropriate to pay somewhat more attention to the truth definition of the future operator F. For, the intuitive meaning of $F\varphi$, namely 'it will be the case that φ,' is now more ambiguous than in linear flows of time. Recall that the interpretation of $F\varphi$ that can be calculated from the truth definition (10.1) yields 'φ holds at some future moment of some possible course of events.' But it does not seem to be unreasonable to assume that 'it will be the case that φ' expresses the speaker's conviction that φ will be the case, in the *actual* course of events, or perhaps *no matter what* course of events. These two interpretations give rise to respectively the Ockhamist and Peircean schools in branching time logic.

To compare these two approaches, assume our flows of time to be *trees*, i.e., connected strict partial orders that do not branch to the past. (Connectedness forbids, for instance, parallel time lines.) A *branch* of a tree $\mathcal{T} = (T, <)$ is a maximal linearly ordered subset of T; the intuitive idea is that each branch through t represents a possible course of events (for a point t and a branch b, t is said to *lie on* b or that b *goes* through t if t belongs to b). In this way, one can imagine a *possible future* of t as the set of all *later* points on some fixed branch b through t; since $\mathcal{T}$ is a tree, each point will have a unique past.

Now Peircean branching time logic interprets the proposition 'it will be the case that φ' in the second way indicated above, namely that φ is bound to happen in every possible future. To make this more precise, define the Peircean tense language as the extension of the Priorean one with the future operator $F_\square$; this operator has a second-order definition, involving a quantification over all branches through the actual time point:

$$\mathcal{M}, t \Vdash F_\square \varphi \text{ if for every branch passing through } t$$
$$\text{there is some } s > t \text{ with } \mathcal{M}, s \Vdash \varphi \qquad (10.4)$$

In the Ockhamist approach on the other hand, it is *meaningless* to ask about the truth value of formulas of the form $F\varphi$ or $G\varphi$ at a time point t, unless one has specified which of the possible futures of t one has in mind. To be able to express that something that will be the case no matter what form the future will take, Ockhamists extend the language with an alethic modal operator $\square$. Ockhamist temporal logic is thus an interesting combination of modal and temporal logic; perhaps the easiest way to work out the idea formally, is to require that in Ockhamist semantics the truth value of *any* formula is evaluated at a *pair* consisting of a time point and a branch through this point (representing the actual course of events). This leads to the following truth definition.

$\mathcal{M}, t, b \Vdash q$ if $\pi(t)(q) = 1$

$\mathcal{M}, t, b \Vdash \neg\varphi$ if not $\mathcal{M}, t, b \Vdash \varphi$

$\mathcal{M}, t, b \Vdash \varphi \wedge \psi$ if $\mathcal{M}, t, b \Vdash \varphi$ and $\mathcal{M}, t, b \Vdash \psi$

$\mathcal{M}, t, b \Vdash G\varphi$ if $\mathcal{M}, s, b \Vdash \varphi$ for all s on b with $t < s$

$\mathcal{M}, t, b \Vdash H\varphi$ if $\mathcal{M}, s, b \Vdash \varphi$ for all s on b with $t > s$

$\mathcal{M}, t, b \Vdash \square\varphi$ if $\mathcal{M}, t, c \Vdash \varphi$ for all branches c through t (10.5)

It is interesting to note that the Peircean language can be seen as a *fragment* of the Ockhamist one; consider the inductively defined translation $(\cdot)^o$ mapping Peircean formulas to Ockhamist ones. The only non-trivial clause of this map concerns the future operators:

$$(F_\square\varphi)^o = \square F\varphi^o \quad \text{and} \quad (G\varphi)^o = \square G\varphi^o$$

It is straightforward to prove that, for all tree models $\mathcal{M}$, all points t in $\mathcal{M}$ and all branches b through t

$\mathcal{M}, t \Vdash \varphi$ iff $\mathcal{M}, t, b \Vdash \varphi^o$

Many results are known concerning Peircean and Ockhamist logic; for instance, axiomatizations have been found for the Peircean logic of the class of all trees. This logic is also known to be decidable, as is its Ockhamist alternative. It is an open problem to find an explicit axiomatization for the Ockhamist tree logic.

Finally, it is obvious that one can extend these branching time logics even further, for instance with the Since and Until operators defined earlier. The 'future fragment' of such systems is closely related to so-called *computational tree logics* that have been developed within theoretical computer science for the purpose of reasoning about paths through labeled transition systems, which in their turn form perhaps the simplest mathematical models of the notion of computation. It is interesting to note that the Peircean and the Ockhamist approaches in philosophical logic find (much more technically inspired) counterparts in the development of the computational tree logics: CTL and CTL*, respectively.

10.5. Time Periods

So far time has been represented by a point-based paradigm. Nevertheless, it seems that, in every field where temporal logics are used or studied, at a certain moment systems are designed in which *periods*, rather than points, are the central entities, or at least, play a more prominent role.

10.5.1. Motivations

The point-based perspective has never been without philosophical objections. For instance, Zeno's paradox of the flying arrow, which, it is argued, cannot change position at a isolated moment of time and thus cannot move at all, makes it clear that there is something problematic about representing time as a series of durationless moments if one wants to describe the concept of movement. Some temporal predicates seem simply not to apply to time points. Suppose that p is a proposition formalizing the statement that Zeno's arrow moves. Obviously, the flying of an arrow is an activity that is extended in time; hence, one might argue that it is pointless to evaluate the truth of p at moments of time. It thus seems that, at least, one needs the existence of time periods for the evaluation of certain expressions.

Apart from such semantic considerations, it is clear that time points are not the kind of objects that one can directly perceive. Due to years of exposure to the scientific view on time it may not be possible always to realize this, but if one wants to base reality on direct experience, then time points will come out as highly abstract and complex artifacts. Thus, it has been argued, it is a dubious enterprise to take points as having primitive ontological status; periods form a far sounder base. This second argument has been taken up, with a more practical twist, within AI. Here the idea has been advocated that period-based representations of time are simpler and more natural in formalizing common sense reasoning than the standard scientific models. (Obviously, this argument may be pushed further, questioning the Newtonian perspective in which absolute Time exists regardless of anything happening in it. Such objections may lead to *event-based* ontologies which due to lack of space cannot be discussed here.)

Finally, in our discussion until now it has been assumed that there is a clear and intuitive distinction between points and periods. This is questionable as well, however; one can quite convincingly argue that there is a notion of *granularity* involved here. A good example can be taken from computer science, where the multiplication of two numbers may be taken as an atomic, durationless action of a high-level programming language, whereas it may be implemented in terms of many operations on the lower level of the machine language.

10.5.2. Time in periods

It is important to observe that the need for a more prominent role of periods does not necessarily commit one to model time in structures in which periods are *primitive* entities; they might as well be *derived* objects.

Indeed, one could well start from a flow of time $T = (T, <)$ as described earlier, and then consider the question how to represent chunks of time within such a structure. For instance, periods could be defined as *convex* sets: subsets C of T that are uninterrupted in the sense that whenever s and a later point t belong to C, then so does any point between s and t. A set-theoretically slightly simpler option is to only consider (closed) intervals; in this approach, the period $\{u \in T \mid s \leq u \leq t\}$ can simply be represented as the *pair* $[s, t]$. Observe that this approach has the advantage that properties of periods can be expressed by binary predicates in the first-order frame language, whereas for convex sets some kind of higher-order logic has to be used [see chapter 2].

If one opts for periods as primitive entities, the simplest mathematical modeling will involve structures consisting of a set P of periods equipped with a collection of natural relations on P. But, in contrast to the point-based approach where the temporal precedence relation is *the* candidate for such a relation, there are now many options. For instance, since one is obviously still interested in temporal precedence, the relation $<$, with $p < q$ holding if the entire period p precedes the entire period q, is a natural candidate, but so is the inclusion relation $\sqsubset$, with $p \sqsubset q$ holding if p is a proper part of q. And in fact, one widespread period-based modeling of time is that in structures of the form $\mathcal{P} = (P, <, \sqsubset)$. But $<$ and $\sqsubset$ are not the only candidates. If one is interested in relations that are close to common sense experience, then the relation of one period overlapping with another is quite relevant as well. And this need not be confined to binary relations at all: a unary predicate may be needed to determine whether a period is of zero duration (and hence, point-like), whereas there are also interesting ternary relations such as the relation C holding of a triple p, q, r if p can be 'chopped' into the two pieces q and r. Of course, just like in the point-based case, one needs to impose conditions on period structures to make them useful as models of time. For instance, in a structure of the kind $\mathcal{P} = (P, <, \sqsubset)$ one will want $<$ and $\sqsubset$ to be strict partial orders that are related by conditions like $\forall xyz(x \sqsubset y < z \rightarrow x < z)$ and others.

The reader may have realized how hard it is to gather one's intuitions and make a complete list of such conditions without taking resort to talking about points after all. The concept of a point in time has obviously been very useful in our thinking about time. Hence, even if periods are to be taken as the primitive entities of one's ontology, it is at least interesting, if not a test for the viability of the proposal, to see whether one can *construct* point-based flows of time from period structures. Various ways have been worked out for this purpose. Perhaps the simplest method is to take as points those periods that have zero duration – of course, this only works if such entities are around and there is access to this information (for instance, through a zero-duration predicate as mentioned above). But even if the period structure does not have atomic periods, there are ways to extract a point structure from it, for instance, by defining a point to be any maximal set of mutually overlapping pairs of periods. Finally, once there are ways to construct point structures from period structures and vice versa, the obvious question is to see how such constructions interact. This line of research has been taken up with great mathematical sophistication, in a number of cases even leading to interesting categorical dualities.

10.5.3. Interval-based temporal logic

Just as in the case for point-based temporal logics, one may choose a class of period structures, design a formal language to talk about it, and study the resulting temporal logic.

For instance, imagine working with intervals in point-based flows of time, as described above. Taking the modal approach, one is presented with a multi-dimensional setting; i.e., one wants to evaluate formulas at *pairs* of points representing the beginning and the end point of the interval, respectively. Typical modal operators are $\langle D \rangle$ and $\circ$ with rules of truth given by

$$\mathcal{M}, [s, t] \Vdash \langle D \rangle \varphi \quad \text{if } \mathcal{M}, [u, v] \Vdash \varphi \text{ for some } t, u \text{ with } s \le u \le v \le t$$

$$\mathcal{M}, [s, t] \Vdash \varphi \circ \psi \quad \text{if } \mathcal{M}, [s, u] \Vdash \varphi \text{ and } \mathcal{M}, [u, t] \Vdash \psi \text{ for some } u \text{ with } s \le u \le t$$

In words, $\langle D \rangle \varphi$ holds at an interval if φ holds at some interval *during* it, while $\varphi \circ \psi$ holds at an interval if it can be chopped into a φ- and a ψ-part. In period terms, one would say that $\sqsubseteq$ and C are the accessibility relations of $\langle D \rangle$ and $\circ$, respectively.

For such modal systems, one may investigate meta-logical properties like completeness and decidability. The general picture here is that one has a price to pay for the increase in expressivity: complete axiomatizations are scarce and hard to find, and undecidability is the rule rather than the exception. On a technical level, the modal logic of time periods thus seems to be more complex (and hence, more intriguing) than point logics over the same flows of time, but the *kinds* of questions that are asked do not differ much.

Hence, to finish, this section mentions some issues that are of specific interest to period logics. To start with, period logics differ from point logics in the sense that, in many cases, it is natural to correlate the interpretation of atomic propositions. A condition that one often encounters is that of *homogeneity* requiring that an atomic proposition holds at a period iff it holds at each of its parts. It is obvious that such a condition only has intuitive appeal for the propositions corresponding to the event categories of states and activities. And even in the latter case, one may raise objections to the 'only if' part of this condition: I can truthfully say that I have been *walking* through town for hours when in fact, I have paused a couple of times to take a coffee.

Now suppose that this condition is being implemented on some interval structure $I(\mathcal{T})$ induced by the flow of time $\mathcal{T}$ by demanding that for each propositional variable p and each point-based valuation π we have

$$(I(\mathcal{T}), \pi), [s, t] \Vdash p \text{ iff } \pi(u)(p) = 1 \text{ for all } u \text{ with } s \le u \le t \tag{10.6}$$

Observe that thus we have effectively reduced period predicates to point predicates. Such a reduction would have considerable computational advantages, something that can easily be explained by taking a first-order perspective. It is obvious that the particular proposal (10.6) is rather naive: Zeno's moving arrow will lead one into trouble. But perhaps there are more inventive modelings in which formulas can be evaluated at periods, while the valuations remain point-based?

In any case, regardless of the technical advantages of reducing period predicates to point predicates, it is clear that there is a rather general philosophical issue at stake here, namely the problem of which *kinds* of predicates apply to periods and points, respectively, and how these are correlated. This issue is in fact a matter of ongoing, and at times heated, debate.

10.6. Temporal Logic Now

As mentioned before, temporal logic has become a vast and active research area with applications in many disciplines. This section briefly sketches some of these recent developments. Since not all of the work mentioned here is covered by the monographs mentioned in the Suggested Further Reading, references are provided to the literature.

10.6.1. Richer ontological structures

One common trend in temporal logic is to study logics of richer ontological structures since it is obvious that for serious real-world applications the kind of temporal logics that have been described so far are too simple. For example, one shortcoming of standard temporal logics is that they only deal with qualitative timing properties, whence they are inadequate for applications such as reasoning about real-time behavior of software. To overcome this deficiency, people have designed logics for describing two-sorted structures consisting of a linear flow of time connected with some metric domain. Such approaches can be found both in the point-based (Montanari and de Rijke, 1997) and in the period-based (Hansen and Chaochen, 1997) paradigm. Another example of a multiple sorted ontology has already been met in the semantics of Ockhamist branching time logic, where branches appeared as a second kind of entities, next to points. One might vary on this 'standard' Ockhamist logic by admitting only some instead of all branches, perhaps a collection satisfying some addition constraints (Zanardo, 1996). Applying this idea of using multiple sorted temporal ontologies to the discussion of the previous section, one can envisage structures in which points, periods and events co-exist, linked by suitable relations (Gardent et al., 1994). One possibility for such a link involves the notion of granularity: atomic objects might suddenly turn out to be divisible when approached at a different level. This obviously ties up with the way of classifying periods of time (months, weeks, days); modal logics for such layered structures are described by Montanari (1996).

10.6.2. Temporal logic at work

Turning temporal logics into actual working systems has created a number of interesting problems and challenges. For instance, one of the most fundamental contributions that AI has made to the field of temporal logic, is that of identifying the *frame problem*. This is the problem of formalizing the properties of an application area that are unaffected by the performance of some action without explicitly summing up *all* such properties. This problem appears to be independent of the particular formalism employed, and has to be faced by anyone wishing to give a formal account of reasoning about change (Sandewall and Shoham, 1995). The computer science literature on modal logics of time has yielded an interesting perspective on the modal truth relation ($\mathcal{M}, t \Vdash \varphi$) between a model $\mathcal{M}$, which is supposed to be finite, and a formula φ; in this perspective φ represents some property of a program and $\mathcal{M}$ some implementation of the program. For obvious reasons then, a considerable amount of effort has been devoted to finding fast *model checking* algorithms deciding whether a given formula holds in a given finite model (Stirling, 1999). As a last example, notice the *dynamic turn* which research in the semantics of natural language has taken. In this way of thinking, the meaning of a formula does not lie so much in its truth condition; linguistic expressions are rather like programs that update the information state of some agent. For instance, in *Discourse Representation Theory* (Kamp and Reyle, 1993) [see chapter 20] temporal expressions in natural language are used to extend and refine temporal representations of the discourse; these representations in their turn are syntactic items themselves that can be interpreted in standard models.

10.6.3. *Temporal logic in context*

There is an increasing tendency to study modal formalisms not as isolated systems but in connection with other branches of logic, as in *Correspondence Theory* which relates modal logic to first- and second-order logic. For instance, the use of game-theoretic methods has deepened our understanding of the relative expressive power of modal logics of time: in particular, variants of Ehrenfeucht–Fraïssé games have provided an interesting perspective on expressive completeness results such as Theorem 10.5 (Immerman and Kozen, 1987; Venema, 1990). Recent approaches to decidability questions concerning modal and temporal logics use insights from algebraic logic and automata theory. This has led to the identification of a variety of decidable fragments of first-order logic, each of which is obtained from atomic formulas using all Boolean connectives but allowing only a specific, guarded pattern of quantification (Andréka et al., 1998). Finally, notice the emergence of so-called hybrid languages which aim to boost the expressive power of modal languages by adding some features from first-order logic like 'names' (special variables that are to be true at a single state), over which quantification is allowed (Blackburn and Tzakova, 1999; Goranko, 1994).

10.7. Epilogue

What then, is temporal logic?

In the narrowest sense, temporal logic comprises the design and study of specific systems for representing and reasoning about time, such as Prior's tense logic. These enterprises may have both an applied and a theoretical side, the former consisting of designing a system (i.e., making choices in the fields of ontology, syntax and semantics), formalizing temporal phenomena in it, and then putting it to work (perhaps through implementing it). On the theoretical side, one aims to prove formal properties of the system, such as completeness or decidability.

On a slightly wider scale, temporal logicians may thus provide a supply of general tools and techniques for answering questions pertaining to specific systems. As an example, note the method of filtration which is a quite general method of proving decidability of a temporal logic, and the canonical model method which is very useful in proving completeness results.

A more ambitious aim for temporal logicians is to devise frameworks for comparing and connecting different modelings of time. This aim can be realized both at a technical and at a philosophical level. As an example of the first, think of the game-theoretic analysis of the expressive power of modal languages, or of the duality between point and period-based representations of time, respectively. On a philosophical level, a thorough classification of event types and of the correlation between predicates pertaining to points and to periods, respectively, would be an extremely useful tool in any discussion on formal representations of temporal phenomena.

Since all of this is relevant for each of the disciplines where formal reasoning about time is needed, temporal logic forms a prime example of the growing role of logic as a source and channel of ideas and techniques applicable in related disciplines. Ultimately, one would hope that temporal logic can provide a unifying perspective on our sometimes confusing thoughts about this highly puzzling thing we call time.

Suggested further reading

This chapter has only scratched the surface of temporal logic. The following monographs, each surveying part of the field of temporal logic, would form a good start for a bibliography. Concerning the philosophy of time, I do not believe there is one standard reference, but Whitrow (1980) offers a very comprehensive study of the concept of time, while Le Poidevin and MacBeath (1993) bring together some seminal articles on the subject. Øhstrøm and Hasle (1995) give a good treatment of philosophical aspects of temporal logic from a historical perspective. Goldblatt (1987) provides the reader with a concise and very accessible treatment of the most important modal logics of time; Gabbay et al. (1994) give a more extensive mathematical treatment. Manna and Pnueli (1991) have produced a classic on applications of temporal logic in computer science; Gabbay et al. (1995) give a good overview of the applications of temporal logic in AI. There seems to be no monograph on the treatment in formal linguistics of temporal aspects of natural language, but Steedman (1997) surveys the field well. Van Benthem (1991) offers a stimulating blend of much of the above. Finally, for an overview of recent developments in temporal logic, the reader is referred to the proceedings of the first two conferences devoted solely to temporal logic, ICTL'94 (Gabbay and Ohlbach, 1994) and ICTL'97 (Barringer et al., 1999).

Acknowledgments

The research of the author has been made possible by a fellowship of the Royal Netherlands Academy of Arts and Sciences. Personal thanks are due to Johan van Benthem for helpful comments on a draft version of this chapter, to Marco Aiello for a scrutinous reading of the manuscript, and to Lou Goble for extensive help in cutting the manuscript to an acceptable size.

References

Andréka, H., van Benthem, J. and Németi, I. 1998: "Modal Logics and Bounded Fragments of Predicate Logic," *Journal of Philosophical Logic*, 27, 217–74.

Barringer, H., Fisher, M., Gabbay, D. and Gough, G. (eds.) 1999: *Proceedings of the Second International Conference on Temporal Logic*, (Kluwer Academic Press, Dordrecht).

van Benthem, J. 1991: *The Logic of Time*, 2nd edn., (Kluwer, Dordrecht).

Blackburn, P. and Tzakova, M. 1999: "Hybrid Languages and Temporal Logic," *Logic Journal of the IGPL*, 7, 27–54.

Gabbay, D. M. and Ohlbach, H. J. (eds.) 1994: *Temporal Logic. Proceedings of the First International Conference, ICTL '94*, vol. 827 of *Lecture Notes in Computer Science*, (Springer-Verlag, Berlin).

Gabbay, D. M., Hodkinson, I. and Reynolds, M. 1994: *Temporal Logic: Mathematical Foundations and Computational Aspects*, (Oxford University Press, Oxford).

Gabbay, D. M., Hogger, C. J. and Robinson, J. A. (eds.) 1995: *Handbook of Logic and AI and Logic Programming*, vol 4 (Epistemic and Temporal Reasoning), (Oxford University Press, Oxford).

Gardent, C., Blackburn, P. and de Rijke, M. 1994: "Back and Forth through Time and Events," in Gabbay and Ohlbach (1994, 225–37).

Goldblatt, R. 1987: "Logics of Time and Computation," *CSLI Lecture Notes*, 2nd edn, (Center for the Study of Language and Information, Standford University).

Goranko V. 1994: "Temporal Logic with Reference Pointers," in Gabbay and Ohlbach (1994, 133–48).

Hansen, M. and Chaochen, Z. 1997: "Duration Calculus: Logical Foundations," *Formal Aspects of Computing*, 9, 283–330.

Immerman, N. and Kozen, D. 1987: "Definability with Bounded Number of Bound Variables," in *Proceedings of the Conference on Logic in Computer Science (LICS '87)*, (Computer Society Press, Washington), 236–44.

Kamp, H. and Reyle, U. 1993: *From Discourse to Logic*, (Kluwer, Dordrecht).

Le Poidevin, R. and MacBeath, M. (eds.) 1993: *The Philosophy of Time*, (Oxford University Press, Oxford).

Manna, Z. and Pneuli, A. 1991: *The Temporal Logic of Reactive and Concurrent Systems*, (Springer-Verlag, Berlin).

Montanari, A. 1996: "Metric and Layered Temporal Logic for Time Granularity," PhD thesis, Institute for Logic, Language and Computation, University of Amsterdam.

Montanari, A. and de Rijke, M. 1997: "Two-Sorted Metric Temporal Logic," *Theoretical Computer Science*, 183, 187–214.

Øhrstrøm, P. and Hasle, P. 1995: *Temporal Logic: From Ancient Ideas to Artificial Intelligence*, Studies in Linguistics and Philosophy, (Kluwer, Dordrecht).

Sandewall, E. and Shoham, Y. 1995: "Non-Monotonic Temporal Reasoning" in Gabbay, Hogger, and Robinson (1995, 439–98).

Steedman, M. 1997: "Temporality," in *Handbook of Logic and Language*, J. van Benthem and A. ter Meulen, eds., (Elsevier Scientific Publishers, Amsterdam), 895–938.

Stirling, C. 1999: "Bisimulation, Modal Logic, and Model Checking Games," *Logic Journal of the IGPL*, 7, 103–24.

Venema, Y. 1990: "Expressiveness and Completeness of an Interval Tense Logic," *Notre Dame Journal of Formal Logic*, 31, 529–47.

Whitrow, G. J. 1980: *The Natural Philosophy of Time*, (Clarendon Press, Oxford).

Zanardo, A. 1996: "Branching-Time Logic with Quantification over Branches," *Journal of Symbolic Logic*, 61, 1–39.

Chapter 11

Intuitionistic Logic

Dirk van Dalen

11.1. Basic Principles

There are basically two ways to view intuitionistic logic: as a philosophical–foundational issue in mathematics; or as a technical discipline within mathematical logic. Considering first the philosophical aspects, for they will provide the motivation for the subject, this chapter follows L. E. J. Brouwer, the founding father of intuitionism. Although Brouwer himself contributed little to intuitionistic logic as seen from textbooks and papers, he did point the way for his successors.[1]

Logic in Brouwer's intuitionism takes a secondary place; the first is reserved for mathematics, which should be understood in the widest possible sense, as the constructional mental activity of the individual.[2] The role of logic is to note and systematically study certain regularities in the mathematical constructional process. Contrary to traditional views, logic is thus dependent on mathematics and not vice versa.

Mathematical practice shows that a relatively few logical connectives suffice for an efficient treatment of arguments. In the case of intuitionism, the meaning of the connectives has to be explained in terms of the basic mathematical notion: construction. A fact A is established by means of a construction. An easy example is $3 + 2 = 5$, which is established by the following construction: construct 3, construct 2 and compare the outcome with the result of the construction of 5. The outcome is a confirmation of the above equation.

The construction criterion for 'truth' also yields an interpretation of the connectives.[3] Write '$a : A$' for 'a is a construction that establishes A'; then this a a called a *proof* of A.

A proof of $A \wedge B$ is simply a pair of proofs a and b of A and B. For convenience, here is a notation for the pairing of constructions, and for the inverses (projections): (a, b) denotes the pairing of a and b, and $(c)_0$, $(c)_1$, are the first and second projection of c. The proof of a disjunction $A \vee B$ is a pair (p, q) such that p carries the information of which disjunct is correct, and q is the proof of it. Stipulate that $p \in \{0, 1\}$, so $p = 0$ and $q : A$ or $p = 1$ and $q : B$. Note that this disjunction is *effective*, in the sense that the disjunct is specified; this contrasts with classical logic, where one does not have to know which disjunct holds.

Negation is also defined by means of proofs: '$p : \neg A$' says that each proof a of A can be converted by the construction p into a proof of an absurdity, say $0 = 1$. A proof of $\neg A$ thus tells us that A has no proof!

The most interesting propositional connective is implication. The classical solution, i.e., $A \rightarrow B$ is true if A is false or if B is true, cannot be used because this uses classical disjunction; moreover, it assumes that the truth values of A and B are known before one can settle the status of $A \rightarrow B$. Heyting, however, showed that this is asking too much. Consider

A = 'there occur twenty consecutive 7s in the decimal expansion of π'

and

B = 'there occur nineteen consecutive 7s in the decimal expansion of π'

Then $\neg A \lor B$ does not hold constructively, but the implication, $A \rightarrow B$ is obviously correct.

The intuitionistic approach, based on the notion of proof, demands a definition of a proof a of the implication $A \rightarrow B$ in terms of (possible) proofs of A and B. The idea is quite natural: $A \rightarrow B$ is correct if one can show the correctness of B as soon as the correctness of A has been established. Thus: $p : A \rightarrow B$ if p transforms each proof $q : A$ into a proof $p(q) : B$. The meaning of the quantifiers is specified along the same lines. Assume a given domain D of mathematical objects. A proof p of $\forall x A(x)$ is a construction which yields for every object $d \in D$ a proof $p(d) : A(d)$. A proof p of $\exists x A(x)$ is a pair (p_0, p_1) such that $p_1 : A(p_0)$. Thus the proof of an existential statement requires an instance plus a proof of this instance.

The full list is given in Table 11.1. (Observe that an equivalent characterization of the disjunction can be given: $a = (a_1, a_2)$, where $a_1 = 0$ and $a_2 : A$ or $a_1 = 1$ and $a_2 : B$.)

This *proof interpretation* is now demonstrated for a few statements:

1 $A \rightarrow (B \rightarrow A)$

An operation p is needed that turns a proof $a : A$ into a proof of $B \rightarrow A$. But if there is already a proof $a : A$, then there is a simple transformation that turns a

Table 11.1

$a : A$	Conditions
$a : \perp$	false
$a : A \land B$	$a = (a_1, a_2)$, where $a_1 : A$ and $a_2 : B$
$a : A \lor B$	$a = (a_1, a_2)$, where $a_2 : A$ if $a_1 = 0$ and $a_2 : B$ if $a_1 = 1$
$a : A \rightarrow B$	for all p with $p : A$, $a(p) : B$
$a : \exists x A(x)$	$a = (a_1, a_2)$ and $a_2 : A(a_1)$
$a : \forall x A(x)$	for all $d \in D$, $a(d) : A(d)$ where D is a given domain
$a : \neg A$	for all $p : A$, $a(p) : \perp$

proof $q : B$ into a proof of A, i.e., the constant mapping $q \mapsto a$, which is denoted by $\lambda q \cdot a$. And so the construction that takes a into $\lambda q \cdot a$ is $\lambda a \cdot (\lambda q \cdot a)$, or in an abbreviated notation $\lambda a \lambda q \cdot a$. Hence $\lambda a \lambda q \cdot a : A \rightarrow (B \rightarrow A)$.

2 $A \rightarrow \neg\neg A$

A proof q of $\neg\neg A$ is a proof of $\neg A \rightarrow \perp$. Assume $p : A$, and $q : \neg A$. Then $q(p) : \perp$, so $\lambda q \cdot q(p) : \neg\neg A$. Hence $\lambda p \lambda q \cdot q(p) : A \rightarrow \neg\neg A$.

3 $A \vee \neg A$

$p : A \vee \neg A \Leftrightarrow (p)_0 = 0$ and $(p)_1 : A$ or $(p)_0 = 1$ and $(p)_1 : \neg A$. However, for an arbitrary proposition A it is not known whether A or $\neg A$ has a proof, and hence $(p)_0$ cannot be computed. So, in general, there is no proof of $A \vee \neg A$.

4 $\neg \exists x A(x) \rightarrow \forall x \neg A(x)$

$p : \neg \exists x A(x) \Leftrightarrow p(a) : \perp$ for a proof $a : \exists x A(x)$. One has to find $q : \forall x \neg A(x)$, i.e. $q(d) : A(d) \rightarrow \perp$ for any $d \in D$. So pick an element d and let $r : A(d)$, then $(d, r) : \exists x A(x)$ and so $p((d, r)) : \perp$. Therefore put $(q(d))(r) = p((d, r))$, so $q = \lambda r \lambda d \cdot p((d, r))$ and hence $\lambda p \lambda r \lambda d \cdot p((d, r)) : \neg \exists x A(x) \rightarrow \forall x \neg A(x)$.

Brouwer himself handled logic in an informal way, often showing the untenability of certain classical principles by a reduction to unproven statements, usually regarding the decimal expansion of π.[4] This technique, which goes by the name of 'Brouwerian counterexample', is illustrated with the following examples.

First, compute simultaneously the decimals of π and the members of a Cauchy sequence. Use $N(k)$ as an abbreviation for 'the decimals $p_{k-89}, \ldots, p_k$ of π are all 9.' Now define:

$$a_n = \begin{cases} (-2)^{-n} & \text{if } \forall k \leq n \neg N(k) \\ (-2)^{-k} & \text{if } k \leq n \text{ and } N(k) \end{cases}$$

a_n is an oscillating sequence of negative powers of -2 until a sequence of 90 nines occurs in π, from then onwards the sequence is constant:

$$1, -\tfrac{1}{2}, \tfrac{1}{4}, -\tfrac{1}{8}, \tfrac{1}{16}, -\tfrac{1}{32}, \ldots, (-2)^{-k}, (-2)^{-k}, (-2)^{-k}, (-2)^{-k}, \ldots$$

The sequence determines a real number a, in the sense that it satisfies the Cauchy condition. The sequence is well-defined, and $N(n)$ can be checked for each n (at least in principle). For this particular a, however, one cannot say that it is positive, negative or zero.

$a > 0 \Leftrightarrow N(k)$ holds for the first time for an even number

$a < 0 \Leftrightarrow N(k)$ holds for the first time for an odd number

$a = 0 \Leftrightarrow N(k)$ holds for no k

Since there is no effective information on the status of the occurence of $N(k)$s, one cannot affirm the trichotomy law; i.e., $\forall x \in \mathbb{R}(x < 0 \vee x = 0 \vee x > 0)$, cannot be said to have a proof. The above number a cannot be irrational, for then $N(k)$ would never apply, and hence $a = 0$. Contradiction. Hence it has been shown $\neg\neg(a$ is rational). But there is no proof that a is rational. So $\neg\neg A \to A$ fails. One also easily sees that $a = 0 \lor a \neq 0$ fails to have proof.

Such Brouwerian counterexamples are *weak* in the sense that they show that some proposition has as yet no proof, but it is not excluded that eventually a proof may be found. In formal logic, there is a similar distinction between $\nvdash A$ and $\vdash \neg A$. The Brouwerian counterexamples are similar to the first case, and strong counter-examples cannot always be expected. For example, although there are instances of the Principle of the Excluded Middle (PEM) where no proof has been provided, the negation cannot be proved. For $\neg(A \lor \neg A)$ is equivalent to $\neg A \land \neg\neg A$, which is a contradiction! Some strong refutations of classical principles are given in later sections.

11.2. Formalization of Intuitionistic Logic

In 1928, the Dutch Mathematics Society posed in its traditional prize contest a problem asking for a formalization of Brouwer's logic. Heyting sent in an essay, with the motto 'stones for bread,' in which he provided a formal system for intuitionistic predicate logic. The system was presented in 'Hilbert style' (as it is called now), i.e., a system with only two derivation rules and a large number of axioms. Heyting had patiently checked the system of Whitehead's and Russell's (1910–13) *Principia Mathematica*, and isolated a set of intuitionistically acceptable axioms. His system was chosen in such a way that the addition of PEM yields full classical logic. Here is a list of axioms for **IQC** taken from Troelstra and van Dalen (1988, p. 68).[5] (In this language negation, $\neg A$, is defined as $A \to \bot$.)

$A \land B \to A,\ A \land B \to B$

$A \to (B \to (A \land B))$

$A \to A \lor B,\ B \to A \lor B$

$(A \to C) \to ((B \to C) \to (A \lor B \to C))$

$A \to (B \to A)$

$(A \to (B \to C)) \to ((A \to B) \to (A \to C))$

$\bot \to A$

$A(t) \to \exists x A(x)$

$\forall x(A(x) \to B) \to (\exists x A(x) \to B)$

$\forall x A(x) \to A(t)$

$\forall x(B \to A(x)) \to (B \to \forall x A(x))$

(The quantifier axioms are subject to the usual conditions: t is free for x in $A(x)$ and x does not occur free in B.) There are two derivation rules: the well-known *modus ponens* (i.e., $\to E$, see below) and the rule of generalization:

$$\vdash_i A(x) \Rightarrow \vdash_i \forall x A(x)$$

where $\vdash_i$ stands for intuitionistic derivability. (When no confusion arises, $\vdash_i$ will simply be writen as $\vdash$.) The $\forall I$-rule (see below) would also have done just as well.

Gentzen (1935) introduced two new kinds of formalization of logic. Both of these are eminently suited for the investigation of formal derivations as objects in their own right. The first is the system of *Natural Deduction*, which is described here. His second kind, the *Sequent Calculus*, is not discussed although it too has important proof-theoretical applications.

In the system of Natural Deduction, there are introduction and elimination rules for the logical connectives that reflect their meanings. The rules are given here in an abbreviated notation.

$$\wedge I \qquad \frac{A \quad B}{A \wedge B}$$

$$\wedge E \qquad \frac{A \wedge B}{A} \qquad \frac{A \wedge B}{B}$$

$$\vee I \qquad \frac{A}{A \vee B} \qquad \frac{B}{A \vee B}$$

$$\vee E \qquad \frac{A \vee B \quad \overset{\displaystyle [A]}{\underset{\displaystyle C}{\mathcal{D}}} \quad \overset{\displaystyle [B]}{\underset{\displaystyle C}{\mathcal{D'}}}}{C}$$

$$\to I \qquad \frac{\overset{\displaystyle [A]}{\underset{\displaystyle B}{\mathcal{D}}}}{A \to B}$$

$$\to E \qquad \frac{A \quad A \to B}{B}$$

$$\perp E \qquad \frac{\perp}{A}$$

$$\forall I \qquad \frac{\overset{\displaystyle \mathcal{D}}{A(x)}}{\forall x A(x)}$$

$$\forall E \qquad \frac{\forall x A(x)}{A(t)}$$

$$\exists I \qquad \frac{A(t)}{\exists x\, A(x)}$$

$$\exists E \qquad \frac{\exists x\, A(x) \qquad \begin{array}{c}[A(x)]\\ \mathcal{D}\\ C\end{array}}{C}$$

There are a few conventions for the formulation of the natural deduction system.

(i) A hypothesis of a derivation between square brackets is cancelled, that is to say, it no longer counts as a hypothesis. Usually all of the hypotheses are cancelled simultaneously. This is not really required, and it may even be be necessary to allow for 'selective' cancellation (Troelstra and van Dalen, 1988, p. 559, and p. 568). For most practical purposes, however, it is a convenient convention.

(ii) For the quantifier rules, there are some natural conditions on the free variables of the rule. In $\forall I$, the variable x may not occur free in the hypotheses of $\mathcal{D}$. In $\forall E$ and $\exists I$, the term t must be free for x in $A(x)$. Finally, in $\exists E$, the variable x may not occur in C or in the remaining hypotheses of $\mathcal{D}$. For an explanation, see van Dalen (1997).

(It is worth noting that strengthening the rule $\perp E$ to the *classical absurdity rule*

$$\perp_c \quad \frac{\begin{array}{c}[\neg A]\\ \mathcal{D}\\ \perp\end{array}}{A}$$

suffices for classical logic [see chapter 1]. This rule is equivalent to having axioms of the form $\neg\neg A \to A$ or a rule of double-negation elimination. It enables the classical principle of the excluded middle, PEM, $A \vee \neg A$, to be proved.)

The intuitionistic rules above are instructive for more than one reason. In the first place, they illustrate the idea of the proof-interpretation described above. Recall that $p : A \to B$ stands for 'for every $a : A$ $(p(a) : B)$'. Now $\to E$ says that if one has a derivation $\mathcal{D}$ of A and a derivation $\mathcal{D}'$ of $A \to B$, then the combination

$$\to E \qquad \frac{\begin{array}{cc}\mathcal{D} & \mathcal{D}'\\ A & A \to B\end{array}}{B} = \frac{\mathcal{D}''}{B}$$

is a derivation of B. So there is an automatic procedure that, given $\mathcal{D}'$, converts $\mathcal{D}$ into a derivation $\mathcal{D}''$ of B.

The introduction rule also illustrates the transformation character of the implication.

$$
\text{Let } \mathcal{D} \text{ be given, then} \rightarrow I \text{ yields}
\quad
\begin{array}{c}
A \\
\mathcal{D} \\
B
\end{array}
\qquad
\begin{array}{c}
[A] \\
\mathcal{D} \\
B \\
\hline
A \rightarrow B
\end{array}
$$

The first derivation shows that by adding a proof $\mathcal{D}'$ of A, one automatically gets a proof of B. So the rules say that there is a particular construction, converting proofs of A into proofs of B. This is exactly the justification for the derivation of $A \rightarrow B$. For the conjunction rules, the analogy is even more striking. Furthermore, as will be seen below, the correspondence can be made even more explicit in the Curry–Howard isomorphism.

Both Martin-Löf (1984) and Dummett (1977) have argued that the introduction and elimination rules of a natural deduction system determine the meanings of the connectives by their use. For example, $\wedge I$ says that if one knows (has evidence for) A and B, then one also knows $A \wedge B$. So $\wedge I$ specifies what one has to require for $A \wedge B$. The elimination rule says what one may claim on the grounds of evidence for $A \wedge B$. If one knows $A \wedge B$ then one also knows A and likewise B. These rules have been chosen so that they are 'in harmony.' The evidence required in $\wedge I$ is exactly the evidence one can derive in $\wedge E$. Dummett (1975) used this feature of the rules to support his claim that intuitionistic logic fits the requirement that 'meaning is use,' insisting that mathematical knowledge be demonstrable. "The grasp of the meaning of a mathematical statement must, in general, consist of a capacity to use that statement in a certain way, or to respond in a certain way to its use by others." As a consequence the traditional, Platonistic, notion of truth has to be replaced by something more palpable; the notion of proof is exactly what will fill the need for communicability and observability. Hence the slogan "a grasp of the meaning of a statement consists in a capacity to recognize a proof of it when one is presented to us." This, of course, is in complete accord with intuitionistic practice. The rejection of the Platonistic notion of truth is indeed an aspect of Dummett's anti-realism. Brouwer had always denied the realistic thesis, that there is an outer world independent of us.

As noted above, while Hilbert designed his proof theory for the purpose of consistency proofs, Gentzen considered the structure of derivations themselves to be objects for study, and, by means of ingenious proof-theoretic techniques, a number of striking intuitionistic features can be shown, e.g., effective versions of the disjunction and existence properties for a number of theories. (These properties are discussed in section 11.3.) Moreover, these proof-theoretic methods have the advantage over the semantical approach to be discussed in section 11.3 in that these results are directly constructive.

Since natural deduction is so close in nature to the proof interpretation, it is perhaps not surprising that a formal correspondence between a term calculus and natural deduction can be established. This will be demonstrated for a small fragment, containing only the connective $\rightarrow$. Consider an $\rightarrow$ introduction:

$$\frac{\begin{array}{c}[A]\\ \mathcal{D}\\ B\end{array}}{A \rightarrow B} \qquad \frac{\begin{array}{c}[x:A]\\ \mathcal{D}\\ t:B\end{array}}{\lambda x \cdot t : A \rightarrow B}$$

Assign in a systematic way λ-terms to formulas in the derivation. Since A is an assumption, it has a hypothetical proof term, say x. On discharging the hypotheses; introduce a λx in front of the (given) term t for B. By binding x, the proof term for $A \rightarrow B$ no longer depends on the hypothetical proof x of A. Similarly, the elimination runs as follows:

$$\frac{A \rightarrow B \qquad A}{B} \qquad \frac{t:A \rightarrow B \qquad s:A}{t(s):B}$$

Observe the analogy to the proof interpretation. Consider a particular derivation.

$$\frac{\dfrac{[A]}{B \rightarrow A}}{A \rightarrow (B \rightarrow A)} \qquad \frac{\dfrac{[x:A]}{\lambda y \cdot x : B \rightarrow A}}{\lambda x \cdot \lambda y \cdot x : A \rightarrow (B \rightarrow A)}$$

Thus the proof term of $A \rightarrow (B \rightarrow A)$ is $\lambda xy \cdot x$, which is the Curry combinator **K**. Note that the informal argument of pages 225–6 is faithfully reflected.

Now consider a cut elimination conversion:

$$\frac{\dfrac{\begin{array}{c}x:B\\ \mathcal{D}\\ t:A\end{array}}{\lambda x \cdot t : B \rightarrow A} \qquad \dfrac{\mathcal{D}'}{s:B}}{(\lambda x \cdot t)(s):A} \qquad \text{reduces to} \qquad \frac{\dfrac{\mathcal{D}'}{s:B}}{\dfrac{\mathcal{D}[s/x]}{t[s/x]:A}}$$

The proof theoretic conversion thus corresponds to the β-reduction of the λ-calculus.

To deal with full predicate logic, specific operations need to be introduced to render the meaning of the connectives and their derivation rules. Here is a list:

$$\begin{cases} p & \text{pairing} \\ p_0, p_1 & \text{projections} \end{cases}$$

$$\begin{cases} D & \text{discriminator ('case dependency')} \\ k & \text{case obliteration} \end{cases}$$

E Witness extractor

$\bot$ *ex falso* operator

$\wedge I$ $\quad \dfrac{t_0:A_0 \quad t_1:A_1}{p(t_0,t_1):A_0 \wedge A_1}$

$\wedge E$ $\quad \dfrac{t:A_0 \wedge A_1 \ (i \in \{0, 1\})}{p_i(t):A_i}$

$\vee I$ $\quad \dfrac{t:A_i \ (i \in \{0, 1\})}{k_i:A_0 \vee A_1}$

$\vee E$ $\quad \dfrac{t:A \vee B \quad t_0[x^A]:C \quad t_1[x^B]:C}{D_{u,v}(t, t_0[u], t_1[v]) \cdot C}$

$\rightarrow I$ $\quad \dfrac{t[x^A]:B}{\lambda y^A \cdot t[y^A]:A \rightarrow B}$

$\rightarrow E$ $\quad \dfrac{t:A \rightarrow B \quad t':A}{t(t'):B}$

$\perp E$ $\quad \dfrac{t:\perp}{\perp_A(t):A}$

$\forall I$ $\quad \dfrac{t[x]:A(x)}{\lambda y \cdot t[y]:\forall y A(y)}$

$\forall E$ $\quad \dfrac{t:\forall x A(x)}{t(t'):A(t')}$

$\exists I$ $\quad \dfrac{t_1:A(t_0)}{p(t_0, t_1):\exists x A(x)}$

$\exists E$ $\quad \dfrac{t:\exists x A(x) \quad t_1[y, z^{A(y)}]:C}{E_{u,v}(t, t_1[u, v]):C}$

There are a number of details to mention:

(i) In $\rightarrow I$, the dependency on the hypothesis has to be made explicit in the term. This is done by assigning to each hypothesis its own variable, e.g., $x^A : A$.

(ii) In $\vee E$ (and similarly $\exists E$) the dependency on the particular (auxiliary) hypotheses A and B disappears. This is done by a variable binding technique. In $\vee E$ and $\exists E$, $D_{u,v}$ and $E_{u,v}$ bind the variables u and v.

(iii) In the falsum rule, the result, of course, depends on the conclusion A. So A has its own *ex falso* operator $\perp_A$.

Now the conversion rules for the derivation automatically suggest the conversion for the term.[6]
    Given the correspondence between the term calculus and the natural deduction system, one may see a correspondence between proofs and propositions on the one hand and elements (given by the terms) and types (the spaces where these terms are to be found). This was first observed for the implication fragment by Curry

(Curry and Feys, 1958, ch. 9, section E), and extended to full intuitionistic logic by Howard (1980). Here is a simple case, the fragment considered by Curry.

Since the meaning of a proposition is expressed in terms of possible proofs – one knows the meaning of A if one knows what things qualify as its proofs – one may take an abstract view and consider a proposition as its collection of proofs. From this viewpoint, there is a striking analogy between propositions and sets. A set has elements, and a proposition has proofs. As seen, proofs are actually a special kind of construction, and they operate on each other. For example, if there is a proof $p : A \rightarrow B$ and a proof $q : A$ then $p(q) : B$. So proofs are naturally typed objects.

Similarly, one may consider sets as being typed in a specific way. If A and B are typed sets then the set of all mappings from A to B is of a higher type, denoted by $A \rightarrow B$ or B^A. Starting from certain basic sets with types, one can construct higher types by iterating this 'function space'-operation. Denote 'a is in type A' by $a \in A$. Then there is the striking parallel shown in Table 11.2.

Table 11.2

Propositions	Types
$a : A$	$a \in A$
$p : A \rightarrow B$, $q : A \Rightarrow p(q) : B$	$p \in A \rightarrow B$, $q \in A \Rightarrow p(q) \in B$
$x : A \Rightarrow t(x) : B$ then $\lambda x \cdot t : A \rightarrow B$	$x : A \Rightarrow t(x) \in B$ then $\lambda x \cdot t \in A \rightarrow B$

It now is a matter of finding the right types corresponding to the remaining connectives. For $\wedge$ and $\vee$, a product type and a disjoint sum type are introduced. For the quantifiers, generalizations are available. The reader is referred to the literature: Gallier (1995) and Howard (1980).

The main aspect of the Curry–Howard isomorphism (also known as 'formulas – or propositions – as types') is the faithful correspondence:

$$\frac{\text{proofs}}{\text{propositions}} = \frac{\text{elements}}{\text{types}}$$

with their conversion and normalization properties. [See chapter 13, section 13.8, for some related discussion.]

Martin-Löf was the first logician to see the full importance of the connection between intuitionistic logic and type theory. Indeed, in his approach, the two are so closely interwoven that they actually merge into one master system. His type systems are no mere technical innovations, but they intend to catch the foundational meaning of intuitionistic logic and the corresponding mathematical universe. Expositions can be found in, for example, Martin-Löf (1975, 1984).

Constable and his collaborators have based a proof checking system on natural deduction and Martin-Löf's type theory. It is a tool for computer assisted development of proofs in intuitionistic systems, and it provides proof terms for provable sentences. An early exposition may be found in Constable et al. (1986); the reader should consult the modern literature for updated versions. There are a number of proof checking systems available, e.g. the system **Coq** of Coquand.

11.3. Semantics

The study of interpretations is called semantics; from this viewpoint, formulas denote certain things. Frege already pointed out that propositions denote truth values, namely 'true' and 'false', conveniently denoted by 1 and 0, and the interpretations of logic under this two-valued semantics is handled by the well-known truth-tables (van Dalen, 1997) [see chapter 1].

This method has a serious drawback: all propositions are supposed to be true or false, and PEM automatically holds (though some might perhaps see this as an advantage rather than a drawback). It certainly is too much of a good thing for intuitionistic logic. By our choice of axioms (or rules), intuitionistic logic is a subsystem of classical logic, so the two-valued semantics obliterates the distinction between the two logics: too many propositions become true!

One might say that there is no need to worry about the problem of semantics, since one already has the intended proof interpretation. Although this certainly is the case, the proof interpretation is not specific enough to yield sharp decisive results, as one would like in model theory. One would need more assumptions about 'construction', before technical problems can be settled.

All of the formal semantics discussed below are strongly complete for intuitionistic predicate and propositional logic, in the sense that

$$\Gamma \vdash_i A \Leftrightarrow \Gamma \vDash A$$

where $\vDash$ is the semantical consequence relation in the particular semantics.

11.3.1. The topological interpretation

In the mid-1930s, a number of systematic semantics were introduced that promised to do for intuitionistic logic what the ordinary truth-tables did for classical logic. Heyting had already introduced many-valued truth-tables in his formalization papers, e.g., to establish non-definability of the connectives. Then Jaśkowski (1936) presented a truth-table family that characterized intuitionistic propositional logic. Gödel (1932) had dispelled the expectation that intuitionistic logic was the logic of some specific finite truth value system.

An elegant interpretation was introduced by Tarski (1938). It was, in fact, a generalization of the Boolean valued interpretation of classical logic. Ever since Boole, it was known that the laws of that logic correspond exactly to those of

Boolean algebra (think of the powerset of a given set with $\cap$, $\cup$ and ^{c} as operations, corresponding to $\vee$, $\wedge$ and $\neg$). Now one wants a similar algebra with the property that $U^{cc} \neq U$ (for $\neg\neg A$ and A are not equivalent). By Brouwer's theorem ($\neg\neg\neg A \leftrightarrow \neg A$), one expects $U^{ccc} = U^c$. The remaining laws of logic demand that

$$(U \cap V)^{cc} = U^{cc} \cap V^{cc}$$

and

$$(U \cup V)^{cc} \subseteq U^{cc} \cup V^{cc}$$

This suggests that the operator ^{cc} behaves as a closure operator in topology. It turns out that it is a good choice to let the open sets in a topological space X play the role of arbitrary sets in the power set of X. So the family $O(X)$ plays the role of $\wp(X)$.

Here is the notation: $\llbracket A \rrbracket$ is the open set of X assigned to A. The valuation $\llbracket \cdot \rrbracket : PROP \to O(X)$ is defined inductively for all propositions; let $\llbracket A \rrbracket$ be given for all atomic A, where $\llbracket \bot \rrbracket = \varnothing$, then

$$\llbracket A \wedge B \rrbracket = \llbracket A \rrbracket \cap \llbracket B \rrbracket$$
$$\llbracket A \vee B \rrbracket = \llbracket A \rrbracket \cup \llbracket B \rrbracket$$
$$\llbracket A \to B \rrbracket = Int(\llbracket A \rrbracket^c \cup \llbracket B \rrbracket)$$
$$\llbracket \neg A \rrbracket = Int(\llbracket A \rrbracket^c)$$

Here $Int(K)$ is the interior of the set K (i.e., the largest open subset of K). Note that this looks very much like the traditional Venn diagrams, with the extra requirement that negation is interpreted by the interior of the complement. This is necessary if one wants open sets all the way. A simple calculation shows that

$$\vdash_i A \Rightarrow \llbracket A \rrbracket = X$$

Since X is the largest open set in $O(X)$, it is plausible to call A true in $O(X)$ if $\llbracket A \rrbracket = X$.

This interpretation can be used to show underivability of propositions. Consider, for example, $O(\mathbb{R})$, the open sets of real numbers. Assign to the atom A the set $(\mathbb{R} - \{0\})$. Then

$$\llbracket A \rrbracket = \mathbb{R} - \{0\}$$
$$\llbracket \neg A \rrbracket = Int(\{0\}) = \varnothing$$
$$\llbracket \neg\neg A \rrbracket = \mathbb{R}$$

So

$$\llbracket \neg\neg A \to A \rrbracket = Int\llbracket \neg\neg A \rrbracket^c \cup A$$
$$= \emptyset \cup A = A \neq \mathbb{R}$$

Hence $\not\vDash_i \neg\neg A \to A$. Similarly $\not\vDash_i A \vee \neg A$, for $\llbracket A \vee \neg A \rrbracket = A \neq \mathbb{R}$.

The topological interpretation can be extended to predicate logic. Let a domain D be given, then

$$\llbracket \exists x A(x) \rrbracket = \cup \{\llbracket A(d) \rrbracket \mid d \in D\}$$
$$\llbracket \forall x A(x) \rrbracket = Int(\cap \{\llbracket A(d) \rrbracket \mid d \in D\})$$

The topological interpretation is indeed *complete* for intuitionistic logic. Suppose that A is true in $O(X)$ if $\llbracket A \rrbracket = X$ for all assignments of open sets to atoms. *A is true* if A is true under all topological interpretations. Completeness can now be formulated as usual: $\vdash_i A \leftrightarrow A$ is true. Classical logic appears as a special case when one provides a set X with the trivial topology: $O(X) = \wp(X)$.[7]

The algebra of open subsets of a topological space is a special case of a *Heyting algebra*, which is defined, much like Boolean algebras, by axioms for the various operations. It has binary operations $\wedge$, $\vee$, $\to$, a unary operation $\neg$ and two constants, 0, 1. The laws are:

$$a \wedge b = b \wedge a$$
$$a \vee b = b \vee a$$
$$a \wedge (b \wedge c) = (a \wedge b) \wedge c$$
$$a \vee (b \vee c) = (a \vee b) \vee c$$
$$a \wedge (b \vee c) = (a \wedge b) \vee (a \wedge c)$$
$$a \vee (b \wedge c) = (a \vee b) \wedge (a \vee c)$$
$$1 \wedge a = a$$
$$1 \vee a = 1$$
$$0 \wedge a = 0$$
$$0 \vee a = a$$
$$a \to a = 1$$
$$a \wedge (a \to b) = a \wedge b$$
$$b \wedge (a \to b) = b$$
$$a \to (b \wedge c) = (a \to b) \wedge (a \to c)$$
$$\neg a = a \to 0$$

Since it is necessary for the interpretation of predicate logic to allow infima and suprema of collections of elements, one often considers *complete* Heyting algebras, i.e., algebras with the property that, for a collection $\{a_i | i \in I\}$ of elements, there is a supremum $\bigvee_{i \in I} a_i$ (the unique least element majorizing all a_i), and an infimum $\bigwedge_{i \in I} a_i$. For a complete Heyting algebra, the laws can be simplified somewhat. Adopt the standard axioms for a lattice and add

$$a \wedge \bigvee S = \bigvee \{a \wedge s \mid s \in S\}$$

11.3.2. Beth–Kripke semantics

Elegant as the topological interpretation may be, it is not as flexible as two later interpretations introduced by Beth and Kripke, both of which have excellent heuristics. This section considers a hybrid semantics, Beth–Kripke models, introduced in van Dalen (1984).

The basic idea is to mimic the mental activity of Brouwer's individual, who creates all of mathematics by himself. This idealized mathematician, also called the *creating subject* by Brouwer, is involved in the construction of mathematical objects, and in the construction of proofs of statements. This process takes place in time. So, at each moment, he may create new elements, and, at the same time, he observes the basic facts that hold for his universe so far. In passing from one moment in time to the next, he is free to choose how to continue his activity, so the picture of his possible activity looks like a partially ordered set (even like a tree). At each moment, there is a number of possible next stages. These stages have become known as *possible worlds*.

Consider, for the moment, the first-order case; that is to say, consider elements of one and the same sort, and a finite number of relations and functions (as in a standard first-order language). The stages for the individual form a partially ordered set $\langle K, \leq \rangle$. View $k \leq \ell$ as 'k is before ℓ or coincides with ℓ.' For each $k \in K$, there is a local domain of elements created so far, denoted by $D(k)$. It is reasonable to assume that no elements are destroyed later, so $k \leq \ell \Rightarrow D(k) \subseteq D(\ell)$.

A path in the poset K is a maximal ordered subset. For a node k in K, a bar **B** is a subset with the property that every path through k intersects **B**. Now, to stipulate how the individual arrives at the atomic facts: He does not necessarily establish an atomic fact A 'at the spot,' but he will, no matter how he pursues his research, establish A eventually. This means that there is a bar **B** for k such that, for all nodes ℓ in **B**, the statement A holds at ℓ. Note that the individual does not (have to) observe composite states of affairs. The next step is to interpret the connectives (Table 11.3). Write '$k \Vdash A$' for 'A holds at k.' The technical terminology is 'k forces A.' For atomic A, $k \Vdash A$ is already given, and $\perp$ is never forced.

Observe that the 'truth' at a node k depends essentially on the future. This is an important feature in intuitionism (and in constructive mathematics, in general). The dynamic character of the universe demands that the future is taken into account. This is particularly clear for $\forall$. If we claim that

All dogs are friendly.

Table 11.3

$k \Vdash A \wedge B$	$k \Vdash A$ and $k \Vdash B$
$k \Vdash A \vee B$	$\exists \mathbf{B} \forall \ell \in \mathbf{B} \; \ell \Vdash A$ or $\ell \Vdash B$
$k \Vdash A \rightarrow B$	$\forall \ell \geq k (\ell \Vdash A \Rightarrow \ell \Vdash B)$
$k \Vdash \neg A$	$k \Vdash A \rightarrow \perp$ $\forall \ell \geq k (\ell \Vdash A \Rightarrow \ell \Vdash \perp)$ $\forall \ell \geq k (\ell \nVdash A)$
$k \Vdash \exists x A(x)$	$\exists \mathbf{B} \forall \ell \in \mathbf{B} \exists a \in D(\ell) \; \ell \Vdash A(a)$
$k \Vdash \forall x A(x)$	$\forall \ell \geq k \forall a \in D(\ell) \; \ell \Vdash A(a)$

then *one* unfriendly dog in the future may destroy the claim.

An individual model over a poset K is denoted by $\mathcal{K}$. We say that 'A is true in a Beth–Kripke model $\mathcal{K}$' if for all $k \in K$, $k \Vdash A$. 'A is true' if A is true in all Beth–Kripke models. 'Semantical consequence' is defined as $\Gamma \Vdash A$ iff (if and only if) for all Beth–Kripke models $\mathcal{K}$ and all $k \in K$, $k \Vdash C$ for all $C \in \Gamma \Rightarrow k \Vdash A$.

A Beth–Kripke model with the property that the bar $\mathbf{B}$ in all the defining clauses is precisely the node k itself, is called a *Kripke model*. And if all the local domains $D(k)$ are identical, we have a *Beth model*. Beth–Kripke-, Kripke- and Beth-semantics are all strongly complete for intuitionistic logic: $\Gamma \vdash_i A \Leftrightarrow \Gamma \Vdash A$ (special case: $\vdash_i A \Leftrightarrow A$ is true).

There are a number of simple properties that can easily be shown, e.g., forcing is monotone, i.e., $k \Vdash A$, $k \leq \ell \Rightarrow \ell \Vdash A$, and in Beth–Kripke and Beth models

$$k \Vdash A \Leftrightarrow \exists \mathbf{B} \forall \ell \in \mathbf{B} \; \ell \Vdash A$$

Similarly Kripke models easily demonstrate examples like these: (Note, first, that $k \Vdash \neg A$ if $\forall \ell \geq k (l \nVdash A)$, i.e., A is not forced after k. $k \nVdash \neg A$ iff for some $\ell \geq k$, $\ell \Vdash A$. So $k \Vdash \neg \neg A$ if for each $\ell \geq k$, there is an $m \geq l$ with $m \Vdash A$.)

(a) Consider an atomic A and let $k_1 > k_0$, $k_1 \Vdash A$, but $k_0 \nVdash A$. By the above remark, note that $k_0 \Vdash \neg \neg A$. Hence $k_0 \nVdash \neg \neg A \rightarrow A$. Furthermore $k_0 \nVdash \neg A$, so $k_0 \nVdash A \vee \neg A$.

(b) $k_1 > k_0$, $k_2 > k_0$, $k_1 \Vdash A$ and $k_2 \Vdash B$. Note that $k_0 \nVdash \neg A$, $k_0 \nVdash \neg B$, so $k_0 \nVdash \neg A \vee \neg B$. $k_1 \nVdash A \wedge B$, $k_2 \nVdash A \wedge B$, so $k_0 \Vdash \neg (A \wedge B)$. Hence $k_0 \nVdash \neg (A \wedge B) \rightarrow (\neg A \vee \neg B)$ (De Morgan's law fails).

(c) $k_1 > k_0$, $k_0 \nVdash A(0)$, $k_1 \nVdash A(0)$, $k_1 \Vdash A(1)$. Clearly $k_1 \nVdash \forall x A(x)$, so $k_0 \Vdash \neg \forall x A(x)$. If $k_0 \Vdash \exists x \neg A(x)$ then $k_0 \Vdash \neg A(1)$. But this contradicts $k_1 \Vdash A(1)$. Hence $k_0 \nVdash \exists x \neg A(x)$. So $k_0 \nVdash \neg \forall x A(x) \rightarrow \exists x \neg A(x)$.

There is an extensive model theory for Kripke semantics. In particular, there are a large number of results on the structure of the partially ordered sets. For example, intuitionistic predicate logic, **IQC**, is complete for Kripke models over trees, and, for propositional logic, this can even be strengthened to completeness over finite trees (the so-called *finite model property*: if $\nvdash A$, then A is false in a Kripke model over a finite tree).

The completeness over tree models can be used to prove the *disjunction property*

(DP) $\vdash_i A \vee B \Rightarrow \vdash_i A$ or $\vdash_i B$

The proof uses *reductio ad absurdum*. Suppose $\nvdash_i A$ and $\nvdash_i B$, then there is a tree model $\mathcal{K}_1$ where A is not forced, similarly a tree model $\mathcal{K}_2$ where B is not forced. The two models are glued together as follows: put the two models side by side and place a new node k below both. In this new node, no proposition is forced. The result is a correct Kripke model. Since $\vdash_i A \vee B$, then $k \Vdash A \vee B$, and hence $k \Vdash A$ or $k \Vdash B$. But that contradicts the fact that A and B are not forced in $\mathcal{K}_1$ and $\mathcal{K}_2$. Therefore $\vdash_i A$ or $\vdash_i B$.

There is a corresponding theorem for existential sentences, the *existence property*

(EP) $\vdash_i \exists x A(x) \Rightarrow \vdash_i A(t)$ for a closed term t

These theorems lend a pleasing support to the intuitionistic intended meaning of 'existence': if you have established a disjunction, you know that you can establish one of the disjuncts. Similarly for existence: if you have shown the existence of something, you can indeed point to a specific instance.

As shall be seen, the disjunction and existence property hold for a number of prominent theories, the most important being arithmetic. DP and EP are often considered the hallmark of constructive logic; one should, however, not overestimate the significance of a technical result like this.

There is a snag in these conclusions. As the reader has seen, the proof made use of *reductio ad absurdum*, i.e., the result has not been established constructively. What one would like is a method that extracts from a proof of $\exists x A(x)$ a proof of $A(d)$ for some d. Fortunately, there are proof theoretical devices that provide exactly this kind of information; see, for example, van Dalen (1997, p. 211). Smorynski (1982) has shown that in a fairly large number of cases 'semantic' proofs can be made constructive.

Finite Beth models are not interesting for intuitionistic logic. For in each leaf (maximal node) A or $\neg A$ holds, so in each node $A \vee \neg A$ holds, i.e., the logic is classical. Beth's original models (Beth, 1956) are slightly more special; he considered *constant domains*, i.e., $D_k = D_\ell$ for all $k, \ell \in K$. This is a certain drawback when compared to Kripke models. The combinatorics of Beth models is just more complicated than that of Kripke models, although Kripke (1965) showed that Kripke and Beth models can be converted into each other.

Beth models are also easily convertible into topological models. For convenience, Beth models over trees are considered. On a tree, one can define a topology as follows: open sets are those subsets U of the tree that are closed under successors, i.e., $k \in U$ and $k \leq \ell \Rightarrow \ell \in U$. It is easily seen that these sets form a topology.

One also sees that $\{k \mid k \Vdash A\}$ is an open set, therefore suppose $[\![A]\!] = \{k \mid k \Vdash A\}$. Now it is a matter of routine to show that the function $[\![\cdot]\!]$ is a valuation as defined in subsection 11.3.1.

In addition, Beth semantics turn out to be a convenient tool in completeness proofs, see Troelstra and van Dalen (1988, ch. 13), and Dummett (1977). In particular, it is useful for rendering completeness proofs in an intuitionistic metamathematics. Veldman (1976) was the first to consider a modified Kripke semantics, for which he could give an intuitionistically correct completeness proof. Since then De Swart, Friedman, Dummett, and Troelstra have given alternative versions for Beth semantics (Troelstra and van Dalen, 1988, section 13.2). Furthermore, Beth models happen to be better adapted to second-order arithmetic with function variables, the so-called *intuitionistic analysis*. They allow for a very natural interpretations of choice sequences (van Dalen, 1978, 1984).

11.3.3. *Super semantics*

This chapter has presented a number of interpretations of intuitionistic theories, but by no means all of them. There is, for example, a totally different interpretation of intuitionistic logic (and arithmetic) in Kleene's realizability interpretation. This is based on algorithms, and, on the face of it, one could not find a similarity with the above semantics. One might wonder if these semantics are totally unrelated, or whether there is some common ground. The obvious common ground is the logic that they are modeling, but that would not be sufficient to link, say, Kripke models and realizability.

Fortunately, there is a general kind of semantics based on category theory.[8] Historically, these newer interpretations grew out of existing semantics, e.g., Scott (1968, 1970) showed how one could capture strikingly intuitionistic features in his extension of the topological interpretation to second-order systems. This section looks at Scott's original model, adapted to the so-called *sheaf semantics*.

Consider the topology of the real line, $\mathbb{R}$, and take the open sets to be the truth values to interpret the intuitionistic theory of reals. The objects are partial continuous real-valued functions with an open domain. This domain 'measures' the existence of the object: $Ea \in O(\mathbb{R})$. Thus this interpretation forces one to consider the notion of partial object and the notions of 'equivalence' and 'strict equality.' All objects are partial, and a is said to be total if $Ea = \mathbb{R}$. Equality has to be reconsidered in this light:

$$[\![a = b]\!] = Int\{t \in \mathbb{R} \mid a(t) = b(t)\}$$

Observe that $[\![a = a]\!] = Ea$, and in general $[\![a = b]\!] \subseteq E(a) \cap E(b)$.

In addition to the notion of equality, there is a convenient notion of *equivalence*: 'a and b coincide where they exist,' written in symbols as

$$a \simeq b := Ea \vee Eb \to a = b$$

According to the above definition, $[\![a \simeq a]\!] = \mathbb{R}$. The operations on the partial elements are defined pointwise:

$$(a + b)(t) = a(t) + b(t)$$
$$(a \cdot b)(t) = a(t) \cdot b(t)$$

The definition of the inverse is, however, problematic. One can define it pointwise for values distinct from 0, but then there seem to be problems with the invertibility of non-zero elements. The fact is that 'non-zero' is not good enough to have an inverse. Let $a(t) = t$, then

$$[\![a = 0]\!] = Int\{t \mid a(t) = t = 0\} = Int\{0\} = \varnothing$$

So

$$[\![a \neq 0]\!] = [\![\neg a = 0]\!] = Int[\![a = 0]\!]^c = \mathbb{R}$$

This a is non-zero in the model. There is, however, no b such that $[\![a \cdot b = 1]\!] = \mathbb{R}$. This is where *apartness* comes in. It is well-known that a real number has an inverse iff it is apart from 0. So, interpret # in the model:

$$[\![a \# b]\!] = \{t \mid a(t) \neq b(t)\}$$

The condition for an inverse now becomes

$$a \# 0 \rightarrow \exists b(a \cdot b = 1)$$

The model now has an inverse for a. Take $b(t) = t^{-1}$ for $t \neq 0$, then

$$[\![a \# 0]\!] = \mathbb{R} - \{0\} = \cup c[\![a \cdot c = 1]\!] \subseteq [\![a \cdot b = 1]\!] = \mathbb{R} - \{0\}$$

The introduction of an existence predicate, and partial equality, of course, carries obligations for our quantifiers. In particular

$$\exists x A(x) \leftrightarrow \exists x(Ex \wedge A(x))$$

and

$$\forall x A(x) \leftrightarrow \forall x(Ex \rightarrow A(x))$$

The logical axioms, or rules, thus have to be revised. It suffices to consider the quantifier rules and the equality rules:

$$\begin{array}{c} [Ex] \\ \mathcal{D} \\ A(x) \\ \hline \forall x\, A(x) \end{array}$$

$$\frac{\forall x\, A(x) \qquad Et}{A(t)}$$

$$\frac{A(t) \qquad E(t)}{\exists x\, A(x)}$$

$$\begin{array}{cc} & [A(x)][Ex] \\ & \mathcal{D} \\ \exists x\, A(x) & C \\ \hline \multicolumn{2}{c}{C} \end{array}$$

The axiomatization of the equality aspects is simple if the equivalence relation is used instead of identity itself. Add the axioms:

$$x \simeq y \wedge A(x) \to A(y)$$

$$\forall z (x \simeq z \leftrightarrow y \simeq z) \to x \simeq y$$

That is, take $\simeq$ as a primitive, and $=$ is then regained by defining[9]

$$t = s := Et \wedge Es \wedge t \simeq s$$

Scott (1970) also extended his model to a higher-order theory of reals, in which he could show that Brouwer's continuity theorem holds, while Moschovakis (1973) applied the methods of Scott's semantics to intuitionistic analysis in the style of Kleene's **FIM**. Her objects were continuous mappings from Baire space to Baire space (a model with total elements). Van Dalen's (1978) model for analysis is based on Beth's original semantics. It can be translated straightforwardly into a topological model, but its formulation in a Beth model allows for some extra fine tuning so that techniques from set theory can be applied. For example, a model for lawless sequences is constructed by means of forcing. The model also interprets the theory of the creating subject.

Sheaf models, as examples of a *topos*, allow a natural interpretation of higher-order logic. Van der Hoeven and Moerdijk (1984) used a special sheaf model to interpret the theory of lawless sequences. Moreover, since Kripke models and Beth models are built over trees, they carry a natural topology, and so they too can be viewed as sheaf models.

The next generalization after sheaf models is that of categorical model. Certain categories are powerful enough to interpret higher-order intuitionistic logic. In that sense, topos models can be viewed as intuitionistic universes. Categorical models also turned out to be important for typed lambda calculus. (The reader is referred to the literature for details.) It should also be mentioned that the topos semantics has managed to capture most of the known semantics. For example, Hyland (1982) showed that the realizability interpretation fitted into his effective topos; see also Troelstra and van Dalen (1988, ch. 13 section 8).

11.4. First-Order Logic

While there is no special foundational bias towards first-order theories, it is an observed fact that large parts of mathematics lend themselves to formulation in a first-order language. This section looks at a number of first-order theories and points out some of their salient properties.

Intuitionistic predicate logic itself is, just like its classical counterpart, undecidable. Fragments are, however, decidable. For example, the class of prenex formulas is decidable, and, as a corollary, not every formula has a prenex normal form in **IQC** (Kreisel, 1958). On the other hand, although monadic predicate logic is decidable in classical logic, Kripke (1968) showed it is undecidable in intuitionistic logic; see also Orevkov et al. (1965). Likewise, Lifschitz (1967) showed that the theory of equality is undecidable.

In propositional logic, one may impose restrictions on the underlying trees of Kripke models; in predicate logic, one may also put restrictions on the domains of the models. A well-known instance is the *constant domain theory* of Goernemann (1971) who showed that predicate logic plus the axiom

$$\forall x(A(x) \vee B) \to \forall x A(x) \vee B$$

(with x not free in B) is complete for Kripke models with constant domains.

In general, Kripke semantics is a powerful tool for meta-mathematical purposes; its usefulness has already been seen in subsection 11.3.2 in the case of the disjunction property. The key method in the proof was the joining of a number of disjoint Kripke models by placing one extra node (the root of the tree) below the models. This technique has become known as gluing. Following Smorynski, it will be applied to a few theories. (First, however, note that, although a number of intuitionistic first-order theories share their axioms with their classical counterparts, in general, theories are sensitive to the formulation of the axioms, notably in the absence of PEM.)

The theory of equality has the usual axioms: reflexivity, symmetry, transitivity. One can strengthen this theory in many ways, for example, the theory of stable equality is given by

$$\mathbf{EQ}^{\mathrm{st}} = \mathbf{EQ} + \forall xy(\neg\neg x = y \to x = y)$$

And the decidable theory of equality is axiomatized by

$$\mathbf{EQ}^{\mathrm{dec}} = \mathbf{EQ} + \forall xy(x = y \vee x \neq y)$$

where $x \neq y$ abbreviates $\neg x = y$

In intuitionistic mathematics, there is also a strong notion of inequality: apartness, #, as mentioned above. This was introduced by Brouwer (1919) and axiomatized by Heyting (1925). The axioms of **AP** are given by **EQ** and the following list

$$\forall xyx'y'(x\#y \land x=x' \land y=y' \rightarrow x'\#y')$$

$$\forall xy(x\#y \rightarrow y\#x)$$

$$\forall xy(\neg x\#y \leftrightarrow x=y)$$

$$\forall xyz(x\#y \rightarrow x\#z \lor y\#z)$$

The gluing technique will now be used to show that **AP** has the disjunction and existence properties. Let **AP** $\vdash A \lor B$ and assume **AP** $\nvdash A$ and **AP** $\nvdash B$. Then, by the strong completeness theorem, there are models $\mathcal{K}_1$ and $\mathcal{K}_2$ of **AP** such that $\mathcal{K}_1 \nVdash A$ and $\mathcal{K}_2 \nVdash B$. Consider the disjoint union of $\mathcal{K}_1$ and $\mathcal{K}_2$ and place the one-point world k_0 below it. That is to say, designate points a and b in $\mathcal{K}_1$ and $\mathcal{K}_2$ which are identified with the point k_0. The new model obviously satisfies the axioms of **AP**. Hence $k_0 \Vdash A \lor B$ and so $k_0 \Vdash A$ or $k_0 \Vdash B$. Both are impossible on the grounds of the choice of $\mathcal{K}_1$ and $\mathcal{K}_2$. Contradiction. Hence **AP** $\vdash A$ or **AP** $\vdash B$.

For EP, it is convenient to assume that the theory has a number of constants, say $\{c_i \mid i \in I\}$. Now let **AP** $\vdash \exists xA(x)$ and **AP** $\nvdash A(c_i)$ for all i. Then, for each i, there is a model $\mathcal{K}_i$ with $\mathcal{K}_i \nVdash A(c_i)$. As above, the models $\mathcal{K}_i$ can be glued by means of a bottom world $\mathcal{K}^*$ with a domain consisting of just the elements c_i. No non-trivial atoms are forced in k_0 (i.e., only the trivial identities $c_i = c_i$). The identification of the c_j with elements in the models $\mathcal{K}_i$ is obvious. Again, it is easy to check that the new model satisfies **AP**. Hence $k_0 \Vdash \exists xA(x)$, i.e., $k_0 \Vdash A(c_i)$ for some i. But then also $\mathcal{K}_i \Vdash A(c_i)$, contradiction. Hence **AP** $\vdash A(c_i)$ for some i.

The gluing operation thus demonstrates that there are interesting operations in Kripke model theory that make no sense in traditional model theory.

The apartness axioms have consequences for the equality relations. In particular stable equality is obtained:

$$\neg\neg x=y \rightarrow x=y$$

For, $\neg x\#y \leftrightarrow x=y$, so

$$x=y \leftrightarrow \neg\neg\neg x\#y \leftrightarrow \neg\neg x=y$$

Indeed, the equality fragment itself is axiomatized by an infinite set of quasi-stability axioms. Put

$$x \neq_0 y := \neg x=y$$

$$x \neq_{n+1} y := \forall z(z \neq_n x \lor z \neq_x y)$$

For these 'approximations to apartness', formulate quasi-stability axioms:

$$S_n := \forall xy(\neg x \neq_n y \rightarrow x=y)$$

The S_n axiomatize the equality fragment of **AP**. To be precise: **AP** is conservative over **EQ** + $\{S_n | n \geq 0\}$.[10] This shows that even a relatively simple theory like equality is incomparably richer than the classical theory.

Apartness and linear order are closely connected. The theory **LO** of linear order has axioms:

$$\forall xyz(x < y \wedge y < z \rightarrow x < z)$$

$$\forall xyz(x < y \rightarrow z < y \vee x < z)$$

$$\forall xyz(x = y \leftrightarrow \neg x < y \wedge \neg y < z)$$

The second axiom is worth noting, because it tells, so to speak, that $a < b$ means that a is 'far' to the left of b, in the sense that if an arbitrary third point is chosen, it has to be to the right of a or to the left of b. The relation with apartness is given by

$$\mathbf{LO} + \mathbf{AP} \vdash x < y \vee y < x \leftrightarrow x \# y$$

One can also use $x < y \vee y < x$ to define apartness. In a way, this gives the best possible result since **LO** + **AP** is conservative over **LO** (van Dalen, 1997; Smorynski, 1973b).

It is important to note that the atoms, or, in general, the quantifier free part of a theory does not yet determine whether it is classical. There are cases where a decidable equality results in the fact that the theory is classical, e.g., the theory of algebraically closed fields; on the other hand, for arithmetic one can prove that

$$\forall xy(x = y \vee x \neq y)$$

but the theory is not classical.

The best known first-order theory is, of course, arithmetic. Intuitionistic arithmetic, **HA**, named after Heyting (1930a, b), is axiomatized by exactly the same axioms as Peano's arithmetic. The difference is the underlying logic:

$$\mathbf{PA} = \mathbf{HA} + \text{PEM}$$

The gluing technique also works for **HA** although, in this case, one has to do some extra work to check the induction axiom. The result is that for **HA** one has the existence property for numerals:

$$\mathbf{HA} \vdash \exists x A(x) \Rightarrow \mathbf{HA} \vdash A(n) \text{ for some } n$$

And, while the disjunction property is an obvious consequence of the existence property, as $\vee$ is definable in terms of $\exists$:

$$\mathbf{HA} \vdash (A \vee B) \leftrightarrow \exists x((x = 0 \rightarrow A) \wedge (x \neq 0 \rightarrow B))$$

it would seem rather unlikely that the existence property is a consequence of the disjunction property. Yet, to the surprise of the insiders, Friedman (1975) proved that this is indeed the case for **HA** and a number of related systems.

Intuitionistic arithmetic is, of course, even more incomplete than classical arithmetic because it is a subsystem of **PA** [see chapter 4]. In fact **PA** is an unbounded extension of **HA**.

There are a number of interesting extensions of intuitionistic arithmetic formed by adding principles that have a certain constructive motivation. One such is Markov's Principle:

$$(\text{MP}) \qquad \forall x(A(x) \vee \neg A(x)) \wedge \neg\neg \exists x A(x) \to \exists x A(x)$$

This principle is a generalization of the original formulation of Markov (1971 [1962]), who considered the halting of a Turing machine. Such a machine is an abstract computing device that operates on a potentially infinite tape. The key question for Turing machines is: Does the machine, when presented with an input on the tape, eventually halt (and hence produce an output)? Suppose now that someone says that it is impossible that the machine never halts, does one know that it indeed halts? Markov argued: "Yes." The decision procedure for the halting in this case consists of turning on the machine and waiting for it to halt. An intuitionist would not buy the argument, however. When somebody claims that a Turing machine will stop, the natural question is: "When?" One wants an actual bound on the computation time. Reading 'the machine halts at time x' for $A(x)$, the above formulation exactly covers Markov's argument. In fact, in Markov's case $A(x)$ is primitive recursive.

A simple Kripke model shows that **HA** $\nvdash$ MP. Consider a model with two nodes k_0, k_1, where $k_0 < k_1$. In the bottom node, put the standard model of natural numbers; in the top node, put a (classical) non-standard model $\mathcal{M}$ in which the negation of Gödel's sentence

I am not provable in **PA**.

i.e., the proper sentence of the form $\exists x A(x)$, is true. So $k_1 \Vdash \exists x A(x)$ and hence $k_0 \Vdash \neg\neg\exists x A(x)$. But $k_0 \Vdash \exists x A(x)$ would ask for an instance $A(n)$ to be true in the standard model, and hence would yield a conflict with the independence of the Gödel sentence from **PA**. Since, clearly, $k_0 \Vdash \forall x(A(x) \vee \neg A(x))$, the model refutes MP.

Although Markov's principle may be unprovable in **HA**, its companion, *Markov's rule*, has a stronger position. Given a statement of the form $A \to B$, one may formulate a corresponding rule

$$\Gamma \vdash A \Rightarrow \Gamma \vdash B$$

which is, in general, weaker than

$$\Gamma \vdash A \to B$$

For example: Markov's rule MR with respect to **HA** says:

$$\mathbf{HA} \vdash \forall x(A(x) \vee \neg A(x) \wedge \neg\neg\exists x A(x) \Rightarrow \mathbf{HA} \vdash \exists x A(x)$$

HA is said to be *closed under Markov's rule*. The heuristic argument is that there is more information in this case; there is a proof of $\neg\neg\exists x A(x)$, from this extra evidence one may hope to draw a stronger conclusion. Markov's rule is indeed correct; see, for example Troelstra and van Dalen (1988, p. 129, and p. 507). Note that $A(x)$ may contain more free variables. For closed $\exists x A(x)$, the proof of closure under Markov's rule is particularly simple: if **HA** $\vdash \neg\neg\exists x A(x)$, then **PA** $\vdash \exists x A(x)$, and hence $A(n)$ is true in the standard model for some n. Now **HA** $\vdash A(n) \vee \neg A(n)$ and, by DP, **HA** $\vdash A(n)$ or **HA** $\vdash \neg A(n)$. The latter is impossible, hence **HA** $\vdash A(n)$, and *a fortiori* **HA** $\vdash \exists x A(x)$ (Smorynski, 1973a, p. 366).

Since the theory of natural numbers is at the very heart of mathematics, it is no surprise that a great deal of research has been devoted to the subject. In the early days of intuitionism, people wondered to what extent **HA** was safer that **PA**. This was settled in 1933 by Gödel (and independently by Gentzen), who showed that **PA** can be translated into **HA**. Gödel defined a translation, which from the intuitionistic viewpoint weakened statements. This was basically done by a judicious distribution of negations. Here is the formal definition:

$$A^\circ = \neg\neg A, \text{ for atomic } A$$
$$(A \wedge B)^\circ = A^\circ \wedge B^\circ$$
$$(A \vee B)^\circ = \neg(\neg A^\circ \wedge \neg B^\circ)$$
$$(A \to B)^\circ = A^\circ \to B^\circ$$
$$(\forall x A(x))^\circ = \forall x A^\circ(x)$$
$$(\exists x A(x))^\circ = \neg\forall x \neg A^\circ(x)$$

This Gödel translation gives

$$\mathbf{PA} \vdash_c A \Leftrightarrow \mathbf{HA} \vdash_i A^\circ$$

and hence

$$\mathbf{PA} \vdash_c 0 = 1 \Leftrightarrow \mathbf{HA} \vdash_i \neg\neg 0 = 1 \Leftrightarrow \mathbf{HA} \vdash_i 0 = 1$$

So **PA** is consistent iff **HA** is so. In other words, no deep philosophical insight can be expected here.

It is an easy consequence of the Gödel translation theorem that the universal fragment of **PA** is conservative over **HA**. Of course, the Gödel translation also works for predicate logic:

$$\Gamma \vdash_c A \Leftrightarrow \Gamma^\circ \vdash_i A^\circ$$

where $\Gamma^\circ = \{B^\circ \mid B \in \Gamma\}$ (van Dalen, 1997, p. 164).

The result of the Gödel translation may be improved for certain simple formulas. Kreisel showed that **PA** and **HA** prove the same Π_2^0 sentences,

$$\mathbf{PA} \vdash_c \forall x \exists y A(x, y) \Leftrightarrow \mathbf{HA} \vdash_i \forall x \exists y A(x, y)$$

where $A(x, y)$ is quantifier free.

The proof of this has some quite interesting features. First, note that a quantifier free formula $A(x, y)$ is equivalent in **HA** to an equation $t(x, y) = 0$ (where it is assumed that **HA** has defining equations for the primitive recursive functions). Next, introduce the *Friedman translation*: for a given formula F, obtain A^F from A by replacing all atoms P by $P \vee F$. It is a routine exercise to show that

(i) $\Gamma \vdash_i A \Rightarrow \Gamma^F \vdash_i A^F$
(ii) $A \vdash_i A^F$
(iii) $\mathbf{HA} \vdash_i A \Rightarrow \mathbf{HA} \vdash_i A^F$

Now consider a term t and let

$$\mathbf{HA} \vdash \neg\neg \exists x (t(x, y) = 0)$$

We apply the Friedman translation with respect to $F := \exists x (t(x, y) = 0)$.

$$((\exists x(t(x, y) = 0) \to \bot) \to \bot)^{\exists x(t(x,y)=0)} = ((\exists x(t(x, y) = 0) \vee \exists x(t(x, y) = 0)) \to$$
$$(\bot \vee \exists x(t(x, y) = 0)) \to (\bot \vee \exists x(t(x, y) = 0)))$$

This formula is equivalent to $\exists x(t(x, y) = 0)$. Hence $\mathbf{HA} \vdash_i \exists x(t(x, y) = 0)$.

Observe that one now has closure under Markov's rule with numerical parameters. It is just one step further to reach Kreisel's theorem. From (formalized) recursion theory, it is known that a function f is provably recursive in **HA** with index e if

$$\mathbf{HA} \vdash \forall x \exists y T(e, x, y)$$

where T is Kleene's T-predicate, which formalizes the notion y is a (halting) computation on input x (strictly speaking 'y is the code of a computation ...'). Now

$$\mathbf{PA} \vdash \forall x \exists y T(e, x, y) \Leftrightarrow \mathbf{PA} \vdash \exists y T(e, x, y)$$

$\Leftrightarrow$ (Gödel translation) $\mathbf{HA} \vdash \neg\neg \exists y T(e, x, y)$

$\Leftrightarrow$ (closure under Markov's Rule) $\mathbf{HA} \vdash \exists y T(e, x, y)$

$\Leftrightarrow \mathbf{HA} \vdash \forall x \exists y T(e, x, y)$

(Friedman (1977) showed that this fact also holds in intuitionistic set theory, **IZF**.)

Finally it is worth mentioning that Gödel also introduced a translation of intuitionistic logic into modal logic; in this translation, the necessity operator has the flavour of 'is provable.' (Recently Artemov (2001) made the provability explicit in a refined version.)

11.4.1. Set theories

Following the tradition in set theory, the various intuitionistic modifications of **ZF** are also first-order. For most classical theories, one can consider one or more corresponding intuitionistic theories. In some cases, it suffices to omit PEM from the logical axioms, although one has to be careful when some non-logical axioms are by themselves strong enough to imply PEM.

Here is an example: the full axiom of choice implies PEM. Let A be a statement, define

$$P = \{n \in \mathbb{N} \mid n = 0 \vee (n = 1 \wedge A)\}$$
$$Q = \{n \in \mathbb{N} \mid n = 1 \vee (n = 0 \wedge A)\}$$
$$S = \{X, Y\}$$

Since obviously

$$\forall X \in S \exists x \in \mathbb{N}(x \in X)$$

AC would yield a choice function F such that

$$\forall X \in S(F(x) \in X)$$

Observe that $F(P), F(Q) \in \mathbb{N}$, so

$$F(P) = F(Q) \vee F(P) \neq F(Q)$$

If $F(P) = F(Q)$, then A holds. If, on the other hand $F(P) \neq F(Q)$, then $\neg A$. So, $A \vee \neg A$.[11]

Friedman studied **IZF**, an intuitionistic version of **ZF**; for a formulation, see Beeson (1985, ch. 8, section 1). The axioms for sets are modifications of the traditional **ZF** ones [see chapter 3], but the theory is very sensitive to the formulation: a wrong choice of axiom may introduce unwanted logical principles. For example, $\in$-induction is used rather than Foundation, and similarly the Axiom of Collection takes the place of the Replacement axiom. As noted above, Friedman (1973) showed that the Gödel translation theorem works for a suitable formulation of intuitionistic set theory.

Aczel considered another version of constructive set theory, **CZF**. This set theory has the attractive feature that it is interpretable in a particular type theory of Martin-Löf (Troelstra and van Dalen, 1988, p. 624).

Set theory under the assumption of Church's Thesis was extensively studied by McCarty (1984, 1986, 1991). He built a model of cumulative constructive set theory in which a number of interesting phenomena can be observed, e.g., in Kleene's realiazability universe sets with apartness are subcountable (i.e., the range of a function on $\mathbb{N}$).

11.5. Second-Order Logics

Whereas first-order intuitionistic logic is a subsystem of classical logic, higher-order logic may contain rules or axioms that are constructively justified, but which contradict classical logic. In practice, there are two ways to formulate second-order logic: with set variables and with function variables.

11.5.1. IQC^2

Second-order logic with set variables is a straightforward adaptation of the classical formulation [see chapter 2]; see van Dalen (1997) and Troelstra and Schwichtenberg (1996, ch. 11). It is a surprising fact that in $\mathbf{IQC}^2$ the connectives are not independent as in first-order logic. Prawitz (1965) showed that one can define the connectives in $\forall^1$, $\forall^2$ and $\rightarrow$ where X is a 0-ary predicate,

$$\bot \;\leftrightarrow\; \forall^2 X.X$$
$$A \wedge B \;\leftrightarrow\; \forall^2 X((A \rightarrow (B \rightarrow X)) \rightarrow X)$$
$$A \vee B \;\leftrightarrow\; \forall^2 X((A \rightarrow X) \wedge (B \rightarrow X) \rightarrow X)$$
$$\exists^1 y A \;\leftrightarrow\; \forall^2 X(\forall^1 y(A \rightarrow X) \rightarrow X)$$
$$\exists^2 Y A \;\leftrightarrow\; \forall^2 X(\forall^2 Y(A \rightarrow X) \rightarrow X)$$

Classically, sets and functions are interdefinable as each set has a characteristic function, but, intuitionistically, S has a characteristic function if its membership is decidable:

$$\begin{cases} a \in S \Leftrightarrow k_S(a) = 1 \\ a \notin S \Leftrightarrow k_S(a) = 0 \end{cases}$$

Since

$$k_S(a) = 1 \vee k_S(a) = 0$$

one has $a \in S \vee a \notin S$. The moral is that there are lots of sets without characteristic functions. Note that the 'set'-approach and the 'function'-approach to second-order logic (arithmetic) yield diverging theories. Generally speaking, total functions, with their 'input–output' behavior are more tractable than sets. That is a good reason to study second-order arithmetic with function variables. Another reason is that this formulation is a natural framework for treating Brouwer's choice sequences.[12]

11.5.2. The theory of choice sequences

For the practice of intuitionistic mathematics, second-order arithmetic with function variables is even more significant than the version with set variables. The reason is that this theory allows one to capture the properties of Brouwer's choice sequences. Since this survey is about logic, the topic is not quite within its scope. This section therefore just briefly notes the main points; for more information, the reader is referred to the literature.

Brouwer's chief contribution to this part of intuitionistic logic is that he realized that particular quantifier combinations are given a specific reading. Choice sequences of, say, natural numbers are infinite sequences, α, of natural numbers, chosen more or less arbitrarily. That is to say, in general, there is no law that determines future choices. Suppose now that it has been shown that $\forall\alpha\exists nA(\alpha, n)$ for some formula A; this means that when a choice sequence α is generated, one will eventually be able to compute the number n, such that $A(\alpha, n)$ holds. Roughly speaking, this says that, at some stage, in the generation of α, all the information needed for the computation of n is available, but then no further information is needed, and any β that coincides so far with α will yield the same n. This sketch is necessarily somewhat simplified; for an extensive analysis see van Atten and van Dalen (2000).

This, in a nutshell, is *Brouwer's Continuity Principle*:

$$\forall\alpha\exists xA(\alpha, x) \rightarrow \forall\alpha\exists xy\forall\beta((\bar{\alpha}(y) = \bar{\beta}(y) \rightarrow A(\beta, x))$$

Here $\bar{\gamma}(y)$ stands for the initial segment of length y of a sequence γ. On the basis of this principle, formulated for $\forall\alpha\exists!x$ in Brouwer (1918), already a number of intuitionistic facts, conflicting with classical mathematics, can be derived. It allows, for example, a simple rejection of PEM.

In later papers, Brouwer further investigated the continuity phenomenon. He added a powerful induction principle, which enabled him to show his famous *Continuity Theorem*: all total real functions on the continuum are locally uniformly continuous (Brouwer, 1924b). As a corollary, the continuum cannot be decomposed into two inhabited parts. Another well-know consequence is the *Fan theorem* (basically the compactness of the Cantor space).

In the 1920s, Brouwer introduced an extra strengthening of analysis, the details of which were published only after 1946. The new idea, known by the name 'the creating subject', was formulated by Kreisel in terms of a tensed modal operator. Subsequently, Kripke simplified the presentation by introducing a choice sequence α that 'witnesses' a particular statement A. α keeps track of the success of the subject in establishing A; it produces zeros as long as the subject has not established A, and when A is proved, or experienced, α produces a single 'one' and goes on with zeros. The existence of such a α is the content of Kripke's schema:

KS $\quad \exists\alpha(A \leftrightarrow \exists x\alpha(x) = 1)$

Brouwer used the creating subject (and implicitly Kripke's schema) to establish strong refutations, which go beyond the already existing Brouwerian counterexamples.

He showed (Brouwer, 1949), for example, that

$$\neg \forall x \in \mathbb{R}(\neg\neg x > 0 \rightarrow x > 0)$$

and

$$\neg \forall x \in \mathbb{R}(x \neq 0 \rightarrow x \# 0)$$

See also Hull (1969).

Kripke's schema has significant consequences for the nature of the mathematical universe. It conflicts, for example, with $\forall \alpha \exists \beta$-continuity, i.e.,

$$\forall \alpha \exists \beta A(\alpha, \beta) \rightarrow \exists F \forall \alpha A(\alpha, F(\alpha))$$

where F is a continuous operation (Myhill, 1966). Using KS, van Dalen (1999b) showed that Brouwer's indecomposability theorem for $\mathbb{R}$ can be extended to all dense negative subsets of $\mathbb{R}$ ($A \subseteq \mathbb{R}$ is *negative* if $\forall x(x \in A \leftrightarrow \neg\neg x \in A)$). So, for example, the set of not-not-rationals is indecomposable.

The technique of the creating subject is used here to demonstrate that, under the assumption of Kripke's schema, one can show a converse of Brouwer's indecomposability theorem: $KS + \mathbb{R}$ is indecomposable $\Rightarrow$ there are no discontinuous real functions.

Proof Let f be discontinuous in 0, and $f(0) = 0$. It follows that

$$\exists k \forall n \exists x(|x| < 2^{-n} \wedge |f(x)| > 2^{-k})$$

Hence there are x_n with $|f(x_n)| > 2^{-k}$ and $|x| < 2^{-n}$. Let α be the Kripke sequence for $r \in \mathbb{Q}$, and β for $r \notin \mathbb{Q}$. Put

$$\begin{cases} \gamma(2n) & = \alpha(n) \\ \gamma(2n + 1) & = \beta(n) \end{cases}$$

$$c_n = \begin{cases} x_n & \text{if } \forall p \leq n, \gamma(p) = 0 \\ x_p & \text{if } p \leq n \text{ and } \gamma(p) = 1 \end{cases}$$

$$c = \lim(c_n).$$

Now, $f(c) < 2^{-k} \vee f(c) > 0$. If $f(c) < 2^{-k}$ then $f(c) = 0$, so $\forall p(\gamma(p) = 0)$. Contradiction. If $f(c) > 0$, then $r \in \mathbb{Q} \vee r \notin \mathbb{Q}$. Hence $\forall r(r \in \mathbb{Q} \vee r \notin \mathbb{Q})$. This contradicts the indecomposability of $\mathbb{R}$. QED

The theory of choice sequences has received a great deal of attention since Kleene and Kreisel formulated suitable formalizations. Some notions, such as 'lawless sequence,' have found important applications in metamathematics; see, for example, Brouwer (1981, 1992) or van Dalen (1986) or Troelstra and van Dalen (1988) and the references cited there. There is also an extensive literature on the semantics of second-order arithmetic; see, for example, the references cited in subsection 11.3.3.

Suggested further reading

For a more comprehensive treatment of intuitionistic logic, the reader may want to consult the author (van Dalen, 1986, 1997) or Kleene (1952). For the more mathematical and meta-mathematical aspects, see also Troelstra and van Dalen (1988), and Heyting (1934, 1956), Dummett (1977), Bridges and Richman (1987), as well as *Philosophia Mathematica*, vol 6 – Special Issue: Perspectives on Intuitionism (ed. R. Tieszen). In addition to these works, for proof theory, the reader might consult Beeson (1985), Buss (1998), Girard (1989), Martin-Löf (1984), or Troelstra and Schwichtenberg (1996). Similarly, for more on semantics, see, for example, Dragalin (1988), Fitting (1969), Fourman and Scott (1979), Gabbay (1982), MacLane and Moerdijk (1992), Rasiowa and Sikorski (1963), and Smorynski (1973a). The works of Dummett, Gabbay, Kleene, Smorynski, and Troelstra and van Dalen just cited are also useful for material on first-order theories. Finally, second-order logic and choice sequences are further treated in Brouwer (1981, 1992), Kleene and Vesley (1965), and Troelstra (1977), as well as works already mentioned, e.g., van Dalen (1986), Dummett (1977) and Troelstra and van Dalen (1988).

Notes

1 Even though Brouwer did not develop logic for its own sake, he was the first to establish a non-trivial result: $\neg A \leftrightarrow \neg\neg\neg A$ (Brouwer, 1920).

2 For a survey of the Brouwerian global philosophy of man and his mathematical enterprise, see van Dalen (1999a).

3 This kind of interpretation of the connectives in terms of proofs was made explicit by Heyting (1934). Kolmogorov (1932) had given a similar interpretation in terms of *problems* and *solutions*. The formulations are, up to terminology, virtually identical.

4 Brouwer (1924a) considered various sequences in this expansion. For one of them, the occurrence has been established: 01234567890 does indeed occur among the decimals of π (Borwein, 1998). Nevertheless, in spite of considerable computational power, there are still enough open questions concerning the occurrence of specific sequences of decimals.

5 Heyting's formalization was published in 1930, Glivenko (1929) and Kolmogorov (1925) had already published similar formalizations, which, however, did not cover full intuitionistic logic (Troelstra, 1978).

6 Normalization and cut-elimination for second-order logic is far more complicated because of the presence of the comprehension rule, which introduces an impredicativity. The proof of a normalization theorem was a spectacular breakthrough; the names to mention here are Girard, Prawitz and Martin-Löf; see their papers in Fenstad (1971).

7 The theory of topological interpretations is treated extensively in Rasiowa and Sikorski (1963).

8 The pioneer in this area was Lawvere, who saw the possibilities for treating logical notions in a categorical setting; see, for example Lawvere (1971). He, in particular, discovered the significance of adjointness for logic.

9 Details of the logic can be found in Troelstra and van Dalen (1988) and Scott's original (1979).

10   This result was first established by proof theoretic means in van Dalen and Statman (1978), and subsequently an elegant model theoretic proof was given in Smorynski (1973b).
11   This fact was discovered by Diaconescu (1975); the proof given here is Goodman and Myhill's (1978).
12   For the proof theory of $\mathbf{IQC}^2$, see Prawitz (1970), Troelstra and Schwichtenberg (1996), and Troelstra (1973).

References

Artemov, S. 2001: "Explicit Provability and Constructive Semantics," *Bull. Symbolic Logic*, 7, 1–36.

van Atten, M. and van Dalen, D. 2000: "Arguments for Brouwer's Continuity Principle," *Logic Group Preprint Series*, 199, (Zeno Institute of Philosophy, Utrecht University).

Beeson, M. 1985: *Foundations of Constructive Mathematics*, (Springer-Verlag, Berlin).

Beth, E. W. 1956: "Semantic Construction of Intuitionistic Logic," *Kon. Nederlandse Ac. Wetenschappen afd. Letteren:Mededelingen*, 19/11, 357–88.

Borwein, J. M. 1998: "Brouwer–Heyting Sequences Converge," *Math. Intelligencer*, 20, 14–15.

Bridges, D. and Richman, F. 1987: *Varieties of Constructive Mathematics*, (Cambridge University Press, Cambridge).

Brouwer, L. E. J. 1918: "Begründung der Mengenlehre unabhängig vom logischen Satz vom ausgeschlossenen Dritten. Erster Teil, Allgemeine Mengenlehre," *Kon Ned Ak Wet Verhandelingen*, 5, 1–43.

Brouwer, L. E. J. 1919: "Begründung der Mengenlehre unabhängig vom logischen Satz vom ausgeschlossenen Dritten. Zweiter Teil, Theorie der Punktmengen," *Kon Ned Ak Wet Verhandelingen*, 7, 1–33.

Brouwer, L. E. J. 1920: "Intuitionistische Mengenlehre," *Jahresber. Dtsch. Math. Ver.*, 28, 203–8.

Brouwer, L. E. J. 1924a: "Über die Bedeutung des Satzes vom ausgeschlossenen Dritten in der Mathematik insbesondere in der Funktionentheorie," *J. Reine Angew Math.*, 154, 1–8.

Brouwer, L. E. J. 1924b: "Beweis dass jede volle Funktion gleichmässig stetig ist," *Nederl Ak Wetensch Proc*, 27, 189–93.

Brouwer, L. E. J. 1949: "Essentieel negatieve eigenschappen," *Ind. Math.*, 10, 322–3.

Brouwer, L. E. J. 1981: *Brouwer's Cambridge Lectures on Intuitionism*, D. van Dalen, ed., (Cambridge University Press, Cambridge).

Brouwer, L. E. J. 1992: *Intuitionismus*, D. van Dalen, ed., (Bibliographisches Institut, Wissenschaftsverlag, Mannheim).

Buss, S. 1998: *Handbook of Proof Theory*, (Elsevier, Amsterdam).

Constable, R. L. et al., 1986: *Implementing Mathematics with the Nuprl Proof Development System*, (Prentice Hall, Englewood Cliffs, NJ).

Curry, H. B. and Feys, R. 1958: *Combinatory Logic. Vol. I*, (North-Holland, Amsterdam).

van Dalen, D. 1978: "An Interpretation of Intuitionistic Analysis," *Ann. Math. Log*, 13, 1–43.

van Dalen, D. 1984: "How to Glue Analysis Models," *J. Symb. Logic*, 49, 1339–49.

van Dalen, D. 1986: "Intuitionistic Logic," in *Handbook of Philosophical Logic, Vol. III*, D. Gabbay and F. Günthner, eds., (D. Reidel, Dordrecht), 225–340.

van Dalen, D. 1997: *Logic and Structure*, 3rd edn, (Springer-Verlag, Berlin).

van Dalen, D. 1999a: *Mystic, Geometer, and Intuitionist: The Life of L. E. J. Brouwer. The Dawning Revolution*, (Oxford University Press, Oxford).

van Dalen, D. 1999b: "From Brouwerian Counter Examples to the Creating Subject," *Studia Logica*, 62, 305–14.

van Dalen, D. and Statman, R. 1978: "Equality in the Presence of Apartness," in *Essays on Mathematical and Philosophical Logic*, J. Hintikka, I. Niiniluoto and E. Saarinen, eds., (D. Reidel, Dordrecht), 95–116.

Diaconescu, R. 1975: "Axiom of Choice and Complementation," *Proc. American Math. Soc.*, 51, 176–8.

Dragalin, A. 1988: *Mathematical Intuitionism*, (American Mathematical Society, Providence, RI).

Dummett, M. 1975: "The Philosophical Basis of Intuitionistic Logic," in Rose and Shepherdson (1975, 5–40).

Dummett, M. 1977: *Elements of Intuitionism*, (Oxford University Press, Oxford).

Fenstad, J. E. (ed.) 1971: *Proceedings of the Second Scandinavian Logic Symposium*, (North-Holland, Amsterdam).

Fitting, M. 1969: *Intuitionistic Model Theory, and Forcing*, (North-Holland, Amsterdam).

Fourman, M. P. and Scott, D. S. 1979: "Sheaves and Logic," in Fourman, Mulvey and Scott (eds.) (1979, 302–401).

Fourman, M. P., Mulvey, C. J. and Scott, D. S. (eds.) 1979: *Applications of Sheaf Theory to Logic, Algebra, and Analysis*, (Springer-Verlag, Berlin).

Friedman, H. 1973: "Some Applications of Kleene's Methods for Intuitionistic Systems," in *Cambridge Summer School in Mathematical Logic*, A. Mathias and H. Rogers, eds., (Springer-Verlag, Berlin), 113–70.

Friedman, H. 1975: "The Disjunction Property Implies the Numerical Existence Property," *Proc. Nat. Acad. Science USA*, 72, 2877–8.

Friedman, H. 1977: "Set Theoretic Foundations for Constructive Analysis," *Ann. Math.*, 105, 1–28.

Gabbay, D. M. 1982: *Semantical Investigations in Heyting's Intuitionistic Logic*, (D. Reidel, Dordrecht).

Gallier, J. H. 1995: "On the Correspondence between Proofs and λ-Terms," in *The Curry–Howard Isomorphism*, Ph. de Groote, ed., (Academia, Louvain-la-Neuve), 55–138.

Gentzen, G. 1935: "Untersuchungen über das Logische Schliessen I, II," *Math. Zeitschr*, 39, 176–210, 405–31.

Girard, J.-Y. 1989: *Proofs and Types*, trans. by P. Taylor, and Y. Lafont, (Cambridge University Press, Cambridge).

Glivenko, V. I. 1929: "Sur quelques points de la Logique de M. Brouwer," *Bull. Soc. Math. Belg.*, 15, 183–8.

Gödel, K. 1932: "Zum intuitionistischen Aussagenkalkül," *Anzeiger der Akademie der Wissenschaften in Wien*, 69, 65–6. (Coll. Works I, pp. 222–5).

Goernemann, S. 1971: "A Logic Stronger than Intuitionism," *J. Symb Logic*, 36, 249–61.

Goodman, N. D. and Myhill, J. R. 1978: "Choice Implies Excluded Middle," *Z. Math. Logik Grundlagen Math.*, 24, 461.

Heyting, A. 1925: "Intuïtionistische Axiomatiek der Projectieve Meetkunde," PhD thesis, Amsterdam.

Heyting, A. 1930a: "Die Formalen Regeln der Intuitionistischen Logik," *Die Preussische Akademie der Wissenschaften. Sitzungsberichte. Physikalische-Mathematische Klasse*, 42–56.

Heyting, A. 1930b: "Die Formalen Regeln der Intuitionistischen Mathematik II, III," *Die Preussische Akademie der Wissenschaften. Sitzungsberichte. Physikalische-Mathematische Klasse*, 57–71, 158–69.

Heyting, A. 1934: *Mathematische Grundlagenforschung. Intuitionismus, Beweistheorie*, (Springer-Verlag, Berlin).

Heyting, A. 1956: *Intuitionism, an Introduction*, (North-Holland, Amsterdam).

Hoeven, G. F. and Moerdijk, I. 1984: "Sheaf Models for Choice Sequences," *Ann. Pure Appl Logic*, 27, 63–107.

Howard, W. A. 1980: "The Formulas-as-Types Notion of Construction," in *To H. B. Curry: Essays on Combinatory Logic, Lambda Calculus and Formalism*, J. R. Hindley and J. P. Seldin, (eds.), (Academic Press, New York), 479–90.

Hull, R. G. 1969: "Counterexamples in Intuitionistic Analysis Using Kripke's Schema," *Zeitschr. Math. Logik*, 15, 241–6.

Hyland, J. M. E. 1982: "The Effective Topos," in Troelstra and van Dalen (1982, 165–216).

Jaśkowski, S. 1936: "Recherches sur le Système de la Logique Intuitioniste," *Actes du Congrès International de Philosophie Scientifique, VI*, (Hermann, Paris), 58–61.

Kleene, S. C. 1952: *Introduction to Metamathematics*, (North-Holland, Amsterdam).

Kleene, S. C. and Vesley, R. E. 1965: *The Foundations of Intuitionistic Mathematics Especially in Relation to Recursive Functions*, (North-Holland, Amsterdam).

Kolmogorov, A. N. 1925: "On the Principle of Excluded Middle" (Russian), *Mathematics of the USSR, Sbornik*, 32, 646–67. English translation in 1967: *From Frege to Gödel: A Source Book in Mathematical Logic, 1879–1931*, J. van Heijenoord, ed., (Harvard University Press, Cambridge MA), 414–37.

Kolmogorov, A. N. 1932: "Zur Deutung der Intuitionistischen Logik," *Math. Zeitschr*, 35, 58–65.

Kreisel, G. 1958: "Elementary Completeness Properties of Intuitionistic Logic with a Note on Negations of Prenex Formulae," *J. Symb. Logic*, 23, 317–30.

Kripke, S. A. 1965: "Semantical Analysis of Intuitionistic Logic I," in *Formal Systems and Recursive Functions. Proc. of the Eighth Logic Colloquium, Oxford*, M. A. E. Dummett and J. N. Crossley, eds., (North-Holland, Amsterdam), 92–130.

Kripke, S. A. 1968: "Semantical Analysis of Intitionistic Logic II," unpublished.

Lawvere, W. 1971: "Quantifiers and Sheaves," in *Actes du Congrès International de Mathématiciens, 1–10 Septembre 1970, Nice, France*, Vol. I, (Gautier-Villors, Paris), 329–34.

Lifschitz, V. 1967: "The Decision Problem for Some Constructive Theories of Equality," *Seminar Math. Institute Steklov*, 4, 29–31.

MacLane, S. and Moerdijk, I. 1992: *Sheaves in Geometry and Logic. A First Introduction to Topos Theory*, (Springer-Verlag, Berlin).

Markov, A. A. 1971: "On Constructive Mathematics," *AMS Transl.*, 98, 1–9. (Original Trudy Mat. Inst. Steklov. 67 (1962).)

Martin-Löf, P. 1975: "An Intuitionistic Theory of Types," in Rose and Shepherdson (1975, 73–118).

Martin-Löf, P. 1984: *Intuitionistic Type Theory*, (Bibliopolis, Napoli).

McCarty, D. 1984: "Realizability and Recursive Mathematics," PhD thesis, Oxford.

McCarty, D. 1986: "Realizability and Recursive Set Theory," *Ann. Pure Appl. Logic*, 32, 153–83.

McCarty, D. 1991: "Polymorphism and Apartness," *Notre Dame Journal of Formal Logic*, 32, 513–32.

Moschovakis, J. 1973: "A Topological Interpretation of Intuitionistic Analysis," *Comp. Math.*, 26, 261–75.

Myhill, J. R. 1966: "Notes towards an Axiomatization of Intuitionistic Analysis," *Logique et Analyse*, 9, 280–97.

Myhill, J. R., Kino, A. and Vesley, R. (eds.) 1970: *Intuitionism and Proof Theory*, (North-Holland, Amsterdam).

Orevkov, V. P., Maslov, S. Yu. and Mints, G. 1965: "Unsolvability in the Constructive Predicate Calculus of Certain Classes of Formulas Containing only Monadic Predicate Variables," *Soviet Mat. Dokl.*, 6, 918–20.

Prawitz, D. 1965: *Natural Deduction. A Proof-Theoretical Study*, (Almqvist & Wiksell, Stockholm).

Prawitz, D. 1970: "Some Results for Intuitionistic Logic with Second Order Quantification," in Myhill, Kino, and Vesley (1970, 259–69).

Rasiowa, H. and Sikorski, R. 1963: *The Mathematics of Metamathematics*, (Panstowe Wydawnictwo Naukowe, Warsaw).

Rose, H. E. and Shepherdson, J. (eds.) 1975: *Logic Colloquium '73*, (North-Holland, Amsterdam).

Scott, D. S. 1968: "Extending the Topological Interpretation to Intuitionistic Analysis," *Comp. Math.*, 20, 194–210.

Scott, D. S. 1970: "Extending the Topological Interpretation to Intuitionistic Analysis II," in Myhill, Kino, and Vesley (1970, 235–55).

Scott, D. S. 1979: "Identity and Existence in Intuitionistic Logic," in Fourman, Mulvey and Scott (1979, 660–96).

Smorynski, C. S. 1973a: "Applications of Kripke models," in Troelstra (1973, 324–91).

Smorynski, C. S. 1973b: "On axiomatizing fragments," *J. Symb. Logic*, 42, 530–44.

Smorynski, C. S. 1982: "Nonstandard Models and Constructivity," in Troelstra and van Dalen (1982, 459–64).

Tarski, A. 1938: "Der Aussagenkalkül und die Topologie," *Fund. Math.*, 31, 103–34.

Troelstra, A. S. 1973: *Metamathematical Investigation of Intuitionistic Arithmetic and Analysis*, (Springer-Verlag, Berlin).

Troelstra, A. S. 1977: *Choice Sequences. A Chapter of Intuitionistic Mathematics*, (Clarendon Press, Oxford).

Troelstra, A. S. 1978: "Heyting, 'Die formale Regeln der intuitionistischen Logik' (1930). Commentary," in *Two Decades of Mathematics in the Netherlands*, E. M. J. Bertin, H. J. M. Bos, and A. W. Grootendorst, eds., (Mathematical Centre, Amsterdam), 153–75.

Troelstra, A. S. and van Dalen, D. (eds.) 1982: *The L. E. J. Brouwer Centenary Symposium*, (Elsevier, Amsterdam).

Troelstra, A. S. and van Dalen, D. 1988: *Constructivism in Mathematics, I, II*, (North-Holland, Amsterdam).

Troelstra, A. S. and Schwichtenberg, H. 1996: *Basic Proof Theory*, (Cambridge University Press, Cambridge).

Veldman, W. 1976: "An Intuitionistic Completeness Theorem for Intuitionistic Predicate Calculus," *J. Symb. Logic*, 41, 159–66.

Whitehead, A. N. and Russell, B. 1910–13: *Principia Mathematica*, 3 vols, (Cambridge University Press, Cambridge).

— Chapter 12 —

Free Logics

Karel Lambert

12.1. Preliminary Remarks

The expression 'free logic,' coined by the author in 1960, is an abbreviation for 'logic free of existence assumptions with respect to its terms, singular and general, but whose quantifiers are treated exactly as in standard quantifier logic.' In more traditional language, such logics do not presume that either singular or general terms – the two distinct categories of terms emphasized in modern logical grammar – have existential import. A singular term 't' has existential import just in case t exists (or, equivalently, there exists an object the same as t) and a general term (or predicate) 'G' has existential import just in case G exist (or, equivalently, there exists an object that is G).[1] Examples from colloquial English customarily taken to be singular terms are expressions such as 'Socrates', 'the planet causing perturbations in the orbit of Mercury', '5', '5/0', 'the square of 3' and 'having a heart'. Some of these do not have existential import – in particular, '5/0' and 'the planet causing perturbations in the orbit of Mercury'. Examples from colloquial English customarily taken to be general terms are expressions such as 'is a philosopher', 'is a planet causing perturbations in the orbit of Mercury', 'number', 'is divisible by 0', and 'has a heart'. Some of these general terms do not have existential import – in particular, 'is a planet causing perturbations in the orbit of Mercury' and 'is divisible by 0'. To say that the quantifers are treated exactly as in standard quantifier logic is to say, roughly, that the operator symbol '∃' (the existential quantifier) reads: 'There exists an object', and the operator symbol '∀' (the universal quantifier) reads: 'Every existent object'.

A distinctive property of free logics is rejection of the principle of standard first-order quantificational logic called universal specification (or its inferential counterpart, the rule of universal instantiation) [see chapter 1]. An instance of universal specification is

$$\forall x(P(x)) \supset P(t) \tag{12.1}$$

where 'P' is a general term (or, in this case, a one-place predicate), 't' is a singular term (a name or definite description), and '$\supset$' is the indicative conditional 'if... then __'. For instance, (12.1) might be the statement

If every existent object (x is such that x) perishes, then Caesar perishes. (12.1*)

Similarly, an instance of rule of universal instantiation is

$$\forall x(P(x)); \text{ so } P(t) \tag{12.2}$$

For example, (12.2) might be the inference

Every existent object (x is such that x) perishes; so Caesar perishes. (12.2*)

Typically, instead of these, free logics adopt a restricted principle of universal specification (or its inferential counterpart, restricted universal instantiation). For instance, in place of (12.1), one customarily finds

(Res 1) $\quad \forall x(P(x)) \supset (t \text{ exists} \supset P(t))$

where an instance of (Res 1) would be

(Res 1*) If every existent object (x is such that x) perishes, then Caesar perishes provided Caesar exists.

Similarly, in place of (12.2), one typically finds

(Res 2) $\quad \forall x(P(x)); \text{ so } (t \text{ exists} \supset P(t))$

For example,

(Res 2*) Every existent object (x is such that x) perishes; so Caesar perishes provided Caesar exists.

As suggested in the first paragraph above, if identity is in the language, 't exists' can be eliminated in favor of '$\exists x(x=t)$'. In particular, 'Caesar exists' can be taken as shorthand for 'There exists an object x (such that x) is the same as Caesar'.

Some, but not all, free logics are *universally* free. In universally free logics, statements such as

$$\forall x(P(x)) \supset \exists x(P(x)) \tag{12.3}$$

are not regarded as logically true because they require the assumption that there exists at least one object, or, in more conventional parlance, they require the assumption that the domain (or universe) of discourse (construed as the set of existent objects) is nonempty. But it is important to notice that rejection of the logical truth of a statement like (12.1*), and acceptance of the logical truth of a statement like (Res 1*), concerns their constituent singular terms; it is presumed only that their constituent singular terms have existential import. They do not, as does acceptance of (12.3) as a logical truth, require the domain (or universe) of discourse to be nonempty. Indeed it is common to see statements such as (12.3) adopted as a logical truth in many systems of free logic. Such free logics, thus, are not universally free.

Free logics are compatible with a pair of conflicting world pictures (essentially, interpreted model structures). One kind, the actualist world picture, depicts the inhabitants of a world (members of the domain, or universe of discourse, of a model structure) to be of only one kind, the existent objects. An exponent of this kind of world picture is the British philosopher Bertrand Russell. The second kind, the nonactualist world picture, depicts the inhabitants to be of two kinds, those that exist and those that do not exist. An exponent of this kind of world picture is the Austrian Philosopher Alexius Meinong. In the first kind of world picture, to say that a singular term has existential import amounts to saying that its purported referent is an inhabitant, but this is not so in the second kind of world picture. For singular terms, not having existential import is not necessarily to be equated with not having a referent or not denoting.

Free logics can be divided into three classes depending on how atomic statements containing singular terms not having existential import are evaluated for truth-value. *Negative free logics* are those free logics in which all atomic statements containing at least one singular term not having existential import are evaluated false. This species of free logic has become a very common logical foundation for certain kinds of programming languages. *Positive free logics* are free logics in which some atomic statements containing singular terms not having existential import are evaluated true. This species of free logic also serves as a logical foundation for some programming languages, LISP, for example. *Neutral free logics* are free logics in which atomic statements, except perhaps those of the form '*t* exists', containing at least one singular term not having existential import, are evaluated as truth-valueless. Those who do not accept a Meinongian world picture consider this species of free logic more congenial to normal inference obeying the Fregean principle that the value of a complex expression is a function of the values of its parts; see, for example, Lehmann (1994).

How the truth-value of atomic sentences containing singular terms without existential import are to be evaluated affects quite dramatically one's account of logical truth and valid inference. For instance, consider Descartes's *Cogito ergo sum*. In negative free logics, the conditional 'If I think, then I am' is logically true and the inference from 'I think' to 'I am' is valid, but in positive free logics (based on a nonactualist world picture), the conditional in question is not logically true and the inference is invalid. In the negative free logic case, any substitution instance for the singular term 'I' that does not have existential import, in 'I think' will make the premise false, and hence the inference valid. But, in the case of positive free logics, substitution, for example, of the grammatically proper name 'Vulcan', a singular term not having existential import, for 'I' in both premise and conclusion of the inference in question and 'is the same as' for 'think' in the premise, yields a true premise, but a false conclusion. On the other hand, there are positive free logics based on actualist world pictures in which the inference from 'I think' to 'I am' is valid, but the conditional 'if I think, then I am' is not logically true (Bencivenga et al., 1991, pp. 115–16).

Free logics do not presume that those singular terms falling in the class of grammatically proper names are reducible to definite descriptions. They do not presume that 'exists' in singular statements such as 'Caesar exists' is a predicate, for there may be free logics in which the expression 'exists' does not even occur in the language (Lambert, 1963a). They do not presume that the interpretation of the quantifiers is objectual, i.e., that the truth of quantificational statements is given by clauses appealing to the values of the variables; such clauses might instead appeal to a subclass of the substituends of the variables, namely, those that have existential import. Finally, to re-emphasize a point made above, free logics do not presume there is any intimate connection between a singular term 't' having existential import and 't' referring.

Despite anticipations in the first half of the twentieth century, e.g., by Rosser (1939), concentrated technical and philosophical study of free logics dates only from the mid-1950s.[2] Their genesis and leading principles may be explained as follows.

12.2. Genesis and Leading Principles

Let 'S' and 'P' be place holders for general terms, expressions purporting to be true (or false) of each of possibly many objects. The Port Royal theory of immediate inference, a theory that flourished in the vicinity of 1662 and which derived ultimately from Aristotle, counted the inferences of the following forms valid:

     (A)   All S are P

∴ (I)   Some S are P

and

     (E)   No S are P

∴ (O)   Some S are not P

Moreover, that theory classified as valid inferences from an (A) statement to the negation of an (O) statement, and vice versa, and from an (E) statement to the negation of an (I) statement, and vice versa.

It is a commonplace that these inferences break down when (A) and (E) statements are interpreted as universal conditionals and (I) and (O) statements are interpreted as existential conjunctions, unless at least the placeholder 'S' is restricted to general terms having existential import – general terms true of at least one existent object. For corroboration, let 'S' be the general term 'planets between the Earth and the Moon', a general term without existential import, and let 'P' be the general term 'in solar orbit', a general term that does have existential import. In the language of traditional logic, the validity of the inferences described earlier is preserved by requiring that all statements of the four basic forms have existential import with respect to their constituent general terms.

This policy has adverse consequences. First, the scope of the Port Royal theory of immediate inference is thereby restricted, which thus precludes its use in assessing the validity of inferences containing general terms without existential import in subject position. For instance, under the current interpretation of the four basic statement forms, the theory cannot be applied to many inferences containing statements of physical law. The statement

> All bodies on which no external forces are acting move uniformly in a given direction

is such a statement because the general term 'bodies on which no external forces are acting' lacks existential import. Second, the Port Royal theory allows no distinction between inferences whose validity requires the assumption that at least its general terms in subject position in the various statements making up the inference have existential import from that inferences whose validity requires no such assumptions. For example, inferences from (A) statements to the negation of (O) statements, and vice versa, require no such assumption, but inferences from (A) statements to (I) statements do.

In the modern logic dating from Frege, object language counterparts of general terms (or predicates) with and without existential import became available: a general term (or predicate) has existential import just in case there exists an object x such that x is S, otherwise it does not have existential import. (A) to (I) and (E) to (O) inferences are modified to hold on to the additional assumption that there is an object x such that x is S, but the mutual inferability between (A) statements and the negation of the corresponding (O) statements, and between (E) statements and the negation of the corresponding (I) statements do not require any such assumption. Given these object language counterparts of general terms (or predicates) with (and without) existential import, it is now customary to say that the modern theory, in contrast to the Port Royal theory of immediate inference, purports to be "free of existence assumptions with respect to its general terms."[3]

Nevertheless, the modern logic also faces a similar problem, but in its treatment of singular inference. Where 't' is a singular term, the following inference (called 'universal instantiation,' UI, after its rule counterpart):

UI   For all objects x, x is such that x is S

∴ t is S

is valid in the modern logic. But, as has often been noted, the validity of this inference is threatened by singular terms without existential import. Let 't' be the singular term 'Vulcan', an expression purporting to name a certain planet causing the perturbations in the orbit of Mercury, and let 'S' be 'there is a object y such that x is the same as y'. Then the premise

For all objects x, there is an object y such that x is the same as y

of UI is true but its conclusion,

There is an object y such that Vulcan is the same as y

is false. Indeed, in a dialogue with Frege in the late 1800s, the validity of UI was challenged on similar grounds by Punjer. Frege's response (1969) has become the standard response when 'Vulcan' is taken to be a genuine singular term, namely, that in logic expressions that occupy the place of 't' are presumed to have existential import.

This policy on singular inference suffers from essentially the same difficulties previously noted with respect to the Port Royal theory of immediate inference. First, it restricts the scope of the modern theory of singular inference. For instance, the modern theory of singular inference cannot be applied to the inferential ruminations of astronomers prior to the discovery of Leverrier that there is no object that is Vulcan; it cannot adjudicate the worth of the inference

Vulcan is the planet causing the perturbations in the orbit of Mercury.

That planet will be at location L at 10.00 PM.

So, Vulcan will be at location L at 10.00 PM.

Second, it cannot discriminate between inferences, like that just depicted, whose validity does not require that their constituent singular terms have existential import from those, like UI above, whose validity does.

In the modification of the modern theory of singular inference called free logic, object language counterparts of singular terms with and without existential import is readily available; a singular term 't' has existential import just in case there exists an object x such that x is t (or, more briefly, just in case t exists). The inference UI is valid only with the additional premise that t exists. That is, the restriction that 't' must have existential import is lifted in free logic, and the inference UI is replaced by

RUI   For all objects x, x is such that x is S.

t exists.

∴ t is S.

This restricted form of universal instantiation is a characteristic feature of free logics. (Indeed, it is easily shown that UI above is valid just in case

There exists an object x, such that x is t.

is valid.)

It is appropriate, then, to say that just as the modern logic of general inference purports to be free of existence assumptions with respect to its general terms, free logics are free of existence assumptions with respect to their general *and* singular terms. It may thus be construed as the culmination of an attitude toward the logic of terms most fully expressed in the logic dating from Frege, and, indeed, implicit in his response above to Punjer.

12.3. Proof Theory

Proof theoretical developments of free logic typically are of two sorts depending on whether the primitive predicate of singular existence, 'E!', is available. For convenience, axiomatic formulations of both sorts will be presented here. It should be noted, however, that natural deduction and tableau (or tree) versions of every species of free logic are widespread.[4]

The vocabulary and grammar of a (first-order) free logic is not essentially different from that of a standard (first-order) predicate logic [see chapter 1] except for the possible presence of a singular existence symbol, 'E!', whereby 'E!t' would be well-formed when 't' was any individual term. 'a', 'b', 'c', etc. represent singular terms (individual constants); 'x', 'y', 'z', etc. represent individual variables; 's', 't', etc. may refer to any individual term, constant or variable; and unless specified otherwise, 'A', 'B', 'C', ..., etc. represent formulas with or without free variables. Statements are closed formulas. '$A(s/t)$' refers to the result of substituting 's' for 't' in A.

The *transformation* rules of the formal system PFL_1 without 'E!' in its primitive vocabulary are these. An *axiom* of PFL_1 is a tautology or any closed statement of the following forms:

MA1 $A \supset \forall x A$

MA2 $\forall x(A \supset B) \supset (\forall x A \supset \forall x B)$

MA3 $\forall y(\forall x A \supset A(y/x))$

MA4 $\forall x \forall y A \supset \forall y \forall x A$

MA5 $\forall x A(x/a)$ if A is an axiom[5]

The only rule of inference is

D   From A, $A \supset B$, infer B.

As usual, a *derivation* of a statement A from a set of statements S is a sequence $\langle A_1, \ldots, A_n \rangle$ such that

(i) $A = A_n$
(ii) A_i is a member of S, or A_i is an axiom, or A_i is the result of previous members of the sequence in accordance with D.

If S is empty, A is a *theorem* in PFL_1 and the sequence $\langle A_1, \ldots, A_n \rangle$ is a *proof* of A in PFL_1.

When the vocabulary of PFL_1 contains an identity predicate and formulas $s = t$, then if the transformation rules of PFL_1 are supplemented by at least

MA6 $a = b \supset (A \supset A(b//a))$

where '$A(b//a)$' is the result of replacing a at one or more places in A by b, if at all, then the restricted principle of universal specification – the statement counterpart of the rule of restricted universal instantiation –

RUS $\forall x A \supset (E!a \supset A(a/x))$

is derivable with the help of the definition

Def1 $E!t =_{df} \exists x(x = t)$

Moreover MA4, the principle of universal quantifier permutation, is also eliminable from the primitive frame of PFL_1. This system ($PFL_{1=}$) is philosophically interesting because it provides a non-modal motivation for the principle MA3, a principle independently recommended in Kripke's treatment of quantified modal logic [see chapter 7].

Another formulation, PFL_2, in which 'E!' is a primitive symbol without identity, is readily obtainable from the core of PFL_1.[6] To obtain the most typical version, *sans* identity, it is sufficient to replace MA3 and MA4 in the primitive frame of PFL_1, respectively, by RUS (= MA3*) and

MA4* $\forall x E!x$

To obtain the standard version of PFL_2 with identity ($PFL_{2=}$), it is sufficient to supplement PFL_2 with MA6 and

MA7 $a = a$

See, for example, Meyer and Lambert (1968). One consequence of this formulation is a formal justification for the definition Def1, as Hintikka (1959) was the first to show; i.e., the biconditional

HT $E!a \equiv \exists x(x = a)$

is derivable in $PFL_{2=}$. Hintikka's discovery assumes greater importance in developments like PFL_2 (and indirectly in PFL_1) given the discovery by Meyer et al. (1982) that $E!a$ is indefinable in PFL_2 itself. Much tradition to the contrary notwithstanding, these two results show that the assertion (or denial) of, say, the planet Vulcan's existence can only be effected, in standard logics *sans* identity but freed of existence assumptions with respect to their terms, by use of the general term 'exists'.

The formal systems above are positive free logics, intuitively reflecting, on appropriate interpretation, that some atomic sentences containing singular terms without existential import are true. There are, however, formal systems of free logic – negative free logics – which are intended to reflect the intuition that all such sentences are false. To represent this in the object language, virtually all versions of negative free logic (NFL) have a primitive existence symbol if identity is not available in the language.[7] So, corresponding to $PFL_{1=}$, there is the system of negative free logic $NFL_{1=}$. It is obtained from $PFL_{1=}$ by substituting for the meta-axioms MA4* and MA7, respectively, the meta-axioms

MA4** $\forall x \exists y (x = y)$

MA7* $\forall x (x = x)$

and adding the meta-axiom

MA5+ $A(a_1, \ldots, a_n) \supset (\exists x (x = a_1) \,\&\, \cdots \,\&\, \exists x (x = a_n))$, where $n \geq 1$ and $A(a_1, \ldots, a_n)$ is atomic.

This system, due in essentials to Burge (1991 [1974], p. 192), permits contexts of the form '$E!t$' to be introduced as in Def1 or, alternatively, by the definition

Def2 $E!t =_{df} t = t$

Also, as in $PFL_{1=}$, RUS can be reduced to the status of a derived principle. MA7 no longer holds – failing, in virtue of MA5+, when t is a singular term not having existential import. Of special note is the fact that

$A(a/x) \supset \exists x A$ if $A(a/x)$ is atomic

is derivable, a principle which is not derivable (nor is logically true) in any positive free logic. This is, perhaps, the most important difference between negative and positive free logics.

When '$E!$' is taken as primitive, corresponding to PFL_2 is the system of negative free logic NFL_2. It is obtained by appending to the set of meta-axioms in PFL_2, the meta-axiom

MA5+* $A(a_1, \ldots, a_n) \supset (E!a_1 \,\&\, \cdots \,\&\, E!a_n)$, where $n \geq 1$ and $A(a_1, \ldots, a_n)$ is atomic.[8]

Similarly, corresponding to the system $PFL_{2=}$, there is the system of negative free logic $NFL_{2=}$. It is obtained by adding to NFL_2 the meta-axiom MA6, and substituting the meta-axiom

MA7* $\forall x (x = x)$

for MA7 of $PFL_{2=}$. See Scales (1969, esp. pp. 11–12).

12.4. Model Theory

Typically, model structures for free logics are of two kinds. The simplest kind – an FM_1 model structure – is an ordered pair $\langle D, f \rangle$, where the domain D is a (possibly empty) set of objects, and the interpretation function f is a function such that

(i)   where a is singular term, $f(a)$ is a member of D, if $f(a)$ is defined
(ii) where P is an n-adic predicate, $f(P)$ is a set of n-tuples of members of D
(iii) every member of D has a name.

Customarily D is construed as the set of existent objects, and hence this represents the actualist or 'Russellian' ontological picture described above. In the characterization of an FM_1 model structure, (i) reveals f to be to be a partial function;[9] it typically represents the possibility that a singular term may not have existential import. (iii) is merely a convenience to enable the clause for the universal quantifier in the ensuing definition of truth in an FM_1 model to be given a substitutional characterization; it is adequate for most logical purposes.

Models of the FM_1 variety are exploited in all three kinds of free logic, positive, negative and neutral. To illustrate this, consider first the definition of truth for a negative free logic with identity such as $NFL_{1=}$.

A statement is true (or false) in an FM_1 model just in case these conditions obtain (Burge, 1991 [1974], p. 194):

(i)   If A has the form $P(a_1, \ldots, a_n)$ then A is true in an FM_1 model if each of $f(a_1), \ldots, f(a_n)$ is defined and $\langle f(a_1), \ldots, f(a_n) \rangle$ is a member of $f(P)$; otherwise A is false in that model.
(ii) If A has the form $a = b$, then A is true in an FM_1 model if $f(a)$ and $f(b)$ are defined and $f(a)$ is the same as $f(b)$; otherwise A is false in that model.
(iii) If A has the form $\sim B$, then A is true in a FM_1 model if B is false in that model; otherwise A is false in that model.
(iv) If A has the form $B \supset C$, then A is true in an FM_1 model if B is false in that model or C is true in that model; otherwise A is false in that model.
(v)   If A has the form $\forall x B$, then A is true in an FM_1 model if $B(a/x)$ is true in that model for all a such that $f(a)$ is a member of D; otherwise A is false in that model.

To obtain a definition of truth in an FM_1 model for a negative free logic with a primitive existence symbol but without identity – such as NFL_2 above – it suffices to replace clause (ii) in the definition above by

(ii*) If A has the form $E!a$, then A is true in an FM_1 model iff $f(a)$ is defined in that model; otherwise A is false in that model.

Soundness and completeness of $NFL_{2=}$ (with and without the primitive symbol E!) based essentially on this kind of semantics has been readily established (Schock, 1968).

For a system of positive free logic like PFL$_{2=}$ above, another kind of definition of truth based ultimately on an FM$_1$ kind of model structure utilizes van Fraassen's widely exploited notion of 'supervaluation.' Here it is presented as augmented by Bencivenga (1991 [1980]); see the references there to van Fraassen's original work.

First, the notion of a classical model structure is needed. A classical model structure is exactly like an FM$_1$ model structure minus the provision 'if f(a) is defined' in clause (i). In short, in classical models, every singular term is assigned some member of the domain D; there are no terms without existential import.[10] Nevertheless, in this approach, under the constraint of the facts, such models can be used to help to assess the truth-value of statements containing singular terms that do lack existential import because they can be viewed as ways of completing an FM$_1$ model.

Second, a complete model structure FM$_1^c$ *based on* an (incomplete) *model structure* FM$_1 = \langle D, f \rangle$ may now be defined as a pair $\langle D^c, f^c \rangle$ such that

(i) D^c is nonempty and has D as a subset

and the interpretation function f^c obeys the conditions that

(ii)   f^c(a) is a member of D^c
(iii) f^c(a) = f(a) wherever f(a) is defined
(iv)   f(P) ⊆ f^c(P) for every *n*-adic predicate P.

A complete model structure FM$_1^c$ based on FM$_1$ is a *completion* of FM$_1$.

Third, the truth-value of a statement (true, false, or neither) in an FM$_1$ model $\langle D, f \rangle$ can now be defined progressively in stages, the third and last of which invokes the notion of a supervaluation.

Where *A* is an atomic statement of the language:

(i)   if *A* has the form P($a_1, \ldots, a_n$), and if all of f(a_1), ..., f(a_n) are defined, then *A* is true in the FM$_1$ model just in case $\langle f(a_1), \ldots, f(a_n) \rangle$ is a member of f(P), and otherwise *A* is false therein
(ii)   if *A* has the form in (i), and at least one of f(a_1), ..., f(a_n) is undefined, then *A* has no truth-value
(iii) if *A* has the form E!a, then *A* is false in the FM$_1$ model iff (if and only if) f(a) is undefined
(iv)   if both of f(a) and f(b) are defined, and *A* has the form a = b, then *A* is true in the FM$_1$ model if f(a) is the same as f(b), and otherwise *A* is false therein
(v)   if exactly one of f(a) and f(b) is undefined, and *A* has the form a = b, then *A* is false in an FM$_1$
(vi)   if neither of f(a), f(b) are defined, and *A* has the form a = b, then *A* has no truth-value in an FM$_1$ model.

Intuitively, the foregoing definition may be construed as providing the basic factual information upon which to calculate the truth-value of any statement in the formal language. Clauses (iii) and (v) are important because they show statements which are factually false, in some uncontroversial sense of 'factual', even when containing a singular term without existential import. The next definition takes seriously the notion of a completion of an FM_1 model into consideration.

Where A is a statement of the language, and M* is a completion of an FM_1 model M, A is true or false in M* *vis-à-vis* M under the following conditions:

(i) if A is an atomic statement and has a truth-value in M, then the truth-value of A in M* *vis-à-vis* M is the same as the truth-value of A in M

(ii) if A is a truth-valueless atomic statement in M, then the truth-value of A in M* *vis-à-vis* M is the same as the truth-value of A in M*

(iii) if A has the form of $\sim B$, then A is true in M* *vis-à-vis* M iff B is false in M* *vis-à-vis* M

(iv) if A has the form $B \supset C$, then A is true in M* *vis-à-vis* M iff B is false in M* *vis-à-vis* M or C is true in M* *vis-à-vis* M

(v) if A has the form of $\forall x B$, then A is true in M* *vis-à-vis* M iff $B(a/x)$ is true in M* *vis-à-vis* M for all singular terms a such that E!a is true in M* *vis-à-vis* M.

Clause (i) in this definition shows that the facts cannot be overridden in a completion. For example, if E!a should turn out false in an FM_1 model M in virtue of the singular term 'a' having no existential import, it has the same value in M* *vis-à-vis* M even though in M* (a kind of model in which all singular terms have existential import) E!a is true. This is the formal force of the phrase 'under the constraint of the facts' above.

Given a FM_1 model M, the *supervaluation* S *over* M is the set of all completions of M. Truth, falsity and neither in a *supervaluation* can now be defined as follows:

Where A is a statement of the formal language, and S_M is the supervaluation S over the FM_1 model M, then:

(i) A is true in S_M iff A is true in M* *vis-à-vis* M for every completion M* based on M

(ii) A is false in S_M iff A is false in M* *vis-à-vis* M for every completion M* based on M

(iii) A is neither true nor false in S_M iff A is true in M* *vis-à-vis* M for some M* based on M and A is false *vis-à-vis* M in others

In this kind of semantics, supervaluations are the admissable valuations, i.e., they are the valuations in terms of which logical truth and validity are defined.[11] Soundness and (weak) completeness of essentially $PFL_{2=}$ with a primitive existence symbol are readily available.[12]

Finally, a definition of truth based of an FM_1 kind of model for neutral free logic is also possible. Following Lehmann (1994), '$\vee$' and '$\exists$' replace '$\supset$' and '$\forall$' as primitive signs in what follows:

(i) If A has the form $P(a_1, \ldots, a_n)$, then if $f(a_1), \ldots, f(a_n)$ are defined, then A is true (false) in an FM_1 model if $\langle f(a_1), \ldots, f(a_n) \rangle$ is a member of $f(P)$ (is not a member of $f(P)$); otherwise A has no truth-value therein.

(ii)   If A has the form $a = b$, then A is true (false) in an FM_1 model if $f(a)$ and $f(b)$ are defined and $f(a)$ is the same as $f(b)$ (are not the same); otherwise A has no truth-value therein.

(iii)   If A has the form $\sim B$, then A is true (false) in an FM_1 model if B is false (true) therein; otherwise A has no truth-value therein.

(iv)   If A has the form $(B \vee C)$, then A is true in an FM_1 model just in case B is true and C is true, or B is false and C is true, or B is true and C is false; A is false therein if both B and C are false; otherwise A has no truth-value therein.

(v)   If A has the form $\exists x B$, then A is true in an FM_1 model if $B(a/x)$ is true therein for some singular term a such that $f(a)$ is defined; otherwise A is false therein.

This definition of truth is a more conventional adaptation of Lehmann's semantics. It yields, indirectly, a soundness and completeness proof of the Jeffrey-like tree rules in Lehmann's formulation of the proof theory for his version of neutral free logic.[13]

The second kind of model structure, FM_2, that one finds in treatments of free logics takes M to be a triple $\langle D_o, D_i, f \rangle$, where D_o (the outer domain) is a possibly empty set, D_i (the inner domain) is a possibly empty set disjoint from D_o, whose union $D_o \cup D_i$ is nonempty, and an interpretation function f such that

(i) $f(a)$ is a member of $D_o \cup D_i$
(ii) $f(P)$, where P is an n-adic predicate, is a set of n-tuples of members of $D_o \cup D_i$
(iii)   every member of $D_o \cup D_i$ has a name.

Typically, the inner domain is interpreted as the set of existent objects, and the outer domain is construed as the set of nonexistent objects, and thus an FM_2 model represents the inhabitants of the nonactualist, or Meinongian, ontology.[14] Inner domain–outer domain model structures, as these kinds of model structures have come to be known,[15] are used most widely in the semantical developments of positive free logics, and much less frequently in negative free logics; there are no known cases of such structures in semantical treatments of neutral free logics. It is to be noted that, in the typical construal, the interpretation function f defined on the singular terms is total, and, hence, that a singular term can refer even when it is devoid of existential import.

A statement A (of the formal language) is true (or false) in an FM_2 model under the following conditions:

(i)   If A has the form $P(a_1, \ldots, a_n)$, then A is true in an FM_2 model if $\langle f(a_1), \ldots, f(a_n) \rangle$ is a member of $f(P)$; otherwise A is false therein.

(ii)   If A has the form $\sim B$, then A is true in an FM_2 model just in case B is false; otherwise A is false therein.

(iii)   If A has the form $B \supset C$, then A is true in an FM_2 model if B is false therein or C is true therein; otherwise A is false therein.

(iv)   If A has the form $\forall x B$, then A is true in an FM_2 model if $B(a/x)$ is true therein for all singular terms a such that $f(a)$ is a member of D_i; otherwise A is false therein.

Essentially, this semantics yields soundness and completeness (weak and strong) for PFL_1.[16] When identity is added to the language, as in $PFL_{1=}$, it is necessary to add the condition

(v)   If A has the form $a = b$, then A is true in an FM_2 model if $f(a)$ and $f(b)$ are the same; otherwise A is false therein.

to extend the completeness proof (Leblanc, 1982). For a formulation such as PFL_2, to obtain soundess and completeness, it is necessary to add

(v*)   If A has the form $E!a$, then A is true in an FM_2 model if $f(a)$ is a member of D_i; otherwise A is false therein.

in place of (v). Given the addition of (v) and (v*) to the truth definition above, the soundness and completeness (weak and strong) of $PFL_{2=}$ are straightforward enough (Meyer and Lambert, 1968).

FM_2 model structures have also been used in negative free logic, especially $NFL_{2=}$.[17] The only difference from the definition of truth given above for positive free logic lies in clauses (i) and (v). These are replaced, respectively, by

(i*)   if A has the form $P(a_1, \ldots, a_n)$, then A is true in an FM_2 model if each of $f(a_1), \ldots, f(a_n)$ is a member of D_i, and $\langle f(a_1), \ldots, f(a_n) \rangle$ is a member of $f(P)$; otherwise A is false therein

(v⁺)   if A has the form $a = b$, then A is true in an FM_2 model if $f(a)$ and $f(b)$ are members of D_i and $f(a)$ is the same as $f(b)$: otherwise A is false therein.

The import of (i*) and (v⁺) is to make false any atomic statement containing a singular term without existential import, for example, 'Vulcan is a planet' and 'Vulcan = Vulcan', in contrast to the definition of truth in an FM_2 model for a positive free logic like $PFL_{2=}$. Soundness and completeness are readily established for $NFL_{2=}$ in this semantic development.[18]

12.5.   Some Applications and Implications

Applications of free logics are wide and varied, ranging from the philosophy of religion at one extreme to programming languages at the other. A few of the more important are discussed below.

12.5.1.   Definite descriptions

The earliest and most well known application is to the (logical) theory of definite descriptions. Free logics have provided, for the first time in nearly a half century, new foundations for such theories, foundations differing from those provided by

Russell, Frege, and Hilbert and Bernays. Virtually all free theories of definite descriptions add the following minimal principle to the underlying free logic with identity.[19] Where '$\imath$' is the definite description operator,

MFD $\qquad \forall x(x = \imath y A \equiv \forall y(A \supset y = x))$

MFD does not hold in standard predicate logic, yet, in negative free logic with identity, it yields the analogs of the famous pair of definitions in Russell's theory of definite descriptions for atomic contexts as theorems without having to reject the singular term status of expressions of the form '$\imath y A$'. Moreover, if a complex predicate forming operator is added to the language, so that scope distinctions can be made, then the analogs of the Russell definitions extended to all contexts can be derived as theorems (Burge, 1991 [1974]; Scales, 1969). Similarly, in positive free logics, the famous elimination theorem of Frege can be derived with the help of the additional extensionality principle,

SText $\qquad \forall x(x = t \equiv x = s) \supset t = s$

where 's' and 't' are singular terms (names or definite descriptions). The system containing this pair of principles, MFD and SText, is known as FD2 in the literature (Lambert, 1963b, 1964; Scott, 1991 [1967]; van Fraassen and Lambert, 1967). Indeed, in positive free logics with identity, a whole hierarchy of definite description theories has emerged between the theory containing only MFD as the minimal theory and FD2 as the maximal theory. The exact nature of this hierarchy is not yet well understood.[20] Finally, it has recently been shown that the four major traditions in the logical treatment of definite descriptions can be seen as reactions to the unsoundness of the very natural principle MFD in standard predicate logic in the same way that various treatments of sets can be seen as reactions to the unsoundness of the principle of set abstraction in naive set theory (as Russell was the first to show) (Lambert, 1991b).

12.5.2. Presupposition

The importance of the semantic notion of presupposition in modern philosophical endeavors is hard to exaggerate. Two examples will suffice. First, Brittan's reconstruction of Kant's theory of science relies heavily on the oft heard language that the (basic propositions of the) Categories 'presuppose' the propositions of (the current) mathematics (e.g., Euclidean geometry) and (the current) natural science (Brittan, 1978, esp. pp. 28–42). Brittan treats that notion in the Frege–Strawson sense and argues

1   it is consistent with much Kantian text, and
2   allows Kant to escape, for example, the criticism that his metaphysical views are falsified by the subsequent development of non-Euclidean geometries.

Second, Lambert's reconstruction of Reichenbach's treatment of the logic for quantum mechanics dispenses with Reichenbach's third truth-value and, in effect, treats elementary statements about definite position (or definite momentum) as presupposing certain measurement conditions. Since the presuppositions must fail, according to the laws of modern quantum mechanics, elementary statements about definite position (or momentum) are 'meaningless', i.e., have no truth-value, *à la* the Copenhagen interpretation (Lambert, 1969a). In both of these examples, the notion of presupposition is treated as a semantical notion, and has received rigorous treatment in some positive free logics and in neutral free logics.

In the supervaluational treatment of positive free logic (van Fraassen, 1991 [1968]), the Frege–Strawson notion of presupposition is analyzed as a metalogical relation:

PRE$_{f\text{-}s}$ A presupposes $B =_{df}$ Neither A nor $\sim A$ is true if B is false.

This relation is distinct from the relation of logical implication and leads to no inconsistency in the van Fraassen–Bencivenga treatment of supervaluations because, though the law of excluded middle is a logical truth, the principle of bivalence that every statement is true or false, does not hold. In Woodruff's version of neutral free logic, which contains a truth operator in the object language, the Frege–Strawson notion is treated as an object language relation as follows:

PRE$_r$ A presupposes $B =_{df} T(A) \vee F(A) \rightarrow B$

where '$\rightarrow$' means '$T(A) \supset T(B)$' (Woodruff, 1970, pp. 134–7). The choice between the two approaches depends on one's preference for the non-truth-functional supervaluational approach versus the truth-functional Frege-inspired approach favored in most semantical versions of neutral free logic. In either foundation for free logic, it follows that many, if not most, predications containing a singular term without existential import – for example, 'Vulcan revolves around the sun' – will have no truth-value because they presuppose a false statement like 'Vulcan exists.'

12.5.3. *Partial functions and programming*

The most recent and flourishing nonphilosophical application of free logics has been in the treatment of partial functions *vis-à-vis* the development of programming languages and program verification. Lambert and van Fraassen (1972, pp. 209–210), noted that one of the obvious applications for free logic lay in the development of a natural theory of partial functions, functions which yield no values for some arguments. Later, Beeson (1985) utilized, in effect, a negative free logic for just this purpose; see also Troelstra and van Dalen (1988, esp. ch. 2, section 2). More recently, Feferman (1995) has used negative free logic for reasoning about expressions which may or may not have a value, especially in complex computational languages, and Farmer (1995) has used a negative free logic in the development of the programming language IMPS for use in reasoning about partial functions. Parnas (1995), likewise, has employed a negative free logic in the development of a technical language for use in the description of software, while Gumb (1989, ch. 5), uses a positive free logic to express information about execution-time errors in programs.

The issue in most of these cases concerns the truth-value to be assigned to identities containing partial function names, for example,

$$5/0 = 5/0$$

where '/' is the two-place partial function sign for division. This sentence is false in all negative free logics, and, indeed, that is the policy most often followed in free logical treatments of partial functions. Recently, however, Gumb and Lambert (1997) have argued that for certain programming languages this policy would be disastrous, for example, as in ALGOL60 and LISP. It is essential in such programming languages that a sentence like

$$5 = \text{if } 5 = 5 \text{ then } 5 \text{ else } 5/0$$

turn out true, and, hence, they have argued that, at least for certain programming languages, the underlying free logic must be positive.

12.5.4. Extensionality

Turning, finally, to one of the most important philosophical applications of free logic, it is necessary, first, to say what it means for a language to be completely extensional in the sense of *salva veritate* substitution. A language is completely extensional if the truth-value of every statement composed of singular terms and/or predicates and/or statements is preserved when co-referential singular terms are substituted for each other, co-extensive predicates are substituted for each other, and co-valent statements are substituted for each other, in those statements. Every free logic fails this test, and hence is not completely extensional. In particular, what fails is the principle that co-extensive predicates always substitute for each other *salva veritate*. This result follows from the fact that the principle of universal specification, rejected in free logics, is logically equivalent to the principle

CP $\forall x(A \equiv B) \supset (A(t/x) \equiv B(t/x))$

where 't' is a singular term (name or definite description) (Lambert, 1974). Indeed, if 't' is 'Vulcan', 'A' is '$x = x$' and 'B' is 'E!x & $x = x$' (or 'E!$x \supset x = x$') one obtains from CP

Vulcan = Vulcan $\equiv$ (E!Vulcan & Vulcan = Vulcan)
(or E!Vulcan $\supset$ Vulcan = Vulcan)

But no matter what truth-value the left-hand side of this biconditional has (including none at all), the right-hand side will have a different truth-value depending on the choice for 'B'.[21]

This failure can have dramatic philosophical consequences. For example,

(i)   it is instrumental to the proof that the theory of predication in Quine's (1960) *Word and Object*, a cornerstone of his theory of referential opacity, is unsound,[22] and

(ii) it is essential to the proof that extensionality *qua* truth-value preservation and extensionality *qua* truth-value dependence are not equivalent even in a predicate logic with singular terms having no existential import and only identity (Lambert, 1997b).

There are those who imagine that failures of various extensionality principles, in the truth-preservation sense, have to do with the addition of operators like 'it is possible that' and 'believes that' to the standard theory of general inference. But with the advent of free logics, there is another kind of addition that takes on special significance *vis-à-vis* extensionality. Just as the addition of modal operators to the standard theory of inference can threaten the substitutivity of co-referential singular terms, so can the addition of singular terms without existential import to the standard theory of inference threaten the substitutivity of co-extensive predicates.

Suggested further reading

An especially readable motivation for free logic is the author's recent *Free Logics: Their Foundations, Character, and Some Applications Thereof* (Lambert, 1997a). Another is Bencivenga's (1989) essay, "Why Free Logic?" in his book *Loose Ends*. Other useful introductions to the subject are Schock (1968), Lambert and van Fraassen (1972) and Bencivenga et al. (1991). More recent technical work can be found in a variety of sources, published and forthcoming, including the proof theory in Lehmann's (1994) paper and a forthcoming essay by Antonelli entitled "Proto-semantics for Positive Free Logic" and various essays in the forthcoming volume *New Directions in Free Logic*, a set of essays edited by E. Morscher. Further technical work can be found in the three papers by Feferman (1995), Farmer (1995), and Parnas (1995), all in volume 43 of *Erkenntnis*; these concern the use of essentially negative free logic to provide a foundation for a natural theory of partial functions. More philosophically oriented work can be found in two recent essays by the author (Lambert 1997b, 1998). Finally, the volume *Philosophical Applications of Free Logic* (Lambert, 1991a) contains an especially wide array of applications of free logics, old and new, from the philosopy of religion to the philosophy of mathematics.

Notes

1   Thus the property of existential import is a property of terms, not of quantifiers. For a more detailed discussion, see Eaton (1931, pp. 223–6).

2   The pivotal paper in the development of free logic is that of Leonard (1956). Other pioneering studies include Hintikka (1959); Leblanc and Hailperin (1959); Smiley (1960); Lambert (1963a, b; 1964); Schock (1964); van Fraassen (1966); Cocchiarella (1966); and Meyer and Lambert (1968).

3   Not quite, however, because in the modern logic general terms of the form 'is the same as *t*' must have existential import, where '*t*' is a singular term.

4   For 'natural deduction' versions see Hintikka (1959), Schock (1968), and Lambert and van Fraassen (1972). For tableau (or tree) versions see Bencivenga et al. (1991), and Lehmann (1994).

5   This set of meta-axioms, essentially an augmentation of the set in the purely quantificational fragment of Lambert (1963a) is due to Leblanc and Meyer (1970); Fine (1983) proved that MA4 is independent of the other meta-axioms in this set.

6   The first such formulation is due to Lambert (1967).

7   Nevertheless, a version of NFL_1 paralleling PFL_1 might be obtained by adding to PFL_1 the meta-axiom: $A(a/x) \supset \exists x A$, provided $A(a/x)$ is atomic. Though incomplete, as is the purely quantificational fragment of Lambert's (1963a) system (see note 5 above), when appropriate meta-axioms for identity are added, as in the formulation of Burge below, completeness is easily obtained.

8   This is essentially the system of Scales (1969, p. 11) minus his apparatus for complex predicates. The language of the provision in MA5+*, however, is closer to Burge (1991 [1974]).

9   There are model structures similar to FM_1 model structures but in which f is a total function, that is, (i) may be replaced by something like (i*): $f(a)$ is a member of D or $f(a) = D$. In this kind of development, singular terms without existential import, for example, 'Vulcan,' are assigned D, and hence, under the conventional rendition of identity, 'Vulcan = Vulcan' turns out true. Hence, this yields a positive free logic (Scott, 1991 [1967]).

10 The reason the Scott-ish model described in note 9 is not a classical model is this: though every singular term is assigned something, not every singular term is assigned something *in* the domain D. In fact, those singular terms without existential import are just those singular terms assigned to D itself.

11 The current statement of supervaluations follows very closely the account in Bencivenga et al. (1991). There is a more lengthy statement of motivations underlying this kind of semantic development in Lambert (1997a). Skyrms (1968) offered a way of augmenting van Fraassen's idea of supervaluations to make them sensitive to differences of structure in atomic statements. It too is a positive free logic. In an informal note to Skyrms, David Kaplan showed that the evaluation rules were not recursively axiomatizable.

12 See, for example, Bencivenga (1991 [1980]). Woodruff (1984) showed that neither compactness nor strong completeness can be proved for $PFL_{2=}$ (with or without a primitive existence symbol) based on supervaluations.

13 Lehmann (1994, sections 2–4). As Lehmann notes, his particular semantics was anticipated by Smiley (1960), though Smiley presented no proof theory. Lehmann's paper contains the only published soundness and completeness proof for neutral free logic. Woodruff offered a proof theory, containing a truth operator, and semantics for a neutral free logic, but it turned out be unsound (as Woodruff himself noted), see Woodruff (1970, esp. p. 142). There is also an excellent discussion of the various semantical approaches for (positive and neutral) free logics permitting truth value gaps in Lehmann (1994). I am grateful to Lehmann for his advice in the adaptation of his original semantics.

14 But not always. In the treatment by Meyer and Lambert (1968), the outer domain (the semantical domain) is stipulated to be a set of expressions. The ontological picture is that of a set of nominalized second intensions *à la* Goodman. So FM_2 there does not reflect the essential ingredient of a Meinongian ontology because the objects (expressions) in the outer domain exist.

15 This kind of model structure (and essentially the ensuing truth definition) was independently invented by Lambert and by Belnap, and presented in lectures by them during the

late 1950s. Lambert's inner domain–outer domain model structure (but not the ensuing truth definition) is reflected in Meyer and Lambert (1968). The most extensive and detailed published treatment of the use of inner domain–outer domain semantics in (positive) free logic is by Leblanc and Thomason (1968).

16 See Leblanc (1982, pp. 58–75). Independently, Gumb (1979) (in a positive free logic without function names) and Dwyer (1988) (in a positive free logic with function names) have demonstrated that Craig's interpolation lemma and Beth's definability theorem [see chapter 1] extend to positive free logics. (The same pair of results extend to negative free logic if definitions are understood as in Schock (1968). I owe this observation to Ray Gumb.)

17 See the formulation, minus the addition of the complex predicate forming operator 'λ,' in Scales (1969, pp. 11–17).

18 Scales' proof (1969, p. 124) is indirect, proceeding via an equivalent formulation in terms of tableau rules. To accommodate $NFL_{2=}$, it suffices to drop the tableau rules involving the complex predicate operator 'λ' in Scales' proof.

19 The only exceptions may be a system proposed by Robinson (1979), and the system in Stenlund (1973). Most, if not all, free definite description theories take as their underlying foundation either a positive or negative free logic (with identity). The first sound and complete free definite description theory was proposed by Lambert, (1963b, 1964). It was in the first of this pair of papers that the basic principle of free definite description theories, MFD, was proposed; it is now called 'Lambert's Law' among free logicians. Of free definite description theories that have been proposed and/or further studied, the more prominent are those in Bencivenga (1980), Burge (1991 [1974]), Grandy (1991 [1972]), Scales (1969), Schock (1968), Scott (1991 [1967]), and van Fraassen and Lambert (1967).

20 See Lambert (1997a, chs 6 and 7) for a fuller account of free theories of definite descriptions and the problem of the hierarchy of positive free definite description theories.

21 In the case of Lehmann's semantics, the counter-example to CP requires different instances of both 'A' and 'B,' namely, '$E!x$' and '$E!x \supset E!x$,' respectively.

22 The proof in question is in Lambert (1998). In this same paper, it is argued that if a predicate forming operator is added to the language of negative free logic, as in Scales (1969), and predications taken as just a subset of the atomic sentences, it may be possible to save a CP-like principle at least in negative free logics. For a realization of this possibility in positive free logic, see Lambert and Bencivenga (1986).

References

Beeson, M. 1985: *Foundations of Constructive Mathematics*, 3. Folge, Band 6, (Springer-Verlag, Berlin).

Bencivenga, E. 1980: "Free Semantics for Definite Descriptions," *Logique et Analyse*, 92, 393–405.

Bencivenga, E. 1989: "Why Free Logic?," in *Loose Ends*, Bencivenga, E. (ed.), (University of Minnesota Press, Minneapolis).

Bencivenga, E. 1991: "Free Semantics," *Boston Studies in the Philosophy of Science*, 47 (1980), 31–48; reprinted with revisions in Lambert (1991a, 98–111).

Bencivenga, E., Lambert K. and van Fraassen, B. 1991: *Logic, Bivalence and Denotation*, 2nd ed., (Ridgeview, Atascadero, CA).

Brittan, G. 1978: *Kant's Theory of Science*, (Princeton University Press, Princeton, NJ).

Burge, T. 1991: "Truth and Singular Terms," *Noûs*, 8 (1974), 309–25; reprinted in Lambert (1991a, 189–204).

Cocchiarella, N. 1966: "A Logic for Possible and Actual Objects," *Journal of Symbolic Logic*, 31, 688–9, (Abstract).

Dwyer, R. 1988: "Denoting and Defining," PhD thesis, University of California, Irvine.

Eaton, R. M. 1931: *General Logic*, (Charles Scribners' Sons, New York).

Farmer, W. 1995: "Reasoning about Partial Functions with the Aid of a Computer," *Erkenntnis*, 43, 279–94.

Feferman, S. 1995: "Definedness," *Erkenntnis*, 43, 295–320.

Fine, K. 1983: "The Permutation Principle in Quantificational Logic," *Journal of Philosophical Logic*, 12, 33–7.

Frege, G. 1969: "Dialog mit Punjer über Existenz. I. Der Dialog," in *Nachgelassene Schriften*, (Felix Meiner Verlag, Hamburg), 60–8.

Grandy, R. 1991: "A Theory of Truth with Intensional Definite Description Operators," *Journal of Philosophical Logic*, 1 (1972), 137–55; reprinted in Lambert (1991a, 171–88).

Gumb, R. 1979: "An Extended Joint Consistency Theorem for Free Logic with Equality," *Notre Dame Journal of Formal Logic*, 20, 321–35.

Gumb, R. 1989: *Programming Languages: An Introduction to Verification and Semantics*, (Wiley, New York).

Gumb, R. and Lambert, K. 1997: "Definitions in Nonstrict Positive Free Logic," *Modern Logic*, 7, 25–56. (Corrections of printing errors can be found in *CSLI Technical Report* CSLI-96-199.)

Hintikka, J. 1959: "Existential Presuppositions and Existential Commitments," *Journal of Philosophy*, 56, 125–37.

Lambert, K. 1963a: "Existential Import Revisited," *Notre Dame Journal of Formal Logic*, 4, 288–92.

Lambert, K. 1963b: "Notes on E!III: A Theory of Descriptions," *Philosophical Studies*, 13, 51–9.

Lambert, K. 1964: "Notes on E!IV: A Reduction in Free Quantification Theory with Identity and Definite Descriptions," *Philosophical Studies*, 15, 85–8.

Lambert, K. 1967: "Free Logic and the Concept of Existence," *Notre Dame Journal Of Formal Logic*, 8, 133–44.

Lambert, K. 1969a: "Logical Truth and Microphysics," in Lambert (1969b, 93–117).

Lambert, K. 1969b: *The Logical Way of Doing Things*, (Yale University Press, New Haven).

Lambert, K. 1974: "Predication and Extensionality," *Journal of Philosophical Logic*, 3, 255–64.

Lambert, K. 1991a: *Philosophical Applications of Free Logic*, (Oxford University Press, New York and London).

Lambert, K. 1991b: "A Theory about Logical Theories of 'Expressions of the Form "the so and so" where "the" Is in the Singular'," *Erkenntnis*, 35, 337–46.

Lambert, K. 1997a: *Free Logics: Their Foundations, Character, and Some Applications Thereof*, (Academia Verlag, Sankt Augustin, Germany).

Lambert, K. 1997b: "Nonextensionality," in *Das weite Spektrum der analytischen Philosophie*, W. Lenzen, ed., (de Gruyter, Berlin), 135–49.

Lambert, K. 1998: "Fixing Quine's Theory of Predication," *Dialectica*, 52, 153–61.

Lambert, K. and Bencivenga, E. 1986: "A Free Logic with Simple and Complex Predicates," *Notre Dame Journal of Formal Logic*, 27, 247–56.

Lambert, K. and van Fraassen, B. 1972: *Derivation and Counterexample*, (Dickenson, Encino, CA).

Leblanc, H. 1982: *Existence, Truth and Provability*, (SUNY Press, Albany).

Leblanc, H. and Hailperin, T. 1959: "Nondesignating Singular Terms," *Philosophical Review*, 68, 129–36.

Leblanc, H. and Meyer, R. K. 1970: "On Prefacing $\forall xA \supset A(y/x)$ with $(\forall y)$: A Free Quantification Theory without Identity," *Zeitschrift für mathematische Logik und Grundlagen der Mathematik*, 16, 447–62.

Leblanc, H. and Thomason, R. 1968: "Completeness Theorems for Some Presupposition-Free Logics," *Fundamenta Mathematicae*, 62, 125–64.

Lehmann, S. 1994: "Strict Fregean Free Logic," *Journal of Philosophical Logic*, 23, 307–36.

Leonard, H. S. 1956: "The Logic of Existence," *Philosophical Studies*, 7, 49–64.

Meyer, R. K. and Lambert, K. 1968: "Universally Free Logic and Standard Quantification Theory," *Journal of Symbolic Logic*, 33, 8–26.

Meyer, R. K., Bencivenga, E. and Lambert, K. 1982: "The Ineliminability of E! in Free Quantification Theory without Identity," *Journal of Philosophical Logic*, 11, 229–31.

Parnas, D. 1995: "A Logic for Describing, Not Verifying, Software," *Erkenntnis*, 43, 321–38.

Quine, W. V. O. 1960: *Word and Object*, (Wiley, New York).

Robinson, A. 1979: "On Constrained Denotation," in *Selected Papers, Vol. 2*, H. Keisler, S. Körner, W. Luxemberg and A. Young, eds., (Yale University Press, New Haven), 493–504.

Rosser, J. B. 1939: "On the Consistency of Quine's *New Foundations for Mathematical Logic*," *Journal of Symbolic Logic*, 4, 15–24.

Scales, R. 1969: "Attribution and Existence," PhD thesis, University of California, Irvine.

Schock, R. 1964: "Contributions to Syntax, Semantics, and the Philosophy of Science," *Notre Dame Journal of Formal Logic*, 5, 241–90.

Schock, R. 1968: *Logics Without Existence Assumptions*, (Almqvist and Wiksells, Uppsala).

Scott, D. S. 1991: "Existence and Description in Formal Logic," in *Bertrand Russell: Philosopher of the Century*, R. Schoenman, ed. (Little, Brown and Co., Boston), 1967, 181–200; reprinted in Lambert (1991a, 28–48).

Skyrms, B. 1968: "Supervaluations: Identity, Existence and Individual Concepts," *Journal of Philosophy*, 64, 477–83.

Smiley, T. 1960: "Sense without Denotation," *Analysis*, 20, 125–35.

Stenlund, S. 1973: *The Logic of Descriptions and Existence*, (Filosofiska Studier, Uppsala).

Troelstra, A. S. and van Dalen, D. 1988: *Constructivism in Mathematics: An Introduction*, Vol. 1, (North Holland: Amsterdam).

van Fraassen, B. 1966: "The Completeness of Free Logic," *Zeitschrift für Mathematische Logik und Grundlagen der Mathematik*, 12, 219–34.

van Fraassen, B. 1991: "Presupposition, Implication and Self-Reference," *The Journal of Philosophy*, 65 (1968), 136–52; reprinted in Lambert (1991a, 205–21).

van Fraassen, B. and Lambert, K. 1967: "On Free Description Theory," *Zeitschrift für Mathematische Logik und Grundlagen der Mathematik*, 13, 225–40.

Woodruff, P. 1970: "Logic and Truth-Value Gaps," in *Philosophical Problems in Logic*, K. Lambert, ed., (D. Reidel: Dordrecht), 121–42.

Woodruff, P. 1984: "On Supervaluations in Free Logic," *Journal of Symbolic Logic*, 49, 943–50.

Chapter 13

Relevant Logics

Edwin D. Mares and Robert K. Meyer

Once upon a time, modal logic was castigated because it 'had no semantics.' Kripke, Hintikka, Kanger, and others changed all that. In a similar way, when Relevant Logic was introduced by Anderson and Belnap, it too was castigated for 'having no semantics.' Then Routley and Meyer (1982a [1973]) changed all that, along with Urquhart (1992a [1972]), Fine (1992b [1974]), and others. The present overview marks a culmination of that effort. The semantic approach described here brings together a number of hitherto disparate efforts to set out formal systems for logics of relevant implication and entailment. It also makes clear (despite some of our hopes and utterances) that the One True Logic *does not exist*. This is as true for relevant logics as Kripke et al., showed it to be for modal logics. In both cases, subtle (and not so subtle) variations on semantical postulates produce different logics in the same family. The question of which semantical postulates are correct makes no sense without further context, i.e., the questioner needs to answer the question: Correct for what? The question that does remain is: What motivates the relevant *family* of logics? And this is the question that is the main job for this chapter to investigate.

13.1. A Little History

Entailment, one would think, is a *relation*. It is the relation that holds between the *premises* of a valid argument and its *conclusion*. Yet modern symbolic logic, which at least since DeMorgan and Peirce has prided itself on taking relations seriously, failed to do so with respect to the central notion of *logical consequence* that is its business to analyze. Here and later we shall insist on the essentially relational character of a good implication.

The modern history of relevant logics begins at the same point as the history of modal logics – namely, with the disquiet over the thought that the material ⊃ is a decent implication.[1] With the ink scarcely dry on the first edition of Whitehead and Russell's *Principia Mathematica* (1910–13), C. I. Lewis (1918) was already in print, decrying the paradoxes of 'implication.' The chief ones say (in English),

P–   A false proposition implies anything.

P+   Anything implies a true proposition.

P– and P+ reflect the well-known truth table for $\supset$, which looks like

$\supset$	F	T
F	T	T
T	F	T

Now what, honestly, would induce a sane human being to suppose that this table captures 'implies'? (Or even, as has sometimes been urged instead, 'if ... then'?) Until they have been brainwashed with sophistries, elementary logic students grasp the point at once. This table is silly. No, Bertie, 'France is in Australia' does not imply 'The sea is sweet'. And no, Van, it is equally false to say 'If France is in Australia then the sea is sweet'.

To be sure, Logic is the *science* of argument, and like any other science, Logic has a right to simplifying assumptions and a formalism of its own. But it also has the obligation to enrich that formalism, the better to separate good arguments from bad.

Lewis saw it that way, introducing several systems of strict implication to overcome the deficiencies of P– and P+, and, as shall be seen a little later, Lewis' original rejection of material implication is based on ideas very close to those of relevant logicians. Beginning with negation $\sim$ and a binary consistency operator $\circ$, Lewis defined strict implication (our $\rightarrow$), via the rubric

D$\rightarrow$ $A \rightarrow B =_{df} \sim(A \circ \sim B)$

That is, A (strictly) implies B just in case A is inconsistent with the negation of B. The task of formalizing a good theory of implication then becomes one of finding the right postulates for the *binary* possibility operator.

In a certain sense, of course, Lewis believed that P– and P+ are true. He agreed that

CP– $\sim A \supset (A \supset B)$

CP+ $A \supset (B \supset A)$

are logical truths. But he also held that "[t]he relation $A \supset B$ in this calculus has not quite the usual meaning of 'A implies B,' due to the fact that relations of the system are those of extension" (Lewis and Langford, 1959, p. 85). Lewis had no objection to CP– and CP+ as material logical truths. He had no qualm with accepting the material hook (or horseshoe) as a legitimate connective. But he objected to the identification of the hook with *implication*. Pleasantly (as Lewis and his later co-author Langford saw it), CP– and CP+ are not theorem schemes of any of the systems of theirs (1959), when formulated with strict implication replacing material $\supset$.

Less welcome to many later logicians were the paradoxes of strict implication, which Lewis and Langford (1959) considered ineluctable. These say, again in English,

SP−   An impossible proposition implies anything.

SP+   Anything implies a necessary truth.

Paradigmatic formal counterparts for Lewis of SP− and SP+ were the following:

XP− $(A \wedge \sim A) \to B$

XP+ $A \to (B \vee \sim B)$

So important were XP− and XP+ to Lewis that he and Langford gave 'independent arguments' for them. Here is a version for XP− based on that of Lewis and Langford (1959, p. 250):

1	$A \wedge \sim A$	Hypothesis
2	A	1, ∧Elim
3	$\sim A$	1, ∧Elim
4	$A \vee B$	2, ∨Intro
5	B	3, 4, Disjunctive Syllogism
6	$(A \wedge \sim A) \to B$	1–5, →Intro

The argument is simple, perhaps even familiar, but is it any good? Is each line really entailed by its premises?[2] It seems that in his 1917 article "The Issues Concerning Material Implication" Lewis had already seen why it is fallacious. There he sets out a dialogue between two characters: X and himself (L). Here is a relevant part of that dialogue (Lewis, 1917, p. 355):

> *L.* But tell me: do you admit that "Socrates was a solar myth" materially implies $2 + 2 = 5$?
> *X.* Yes; but only because Socrates was *not* a solar myth.
> *L.* Quite so. But if Socrates were a solar myth, would it be true that $2 + 2 = 5$? If you granted some paradoxer his assumption that Socrates was a solar myth, would you feel constrained to go on and grant that $2 + 2 = 5$?
> *X.* I suppose you mean to harp on "irrelevant" some more.

In his and Langford's 'independent argument' for XP−, they do not "grant the paradoxer his assumption" that a contradiction holds. What is needed is a way to deal non-trivially with impossible assumptions, like contradictions or Socrates' being a solar myth. Section 13.4 returns to the treatment of impossibilities in relevant logic. The next section 13.2 turns to another aspect of the relevant analysis of the paradoxes.

13.2. Variable Sharing

What *in general* is wrong with the paradoxes of implication? It would seem that, in each, there is an insufficient tie between antecedent and consequent or premise and conclusion. As Lewis says in the dialogue given above, there is a lack of *relevance* here.

Relevant logics ensure that logically true implications do not have antecedents that are completely irrelevant to their consequents. As Ackermann (1956), the father of the theory of relevant entailment, wrote, there should be a connection between the content of the antecedent and the content of the consequent. This connection might seem difficult to enforce. For *content* is a semantic notion. The notion of a logic, on the other hand, is usually taken to be a syntactic concept, specified either in terms of a set of valid proofs or of a set of theorems. The gap between the semantic and the syntactic is bridged in part, however, by the *variable sharing constraint*. A logic, **L**, satisfies the variable sharing constraint iff (if and only if) whenever $A \rightarrow B$ is a theorem of **L**, A and B share at least one propositional variable.[3] The variable sharing constraint forces the antecedent and consequent to share some content, for then they are, in part, both about at least one or two or more propositions. Thus, they cannot be *absolutely* semantically irrelevant to one another.

A form of the variable sharing constraint was discovered early in the development of modern logic. Russell's book, *The Principles of Mathematics*, begins in its first chapter with a version of variable sharing (1903, p. 3):

> Pure mathematics is the class of all propositions of the form "*p* implies *q*," where *p* and *q* are propositions containing one or more variables, the same in the two propositions, and neither *p* nor *q* contains any constants except logical constants.[4]

It is not remarkable that Russell demands that all statements of mathematics be implications, since it is well-known that Russell (following Peano) believed that statements of mathematics are formal implications. What is interesting, however, is that Russell demands that the two propositions in an implication of mathematics contain exactly the same variables. The variables discussed here are not usually propositional variables, as they are in the relevant logicians' variable sharing constraint, but Russell does seem to desire that the formal implications of mathematics connect propositions that have content in common. These propositions are supposed to be about the same things (Russell, 1903, section 5).

The variable sharing constraint by itself, however, does not yield an analysis of relevance. Although it is a necessary condition for a logic to be a relevant logic, it is not sufficient. For suppose that one merely accepted all of the theorems of classical logic that satisfied this constraint. One would then still be left with

$$p \rightarrow (q \rightarrow p)$$

$$\sim(p \rightarrow q) \rightarrow (q \rightarrow r)$$

as well as many other paradoxes.

13.3. The Deduction Theorem

Relevant logics are supposed to capture the relation of entailment or that of implication between propositions. The philosophical notion of entailment was first developed by G. E. Moore in approximately 1920. He defines 'p entails q' to mean 'q is deducible from p' (Moore, 1922, p. 291). Thus, where '$\vdash$' represents the relation of deducibility, the following captures the logics of entailment:

> If $A \vdash B$, then it is a theorem of the logic that A *entails* B.

Since implication is logically weaker than entailment, this relationship should also hold for implication. The above condition is known as the *single premise deduction theorem*.

To understand the importance of the deduction theorem in this context, a little more needs to be said about the notion of relevant deducibility. One standard condition on deducibility relations is that, if a proposition is a premise then it can also be a conclusion. For example, classical logicians and intuitionists take

> (PP) $p, q \vdash p$

to be a valid deduction. But relevant logicians do not. For, consider the full deduction theorem:

> If $A_1, \ldots, A_n, A \vdash B$, then $A_1, \ldots, A_n \vdash A \rightarrow B$

If one were to accept (PP), then, by two applications of the deduction theorem, one would have to accept

> $\vdash p \rightarrow (q \rightarrow p)$

This says that $p \rightarrow (q \rightarrow p)$ is a theorem. But it is a paradox of implication, and it is not wanted. So one cannot accept this standard condition on deducibility.

Instead, relevant logicians have developed a notion of deduction due to Moh Shaw-Kwei (1950) and Church (1951). On this conception of deducibility, $A_1, \ldots, A_n \vdash B$ is *relevantly valid* only if $A_1, \ldots, A_n$ may *all* be really used in the deduction of B. In (PP), q is *not* used in the deduction of p, hence relevant logicians claim that (PP) is not a valid inference.[5]

The requirement that it is *possible* to use all premises in a relevant deduction needs itself to be fleshed out. One means, in natural deduction systems, is the method of 'relevance indices.' Such systems are not dealt with here,[6] but the main point can be put briefly. Hypotheses in a proof are tagged, and other steps are indexed by the tags on the hypotheses that are used to produce them. For a tagged hypothesis A to be discharged in a conditional sub-proof, the conclusion C of that sub-proof *must bear* (perhaps among others) the tag on the hypothesis A; if it does, $A \rightarrow C$ is inferred by *discharging* A, ending the sub-proof. After this application of the $\rightarrow$ I rule, the tag on the discharged hypothesis A is removed from the indices on $A \to C$, which inherits its remaining tags, if any, from the conclusion C of the conditional proof. If a tag on a hypothesis does not appear in the steps on which the conditional proof is based, then the hypothesis cannot be discharged in that proof. Thus only hypotheses that are really used can be discharged.

In sequent systems for relevant logics, the real use requirement is enforced by treating premises and their relation to conclusions in a very intensional manner. A sequent (or consecution) is a structure of the form $A_1, \ldots, A_n \vdash B$. And a sequent calculus (also known as a 'consecution calculus' or 'Gentzen system') is a logic for inferring sequents from sequents. Consider the classically and intuitionistically valid inference on sequents from (13.1) to (13.2):

$$B \vdash C \tag{13.1}$$

$$A, B \vdash C \tag{13.2}$$

This inference – the so-called 'weakening' rule – obviously allows one to add arbitrary premises, even those that *cannot* be used in any intuitive sense. True, there is a way to concede that classical or intuitionist logicians who appeal to the weakening rule know what they are talking about. For they interpret the structural ',' as extensional conjunction '$\wedge$'. Following Dunn (1975b [1973]) and Mints (1976), *another* structural connective is introduced, ':', to do this job. So the standard logician does have a good argument to justify weakening. But it applies to ':', and not to ','. So from (13.1), one can justifiably conclude, not (13.2), but

$$A : B \vdash C \tag{13.3}$$

On the Dunn–Mints plan, this leads immediately to

$$A \wedge B \vdash C \tag{13.4}$$

Relevant logicians deny that (13.2) and (13.3) are equivalent. That is, they deny that the premises in a relevantly valid argument are conjoined to one another with standard conjunction. Rather, they think an inference $A_1, \ldots, A_n \vdash B$ is equivalent to $\vdash A_1 \to (\ldots (A_n \to B) \ldots)$. Moreover, the latter is *not* equivalent to $\vdash (A_1 \wedge \cdots \wedge A_n) \to B$ in relevant logics. Instead of taking premises in an inference as bound together by standard extensional conjunction (i.e. whose truth conditions are determined by a truth-table), relevant logicians have introduced another form of conjunction. This is the intensional conjunction that was briefly introduced in section 13.1. It is called *fusion*, written '∘', and goes back (at least) to Church (1951). The central requirement of fusion is that it obey *residuation*:

$$A \circ B \vdash C \text{ iff } A \vdash B \to C$$

In short, fusion needs to satisfy the deduction theorem.[7]

To sum up what has been said so far, relevant logics should satisfy three conditions:

1 They should avoid the paradoxes of implication and, in particular, give a way of dealing with contradictions and other impossibilities non-trivially.
2 They should satisfy the variable sharing constraint.
3 They should contain a deducibility relation that requires all premises in a valid deduction to be capable of being used in that deduction and they should satisfy a deduction theorem.

13.4. The Ubiquity of Inconsistency

Relevant logics avoid XP–. This makes them *paraconsistent* logics. A paraconsistent logic is a logic that somehow tolerates contradictions. This is a very good feature. For contradictions are everywhere. Sad though this fact may be for any pursuit of rationality, candor compels its admission. Here are some of the spots at which inconsistencies break through:

- *Natural science* A theory is said to be 'in difficulties' when it conflicts with the results of observation or with another well-accepted theory. Combined with classical physics, Bohr's early theory of the atom predicts that electrons would radiate energy and fall into nuclei, and that they would not.
- *Foundations of Mathematics* From infinitesimal analysis through the summation of infinite series to the contradictions of set theory, mathematics too has ever been 'in difficulties.'
- *Bad data* A recent census reported one million more married women than married men in the USA. This is unlikely.
- *Metaphysics* Is not Zeno's arrow always both at rest and in motion?
- *Theology* God is three. God is one. Is He off by two?

This is not to suggest that the contradictions in all (or even any) of these cases is ineluctable. Great efforts have been made to resolve (or at worst live with) the associated problems. But no one takes XP– above at face value, to deduce whatever they want (and don't want) from present mistakes (if mistakes they be).

Rather, as Belnap has urged, people reason around any inconsistency in their present beliefs. This section now tries to find some theoretical ground on which to do so. Building on algebraic and semantic work by Białnicki-Birula and Rasiowa (1975), Dunn (1975a [1966]) and others, Routley and Routley (1972) introduced a unary operation on what are called 'worlds' or, more soberly, 'theories', 'set-ups' or 'situations'. Where a is a world, Routley and Routley postulate a companion world a^* such that

T~ $I(\sim A, a) = true$ iff $I(A, a^*) = false$

where I is an interpretation in a model. Two ways to understand the 'Routley star operator' are discussed in section 13.6 below. Given this formalism, however, it is immediately clear how Routley and Routley (renamed Sylvan and Plumwood) provide a semantic refutation of XP–. Here $(p \wedge \sim p) \rightarrow q$ is refuted. Fixing a, set $I(p, a) = true$ and $I(p, a^*) = I(q, a) = false$. Applying T$\sim$ this makes the premise (of XP–) true at a but its conclusion false at a. And a purported implication that fails to preserve truth is surely no just candidate to ground a theory of logical consequence.[8]

13.5. Model Theoretic Semantics

Section 13.4 introduced worlds and the Routley star operator. Now it is time to present a semantics for relevant logic in almost all its glory. Some its finer technical details are omitted, and discussion is limited to its philosophically more interesting aspects.

Like Kripke's semantics for modal logics [see chapter 7], the semantics for relevant logic is a world-based semantics. Our frames start with a set of worlds, K. Of these worlds, some are distinguished, and called N ('normal worlds'). A formula is valid in a frame iff it is true on all normal worlds on all interpretations. Like Kripke, there is also an accessibility relation, R, between worlds. His accessibility relation, however, is meant to deal with a unary operator, necessity. Instead, R deals with a binary relation, implication. According to Jónsson and Tarski (1951), it makes formal sense to treat a unary connective by means of a binary relation and to treat a binary connective using a ternary relation.

The truth condition for relevant implication is

T$\rightarrow$ $I(A \rightarrow B, a) = true$ iff for all b, c such that $Rabc$, if $I(A, b) = true$, then $I(B, c) = true$.

Notice how this truth condition allows one to avoid, e.g., the paradoxical $A \rightarrow (B \rightarrow B)$ since it does not force $B \rightarrow B$ to hold at all worlds.

To handle negation, there is the Routley star operator, introduced above. The truth conditions for extensional conjunction and disjunction are straightforward:

T$\wedge$ $I(A \wedge B, a) = true$ iff $I(A, a) = true$ and $I(B, a) = true$.

T$\vee$ $I(A \vee B, a) = true$ iff $I(A, a) = true$ or $I(B, a) = true$.

Intensional conjunction, or fusion, discussed above, has a more technical condition:

T$\circ$ $I(A \circ B, a) = true$ iff there are some worlds b, c, such that $Rbca$ and $I(A, b) = true$ and $I(B, c) = true$.

This condition looks a bit forbidding, but it can be understood if one follows Lewis in thinking of fusion as a type of binary relative possibility connective. $I(A \circ B, a) = true$ says that, A and B are jointly possible at a in the sense that a recognizes the combination of worlds in which A and B obtain.

The relationship between non-normal worlds and normal worlds in the Routley–Meyer – henceforth *relational* – semantics is also interesting and important. Define a relation on worlds ≤ such that

a ≤ b iff there is some world n in N such that Rnab

and postulate that ≤ is reflexive and transitive. Also, place certain constraints on frames and on interpretations so that *hereditariness* holds, namely,

If I(A, a) = *true* and a ≤ b, then I(A, b) = *true*.

It is traditional in logic to identify an entailment *relation* on sentences with the truth of → statements at one or more points. This tradition is reflected in the relational semantics via the semantical entailment fact below. Given an interpretation I, it is said that

A entails B iff, for all worlds a, if I(A, a) = *true* then I(B, a) = *true*.

Entailment thus being (as usual) truth-preservation over *all* worlds, the matching true → statements are those true at all normal worlds n in N. That is, given I,

A *normally implies* B iff, for all n in N, I(A → B, n) = *true*.

And now by hereditariness and reflexivity of ≤, this important *semantical entailment fact* obtains, for every frame and every interpretation I therein:

Fact (SemEnt):   *A entails B iff A normally implies B.*

The proof is simple, and so is left to the reader.

This fact simplifies soundness proofs for relevant logics. Suppose that one wants to verify a theorem of the form 'A → B'. Assuming that at an arbitrary world a, I(A, a) = *true*, one then shows I(B, a) = *true*. Applying SemEnt, A → B is true on every normal world in the model. Generalizing, A → B is true on every normal world in every model structure, hence it is valid. The reader should keep this use of SemEnt in mind when the various semantical postulates that are placed on models in coming sections are discussed. This clarifies greatly the relationship between the postulates and their corresponding axioms.

13.6.   Interpreting the Semantics

How is one to understand the various features of the semantics? We do not think that there is a single right answer to this question. Different relevant logics, we think, formalize different notions of entailment or implication. For these, different interpretations of their corresponding semantics are appropriate.

Consider the relation R. One interpretation, due to Barwise (1993) and developed by Restall (1996), takes worlds to be 'sites and channels.' A channel transmits information from site to site. In addition, channels can also be sites and sites can be channels. Where a, b and c are sites, they read $Rabc$ as saying that a is a channel between b and c, and thus $I(B \to C, a) = true$ as saying that all pairs of sites b, c connected by channel a are such that if B is information available in b, then C is information available in c. For example, for two sites connected by a telephone wire (the channel), what one person says in one site causes a person in the second site to hear certain sounds.

Mares (1996) presents another interpretation that adapts Israel and Perry's (1990) theory of information to the relational semantics. On this, the worlds in frames are situations, in the sense of Barwise and Perry's situation semantics (1983). [See chapter 20.] Situations contain information. A piece of information – an *infon*, to use Devlin's (1991) term – might be about the physical things in the situation, or it might be about connections between other infons. In particular, an infon might be about what information other infons carry. For example, an infon might carry the information that a red light showing on a stove carries the information that the oven is on. These infons that present information about connections between other infons, can be called *informational links*. The accessibility relation R represents the links in situations. If there is a link in a situation a that says that an infon σ carries the information that the infon π also holds, then if $Rabc$ and b contains the infon σ, then c contains the infon π. Links are not only included among the information in a situation, but also impose closure constraints on the set of infons in the situation. For example, if the 'law of nature'

All bodies attract one another

is a link in a and i and j are bodies in a, then i and j attract one another in a. Thus, on the link-interpretation, add the following postulate to the definition of a frame:

$Raaa$

which says that every situation is closed under informational links. And note that the link interpretation demands this closure. On the channel theoretic interpretation, on the other hand, this is an unnatural postulate, for not every channel carries information from itself to itself.

On to the other aspects of the semantics: As has been seen, the relational semantics divides worlds into normal and non-normal worlds. For some logics, the normal worlds (those at which we verify theorems) can be interpreted as possible worlds in the metaphysicians' sense. For these logics, the normal worlds can be taken to be complete (i.e. to satisfy the principle of excluded middle) and to be consistent. But not all relevant logics are characterized by a class of frames that have these properties. Only those logics which have excluded middle as a theorem and for which the rule gamma (γ) is admissible (see section 13.9) have a model theory of this sort.

The star operator has been controversial, but it can be given various reasonable interpretations. First, start with a linguistic interpretation from Meyer and Martin

(1986). The underlying idea here is that there is a distinction between what one actually *asserts* and what one fails to deny (thus what one *weakly asserts*). Here are a couple of sentences of recent interest:

P: In December 1999, NASA listened in vain for signals from the Mars polar lander.

Q: Martians interfered in 1999 with the transmission from their polar region.

All of us, probably, will agree with P. But what of Q? Only supermarket tabloids are likely actually to assert it, perhaps citing P as evidence. But one might, if one pleases, *weakly assert* Q, lacking evidence to support its denial. On this interpretation, a^* comprises the sentences weakly asserted at a.

Another interpretation, due to Dunn (1993), suggests one thinks of two worlds as containing compatible or incompatible information. Suppose that a says that a particular table is round and according to b that table is square. Then a and b can be said to be incompatible with one another. On the other hand, if there are no such conflicts, then the two worlds are compatible. In the language of our formal semantics *Cab* says that a and b are compatible. The truth condition for negation can be explicated in terms of compatibility alone, namely,

C~ $I(\sim A, a) = true$ iff for all b such that *Cab*, $I(A, b) = false$.

In other words, $\sim A$ is true at a if A's being true is somehow incompatible with the other information contained in a. Worlds can be incompatible with themselves; any inconsistent world is. The star operator can now be understood in terms of compatibility, for a^* can be taken to be the maximal world such that a is compatible with it. That is, for any world a, a^* is the world such that

(i)   *Caa** and
(ii) for any world b, if *Cab*, then $b \leq a^*$.

Of course, this definition assumes that, for any world, there always is a maximal world compatible with it.[9]

13.7.   Some Main Systems of Relevant Logic

This section presents some of the central systems of relevant logic. It does not present all the systems that people have proposed or on which important work has been done. Rather, it looks at only enough to give the reader the flavor of the systems and an idea of the range of relevant logics.

From the outset here, a relevant $\rightarrow$ has been considered *essentially relational*. Before going into the details of specific systems, one might pause to think about relations. The most famous ones are *binary* (2-place), e.g., *brother, sister, parent, child* – not to mention =, $\in$, $<$. Even modal logics have a philosophically motivated (Kripke) binary relational semantics [see chapter 7]. Yet the *key to the universe*, discussed below, involves a step up, at least to ternary (3-place) relations. (There are more than a few of these as well, e.g., *between, sum, product, jealous*.) Consider now relational *composition*. Use '*B*', '*P*', '*U*' respectively for *brother, parent*, and *uncle*. Then x is the uncle of y iff $\exists z(Bxz \wedge Pzy)$. The notation for this will set

$$Uxy =_{df} P(Bx)y$$

which one can abbreviate, on the obvious convention, to

$$Uxy =_{df} PBxy$$

Thus, the result of composing two binary relations is another binary relation. Things become more interesting when composing general n-ary relations. For one thing, composing two 3-place relations yields a 4-place one (and so on, pushing n as high as one likes). For another thing, the order in which 3-place relations are composed definitely matters. For it is important to distinguish $\exists x(Rabx \wedge Rxcd)$ from $\exists x(Raxd \wedge Rbcx)$. This can be done by extending the conventions just introduced in the 2-place case and writing:

$$Rabcd =_{df} R(Rab)cd =_{df} \exists x(Rabx \wedge Rxcd)$$
$$Ra(bc)d =_{df} Ra(Rbc)d =_{df} \exists x(Raxd \wedge Rbcx)$$

(thus, employing again the device of associating the composed relations *to the left*, inserting explicit parentheses otherwise. The iterated occurrences of R can also be dropped, which

(a) reduces visual clutter and
(b) clarifies connections between candidate logical axioms and matching combinators
 – *the key to the universe*, discussed below.)

Now for some systems: Start with the logic **B**. This system (or at least its *positive* part **B+**) may be taken as a base system in much the same sense as the logic **K** is taken to be the base normal modal logic. The language used, and that has been assumed throughout this chapter, includes the unary connective $\sim$ (for negation), the binary connectives $\wedge$ (extensional conjunction) and $\rightarrow$ (implication or entailment). Extensional disjunction, $\vee$, is another primitive for **B+**; otherwise it is defined, along with $\leftrightarrow$, as usual:

$$A \vee B =_{df} \sim(\sim A \wedge \sim B)$$
$$A \leftrightarrow B =_{df} (A \rightarrow B) \wedge (B \rightarrow A)$$

The axiom schemes and rules for **B** are as follows:

1     $A \rightarrow A$

2     $(A \wedge B) \rightarrow A$

3     $(A \wedge B) \rightarrow B$

4     $((A \rightarrow B) \wedge (A \rightarrow C)) \rightarrow (A \rightarrow (B \wedge C))$

5     $((A \rightarrow C) \wedge (B \rightarrow C)) \rightarrow ((A \vee B) \rightarrow C))$

6     $A \rightarrow (A \vee B)$

7     $B \rightarrow (A \vee B)$

8     $(A \wedge (B \vee C)) \rightarrow ((A \wedge B) \vee (A \wedge C))$

9     $\sim\sim A \rightarrow A$

$$\textit{Modus Ponens} \quad \frac{\vdash A \rightarrow B \\ \vdash A}{\vdash B}$$

$$\textit{Adjunction} \quad \frac{\vdash A \\ \vdash B}{\vdash A \wedge B}$$

$$\textit{Affixing} \quad \frac{\vdash B \rightarrow B' \\ \vdash A' \rightarrow A}{\vdash (A \rightarrow B) \rightarrow (A' \rightarrow B')}$$

$$\textit{Contraposition} \quad \frac{\vdash A \rightarrow \sim B}{\vdash B \rightarrow \sim A}$$

To form the positive fragment **B**+ of **B**, chop axiom 9 and the contraposition rule. To these systems, relevant logicians add various axiom schemes. For example, the logic **R** results from adding to **B** the schemes:

10     $(A \rightarrow B) \rightarrow ((B \rightarrow C) \rightarrow (A \rightarrow C))$ (*Suffixing*)

11     $(A \rightarrow (A \rightarrow B)) \rightarrow (A \rightarrow B)$ (*Contraction*)

12     $(A \rightarrow (B \rightarrow C)) \rightarrow (B \rightarrow (A \rightarrow C))$ (*Permutation*)

13     $(A \rightarrow \sim B) \rightarrow (B \rightarrow \sim A)$ (*Contraposition*)

14     $(A \rightarrow \sim A) \rightarrow \sim A$ (*Reductio*)

With the addition of these schemes, there is no need for the affixing and contraposition rules – they can be derived. (Adding these axiom schemes to **B**+ yields the positive fragment **R**+ of **R**, and similarly for the other logics mentioned below.)

    E results from adding to **B** suffixing, contraction, contraposition, reductio and another axiom, e.g.,

15     $(((A \rightarrow A) \wedge (B \rightarrow B)) \rightarrow C) \rightarrow C$

E was supposed to formalize the notion of entailment – 'the converse of deducibility.'
Entailment was motivated as *both* relevant and necessary. **R** was supposed to be the
'demodalized,' but nonetheless *relevant* version of **E**. The thought was that **R** has
approximately the same relationship to **E** that classical propositional logic has to **S4**.
A natural hope was that by adding an **S4**-like necessity, **R** could be extended to a
system **NR** that would prove equivalent to **E**, parsing the entailment of **E** as *strict*
relevant implication (Routley and Meyer, 1982b [1972]). Although Kripke and
others confirmed this for some fragments of **E**, the project unfortunately collapsed
when Maksimova (1973) exhibited a *non-theorem* of **E** which is nonetheless *provable*
on **NR** translation.

The system **T** of 'ticket entailment' results from adding to **B** suffixing, contraction,
and prefixing, which is

16     $(B \rightarrow C) \rightarrow ((A \rightarrow B) \rightarrow (A \rightarrow C))$

as well as contraposition (axiom 13) and reductio (axiom 14). Here an arrow
formula is taken as an inference ticket, '$A \rightarrow B$', saying that the inference from A to
B is justified (Anderson and Belnap, 1975, section 6).

Using the abbreviations introduced above, table 13.1 presents some correspondences between propositional theses and semantic theses in the relational semantics.
Also listed are the names of *associated combinators*, whose significance becomes clear
in section 13.8.

Table 13.1

Combinator	Thesis name	Thesis	Semantic postulate
B	Prefixing	$(B \rightarrow C) \rightarrow ((A \rightarrow B) \rightarrow (A \rightarrow C))$	$Rabcd \Rightarrow Ra(bc)d$
B'(= CB)	Suffixing	$(A \rightarrow B) \rightarrow ((B \rightarrow C) \rightarrow (A \rightarrow C))$	$Rabcd \Rightarrow Rb(ac)d$
W	Contraction	$(A \rightarrow (A \rightarrow B)) \rightarrow (A \rightarrow B)$	$Rabc \Rightarrow Rabbc$
C	Permutation	$(A \rightarrow (B \rightarrow C)) \rightarrow (B \rightarrow (A \rightarrow C))$	$Rabcd \Rightarrow Racbd$
C*(= CI)	Assertion	$A \rightarrow ((A \rightarrow B) \rightarrow B)$	$Rabc \Rightarrow Rbac$
K	Weakening 1	$A \rightarrow (B \rightarrow A)$	$Raba$
K*(= KI)	Weakening 2	$A \rightarrow (B \rightarrow B)$	$Rabb$
	Double negation	$\sim\sim A \rightarrow A$ and $A \rightarrow \sim\sim A$	$a^{**} = a$
	Contraposition	$(A \rightarrow \sim B) \rightarrow (B \rightarrow \sim A)$	$Rabc \Rightarrow Rac^*b^*$

13.8. Combinators: Connecting Proof Theory to Semantics

This section presents the mathematical motivations behind the various semantical
postulates. Clearly, the immediate mathematical motivation in each case is that the

postulate works – it does define a class of frames which characterizes the corresponding logical system. But, there is much more to it than this. There is an elegant
relationship between the conditions on relational frames and the branches of mathematics called 'combinatory logic' (**CL**) and 'lambda calculus' (**LC**).[10]

Combinatory logic was devised by Curry in approximately 1930 as a very general
way to represent and study operators and combinations of operators.[11] For example,
from (Hindley and Seldin, 1986, p. 20), consider the arithmetic operation of addition. Addition is commutative, i.e., $x + y = y + x$. Let the addition function be represented by +. Then $+(x, y) = +(y, x)$. Adopting the usual conventions of **CL**, all
functions may be treated as 1-place and parentheses and commas dropped while
associating to the left: $+xy = +yx$. Now introduce an operator **C** such that, for any
function f, $Cfxy = fyx$. Then it can be said of the addition operator that $+ = C+$.

Combinatory logic studies operators, called *combinators*, that, like **C**, describe the
behavior of functions. It begins with a small stock of combinators, and defines other
combinators from them. For example, there is another combinator that describes
how functions are composed. This is the combinator **B**, and it obeys the equation:

$$B(f, g)x = f(g(x))$$

where f and g are functions. **B** says that the result of applying the composition of
two functions to an object is the same as the result of the application of the first
function to the result of applying the second function to the object.

Instead of using special notation for functions, combinatory logic attempts to be
perfectly general, not distinguishing notationally between functions and other entities. To this end, '$Bxyz > x(yz)$' will be written to represent the above reduction
rule.[12]

In addition to the combinators themselves, one needs to understand the *type
schemes* of combinators.[13] A type scheme will be interpreted as a schematic formula.
In a 'Curry type,' the only pieces of logical notation are type variables p, etc., and
formulas A, etc., built out of these variables by implication $\rightarrow$ (and parentheses). For
example, the scheme $A \rightarrow B$ is the type of a combinator which takes entities of type
A to entities of type B. An easy combinator to type is the identity combinator, **I**,
whose reduction rule is $Ix > x$. Clearly, it takes entities of any type A and returns an
entity of the same type. So its type scheme is $A \rightarrow A$. The type of **K** is also easy to
understand. Its reduction rule is $Kxy > x$. (Kx) applied to any entity returns x. So,
it is a function from a thing of type A to a function from any entity to a thing of
type A. Consider $K3$, where 3 is the third positive integer. This is a *constant
function*, which returns the value 3 for any argument of any type. So **K** itself is of
the type $A \rightarrow (B \rightarrow A)$. Table 13.2 lists some combinators with their reduction rules
and principle type schemes.

A logic can be thought of in terms of a set of combinators. The relevant logic **R**,
for example, can be thought of as **B**, **C**, **I**, **W** logic because it contains as axiom
schemes the type schemes of these combinators. In addition, **R** contains as theorems
all the type schemes for the combinations of these combinators. For instance, the
type scheme of **CI** is $A \rightarrow ((A \rightarrow B) \rightarrow B)$, which is a theorem of **R**.

Table 13.2

Combinator (Name)	Reduction rule	Type-scheme
I (Identity)	$Ix > x$	$A \to A$
B (Composition)	$Bxyz > x(yz)$	$(B \to C) \to ((A \to B) \to (A \to C))$
B'	$B'xyz > y(xz)$	$(A \to B) \to ((B \to C) \to (A \to C))$
C	$Cxyz > xzy$	$(A \to (B \to C)) \to (B \to (A \to C))$
W (Diagonalization)	$Wxy > xyy$	$(A \to (A \to B)) \to (A \to B)$
K (Constant function)	$Kxy > x$	$A \to (B \to A)$
S (Strong composition)	$Sxyz > xz(yz)$	$(A \to (B \to C)) \to ((A \to B) \to (A \to C))$

To understand the relationship between combinators and the relational semantics, the notion of a *theory* is needed. The language used is a fragment of propositional language. For now, only formulas containing propositional variables, parentheses, extensional conjunction and relevant implication are considered. Then a theory of a logic **L** is defined to be a set of formulas X such that

(i) (*adjunction*) if A is in X and B is in X, then $A \wedge B$ is in X and
(ii) (*entailment*) if $A \to B$ is in **L** then, if A is in X, then B is also in X.

Then a model may be created out of the set of theories of **L**. The ternary accessibility of relation on this set will be defined later. Now, introduce a *fusion operator* on theories, ∘. (This is the same symbol as was used for intensional conjunction in the syntax; that will be explained later.) Fusion is defined on theories as:

If X and Y are theories of **L**, then $X \circ Y =_{df} \{B: \exists A (A \to B \in X \,\&\, A \in Y)\}$.

It can be shown that for any relevant logic that contains the implication–conjunction fragment of **B**, the fusion of two theories is also a theory.[14] The properties that fusion has in a structure of this sort depend on the choice of relevant logic for **L**, but here is one general property of fusion that will be needed later:

Fusion Fact   If $X \subseteq Y$, then $X \circ W \subseteq Y \circ W$.

(The proof of this fact is easy and is left to the reader.)

One way of looking at the variations between the structure of theories of different logics is by investigating the combinators under which they are closed. To explain: take the combinator *C*. For ease of expression omit the fusion operator and merely write '*xy*' for the fusion of x and y; and associate to the left as above. Applied to theories, the combinator equation for *C* says that $Cxyz = xzy$. Closure of a structure of theories under *C* means that for any theories x, y and z of **L**, $xyz = xzy$.

Now for the fun part: Recall that the principle type scheme for *C* is the permutation scheme $(A \to (B \to C)) \to (B \to (A \to C))$. One can prove that the theory structure for **L** is closed under *C* iff all instances of that type scheme are theorems of **L**. This might seem to be an amazing coincidence, but it is not merely a coincidence. It is, as promised, *the key to the universe*. The same correspondence holds for all the combinators listed above.

There's more! *Curry types* (near enough, pure → formulas) were assigned to combinators above. Types become more interesting if ∧ along with → are thrown in. This fact was independently discovered by workers in **LC** in the late 1970s, led by Coppo et al. (1980); but it is already reflected in the behavior of relevant theories under *fusion*. Here's the scoop.

Think again about formulas of the form $(A \rightarrow (B \rightarrow C)) \rightarrow (B \rightarrow (A \rightarrow C))$, which according to us (and Curry) are mates of the combinator *C*. This is not, however, a theorem scheme of the basic relevant logic **B**; but it does give rise to a *theory* – namely, the set of all formulas which are provably entailed in the basic relevant logic by conjunctions of permutation principles. It is this theory – call it *C* also – which so wonderfully interacts with the fusion operation ∘ on theories. Other cases are similar.

There are profound semantical and combinatorial facts underlying these correspondences. Check again the postulates in table 13.1 on the relevant accessibility relation *R* induced by various candidate axiom schemes. Note that, in the abbreviated relational notation, the postulates *look like* the matching reduction rules for corresponding combinators, as listed in table 13.2. Think yet again of *C*. Its combinatorial reduction rule sets *Cxyz* = *xzy*. In section 13.7, in table 13.1, the permutation axiom scheme was matched with the semantic postulate (often called 'Pasch') $Rxyzw \Rightarrow Rxzyw$. Note that the second and the third arguments are *reversed*, just as they are in the **CL** equality governing *C*. Combinator fans will note similar linkages with the other suggested postulates and axioms, such as *B′*, *W*, *CI*.

Meyer and Routley (1972) were already in print with a *key to the universe* remark, induced by the shape of relevant semantics and the corresponding algebras. They knew even then of the formulas-as-(Curry) types connections between combinators and theorems of pure → intuitionist logic. But there were other candidate relevant axioms that appeared as though they should fit into the scheme; but which did not do so. Table 13.3 extends the two preceding tables (13.1 and 13.2) by incorporating columns from both.

Both of these candidate axiom schemes contain ∧ along with →. *W** is also known as *WI*, *SII*, or λ*x* · *xx*. It has no Curry type. Yet the principles with which it has been mated – conjunctive *modus ponens* deductively and total reflexivity of the 3-place

Table 13.3

Combinator (name)	Reduction rule	Semantic postulate	Type-scheme
*W** (Duplication)	$W^*x > xx$	$Raaa$	$((A \rightarrow B) \wedge A) \rightarrow B$
WB	$WBxy > x(xy)$	$Rabc \Rightarrow Ra(ab)c$	$((B \rightarrow C) \wedge (A \rightarrow B)) \rightarrow (A \rightarrow C)$

relation R semantically – are natural (and famous). **WB** *does* have a Curry type – but it is the dull $(A \to A) \to (A \to A)$, not the more exciting conjunctive syllogism here.

These correspondences point to a deep relationship between theories, fusion and combinators. Return to our minimal positive logic **B+**; more particularly, to its implication–conjunction part **B∧**, pronounced 'Band,' which is determined by the $\to\land$ axioms 1–4 of section 13.7, with the *modus ponens*, adjunction and affixing rules governing these particles. For technical reasons (largely having to do with modeling the *bad* combinator K), it is useful to extend **B∧** to include also the *Church constant T*, subject to the axiom schemes

$(T1) \qquad A \to T$

$(T2) \qquad T \to (T \to T)$

The truth-condition on T is that it shall be marked *true* at every world, which is a dull (and mainly silly) thing to do.[15] The resulting system is called $\mathbf{B \land T}$ (say 'Bat'). Then, applying Barendregt et al. (1983) it can be seen that there is a model of **LC** (and hence of **CL**) in the theories of $\mathbf{B \land T}$.[16] For the *filters* of the **LC** algebraists are nothing but the *theories* of the relevant logicians. And the non-empty theories of $\mathbf{B \land T}$ have all the right properties, along the lines explored above, to make true the provable equalities of **CL**. Identify each combinator (B, C, W, K, S, W^*, I, etc.) with the set of all formulas of the corresponding scheme, closed in the appropriate way to make it a theory of $\mathbf{B \land T}$.

To be specific: Consider the combinator I, whose type scheme is $A \to A$. Since a theory is closed under the adjunction condition (i) on page 295 everything of the form $(A \to A) \land (B \to B)$ will also belong to the theory I. And since theories are closed under the condition of provable entailment (ii) on page 295 I will contain yet further members. Trivially, the top truth T is one such member; more interestingly, formulas entailed by members of I, like any $(A \land B) \to A$, also belong to I. In a nutshell, as readers may verify, I will consist *exactly* of the theorems of our minimal relevant logic. It follows, as night follows day, that, for every theory x, $Ix = x$.

Other combinators are similar – except that, since their corresponding schemes are only *sometimes* available, only those logics for which the schemes are valid will be closed under them. For illustrative purposes, consider the 'wicked' combinator K. Its reduction rule is $Kxy = x$. While hopefully one has by now excluded its mate $A \to (B \to A)$ from one's own preferred logic, the displayed equality holds already for all non-empty theories x, y at the $\mathbf{B \land T}$ level. For let $A \in x$. By definition of K, $B \to A \in Kx$ for *all* B. Something B belongs to the non-empty theory y – at least T, if nothing more salutary shows up. (And *that* is why T was added to **B∧**.) Detaching, $A \in Kxy$, which establishes the inclusion from right to left. The converse inclusion is also demonstrable. Using the ideas of Dezani, Motohama and their colleagues – especially Proposition 9.6 of Dezani-Ciancaglini et al. (1998, p. 70) – all the other demonstrable equalities of the $\lambda\beta$-calculus (and hence of its definable **CL** subsystem) are likewise modeled in the theories of $\mathbf{B \land T}$.

That **CL** is the key to the (relevant semantical) universe means, so far, that

(a) there is a minimal relevant logic **B**∧ based on → and ∧
(b) the non-empty theories of this logic (with T) constitute a model for **CL**
(c) the fusion of theories models functional application in **CL**
(d) combinators are the theories determined by their 'types'
(e) all combinator laws hold as equalities in the calculus of theories.

Much has been made by **CL** and **LC** theorists about the interpretations of *formulas-as-types*. Relevant logics turn this so-called *Curry–Howard isomorphism* on its head [see chapter 11]. We interpret *types-as-formulas*. And our formulas really *are* formulas – the formal sentences of some logical language. Aggregations of formulas are bound into theories by conjunction and entailment. And it turns out, as Fine (1992b [1974]) also emphasized, both that

(i) whole theories are the underlying ingredients of relevant semantical analysis, and
(ii) the shape of the semantics for any particular relevant logic will be determined by the combinators that correspond to its axioms.

Passing now to the analysis of further logical particles beyond → and ∧, and stronger relevant logics than **B** and its kin, the disjunction ∨ poses immediate problems. One prefers (and *ought* to prefer) *prime* theories x, which satisfy, for all A, B, the primeness condition:

Primeness Condition If $A \vee B \in x$ then $A \in x$ or $B \in x$.

This is wanted because it corresponds to the truth-condition on ∨, on which the truth at x of a disjunction requires the truth at x of a disjunct. But prime theories are not always easy to come by. Worse, even when each of the theories x, y is prime, there is no guarantee that their fusion xy will be prime.

Nonetheless, there remains a strong relationship between combinators and the relational semantics. For the *canonical* ternary accessibility relation is definable on the structure of prime theories as

$Rxyz$ iff $xy \subseteq z$

And it turns out that, using the combinator facts about the calculus of theories (for a given logic **L**), the necessary semantical postulates on the relation R almost suggest themselves. So, think briefly (but only by example) about what makes the relational semantics sound and complete. Suppose the familiar example, the C scheme $(A \to (B \to C)) \to (B \to (A \to C))$, is an axiom scheme of the logic **L**. Its mated relational (Pasch) postulate is $Rxyzw \Rightarrow Rxzyw$, whose correspondence to the combinator C has also been observed. To show that the postulate suffices to verify the axiom – hence the closure of the theory structure of **L** under C – one simply applies the SemEnt fact of section 13.5. (This is left for the reader to check.)

This illustrates the *soundness* of the ternary relational semantics for logics **L**. On the side of *completeness*, the converse for the same case will be shown. Assuming that all instances of the permutation scheme are theorems of **L**, – equivalently, that the structure of theories of **L** is closed under **C** – it will be shown that the Pasch postulate holds for the canonical ternary relation R defined above on the structure of prime theories of **L**.

In the first place, closure of *all* theories x of **L** under provable entailment still means that $Cx = x$, in the presence of permutation as a theorem scheme. Hence, $xyz = Cxyz = xzy$ for all theories x, y, z of **L**. (The presence of $\vee$, or even $\sim$, in the vocabulary makes no difference to this situation.) But it needs to be shown that permutation forces Pasch for the structure of prime theories of **L**. This, however, follows from the squeezing lemma which holds for any of our logics **L** (Anderson et al., 1992; Routley and Meyer, 1982a [1973]; Routley et al., 1982):

> **Squeezing Lemma** Let x, y be theories, and let z' be a prime theory of **L**. Suppose $xy \subseteq z'$. Then there exist prime theories x', y' of **L**, such that $x'y \subseteq z'$ and $xy' \subseteq z'$, where $x \subseteq x'$ and $y \subseteq y'$

Then, to verify Pasch, given that the structure of theories of **L** is closed under **C**, assume that there are prime theories x', y', a', z', w' such that

(i) $x'y' \subseteq a'$ and
(ii) $a'z' \subseteq w'$.

To prove that there is a prime theory u' such that $x'z' \subseteq u'$ and $u'y' \subseteq w'$:

1	$x'y' \subseteq a'$	Hypothesis (i)
2	$x'y'z' \subseteq a'z' \subseteq w'$	1, Fusion fact, Hypothesis (ii), Transitivity of $\subseteq$
3	$x'z'y' = x'y'z' \subseteq w'$	2, Closure under **C**
4	Set $u = x'z'$	Definition (but u may *not* be prime)
5	$uy' \subseteq w'$	3, 4

But then, by the Lemma, there exists a prime theory u' of **L**, $u \subseteq u'$, such that

6	$u'y' \subseteq w'$	5, Squeezing lemma
7	$x'z' = u \subseteq u'$	4

The conjunction of steps 7 and 6 verifies the conclusion of the Pasch postulate, on the antecedent hypotheses (i) and (ii). So, given that **L** provides permutation, the canonical ternary relation R on prime theories delivers Pasch, as promised. Other cases are similar.

Thus there is a mathematically elegant relationship between combinatory logic and relational semantics. This, however, is a point about the relational semantics in general, rather than a feature of relevant logics. For one can give a ternary relational semantics for non-relevant logics (Routley and Meyer, 1976). For example, if a structure of theories is closed under K, this is not very relevant!

13.9. Relevant Results

To understand a logic, one needs to understand a few of its mathematical properties. This section presents, in a non-technical way, some technical results about relevant logics.

13.9.1. The admissibility of gamma

When Anderson and Belnap (1975) reformulated Ackermann's logic Π' (1956) as their system **E**, they omitted Ackermann's third rule of inference, named γ:

$$\vdash \sim A \vee B$$
$$\frac{\vdash A}{\vdash B}$$

Anderson and Belnap argue that a logic should not include a rule unless it includes the corresponding theorem scheme. In this case, the corresponding theorem scheme is

$$((\sim A \vee B) \circ A) \to B \qquad \text{or} \qquad ((\sim A \vee B) \wedge A) \to B$$

Adding the latter to **E**, by virtue of the Lewis argument given in section 13.1 above, makes XP− valid in **E**. And so adding it would remove **E** from the class of relevant logics. Luckily, as Meyer has shown with Dunn (1975 [1969]) by algebraic means and then on his own by a technique called 'metavaluations' (Meyer, 1975 [1976]), the theorems of **E** are closed under γ. Thus, Anderson and Belnap's **E** has the same theorems as Ackermann's logic.

The importance of the admissibility of γ goes far beyond proving the coincidence of **E** and Π'. It shows that a logic is characterized by its class of 'normal' theories. A *normal theory* is a theory that contains all the theorems of the logic, is consistent and is prime.

Sometimes admitting γ also shows that a relevant logic contains the corresponding logic based on the classical propositional calculus. Using γ, one can show that **R** and **E** contain all of classical propositional logic (phrased in terms of negation, conjunction and disjunction) and that various modal relevant logics contain all the theorems of the corresponding classically based logics (Mares and Meyer, 1992). Unfortunately, Meyer's relevant Peano arithmetic (the system **R#**) was shown by Friedman and Meyer (1992) not to admit γ. In the process, it was also shown not to contain all of the theorems of classical Peano arithmetic.

13.9.2. *The undecidability of R and E*

Urquhart (1992b [1984]) proved that the logics **E**, **R** and **T** are undecidable. This result is important and the proof is very clever. Most philosophically motivated propositional logics are decidable – for instance, classical propositional logic, intuitionist logic and the standard normal modal logics. In fact **E**, **R** and **T** are the first philosophically motivated propositional logics to have been proven undecidable.

The proof of undecidability is an extraordinary piece of work. Urquhart shows that there is an interesting and important link between the relational semantics for these relevant logics and projective spaces (of projective geometry). He then uses the fact that the word problem for a particular class of infinite-dimensional projective spaces is unsolvable to prove that the logics are undecidable.

13.9.3. *The failure of interpolation in R and E*
(and a host of other systems)

Another difficult and interesting proof due to Urquhart is his theorem that interpolation fails in **E** and **R** as well as in **T** and a range of other logics.

What is interesting about interpolation from a relevant point of view is that some relevant logics satisfy what Anderson and Belnap call the 'Perfect Interpolation Theorem.' Consider Craig's interpolation theorem as stated for classical propositional logic [see chapter 1, page 31]:

Suppose that C is derivable from A. Then,

   (Cop-out) if A is not a contradiction and C is not a tautology

there is some formula B such that

(a) B contains only propositional variables that occur in both A and C;
(b) B is derivable from A; and
(c) C is derivable from B.

The Perfect Interpolation Theorem is the same as Craig's theorem with the omission of the qualification Cop-out.

Some relevant logics do satisfy the Perfect Interpolation Theorem. For example, McRobbie (1979) showed that the system **OR** (which is **R** without the distribution axiom, Axiom 8, given on page 292) is perfectly interpolable. But Urquhart (1993) again used the relationship between projective geometry and the relational semantics to show that a range of relevant logics around and including **E**, **R** and **T** do not interpolate.[17]

13.9.4. *Boolean conservative extension results*

Meyer and Routley (1982 [1973]) show that one can add a second, Boolean, negation to certain relevant logics without altering the stock of theorems that the logic has in the old vocabulary. This is what is called a *conservative extension result.* Boolean negation, ¬, is governed by some very unrelevant looking principles, such as

$(\neg A \wedge A) \rightarrow B$

$B \rightarrow (\neg A \vee A)$

This extension is interesting for a variety of reasons, mathematical and philosophical. First, it allows one to use what is sometimes called 'denial negation' (a negation that expresses the failure of something to be true) in relevant logic. Second, the conservative extension result has enabled Belnap (1992b [1982]) to prove the correctness of his elegant proof theory – Display Logic – for a range of relevant logics.

The conservative extension result holds for a wide range of logics, including **B** and **R**. But it does not hold for **E** (Mares, 2000) nor for **NR**, mentioned above (Meyer and Mares, 1993). (Recently Ross Brady has proved that quantified **R** is conservatively extended by the addition of Boolean negation. As of the writing of this chapter, he has not yet published this result.)

13.9.5. *The consistency of relevant set theories*

Brady (1983) showed that a class theory with a naïve comprehension axiom, based on a weak relevant logic, is consistent. The comprehension axiom is

$\exists Y \forall X (X \in Y \leftrightarrow A)$

where X and Y are variables ranging over classes. This says that for each open sentence A, there is a set that is its extension. This axiom was restricted in classical set theory because it enabled the derivation of Russell's paradox [see chapter 3]. But, using his logic, **DJ^{d}Q**, as a base, Brady (1989) shows that a theory of classes – and in Brady (2001), a theory of sets – that incorporates naïve comprehension is consistent.

13.9.6. *The completeness and incompleteness of quantified relevant logic*

Fine (1992a [1989]) shows that the quantified relevant logic, **RQ**, is not complete over its *constant domain semantics*. According to the constant domain semantics, each world has the same stock of individuals and the truth condition for the universal quantifier is the standard clause from modal logic [see chapter 7], namely,

$I_v(\forall x A, a) = true$ iff $I_u(A, a) = true$, for every u, x-variant of v

Fine shows that there is a thesis valid over the class of constant domain models for
R that is not provable in the logic **RQ**. How to axiomatize a logic complete over
the constant domain semantics is still an open question.

Fine (1992c [1988]) developed a variable domain semantics for **RQ**. The semantics
is quite complicated and appeals to a special notion of arbitrary objects; but one
can make contact with more familiar terrain by linking Fine's ideas to central ones
from Kripke's model theory for intuitionistic logic [see chapter 11]. Altering Fine's
notation slightly, each world is linked to other worlds with larger domains of individuals by a relation, Q. Thus, Qab only if $D(a) \subseteq D(b)$. Fine's truth condition for
the quantifier may be put as

$$I_v(\forall xA, a) = true \text{ iff } I_u(A, b) = true, \text{ for all } b \text{ that } Qab \text{ and every } u, x\text{-variant of } v$$

In effect, this says that a universally quantified sentence, $\forall xA$, is true at a world, a,
iff the open sentence A is true of everything in every world b larger than a.

13.9.7. The **P–W** problem

The logic **P–W**, as it is usually called (or **T$_\to$–W** as it should be called) has implication as its sole connective. It contains as axiom schemes the type schemes for the
combinators **B**, **B'** and **I** and is closed under *modus ponens*. Belnap had conjectured
that, for formulas A and B, the only cases in which both $A \to B$ and $B \to A$ are
provable in **P–W** are those in which A and B are the same formula. In the late
1960s, Larry Powers showed that this conjecture is equivalent to the conjecture that
no formula of the form $A \to A$ can be proved in the logic **S**, which is the closure
under *modus ponens* of the schemes **B** and **B'** *alone*. Martin (1992 [1978]), and
Martin and Meyer (1982) proved Powers' **S** conjecture. So Martin solved the **P–W**
problem (which had been shaping up as the *Fermat's Last Theorem* of the area).

Martin's solution of the **P–W** problem is a wonderful example of technical inge-
nuity and philosophical insight going hand in hand in the advancement of relevant
logic. For one now has a logic that does not make valid any form of circular
reasoning. It has been thought since the beginning of logic that deriving a proposition from itself is not only useless but also fallacious. In **S** one has a logic that rejects
(root and branch) all forms of circular reasoning. Thus it serves as a test-bed for
ideas about circularity and how to avoid it.[18]

13.10. But There's So Much More to Say

This chapter has provided the reader with a brief look at the motivation for and
some of the technical and philosophical aspects of relevant logic. But it has only
scratched the surface of this vibrant field of logic that has been the focus of fairly
intense mathematical scrutiny and philosophical debate in the past four decades.
It has not touched on the use of relevant logic in automated theorem proving,

(Thistlewaite et al., 1988), or its relationship to linear logic or to computing more generally. Nor has it discussed the sometimes heated debate over the status of disjunctive syllogism (Read, 1988). And there is so much more. There are areas in relevant logic that are just now beginning to be explored: The relationship between these logics and logics of natural language conditionals, the use of relevant logic in non-monotonic reasoning, among others. Hopefully, this chapter will inspire readers to delve into these areas on their own, sadly without our guidance.

Suggested further reading

The best detailed introduction to relevant logic is Dunn (1984), which has recently been updated (Dunn and Restall, 2001). For the philosophical debates surrounding relevant logic, Routley, et al., (1982) and Read (1988) are good places to start. A fine and very readable introduction to substructural logics, with much about relevant logics, is Restall (2000). Mares (2002) introduces relevant logic through natural deduction. For the reader who wants technical details and proofs of theorems, Anderson and Belnap (1975) and Anderson et al. (1992) are excellent sources. Anderson et al. (1992) contains a detailed, although now out of date, bibliography of work on relevant logic, compiled by Robert G. Wolf.[19]

Notes

1 For the pre-history and history of relevant logics, a good source is Read (1988).
2 Relevant logic locates the fallacy at line 5, denying the entailment $(\sim A \wedge (A \vee B)) \rightarrow B$. See Anderson and Belnap (1975, section 16.1) or Read (1988) for discussion of this issue.
3 This holds for propositional relevant logics without so-called Ackermann constants t and f or Church constants T and F (see section 13.8).
4 We are very grateful to Nicholas Griffin for pointing out this passage to us.
5 For a clear presentation of the relevant deduction theorem, see Dunn (1984).
6 There are several good introductions to natural deduction for relevant logics, such as Anderson and Belnap (1975), Dunn (1984), and Mares (2002).
7 As for other properties of fusion, these vary among relevant logics. Not all relevant logics allow fusions to commute. That is, there are relevant logics in which $A \circ B$ is not equivalent to $B \circ A$, but there are others, like $\mathbf{R}$, where $\vdash A \circ B \rightarrow B \circ A$. Fusion is not idempotent in *most* relevant logic, i.e., in systems like $\mathbf{R}$ and $\mathbf{E}$, $A \circ A$ is not equivalent to A. And so on.
8 This is what Meyer and Martin (1986) call the *Australian plan* of relevant semantical analysis. There is a contrasting *American Plan*, developed by Dunn (1992 [1976], 1969) and championed and augmented by Belnap (1977, 1992a [1977]), that utilizes a natural four-valued semantics to refute XP–. For simplicity's sake, in what follows we discuss only the two-value semantics with the Routley star. Interested readers should consult Routley et al. (1982) for the technical details of the completed American plan.
9 There is another interpretation of negation that uses the compatibility relation, but for it this relation is not a semantical primitive. This is the implicational interpretation of negation of Mares (1995). On this semantics, there is a falsum, f, that is taken to be true at all and only impossible worlds (impossible worlds too can be defined in terms of other primitives). On this semantics, one can define Cab to hold iff there is some world c, such that $Rabc$, and c is not impossible. In other words, two worlds are taken to be compatible if they can be combined (in the sense of fusion) in a possible world.

10 We do not try to give a full account of combinatory logic here. We just want to give the reader the flavor of the theory. For a more detailed introduction, see Hindley and Seldin (1986), *q.v.* for further bibliographical references to **CL** and **LC**.

11 Curry was anticipated in 1924 by Schönfinkel. Church invented the kindred **LC** *circa* 1932.

12 Strictly speaking we should distinguish the general reduction relation $>$, which is reflexive, transitive and satisfies positive monotonic replacement, from $>_1$ of immediate (one-step) reducibility. Equality, '=,' is the symmetric transitive closure of $>$.

13 For an introduction to types, with references and especially in **LC**, see Takahashi et al. (1998).

14 For technical reasons, we will add a (top) Church constant T below; it is a member of all *non-empty* theories. Then the fusion of two non-empty theories in $\rightarrow$, $\wedge$, T (at least) is also a non-empty theory.

15 But it does correspond to the constant ω which is the *whole domain* of the models of **LC** discussed in Barendregt et al. (1983) and Dezani et al. (1998). While we prefer the more natural *Ackermann constant t* in relevant logics, T continues to make some sense as the trivial truth implied by absolutely everything. Ackermann t, when present, admits the 2-sided rule $\vdash A$ iff $\vdash t \rightarrow A$. Think of t as a *conjunction* of truths (interesting) but T as a corresponding *disjunction* (boring, but that many logics *confuse t* and $T!$).

16 In essence, the **LC** investigators had rediscovered the basic positive relevant logic of, e.g., Meyer and Routley (1972). Alas, they thought that they had invented a *type theory*, and were not aware that they had stumbled on a *relevant logic*. When Meyer first met Barendregt in 1990, he pointed this out, Barendregt conceded that, while he had not previously thought much of relevant logics, perhaps it was time to change his tune; for now it was clear that he had been involved (with members of the Torino group) in the (re)invention of one.

17 This means, in McRobbie's lingo, that **E** is *not* reasonable in the sense of Anderson and Belnap.

18 More accurately we have such a logic in $\mathbf{S}_\rightarrow$ (and, thanks to more joint work by Fine and Martin (2001), in $\mathbf{S}_{\rightarrow\wedge}$ as well). Further particles (and, it may be, further axioms) await. We add that it is a pity that the elegantly combinatorial Martin insights are as yet insufficiently appreciated.

19 Thanks are due to Neil Leslie, who commented extensively on an earlier draft, as did Lou Goble, Katalin Bimbó, Chris Mortensen and Beate Elsner.

References

Ackermann, W. 1956: "Begrundung einer strenge Implikation," *Journal of Symbolic Logic*, 21, 113–28.

Anderson, A. R. and Belnap, N. D., Jr. 1975: *Entailment. The Logic of Relevance and Necessity*, Vol. I, (Princeton University Press, Princeton, NJ).

Anderson, A. R., Belnap, N. D., Jr. and Dunn, J. M. 1992: *Entailment. The Logic of Relevance and Necessity*, Vol. II, (Princeton University Press, Princeton, NJ).

Barendregt, H. P., Coppo, M. and Dezani-Ciancaglini, M. 1983: "A Filter Lambda Model and the Completeness of Type Assignment," *Journal of Symbolic Logic*, 48, 931–40.

Barwise, J. 1993: "Constraints, Channels and the Flow of Information," in *Situation Theory and Its Applications*, Vol. 3, P. Aczel, D. Israel, Y. Katagiri and S. Peters, eds., (CSLI, Stanford), 3–27.

Barwise, J. and Perry, J. 1983: *Situations and Attitudes*, (MIT Press, Cambridge, MA).

Belnap, N. D., Jr. 1977: "How a Computer Should Think," in *Contemporary Aspects of Philosophy*, G. Ryle, ed., (Oriel Press, Stocksfield), 30–55.

Belnap, N. D., Jr. 1992a: "A Useful Four-Valued Logic," in *Modern Uses of Many-Valued Logic*, J. M. Dunn and G. Epstein, eds., (D. Reidel, Dordrecht), 1977, 8–37; reprinted in Anderson, Belnap and Dunn (1992, section 81).

Belnap, N. D., Jr. 1992b: "Display Logic," *Journal of Philosophical Logic*, 11 (1982), 375–417; substantially reprinted in Anderson, Belnap, and Dunn (1992, section 62).

Białnicki-Birula, A. and Rasiowa, H. 1975: "On the Representation of Quasi-Boolean Algebras," *Bulletin de l'Acadamie Polonaise des Science*, 5, 259–61.

Brady, R. T. 1983: "The Simple Consistency of a Set Theory Based on the Logic CSQ," *Notre Dame Journal of Formal Logic*, 24, 431–49.

Brady, R. T. 1989: "The Non-Triviality of Dialectical Set Theory," in *Paraconsistent Logic*, G. Priest, R. Routley and J. Norman, eds., (Philosophia Verlag, Munich), 437–71.

Brady, R. T. 2001: Universal Logic, (CSLI Press, Stanford), forthcoming.

Church, A. 1951: "The Weak Theory of Implication," in *Kontrolliertes Denken, Untersuchungen zum Logikkalkül und zur Logik der Einzelwissenschaften*, A. Menne, A. Wilhelmy and H. Angsil, eds., (Kommissions-Verlag Karl Alber, Munich), 22–37.

Coppo, M., Dezani-Ciancaglini, M. and Vennari, B. 1980: "Principle Type Schemes and λ-Calculus Semantics" in *To H. B. Curry, Essays in Combinatory Logic, Lambda-Calculus and Formalism*, R. Hindley and J. P. Seldin, eds., (Academic Press, NY), 535–60.

Devlin, K. 1991: *Logic and Information* (Cambridge University Press, Cambridge, UK).

Dezani-Ciancaglini, M., Giovannetti, E. and de'Liguoro, U. 1998: "Intersection Types, λ-Models, and Böhm Trees," in Takahashi et al. (1998, 45–97).

Dunn, J. M. 1969: "Natural Language versus Formal Language," presentation made to the Joint American Philosophical Association–Association of Symbolic Logic Symposium at New York, 27 December.

Dunn, J. M. 1975a: "The Algebra of Intensional Logics," PhD dissertation, University of Pittsburgh, Pittsburgh 1966. Some results from this are in Anderson and Belnap (1975, 180–206, 352–73).

Dunn, J. M. 1975b: "A 'Gentzen System' for Positive Relevant Implication," *The Journal of Symbolic Logic* 38 (1973), 356–7. For a complete treatment of this system, see Anderson and Belnap (1975, 381–91).

Dunn, J. M. 1984: "Relevant Logic and Entailment," in *Handbook of Philosophical Logic*, Vol. III, D. Gabbay and F. Guenthner, eds., (D. Reidel, Dordrecht), 117–224.

Dunn, J. M. 1992: "Intuitive Semantics for First-Degree Entailments and 'Coupled Trees'," *Philosophical Studies*, 29 (1976), 149–68; reprinted in Anderson, Belnap and Dunn (1992, 193–208).

Dunn, J. M. 1993: "Star and Perp: Two Treatments of Negation," *Philosophical Perspectives*, 7, 331–57.

Dunn, J. M. and Restall, G. 2001: "Relevance Logic and Entailment," in *Handbook of Philosophical Logic*, Vol. 8, 2nd edn., D. Gabbay, ed., (Kluwer, Dordrecht), 1–128. (Revision of Dunn (1984).)

Fine, K. 1992a: "Incompleteness for Quantified Relevant Logic," in *Directions in Relevant Logic*, J. Norman and R. Sylvan, eds., (Kluwer, Dordrecht), 1989, 205–25. Reprinted in Anderson, Belnap and Dunn (1992, 231–5).

Fine, K. 1992b: "Models for Entailment" *Journal of Philosophical Logic*, 3 (1974), 347–72. Reprinted in Anderson, Belnap and Dunn (1992, 208–31).

Fine, K. 1992c: "Semantics for Quantified Relevant Logic," *Journal of Philosophical Logic*, 17 (1988), 27–59. Reprinted in Anderson, Belnap and Dunn (1992, 235–62).

Fine, K. and Martin, E. P. 2001: "Positive Logic and Conjunction," in *From a Non-Classical Point of View*, E. D. Mares and G. Restall, eds., forthcoming.

Friedman, H. and Meyer, R. K. 1992: "Whither Relevant Arithmetic?," *Journal of Symbolic Logic*, 57, 824–31.

Hindley, J. R. and Seldin, J. P. 1986: *Introduction to Combinators and λ-Calculus*, (Cambridge University Press, Cambridge).

Israel, D. and Perry, J. 1990: "What is Information?," in *Information, Language, and Cognition*, P. Hanson, ed., (University of British Columbia Press, Vancouver, B. C.), 1–19.

Jónsson, B. and Tarski, A. 1951: "Boolean Algebras with Operators," *American Journal of Mathematics*, 73, 891–939.

Lewis, C. I. 1917: "The Issues Concerning Material Implication," *Journal of Philosophy, Psychology and Scientific Methods*, 14, 350–6.

Lewis, C. I. 1918: *A Survey of Symbolic Logic*, (University of California Press, Berkeley).

Lewis, C. I. and Langford, C. H. 1959: *Symbolic Logic*, 2nd edn., (Dover, New York), (1st edn., 1932).

Maksimova, L. L. 1973: "A Semantics for the Calculus E of Entailment," *Bulletin of the Section of Logic*, 2, 18–21.

Mares, E. D. 1995: "A Star-Free Semantics for **R**," *Journal of Symbolic Logic*, 60, 579–90.

Mares, E. D. 1996: "Relevant Logic and the Theory of Information," *Synthese*, 109, 345–60.

Mares, E. D. 2000: "CE is Not a Conservative Extension of **E**" *Journal of Philosophical Logic*, 29, 263–75.

Mares, E. D. 2002: "Relevance Logic," in *Companion to Philosophical Logic*, D. Jacquette, ed., (Blackwell, Oxford), forthcoming.

Mares, E. D. and Meyer, R. K. 1992: "The Admissibility of γ in **R4**," *Notre Dame Journal of Formal Logic*, 33, 197–206.

Martin E. P. 1992: "The P–W Problem," PhD dissertation, Australian National University, Canberra, 1978. Reprinted substantially in Anderson, Belnap and Dunn (1992, section 66).

Martin E. P. and Meyer, R. K. 1982: "Solution to the P–W Problem," *Journal of Symbolic Logic*, 47, 869–86.

McRobbie, M. 1979: "A Proof Theoretic Investigation of Relevant and Modal Logics," PhD dissertation, Australian National University, Canberra.

Meyer, R. K. 1975: "Metacompleteness," *Notre Dame Journal of Formal Logic*, 17 (1976), 501–16. Substantially reprinted in Anderson and Belnap (1975, 263–71).

Meyer, R. K. and Dunn, J. M. 1975: "**E**, **R** and γ" *Journal of Symbolic Logic*, 34 (1969), 460–74. Reprinted in Anderson and Belnap (1975, section 25.2).

Meyer, R. K. and Mares, E. D. 1993: "The Semantics of Entailment 0," in *Substructural Logics*, P. Schröder-Heister and K. Došen, eds., (Oxford University Press, Oxford), 239–58.

Meyer, R. K. and Martin, E. P. 1986: "Logic on the Australian Plan," *Journal of Philosophical Logic*, 15, 305–32.

Meyer, R. K. and Routley, R. 1972: "Algebraic Analysis of Entailment I," *Logique et Analyse*, 15, 407–28.

Meyer, R. K. and Routley, R. 1982: "Classical Relevant Logics (I)," *Studia Logica*, 32 (1973), 51–66; Reprinted substantially in Routley et al. (1982).

Mints, G. E. 1976: "Cut-Elimination Theorem in Relevant Logics," *J. Sov. Math.*, 6, 422–8.

Moh Shaw-Kwei 1950: "The Deduction Theorems and Two New Logical Systems," *Methodos*, 2, 56–75.

Moore, G. E. 1922: *Philosophical Studies*, (Routledge and Kegan Paul, London).

Read, S. 1988: *Relevant Logic*, (Blackwell, Oxford).

Restall, G. 1996: "Information Flow and Relevant Logics," in *Logic, Language and Computation*, Vol. 1, J. Seligman and D. Westerståhl, eds., (CSLI Press, Stanford), 463–77.

Restall, G. 2000: *An Introduction to Substructural Logics*, (Routledge, London and New York).

Routley, R. and Meyer, R. K. 1976: "Every Sentential Logic has a Two-Valued Semantics," *Logique et Analyse*, n.s. 19, 345–65.

Routley, R. and Meyer, R. K. 1982a: "The Semantics of Entailment," in *Truth, Syntax and Modality*, H. Leblanc, ed., (North Holland, Amsterdam), 1973, 199–243; reprinted substantially in Routley et al. (1982).

Routley, R. and Meyer, R. K. 1982b: "The Semantics of Entailment II," *Journal of Philosophical Logic*, 1 (1972), 53–73: reprinted substantially in Routley et al. (1982).

Routley, R. and Routley, V. 1972: "Semantics of First Degree Entailment," *Noûs*, 6, 335–59.

Routley, R., Meyer, R. K., Brady, R. T. and Plumwood, V. 1982: *Relevant Logics and Their Rivals I*, (Ridgeview Press, Atascadero, CA).

Russell, B. 1903: *Principles of Mathematics*, (Norton and Norton, New York).

Takahashi, M., Okada, M. and Dezani-Ciancaglini, M. (eds) 1998: *Theory of Types and Proofs*, *MSJ Memoirs 2*, (Mathematical Society of Japan, Tokyo).

Thistlewaite, P. B., McRobbie, M. A. and Meyer, R. K. 1988: *Automated Theorem Proving in Non-Classical Logics*, (Pitman, London).

Urquhart, A. 1992a: "Semantics for Relevant Logics," *Journal of Symbolic Logic*, 37 (1972), 159–69: substantially reprinted in Anderson, Belnap and Dunn (1992, section 47).

Urquhart, A. 1992b: "The Undecidability of Entailment and Relevant Implication," *Journal of Symbolic Logic*, 49 (1984), 1059–73; reprinted in Anderson, Belnap and Dunn (1992, section 65).

Urquhart, A. 1993: "Failure of Interpolation in Relevant Logics," *Journal of Philosophical Logic*, 22, 449–79.

Whitehead, A. N. and Russell, B. 1910–13: *Principia Mathematica*, 3 vol, (Cambridge University Press, Cambridge).

$$\text{Chapter 14}$$

Many-Valued Logics

Grzegorz Malinowski

Classical logic is based on the *principle of bivalence*, that every proposition has exactly one of the two logical values *truth* or *falsity*. This finds expression in the two laws: the *law of the excluded middle*

(EM) $p \vee \neg p$

and the *law of non-contradiction*,

(CP) $\neg(p \wedge \neg p)$

With the classical understanding of the connectives, EM and CP may be read as stating that of the two propositions p and $\neg p$, at least one is true and at least one is false, respectively.

The most natural and straightforward step beyond two-valued logic is to introduce more logical values, thereby rejecting the principle of bivalence. Another, indirect, way consists in challenging the classical laws concerning the sentence connectives and introducing other non-two-valued connectives into the language. Either way, propositional logic seems fundamental to many-valuedness, rather than its first-order extension. Hence, although there has been interesting research into first-order many-valued logics, we shall confine our discussion here to the 0-order case.

While the roots of many-valued logics can be seen in Aristotle – with his famous concern for future contingents and the 'sea-battle tomorrow' – and traced through the middle ages and the nineteenth century, the real 'era of many-valuedness' began in 1920 with the work of Łukasiewicz and Post. This chapter looks at each in turn, and then some others.

14.1. Łukasiewicz Three-Valued Logic

Łukasiewicz first introduced a third logical value – which can be called $\frac{1}{2}$, in addition to 0 and 1 for falsehood and truth – as a result of philosophical investigation into ideas of freedom, indeterminism, future contingents, modality, and also the paradoxes of set theory. With Aristotle, he argued that a sentence like

I shall be in Warsaw at noon on 21 December of the next year.

is, at the time of its utterance, neither true nor false, since otherwise fatalist conclusions about necessity or impossibility of contingent future events would follow. The value $\frac{1}{2}$ was to apply to such cases. Initially, Łukasiewicz interpreted this third logic value, $\frac{1}{2}$, as 'possibility' or 'indeterminacy', and, following his intuitions about these concepts, he extended the classical interpretation of negation and implication according to the tables:[1]

α	$\neg\alpha$
0	1
$\frac{1}{2}$	$\frac{1}{2}$
1	0

$\rightarrow$	0	$\frac{1}{2}$	1
0	1	1	1
$\frac{1}{2}$	$\frac{1}{2}$	1	1
1	0	$\frac{1}{2}$	1

The other connectives of disjunction, conjunction and equivalence were introduced through the definitions:

$$\alpha \vee \beta =_{df} (\alpha \rightarrow \beta) \rightarrow \beta$$

$$\alpha \wedge \beta =_{df} \neg(\neg\alpha \vee \neg\beta)$$

$$\alpha \equiv \beta =_{df} (\alpha \rightarrow \beta) \wedge (\beta \rightarrow \alpha)$$

Their tables are:

$\vee$	0	$\frac{1}{2}$	1
0	0	$\frac{1}{2}$	1
$\frac{1}{2}$	$\frac{1}{2}$	$\frac{1}{2}$	1
1	1	1	1

$\wedge$	0	$\frac{1}{2}$	1
0	0	0	0
$\frac{1}{2}$	0	$\frac{1}{2}$	$\frac{1}{2}$
1	0	$\frac{1}{2}$	1

$\equiv$	0	$\frac{1}{2}$	1
0	1	$\frac{1}{2}$	0
$\frac{1}{2}$	$\frac{1}{2}$	1	$\frac{1}{2}$
1	0	$\frac{1}{2}$	1

A valuation of formulas in Łukasiewicz three-valued logic is any function v: *For* $\rightarrow \{0, \frac{1}{2}, 1\}$ compatible with the above tables, where *For* is the set of formulas of the language. A *tautology* is a formula which takes the *designated value* 1 under any valuation v.

The set L_3 of tautologies of this three-valued logic of Łukasiewicz differs from the set of two-valued tautologies *TAUT* of classical logic. For instance, neither the law of the excluded middle, nor the principle of contradiction is in L_3. To see this, assign $\frac{1}{2}$ to p: any such valuation also associates $\frac{1}{2}$ with EM and CP. The thorough-going refutation of these two laws was intended, in Łukasiewicz's opinion, to codify the principles of indeterminism.

Another property of new semantics is that some classically inconsistent formulas are no longer contradictory in L_3. One such:

(*) $\quad p \equiv \neg p$

is connected with the famous Russell paradox of the 'set of all sets that are not their own elements' [see chapter 3]. *Russell's set* is defined by the equation

$$Z = \{x : x \notin x\}$$

And the resulting paradox

$$Z \in Z \equiv Z \notin Z$$

is an instance of (*). Russell's paradox ceases to be an antinomy in L_3, however, since putting $\frac{1}{2}$ for p makes the formula true and therefore (*) is non-contradictory. Łukasiewicz found this to be a strong argument in favor of his three-valued logic.

Łukasiewicz also sought to formalize the modal functors of possibility M and necessity L. Aware of the impossibility of representing these functors in truth-functional classical logic, he proposed taking the three-valued logic as their basis instead. In 1921, Tarski (Łukasiewicz, 1967 [1930]) produced simple definitions, using negation and implication, of these two connectives that would meet Łukasiewicz's requirements, namely:

x	Mx
0	0
$\frac{1}{2}$	1
1	1

x	Lx
0	0
$\frac{1}{2}$	0
1	1

$$M\alpha =_{\text{df}} \neg\alpha \rightarrow \alpha$$
$$L\alpha =_{\text{df}} \neg M\neg\alpha = \neg(\alpha \rightarrow \neg\alpha)$$

The first known axiomatization of a system of many-valued logic was Wajsberg's (1967 [1931]) axiomatization of L_3, namely, for the $(\neg, \rightarrow)$-version of Łukasiewicz's three-valued propositional calculus:

W1 $\quad p \rightarrow (q \rightarrow p)$

W2 $\quad (p \rightarrow q) \rightarrow ((q \rightarrow r) \rightarrow (p \rightarrow r))$

W3 $\quad (\neg p \rightarrow \neg q) \rightarrow (q \rightarrow p)$

W4 $\quad ((p \rightarrow \neg p) \rightarrow p) \rightarrow p$

with the rules *modus ponens* (MP) and universal substitution (SUB). The result obviously applies to the whole L_3 since the other Łukasiewicz connectives are definable in terms of negation and implication.

14.2. Post Logics

As an outcome of his research on the classical propositional logic, Post (1920, 1921) construed a family of finite-valued propositional logics. This was inspired by the formalization of the classical propositional calculus, CPC, presented in *Principia*

Mathematica of Whitehead and Russell (1910), by the method of truth tables, and by Post's own results concerning functional completeness for classical logic.

Following *Principia Mathematica*, Post takes negation, $\neg$, and disjunction, $\vee$, as primitive connectives. For any natural $n \geq 2$, he considers a linearly ordered set of objects

$$P_n = \{t_1, t_2, \ldots, t_n\}$$

$t_n < t_j$ iff (if and only if) $i < j$, equipped with two operations corresponding to connectives; unary *rotation* (or *cyclic negation*) $\neg$ and binary *disjunction* $\vee$ defined as:

$$\neg t_i = \begin{cases} t_{i+1} & \text{if } i \neq n \\ t_1 & \text{if } i = n \end{cases}$$

$$t_i \vee t_j = t_{\max\{i,j\}}$$

These equations define, for a given $n \geq 2$, n-element truth tables of negation and disjunction. Thus, e.g., for $n = 5$, the tables are:

x	$\neg x$		$\vee$	t_1	t_2	t_3	t_4	t_5
t_1	t_2		t_1	t_1	t_2	t_3	t_4	t_5
t_2	t_3		t_2	t_2	t_2	t_3	t_4	t_5
t_3	t_4		t_3	t_3	t_3	t_3	t_4	t_5
t_4	t_5		t_4	t_4	t_4	t_4	t_4	t_5
t_5	t_1		t_5	t_5	t_5	t_5	t_5	t_5

It is easy to see that for $n = 2$, Post logic coincides with the negation-disjunction version of the classical logic: the set $P_2 = \{t_1, t_2\}$ may be identified as containing 0 and 1, respectively, and then the Post negation and disjunction are isomorphic variants of the classical connectives.[2] The relation to CPC breaks down for $n > 2$. In all these cases, the truth table of negation is not compatible with the classical one. To see that, remark that due to the properties of disjunction, t_1 always corresponds to 0 and t_n to 1. Though $\neg t_n = t_1$, $\neg t_1$ equals t_2, which is not t_n. Accordingly, it can be said that the n-valued Post algebra

$$\mathbf{P}_n = (\{t_1, t_2, \ldots, t_n\}, \neg, \vee)$$

either coincides with the negation-disjunction algebra of CPC ($n = 2$), or the latter algebra is not a subalgebra of it ($n > 2$).

Post considers the 'highest' value t_n as the distinguished element. It is remarkable that among the laws of all its logics ($n > 2$) generalizations of some significant tautologies of the classical logic expressed in terms of negation and disjunction are still present. For example, this counterpart of the law of the excluded middle:

$$p \vee \neg p \vee \neg\neg p \vee \cdots \vee \underbrace{\neg\neg \cdots \neg p}_{(n-1) \text{ times}}$$

is such a formula. By contrast, applications of classical definitional patterns for other standard connectives, like conjunction, implication and equivalence, lead to very strange results. For example, the definition of conjunction using the DeMorgan law

$$\alpha \wedge \beta = \neg(\neg\alpha \vee \neg\beta)$$

results in a non-associative connective $\wedge$! The source of unexpected properties is, manifestly, the rotate character of Post negation.

The most important property of Post algebras is their functional completeness: Every finite–argument function on P_n can be defined by means of the two primitive functions. In particular, then, also the constant functions and hence the 'logical values' $t_1, t_2, \ldots, t_n$, themselves. Establishing functional completeness was one of Post's primary aims.

Post's original construction, definitely algebraic, was eventually provided with an interesting semantic interpretation. Post suggests regarding the elements of P_n as objects corresponding to special $(n-1)$-element tuples $P = (p_1, p_2, \ldots, p_{n-1})$ of ordinary two-valued propositions $p_1, p_2, \ldots, p_{n-1}$. More specifically, P_n is replaced with the 'space' E^{n-1} of such tuples subject to the condition that the true propositions are listed before the false. The connectives on E^{n-1} are defined as:

($\neg$) $\neg P$ is formed by replacing the first false element by its denial, but if there is no false element in P, then all are to be denied, in which case $\neg P$ is a sequence of false propositions.

($\vee$)   When $P = (p_1, p_2, \ldots, p_{n-1})$ and $Q = (q_1, q_2, \ldots, q_{n-1})$, then $P \vee Q = (p_1 \vee q_1, p_2 \vee q_2, \ldots, p_{n-1} \vee q_{n-1})$.

The mapping $\mathbf{i} : E^{n-1} \rightarrow P_n$

$i(P) = t_i$ iff P contains exactly $(i-1)$ true propositions

establishes an isomorphism of $(E^{n-1}, \vee, \neg)$ onto the Post algebra $\mathbf{P}_n$. For example, the universe E^4, corresponding to the case of five-valued Post logic considered before, consists of these 4-tuples:

$(0, 0, 0, 0)$	t_1
$(1, 0, 0, 0)$	t_2
$(1, 1, 0, 0)$	t_3
$(1, 1, 1, 0)$	t_4
$(1, 1, 1, 1)$	t_5

This interpretation of logic values and its algebra shows, among other things, that the values in different Post logics should be understood differently.

Post (1921) also defined a family of purely implicative n-valued logics. The family is fairly extensive and it covers implications designed by other authors, e.g. Łukasiewicz and Gödel. The novelty of this truth-table proposal was that Post designated many logical values at a time. That possibility, quite natural nowadays, was not considered by many of the originators of many-valued logics.

14.3. Three-Valued Logic of Kleene

Kleene (1938, 1952) is the author of two systems of three-valued propositional and predicate logic designed to allow for the indeterminacy of some propositions at a certain stage of investigation. These were particularly inspired by research in the foundations of mathematics and the theory of recursion, where there was need for tools that render the analysis of partially defined predicates, or propositional functions, possible.

To be aware of the necessity for such logic(s), consider a simple example of such a predicate, the mathematical property P defined by the equivalence

$$P(x) \text{ iff } 1 \le \frac{1}{x} \le 2$$

where x is a variable ranging over the set of real numbers. It is apparent that the propositional function $P(x)$ is undetermined when $x = 0$. More precisely,

$$\text{Proposition } P(a) \text{ is } \begin{cases} \text{true} & \text{if } \frac{1}{2} \le a \le 1 \\ \text{undetermined} & \text{if } a = 0 \\ \text{false} & \text{otherwise} \end{cases}$$

The starting point of Kleene's (1938) construction consists in considering also the propositions whose logical value of truth (T) or falsity (F) is undefined, undetermined by means of accessible algorithms, or not essential for actual consideration. The third logical value of undefiniteness (U) is reserved for this category of propositions. Kleene's counterparts of the standard connectives are defined by these tables:

α	¬α
F	T
U	U
T	F

→	F	U	T
F	T	T	T
U	U	U	T
T	F	U	T

∨	F	U	T
F	F	U	T
U	U	U	T
T	T	T	T

∧	F	U	T
F	F	F	F
U	F	U	U
T	F	U	T

≡	F	U	T
F	T	U	F
U	U	U	U
T	F	U	T

One may easily notice that, as in Łukasiewicz logic, the connectives' behavior towards the classical logical values T and F remains unchanged. Furthermore, the classical interdefinability of $\alpha \rightarrow \beta$ and $\neg \alpha \vee \beta$ is preserved.

Kleene takes T as the only distinguished value, with the result that that no formula is a tautology. This follows from the fact that any valuation which assigns U to every propositional variable also assigns U to any formula. It is striking that a 'conservative' extension of the two-valued logic should reject all classical tautologies, even $p \to p$ and $p \equiv p$.

Körner (1966) provided the most accurate and compatible interpretation of Kleene's connectives, defining the notion of an inexact class of a given non-empty domain A generated by a partial definition $D(P)$ of some property P (of elements of A) to be a three-valued 'characteristic function' $X_P : A \to \{-1, 0, +1\}$:

$$X_P(a) = \begin{cases} -1 & \text{when } P(a) \text{ is false according to } D(P) \\ 0 & \text{when } P(a) \text{ is } D(P)\text{-undecidable} \\ +1 & \text{when } P(a) \text{ is true according to } D(P) \end{cases}$$

Any family of inexact classes of a given domain A forms a *DeMorgan lattice*, whose algebraic operations $\cup$, $\cap$ and $-$:

$$(X \cup Y)(a) = \max\{X(a), Y(a)\}$$
$$(X \cap Y)(a) = \min\{X(a), Y(a)\}$$
$$(-X)(a) = -X(a)$$

are counterparts of the Kleene connectives. Körner's ideas have recently been revitalized in the theory of *rough sets* of Pawlak (1991) and the *approximation logic* based on it (Rasiowa, 1991; Bolc and Borowik, 1992).

Kleene (1952) refers to these connectives as 'strong' and introduces another set of 'weak' connectives. With negation and equivalence the same, he defines the three others by the tables

$\to$	F	U	T
F	T	U	T
U	U	U	U
T	F	U	T

$\vee$	F	U	T
F	F	U	T
U	U	U	U
T	T	U	T

$\wedge$	F	U	T
F	F	U	F
U	U	U	U
T	F	U	T

The new truth-tables are to describe the employment of logical connectives with respect to those arithmetical propositional functions whose decidability depends on effective recursive procedures. They are constituted according to the rule that any single appearance of U results in the whole context taking U, the motivation being that indeterminacy occurring at any stage of computation makes the entire procedure undetermined.

14.4. Bochvar Logic and Beyond

Bochvar's (1938) conception of the three-valued logic is based on the division of propositions into sensible and senseless, and then 'mapping' that into a two-level formal language. A proposition is *meaningful* if it is either *true* or *false*, all other sentences are considered as *meaningless* or *paradoxical*. This approach was designed for solving paradoxes that emerge from classical logic and set theory based on it.

The propositional language of Bochvar logic has two levels, which correspond to object language and metalanguage. Both levels have their own connectives that are counterparts of negation, implication, disjunction, conjunction and equivalence. The two planes of Bochvar construction correspond to Kleene weak logic (internal) and to classical logic (external), respectively. The *internal* connectives are conservative three-valued generalizations of the classical ones; they are denoted here as ¬, →, ∨, ∧ and ≡. The *external* connectives are devised to characterize the relations between logical values of propositions. They are 'metalinguistic' and incorporate the expressions '. . . is true' and '. . . is false.' These are marked as starred counterparts of the standard connectives, and understood in the following way:

external negation: ¬* α   α is false

external implication: α →* β   if α is true, then β is true

external disjunction: α ∨* β   α is true or β is true

external conjunction: α ∧* β   α is true and β is true

external equivalence: α ≡* β   α is true iff β is true

The truth tables of internal connectives have been compiled according to the rule which follows Kleene's principle: "every compound proposition including at least one meaningless component is meaningless; in other cases, its value is determined classically." Thus, the internal Bochvar connectives coincide with Kleene's weak connectives, as given by the tables from the last section, but with U now for the value 'meaningless.' The truth-table description of the second collection of Bochvar connectives is:

α	¬* α
F	T
U	T
T	F

→*	F	U	T
F	T	T	T
U	T	T	T
T	F	F	T

∨*	F	U	T
F	F	F	T
U	F	F	T
T	T	T	T

∧*	F	U	T
F	F	F	F
U	F	F	F
T	F	F	T

≡*	F	U	T
F	T	T	F
U	T	T	F
T	F	F	T

An important property of Bochvar construction, which makes it more natural, is the compatibility of two levels. The passage from the internal to external level is assured by the so-called *external assertion* 'α is true,' *A**. The truth-table for this connective, and the intuitively justified definitions of the external connectives, is:

α	$A^*\alpha$
F	F
U	F
T	T

Where

$$\neg^*\alpha =_{df} \neg A^*\alpha$$
$$\alpha \rightarrow^* \beta =_{df} A^*\alpha \rightarrow A^*\beta$$
$$\alpha \vee^* \beta =_{df} A^*\alpha \vee A^*\beta$$
$$\alpha \wedge^* \beta =_{df} A^*\alpha \wedge A^*\beta$$
$$\alpha \equiv^* \beta =_{df} A^*\alpha \equiv A^*\beta$$

Bochvar takes T as the designated value and thus obtains a construction that coincides with the Kleene weak logic. Like that, Bochvar's *internal logic* has no tautologies. Finally, the *external logic* is classical logic; this is due to the fact that the truth tables of all external connectives 'identify' the values U and F, while the behavior of these connectives with regard to F and T is classical.

Several authors have taken up Bochvar's idea so as to develop systems appropriate for dealing with vagueness or of the logic of nonsense. Halldén (1949), for example, rediscovered Bochvar logic for these purposes. Halldén adopts three logic values: falsity (F), truth (T) and 'meaningless' (U), and the same rules for the connectives of negation and conjunction as in Bochvar's internal logic.[3] Halldén's system, however, differs from the latter. First, it has a new one-argument connective + serving to express meaningfulness of propositions. Thus, if α is meaningless, then $+\alpha$ is false. Otherwise, $+\alpha$ is true. Second, Halldén distinguishes two logical values U and T. Therefore, a formula is valid if it never takes F. In consequence, the set of valid formulas not containing + coincides with the set of tautologies of CPC. The construction, however, differs from classical logic by its inference properties. The logic of nonsense heavily restricts several rules of inference, including *modus ponens*. Thus, in general, q does not follow from $p \rightarrow q$ and p. To see that, it suffices to consider a valuation for which p is meaningless and q is false. Under such valuation, q is not designated, while the premises as meaningless are both designated.

Halldén provides a readable axiomatization of his logic. To this aim, he introduces the connectives of implication, $\rightarrow$, and equivalence, $\equiv$, accepting standard classical definitions and two standard inference rules MP and SUB

H1	$(\neg p \rightarrow p) \rightarrow p$
H2	$p \rightarrow (\neg p \rightarrow q)$
H3	$(p \rightarrow q) \rightarrow ((q \rightarrow r) \rightarrow (p \rightarrow r))$
H4	$+p \equiv +\neg p$
H5	$+(p \wedge q) \equiv +p \wedge +q$
H6	$p \rightarrow +p$

In this framework, it is easy to define a dual to the + connective, putting: $-\alpha =_{df} \neg +\alpha$. Thus, as $+\alpha$ corresponds to 'α is meaningful,' $-\alpha$ stands for 'α is meaningless.'

Further elaboration of Halldén's approach is made by Åqvist (1962) and Segerberg (1965). Starting with problems arising with normative sentences, Åqvist created a propositional calculus that is a minor variant of Łukasiewicz three-valued logic, or a fragment of Kleene strong logic. The three primitives of Åqvist's logic are: negation, $\neg$, disjunction, $\vee$, and a special connective, #. Their tables use the three values: F, U, T (in our notation), where the intended meaning of F and T is standard and T is the only designated value. Finally, the tables of negation and disjunction are the same, modulo notation, as the truth-tables of Łukasiewicz three-valued connectives. In turn, # is defined as:

$$\#(F) = \#(U) = F \qquad \text{and} \qquad \#(T) = T$$

As a result, this coincides with the Łukasiewicz 'necessity' operator L (see section 14.1).

Given the philosophical application of his formal approach, Åqvist defines three 'characteristic' functors of the system:

$$F\alpha =_{df} \#\neg\alpha \qquad L\alpha =_{df} \#\alpha \vee F\alpha \qquad M\alpha =_{df} \neg L\alpha$$

whose intuitive reading is: 'α is false' ($F\alpha$), 'α is meaningful' ($L\alpha$) and 'α is meaningless' ($M\alpha$).

14.5. Logic Algebras and Matrices

The algebraic approach is an efficient tool of logical investigation; See, for example, Rasiowa (1974) and Wójcicki (1988). Its use in the case of many-valued logic is especially natural, and it enables a better insight into problems of many-valuedness. A *propositional language* is viewed as an algebra of formulas

$$L = (For, F_1, \ldots, F_m)$$

freely generated by the set of propositional variables $Var = \{p, q, r, \ldots\}$; the connectives $F_1, \ldots, F_m$ being finitary operations on For. An interpretation structure A for L is an algebra

$$A = (A, f_1, \ldots, f_m)$$

similar to it. Any mapping $s: Var \to A$, may be extended uniquely to the homomorphism $h_s: L \to A$, $h_s \in Hom(L, A)$. Interpretation structures equipped with a distinguished subset of elements to correspond to propositions of a specified kind (e.g., true sentences) are called logical matrices. More specifically, a pair

$$M = (A, D)$$

with A being an algebra similar to a language L and $D \subseteq A$, will be referred to as a *matrix* for L. Elements of D will be called *designated* (or, *distinguished*) elements of M. The set of formulas which take designated values only:

$$E(M) = \{\alpha \in For : h\alpha \in D \text{ for any } h \in Hom(L, A)\}$$

is called the *content* of M. The relation $\vDash_M$ is said to be a *matrix consequence relation* of M provided that, for any $X \subseteq For$, $\alpha \in For$,

$$X \vDash_M \alpha \text{ iff for every } h \in Hom(L, A), h\alpha \in D \text{ whenever } hX \subseteq D$$

The content of a matrix is a counterpart of the set of tautologies and the entailment relation $\vDash_M \subseteq 2^{For} \times For$ is a natural generalization of the relation of classical consequence.

To illustrate these concepts, the language of classical logic is most familiar:

$$L = (For, \neg, \rightarrow, \vee, \wedge, \equiv)$$

Then, the two-element *algebra of the classical logic* is of the form

$$A_2 = (\{0, 1\}, \neg, \rightarrow, \vee, \wedge, \equiv)$$

(The same symbols $\neg$, $\rightarrow$, $\vee$, $\wedge$, $\equiv$ may be used as for connectives to denote corresponding operations on $\{0, 1\}$ as determined by the truth-tables.) The classical matrix has the form

$$M_2 = (\{0, 1\}, \neg, \rightarrow, \vee, \wedge, \equiv, \{1\})$$

and the classical consequence relation in this notation is characterized as follows:

$$X \vDash_2 \alpha \text{ iff, for every } h \in Hom(L, A_2), h\alpha = 1 \text{ whenever } hX \subseteq \{1\}$$

Notice that the set of tautologies is the content of M_2 and it consists of formulas that are 'consequences' of the empty set, $TAUT = E(M_2) = \{\alpha : \varnothing \vDash_2 \alpha\}$. The so-called *deduction theorem* for classical logic expressed semantically in terms of $\vDash_2$ says now that for any set of formulas X and α, $\beta \in For$,

(*ded$_2$*) $X, \alpha \vDash_2 \beta$ iff $X \vDash_2 \alpha \rightarrow \beta$

To see how the framework of matrices and consequence relations works for many-valued logic, consider a few properties of three-valued logics already presented. First, the matrix of the three-valued logic of Łukasiewicz:

$$M_3 = (\{0, \tfrac{1}{2}, 1\}, \neg, \rightarrow, \vee, \wedge, \equiv, \{1\})$$

with the connectives set by the tables in section 14.1. It is now possible to check that L_3 has the deduction theorem in this form

(ded_3) $X, \alpha \vDash_3 \beta$ iff $X \vDash_3 \alpha \to (\alpha \to \beta)$

The left to right direction is essential. To see why the antecedent α appears twice, it suffices to consider a valuation h, which sends all formulas from X into $\{1\}$ and such that $h\alpha = \frac{1}{2}$, $h\beta = 0$. For the same reasons, (ded_2) fails in this case.

The last example shows that a many-valued logic may differ not only on the level of tautologies, but also with respect to the rules of consequence relation and, ultimately, by the set of inference rules. Another case where the consequence relation is important, occurs when the logic has the empty set of tautologies, such as one finds with Kleene and Bochvar logics. The matrix of the weak Kleene logic and, thus, the internal Bochvar logic is

$$K_3 = (\{F, U, T\}, \neg, \to, \vee, \wedge, \equiv, \{T\})$$

with the second collection of operations in section 14.3. It was already stated that this logic is non-tautological, $E(K_3) = \varnothing$. However, Kleene logic is non-trivial since the consequence $\vDash_{K_3}$ determined by its matrix is not. It is noteworthy that the set of rules of $\vDash_{K_3}$ consists of some special rules of the classical logic. Namely, for any classically consistent $X \subseteq For$, i.e. such that for some valuation $h \in Hom(L, A_2)$ $hX \subseteq \{1\}$,[4]

$X \vDash_{K_3} \alpha$ iff $X \vDash_2 \alpha$ and $Var(\alpha) \subseteq Var(X)$

The use of logical matrices is undoubtedly the most natural way of achieving many-valuednes i.e. consequence relations different from $\vDash_2$. Two cases of obtaining a genuine logic of this kind have already been discussed. Nevertheless, taking a multiple-element matrix as a base for the logical construction does not guarantee its many-valuedness. Also, there are different kinds of many-valuedness. Consider, for instance, the matrix

$$W_3 = (\{0, T, 1\}, \neg, \to, \vee, \wedge, \equiv, \{T, 1\})$$

with operations defined by the tables

x	$\neg x$		$\to$	0	T	1		$\vee$	0	T	1		$\wedge$	0	T	1		$\equiv$	0	T	1
0	1		0	1	T	1		0	0	T	1		0	0	0	0		0	1	0	0
T	0		T	0	T	T		T	T	T	1		T	0	T	T		T	0	T	T
1	0		1	0	T	1		1	1	1	1		1	0	T	1		1	0	T	1

Notice, that with every $h \in Hom(L, W_3)$ the valuation $h^* \in Hom(L, M_2)$ corresponds in a one-to-one way such that $h\alpha \in \{T, 1\}$ iff $h^*\alpha = 1$. Therefore, $\vDash_{W_3} = \vDash_{M_2}$ and W_3 is nothing more then a three-element model of the two-valued logic.[5]

The last, somewhat striking, case is when a multiple-element matrix retains all classical tautologies, i.e. its content coincides with *TAUT*, but its consequence relation differs from the classical by some rules of inference. The matrix

$$K_{3*} = (\{F, U, T\}, \neg, \rightarrow, \vee, \wedge, \equiv, \{U, T\})$$

is like the Kleene–Bochvar matrix K_3 but having two elements U and T designated; it has this property. Its consequence operation $\vDash_{3*}$ falsifies MP, since the inference $\{p \rightarrow q, p\} \vDash_{3*} q$ does not hold.

14.6. Functional Completeness

A logic algebra is functionally complete when all finitary operations on its universe are definable by use of its original operations. Classical propositional logic is functionally complete in this sense. In the terminology just adopted one may say equivalently that the algebra A_2 and, consequently, the matrix M_2 have this property.

Where $n \geq 2$ is a given natural number, put $E_n = \{1, 2, \ldots, n\}$ and by U_n denote any algebra of the form

$$U_n = (E_n, f_1, \ldots, f_m)$$

with $f_1, \ldots, f_m$ being finitary operations on E_n. U_n will be called *functionally complete* if every finitary mapping $f \colon E_n^k \rightarrow E_n$ ($k \geq 0$, k finite)[6] can be represented as a composition of the operations $f_1, \ldots, f_m$.

This definition of functional completeness is due to Post (1921), who reduced the complexity of the problem to a small number of connectives. If one requires only that for some finite m any k-argument operation on E_n, where $k \leq m$, is definable then U_n is said to be *functionally complete for m variables*. The logical counterpart of the last definition is that it warrants definability of all at most *m-argument* connectives.

> **Theorem 14.1** (Post, 1921). If U_n is functionally complete for m variables, where $m \geq 2$, then is also functionally complete for $m + 1$ variables and hence also functionally complete.

Note that theorem 14.1 reduces the functional completeness of A_2 to the definability of all 4 unary and 16 binary connectives. In turn, it is easy to show that the connectives of the standard language define all twenty. Post himself provided several other small collections to do the same and there is also a 'minimalist' reduction of all classical connectives to a single one, the so-called Sheffer stroke.

Obtaining the functional completeness of *n element* algebras of logic was another motivation for building many-valued logic. Post was the first to give such an algebra generating two functions: the one-argument cyclic *rotation* (negation) and the two-argument *maximum* function (disjunction) of section 14.2. In the present notation, these look like

$$\neg_n x = \begin{cases} i + 1 & \text{if } x = i \neq n \\ 1 & \text{if } x = n \end{cases} \qquad x \vee y = \max(x, y)$$

Consequently, every *Post algebra*

$$P_n = (E_n, \neg_n, \vee)$$

is functionally complete (Post, 1921). It is of interest to notice that

$$P_2 = (E_2, \neg_2, \vee)$$

is the $(\neg, \vee)$-reduct of the algebra A_2.

The functional completeness of the n-valued logic algebras is important because propositional logics founded on such algebras are logics of all possible extensional n-valued connectives (truth functional when $n = 2$) and, for every n, they are, in a sense, unique. Since functional completeness is not a frequent property, several criteria have been formulated which might help to determine its presence.

Theorem 14.2 (Słupecki, (1939a) An n-valued algebra $U_n (n \geq 0, n$ finite) is functionally complete iff in U_n there are definable:

(i) all one-argument operations on E_n
(ii) at least one two-argument operation $f(x, y)$ whose range consists of all values i for $1 \leq i \leq n$.

Using theorem 14.2, one may easily establish the functional incompleteness of all the three-valued logics described above, excepting, of course, the Post logic. Thus, for example, for the Łukasiewicz three-valued logic L_3, it suffices that the one-argument constant function $T: Tx = \frac{1}{2}$ for any $x \in \{0, \frac{1}{2}, 1\}$ is not definable in terms of the basic operations (connectives) in L_3. For consider any compound function of one-argument and assume that $x \in \{0, 1\}$, then, due to the tables of the primitive connectives, the output value cannot be equal to $\frac{1}{2}$. On the other hand, the same criterion implies that adding T to the stock of functions of L_3 leads to the functionally complete logic algebra (Słupecki, 1967 [1936]). Furthermore, Słupecki proved that the set of axioms W1–W4 of Wajsberg (see section 14.1) together with

W5 $\quad Tp \rightarrow \neg Tp$

W6 $\quad \neg Tp \rightarrow Tp$

axiomatize the functionally complete version of Łukasiewicz's three-valued logic.

Słupecki (1939b) also constructed the largest possible class of functionally complete logics and gave a general method of their axiomatization. The Słupecki matrix S_{nk} (n being a given natural number, $1 \leq k < n$) is of the form

$$S_{nk} = (\{1, 2, \ldots, n\}, \rightarrow, R, S, \{1, 2, \ldots, k\})$$

where $\rightarrow$ is a binary (implication), and R, S unary operations defined by

$$x \rightarrow y = \begin{cases} y & \text{if } 1 \le x \le k \\ 1 & \text{if } k < x \le n \end{cases}$$

$$R(x) = \begin{cases} x + 1 & \text{if } 1 \le x \le n - 1 \\ 1 & \text{if } x = n \end{cases}$$

$$S(x) = \begin{cases} 2 & \text{if } x = 1 \\ 1 & \text{if } x = 2 \\ x & \text{if } 3 \le x \le n \end{cases}$$

Here the similarity to Post logics is evident: R is the Post negation and S a sort of 'permutation' function. Finally, the classical properties of implication enabled Słupecki's original axiomatization of the class of logics defined by the above matrices.

The next section looks briefly at some infinite-valued logical constructions. These are all functionally incomplete, due to the fact that the set of possible functions of any algebra of this kind in uncountably infinite, while using a finite number of original operations one may define, at most, a countable family of functions.

14.7. Łukasiewicz Logics

In 1922, Łukasiewicz generalized his three-valued logic and defined a family of many-valued logics, both finite and infinite-valued. (Łukasiewicz, 1970c, p. 140.) A *Łukasiewicz n-valued matrix* has the form

$$M_n = (L_n, \neg, \rightarrow, \vee, \wedge, \equiv, \{1\})$$

where, for N the set of natural numbers

$$L_n = \begin{cases} \{0, \frac{1}{n-1}, \frac{2}{n-1}, \ldots, \frac{n-2}{n-1}, 1\} & \text{if } n \ge 2, n \in N \\ \{s/w: 0 \le s \le w; s, w \in N \text{ and } w \ne 0\} & \text{if } n = \aleph_0 \\ [0, 1] & \text{if } n = \aleph_1 \end{cases}$$

and the functions are defined on L_n as

(i) $\neg x = 1 - x$
       $x \rightarrow y = \min(1, 1 - x + y)$
(ii) $x \vee y = (x \rightarrow y) \rightarrow y = \max(x, y)$
       $x \wedge y = \neg(\neg x \vee \neg y) = \min(x, y)$
       $x \equiv y = (x \rightarrow y) \wedge (y \rightarrow x) = 1 - |x - y|$

The introduction of these new many-valued logics was not supported by any separate argumentation – Łukasiewicz did not give new reasons for the choice of more logical values. He merely underlined that the generalization was correct since for $n = 3$ one obtains exactly the matrix of his 1920 three-valued logic. Later history has shown, however, that the Łukasiewicz logics have many properties that make them among the most important logical constructions.

First, the Łukasiewicz matrix M_2 coincides with the matrix of the classical logic. Moreover, the set $\{0, 1\}$ is closed with respect to all Łukasiewicz connectives, which is another expression of conservative character of the generalization. Consequently, A_2 is a subalgebra of any algebra $(L_n, \neg, \rightarrow, \vee, \wedge, \equiv)$ and M_2 is a *submatrix* of M_n. Therefore, all tautologies of Łukasiewicz propositional calculi are included in the classical *TAUT*

$$E(M_n) \subseteq E(M_2) = TAUT$$

Next, the relations between the contents of finite matrices are established by the famous Lindenbaum condition (Łukasiewicz and Tarski, 1930):

Theorem 14.3   For finite n, $m \in N$, $E(M_n) \subseteq E(M_m)$ iff $m - 1$ is a *divisor* of $n - 1$.

The proof of the last property may be based on the 'submatrix' properties, mentioned above, of the family of the finite matrices of Łukasiewicz. Using the same argument one may also prove the counterpart of theorem 14.3 for matrix consequence relations $\vDash_n$ of M_n:

Theorem 14.4   For finite n, $m \in N$, $\vDash_n \subseteq \vDash_m$ iff $m - 1$ is a *divisor* of $n - 1$.

The most interesting property of the infinite Łukasiewicz matrices is that they have the same set of tautologies, i.e., a common content, which is equal to the intersection of the contents of all finite matrices:

Theorem 14.5 $E(M_{\aleph_0}) = E(M_{\aleph_1}) = \cap\{E(M_n) : n \geq 2, n \in N\}$

Łukasiewicz n-valued logics L_n are not functionally complete. All of what was established for $n = 3$ applies for each finite n. First, no constant except 0 and 1 is definable in $(L_n, \neg, \rightarrow, \vee, \wedge, \equiv)$. Second, adding the constants to the stock of connectives makes this algebra functionally complete (compare theorem 14.2). And, since M_n is generated, either by $1/(n-1)$ or by $(n-2)/(n-1)$, adding only one of them will do the job as well. McNaughton (1951) formulated and proved an ingenious definability criterion for Łukasiewicz matrices, both finite and infinite, showing the mathematical beauty of Łukasiewicz's logic constructions.

A proof that finite matrices are axiomatizable was given in Łukasiewicz and Tarski (1930). However, the problem of formulation of a concrete axiom system for finite Łukasiewicz logics for $n > 3$ remained open until Rosser's and Turquette's (1952) general method of axiomatization of n-valued logics with connectives satisfying the so-called standard conditions. This method can be applied, among others, to L_n since such connectives are either primitive or definable in Łukasiewicz finite matrices. Hence, for every n an axiomatization of Łukasiewicz's n-valued propositional calculus can be obtained. The axiomatization, however, becomes very complicated due to the high generality of the method given by Rosser and Turquette.

In 1930, Łukasiewicz (Łukasiewicz and Tarski, 1930) conjectured that his $\aleph_0$-valued logic was axiomatized by:

L1 $p \rightarrow (q \rightarrow p)$

L2 $(p \rightarrow q) \rightarrow ((q \rightarrow r) \rightarrow (p \rightarrow r))$

L3 $((p \rightarrow q) \rightarrow q) \rightarrow ((q \rightarrow p) \rightarrow p)$

L4 $(\neg p \rightarrow \neg q) \rightarrow (q \rightarrow p)$

L5 $((p \rightarrow q) \rightarrow (q \rightarrow p)) \rightarrow (q \rightarrow p)$

together with the rules MP and SUB. According to Łukasiewicz, this hypothesis was confirmed by Wajsberg in 1931.[7] Next comes the reduction of the axiom set: Meredith (1958) and Chang (1958) independently showed that axiom L5 is dependent on the others. There are two main accessible completeness proofs of L1–L4 (with MP and SUB): by Rose and Rosser (1958) based on syntactic methods and linear inequalities, and by Chang (1959) with purely algebraic methods.

Several axiomatizations for finite-valued Łukasiewicz logics ($n > 3$) have been obtained by extending the axiom system L1–L4 in different ways; see, for example, Grigolia (1977) and Tokarz (1974).

14.8. Background to Formalization

Rosser and Turquette (1952) determined the conditions that make finitely many-valued propositional logics resemble CPC, thereby simplifing the problem of axiomatization (and the question of their extension to predicate logics, which we shall not discuss). Begin with the pattern of interpretation discussed in section 14.4, with matrices of the form

$$M_{n,k} = (U_n, D_k)$$

where

$U_n = (E_n, f_1, \ldots, f_m)$

$E_n = \{1, 2, \ldots, n\}$

$D_k = \{1, 2, \ldots, k\}$

with $n \geq 2 \in N$ and $1 \leq k < n$. The natural number ordering conveys decreasing degree of truth so that 1 always refers to 'truth' and n takes the role of falsity.

Next come the conditions concerning propositional connectives, which in $M_{n,k}$ have to represent negation, $\neg$, implication, $\rightarrow$, disjunction, $\vee$, conjunction, $\wedge$, equivalence, $\equiv$, and special one-argument connectives $j_1, \ldots, j_n$. Assume that the same symbols are used to denote the corresponding functions of U_n and that a given $M_{n,k}$ is the interpretation structure. Then the respective connectives are said to satisfy the *standard conditions* if for any $x, y \in E_n$ and $i \in \{1, 2, \ldots, n\}$

$$\neg x \in D_k \quad \text{iff} \quad x \notin D_k$$

$$x \rightarrow y \notin D_k \quad \text{iff} \quad x \in D_k \text{ and } y \notin D_k$$

$$x \vee y \in D_k \quad \text{iff} \quad x \in D_k \text{ or } y \in D_k$$

$$x \wedge y \in D_k \quad \text{iff} \quad x \in D_k \text{ and } y \in D_k$$

$$x \equiv y \in D_k \quad \text{iff} \quad \text{either } x, y \in D_k \text{ or } x, y \notin D_k$$

$$j_i(x) \in D_k \quad \text{iff} \quad x = i$$

Each matrix $M_{n,k}$ having standard connectives as primitive or definable is called *standard*. When only some of them are present, the term 'Q-standard' is used, where Q is a subset of the set of all standard connectives.

All Post and all finite Łukasiewicz matrices are standard. The first case is easy. Post matrices are based on functionally complete algebras, see section 14.6, and thus any possible connective is definable. A given n-valued Łukasiewicz matrix may be isomorphically transformed onto a matrix of the form $M_{n,1}$: the isomorphism is established by the mapping $f(x) = n - (n-1)x$ of the set

$$\{0, \tfrac{1}{n-1}, \tfrac{2}{n-1}, \ldots, \tfrac{n-2}{n-1}, 1\}$$

onto $\{1, 2, \ldots, n\}$. A moment's reflection shows that original Łukasiewicz disjunction and conjunction satisfy standard conditions. In turn, the other required connectives are definable in M_n. Thus,

$$x \Rightarrow y =_{df} x \rightarrow (x \rightarrow \cdots \rightarrow (x \rightarrow y))$$
$$\underset{(n-1) \text{ times}}{}$$

$$x \approx y =_{df} (x \Rightarrow y) \wedge (y \Rightarrow x)$$

define the standard implication and equivalence ($\rightarrow$ appearing on the right is the original Łukasiewicz connective). The definability of j's, $j_i(x) = 1$ iff $x = i$ follows easily from the McNaughton (1951) criterion; see also Rosser and Turquette (1952).

Using their framework, Rosser and Turquette solved the problem of axiomatizing known systems of many-valued logic, including n-valued Łukasiewicz and Post logics. Any logic determined by a $\{\rightarrow, j_1, j_2, \ldots, j_n\}$-standard matrix $M_{n,k}$ is axiomatized by means of the rule MP and SUB and the following set of axioms:

A1 $p \rightarrow (q \rightarrow p)$

A2 $(p \rightarrow (q \rightarrow r)) \rightarrow (q \rightarrow (p \rightarrow r))$

A3 $(p \rightarrow q) \rightarrow ((q \rightarrow r) \rightarrow (p \rightarrow r))$

A4 $(j_i(p) \rightarrow (j_i(p) \rightarrow q)) \rightarrow (j_i(p) \rightarrow q)$

A5 $(j_n(p) \rightarrow q) \rightarrow ((j_{n-1}(p) \rightarrow q) \rightarrow (\cdots \rightarrow ((j_1(p) \rightarrow q) \rightarrow q) \ldots))$

A6 $j_i(p) \rightarrow p$ for $i = 1, 2, \ldots, k$

A7 $j_{i(r)}(p_r) \rightarrow (j_{i(r-1)}(p_{r-1}) \rightarrow (\cdots \rightarrow (j_{i(1)}(p_1) \rightarrow j_f(F(p_1, \ldots, p_{r-1}, p_r))) \ldots))$
       where $f = f(i(1), \ldots, i(r))$

where the symbols f and F used in A7 represent, respectively, an arbitrary function of the matrix $M_{n,k}$ and a propositional connective associated with it (Rosser and Turquette, 1952).

The axiom system A1–A7 consists of the two parts: A1–A3 and A4–A7. The first group of axioms describes the properties of pure classical implication sufficient to present the deduction theorem in its classical version, (ded_2), cf. section 14.5. The second group contains formulas, which, due to the properties of the j connectives and implication, bridge semantic and syntactic properties. Checking the soundness of the axioms is easy, drawing on procedures from classical logic. The completeness proof, however, requires much calculation and involves quite a complicated induction.

14.9. Interpretation and Justification

Problems of the philosophical interpretation and intuitive explanation of many-valuedness are vexed questions of logic. Through time, even those motivations that were once accepted have undergone revision. Only some algebraic interpretations remain untouched, mostly due to the mathematical properties and their usefulness for solving further formal problems. This section concentrates on selected aspects of the topic.

Recall from section 14.1 how Łukasiewicz (1970b [1920]) was initially concerned with 'future contingents' and interpreted the value $\frac{1}{2}$ as 'possibility' or undetermination of the 0–1 status of a proposition. Yet, as Gonseth (1941) argued, this way of interpreting the third value is incompatible with other principles of the Łukasiewicz logic. Consider two propositions α and $\neg\alpha$; whenever α is undetermined, so is $\neg\alpha$ and then, according to the table of conjunction $\alpha \wedge \neg\alpha$ is undetermined. This, however, contradicts the intuition that $\alpha \wedge \neg\alpha$ is false, independent of α's content. This reveals how Łukasiewicz's original interpretation neglects the mutual dependence of some 'possible' propositions.

Furthermore, Haack (1978, p. 209) argued that even Łukasiewicz's motivation in rejecting the law of bivalence so as to avoid the fatalist conclusion depends on a modal fallacy, inferring

If α, then it is necessary that β.

from

It is necessary that (if α, then β).

Urquhart (1986) presents another interesting criticism of Łukasiewicz implication. Taking the third logical value as the set {0, 1} of two 'potential' classical values of a future contingent sentence, he defines implication in a natural way so that an implication having 0 as antecedent always has the value 1, an implication from 1 to {0, 1} has the value {0, 1} and, finally the implication from {0, 1} to {0, 1} has the value {0, 1}. The last point is inconsistent with the Łukasiewicz stipulation, however, since that would make the output be 1. Therefore, Urquhart claims, the Łukasiewicz table is wrong.[8]

Reichenbach (1944) argued that adoption of three-valued logic would provide a solution to some problems raised by quantum mechanics. To avoid 'causal anomalies,' Reichenbach presents an extended version of the Łukasiewicz logic, adding further negation and implication connectives. He refers to the third logical value as 'indeterminate' and assigns it to anomalous statements of quantum mechanics, primarily sentences indicating both the position and the momentum of a particle at a given time, which, according to Bohr and Heisenberg, are to be regarded as meaningless. The weak point of Reichenbach's (1944, p. 166) proposal is that certain laws, such as the principle of energy, are also classified as 'indeterminate.' (See Haack (1996) for criticism of other interpretations of three-valued logic.)

The mathematical probability calculus resembles a many-valued logic, and so the question of a connection between probability and many-valuedness naturally arises. [See chapter 16.] Łukasiewicz (1970a [1913]) himself invented a theory of *logical probability*, whose distinguishing feature was that it referred probability to propositions, rather than events. Reichenbach (1949) and Zawirski (1934), among others, continued this conception attempting to create a many-valued logic in which logical probability could find a satisfactory interpretation. The Reichenbach–Zawirski conception is based on the assumption that there is a function *Pr* ranging over the set of propositions of a given standard propositional language, with values from the real interval [0, 1]. The postulates for *Pr* are as follows:

P1 $0 \leq Pr(p) \leq 1$

P2 $Pr(p \vee \neg p) = 1$

P3 $Pr(p \vee q) = Pr(p) + Pr(q)$ if p and q are mutually exclusive
        (i.e., $Pr(p \wedge q) = 0$)

P4 $Pr(p) = Pr(q)$ when p and q are logically equivalent

From P1–P4, it is possible to infer other expected properties of *Pr*. Identifying the logical value $v(p)$ with the measure of probability $Pr(p)$, then, for $Pr(p) = \frac{1}{2}$ from the properties mentioned, gives

$$\tfrac{1}{2} \vee \tfrac{1}{2} = Pr(p \vee \neg p) = 1$$

and

$$\tfrac{1}{2} \vee \tfrac{1}{2} = Pr(p \vee p) = Pr(p) = \tfrac{1}{2}$$

Consequently, logical probability must not be identified with logical values of any ordinary extensional many-valued logic. Giles (1974), however, presents a plausible interpretation of $\aleph_0$-valued Łukasiewicz logic in terms of dialogue logic with risk values being associated with subjective probabilities.

Another early goal of many-valued logicians, including Łukasiewicz and Bochvar, was to eliminate the Russell paradox. (See section 14.1.) The problem concerns the *Comprehension Axiom* (CA), which states the existence of all sets bearing logically expressible properties. [See chapter 3.] Russell's discovery excludes the acceptance of CA in set theory based on first-order classical logic. This raises the question whether CA could be incorproated in Łukasiewicz logics. Moh Shaw-Kwei (1954) proved the impossibility of this for finite systems. Skolem (1957) hypothesized, however, that CA was consistent in $\aleph_1$-valued Łukasiewicz logic. Although this is an active area of research, with several interesting results, the question in its full generality remains open.[9]

Scott (1973) presented an interesting interpretation of finite-valued logical matrices. Aware of the deficiency of all known interpretations of non-classical logical values, he proposed replacing more values by more valuations. In each case, a definite number of bivalent valuations generates a partition of the set of propositions into types corresponding to the original logical values – Scott refers to them as *indexes*. Formally, valuations are arbitrary functions from the set of formulas to the two classical values of the truth and falsity, $v_i: For \rightarrow \{T, F\}$. An n-element set of valuations can thus induce maximally 2^n types. The actual number of types depends on limiting conditions imposed on valuations. An accurate choice of these conditions leads to a relatively simple characterization of the connectives of the logic under consideration. Applying this method, Scott obtains a description of the n-valued Łukasiewicz negation and implication connectives through an $(n-1)$-element set of valuations $\{v_0, v_1, \ldots, v_{n-2}\}$. He suggest that equalities of the form '$v_i(\alpha) = T$' should be read as '(the statement) α is true to within the degree i.' Thus, the numbers $0, 1, \ldots, n-2$ stand for *degrees of error in deviation from the truth*. Degree 0 is the strongest and corresponds to 'perfect' truth or no error: All Łukasiewicz tautologies are schemes of the statements having 0 as their degree of error. Łukasiewicz implication may also be conveniently explained in these terms: The measure of error of the whole implication expresses the amount of *shift* of error between the degree of hypothesis and that of the conclusion.

Urquhart (1973) independently suggested an interpretation motivated by the logic of tenses that is formally equivalent to the Scott's interpretation. Let $\vdash$ be a relation between natural numbers of the set $S_n = \{0, 1, \ldots, n-2\}$ and formulas, with '$x \vdash \alpha$' to be read 'α is true at x'. Urquhart assumes that

If $x \vdash \alpha$ and $x \leq y \in S_n$, then $y \vdash \alpha$

and then adapts ⊢ to particular logics, specifying *n*, the language, and recursive conditions that establish the meaning of connectives. Accordingly, each case results in a Kripke-style semantics having a finite number of 'reference points' S_n. The meaning of elements of S_n depends on the properties of the logic under consideration. For Łukasiewicz and Post logics, Urquhart suggest a temporal interpretation: 0 is the present moment and all other points of reference are future moments. The interpretation of Post logic is entirely compatible with the original interpretation envisaged by Post himself. The temporal way of understanding Łukasiewicz negation and implication exhibits the sources of difficulties in obtaining plausibly intuitive interpretation of many-valued Łukasiewicz logic. Urquhart eventually indicates clauses which 'natural' connectives of negation and implication should satisfy.

14.10. Applications

Many-valued logic has always been motivated by anticipated applications. To what extent these expectations have been fulfilled is difficult to say, but this section briefly mentions some of the proposed concrete applications, especially for philosophical logic and such practical areas as switching theory and computer science. Unfortuntely, there is not room enough here to describe them in detail.

Many-valued matrices have been applied to the formalization of intensional functions, to the approximation of syntactically based non-classical logics, and to testing the independence of the axioms of logical systems. As seen in section 14.1, Łukasiewicz himself sought to formalize possibility and necessity within three-valued logic. Later, he proposed a four-valued system of modal logic (Łukasiewicz, 1953). Although, from the philosophical point of view, such finite-valued interpretations of modalities have no particular value, since, as Dugundji (1940) proved, for no reasonable non-trivial modal logic is there an adequate finite matrix such that the logic coincides with the content of the matrix, nevertheless, their counterparts in Post algebras have proved crucial for the computer science applications.

The matrix approach has, to some extent, been important for intuitionistic logic [see chapter 11]. Although its creators were not guided by the idea of introducing supplementary logical values and rendering that idea axiomatically, it turns out that intuitionistic logic can be characterized exclusively by means of an infinite class of infinite-valued matrices (Jaśkowski, (1975 [1936]). At an early stage, Heyting approximated the laws of intuitionism *INT* by the content of a three-valued matrix, now called the *Heyting matrix*. This approximation was refined by Gödel (1932), who showed that *INT* cannot be described by a finite matrix, nor by a finite set of finite matrices. An essential part of Gödel's reasoning consists of the construction of a sequence of finite matrices approximating *INT*, which have their own interest, defining interesting implicative systems. Keeping the original definitions of Gödel's connectives, one may define an infinite-valued logic. Dummett (1959) showed that this was axiomatizable by extending *INT* with the axiom $(p \rightarrow q) \vee (q \rightarrow p)$. This version of intuitionism and its relation to the original have been of special importance in the development of intuitionistic logic and its other formlizations.

Łoś (1948) applied many-valuedness in the formalization of epistemic functions, such as 'John believes that p' or, more accurately, 'John asserts that p.' Such propositions are instances of the schema 'x asserts that p,' whose formal counterpart is a function Lxp with two different arguments: nominal and propositional. Consider a case with two persons and a set of propositions which they either accept or deny. There are then four possible evaluations in terms of pairs of classical logical values, i.e., truth and falsity, that divide the propositions into four kinds, those that both deny, that one accepts and the other denies, that the first denies and the second accepts, and those that both accept. These four types of proposition will correspond to four non-classical values. The connectives of negation and implication defined 'naturally' with respect to their classical counterparts for each person, will behave classically. Accordingly, the content of the negation-implication fragment of the characteristic four-valued matrix coincides with the set of classical ($\neg$, $\rightarrow$)-tautologies. On the base of this four-valued version of CPC, the belief operators are formalized. This may be extended to the case with any number of persons, which results in other formal many-valued interpretations of the classical logic with additional operators. Łoś's construction thus shows how it is possible to obtain a many-valued interpretation of some special intensional functions while simultaneously adhering to the intuition of bivalence. Since, however, the many-valuedness thus obtained depends on a certain relation between two categorially different arguments, a person and a proposition, it has to be considered an atypical semantics.

A very natural application of many-valuedness is for the analysis of vagueness and inexactness and their associated paradoxes, like the Sorites Paradox (Körner, 1966; Williamson, 1994). This application gave rise to fuzzy set theory (Zadeh, 1965), and ultimately to the theory of fuzzy logics (Zadeh, 1975), which has become an autonomous research discipline, with use in artificial intelligence (AI), computer science and steering theory (Turner, 1984, and Gottwald, 1981).

Just as classical logic and Boolean algebras have been successfully used in switching theory and computer science for the analysis, synthesis and minimalization of multiplex networks, so there has been interest in the possibility of applying many-valued logics for similar purposes. These have resulted in several techniques for the analysis and synthesis of electronic circuits and relays based mainly on Moisil and Post algebras (Rine, 1977). The *practical* switchover of two oppositely oriented contacts positioned in parallel branches of a circuit that must change their positions simultaneously, is the simplest possible electronic circuit to consider within a three-valued framework. Since there are good reasons to drop the idealistic assumption that effecting the circuit, e.g., using relays, would really change the positions of both contacts instantly, i.e. that the circuit would pass from the state 1 to the state 0, then, obviously, there is a third state that might also obtain. A generalization of this construction for any number of contacts similarly results in n states. Finally, obtaining a description of networks composed of such switchovers is possible within an appropriate algebraic base. For this, many-valued algebras with 'modal' functions – Moisil algebras, i.e., Łukasiewicz n-valued algebras, and Post algebras – appear useful. The most important advantage of the many-valued approach is the possibility of eliminating possible switching disturbances through the algebraic synthesis of the networks. (Moisil, 1966, 1972)

Logical many-valuedness has also been used successfully in computer science, in both hardware and software. Full-scale ternary computers were even completed twice: in the USSR (*SETUN*, 1958) and in the USA (*TERNAC*, 1973). These attempts, however, showed technical difficulties that were too big compared to the gain. So, efforts aimed at full hardware realization of many-valued computers have been reduced and attention directed instead towards the synthesis and construction of digital devices, e.g. memories, using many-valued algebras, especially Post algebras (Epstein et al., 1974; Rasiowa, 1977.)

Suggested further reading

For a more complete discussion of the topics discussed here, see Malinowski (1993). As further readings, the following items are also recommended: Bolc and Borowik (1992), Haack (1996), Łukasiewicz (1970c), Rine (1977), Rosser and Turquette (1952), Turner (1984) and Urquhart (1986).

Notes

1 The truth-tables of binary connectives * are viewed as follows: the value of α is placed in the first vertical line, under the connective, the value of β in the first horizontal line, beside the connective, and the value of $\alpha * \beta$ at the intersection of the two lines.
2 Recall that this set of connectives is sufficient to define all other classical connectives and thus warrants functional completeness of the underlying algebra and logic.
3 The coincidence with Bochvar is striking. However, Halldén's work is independent and original; compare, e.g., Williamson (1994).
4 $Var(\alpha)$ and $Var(X)$ are the sets of variables appearing in the formula α and in the formulas of X, respectively.
5 Similar n-element models (any $n \geq 2$) of the classical logic may be provided using matrices having standard connectives described in section 14.8.
6 The 0-ary operations are constants, i.e., elements of E_n.
7 Łukasiewicz (1970c, p. 144); no publication on the topic by Wajsberg exists.
8 Note that Urquhart's table gives the Kleene strong implication.
9 See Malinowski (1993, pp. 81–3) for a more detailed account.

References

Åqvist, L. 1962: "Reflections on the Logic of Nonsense," *Theoria*, 28, 138–58.
Bochvar, D. A. 1938: "Ob odnom tréhznacnom iscislénii i égo priménénii k analizu paradosov klassičéskogo rasširennogo funkcjonal'nogo isčislénia," ("On a Three-Valued Calculus and its Application to Analysis of Paradoxes of Classical Extended Functional Calculus"), *Matématicéskij Sbornik*, 4, 287–308.
Bolc, L. and Borowik, P. 1992: *Many-Valued Logics. 1. Theoretical Foundations*, (Springer-Verlag, Berlin and Heldelberg).
Chang, C. C. 1958: "Proof of an Axiom of Łukasiewicz," *Transactions of the American Mathematical Society*, 87, 55–6.

Chang, C. C. 1959: "A New Proof of the Completeness of the Łukasiewicz Axioms," *Transactions of the American Mathematical Society*, 93, 74–80.

Dugundji, J. 1940: "Note on a Property of Matrices for Lewis and Langford's Calculi of Propositions," *Journal of Symbolic Logic*, 5, 150–1.

Dummett, M. 1959: "A Propositional Matrix with Denumerable Matrix," *Journal of Symbolic Logic*, 24, 97–106.

Epstein, G., Frieder, G. and Rine, D. C. 1974: "The Development of Multiple-Valued Logic as Related to Computer Science," *Computer*, 7, 20–32.

Giles, R. 1974: "A Non-Classical Logic for Physics," *Studia Logica*, 33, 397–416.

Gödel, K. 1932: "Zum intuitionistischen Aussagenkalkül," in *Akademie der Wissenschaften in Wien*, (Mathematisch-naturwissenschaftliche Klasse), LXIX, 65–6.

Gonseth, F. (ed.) 1941: *Les Entretiens de Zurich sur les Fondements et la Méthode des Sciences Mathématiques 6–9 Décembre 1938*, (S. A. Leemon frères & Cie, Zurich).

Gottwald, S. 1981: "Fuzzy-Mengen und ihre Anwendungen. Ein Überblick," *Elektronische Informationsverarbeitung und Kybernetik*, 17, 207–33.

Grigolia, R. 1977: "Algebraic Analysis of Łukasiewicz–Tarski's *n*-Valued Logical Systems," in *Selected Papers on Łukasiewicz Sentential Calculi*, R. Wójcicki and G. Malinowski, eds., (Ossolineum, Wroclaw), 81–92.

Haack, S. 1978: *Philosophy of Logics*, (Cambridge University Press, Cambridge).

Haack, S. 1996: *Deviant Logic. Fuzzy Logic. Beyond the Formalism*, (University of Chicago Press, Chicago and London).

Halldén, S. 1949: *The Logic of Nonsense*, (Uppsala Universitets Arsskrift, Uppsala).

Jaśkowski, S. 1975: "Recherches sur le Systéme de la Logique Intuitioniste," *Actes du Congrés International de Philosophie Scientifique VI*, 393, (Herman, Paris), 1936, 58–61; translated in *Studia Logica*, 34, 117–30.

Kleene, S. C. 1938: "On a Notation for Ordinal Numbers," *Journal of Symbolic Logic*, 3, 150–5.

Kleene, S. C. 1952: *Introduction to Metamathematics*, (North-Holland, Amsterdam).

Körner, S. 1966: *Experience and Theory*, (Routledge and Kegan Paul, London).

Łoś, J. 1948: "Logiki wielowartościowe a formalizacja funkcji intensjonalnych," ("Many-Valued Logics and the Formalization of Intensional Functions"), *Kwartalnik Filozoficzny*, 17, 59–78.

Łukasiewicz, J. 1953: "A System of Modal Logic," *Journal of Computing Systems*, 1, 111–49.

Łukasiewicz, J. 1967: "Philosophische Bemerkungen zu Mehrwertigen Systemen des Aussagenkalküls," *Comptes Rendus des Séances de la Société des Sciences et des Lettres de Varsovie Cl. III*, 23 (1930), 51–77; English tr. "Philosophical Remarks on Many-Valued Systems of Propositional Logic," in *Polish Logic 1920–1939*, S. McCall, ed., (Clarendon Press, Oxford), 40–65.

Łukasiewicz, J. 1970a: *Die logischen Grundlagen der Wahrscheinlichkeitsrechnung*, (Kraków), 1913; English tr. "Logical Foundations of Probability Theory," in, Łukasiewicz (1970c, 16–63).

Łukasiewicz, J. 1970b: "O Logice Trójwartościowej," *Ruch Filozoficzny*, 5 (1920), 170–1; English tr. "On Three-Valued Logic," in Łukasiewicz (1970c, 87–8).

Łukasiewicz, J. 1970c: *Selected Works*, L. Borkowski, ed., (North-Holland, Amsterdam).

Łukasiewicz, J. and Tarski, A. 1930: "Untersuchungen über den Aussagenkalkül," *Comptes Rendus des Séances de la Société des Sciences et des Lettres de Varsovie Cl. III*, 23, 30–50.

McNaughton, R. 1951: "A Theorem about Infinite-Valued Sentential Logic," *Journal of Symbolic Logic*, 16, 1–13.

Malinowski, G. 1993: *Many-Valued Logics*, (Clarendon Press, Oxford).

Meredith, C. A. 1958: "The Dependence of an Axiom of Łukasiewicz," *Transactions of the American Mathematical Society*, 87, 54.

Moh Shaw-Kwei 1954: "Logical Paradoxes for Many-Valued Systems," *Journal of Symbolic Logic*, 19, 37–40.

Moisil, G. 1966: *Zastosowanie Algebr Łukasiewicza do teorii Układów Przekaźnikowostykowych* (*Application of Łukasiewicz Algebras to the Study of Relay-Contact Networks*), (Ossolineum, Wrocław), (vol. II, 1967 edn.).

Moisil, G. 1972: *Essais sur les Logiques Non-Chrisipiennes*, (Editions de l'Académie de la Republique Socialiste de Roumanie, Bucharest).

Pawlak, Z. 1991: *Rough Sets: Theoretical Aspect of Reasoning about Data*, (Kluwer, Dordrecht).

Post, E. L. 1920: "Introduction to a General Theory of Elementary Propositions," *Bulletin of the American Mathematical Society*, 26, 437.

Post, E. L. 1921: "Introduction to a General Theory of Elementary Propositions," *American Journal of Mathematics*, 43, 163–85.

Rasiowa, H. 1974: *An Algebraic Approach to Non-Classical Logics*, (North-Holland, Amsterdam; PWN, Warsaw).

Rasiowa, H. 1977: "Many-Valued Algorithmic Logic as a Tool to Investigate Programs," in *Modern Uses of Multiple-Valued Logic*, J. M. Dunn and G. Epstein, eds., (D. Reidel, Dordrecht), 79–102.

Rasiowa, H. 1991: *On Approximation Logics: A Survey*, (Institute of Mathematics, University of Warsaw).

Reichenbach, H. 1944: *Philosophical Foundations of Quantum Mechanics*, (University of California Press, Berkeley and Los Angeles, CA).

Reichenbach, H. 1949: *Wahrscheinlichkeitslehre*, (A. W. Sijthoff, Leiden), 1935; English tr. *The Theory of Probability*, (University of California Press, Berkeley, CA).

Rine, D. C. (ed.) 1977: *Computer Science and Multiple-Valued Logic. Theory and Applications*, (North-Holland, Amsterdam).

Rose A. and Rosser, J. B. 1958: "Fragments of Many-Valued Statement Calculi," *Transactions of the American Mathematical Society*, 87, 1–53.

Rosser, J. B. and Turquette, A. R. 1952: *Many-Valued Logics*, (North-Holland, Amsterdam).

Scott, D. S. 1973: "Background to Formalisation," in *Truth, Syntax and Modality*, H. Leblanc, ed., (Amsterdam, North-Holland), 244–73.

Segerberg, K. 1965: "A Contribution to Nonsense Logic," *Theoria*, 31, 199–217.

Skolem, T. 1957: "Bemerkungen zum Komprehensionsaxiom," *Zeitschrift für Mathematische Logik und Grundlagen der Mathematik*, 3, 1–17.

Słupecki, J. 1939a: "Kryterium Pełności Wielowartościowych Systemów Logiki Zdań," ("A Criterion of Completeness of Many-Valued Systems of Propositional Logic"), *Comptes Rendus des Séances de la Société des Sciences et des Lettres de Varsovie Cl. III*, 32, 102–9.

Słupecki, J. 1939b: "Dowód Aksjomatyzowalności Pełnych Systemów Wielowartościowych Rachunku Zdań," ("Proof of the Axiomatizability of Full Many-Valued Systems of Propositional Calculus"), *Comptes Rendus des Séances de la Société des Sciences et des Lettres de Varsovie Cl. III*, 32, 110–28.

Słupecki, J. 1967: "Der Volle Dreiwertige Aussagenkalkül," *Comptes Rendus des Séances de la Société des Sciences et des Lettres de Varsovie Cl. III*, 29 (1936), 9–11; English tr. "The Full Three-Valued Propositional Calculus," in *Polish Logic 1920–1939*, S. McCall, ed., (Clarendon Press, Oxford), 335–7.

Tokarz, M. 1974: "A Method of Axiomatization of Łukasiewicz Logics," *Bulletin of the Section of Logic*, 3, 21–4.

Turner, R. 1984: *Logics for Artificial Intelligence*, (Ellis Horwood, Chichester).

Urquhart, A. 1973: "An Interpretation of Many-Valued Logic," *Zeitschrift für Mathematische Logik und Grundlagen der Mathematik*, 19, 111–4.

Urquhart, A. 1986: "Many-Valued Logic," in *Handbook of Philosophical Logic*, vol. III, D. Gabbay and F. Guenthner, eds., (D. Reidel, Dordrecht), 71–116.

Wajsberg, M. 1967: "Aksjomatyzacja Trójwartosciowego Rachunku Zdan," *Comptes Rendus de la Société des Sciences et des Lettres de Varsovie Cl. III*, 24 (1931), 126–48; English tr. "Axiomatization of the Three-Valued Propositional Calculus," in *Polish Logic 1920–1939*, S. McCall, ed., (Clarendon Press, Oxford), 264–84.

Whitehead, A. N. and Russell, B. 1910: *Principia Mathematica*, vol. I., (Cambridge University Press, Cambridge).

Williamson, T. 1994: *Vagueness*, (Routledge, London and New York).

Wójcicki, R. 1988: *Theory of Logical Calculi. Basic Theory of Consequence Operations*, (Kluwer Academic Publishers, Dordrecht).

Zadeh, L. A. 1965: "Fuzzy Sets," *Information and Control*, 8, 338–53.

Zadeh, L. A. 1975: "Fuzzy Logic and Approximate Reasoning," *Synthese*, 30, 407–28.

Zawirski, Z. 1934: "Stosunek Logiki Wielowartościowej do Rachunku Prawdopodobieństwa," ("Relation of Many-Valued Logic to the Calculus of Probability), *Prace Komisji Filozoficznej Polskiego Towarzystwa Przyjaciół Nauk*, 4, 155–240.

Chapter 15

Nonmonotonic Logic

John F. Horty

15.1. Introduction

The goal of a logic is to define a consequence relation between a set of formulas Γ and, in most cases, an individual formula A. This definition generally takes one of two forms. From a proof theoretic standpoint, A is said to be a consequence of Γ whenever there is a deduction of A from the set Γ, viewed as a set of premises; from a model theoretic standpoint, A is said to be a consequence of Γ whenever A holds in every model that satisfies each formula in Γ.

Although the detailed inferences sanctioned by particular logics vary widely depending on the connectives present and the properties attributed to them, certain abstract features of the consequence relation are remarkably stable across logics. Among these is the property of *monotonicity*: if A is a consequence of Γ, then A is a consequence of $\Gamma \cup \{B\}$. What this means is that any conclusion drawn from a set of premises will be preserved as a conclusion even if the premise set is supplemented with additional information – that the set of conclusions grows monotonically as the premise set grows.

The monotonicity property flows from assumptions that are deeply rooted in both the proof theory and the semantics, not only of classical logic, but of most philosophical logics as well. From the proof theoretic standpoint, monotonicity follows from the fact that any derivation of the formula A from the premise set Γ also counts as a derivation of that formula from the expanded premises set $\Gamma \cup \{B\}$; the addition of further premises cannot perturb a derivation, since standard inference rules depend only on the presence of information, not its absence. The verification of monotonicity is, if anything, even more immediate from the model theoretic standpoint: since every model of $\Gamma \cup \{B\}$ is a model of Γ, it follows at once, if the formula A holds in every model of Γ, that it must hold also in every model of $\Gamma \cup \{B\}$.

A *nonmonotonic logic* is simply one whose consequence relation fails to satisfy the monotonicity property – where the addition of further premises can lead to the retraction of a conclusion already drawn, so that the conclusion set need not increase monotonically with the premise set. Although certain philosophical logics, such as relevance logic [see chapter 13], could be classified as nonmonotonic in this sense, the phrase is generally reserved for a family of logics originating in the field of artificial intelligence (AI), and aimed at formalizing the patterns of *default reasoning* that seem to guide much of our intelligent behavior.

Without attempting anything like a formal definition, one can think of default reasoning, very roughly, as reasoning that relies on the absence of information as well as its presence, often mediated by rules of the general form: given *P*, conclude *Q* unless there is information to the contrary. It is easy to see why a logical account of this kind of reasoning requires a nonmonotonic consequence relation. Suppose, for example, that the generic truth 'Birds fly' is taken to express such a default: given that *x* is a bird, conclude that *x* flies unless there is information to the contrary. And suppose one is told that Tweety is a bird. Taken alone, these two premises – that birds fly, and that Tweety is a bird – would then support the conclusion that Tweety flies, since the premise set contains no information to the contrary. But now, imagine that this premise set is supplemented with the additional information that Tweety does not fly (perhaps Tweety is a penguin, or a baby bird). In that case, the original conclusion that Tweety flies would have to be withdrawn, since the default leading to this conclusion relied on the absence of information to the contrary, but the new premise set now contains such information.

The field of nonmonotonic logic began in the late 1970s as an attempt to represent this kind of reasoning within a general logical framework. Since then, the area has been the focus of intense activity, giving rise to hundreds of conference and journal papers, most of which, however, are still confined to the AI literature. At this point, it would be impossible to provide a balanced survey of the field in anything less than a full-length monograph. The present chapter is intended, instead, only as an introductory presentation of two of the main lines of approach – a fixed-point theory and a model-preference theory – in a way that is accessible to a philosophical audience, with an emphasis on conceptual rather than implementational issues.

15.2. Some Motivating Problems

Here are some of the problems that led to development of nonmonotonic logics, namely, the *frame problem*, first noticed by McCarthy and Hayes (1969), what is known as the *qualification problem*, and the problems of *closed-world reasoning* and *defeasible inheritance reasoning*.

15.2.1. The frame problem

One of the most important reasoning tasks studied within AI is that of planning – the problem of finding, in the simplest case, a sequence of actions to achieve a specified goal from a specified initial state. Within a logical framework, the planning problem is often studied from the standpoint of the situation calculus, a first-order formalism containing expressions of the form $H[\phi, s]$ to represent the fact that the proposition ϕ holds in the situation s, and allowing also for a description of the effects of various actions.

To illustrate the use of this formalism, imagine that four blocks – A, B, C, and D – are arranged on a table, with blocks A, C, and D set on the table's surface, block B stacked on top of block A, and none of the others having anything on top of them. If this situation is referred to as $s1$, some of the relevant facts from the situation might be depicted through the formulas

$$H[On(B, A), s1]$$

$$H[Clear(B), s1]$$

$$H[Clear(C), s1] \tag{15.1}$$

$$H[Clear(D), s1]$$

which state that the proposition that block B is on block A holds in the situation $s1$, as do the propositions that the blocks B, C, and D are clear. Note that expressions like $On(B, A)$ and $Clear(B)$ are treated grammatically as complex terms referring to propositions or facts, not as sentences.

Suppose then that these blocks must be manipulated using a robot arm that can perform only two primitive actions: stacking one block on another and unstacking one block from another (and placing it on the table). Let $Stack(X, Y)$ and $Unstack(X, Y)$ represent the actions of stacking X on Y and unstacking X from Y, the effects of these actions can be captured through the axioms

$$(H[Clear(X), s] \wedge H[Clear(Y), s] \wedge X \neq Y) \supset H[On(X, Y), Res(\langle Stack(X, Y) \rangle, s)]$$

$$(H[On(X, Y), s] \wedge H[Clear(X), s]) \supset H[Clear(Y), Res(\langle Unstack(X, Y) \rangle, s)]$$
$$\tag{15.2}$$

in which it is assumed that all variables are universally quantified. Where α is a sequence of actions, the expression $Res(\alpha, s)$ denotes the situation that results when the actions in α are executed in turn, beginning with situation s. What the first of these two axioms says, then, is that, as long as the distinct blocks X and Y are both clear in the situation s, the situation that results from s when X is stacked on Y is one in which X is on Y; the second axiom says that, if X is on Y and X is clear in s, then Y is clear in the situation that results from s by unstacking X from Y.

Of course, these two axioms define the effects only of action sequences containing a single action, the base case. The effects of longer sequences can be defined inductively by stipulating that

$$Res(\langle A_1, \ldots, A_n \rangle, s) = Res(\langle A_n \rangle, Res(\langle A_1, \ldots, A_{n-1} \rangle, s)) \tag{15.3}$$

when n is greater than one; the result of executing a sequence of n actions in a situation s is equivalent to the result of executing the last of these actions in the situation that results from executing all but the last.

Now suppose that Γ is a set of sentences containing a description of some initial situation s, as well as axioms specifying the effects of the available actions and perhaps some bookkeeping material, such as the inductive definition of the Res function; and let ϕ represent the proposition desired as a goal. Then the planning problem is the problem of finding an action sequence α whose execution in the initial state s can be proved from the information in Γ to yield a state in which the goal proposition ϕ holds – more formally, a sequence α for which it can be shown that

$$\Gamma \vdash H[\phi,\ Res(\alpha,\ s)]$$

where $\vdash$ is the classical consequence relation.

As a concrete example, imagine that $s1$ above is the initial state, and that Γ contains the statements (15.1)–(15.3): the four sentences describing the initial state, the axioms describing the $Stack$ and $Unstack$ actions, and the inductive specification of the Res function. Now suppose the goal is to achieve a situation in which block A is stacked on top of block C – that is, a situation in which the statement $On(A, C)$ holds. In this simple case, it is easy to find an appropriate plan: first unstack B from A, then stack A on C. More formally, the appropriate plan appears to be $\langle Unstack(B, A),\ Stack(A, C) \rangle$, and it seems intuitively – just thinking about how this sequence of actions should work – that it should be possible to verify the correctness of this plan by establishing that

$$\Gamma \vdash H[On(A, C),\ Res(\langle Unstack(B, A),\ Stack(A, C) \rangle,\ s1)]$$

showing that the plan achieves its goal.

In fact, however, this result cannot be established, and it is important to see why. Because Γ contains the statements $On(B, A)$ and $Clear(B)$, one can indeed conclude from the $Unstack$ axiom that

$$H[Clear(A),\ Res(\langle Unstack(B, A) \rangle,\ s1)]$$

which states that the block A is clear in the situation that results from $s1$ when B is unstacked from A. And because Γ contains $H[Clear(C),\ s1]$, one knows that the block C was already clear in the initial state. Since A is now clear as well, it is reasonable to think that a goal state could now be achieved simply by stacking block A onto block C – that is, that the $Stack$ axiom could be used to derive

$$H[On(A, C),\ Res(\langle Stack(A, C) \rangle,\ Res(\langle Unstack(B, A) \rangle,\ s1))]$$

from which the desired conclusion would then follow by the definition of the Res function. Unfortunately, this application of the $Stack$ axiom would require one to know, not just that C is clear in the original state, but that C remains clear also in the state that results from the $Unstack(B, A)$ action – that is, one would need to be able to establish

$$H[Clear(C),\ Res(\langle Unstack(B, A) \rangle,\ s1)] \tag{15.4}$$

as an intermediate step.

Of course, this intermediate step seems perfectly natural from the standpoint of one's ordinary reasoning about actions: since *C* is clear in the initial state, it is natural to suppose that it would remain clear even after *B* is unstacked from *A*. In fact, however, nothing in Γ allows this intermediate step to be derived – and indeed, the step should not be derivable as a matter of logic, for it is always possible, at least, that the removal of *B* from *A* does interfere with the fact that *C* is clear. (Perhaps blocks *B* and *D* are connected by a wire in such a way that removing *B* from *A* causes *D* to be pulled to the top of *C*; this possibility is consistent with the information in Γ.) What one has here is the notorious *frame problem*, originally noticed by McCarthy and Hayes (1969). When an action is performed, some facts change and some do not. How can one tell which are which, and in particular, how does one propagate those facts that do not change from the original to the resulting situation in a natural way?

15.2.2. The qualification problem

Look again at the axiom governing the *Stack* action. Notice that it does not state that *X* will be on *Y* in any situation that results from a *Stack(X, Y)* action, but only that *X* will be on *Y* as long as *X* and *Y* are distinct blocks that are both clear in the original situation. These qualifications are necessary, of course, because the robot arm cannot reach blocks that are not clear, and because it is impossible to stack a block on top of itself.

But once these qualifications are in place, is the *Stack* axiom then correct? Well, no. What if the block *X* is so slippery that the robot arm cannot pick it up? What if *X* is so heavy that it will crush the block *Y*? What if *Y* is a bomb that will explode if another block is placed on top of it? The difficulty suggested by these peculiar considerations is known as the *qualification problem*: how does one arrive at an accurate, suitably qualified formulation of the axioms governing actions?

One might respond to this problem by deciding simply to fold all the various possible qualifications into the antecedent of the axioms, either explicitly or implicitly. In the present case, for example, one might introduce a new propositional constant *Weird* to represent the occurrence of a weird circumstance that would interfere with the *Stack* action, and then modify the axiom governing this action with the further precondition that no such weird circumstances occur:

$$(H[Clear(X), s] \land H[Clear(Y), s] \land X \neq Y \land \neg Weird)$$
$$\supset H[On(X, Y), Res(\langle Stack(X, Y)\rangle, s)] \tag{15.5}$$

The interfering circumstances imagined in the previous paragraph could then be classified, quite naturally, as weird:

Slippery(X) ⊃ *Weird*

Heavy(X) ⊃ *Weird* (15.6)

Bomb(Y) ⊃ *Weird*

There are, however, two problems with this suggestion. The first – to which I know of no solution – is that the list of circumstances that might interfere with a stacking action is open-ended. No conceivable list of possible interfering circumstances could be complete. What if a meteor hits the laboratory and destroys the robot? Then the stack action would not be successful. What if there is an evil demon in the room that does not want to see X on Y and will knock X out of the hand of the robot arm as it approaches Y?

The second problem is more subtle, and would arise even if there was a relatively exhaustive list of qualifications. The point of placing preconditions in the antecedent of an action axiom is that one must verify that the preconditions are satisfied before concluding that the action is successful. And it does seem reasonable, in the case of the *Stack* axiom, that one should have to verify that the blocks X and Y must both be clear before one can know that the result of stacking X on Y is successful. But it seems less reasonable to suppose that one must actually have to verify that all of the various weird circumstances that might interfere with this action do not occur – that there is no bomb, no meteor, no evil demon, and so on. It would be better to be able simply to assume that weird circumstances like these do not occur unless there is information to the contrary.

15.2.3.   *Closed-world reasoning*

Suppose I ask my travel agent if United Airlines has a direct flight from Washington to Barcelona. The travel agent has access to a database containing flight information. From a logical standpoint, one can think of this database as a set of sentences of the form

Connects(UA354, Baltimore, Boston)

Connects(UA750, Washington, London)   (15.7)

Connects(UA867, London, Barcelona)

and so on; the travel agent answers my question by drawing inferences from these sentences. Suppose I am told: No, there is no direct flight from Washington to Barcelona. How can the travel agent reach this conclusion? The airline database only says what cities are connected by what flights; it does not list the cities that are not connected, and certainly this kind of negative information does not follow as an ordinary logical consequence from the positive information provided.

The answer is that the travel agent's reasoning is governed by a convention known as the *closed-world assumption* (Reiter, 1978), which states, in the simplest case, that all relevant positive information is explicitly listed. Because of this convention, it is legitimate to conclude that a positive proposition is false whenever it is not explicitly present in the database; the travel agent can legitimately conclude, for example, that there is no direct flight between Washington and Barcelona simply because no such flight is listed.

The closed-world assumption applies, of course, not only to the airline database, but to any number of situations in which positive information is overwhelmed by negative information. When I look at a list of people invited to a party, I can conclude, if I am not on the list, that I am not invited to the party; when I look at my desk calendar, I can conclude, if there is no doctor's appointment listed for Thursday at 3:00, that I have no doctor's appointment at that time. Reasoning based on the closed-world assumption exemplifies the general pattern of default reasoning as relying on the absence of information: lacking information to the contrary, one can assume that there is no direct flight between two cities; an entry in the database provides information to the contrary.

15.2.4. Defeasible inheritance reasoning

Returning to the initial example: birds fly, Tweety is a bird, therefore Tweety flies. Reasoning like this is known in AI as inheritance reasoning, and was originally developed in response to the need for an efficient way of representing and accessing taxonomic information. Rather than having to list explicitly the properties of each individual, it is imagined that classes and properties are arranged in a taxonomic hierarchy, and that individuals inherit their properties from the classes to which they belong. It is not necessary to state explicitly that Tweety flies, since this property is inherited from the general class of birds.

This kind of taxonomic reasoning has been familiar since Aristotle, and was explored in some detail by medieval philosophers; what is new in AI is the idea that – again, for reasons of efficiency – the taxonomy is often allowed to represent defeasible as well as strict information. An example of such a defeasible inheritance network is provided in Figure 15.1, known as the Tweety Triangle. Here, strict links are represented by the strong arrow ⇒ and defeasible links by the weak arrow →, so that the displayed network provides the following information: Tweety is a penguin; penguins are birds; as a rule, birds tend to fly, and penguins tend not to.

When these defeasible inheritance networks were first introduced, they were supplied only with a 'procedural' semantics, according to which the meaning of the representations was supposed to be specified implicitly by the inference algorithms operating on them. It was soon realized, however, that these algorithms could lead

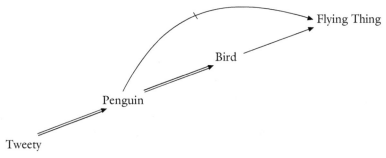

Figure 15.1 The Tweety Triangle

to bizarre and unintuitive results in complicated cases, and researchers felt the need to provide an implementation independent account of the meaning of these network formalisms. One natural idea involved providing a logical interpretation of the networks – interpreting the individual links in the network as logical formulas, and so the entire network as a collection of formulas, whose meaning could then be specified by the appropriate logic. The logical interpretation of strict links, of course, presents no problems: a link like *Tweety* $\Rightarrow$ *Penguin*, for example, could naturally be represented as an atomic statement, such as *Pt*, and a link like *Penguin* $\Rightarrow$ *Bird* as a universal statement of the form $\forall x (Px \supset Bx)$. But there is nothing in ordinary logic to represent the defeasible links *Bird* $\rightarrow$ *Fly* and *Penguin* $\nrightarrow$ *Fly*, carrying the intuitive meaning birds fly and that penguins do not.

15.3. A Fixed-Point Approach: Default Logic

Perhaps the best known and most widely applied formalism for nonmonotonic reasoning is *default logic*, introduced by Reiter (1980). This formalism results from supplementing ordinary logic with new rules of inference, known as *default rules*, and then modifying the standard notion of logical consequence to accommodate these new rules.

15.3.1. Basic ideas

An ordinary rule of inference (with a single premise) can be depicted simply as a premise/conclusion pair, such as (A/B); this rule commits the reasoner to B once A has been established. By contrast, a default rule is a triple, of the form $(A : C/B)$. Very roughly, such a rule commits the reasoner to B once A has been established and, in addition, C is consistent with the reasoner's conclusion set. The formula A is referred to as the *prerequisite* of this default rule, B as its *consequent*, and C as its *justification*.[1] A *default theory* is a pair $\Delta = \langle W, \mathcal{D} \rangle$, in which W is a set of ordinary formulas and $\mathcal{D}$ is a set of default rules.

Before characterizing the new notion of logical consequence defined by Reiter, consider how default logic might be used to represent the initial example, in which one is told that Tweety is a bird and that birds fly. The generic statement that birds fly can reasonably be taken to mean something like: once one learns of an object x that it is a bird, one should conclude that x flies unless there is information to the contrary – unless, that is, this conclusion is inconsistent with one's beliefs. What this suggests is that the generic statement should be represented as a sort of universally quantified default rule, perhaps of the form $\forall x (Bx : Fx/Fx)$, but unfortunately it is no more meaningful to quantify a default rule than it is to quantify an ordinary rule of inference. To avoid this problem, Reiter allows open formulas to occur in defaults, so that the generalization concerning birds can be expressed as $(Bx : Fx/Fx)$. However, to avoid the resulting complexities – involving the application of these open defaults to yield closed formulas – the somewhat simpler approach of representing these defeasible generalizations, not by open defaults, but instead by appropriate instance of these defaults for each object in the domain is adopted here. In the present case, where Tweety is the only object of concern, the only default necessary is $(Bt : Ft/Ft)$, which says that if Tweety is a bird, one should conclude that Tweety flies as long as this is consistent with what is known. The information from this initial example can then be represented through the default theory $\Delta_1 = \langle W_1, \mathcal{D}_1 \rangle$, where $W_1 = \{Bt\}$ and $\mathcal{D}_1 = \{(Bt : Ft/Ft)\}$.

In this example, because one knows that Bt, and because Ft is consistent with one's knowledge, the default rule justifies drawing the conclusion Ft. The appropriate conclusion set based on Δ_1 therefore seems to be $Th(\{Bt, Ft\})$, the logical closure of what one is told to begin with, together with the conclusions of the applicable defaults. If one is told, in addition, that Tweety does not fly, one moves to the default theory $\Delta_2 = \langle W_2, \mathcal{D}_2 \rangle$, with $\mathcal{D}_2 = \mathcal{D}_1$ and $W_2 = W_1 \cup \{\neg Ft\}$. Here the default rule $(Bt : Ft/Ft)$ can no longer be applied, because its justification is now inconsistent with one's knowledge and so the appropriate conclusion set based on Δ_2 is simply $Th(W_2)$.

15.3.2.   Extensions

The discussion of this example illustrates the kind of conclusion sets desired from particular default theories. The task of arriving at a general definition of this notion, however, is not trivial; the trick is to find a way of capturing the meaning of the new component – the justification – present in default rules.

In ordinary logic, the conclusion set associated with a set of formulas W is simply $Th(W)$, the logical closure of W. It might seem, then, that the conclusion set associated with a default theory $\Delta = \langle W, \mathcal{D} \rangle$ should be

$$\mathcal{E} = Th(W) \cup \{C : (A : B/C) \in \mathcal{D}, A \in Th(W), \neg B \notin Th(W)\}$$

the closure of W together with the consequents of those default rules whose prerequisites are entailed by and whose justifications are consistent with W. A moment's thought, however, shows that this suggestion is inadequate. For one thing, the set $\mathcal{E}$ defined in this way is not even closed under logical consequence: the addition of the consequent from some default rule into the set $\mathcal{E}$ may trigger new logical implications that should, intuitively, be included in the conclusion set, or worse still, the addition of the consequent from one default rule may trigger the firing of another. As an example, consider the default theory $\Delta_3 = \langle W_3, \mathcal{D}_3 \rangle$ in which $W_3 = \{A\}$ and $\mathcal{D}_3 = \{(A : B/C), (C : D/E)\}$. The above definition correctly adds the consequent C of the first default rule into the conclusion set $\mathcal{E}$. It seems, though, that the presence of C should then trigger the firing of the second rule, resulting also in the addition of E to the conclusion set, but this statement is not included.

What this example suggests is that the definition of the appropriate conclusion set for a default theory should be iterative. Perhaps one should take the conclusion set of the default theory $\Delta = \langle W, \mathcal{D} \rangle$ to be

$$\mathcal{E} = \overset{\infty}{\underset{i=0}{\cup}} \mathcal{E}_i$$

with

$$\mathcal{E}_0 = \mathcal{W}$$

$$\mathcal{E}_{i+1} = \mathit{Th}(\mathcal{E}_i) \cup \{C : (A : B/C) \in \mathcal{D}, A \in \mathit{Th}(\mathcal{E}_i), \neg B \notin \mathit{Th}(\mathcal{E}_i)\}$$

This suggestion responds to the previous concern, giving $\mathit{Th}(\{A, C, E\})$ as the conclusion set for the default theory Δ_3, as desired. Now, however, there is a new problem, illustrated by the theory $\Delta_4 = \langle \mathcal{W}_4, \mathcal{D}_4 \rangle$, with $\mathcal{W}_4 = \{A, B \supset \neg C\}$ and $\mathcal{D}_4 = \{(A : C/B)\}$. Tracing through the iteration, one can see that the rule $(A : C/B)$ is applicable at the first stage, since its prerequisite belongs to $\mathit{Th}(\mathcal{W}_4)$ and its justification is consistent with this set; hence one has B in $\mathcal{E}_1$. Just a bit of additional reasoning then shows that $\neg C$ must belong to $\mathcal{E}_2$, and so to $\mathcal{E}$, since this formula is a logical consequence of the information contained in $\mathcal{E}_1$. The rule $(A : C/B)$ seems initially to be applicable, since, prior to its application, there is no reason to conclude $\neg C$; but once the rule has been applied, the information it provides does allow us to derive $\neg C$. The rule thus seems to undermine its own applicability.

Of course, a chain of reasoning like this showing that some default rule is undermined can be arbitrarily long; and so one cannot really be sure that a default rule is applicable in some context until one has applied it, along with all the other rules that seem applicable, and then one has surveyed the logical closure of the result. Because of this, the conclusion set associated with a default theory cannot be defined in the usual iterative way, by successively adding to the original data the conclusions of the applicable rules of inference, and then taking the limit of this process.

Instead, Reiter is forced to adopt a fixed-point approach in specifying the appropriate conclusion sets of default theories – which are described as *extensions*. In fact, he actually offers two characterizations of the concept of an extension. The first considered here, although not the official definition, is both more intuitive and more useful in practice. The idea behind this particular characterization is that, given a default theory, one first conjectures a candidate extension for the theory, and then – using this candidate – defines a sequence of approximations to some conclusion set. If this approximating sequence has the original candidate as its limit, the candidate is then certified as an extension for the default theory.

Definition 15.1 The set $\mathcal{E}$ is an *extension* of the default theory $\Delta = \langle \mathcal{W}, \mathcal{D} \rangle$ iff (if and only if) there exists a sequence of sets $\mathcal{E}_0, \mathcal{E}_1, \mathcal{E}_2, \ldots$ such that

$$\mathcal{E} = \overset{\infty}{\underset{i=0}{\cup}} \mathcal{E}_i$$

$$\mathcal{E}_0 = \mathcal{W}$$

$$\mathcal{E}_{i+1} = \mathit{Th}(\mathcal{E}_i) \cup \{C : (A : B/C) \in \mathcal{D}, A \in \mathit{Th}(\mathcal{E}_i), \neg B \notin \mathcal{E}\}$$

Here, of course, the set $\mathcal{E}$ is the candidate, which is certified as a true extension of Δ if it turns out that $\mathcal{E}$ coincides with the union of the approximating sequence

$\mathcal{E}_0$, $\mathcal{E}_1$, $\mathcal{E}_2$. . . . . Note that $\mathcal{E}$ figures in the definition of $\mathcal{E}_{i+1}$: the approximating sequence is defined in terms of the original candidate.

The fixed-point nature of extensions is more apparent in Reiter's official definition, which relies on an operator Γ that uses the information from a particular default theory to map formula sets into formula sets.

Definition 15.2 Where $\Delta = \langle W, \mathcal{D} \rangle$ is a default theory and S is some set of formulas, $\Gamma_\Delta(S)$ is the minimal set satisfying three conditions:

1 $W \subseteq \Gamma_\Delta(S)$
2 $Th(\Gamma_\Delta(S)) = \Gamma_\Delta(S)$
3 For each $(A : B/C) \in \mathcal{D}$, if $A \in \Gamma_\Delta(S)$ and $\neg B \notin S$, then $C \in \Gamma_\Delta(S)$.

The first two conditions in this definition simply state that $\Gamma_\Delta(S)$ contains the information provided by the original theory, and that it is closed under logical consequence; the third condition states that it contains the conclusions of the default rules applicable in S; and the minimality constraint prevents unwarranted conclusions from creeping in. Where $\Delta = \langle W, \mathcal{D} \rangle$ is a default theory, the operator Γ_Δ maps any formula set S into the minimal superset of W that is closed under both ordinary logical consequence and the default rules from $\mathcal{D}$ that are applicable in S. The official definition of extensions – here presented as a theorem – then identifies the extensions of a default theory as the fixed points of this operator.

Theorem 15.1 The set $\mathcal{E}$ is an *extension* of the default theory Δ iff $\Gamma_\Delta(\mathcal{E}) = \mathcal{E}$.

As the reader can verify, the default theories Δ_1 and Δ_2 have, as desired, the respective sets $Th(\{Bt, Ft\})$ and $Th(\{Bt, \neg Ft\})$ as their extensions. It should be clear that the notion of an extension defined here is a conservative generalization of the corresponding notion of a conclusion set from ordinary logic: the extension of a default theory $\langle W, \mathcal{D} \rangle$, in which $\mathcal{D}$ is empty, is simply $Th(W)$. And it can be shown also that default rules themselves cannot introduce inconsistency: any extension of a default theory $\langle W, \mathcal{D} \rangle$ will be consistent as long as the ordinary component W of that theory is consistent.

15.3.3. Default consequence

In contrast to the situation in ordinary logic, however, not every default theory leads to a single extension, a single set of appropriate conclusions. Some default theories have no extensions; Δ_4 is an example. The easiest way to see that this theory has no extensions is to work with the Definition 1 of the notion, and then to suppose that Δ_4 did have an extension – say, $\mathcal{E}$. Evidently, one would then have either $\neg C \in \mathcal{E}$ or $\neg C \notin \mathcal{E}$. Suppose, first, that $\neg C \in \mathcal{E}$. Well, since $\neg C \notin \mathcal{E}_0$, and under the supposition that $\neg C \in \mathcal{E}$ it is easy to see from the definition of the approximating sequence that $\neg C \notin \mathcal{E}_1$, that $\neg C \notin \mathcal{E}_2$, and so on. But since $\mathcal{E}$ is simply the union of $\mathcal{E}_0$, $\mathcal{E}_1$, $\mathcal{E}_2$, and so on, it follows, contrary to assumption, that $\neg C \notin \mathcal{E}$. Next, suppose

$\neg C \notin \mathcal{E}$. In that case, it is easy to see that $\neg C \in \mathcal{E}_2$, and since $\mathcal{E}_2$ is a subset of $\mathcal{E}$, that $\neg C \in \mathcal{E}$, which again contradicts the assumption.

Default theories without extensions are often viewed as incoherent, and can perhaps be dismissed simply as anomalous. But there are also perfectly coherent default theories that allow multiple extensions. A standard example arises when one tries to encode as a default theory the inheritance network depicted in Figure 15.2, known as the Nixon Diamond, and representing the following set of facts:

- Nixon is a Quaker.
- Nixon is a Republican.
- Quakers tend to be pacifists.
- Republicans tend not to be pacifists.

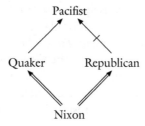

Figure 15.2   The Nixon Diamond

If one instantiates for Nixon the general statements expressed here about Quakers and Republicans, the resulting theory is $\Delta_5 = \langle W_5, \, \mathcal{D}_5 \rangle$, with

$$W_5 = \{Qn, \; Rn\}$$

and

$$\mathcal{D}_5 = \{(Qn : Pn/Pn), \; (Rn : \neg Pn/\neg Pn)\}$$

This theory allows both $Th(W_5 \cup \{Pn\})$ and $Th(W_5 \cup \{\neg Pn\})$ as extensions. Initially, before drawing any new conclusions, both of the default rules from $\mathcal{D}_5$ are applicable, but once one adopts the conclusion of either, the applicability of the other is blocked.

In cases like this, when a default theory leads to more than one extension, it is difficult to decide what conclusions a reasoner should actually draw from the information contained in the theory, and several options have been discussed in the literature. One option is to suppose that the reasoner should arbitrarily select one of the theory's several extensions and endorse the conclusions contained in it; a second option is to suppose that the reasoner should be willing to endorse a conclusion as long as it is contained in some extension of the default theory. These first two options are sometimes said to reflect a *credulous* reasoning strategy. A third option, sometimes described as *skeptical*, is to suppose that the reasoner should endorse a conclusion only if it is contained in every extension of the default theory.[2]

The first of these options – pick an arbitrary extension – really does seem to reflect a rational policy for reasoning in the face of conflicting information: often, given such information, one simply adopts some internally coherent point of view in which the conflicts are resolved in some particular way, regardless of the fact that there are other coherent points of view available in which the conflicts are resolved in a different way. Still, although this reasoning policy is rational, it is hard to see how such a policy could be codified as a formal consequence relation. If the choice of extension really is arbitrary, different reasoners could easily select different extensions, or the same reasoner might select different extensions at different times. Which extension, then, would represent the consequence set of the theory?

The second option – endorse a conclusion whenever it is contained in some extension of the default theory – can indeed be codified as a consequence relation, but it would be a peculiar one. According to this policy, the consequence set of a default theory need not be closed under standard logical consequence, and, in fact, might easily be inconsistent. The consequence set of Δ_5, for example, would contain both Pn and $\neg Pn$, since each of these formulas belongs to some extension of the default theory, but it would not contain $Pn \wedge \neg Pn$. This second option seems to provide a characterization, not so much of the formulas that should be believed on the basis of a default theory, but instead of the formulas that are believable.[3]

Only the third, skeptical option – endorse a conclusion whenever it is contained in every extension of the default theory – results in a natural consequence relation, as follows.

Definition 15.3 Let $\Delta = \langle W, \mathcal{D} \rangle$ be a default theory and A a formula. Then A is a *skeptical consequence* of Δ – written, $\Delta \vdash A$ – just in case $A \in \mathcal{E}$ for each extension $\mathcal{E}$ of Δ.

And it is worth noting explicitly, now that a formal consequence relation has been defined, that it is indeed nonmonotonic in two ways: both adding new factual information to the W-component of a default theory and adding new default information to the $\mathcal{D}$-component can force one to abandon consequences previously supported. The first possibility can be illustrated by referring back to the default theories Δ_1 and Δ_2. Here, $\Delta_1 \vdash Ft$, but it is not the case that $\Delta_2 \vdash Ft$ even though Δ_2 is obtained by adding the new factual information that $\neg Ft$ to the W-component of Δ_1. To illustrate the second case, consider the default theory $\Delta_6 = \langle W_6, \mathcal{D}_6 \rangle$, where $W_6 = W_5$ and $\mathcal{D}_6 = \{(Qn : Pn/Pn)\}$; this theory is like the Nixon Diamond Δ_5, except without the default that Republicans tend not to be pacifists. It is easy to see that Δ_6 has $Th(W_6 \cup \{Pn\})$ as its only extension, so that $\Delta_6 \vdash Pn$. The theory Δ_5, however, has two extensions, one of which does not contain Pn; so it is not the case that $\Delta_5 \vdash Pn$, even though Δ_5 results from the addition of the new default information $(Rn : \neg Pn/\neg Pn)$ to the $\mathcal{D}$-component of Δ_6.

15.3.4. *Examples and non-normal defaults*

Now, how can the motivating examples from section 15.2 be handled from the perspective of default logic?

To begin with, the frame problem appears to have a straightforward solution that results when one supplements the standard logical description of the initial situation and the available actions with default rules which simply say that facts tend to persist. To illustrate, one might encode the problem from section 15.2.1 into the default theory $\Delta_7 = \langle W_7, D_7 \rangle$, as follows. First, the factual component W_7 contains the formulas (15.1) through (15.3), describing the initial situation, the axioms characterizing the effects of the *Stack* and *Unstack* actions, and the inductive description of sequences of actions. Second, the default component D_7 contains all instances of the default rule schema

$$(H[\phi, s] : H[\phi, Res(\alpha, s)]/H[\phi, Res(\alpha, s)])$$

which states that: whenever a fact ϕ holds in a situation s, if it is consistent to conclude that ϕ still holds after the performance of the action α, then one should conclude by default that ϕ still holds after the performance of α.

It is easy to verify that this default theory has a single extension containing the formula (15.4), which is, of course, the intermediate step that was not derivable earlier without the help of frame axioms. Although the proposition that block C is still clear even after B is unstacked from A does not follow from the factual information contained in (15.1) through (15.3) alone, it can be derived with the help of the default rule which says to conclude, unless there is information to the contrary, that facts tend to persist.[4]

Turning to the qualification problem, again a partial solution can be found using default logic by supplementing the statement of the axioms governing actions with default rules which say simply that peculiar circumstances that might interfere with these actions tend not to occur. In the case of the example from section 15.2.2, the relevant information might be formulated through the theory $\Delta_8 = \langle W_8, D_8 \rangle$, in which W_8 contains, in addition to the appropriate background information, the modified *Stack* axiom (15.5) as well as the specifications from (15.6) of the various weird circumstances that might interfere with that action, and in which D_8 contains the single default

$$(\top : \neg Weird/\neg Weird)$$

which says to assume, absent information to the contrary, that no such weird circumstances occur ($\top$ stands for the universally true proposition). Of course, this representation does not help to resolve the first of the two issues presented by the qualification problem – that the list of conditions that might interfere with the *Stack* action is open-ended. The representation does, however, offer a resolution to the second of these issues. Given a list of various peculiar conditions that might conceivably interfere with the *Stack* action, one no longer actually verifies that each of these conditions fails in order to conclude that *Stack* has the desired effects; the default rule allows one simply to assume that these conditions fail unless there is information to the contrary.

Like the frame and qualification problems, the difficulties presented by closed-world reasoning also seem to be amenable to a solution based on default logic. As an initial suggestion, one might represent the information from section 15.2.3, for example, through the default theory $\Delta_9 = \langle W_9,\ D_9 \rangle$, with W_9 containing the factual data from (15.7) and D_9 containing each instance of the default rule schema

$$(\top : \neg Connects(x,\ y,\ z) / \neg Connects(x,\ y,\ z))$$

which says that, in the absence of information to the contrary, one should assume that cities are not connected by a direct flight. This theory will then have a single extension, allowing one to conclude (under reasonable assumptions, such as that all existing flights are named) that there is no direct flight between Baltimore and Barcelona.

Now, step back and notice a common feature in our default logic representation of these various examples illustrating the frame problem, the qualification problem, and closed-world reasoning, as well as in our representation of the Nixon Diamond. Each of these cases relied entirely on default rules of the special form $(A : B/B)$, in which the same formulas occurs as both justification and conclusion. Such default rules are known as *normal defaults*, and theories containing only normal defaults as *normal default theories*. As shown in Reiter (1980), normal default theories possess a number of attractive properties that are not shared by default theories in general – most notably, normal theories are guaranteed to have extensions. Because of these attractive properties, and because, as has been seen, many important examples can be coded into normal theories, Reiter originally conjectured that the full expressive power of default logic might not be needed in realistic applications, and it could be limited to normal theories.

This conjecture, however, was soon seen to be incorrect, as is illustrated by considering the final example – the Tweety Triangle from section 15.2.4. Considering only normal defaults, the information from the Tweety Triangle is naturally represented in the theory $\Delta_{10} = \langle W_{10},\ D_{10} \rangle$ with W_{10} containing the sentences Pt and $\forall x (Px \supset Bx)$, stating that Tweety is a penguin and that all penguins are birds, and with D_{10} containing the defaults $(Bt : Ft/Ft)$ and $(Pt : \neg Ft/\neg Ft)$, instantiating for Tweety the generic truths that birds tend to fly and that penguins tend not to. This default theory, like the representation of the Nixon Diamond as Δ_4, contains two conflicting default rules, and so leads to two extensions:

$$Th(W_{10} \cup \{Ft\}) \quad \text{and} \quad Th(W_{10} \cup \{\neg Ft\})$$

But is this right? In the case of the Nixon Diamond, the multiple extensions are reasonable, since the defaults concerning Quakers and Republicans appear to carry equal weight. But in the case of the Tweety Triangle, it really does seem that the default concerning penguins should be preferred to the default concerning birds, since penguins are a specific kind of bird, and it is always best to reason on the basis of the most specific information available. One way of capturing such preferences among defaults – first explored by Etherington and Reiter (1983) – is to modify the representation so that the reasons that might override the application of a default rule are explicitly built into the statement of that rule. Following this approach, the default concerning birds from the Tweety Triangle, for example, could be represented, not by the normal default rule $(Bt : Ft/Ft)$, but instead by the non-normal rule

$(Bt : [Ft \land \neg Pt]/Ft)$

What this rule says is that, once it is known that Tweety is a bird, if it is consistent with what is known that Tweety flies and that he is not a penguin, then one should presume that he flies.

This appeal to non-normal rules solves the initial problem presented by the Tweety Triangle: when this new, non-normal default is substituted for its normal predecessor in the previous Δ_{10}, the resulting theory now has only the single extension $Th(W_{10} \cup \{\neg Ft\})$, which states unambiguously that Tweety does not fly. Only the default rule $(Pt : \neg Ft/\neg Ft)$ can be applied. The new default $(Bt : [Ft \land \neg Pt]/Ft)$ does not come into play, since Pt is known.

Unfortunately, in solving the previous problem, the strategy of using non-normal rules to express preferences among competing defaults from defeasible inheritance networks now introduces a new difficulty: the new mapping of information from inheritance networks into default rules is holistic – the translation of a particular statement can vary depending on the context in which it is embedded. To illustrate, suppose one was to supplement the Tweety Triangle with the additional information that another class of birds – say, very young birds – does not fly. Of course, one would then have to add to the representation the formula $\forall x(Yx \supset Bx)$, which states that young birds are birds, as well as the default $(Yt : \neg Ft/\neg Ft)$, instantiating for Tweety the statement that young birds tend not to fly. But in addition, since there is now another possible reason present for overriding the default that birds tend to fly, the previous representation of that default must also be replaced with the new rule

$(Bt : [Ft \land \neg Pt \land \neg Yt]/Ft)$

From a computational point of view, this consequence is unattractive because it makes the process of updating a body of information extremely complicated, involving, not only the representation of new information, but also the reformulation of information that was already represented. From a philosophical point of view, the consequence is unattractive for much the same reason that holism is generally unattractive: the meaning of the statement that birds tend to fly seems not to vary from context to context, and so it is odd that its translation should vary.

15.4. A Model-Preference Approach: Circumscription

It was noted in the introduction that the monotonicity property reflects both proof theoretic and model theoretic assumptions of ordinary logic. Default logic results from a modification of the usual proof theoretic assumptions, introducing rules of inference that depend on the absence as well as the presence of information. This section now turns to a theory that results from a modification of the usual semantic assumptions.

Typically, a formula A is said to be a semantic consequence of a set of formulas Γ – written, $\Gamma \Vdash A$ – when A is true in every model of Γ. For many applications, however, one does not really care about all the models of Γ, but only about certain *preferred* models, and it then seems reasonable to modify the usual notion of consequence so that A is said to be a consequence of Γ whenever A is true in all the preferred models of Γ. The theory of circumscription, originally formulated by McCarthy (1980), results from this general preferential framework when the preferred models are defined as those in which certain predicates have minimal extensions.

15.4.1. *Predicate circumscription*

Taking a model as a pair $M = \langle \mathcal{D}, v \rangle$, with $\mathcal{D}$ a domain and v an interpretation of some fixed background language over that domain, begin by defining more precisely the preference ordering on models that forms the semantic background for the theory of circumscription. The general idea is that one model is at least as preferable as another just in case, while agreeing on everything else, the first assigns to some particular predicate P an extension at least as small as that assigned by the second.

Definition 15.4 Where $M_1 = \langle \mathcal{D}_1, v_1 \rangle$ and $M_2 = \langle \mathcal{D}_2, v_2 \rangle$ are models and where P is a predicate, then $M_1 \leq_P M_2$ just in case

(i) $\mathcal{D}_1 = \mathcal{D}_2$
(ii) $v_1(Q) = v_2(Q)$ for every linguistic symbol Q other than P, and
(iii) $v_1(P) \subseteq v_2(P)$.

It should be clear that the weak preference relation $\leq_P$ is a partial ordering, so that a corresponding strong preference relation is definable in the standard way.

Definition 15.5 Where M_1 and M_2 are models and where P is a predicate, then $M_1 <_P M_2$ just in case $M_1 \leq_P M_2$ but $M_1 \neq M_2$.

And one can then define the minimal elements in a class of models – the most preferred elements – as those models from the class for which the class contains no model that is more preferred.

Definition 15.6 Let $\mathcal{K}$ be a set of models and P a predicate. Then M is *P-minimal* in $\mathcal{K}$ just in case $M \in \mathcal{K}$ and there is no $M' \in \mathcal{K}$ such that $M' <_P M$.

Suppose $|\Gamma|$ is the model class of Γ, the set of models that satisfies each member of Γ. Having identified the minimal, or most preferred, models in a class, one can now define McCarthy's original notion of preferential, or minimal, consequence by focusing only on the minimal models of a theory, defining a formula as a consequence of the theory whenever it is true in all those models.

Definition 15.7 Where Γ is a set of formulas, P a predicate, and A a formula, A is said to be a *P-minimal consequence* of Γ – written $\Gamma \Vdash_P A$ – just in case $M \models A$ for every model M that is P-minimal in the set $|\Gamma|$.

And it is easy to see that this notion of minimal consequence is nonmonotonic. As an example, take $\Gamma_1 = \{Pa, a \neq b\}$. Then $\Gamma_1 \Vdash_P \neg Pb$, since the P-minimal models of Γ are those in which P holds only of the single element a, but of course one does not have $\Gamma_1 \cup \{Pb\} \Vdash_P \neg Pb$.

In addition to defining the notion of minimal consequence, McCarthy provides a sound second-order syntactic characterization of the idea through the axiom of circumscription, for which some preliminary notation is needed. Where P and Q are n-ary predicates, take $P \leq Q$ as an abbreviation of the formula

$$\forall x_1 \cdots x_n (P x_1 \ldots x_n \supset Q x_1 \ldots x_n)$$

Likewise, $P < Q$ abbreviates

$$P \leq Q \wedge \neg(Q \leq P)$$

and $P = Q$ abbreviates

$$P \leq Q \wedge Q \leq P$$

Where Γ is a finite theory, $\overline{\Gamma}$ stands for the conjunction of the members of Γ, and $\Gamma^{P/Q}$ stands for the result of substituting the predicate P for the predicate Q throughout Γ.

Using this notation, the *circumscription formula* for the predicate P in the theory Γ – abbreviated $Circ[\Gamma; P]$ – can be expressed quite simply through the second-order sentence

$$\overline{\Gamma} \wedge \neg \exists P'[\overline{\Gamma}^{P'/P} \wedge P' < P]$$

Any model $\mathcal{M}$ that satisfies the first conjunct of this formula, of course, is a model of Γ. But what does the second conjunct say? Well, if there were another model $\mathcal{M}'$ also satisfying Γ and such that $\mathcal{M}' <_P \mathcal{M}$, one could then use the value assigned by $\mathcal{M}'$ to the predicate P to show that $\mathcal{M}$ satisfies the formula $\exists P'[\overline{\Gamma}^{P'/P} \wedge P' < P]$. The force of the second conjunct, then, is simply that there is no such model $\mathcal{M}'$, and so together, what the two conjuncts say is that $Circ[\Gamma; P]$ is satisfied by exactly the P-minimal models of Γ.

Theorem 15.2 Let Γ be a finite set of sentences, P a predicate, and $\mathcal{M}$ a model. Then $\mathcal{M} \vDash Circ[\Gamma; P]$ just in case $\mathcal{M}$ is P-minimal in $|\Gamma|$.

From this result, the soundness of circumscription with respect to minimal consequence follows at once.

Theorem 15.3 Let Γ be a finite set of sentences, P a predicate, and A a formula. Then $\Gamma \Vdash_P A$ whenever $Circ[\Gamma; P] \vdash A$.

The argument is again straightforward. To say that $\Gamma \Vdash_P A$ is to say that every P-minimal model of Γ satisfies A, so let $\mathcal{M}$ be such a model. From the preceding result, it is known that $\mathcal{M} \vDash Circ[\Gamma;\ P]$. Since $Circ[\Gamma;\ P] \vdash A$, the soundness of second-order logic says that $Circ[\Gamma;\ P] \Vdash A$, and so one can conclude that $\mathcal{M} \vDash A$.

Of course, circumscription is not complete with respect to minimal consequence; not every minimal consequence of a theory can be derived from the circumscription formula. But this failure is no surprise, following from the incompleteness of second-order logic itself. It was also noticed early on that the result of circumscribing certain predicates even in consistent theories might lead to inconsistency; a simple example, due to Etherington et al. (1985), results when one considers the theory Γ_2, containing the sentences

$$\exists x[Nx \wedge \forall y(Ny \supset x \neq s(y))]$$

$$\forall x(Nx \supset Ns(x))$$

$$\forall xy(s(x) = s(y) \supset x = y)$$

Any model $\mathcal{M}$ of Γ_2 must assign to N an extension containing a series isomorphic to the natural numbers (with s interpreted as successor); and one can then define another model $\mathcal{M}'$ of Γ_2 simply by deleting from the extension of N the initial element of this series. Evidently, then, $\mathcal{M}' <_N \mathcal{M}$, and so the model class of Γ_2 has no N-minimal elements. Since, as has been seen, $Circ[\Gamma_2;\ N]$ is satisfied by all and only the N-minimal elements of this model class, it follows that the result of circumscribing the predicate N in the theory Γ_2 is not satisfiable.

To illustrate the use of the circumscription formula, consider how circumscribing the predicate P in the earlier example of Γ_1 allows one to derive $\neg Pb$. To begin with, it is most convenient to express the circumscription formula $Circ[\Gamma_1;\ P]$, not exactly in the fashion displayed above, but instead in the logically equivalent form

$$\overline{\Gamma}_1 \wedge \forall P'[(\overline{\Gamma_1^{P'/P}} \wedge P' \leq P) \supset P' = P]$$

The second conjunct of this formula can then be instantiated by identifying P' with the predicate $\lambda x(x = a)$, in which case it is easy to see from the ordinary logic of identity that both the formulas $\overline{\Gamma_1^{P'/P}}$ and $P' \leq P$ are derivable from $\overline{\Gamma}_1$. The second conjunct therefore allows us to derive the formula $P' = P$ – that is, $\forall x(\lambda x(x = a)x \equiv Px)$ – and from this one can conclude at once that $\neg Pb$, since Γ_1 contains the information that $a \neq b$.

15.4.2. Variable circumscription

The inference relation defined by the theory of predicate circumscription allows one, for example, to formalize the kind of closed-world reasoning illustrated in section 5.2.3 by circumscribing the extension of the predicate *Connects*; one could then conclude that there is no direct flight connecting Washington and Barcelona. It turns out, however, that this theory is of severely limited applicability for the simple reason that it never allows new positive conclusions to be drawn by default.

This failure can be illustrated by returning again the initial example. Given the information that Tweety is a bird and that birds fly, how could one use the theory of circumscription to reach the conclusion that Tweety flies? It was suggested by McCarthy that defaults might naturally be represented in the theory through an appeal to explicit abnormality predicates. Where the predicate AB stands for abnormality with respect to flying, for example, the statement that birds fly might be represented through the formula $\forall x((Bx \land \neg ABx) \supset Fx)$ – saying that all birds that are not abnormal in this respect fly. Suppose Γ_3 contains this statement as well as Bt then it might seem that one should be able to reach the conclusion Ft simply by circumscribing the predicate AB, ensuring that there are no more abnormal birds than necessary.

In fact, this is a reasonable idea, but it fails for technical reasons, as can be seen by considering the model $M = \langle D, v \rangle$, with $D = \{t\}$, $v(B) = \{t\}$, $v(AB) = \{t\}$, and $v(F) = \emptyset$. Of course, M does not support the statement Ft, but it turns out that it is an AB-minimal model of Γ_3. The only way of decreasing the extension of the predicate AB, while still modeling Γ_3, would result in increasing the extension of the predicate F – but this violates clause (ii) of definition 15.4, which tells us that models involved in a preference ordering with respect to a particular predicate must agree in their treatment of all other predicates.

Because of this problem, McCarthy (1986) elaborated the basic theory of predicate circumscription into a more flexible theory of variable circumscription, which orders models with respect to a pair of predicates, P and Z. The idea is that those models are preferred that minimize the extension of P while agreeing on everything else, with the possible exception of the predicate Z, whose extension is allowed to vary.

Definition 15.8 Where $M_1 = \langle D_1, v_1 \rangle$ and $M_2 = \langle D_2, v_2 \rangle$ are models and where P and Z are distinct predicates, then $M_1 \leq_{P,Z} M_2$ just in case

(i) $D_1 = D_2$,
(ii) $v_1(Q) = v_2(Q)$ for every linguistic symbol Q other than P and Z, and
(iii) $v_1(P) \subseteq v_2(P)$.

This weak preference ordering is reflexive and transitive, but it is not anti-symmetric, since it is possible for distinct models, agreeing in their interpretation of every predicate but Z, to bear the $\leq_{P,Z}$ relation to one another. Still, one can define a corresponding strong preference ordering between models by requiring the weak ordering to hold in only one direction.

Definition 15.9 Where M_1 and M_2 are models and where P and Z are distinct predicates, then $M_1 <_{P,Z} M_2$ just in case $M_1 \leq_{P,Z} M_2$ and it is not the case that $M_2 \leq_{P,Z} M_1$.

And then the pattern set out above can be followed in defining the P,Z-minimal models in a class, and the corresponding notion of consequence.

Definition 15.10 Let $\mathcal{K}$ be a set of models and P and Z distinct predicates. Then $\mathcal{M}$ is $P;Z$-*minimal* in $\mathcal{K}$ just in case $\mathcal{M} \in \mathcal{K}$ and there is no $\mathcal{M}' \in \mathcal{K}$ such that $\mathcal{M}' <_{P,Z} \mathcal{M}$.

Definition 15.11 Where Γ is a set of formulas and A a formula and P and Z are distinct predicates, A is a $P;Z$-*minimal consequence* of Γ – written $\Gamma \Vdash_{P,Z} A$ – just in case $\mathcal{M} \vDash A$ for every $\mathcal{M}$ that is $P;Z$-minimal in the set $|\Gamma|$.

These ideas can be illustrated by returning once again to the initial example. As already seen, the formula Ft is not an AB-minimal consequence of Γ_3, since the model $\mathcal{M}$ defined above is AB-minimal in the model class of Γ_3 but does not support this statement. One can now, however, define the model $\mathcal{M}' = \langle \mathcal{D}', v' \rangle$, like $\mathcal{M}$ except that $v'(AB) = \emptyset$ and $v'(F) = \{t\}$. It is then easy to see that $\mathcal{M}' <_{AB,F} \mathcal{M}$, so that $\mathcal{M}$ is not $AB;F$-minimal, that $\mathcal{M}'$ is itself $AB;F$-minimal, and that every $AB;F$-minimal model of Γ_3 supports the statement Ft, so that now $\Gamma_3 \Vdash_{AB;F} Ft$.

As before, a sound second-order syntactic characterization of the notion of $P;Z$-minimal consequence can be provided through the following circumscription formula, abbreviated $Circ[\Gamma; P; Z]$ and expressing the result of circumscribing the predicate P in the theory Γ while allowing Z to vary:

$$\overline{\Gamma} \wedge \neg \exists P', Z'[\overline{\Gamma^{P'/P\,Z'/Z}} \wedge P' < P]$$

And again, the variable circumscription formula $Circ[\Gamma; P; Z]$ can be seen to hold in exactly the $P;Z$-minimal models of the theory Γ, from which it follows immediately that variable circumscription is sound with respect to $P;Z$-minimal consequence.

Theorem 15.4 Let Γ be a finite set of sentences, P and Z distinct predicates, and $\mathcal{M}$ a model. Then $\mathcal{M} \vDash Circ[\Gamma; P; Z]$ just in case $\mathcal{M}$ is $P;Z$-minimal in $|\Gamma|$.

Theorem 15.5 Let Γ be a finite set of sentences, P and Z distinct predicates, and A a formula. Then $\Gamma \Vdash_{P,Z} A$ whenever $Circ[\Gamma; P; Z] \vdash A$.

The application of this new variable circumscription formula can be illustrated through the initial example, deriving Ft from Γ_3 by circumscribing AB while allowing F to vary. As before, begin by rewriting $Circ[\Gamma_3; AB; F]$ as

$$\overline{\Gamma}_3 \wedge \forall P' Z'[(\overline{\Gamma_3^{P'/AB\,Z'/F}} \wedge P' \leq AB) \supset P' = AB]$$

Then, the second conjunct of this formula can be instantiated by identifying P' with the empty predicate $\lambda x(x \neq x)$ and identifying Z' with $\lambda x(x = t)$. It is a straightforward matter, using the information from $\overline{\Gamma}_3$, to verify both $\overline{\Gamma_3^{P'/AB\,Z'/F}}$ and $P' \leq AB$, and so one can conclude that $P' = AB$ – i.e., that $\forall x(\lambda x(x \neq x)x \equiv ABx)$. From this it follows at once, of course, that $\neg ABt$, which allows one to conclude, again using the information from $\overline{\Gamma}_3$, that Ft.

15.4.3. *Parallel and prioritized circumscription*

The theory of circumscription set out here has been generalized in a number of ways. Two are sketched – parallel circumscription, which allows several predicates to be circumscribed at once, while several others vary; and prioritized circumscription, which allows some predicates to be circumscribed with higher priority than others.

In fact, the theory of parallel circumscription is best seen simply as a notational elaboration of the previous theory. Suppose that, while allowing $X \subseteq Y$ to carry its usual meaning when X and Y are sets, this notation is generalised so that, when $X = X_1, \ldots, X_n$ and $Y = Y_1, \ldots, Y_n$ are n-tuples of sets, $X \subseteq Y$ means that $X_i \subseteq Y_i$ for each i between 1 and n. Suppose also that, where $P = P_1, \ldots, P_n$ is a tuple of predicates, $v(P)$ represents the tuple $v(P_1), \ldots, v(P_n)$ of extensions assigned to these predicates by the interpretation v. And finally, suppose that, where $P = P_1, \ldots, P_n$ and $Q = Q_1, \ldots, Q_n$ are n-tuples of predicates, with each P_i taking the same number of arguments as the corresponding Q_i, let $P \leq Q$ mean $P_1 \leq Q_1 \wedge \cdots \wedge P_n \leq Q_n$, and take $P < Q$ and $P = Q$ to be defined as before.

Once these notational enhancements are in place, the theory of parallel circumscription can be presented just as before – in definition 15.8 through theorem 1.5.5 – with the sole exception that now P and Z must be disjoint tuples of predicates instead of distinct individual predicates: rather than looking at models in which the individual predicate P is circumscribed, look at models in which the various predicates belonging to the tuple P are circumscribed in parallel.

To illustrate this theory, return to the Nixon Diamond from figure 15.2, here represented through the theory Γ_4, containing the statements Qn and Rn, saying that Nixon is a Quaker and a Republican, as well as the statements

$$\forall x((Qx \wedge \neg AB_1 x) \supset Px)$$

and

$$\forall x((Rx \wedge \neg AB_2 x) \supset \neg Px)$$

saying that Quakers that are normal in one respect are pacifists, and that Republicans normal in an another respect are not. To decide whether to conclude that Nixon is a pacifist, it seems reasonable to minimize both sorts of abnormality in parallel, while allowing the predicate P to vary – focusing, that is, on the AB_1, AB_2;P-minimal models. The reader can then verify that Γ_4 has one AB_1, AB_2;P-minimal model that assigns an empty extension to AB_1 and supports the conclusion Pn, as well as another that assigns an empty extension to AB_2 and supports the conclusion $\neg Pn$. Since neither Pn nor $\neg Pn$ is supported by all AB_1, AB_2;P-minimal models of Γ_4, one can conclude that neither formula is an AB_1, AB_2;P-minimal consequence of this theory. And by the soundness of circumscription with respect to minimal consequence, one can conclude also that neither Pn nor $\neg Pn$ can be derived from the parallel circumscription formula $Circ[\Gamma_4; AB_1, AB_2; P]$.

In the case of the Nixon Diamond, it does seem reasonable to minimize the abnormalities associated with Quakers and Republicans in parallel; but in other cases, when defaults have different degrees of strength, it is more natural to assign a higher priority to the minimization of some abnormalities than others. An example is provided by the Tweety Triangle, from figure 15.1, which can be represented through the theory Γ_5, containing the statements Pt and $\forall x(Px \supset Bx)$, saying that Tweety is a penguin and that all penguins are birds, as well as the statements

$$\forall x((Bx \wedge \neg AB_1 x) \supset Fx)$$

and

$$\forall x((Px \wedge \neg AB_2 x) \supset \neg Fx)$$

saying that birds normally fly but that penguins normally do not. Here, if one minimizes the two abnormalities in parallel, again, as in the Nixon Diamond, there are some minimal models supporting the formula Ft supported and others supporting $\neg Ft$, so that one is unable to draw any conclusions. It seems more natural, however, to minimize the abnormality associated with penguins with a higher priority than that associated with birds, so that all minimal models then support the desired conclusion $\neg Ft$.

To develop the theory of prioritized circumscription leading to this result, first define the relation

$$\langle X_1, X_2 \rangle \sqsubseteq \langle Y_1, Y_2 \rangle$$

to mean that

(i) $X_1 \subseteq Y_1$ and
(ii) if $X_1 = Y_1$ then $X_2 \subseteq Y_2$.

Although this new relation can actually be taken – using the enhanced notation just introduced in connection with parallel circumscription – as holding between pairs of tuples of sets, things can be kept simple by reading it as a relation between pairs of sets, and use it to define the following preference ordering on models.

Definition 15.12   Where $M_1 = \langle D_1, v_1 \rangle$ and $M_2 = \langle D_2, v_2 \rangle$ are models and where P, Q and Z are distinct predicates, then $M_1 \leq_{P>Q;Z} M_2$ just in case

(i) $D_1 = D_2$
(ii) $v_1(R) = v_2(R)$ for every linguistic symbol R other than P, Q, or Z, and
(iii) $\langle v_1(P), v_1(Q) \rangle \sqsubseteq \langle v_2(P), v_2(Q) \rangle$.

The idea behind this weak prioritized ordering is that those models are preferred that minimize the extensions assigned to both the predicates P and Q while allowing Z to vary, but that minimizing P is assigned a higher priority than minimizing Q.

Once this weak prioritized preference ordering has been defined, the development of the theory follows the pattern set out earlier. A corresponding strong ordering can be introduced as in definition 15.9, with $M_1 <_{P>Q;Z} M_2$ taken to mean that $M_1 \leq_{P>Q;Z} M_2$ and it is not the case that $M_2 \leq_{P>Q;Z} M_1$. The minimal elements of a class of models can then be defined as in definition 15.10, with M taken as $P > Q$; Z-minimal in the class $\mathcal{K}$ whenever M belongs to $\mathcal{K}$ and there is no M' from $\mathcal{K}$ such that $M' <_{P>Q;Z} M$. And the appropriate notion of consequence can be defined as in definition 15.11, with A taken to be a $P > Q$; Z-minimal consequence of Γ – written, $\Gamma \Vdash_{P>Q;Z} A$ – whenever $M \vDash A$ for each $P > Q$; Z-minimal model M from $|\Gamma|$. With these definitions in hand, the reader can then verify that $\Gamma_5 \Vdash_{AB_2>AB_1;F} \neg Ft$ – i.e., that the statement $\neg Ft$ follows as a consequence of Γ_5 when the predicate AB_2 is minimized with a higher priority than AB_1, allowing F to vary.

Turning to the proof theory for prioritized circumscription, begin by defining $\langle P_1, P_2 \rangle \leq \langle Q_1, Q_2 \rangle$ as an abbreviation of the statement

$$P_1 \leq Q_1 \wedge (P_1 = Q_1 \supset P_2 \leq Q_2)$$

and then taking $\langle P_1, P_2 \rangle < \langle Q_1, Q_2 \rangle$ to mean that

$$\langle P_1, P_2 \rangle \leq \langle Q_1, Q_2 \rangle \wedge \neg(\langle Q_1, Q_2 \rangle < \langle P_1, P_2 \rangle)$$

The circumscription formula for minimizing P with higher priority than Q in the theory Γ while allowing Z to vary, abbreviated as $Circ[\Gamma; P > Q; Z]$, can now be expressed through the second-order statement

$$\Gamma \wedge \neg \exists P', Q', Z'[\overline{\Gamma^{P/P\,Q'/Q\,Z'/Z}} \wedge \langle P_1, P_2 \rangle < \langle Q_1, Q_2 \rangle]$$

Analogues to theorems 15.4 and 15.5 can be established, saying that $Circ[\Gamma; P > Q; Z]$ holds in exactly the $P > Q$;Z-minimal models of Γ, and therefore, that prioritized circumscription is sound with respect to the appropriate prioritized notion of minimal consequence. And the interested reader can verify that $\neg Ft$ is indeed derivable from the formula $Circ[\Gamma_5; AB_2 > AB_1; F]$.

It should be clear that the theories presented here of parallel and prioritized circumscription can be combined and generalized, so that groups of predicates can be minimized in parallel, but all with higher priority than other groups of predicates. One could, for example, speak of the $P_1, P_2 > P_3 > P_4, P_5$; Z_1, Z_2-minimal models as those obtained by minimizing the predicates P_1 and P_2 in parallel with higher priority than P_3, which is itself minimized with higher priority than P_4, and P_5, all the while allowing Z_1 and Z_2 to vary. Note, however, that – just as with default logic – it is still necessary to specify the preferences among various competing defaults by hand, in this case by explicitly tailoring the priorities involved in the minimization ordering, rather than coding these preferences into non-normal default rules.

Suggested further reading

Many of the original papers on nonmonotonic logic are reprinted in Ginsberg (1987). A more recent collection is Gabbay et al. (1994), which contains several valuable survey articles on different approaches. There have been a number of variations on the general themes introduced in Reiter's default logic; the most readable and comprehensive presentation of these is Delgrande et al. (1994). Another fixed-point theory of nonmonotonic reasoning, closely related to default logic, is the modal approach of McDermott and Doyle (1987 [1980]). This modal approach was refined in Moore (1985); relations to default logic are established in Konolige (1988 [1987]). The best general survey of the theory of circumscription is Lifschitz (1994). Different model-preference approaches, based on different preference orderings can be found in Kautz (1986) and Shoham (1988). A general study of nonmonotonic consequence relations, with a special emphasis on model preference logics, was initiated by Makinson (1989) and Kraus et al. (1990).

Notes

1 Just as ordinary inference rules allow multiple premises, default rules allow multiple prerequisites and also multiple justifications; we limit our attention to default rules in which prerequisites and justification are unique for ease of exposition.

2 The use of the *credulous/skeptical* terminology to characterize these two broad reasoning strategies was first introduced in Touretzky et al. (1987), but the distinction is older than this; it was noted already by Reiter, and was described in McDermott (1982) as the distinction between *brave* and *cautious* reasoning.

3 Reiter provides a proof procedure, sound and complete under certain conditions, for determining whether a formula is believable in this sense on the basis of a default theory. A different interpretation of this second credulous option is provided in Horty (1994), which interprets default logic as a deontic logic allowing for moral conflicts.

4 Unfortunately, although the treatment of the frame problem suggested here does seem to work for the simple example set out in section 15.2.1, it was shown in Hanks and McDermott (1987) that this straightforward kind of nonmonotonic approach delivers anomalous results in situations that are only slightly more complicated. Since then, a number of more sophisticated encodings of actions and their effects in various nonmonotonic logics have been explored, such as those of Lifschitz (1994) and Morgenstern and Stein (1988), as well as renewed attempts to resolve the frame problem in ordinary monotonic logics, such as that of Reiter (1991). The field is now an area of active research; a recent survey can be found in Shanahan (1997).

References

Delgrande, J., Schaub, T. and Jackson, W. K. 1994: "Alternative Approaches to Default Logic," *Artificial Intelligence*, 70, 167–237.

Etherington, D. and Reiter, R. 1983: "On Inheritance Hierarchies with Exception," in *Proceedings of AAAI-83*, (William Kaufman, Los Altos, CA), 104–8.

Etherington, D., Mercer, R. and Reiter, R. 1985: "On the Adequacy of Predicate Circumscription for Closed-World Reasoning," *Computational Intelligence*, 1, 11–15.

Gabbay, D. M., Hogger, C. and Robinson, J. A. (eds.) 1994: *Handbook of Logic in Artificial Intelligence and Logic Programming, Volume 3: Nonmonotonic Reasoning and Uncertain Reasoning*, (Oxford University Press, Oxford).

Ginsberg, M. (ed.) 1987: *Readings in Nonmonotonic Reasoning*, (Morgan Kaufmann, Los Altos, CA).

Hanks, S. and McDermott, D. 1987: "Nonmonotonic Logic and Temporal Projection," *Artificial Intelligence*, 33, 379–412.

Horty, J. 1994: "Moral Dilemmas and Nonmonotonic Logic," *Journal of Philosophical Logic*, 23, 35–65.

Kautz, H. 1986: "The Logic of Persistence," in *Proceedings of AAAI-86*, (Morgan Kaufmann, Los Altos, CA), 401–5.

Konolige, K. 1988: "On the Relation between Default Theories and Autoepistemic Logic," *Artificial Intelligence*, 35, 343–82; also in Ginsberg (1987, 195–226).

Kraus, S., Lehman, D. and Magidor, M. 1990: "Nonmonotonic Reasoning, Preferential Models, and Cumulative Logics," *Artificial Intelligence*, 44, 167–207.

Lifschitz, V. 1994: "Circumscription," in Gabbay et al. (1994, 297–352).

Makinson, D. 1989: "General Theory of Cumulative Inference," in *Proceedings of the Second International Workshop on Nonmonotonic Reasoning*, M. Reinfrank, J. de Kleer, M. Ginsberg and E. Sandewall, eds., Springer-Verlag Lecture Notes in Artificial Intelligence, 346, 1–18.

McCarthy, J. 1980: "Circumscription – A Form of Non-Monotonic Reasoning," *Artificial Intelligence*, 13, 27–39.

McCarthy, J. 1986: "Applications of Circumscription to Formalizing Commonsense Knowledge," *Artificial Intelligence*, 28, 89–116.

McCarthy, J. and Hayes, P. 1969: "Some Philosophical Problems from the Standpoint of Artificial Intelligence," in *Machine Intelligence, volume 4*, B. Meltzer and D. Michie, eds., (Edinburgh Press, Edinburgh), 463–503.

McDermott, D. 1982: "A Temporal Logic for Reasoning about Processes and Plans," *Cognitive Science*, 6, 101–55.

McDermott, D. and Doyle, J. 1987: "Non-Monotonic Logic – I," *Artificial Intelligence*, 13 (1980), 41–72; reprinted in Ginsberg (1987, 111–26).

Moore, R. 1985: "Semantic Considerations on Nonmonotonic Logic," *Artificial Intelligence*, 25, 75–94.

Morgenstern, L. and Stein, L. 1988: "Why Things Go Wrong: A Formal Theory of Causal Reasoning," in *Proceedings of AAAI-88*, (Morgan Kaufmann, Los Altos, CA), 518–23.

Reiter, R. 1978: "On Closed World Data Bases," in *Logic and Data Bases*, H. Gallaire and J. Minker, eds., (Plenum Publishing Corp., New York), 119–40.

Reiter, R. 1980: "A Logic for Default Reasoning," *Artificial Intelligence*, 13, 81–132.

Reiter, R. 1991: "The Frame Problem in the Situation Calculus: A Simple Solution (Sometimes) and a Completeness Result for Goal Regression," in *Artificial Intelligence and Mathematical Theory of Computation: Papers in Honor of John McCarthy*, V. Lifschitz, ed., (Academic Press, Boston), 359–80.

Shanahan, M. 1997: *Solving the Frame Problem*, (The MIT Press, Cambridge, MA).

Shoham, Y. 1988: *Reasoning about Change*, (The MIT Press, Cambridge, MA).

Touretzky, D., Horty, J. and Thomason, R. 1987: "A Clash of Intuitions: The Current State of Nonmonotonic Multiple Inheritance Systems," in *Proceedings of the Tenth International Joint Conference on Artificial Intelligence (IJCAI-87)*, (Morgan Kaufmann, Los Altos, CA), 476–82.

Chapter 16

Probability, Logic, and Probability Logic

Alan Hájek

The true logic of the world is in the calculus of probabilities.

James Clerk Maxwell

16.1. Probability and Logic

'Probability logic' might seem like an oxymoron. Logic traditionally concerns matters immutable, necessary and certain, while probability concerns the uncertain, the random, the capricious. Yet our subject has a distinguished pedigree. Ramsey begins his classic "Truth and Probability" (1980 [1931]) with the words: "In this essay the Theory of Probability is taken as a branch of logic . . . ." De Finetti (1980) speaks of "the logic of the probable." And more recently, Jeffrey (1992) regards probabilities as estimates of truth values, and thus probability theory as a natural outgrowth of two-valued logic – what he calls "probability logic." However the point is put, probability theory and logic are clearly intimately related. This chapter explores some of the multifarious connections between probability and logic, and focuses on various philosophical issues in the foundations of probability theory.

The survey begins in section 16.2 with the probability calculus, what Adams (1975, p. 34) calls "pure probability logic." As will be seen, there is a sense in which the axiomatization of probability presupposes deductive logic. Moreover, some authors see probability theory as the proper framework for *inductive* logic – a formal apparatus for codifying the degree of support a piece of evidence lends a hypothesis, or the impact of evidence on rational opinion.

Fixing a meaning of 'probability' allows more specific connections to logic to be drawn. Thus section 16.3 considers various interpretations of probability. According to the classical interpretation, probability and possibility are intimately related, so that probability becomes a kind of modality. For objective interpretations such as the frequency and propensity theories, probability theory can be regarded as providing the logic of 'chance'. Under the subjective (Bayesian) interpretation, probability can be thought of as the logic of partial belief. And for the logical interpretation, the connection to logic is the most direct, probability theory being a logic of partial entailment, and thus a true generalization of deductive logic.

Kolmogorov's axiomatization is the orthodoxy, the probabilistic analogue of classical logic. However, a number of authors offer rival systems, analogues of 'deviant' logics, as it were. These are discussed in section 16.4, noting some bridges between them and various logics. Probabilistic semantics is introduced in section 16.5. The conclusions of even valid inferences can be uncertain when the premises of the inferences are themselves uncertain. This prompts Adams' version of 'probability logic,' the study of the propagation of probability in such inferences. This, in turn, motivates the discussion in section 16.6 of the literature on probabilities of conditionals, in which probability theory is used to illuminate the logic of conditionals. [See also chapter 17.]

One cannot hope for a complete treatment of a topic this large in a survey this short. The reader who is interested in pursuing these themes further is invited to consult the Suggested Readings and the References at the end.

16.2. The Probability Axioms

Probability theory was inspired by games of chance in seventeenth-century France and inaugurated by the Fermat–Pascal correspondence. Their work culminated in the publication of *The Port Royal Logic*, which offered a 'logic of uncertain expectation' in Jeffrey's (1992) phrase. However, the development of the probability calculus had to wait until well into the twentieth century.

Kolmogorov (1950 [1933]) begins his classic book with what he calls the "elementary theory of probability": the part of the theory that applies when there are only finitely many events in question. Let Ω be a set (the 'universal set'). A *field* (or *algebra*) on Ω is a set of subsets of Ω that has Ω as a member, and that is closed under complementation (with respect to Ω) and finite union. Let Ω be given, and let $\mathcal{F}$ be a field on Ω. Kolmogorov's axioms constrain the possible assignments of numbers, called *probabilities*, to the members of $\mathcal{F}$. Let P be a function from $\mathcal{F}$ to $[0, 1]$ obeying:

Axiom 1 (*Non-negativity*) $P(A) \geq 0$ for all $A \in \mathcal{F}$
Axiom 2 (*Normalization*) $P(\Omega) = 1$
Axiom 3 (*Finite additivity*) $P(A \cup B) = P(A) + P(B)$ for all $A, B \in \mathcal{F}$ such that $A \cap B = \emptyset$

Call such a triple of $(\Omega, \mathcal{F}, P)$ a *probability space*.

Here the arguments of the probability function are sets, probability theory being thus parasitic on set theory. One could, instead, attach probabilities to members of a collection $\mathcal{S}$ of *sentences* of a language, closed under finite truth-functional combinations, with the following counterpart axiomatization:

I $P(A) \geq 0$ for all $A \in \mathcal{S}$.
II If $\top$ is a tautology (of classical logic), then $P(\top) = 1$.

III $P(A \lor B) = P(A) + P(B)$ for all $A \in S$ and $B \in S$ such that A and B are logically incompatible.

Note how these axioms take the notions of 'tautology' and 'logical incompatibility' as antecedently understood. To this extent, one may regard probability theory as parasitic on deductive logic.

Kolmogorov then allows Ω to be infinite. A non-empty collection $\mathcal{F}$ of subsets of Ω is called a *sigma field* (or *sigma algebra*, or *Borel field*) on Ω iff (if and only if) $\mathcal{F}$ is closed under complementation and countable union. Define a *probability measure* $P(-)$ *on* $\mathcal{F}$ as a function from $\mathcal{F}$ to $[0, 1]$ satisfying axioms 1–3, as before, and also:

Axiom 4   (*Continuity*) $E_n \downarrow \varnothing \Rightarrow P(E_n) \to 0$ (where, for every n, $E_n \in \mathcal{F}$)

(As shrinking sets converge to the null set, their probability approaches 0.) Equivalently, we can replace the conjunction of axioms 3 and 4 with a single axiom:

Axiom 3′   (*Countable additivity*)   If $\{A_i\}$ is a countable collection of (pairwise) disjoint sets, each $\in \mathcal{F}$, then

$$P\left(\bigcup_{n=1}^{\infty} A_n\right) = \sum_{n=1}^{\infty} P(A_n)$$

The *conditional probability* of A given B, $P(A \mid B)$, is standardly given by the ratio of unconditional probabilities:

$$P(A \mid B) = \frac{P(A \cap B)}{P(B)} \qquad \text{provided } P(B) > 0.$$

This is often taken to be the definition of conditional probability, although it should be emphasized that this is a technical usage of the term that may not align perfectly with a pretheoretical concept that we might have. For example, it seems that we can make sense of conditional probabilities that are defined in the absence of the requisite unconditional probabilities, or when the condition B has probability 0 (Hájek, 2001).

Various important theorems can now be proved, among them the law of total probability:

$$P(A) = P(A \mid B) \cdot P(B) + P(A \mid -B) \cdot P(-B)$$

Even more importantly, various versions of *Bayes' theorem* can be proved:

$$P(A \mid B) = \frac{P(B \mid A) \cdot P(A)}{P(B)}$$

$$= \frac{P(B \mid A) \cdot P(A)}{P(B \mid A) \cdot P(A) + P(B \mid -A) \cdot P(-A)}$$

These are all of the essentials of the mathematical theory of probability that will be needed here.[1] Jeffrey (1992) stresses various analogies between this 'formal probability logic' and deductive logic. Here is an important one: theorems such as these enable one, given certain probabilities, to calculate further probabilities. However, the probability calculus does not itself determine the probabilities of any sentences, apart from 1 for tautologies and 0 for contradictions. Such values need to be provided 'from the outside,' with probability theory only providing a framework. Compare this with deductive logic, which says which sentences are consistent with others, and which sentences are implied by others, but which does not itself determine the truth values of any sentences, apart from 'true' for tautologies and 'false' for contradictions.

How, then, are probability values determined in the first place? This raises the issue of what probabilities *are* – i.e., the so-called *interpretation* of probability.

16.3. Interpretations of Probability

The mathematics of probability is well understood, but its interpretation is controversial. Kolmogorov's axioms are remarkably economical, and as such they admit of many interpretations. This section briefly presents some of the best known ones, emphasizing various connections to logic along the way.[2]

16.3.1. The classical interpretation

According to the classical interpretation – championed, for example, by Laplace – when evidence equally favors each of various possibilities, or there is no such evidence at all, the probability of an event is simply the fraction of the total number of possibilities in which the event occurs – this is sometimes called the *principle of indifference*. Thus, the modalities of possibility and probability are intimately related. For example, the probability of a fair die landing with an even number showing up is $\frac{3}{6}$. Unfortunately, the prescription can apparently yield contradictory results when there is no single privileged set of possibilities. And even when there is, critics have argued that biases cannot be ruled out *a priori*. Finally, classical probabilities are only finitely additive, so they do not provide an interpretation of the full Kolmogorov calculus.

16.3.2. The logical interpretation

Logical theories of probability are descendants of the classical theory. They generalize the notion that probability is to be computed in the absence of evidence, or on the basis of symmetrically balanced evidence, to allow probability to be computed on the basis of the evidence, whatever it may be. At least in their earlier forms, logical theories saw the probability of a hypothesis given such evidence as objectively and uniquely determined, and thus ideally to be agreed on by all rational agents. If one thinks that there can be, besides deductive implication, a weaker relation of partial implication, then one may also think of logical probability as an analysis of 'degree of implication.' This interpretation more than any other explicitly sees probability as part of logic, namely *inductive* logic.

Early proponents of logical probability include Keynes (1921), W. E. Johnson (1932), and Jeffreys (1939). However, by far the most systematic study of logical probability was by Carnap. He thought of probability theory as an elaboration of deductive logic, arrived at by adding extra rules. Specifically, he sought to explicate 'the degree to which hypothesis h is confirmed by evidence e,' with the 'correct' conditional probability $c(h, e)$ its explication. Statements of logical probability such as '$c(h, e) = x$' were then to be thought of as logical truths.

The formulation of logical probability begins with the construction of a formal language. Carnap (1950) initially considers a class of very simple languages consisting of a finite number of logically independent monadic predicates (that name properties) applied to countably many individual constants (that name individuals) or variables, and the usual logical connectives. The strongest (consistent) statements that can be made in a given language describe all of the individuals in as much detail as the expressive power of the language allows. They are conjunctions of complete descriptions of each individual, each description itself a conjunction containing exactly one occurrence (negated or unnegated) of each predicate letter of the language. Call these strongest statements *state descriptions*.

An *inductive logic* for a language is a specification, for each pair of statements $\langle p, q \rangle$ of the language, a unique probability value, or degree of confirmation $c(p, q)$. To achieve this, begin by defining a probability measure $m(-)$ over the state descriptions. Every sentence h of a given language is equivalent to a disjunction of (mutually exclusive) state descriptions, and its *a priori* probability $m(h)$ is thus determined. m in turn will induce a confirmation function $c(-,-)$ according to the conditional probability formula:

$$c(h, e) = \frac{m(h \& e)}{m(e)}$$

There are obviously infinitely many candidates for such an m, and hence c, even for very simple languages. However, Carnap favors one particular measure, which he calls 'm*'. He argues that the only thing that significantly distinguishes individuals from one another is some qualitative difference, not just a difference in labeling. Define a *structure description* as a maximal set of state descriptions, each of which can be obtained from another by some permutation of the individual names. m* assigns numbers to the state descriptions as follows: first, every structure description is assigned an equal measure; then, each state description belonging to a given structure description is assigned an equal share of the measure assigned to the structure description. From this, one can then define

$$c^*(h, e) = \frac{m^*(h \& e)}{m^*(e)}$$

m* gives greater weight to homogenous state descriptions than to heterogeneous ones, thus 'rewarding' uniformity among the individuals in accordance with putatively reasonable inductive practice. It can be shown that c* allows inductive learning from experience. However, even insisting that an acceptable confirmation function must allow such learning, there are still infinitely many candidates; there is no reason yet to think that c* is the right choice. Carnap realizes that there is some arbitrariness here, but nevertheless regards c* as the proper function for inductive logic – he thinks it stands out for being simple and natural.

He later generalizes his confirmation function to a continuum of confirmation functions c_λ, each of which gives the weighted average (weighted according to a positive real number λ) of an *a priori* value of the probability in question, and that calculated in the light of evidence. Define a *family* of predicates to be a set of predicates such that, for each individual, exactly one member of the set applies. Carnap goes on to explore first-order languages containing a finite number of families of predicates. Carnap (1963) considers the special case of a language containing only one-place predicates. He lays down a host of axioms concerning the confirmation function c, including those induced by the probability calculus itself, various axioms of symmetry (for example, that c(*h*, *e*) remains unchanged under permutations of individuals, and of predicates of any family), and axioms that guarantee undogmatic inductive learning, and long-run convergence to relative frequencies. They imply that, for a family $\{P_n\}$, $n = 1, \ldots, k$, $k > 2$:

$$c_\lambda(\text{individual } s+1 \text{ is } P_j, s_j \text{ of the first } s \text{ individuals are } P_j) = \frac{s_j + \lambda/k}{s+\lambda}$$

where λ is a positive real number. The higher the value of λ is, the less impact evidence has.

The problem remains: what is the correct setting of λ? And problems remain even once one has fixed the value of λ. It turns out that a universal statement in an infinite universe always receives zero confirmation, no matter what the (finite) evidence. Many find this counterintuitive, since laws of nature with infinitely many instances can apparently be confirmed. Hintikka (1965) provides a system of confirmation that avoids this problem.

Recalling an objection to the classical interpretation, the various axioms of symmetry are hardly mere truths of logic. More seriously, one cannot impose further symmetry constraints that are seemingly just as plausible as Carnap's, on pain of inconsistency (Fine, 1973, p. 202). Moreover, Goodman's 'grue' paradox apparently teaches one that some symmetries are better than others, and that inductive logic must be sensitive to the meanings of predicates, strongly suggesting that a purely syntactic approach such as Carnap's is doomed. One could try to specify a canonical language, free of such monstrosities as 'grue', to which such syntactic rules might apply. But traditional logic finds no need for such a procedure, sharpening the suspicion that Carnap's program is *not* merely that of extending the boundaries of logic. Scott and Krauss (1966) use model theory in their formulation of logical probability for richer and more realistic languages than Carnap's. Still, finding a canonical language seems to many to be a pipe dream, at least if one wants to analyze the 'logical probability' of any argument of real interest – either in science, or in everyday life.

16.3.3. Frequency interpretations

The guiding empiricist idea of frequency interpretations, which originated with Venn, is that an event's probability is the *relative frequency* of events of that type within a suitably chosen reference class. The probability that a given coin lands 'heads', for example, might be identified with the relative frequency of 'heads' outcomes in the class of all tosses of that coin. But there is an immediate problem: observed relative frequencies can apparently come apart from true probabilities, as when a fair coin that is tossed ten times happens to land heads every time. Von Mises (1957) offers a more sophisticated formulation based on the notion of a *collective*, rendered precise by Church: a hypothetical infinite sequence of 'attributes' (possible outcomes) of a specified experiment, for which the limiting relative frequency of any attribute exists, and is the same in any recursively specified subsequence. The probability of an attribute A, relative to a collective ω, is then defined as the limiting relative frequency of A in ω. Limiting relative frequencies violate countable additivity, and the domain of definition of limiting relative frequency is not even a field. Thus it does not genuinely provide an interpretation of Kolmogorov's probability calculus.

As well as giving a (hypothetical) limiting relative frequency interpretation of probabilities of events, Reichenbach (1949) gives an interpretation in terms of truth frequencies: the probability of truth of a statement of a certain type is the limiting relative frequency of statements of that type being true in a specified reference class of statements. Out of this definition, he constructs a probability logic with a continuum of truth values, corresponding to the various possible probabilities.

A notorious problem for any version of frequentism is the so-called *problem of the single case*: sometimes non-trivial probabilities are attributed to results of experiments that occur only once, and that indeed may do so of necessity. Moreover, frequentist probabilities are always relativized to a reference class, which needs to be fixed in a way that does not appeal to probability; but most events belong to *many* 'natural' reference classes, which need not agree on the required relative frequency. In this sense, there may be no such thing as *the* probability of a given event – the infamous *reference class problem*. The move to hypothetical infinite sequences of trials creates its own problems: There is apparently no fact of the matter as to what such a hypothetical sequence would be, nor even what its limiting relative frequency for a given attribute would be, nor indeed whether that limit is even defined; and the limiting relative frequency can be changed to any value one wants by suitably permuting the order of trials. In any case, the empiricist intuition that facts about probabilities are simply facts about patterns in the actual phenomena has been jettisoned. Still more sophisticated accounts, frequentist in spirit, uphold this intuition – see, for instance, Lewis (1994). Such accounts sacrifice another intuition: that it is built into the very concept of 'chanciness' that fixing what actually happens does *not* fix the probabilities.

16.3.4. *Propensity interpretations*

Attempts to locate probabilities 'in the world' are also made by variants of the *propensity* interpretation, championed by such authors as Popper (1959b), Mellor (1971) and Giere (1973). Probability is thought of as a physical propensity, or disposition, or tendency of a given type of physical situation to yield an outcome of a certain kind, or to yield a long-run relative frequency of such an outcome. This view is explicitly intended to make sense of single-case probabilities, such as 'the probability that this radium atom decays in 1500 years is $\frac{1}{2}$.' According to Popper, a probability p of an outcome of a certain type is a propensity of a repeatable experiment to produce outcomes of that type with limiting relative frequency p. With its heavy reliance on limiting relative frequency, this position risks collapsing into von Mises-style frequentism. It seems moreover not to be a genuine interpretation of the probability calculus at all, for the same reasons that limiting relative frequentism is not. Giere, on the other hand, explicitly allows single-case propensities, with no mention of frequencies: probability is just a propensity of a repeatable experimental set-up to produce sequences of outcomes. This, however, creates the opposite problem to Popper's: How, then, does one achieve the desired connection between probabilities and frequencies? Indeed, it is not clear why the assignments of such propensities should obey the probability calculus at all. For reasons such as these, propensity accounts have been criticized for being unacceptably vague.

16.3.5. *The subjectivist interpretation (subjective Bayesianism)*

Degrees of belief Subjectivism is the doctrine that probabilities can be regarded as degrees of belief, sometimes called *credences*. It is often called 'Bayesianism' thanks to the important role that Bayes' theorem typically plays in the subjectivist's calculations of probabilities, although the theorem itself is neutral regarding interpretation. Unlike the logical interpretation (at least as Carnap originally conceived it), subjectivism allows that different agents with the very same evidence can rationally give different probabilities to the same hypothesis.

But what is a degree of belief? A standard analysis invokes betting behavior: an agent's degree of belief in A is p iff the agent is prepared to pay up to p units for a bet that pays 1 unit if A, 0 if not A (de Finetti, 1980). It is assumed that the agent is also prepared to sell that bet for p units. Thus, here is an operational definition of subjective probability, and indeed it inherits some of the difficulties of operationalism in general, and of behaviorism in particular. For example, the agent may have reason to misrepresent her true opinion. Moreover, as Ramsey (1980 [1931]) points out, the proposal of the bet may itself alter her state of opinion; and the agent might have an eagerness or reluctance to bet. These problems are avoided by identifying the agent's degree of belief in a proposition with the betting price she regards as fair, whether or not the agent enters into such a bet (Howson and Urbach, 1993). Still, the fair price of a bet on A appears to measure not the agent's probability that A will be the case, but rather the agent's probability that A will be the case *and* that the prize will be paid, which may be rather less – for example, if A is unverifiable. Some think that this commits proponents of the betting interpretation to an underlying intuitionistic logic.

If no restriction is placed on who the agent is, one would not have an interpretation of the probability calculus at all, for there would be no guarantee that the agent's degrees of belief would conform to it. Human agents sometimes violate the probability calculus in alarming ways (Kahneman et al., 1982), and indeed conforming all our degrees of belief to the probability calculus is surely an impossible standard. However, if attention is restricted to ideally rational agents, the claim that degrees of belief are at least finitely additive probabilities becomes more plausible (much as deductive consistency of one's beliefs might be an impossible standard but a reasonable ideal).

So-called *Dutch Book* arguments provide one important line of justification of this claim. A Dutch Book is a series of bets, each of which the agent regards as fair, but which collectively guarantee the agent's loss. De Finetti (1980) proves that if one's degrees of belief are not finitely additive probabilities, then one is susceptible to a Dutch Book. Equally important, and often neglected, is Kemeny's (1955) converse theorem: If an agent's degrees of belief are finitely additive probabilities, then no Dutch Book can be made against the agent.

A related defence of the probability axioms comes from *utility theory*. Ramsey (1980 [1931]) derives both probabilities and utilities (desirabilities) from rational preferences. Specifically, given various assumptions about the richness of the preference space, and certain 'consistency' assumptions, he shows how to define a real-valued utility function of the outcomes – in fact, various such functions will represent the agent's preferences. It turns out that ratios of utility-differences are invariant, the same whichever representative utility function is chosen. This fact allows Ramsey to define degrees of belief as ratios of such differences, and to show that they are finitely additive probabilities. However, it is dubious that *consistency* requires one to have a set of preferences as rich as Ramsey requires. This places strain on Ramsey's claim to assimilate probability theory to logic. However, Howson (1997) argues that a betting interpretation of probability underpins a soundness and completeness proof of the probability axioms, thus supporting the claim that the Bayesian theory does provide a logic of consistent belief.

Savage (1954) likewise derives probabilities and utilities from preferences among options that are constrained by certain putative 'consistency' principles. Jeffrey (1983) refines the method further, giving a 'logic of decision' according to which rational choice maximizes *expected utility*, a certain probability-weighted average of utilities.

Updating probability Suppose that an agent's degrees of belief are initially represented by a probability function $P_{initial}(-)$, and that the agent becomes certain of a piece of evidence E. What should be the agent's new probability function P_{new}? To avoid any gratuitous changes in the agent's degrees of belief that were not prompted by the evidence, P_{new} should be the minimal revision of $P_{initial}$ subject to the constraint that $P_{new}(E) = 1$. The favored updating rule among Bayesians is *conditionalization*: P_{new} is derived from $P_{initial}$ by taking probabilities conditional on E, according to the schema:

(*Conditionalization*) $P_{new}(A) = P_{initial}(A \mid E)$ (provided $P_{initial}(E) > 0$)

Lewis (1998) gives a 'diachronic' Dutch Book argument for conditionalization: if one's updating is rule-governed, one is subject to a Dutch Book (at the hands of a bookie who knows the rule employed) if one does not conditionalize. Equally important is the converse theorem: if one does conditionalize, one cannot be Dutch Booked (Skyrms, 1987a).

Now suppose that, as the result of some experience, the agent's degrees of belief across a countable partition $\{E_1, E_2, \ldots\}$ change to $\{P_{new}(E_1), P_{new}(E_2), \ldots\}$, where none of these values need be 1 or 0. The rule of *Jeffrey conditionalization*, or *probability kinematics*, relates the agent's new probability function to the initial one according to

$$P_{new}(A) = \sum_i P_{initial}(A \mid E_i) P_{new}(E_i)$$

(If the probabilities are only finitely additive, then the partition and sum must be finite.) Conditionalization can be thought of as the special case of Jeffrey conditionalization in which $P(E_i) = 1$ for some i. Jeffrey conditionalization is supported by a Dutch Book argument due to Armendt (1980); it is also the rule that, subject to the constraints on the partition, minimizes a measure of 'distance' in function space between the initial and new probability functions, called 'cross-entropy' (Diaconis and Zabell, 1982).

Orthodox Bayesianism can now be characterized by the following maxims:

B1   The rational agent's 'prior' (initial) probabilities conform to the probability calculus.

B2   The rational agent's probabilities update by the rule of (Jeffrey) conditionalization.

B3   There are no further constraints on the rational agent.

Some critics reject orthodox Bayesianism's radical permissiveness regarding prior probabilities. A standard defense – e.g., Howson and Urbach (1993), and Savage (1954) – appeals to famous 'convergence-to-truth,' and 'merger-of-opinion' results. Roughly, their content is that with probability 1, in the long run, the effect of choosing one prior rather than another is washed out. Successive conditionalizations on the evidence will make a given agent eventually converge to the truth, and thus, initially discrepant agents eventually come to agree with each other (assuming that the priors do not give probability 0 to the truth, and that the stream of incoming evidence is sufficiently rich). In an important sense, at least this much inductive logic is implicit in the probability calculus.

But Bayesianism is a theme that admits of many variations.

Further constraints on subjective probabilities   Against (B3), some less permissive Bayesians also require that a rational agent's probabilities be *regular*, or *strictly coherent*: if $P(A) = 1$, then A is a tautology. Regularity is the converse of axiom II (page 363), again linking probability and logic. It is meant to guard against the sort of dogmatism that no course of learning by (Jeffrey) conditionalization could cure.

Van Fraassen (1995) suggests a further constraint on rational opinion called *reflection*, involving credences about one's own future credences. Here is one formulation:

(*Reflection*) $P_t(A \mid P_{t+\Delta}(A) = x) = x$ $(\Delta > 0)$

where P_t is the agent's probability function at time t. The idea is that when all is well, a certain sort of epistemic integrity requires one to regard one's future opinions as being trustworthy, having arisen as the result of a rational process of learning. A more general version of reflection is presented by Goldstein (1983).

Lewis (1986c [1980]) offers a principle that links objective chance and rational credence:

(*Principal Principle*) $P_t(A \mid ch_t(A) = x \ \& \ E) = x$

where $ch_t(A)$ is the objective chance of A at time t, and E is any information that is 'admissible' at time t (roughly, gives no evidence about the actual truth value of A). For example, the principle says: given that this coin is believed to be fair, and thus has a chance of $\frac{1}{2}$ at the moment of landing heads at the next toss, one should assign credence $\frac{1}{2}$ to that outcome. The principle can, on the other hand, be thought of as giving an implicit characterization of chance as a theoretical property whose distinctive role is to constrain rational credences in just this way. See Lewis (1994), Hall (1994b), and Thau (1994) for refinements of the principle.

Finally, there have been various proposals for resuscitating symmetry constraints on priors, in the spirit of the classical and logical interpretations. More sophisticated versions of the principle of indifference have been explored by Jaynes (1968) and Paris and Vencovská (1997). Their guiding idea is to maximize the probability function's *entropy*, which for an assignment of positive probabilities $p_1, \ldots, p_n$ to n worlds equals $-\Sigma_i \, p_i \log(p_i)$.

Orthodox Bayesianism has also been denounced for being overly demanding: its requirements of sharp probability assignments to all propositions, logical omniscience, and so on have been regarded by some as unreasonable idealizations. This motivates various relaxations of tenets (B1) and (B2) above. (B2) might be weakened to allow other rules for the updating of probabilities besides conditionalization – for example, revision to the probability function that maximizes entropy, subject to the relevant constraints (Jaynes, 1968; Skyrms, 1987a). And some Bayesians drop the requirement that probability updating be rule-governed altogether, e.g., Earman (1992).

The relaxation of (B1) is a large topic, and it motivates some non-Kolmogorovian theories of probability.

16.4. Non-Kolmogorovian Theories of Probability

A number of authors would abandon the search for an adequate interpretation of Kolmogorov's probability calculus, since they abandon some part of his axiomatization.

Abandoning the sigma field sub-structure Fine (1973) argues that requiring the domain of the probability function to be a sigma field is overly restrictive. For example, one might have limited census data on race and gender that gives good information concerning the probability P(M) that a randomly chosen person is male, and the probability P(B) that such a person is black, without giving any information about the probability P(M ∩ B) that such a person is both male and black.

Abandoning sharp probabilities Each Kolmogorovian probability is a single number. But suppose that an agent's state of opinion does not determine a single probability function, but rather is consistent with a multiplicity of such functions. In that case, one might represent the agent's opinion as the *set* of all these functions; see, for example, Jeffrey (1992) and Levi (1980). Each function in this set corresponds to a way of precisifying an agent's opinion in a legitimate way. This approach will typically coincide with interval-valued probability assignments, but it need not. Koopman (1980 [1940]) offers axioms for 'upper' and 'lower' probabilities which may be thought of as the endpoints of such intervals. See also Walley (1991) for an extensive treatment of imprecise probabilities.

Abandoning numerical probabilities altogether In contrast to the 'quantitative' probabilities so far assumed, Fine (1973) sympathetically canvases various theories of comparative probability, exemplified by statements of the form '*A* is at least as probable as *B*' (*A* ≿ *B*). He offers axioms governing '≿,' and explores the conditions under which comparative probability can be given a representation in terms of Kolmogorovian probabilities.

Negative and complex-valued probabilities More radically, physicists such as Dirac, Wigner, and Feynman have countenanced *negative* probabilities. Feynman, for instance, suggests that a particle diffusing in one dimension in a rod has a probability of being at a given position and time that is given by a quantity that takes negative values. Depending on how one interprets probability, however, one may instead want to say that this function bears certain analogies to a probability function, but when it goes negative the analogy breaks down. Cox allows probabilities to take values among the complex numbers in his theory of stochastic processes having discrete states in continuous time. See Mückenheim (1986) for references.

Abandoning the normalization axiom It might seem entirely conventional that the maximal value a probability function can take is 1. However, it has some non-trivial consequences. Coupled with the other axioms, it guarantees that a probability function takes at least two distinct values, whereas setting P(Ω) = 0 would not. More significantly, it is non-trivial that there *is* a maximal value. Other measures, such as length or volume, are not so bounded. Indeed, Renyi (1970) drops the normalization assumption altogether, allowing probabilities to attain the 'value' ∞.

Some authors would loosen the rein that classical logic has on probability, allowing logical/necessary truths to be assigned probability less than one – perhaps because logical or mathematical conjectures may be more or less well confirmed; see, for example, Polya (1968). Furthermore, axiom II (page 363) makes reference to the notion of 'tautology,' with classical logic implicitly assumed. Proponents of non-classical logics may wish to employ instead their favorite 'deviant' notion of 'tautology' (perhaps requiring corresponding adjustments elsewhere in the axiomatization). Thus, *constructivist* theories ground probability theory in intuitionistic logic.

Infinitesimal probabilities Kolmogorov's probability functions are real-valued. A number of philosophers – e.g., Lewis, 1986c [1980], and Skyrms, 1980 – drop this assumption, allowing probabilities to take values from the real numbers of a *non-standard model* of analysis – see Skyrms (1980, App. 4) for the construction of such a model. In particular, they allow probabilities to be *infinitesimal*: positive, but smaller than every (standard) real number. Various non-empty propositions in infinite probability spaces that would ordinarily receive probability zero according to standard probability theory, and thus essentially treated as impossible, may now be assigned positive probability. (Consider selecting at random a point from the [0, 1] interval.) In uncountable spaces, regular probability functions cannot avoid taking infinitesimal values.

Abandoning countable additivity Kolmogorov's most controversial axiom is undoubtedly *continuity* – i.e., the 'infinite part' of countable additivity. He regarded it as an idealization that finessed the mathematics, but that had no empirical meaning. As has been seen, according to the classical, frequency, and certain propensity interpretations, probabilities violate countable additivity. De Finetti (1972) marshals a battery of arguments against it. Here is a representative one: Countable additivity requires one to assign an extremely biased distribution to a denumerable partition of events. Indeed, for any $\varepsilon > 0$, however small, there will be a finite number of events that have a combined probability of at least $1 - \varepsilon$, and thus the lion's share of all the probability.

Abandoning finite additivity Various theories of probability that give up even finite additivity have been proposed – so-called *non-additive* probability theories.

Dempster–Shafer theory begins with a *frame of discernment* Ω, a partition of hypotheses. To each subset of Ω, assign a 'mass' between 0 and 1 inclusive; all the masses sum to 1. Then define a *belief function* Bel(A) by the rule: for each subset A of Ω, Bel(A) is the sum of the masses of the subsets of A. Shafer (1981) gives this interpretation: Suppose that the agent will find out for certain some proposition on Ω. Then Bel(A) is the agent's degree of belief that he will find out A. Bel(A) + Bel($-A$) need not equal 1; indeed, Bel(A) and Bel($-A$) are functionally independent of each other. Belief functions have many of the same formal properties as Koopman's lower probabilities. Mongin (1994) shows that there are important links between epistemic modal logics and Dempster–Shafer theory.

So-called 'Baconian probabilities' represent another non-additive departure from the probability calculus. The Baconian probability of a conjunction is equal to the minimum of the probabilities of the conjuncts. Such 'probabilities' are formally similar to membership functions in fuzzy logic. Cohen (1977) regards them as appropriate for measuring inductive support, and for assessing evidence in a court of law.

For further non-additive probability theories, see (among others) Ghirardato's modeling of ambiguity aversion, Shackle's potential surprise functions, Dubois and Prade's theory of fuzzy probabilities, Schmeidler's and Wakker's respective theories of expected utility, and Spohn's theory of non-probabilistic belief functions. Ghirardato (1993) and Howson (1995) have references and more discussion.

Conditional probability as primitive According to each of the interpretations of probability that have been discussed, probability statements are always at least tacitly relativized. On the classical interpretation, they are relativized to the set of possibilities under consideration; on the logical interpretation, to an evidence statement; on the frequency interpretations, to a reference class; on the propensity interpretation, to a chance set-up; on the subjective interpretation, to a subject (who may have certain background knowledge) at a time. Perhaps, then, it is *conditional* probability that is the more fundamental notion.

Rather than axiomatizing unconditional probability, and later defining conditional probability therefrom, Popper (1959a) and Renyi (1970) take conditional probability as primitive, and axiomatize it directly. Popper's system is more familiar to philosophers. His primitives are:

(i) Ω, the universal set;
(ii)   a binary numerical function p(–,–) of the elements of Ω;
(iii) a binary operation ab defined for each pair (a, b) of elements of Ω;
(iv)   a unary operation $\neg a$ defined for each element a of Ω.

Each of these concepts is introduced by a postulate (although the first actually plays no role in his theory):

Postulate 1   The number of elements in Ω is countable.

Postulate 2   If a and b are in Ω, then p(a, b) is a real number, and the following axioms apply:

A1   *Existence*   There are elements c and d in Ω such that p(a, b) $\neq$ p(c, d).

A2   *Substitutivity*   If p(a, c) = p(b, c) for all c in Ω, then p(d, a) = p(d, b) for all d in Ω.

A3   *Reflexivity*   p(a, a) = p(b, b).

Postulate 3   If a and b are in Ω, then ab is in Ω; and if c is also in Ω, then:

B2   *Monotony*   p(ab, c) $\leq$ p(a, c)

B2   *Multiplication*   p(ab, c) = p(a, bc)p(b, c)

Postulate 4 If a is in Ω, then $\neg a$ is in Ω; and if b is also in Ω, then:

C *Complementation* $p(a, b) + p(\neg a, b) = p(b, b)$, unless $p(b, b) = p(c, b)$ for all c in Ω.

Popper also adds a 'fifth postulate,' which may be thought of as giving the definition of absolute (unconditional) probability:

Postulate AP If a and b are in Ω, and if $p(b, c) \geq p(c, b)$ for all c in Ω, then $p(a) = p(a, b)$.

Here, b can be thought of as a tautology. Unconditional probability, then, is probability conditional on a tautology. Thus, Popper's axiomatization generalizes ordinary probability theory. A function $p(-,-)$ that satisfies the above axioms is called a *Popper function*.

An advantage of using Popper functions is that conditional probabilities of the form $p(a, b)$ can be defined, and can have intuitively correct values, even when b has absolute probability 0, rendering the usual conditional probability ratio formula inapplicable. For example, the probability that a randomly selected point from $[0, 1]$ is $\frac{1}{3}$, given $E =$ 'it is either $\frac{1}{3}$ or $\frac{2}{3}$', is plausibly equal to $\frac{1}{2}$, and a Popper function can yield this result; yet the probability of E is standardly taken to be 0. Popper functions also allow a natural generalization of updating by conditionalization, so that even items of evidence that were originally assigned probability 0 by an agent can be learned. McGee (1994) shows that, in an important sense, probability statements cast in terms of Popper functions and those cast in terms of nonstandard probability functions are inter-translatable.

16.5. Probabilistic Semantics and Probability Propagation

Various notions from standard semantics can be recovered by *probabilistic semantics*. The central idea is to define the logical concepts in terms of probabilistic ones. Alternative axiomatizations of probability will then give rise to alternative logics.

16.5.1. *Probabilistic semantics*

Call a statement A of a first-order language L *logically true in the probabilistic sense* if for all probability functions P, $P(A) = 1$. Where S is a set of statements of L, say that A is *logically entailed by S in the probabilistic sense* if, for all P, $P(A) = 1$ if $P(B) = 1$ for each member B of S. This sense of logical entailment is strongly sound and strongly complete: $S \vdash A$ iff A is logically entailed by S in the probabilistic sense. And taking S to be $\emptyset$, then $\vdash A$ iff A is logically true in the probabilistic sense. Popper functions also permit natural definitions of logical truth and logical entailment, with analogous soundness and completeness results (Kyburg, 1970, pp. 245 ff.).

Van Fraassen (1981) exploits (slightly differently axiomatized) primitive conditional probability functions in providing probabilistic semantics for intuitionistic propositional logic and classical quantifier logic. Probabilistic semantics have been supplied for first-order logic with and without identity, modal logic, and conditional logic. See Leblanc (1983) for a good general survey and for references. Van Fraassen (1983) offers such semantics for relevant logic; Pearl (1991) has a general discussion of probabilistic semantics for nonmonotonic logic.

Probabilistic semantics represent a limiting case of the idea that a valid argument is one in which it is not possible for the probabilities of all of the premises to be high, while the probability of the conclusion is not. More generally, what can be said about the propagation of probability from the premises to the conclusion of a valid argument?

16.5.2. Probability propagation: Adams' probability logic

If the premises of a valid argument are all certain, then so is the conclusion. Suppose, on the other hand, that the premises are not all certain, but probable to various degrees; can one then put bounds on the probability of the conclusion? Or suppose that one wants the probability of the conclusion of a given valid argument to be above a particular threshold; how probable, then, must the premises be? These questions are pressing, since in real-life arguments one typically is not certain of the premises, and it may be important to know how confidently one may hold their conclusions. Indeed, one knows from the lottery paradox that each premise in a valid argument can be almost certain, while the conclusion is certainly false. 'Probability logic' is the name that Adams (1998) gives to the formal study of such questions – the study of the transmission (or lack thereof) of probability through valid inferences. A sketch of his treatment is given here.

The hallmark of his probability logic is that traditional concerns with truth and falsehood of premises and conclusions are replaced with concerns about their probabilities. This, in turn, leads to the nonmonotonic nature of probability logic: a conclusion that is initially assigned high probability and hence accepted may later be retracted in the face of new evidence. Define the *uncertainty* $u(F)$ of a sentence by

$$u(F) = 1 - P(F)$$

Various important results in probability logic are more conveniently stated in terms of uncertainties rather than probabilities. For example:

Valid inference uncertainty theorem (VIUT) The uncertainty of the conclusion of a valid inference cannot exceed the sum of the uncertainties of the premises.

Hence, the uncertainty of the conclusion of a valid inference can only be large if the sum of the uncertainties of the premises is large – witness the lottery paradox, in which many small uncertainties in the premises accumulate to yield a maximally uncertain conclusion. In particular, if each premise has an uncertainty no greater than ε, then there must be at least $1/\varepsilon$ of them for the conclusion to have maximal uncertainty.

The VIUT gives a bound on the uncertainty of the conclusion. Under certain circumstances, the bound can be achieved. Call a premise of a valid inference *essential* if the inference that omits that premise but that is otherwise the same is invalid. We have:

> **Uncertainty bound attainment theorem** Suppose $F_1, \ldots, F_n \therefore F$ is valid, and let $u_1, \ldots, u_n$ be nonnegative, with $\Sigma u_i \leq 1$. If the premises are consistent and all essential, then there is an uncertainty function $u(-)$ such that $u(F_i) = u_i$ for $i = 1, \ldots, n$, and $u(F) = u_1 + \cdots + u_n$.

However, such 'worst case' uncertainties in a conclusion can be reduced by introducing redundancy among the premises from which it is derived. For it can further be shown that, given a valid inference with various premises, different subsets of which entail the conclusion, the conclusion's uncertainty cannot be greater than the total uncertainty of that subset with the smallest total uncertainty. Define a *minimal essential premise set* to be an essential premise set that has no proper subsets that are essential. Suppose that there is a valid inference with premises $F_1, \ldots, F_n$. The *degree of essentialness* of premise F_i, $e(F_i)$, is: $1/k$, where k is the cardinality of the smallest essential set of premises to which F_i belongs, if F_i belongs to some minimal essential set, and 0 otherwise. Intuitively, $e(F_i)$ is a measure of how much 'work' F_i does in a valid inference.

The VIUT can now be generalized:

> **Theorem** If $F_1, \ldots, F_n \therefore F$ is valid, then $u(F) \leq e(F_1)u(F_1) + \cdots + e(F_n)u(F_n)$.

One thus can lower the upper bound on $u(F)$ from that given by the VIUT.

Adams calls an inference *probabilistically valid* iff, for any $\varepsilon > 0$, there exists a $\delta > 0$ such that, under any probability assignment according to which each of the premises has probability greater than $1 - \delta$, the conclusion has probability at least $1 - \varepsilon$. A linchpin of his account of probabilistic validity is his treatment of conditionals. According to him, a conditional has no truth value, and hence sense cannot be made of the probability of its *truth*. Yet conditionals can clearly figure either as premises or conclusions of arguments, and one still wants to be able to assess these arguments. How, then, does one determine the probabilities of conditionals? This leads to another important point of cross-fertilization between probability and logic.

16.6. Probabilities of Conditionals

Probability and logic are intimately intertwined in the study of probabilities of conditionals. In the endeavor to furnish a logical analysis of natural language, the conditional has proved to be somewhat recalcitrant, and the subject of considerable controversy. [See chapter 17.] Meanwhile, the notion of 'conditionality' is seemingly well understood in probability theory, and taken by most to be enshrined in the usual ratio formula for conditional probability. Thus, fecund research programs have been founded on both promoting and parrying a certain marriage between the logic of conditionals and probability theory: the hypothesis that probabilities of conditionals *are* conditional probabilities. More precisely, the hypothesis is that some suitably quantified and qualified version of the following equation holds:

(PCCP) $P(A \rightarrow B) = P(B \mid A)$ for all A, B in the domain of P, with $P(A) > 0$

where '$\rightarrow$' is a conditional connective.

The best known presentations of this hypothesis are due to Stalnaker (1970) and Adams (1975). Stalnaker hoped that a suitable version of it would serve as a criterion of adequacy for a truth-conditional account of the conditional. He explored the conditions under which it would be reasonable for a rational agent, with subjective probability function P, to believe a conditional $A \rightarrow B$. By identifying the probability of $A \rightarrow B$ with $P(B \mid A)$, Stalnaker was able to put constraints on the truth conditions of '$\rightarrow$' (for example, the upholding of conditional excluded middle) that supported his preferred C2 logic. While Adams eschewed any truth-conditional account of the conditional, he was happy to speak of the probability of a conditional, equating it to the corresponding conditional probability. This allowed him to extend his notion of probabilistic validity to arguments that contain conditionals – arguments that in his view lie outside the scope of the traditional account of validity couched in terms of truth values. He argued that the resulting scheme respects intuitions about which inferences are reasonable, and which not.

With these motivations in mind, and for their independent interest, there are four salient ways of rendering precise the hypothesis that probabilities of conditionals are conditional probabilities:

Universal version   There is some $\rightarrow$ such that for all P, PCCP holds.

Rational Probability Function version   There is some $\rightarrow$ such that for all rational subjective probability functions P, PCCP holds.

Universal Tailoring version   For each P there is some $\rightarrow$ such that PCCP holds.

Rational Probability Function Tailoring version   For each rational subjective probability function P, there is some $\rightarrow$ such that PCCP holds.

If any of these versions can be sustained, then important links between logic and probability theory will have been established, just as Stalnaker and Adams hoped. Probability theory would be a source of insight into the formal structure of conditionals; and probability theory, in turn, would be enriched, since one could characterize more fully what the usual conditional probability ratio means, and what its use is.

There is now a host of results – mostly negative – concerning PCCP. Some preliminary definitions will assist in stating some of the most important ones. If PCCP holds (for a given $\rightarrow$ and P) then $\rightarrow$ is said to be a *PCCP-conditional for* P, and P is said to be a *PCCP-function for* →. If PCCP holds for each member P of a class of probability functions $\wp$, then → is said to be a *PCCP-conditional for* $\wp$. A pair of probability functions P and P′ are *orthogonal* if, for some A, $P(A) = 1$ but $P'(A) = 0$. Call a proposition A a *P-atom* iff $P(A) > 0$ and, for all X, either $P(AX) = P(A)$ or $P(AX) = 0$. Finally, a probability function is called *trivial* if it has at most four different values.

The negative results are 'triviality results': only trivial probability functions can sustain PCCP, given certain assumptions. The earliest and most famous results are due to Lewis (1986a [1976]), which he later strengthens (1986b). Their upshot is that there is no PCCP-conditional for any class of probability functions closed under conditionalizing (restricted to the propositions in a single finite partition), or under Jeffrey conditionalizing, unless the class consists entirely of trivial functions. These results refute the Universal version of the hypothesis. They also spell bad news for the Rational Probability Function version, since rationality surely permits having a non-trivial probability function and updating by (Jeffrey) conditionalizing. This version receives its death blow from a result by Hall (1994a) that significantly strengthens Lewis' results:

> *Orthogonality result* Any two non-trivial PCCP-functions for a given → with the same domain are orthogonal.

It follows from this that the Rational Probability Function version is true only if any two rational agents' probability functions are orthogonal if distinct – which is absurd.

So far, the 'tailoring' versions remain unscathed. The Universal Tailoring version is refuted by the following result due to Hájek (1989, here slightly strengthened):

> *Finite probability functions result* Any non-trivial probability function with finite range has no PCCP-conditional.

This result also casts serious doubt on the Rational Probability Tailoring version, for it is hard to see why rationality requires one to have a probability function with infinite range. If one makes a minimal assumption about the logic of the '→,' matters are still worse thanks to another result of Hall's (1994a):

> *No Atoms Result* Given $(\Omega, \mathcal{F}, P)$, suppose that PCCP holds for P and a → that obeys *modus ponens*; then $(\Omega, \mathcal{F}, P)$ does not contain a P-atom, unless P is trivial.

It follows, on pain of triviality, that the range of P, and hence Ω and $\mathcal{F}$, are uncountable. All the more, it is hard to see how rationality requires this of an agent's probability space.

It seems, then, that all four versions of the hypothesis so far considered are untenable. For all that has been said so far, though, a 'tailoring' version restricted to uncountable probability spaces might still survive. Indeed, here there is a positive result due to van Fraassen (1976). Suppose that → distributes over ∩ and ∪, obeys *modus ponens* and centering, and the principle that $A \rightarrow A = \Omega$. Such an → conforms to the logic CE. Van Fraassen shows:

CE tenability result Any probability space can be extended to one for which PCCP holds, with an → that conforms to CE.

Of course, the larger space for which PCCP holds is uncountable. He also shows that → can have still more logical structure, while supporting PCCP, provided one restricts the admissible iterations of → appropriately.

A similar strategy of restriction protects Adams' version of the hypothesis from the negative results. He applies a variant of PCCP to unembedded conditionals of the form $A \rightarrow B$, where A and B are conditional-free. More precisely, he proposes:

Adams' Thesis (AT) For an unembedded conditional $A \rightarrow B$

$$P(A \rightarrow B) = \begin{cases} P(B \mid A) & \text{if } P(A) > 0 \\ 1 & \text{otherwise} \end{cases}$$

Since Adams does not allow the assignment of probabilities to Boolean compounds of conditionals, thus violating the closure assumptions of the probability calculus, 'P' is not strictly speaking a probability function (and thus the negative results, which presuppose that it is, do not apply). McGee (1994) extends Adams' theory to certain more complicated compounds of conditionals. He later refines AT, using Popper functions to give a more nuanced treatment of conditionals with antecedents of probability 0. Finally, Stalnaker and Jeffrey (1994) offer an account of the conditional as a random variable. They recover an analogue of AT, with expectations replacing probabilities, and generalize it to encompass iterations and Boolean compounds of conditionals.

As the recency of much of this literature indicates, this is still a flourishing field of research. The same can be said for virtually all of the points of contact between probability and logic that have been surveyed here.

Suggested further reading

Skyrms (1999) is an excellent introduction to the philosophy of probability. Von Plato (1994) is more technically demanding and more historically oriented, with an extensive bibliography that has references to many landmarks in the development of probability theory this century. Fine (1973) is still a highly sophisticated survey of and contribution to various foundational issues in probability. Billingsley (1995) and Feller (1968) are classic textbooks on the mathematical theory of probability. Mückenheim (1986) surveys the literature on 'extended probabilities' that take values outside the real interval [0, 1]. Eells and Skyrms (1994) is a fine collection of articles on probabilities of conditionals. Fenstad (1980) discusses further connections between probability and logic, emphasizing probability functions defined on formal languages, randomness and recursion theory, and non-standard methods. A vast bibliography of the literature on probability and induction pre-1970 can be found in Kyburg (1970). Also useful for references before 1967 is the bibliography for "Probability" in the *Encyclopedia of Philosophy*. Earman (1992) and Howson and Urbach (1993) have more recent bibliographies, and give detailed presentations of the Bayesian program.[3]

Notes

1 Lebesgue's theory of measure and integration allows a highly sophisticated treatment of various further concepts in probability theory – random variable, expectation, martingale, and so on – all based ultimately on the characterization of the probability of an event as the measure of a set. Important limit theorems, such as the laws of large numbers and the central limit theorem, are beyond the scope of this chapter. The interested reader is directed to references in the suggested further reading.

2 Space limitations preclude discussing various other important approaches, including Dawid's (1992) prequential theory; Fisher's (1973) fiducial probability, explored further by Fisher, Kyburg (1974) and Seidenfeld (1992), those based on fuzzy logic, and those based on complexity theory.

3 This article was written mostly at Cambridge University, and I am grateful to the Philosophy Department and to Wolfson College for the hospitality I was shown there. I also especially thank Jeremy Butterfield, Alex Byrne, Tim Childers, Haim Gaifman, Matthias Hild, Christopher Hitchcock, Colin Howson, Paul Jeffries, Isaac Levi, Vann McGee, Teddy Seidenfeld, Brian Skyrms, Brian Weatherson and Jim Woodward for their very helpful comments.

References

Adams, E. 1975: *The Logic of Conditionals*, (D. Reidel, Dordrecht).

Adams, E. 1998: *A Primer of Probability Logic*, (CSLI, Stanford University, Stanford, California).

Armendt, B. 1980: "Is There a Dutch Book Argument for Probability Kinematics?" *Philosophy of Science*, 47, 583–9.

Billingsley, P. 1995: *Probability and Measure*, 3rd edn., (John Wiley & Sons, New York).

Carnap, R. 1950: *Logical Foundations of Probability*, (University of Chicago Press, Chicago).

Carnap, R. 1963: "Replies and Systematic Expositions," in *The Philosophy of Rudolf Carnap*, P. A. Schilpp, ed., (Open Court, La Salle, Illinois), 966–98.

Cohen, L. J. 1977: *The Probable and the Provable*, (Clarendon Press, Oxford).

Dawid, A. P. 1992: "Prequential Analysis, Stochastic Complexity and Bayesian Inference," in *Bayesian Statistics*, Vol. 4, J. M. Bernardo et al., eds., (Oxford University Press, Oxford), 109–25.

de Finetti, B. 1972: *Probability, Induction and Statistics*, (John Wiley & Sons, London).

de Finetti, B. 1980: "Foresight: Its Logical Laws, Its Subjective Sources," translated in Kyburg and Smokler (1980, 53–118).

Diaconis, P. and Zabell, S. L. 1982: "Updating Subjective Probability," *Journal of the American Statistical Association*, 77, 822–30.

Earman, J. 1992: *Bayes or Bust? A Critical Examination of Bayesian Confirmation Theory*, (MIT Press, Cambridge, MA).

Eells, E. and Skyrms, B. (eds.) 1994: *Probability and Conditionals*, (Cambridge University Press, Cambridge).

Feller, W. 1968: *An Introduction to Probability Theory and Its Applications*, (John Wiley & Sons, New York).

Fenstad, J. E. 1980: "Logic and Probability," in *Modern Logic – A Survey*, E. Agazzi, ed., (D. Reidel, Dordrecht), 223–33.

Fine, T. 1973: *Theories of Probability*, (Academic Press, New York).

Fisher, R. A. 1973: *Statistical Methods and Scientific Inference*, 3rd edn., (Hafner, NY).

Ghirardato, P. 1993: "Non-Additive Measures of Uncertainty: A Survey of Some Recent Developments in Decision Theory," *Rivista Internazionale di Scienze Economiche e Commerciali*, 40, 253–76.

Giere, R. N. 1973: "Objective Single-Case Probabilities and the Foundations of Statistics," in P. Suppes et al., eds., *Logic, Methodology and Philosophy of Science* IV, (North-Holland, New York), 467–83.

Goldstein, M. 1983: "The Prevision of a Prevision," *Journal of the American Statistical Assocociation*, 77, 822–30.

Hájek, A. 1989: "Probabilities of Conditionals – Revisited," *Journal of Philosophical Logic* 18, 423–8.

Hájek, A. 2001: "What Conditional Probability Could Not Be," *Synthese*, forthcoming.

Hall, N. 1994a: "Back in the CCCP," in Eells and Skyrms (1994, 149–60).

Hall, N. 1994b: "Correcting the Guide to Objective Chance," *Mind*, 103, 505–517.

Hintikka, J. 1965: "A Two-Dimensional Continuum of Inductive Methods," in *Aspects of Inductive Logic*, J. Hintikka and P. Suppes, eds., (North-Holland, Amsterdam), 113–32.

Howson, C. 1995: "Theories of Probability," *British Journal of Philosophy of Science*, 46, 1–32.

Howson, C. 1997: "Logic and Probability," *British Journal of Philosophy of Science*, 48, 517–31.

Howson, C. and Urbach, P. 1993: *Scientific Reasoning: The Bayesian Approach*, 2nd edn., (Open Court, Chicago).

Jaynes, E. T. 1968: "Prior Probabilities," *Institute of Electrical and Electronic Engineers Transactions on Systems Science and Cybernetics*, SSC-4, 227–41.

Jeffrey, R. 1983: *The Logic of Decision*, 2nd edn., (University of Chicago Press, Chicago).

Jeffrey, R. 1992: *Probability and the Art of Judgment*, (Cambridge University Press, Cambridge).

Jeffreys, H. 1939: *Theory of Probability*, (Oxford University Press, Oxford). 3rd edn. printed in 1961.

Johnson, W. E. 1932: "Probability: The Deductive and Inductive Problems," *Mind*, 49, 409–23.

Kahneman, D., Slovic, P. and Tversky, A. (eds.) 1982: *Judgment Under Uncertainty: Heuristics and Biases*, (Cambridge University Press, Cambridge).

Kemeny, J. G. 1955: "Fair Bets and Inductive Probabilities," *Journal of Symbolic Logic*, 20, 263–73.

Keynes, J. M. 1921: *Treatise on Probability*, (Macmillan, London). Reprinted in 1962 by Harper and Row, NY.

Kolmogorov, A. N. 1950: "Grundbegriffe der Wahrscheinlichkeitrechnung," *Ergebnisse Der Mathematik*, 2, 3, Berlin, 1933; transl. as *Foundations of Probability*, (Chelsea Publishing Co., New York).

Koopman, B. 1980: "The Bases of Probability," *Bulletin of the American Mathematical Society*, 46 (1940), 763–74; reprinted in Kyburg and Smokler (1980, 119–31).

Kyburg, H. E. 1970: *Probability and Inductive Logic*, (Macmillan, New York).

Kyburg, H. E. 1974: *The Logical Foundations of Statistical Inference*, (D. Reidel, Dordrecht).

Kyburg, H. E. and Smokler, H. E. (eds.) 1980: *Studies in Subjective Probability*, 2nd edn., (Robert E. Krieger Publishing Co., Huntington, New York).

Leblanc, H. 1983: "Alternatives to Standard First-Order Semantics," in *Handbook of Philosophical Logic*, Vol. I., D. Gabbay and F. Guenthner, eds., (D. Reidel, Dordrecht), 189–274.

Levi, I. 1980: *The Enterprise of Knowledge*, (MIT Press, Cambridge, MA).

Lewis, D. 1986a: "Probabilities of Conditionals and Conditional Probabilities," *Philosophical Review*, 85 (1976), 297–315; reprinted with postscripts in D. Lewis, *Philosophical Papers Volume II*, (Oxford University Press, Oxford), 133–56.

Lewis, D. 1986b: "Probabilities of Conditionals and Conditional Probabilities II," *Philosophical Review*, 95, 581–9.

Lewis, D. 1986c: "A Subjectivist's Guide to Objective Chance," in *Studies in Inductive Logic and Probability*, Vol II., R. Jeffrey, ed., (University of California Press, Berkeley), 1980, 263–93; reprinted with postscripts in D. Lewis, *Philosophical Papers Volume II*, (Oxford University Press, Oxford), 83–132.

Lewis, D. 1994: "Humean Supervenience Debugged," *Mind*, 103, 473–90.

Lewis, D. 1998: *Papers in Metaphysics and Epistemology*, (Cambridge University Press, Cambridge).

McGee, V. 1994: "Learning the Impossible," in Eells and Skyrms (1994, 179–99).

Mellor, D. H. 1971: *The Matter of Chance*, (Cambridge University Press, Cambridge, UK).

Mongin, P. 1994: "Some Connections Between Epistemic Logic and the Theory of Nonadditive Probability," in *Patrick Suppes: Scientific Philosopher*, Vol. 1, P. Humphreys, ed., (Kluwer, Dordrecht), 135–71.

Mückenheim, W. 1986: "A Review of Extended Probabilities," *Physics Reports*, 133, 6, 337–401.

Paris, J. and Vencovská, A. 1997: "In Defence of the Maximum Entropy Inference Process," *International Journal of Approximate Reasoning*, 17, 77–103.

Pearl, J. 1991: "Probabilistic Semantics for Nonmonotonic Reasoning," in *Philosophy and AI: Essays at the Interface*, R. Cummins and J. Pollock, eds., (MIT Press, Cambridge, MA), 157–88.

Polya, G. 1968: *Patterns of Plausible Inference*, 2nd edn., (Princeton University Press, NJ).

Popper, K. 1959a: *The Logic of Scientific Discovery*, (Basic Books, New York).

Popper, K. 1959b: "The Propensity Interpretation of Probability," *British Journal of the Philosophy of Science*, 10, 25–42.

Ramsey, F. P. 1980: "Truth and Probability," in *Foundations of Mathematics and other Logical Essays*, R. B. Braithwaite, ed., (Routledge and Kegan Paul, London), 1931 [reprinted 1965], 156–98; reprinted in Kyburg and Smokler (1980, 23–52).

Reichenbach, H. 1949: *The Theory of Probability*, (University of California Press, Berkeley).

Renyi, A. 1970: *Foundations of Probability*, (Holden-Day, Inc., Boca Raton).

Savage, L. J. 1954: *The Foundations of Statistics*, (John Wiley & Sons, New York).

Scott, D. S. and Krauss, P. 1966: "Assigning Probabilities to Logical Formulas," in *Aspects of Inductive Logic*, J. Hintikka and P. Suppes, eds., (North-Holland, Amsterdam), 219–64.

Seidenfeld, T. 1992: "R. A. Fisher's Fiducial Argument and Bayes' Theorem," *Statistical Science*, 7, 358–68.

Shafer, G. 1981: "Constructive Probability," *Synthese*, 48, 1–60.

Skyrms, B. 1980: *Causal Necessity*, (Yale University Press, New Haven).

Skyrms, B. 1987a: "Dynamic Coherence and Probability Kinematics," *Philosophy of Science*, 54, 1–20.

Skyrms, B. 1987b: "Updating, Supposing, and MAXENT," *Theory and Decision*, 22, 225–46.

Skyrms, B. 1999: *Choice and Chance*, 4th edn., (Wadsworth Publishing Company, Belmont, California).

Stalnaker, R. 1970: "Probability and Conditionals," *Philosophy of Science*, 37, 64–80.

Stalnaker, R. and Jeffrey, R. 1994: "Conditionals as Random Variables," in Eells and Skyrms (1994, 31–46).

Thau, M. 1994: "Undermining and Admissibility," *Mind*, 103, 491–503.

van Fraassen, B. 1976: "Probabilities of Conditionals," in *Foundations of Probability Theory, Statistical Inference and Statistical Theories of Science*, Vol. I, W. L. Harper and C. Hooker, eds., (D. Reidel, Dordrecht), 261–301.

van Fraassen, B. 1981: "Probabilistic Semantics Objectified I," *Journal of Philosophical Logic*, 10, 371–94; part II, 495–510.

van Fraassen, B. 1983: "Gentlemen's Wagers: Relevant Logic and Probability," *Philosophical Studies*, 43, 47–61.

van Fraassen, B. 1995: "Belief and the Problem of Ulysses and the Sirens," *Philosophical Studies*, 77, 7–37.

von Mises, R. 1957: *Probability, Statistics and Truth*, revised English edn, (Macmillan, New York).

von Plato, J. 1994: *Creating Modern Probability*, (Cambridge University Press, Cambridge).

Walley, P. 1991: *Statistical Reasoning with Imprecise Probabilities*, (Chapman & Hall, London).

Chapter 17

Conditionals

Dorothy Edgington

A simple statement

It will rain soon.

Mary cooked the dinner.

can have a conditional clause attached, making a conditional statement:

It will rain soon if the clouds don't blow away.

If John didn't cook the dinner, Mary cooked it.

These, traditionally called 'indicative conditionals', are my topic. I do not have space to discuss theories of 'subjunctive' or 'counterfactual' conditionals like

John would have cooked the dinner if Mary had not done so.

If the wind hadn't blown the clouds away, it would have rained.

That there is some difference between indicatives and subjunctives is shown by pairs of examples like

If Oswald didn't kill Kennedy, someone else did.

and

If Oswald hadn't killed Kennedy, someone else would have.

One can accept the first but reject the second (Adams, 1970). That there is not a huge gulf between them is shown by examples like the following:

"Don't go in there," I say, "if you go in you will get hurt."

You look skeptical but stay outside, when there is a loud crash as the ceiling collapses. I say,

You see, if you had gone in you would have been hurt. *I told you so.*

It is controversial how best to classify conditionals. According to some theorists, the forward-looking indicatives (those with a 'will' in the main clause) belong with the subjunctives (those with a 'would' in the main clause), and not with the other indicatives.[1] The easy transition from typical 'wills' to 'woulds' is indeed a datum to be explained. Still, straightforward statements about the past, present or future, to which a conditional clause is attached – the traditional class of indicative conditionals – do (in my view) constitute a single semantic kind. The theories I discuss do not fare better or worse when restricted to a particular subspecies.

17.1. Truth Conditions for Indicative Conditionals

An indicative conditional sentence, 'If *A*, *B*,' has two constituent sentences, or sentence-like clauses, *A* and *B*, called the *antecedent* and *consequent* respectively. It is part of the task of compositional semantics to specify the meaning of a complex sentence as a function of the meanings of its parts. The generally most fruitful and time-honored approach is to specify the truth conditions of the complex sentence as a function of the truth conditions of its parts. A semantics of this kind illuminates the question of the validity of arguments involving the complex sentences, given the conception of validity as necessary preservation of truth [see chapter 6]. This section assumes that this approach to conditionals is correct – that is, it assumes that conditionals have truth conditions. Let *A* and *B* be two sentences such as 'Ann is in Paris' and 'Bill is in Paris.' Our question will be: Does 'If *A*, *B*' have simple, extensional, truth-functional truth conditions, as '*A* and *B*,' '*A* or *B*' and 'It is not the case that *A*' do? That is, do the truth values of *A* and of *B* determine the truth value of 'If *A*, *B*'? Or are they non-truth-functional, like those of '*A* because *B*', '*A* before *B*', 'It is possible that *A*'? That is, do the truth values of *A* and *B*, in some cases, leave open the truth value of 'If *A*, *B*'?

The truth-functional conditional was integral to Frege's new logic (1960). It was taken up enthusiastically by Russell (who called it 'material implication'), Wittgenstein and the logical positivists, and it is now found in every logic text. It is the first theory of conditionals that students of philosophy encounter. Typically, it does not strike students as *obviously* correct: some have been known to paste the truth table for 'if' above their bed as an *aide memoire*. It is logic's first surprise. Yet, as the textbooks testify, it does a creditable job in many circumstances. And it has many defenders. It is a strikingly simple theory: 'If *A*, *B*' is true iff (if and only if) it is not the case that ('*A*' is true and '*B*' is false). It is thus equivalent to

$$\neg(A \;\&\; \neg B)$$

and to

$\neg A \vee B$

'$A \supset B$' has, by stipulation, this truth condition. Our question is whether this is an adequate rendering of 'If A, B'.

It is easy to see that *if* 'if' is truth-functional, this particular truth function, depicted in column (i) of table 17.1, is the correct one. For *sometimes* 'If A, B' is true when 'A' and 'B' are, respectively, (true, true), or (false, true), or (false, false). For instance,

If it's a square, it has four sides.

is true whether the unknown shape is a square, an oblong rectangle, or a triangle. Assuming truth-functionality, it follows that conditionals are *alway* true for these combinations of truth values of their parts. The remaining case, (true, false), is unrealizable in this example. Assuming truth-functionality, the conditional must be false in this case; otherwise, there would be no such thing as a false conditional – all conditionals would be tautologies. This last case is the most obviously correct, anyway. If it were possible to have 'A' true, 'B' false, and 'If A, B' true, it would be unsafe to infer 'B' from 'A' and 'If A, B': *modus ponens* would be invalid. Taking for granted that *modus ponens* is valid for any interpretation of 'If A, B' worth taking seriously, any acceptable interpretation of 'If A, B' must entail $\neg(A \& \neg B)$, i.e., $A \supset B$.

There are different proposals for non-truth-functional truth conditions for 'If A, B.' I am here concerned only with schematic features. I shall use '$A \rightarrow B$' as a generic representation of any such conditional. On some interpretations, '$A \rightarrow B$' differs from '$A \supset B$' only when A is false. For instance, Stalnaker's (1991b [1968]) proposal is of this type. I say

(S) If you strike the match, it will light.

If you do strike it, my remark is true if it lights, false if it does not – in agreement with the truth-functional account. If you don't strike it, the truth-value of S, on this account, depends on whether the match lights in a non-actual possible world in which you do strike it, and which otherwise differs minimally from the actual world. Suppose that actually you don't strike it, and there is a hurricane blowing. In the

Table 17.1

	A	B	Truth-functional (i) $A \supset B$	(ii) $\neg A \supset B$	(iii) $A \supset \neg B$	Non-Truth-functional (iv) $A \rightarrow B$	(v) $\neg A \rightarrow B$	(vi) $A \rightarrow \neg B$
1	T	T	T	T	F	T	T/F	F
2	T	F	F	T	T	F	T/F	T
3	F	T	T	T	T	T/F	T	T/F
4	F	F	T	F	T	T/F	F	T/F

world most like the actual world in which you strike it, it doesn't light. S is false. Suppose that actually you don't strike it, and conditions are ideal for the lighting of matches. In the world most like the actual world in which you strike the match, it lights. S is true.

On other non-truth-functional interpretations, '$A \to B$' may be false not only when A is false, but also when A and B are both true. For instance, if, in some sense of 'necessitate,' the truth of '$A \to B$' requires that A necessitate B, $A \& B$ is not sufficient for $A \to B$. I represent below a non-truth-functional account of Stalnaker's kind, but the argument which follows applies to any non-truth-functional account.

Let A and B be two logically independent propositions. The four lines in table 17.1 represent the four incompatible logical possibilities for the truth values of A and B. 'If A, B,' 'If $\neg A$, B' and 'If A, $\neg B$' are interpreted truth-functionally in columns (i)–(iii), and non-truth-functionally in columns (iv)–(vi). 'T/F' means both truth values are open for the corresponding assignment of truth values to A and B. For instance, line 4, column (iv), represents two possibilities for A, B and $A \to B$, (F, F, T) and (F, F, F).

Column (i) may reasonably be said to specify the meaning of the truth-functional conditional, in terms of the meanings of A and of B. The meanings of A and of B, together with how the world is, determine their truth values. The four lines represent four exclusive and exhaustive ways the world might be. Column (i) shows, whichever way the world is for A and B, how to determine the truth value of $A \supset B$. Column (iv) does not pretend to specify the meaning of a non-truth-functional conditional. Rather, once that meaning has been specified (e.g. in Stalnaker's way), it follows that this array of logically possible combinations of truth values for A, B and $A \to B$ exists.

17.1.1. *Arguments for truth-functionality*

The main argument points to the fact that minimal knowledge that the truth-functional truth condition is satisfied is enough for knowledge that if A, B. In short: suppose there are two balls in a bag, a and b. All that is known about their color is that at least one of them is red. That's enough to know that if a isn't red, b is red. Or: all that is known is that they are not both red. That's enough to know that if a is red, b is not red.

Suppose there is no information to start with about which of the four possible combinations of truth values for A and B obtains. Then compelling reason is acquired to think that $A \lor B$. There is no stronger belief about the matter; in particular, there is no firm belief as to whether or not A. Line 4 is ruled out; the other possibilities remain open. Supposing all that, then, intuitively, one is justified in inferring that if $\neg A$, B. Look at the possibilities for A and B on the left. The possibility that both A and B are false has been eliminated. So if A is false, only one possibility remains: B is true.

The truth-functionalist (call him Hook) gets this right. Look at column (ii). Eliminate line 4 and line 4 only, and the only possibility in which '$\neg A \supset B$' is false has been eliminated. One knows enough to conclude that '$\neg A \supset B$' is true.

The non-truth-functionalist (call him Arrow) gets this wrong. Look at column (v). Eliminate line 4 and line 4 only, and some possibility of falsity must remain in other cases which have not been ruled out. By eliminating just line 4, one does not *ipso facto* eliminate these further possibilities, incompatible with line 4, in which '$\neg A \rightarrow B$' is false.

The same point can be made with negated conjunctions. Suppose for sure that $\neg(A\ \&\ B)$, but nothing stronger than that. In particular, one does not know whether or not A. Line 1 is ruled out; nothing more. One may justifiably infer that if A, $\neg B$. Hook gets this right. In column (iii), if line 1 is eliminated, this leaves only cases in which '$A \supset \neg B$' is true. Arrow gets this wrong. In column (vi), eliminating just line 1 leaves open the possibility that '$A \rightarrow \neg B$' is false.

Intuitively, in evaluating 'If A, $\neg B$,' one supposes that A is true. That is, one supposes that line 1 or line 2 obtains. When it is known that line 1 does not obtain, one concludes that line 2 obtains. If A is true, B is not. End of story. Arrow agrees that '$A \rightarrow \neg B$' is true if line 2 obtains. But, for him, that is not the end of the story. For A may be false, and in this case, '$A \rightarrow \neg B$' may be false. Now there is something counterintuitive about this part of his thought experiment: when considering whether $\neg B$ is true if A is true, why should one have to bother to think about what is the case if A is false?

The same argument renders compelling the thought that if one eliminates *just* $A\ \&\ \neg B$ – nothing stronger, i.e., one does not eliminate A, then there is sufficient reason to conclude that if A, B.

Hook's second argument is in the style of Natural Deduction. The three premisses $\neg(A\ \&\ B)$, A and B entail a contradiction. So, by *reductio ad absurdum*, $\neg(A\ \&\ B)$ and A entail $\neg B$. So, by Conditional Proof (CP), $\neg(A\ \&\ B)$ entails 'If A, $\neg B$.' Substitute $\neg C$ for B, and then, provided Double Negation Elimination is allowed, one has a proof of 'If A, C' from $\neg(A\ \&\ \neg C)$.

Conditional Proof raises no eyebrows. It *seems* sound. 'From X and Y, it follows that Z.' 'From X, it follows that if Y, Z.' The 'if'-clause in the latter sentence seems to function just as the second premiss in the former. Yet, *for no reading of 'if' which is stronger than the truth-functional reading is CP valid* – at least this is so if '&' and '$\neg$' are treated in the classical way and hence one accepts the validity of the inference:

(I) $\neg(A\ \&\ \neg B)$, $A \vdash B$.

Suppose CP is valid for some interpretation of 'If A, B.' Applying CP to (I) gives

$\neg(A\ \&\ \neg B) \vdash$ If A, B.

That is, $A \supset B \vdash$ If A, B.

17.1.2.   *Arguments against truth-functionality*

The best-known objection, one of the 'paradoxes of material implication' is that, according to Hook, the falsity of A is logically sufficient for the truth of 'If A, B'.

[See chapter 13.] Look at the last two lines of column (i). In every possible situation in which A is false, 'If A, B' is true. Can it be right that the falsity of

She ate the apple.

entails the truth of

If she ate the apple, she was ill.

Hook might respond as follows. How can intuitions about the validity of an inference be tested? The direct way is to imagine that one knows for sure that the premiss is true, and to consider what one would then think about the conclusion. Now when one knows for sure that something, A, is true, there is no place for thoughts beginning 'If A is false, ...' When one knows for sure that Harry did it, one does not think or remark 'If Harry didn't do it . . .'. In this circumstance, conditionals have no role to play, and one has no practice in assessing them. The direct intuitive test is, therefore, silent on whether 'If A, B' follows from $\neg A$. If the smoothest, simplest, generally satisfactory theory has the consequence that it does follow, perhaps one should learn to live with this consequence.

There may, of course, be further consequences of this feature of '$\supset$' which jar with intuition. That needs investigating. But, Hook may add, even if one concludes that '$\supset$' does not fit perfectly our natural language use of 'if,' it comes close, and it has the virtues of simplicity and clarity. As has been seen, rival theories also have counterintuitive consequences. Natural language is a fluid affair, and theories cannot be expected to achieve better than approximate fit. Perhaps, in the interests of precision and clarity, in serious reasoning the untidy and unclear 'if' should be replaced with its neat, close relative, '$\supset$.'

This was no doubt Frege's attitude. Frege's primary concern was to construct a system of logic, formulated in an idealized language, which was adequate for mathematical reasoning. If '$A \supset B$' does not translate perfectly our natural language 'If A, B', but plays its intended role, so much the worse for natural language.

Perhaps, for the purpose of doing mathematics, Frege's judgment was correct. The main defects of the truth-functional conditional do not show up in mathematics. There are some peculiarities, but as long as one is aware of them, they can be lived with. And arguably, the gain in simplicity and clarity more than offsets the oddities.

The oddities become less tolerable when considering conditional judgments about empirical matters. The difference is this: in thinking about the empirical world, propositions are often accepted and rejected with degrees of confidence less than certainty.

I think, but am not sure, that A

plays no central role in mathematical thinking. Perhaps, the use of indicative conditionals can be dismissed as unimportant in circumstances in which one is *certain* that the antecedent is false. But the use of conditionals whose antecedent is thought to be likely to be false cannot be ignored. They are used often, some are accepted, others are rejected.

I think I won't need to get in touch, but if I do, I shall need a phone number.

you say, as your partner is about to go away; not

If I do, I'll manage by telepathy.

I think John spoke to Mary; if he didn't, he wrote to her.

not

If he didn't, he shot her.

Hook's theory has the appalling consequence that *all* conditionals with unlikely antecedents are likely to be true. To think it likely that $\neg A$ is to think it likely that a sufficient condition for the truth of $A \supset B$ obtains. Take someone who thinks the Republicans won't win the election, and who does not think that if they do win, they will double income tax (i.e., he rejects that). According to Hook, this person has grossly inconsistent opinions. Not only does Hook's theory fit badly the patterns of thought of competent, intelligent people. It cannot be claimed that one would be better off with '$\supset$.' On the contrary, one would be intellectually disabled: lacking the power to discriminate between believable and unbelievable conditionals whose antecedent is thought to be likely to be false.

Arrow does not have this problem. His theory explicitly avoids it, by allowing that '$A \rightarrow B$' may be false when A is false.

The other paradox of material implication is that, according to Hook, all conditionals with true consequents are true: $B \vdash A \supset B$. This is perhaps less obviously unacceptable: if I'm sure that B, and treat A as an epistemic possibility, I must be sure that if A, B. Again, the problem becomes vivid when considering the case where I'm nearly sure, but not quite sure, that B. I think B *may* be false; and will be false if certain, in my view unlikely, circumstances obtain. For example, I think that Fred is giving a lecture right now. I don't think that if he was seriously injured on his way to work, he is giving a lecture right now. But on Hook's account, the truth of the consequent is a logically sufficient condition for the truth of the conditional: the conditional is false *only if* the consequent is false. So on this account, no one can, without gross irrationality, think that the consequent is likely to be true, but the conditional is unlikely to be true.

17.1.3. *The pragmatic defence of truth-functionality*

Grice famously defended the truth-functional account, in his William James lectures, "Logic and Conversation," delivered in 1967 (Grice, 1989). There are many ways of speaking the truth yet misleading your audience, given the standards to which

you are expected to conform in conversational exchange. One way is to say something weaker than some other relevant thing you are in a position to say. Consider
disjunctions. I am asked where John is. I am sure that he is in the pub, and know
that he never goes near libraries. Inclined to be unhelpful but not wishing to lie,
I say

He is either in the pub or the library.

My hearer naturally assumes that this is the most precise information I am in a
position to give, and also concludes from the truth (let us assume) that I told him

If he's not in the pub he's in the library.

The conditional, like the disjunction, according to Grice, is true if he's in the pub,
but misleadingly asserted on that ground.
    Another example, from David Lewis (1986c [1976], p. 143):

You won't eat those and live.

I say of some wholesome and delicious mushrooms – knowing that you will now
leave them alone, deferring to my expertise. I told no lie – for indeed you don't eat
them – but of course I misled you.
    Grice drew attention, then, to situations in which a person is *justified in believing*
a proposition, which would nevertheless be an unreasonable thing for the person to
say, in normal circumstances. His lesson was salutary and important. He is, I think,
right about disjunctions and negated conjunctions. Believing that John is in the
pub, I can't consistently *disbelieve*

He is either in the pub or the library.

If I have any epistemic attitude to this proposition, it should be one of belief,
however inappropriate it is for me to assert it. Similarly for

You won't eat those and live.

when I believe you won't eat them. But the difficulties with the truth-functional
conditional cannot be explained away in terms of what is an inappropriate conversational remark. They arise at the level of belief. Thinking that John is in the pub,
I may without irrationality disbelieve

If he isn't in the pub, he's in the library.

Thinking you won't eat the mushrooms, I may without irrationality reject

If you eat them you will die.

As facts about the norms to which people defer, these claims can be tested. A good enough test is to take a co-operative person, who understands that you are merely interested in her opinions, as opposed to what would be a reasonable remark to make, and note which conditionals she assents to. Are we really to brand as illogical someone who dissents from both

The Republicans will win.

and

If the Republicans win, income tax will double?

The Gricean phenomenon is a real one. On anyone's account of conditionals, there will be circumstances in which a conditional is justifiably believed, but is liable to mislead if stated. For instance, I believe that the match will be cancelled, because all the players have 'flu. I believe that whether or not it rains, the match will be cancelled: if it rains, the match will be cancelled, and if it doesn't rain, the match will be cancelled. But I would mislead my audience by responding to a query about whether the match will be cancelled by asserting the first of these conditionals. This does not demonstrate that Hook is correct. Although I believe that the match will be cancelled, I don't believe that if all the players make a very speedy recovery, the match will be cancelled.

17.1.4. Compounds of conditionals: Against Hook, and against Arrow

$\neg(A \supset B)$ is equivalent to $A \& \neg B$. Intuitively, one may safely say, of an unseen geometric figure,

It's not the case that if it's a pentagon, it has six sides.

But by Hook's lights, one may well be wrong; for it may not be a pentagon. Another example, due to Gibbard (1981, pp. 235–6): Of a glass that had been held a foot above the floor, I say (having left the scene),

If it broke if it was dropped, it was fragile.

Intuitively this is reasonable. But by Hook's lights, if the glass was not dropped, and was not fragile, my conditional has a true (conditional) antecedent and false consequent, and is hence false. Grice's strategy was to explain why we don't assert certain conditionals which we have reason to believe true. In these two cases, the problem is reversed: there are compounds of conditionals which we confidently assert and accept which, by Hook's lights, we do not have reason to believe true.

Disjunctions are also troublesome. $(A \supset B) \vee (\neg A \supset B)$ is a tautology. If you deny that you will be upset if you are not promoted, you are committed to accepting that you will be upset if you are promoted. And here is my favorite, truth-functionally valid, proof of the existence of God:

> If God does not exist, it's not the case that if I pray, my prayers will be answered.

> I do not pray.

> Therefore God exists.

Arrow does fine with the above examples. But other cases of embedded conditionals count in the opposite direction. Here are two sentence forms which are, intuitively, equivalent:

(i)   If (A & B), C.
(ii) If A, then if B, C.

Try any example:

> If Mary comes then if John doesn't have to leave early we will play Bridge.

> If Mary comes and John doesn't have to leave early we will play Bridge.

> If they were outside and it rained, they got wet.

> If they were outside, then if it rained they got wet.

The intuitive case for Import–Export, as this equivalence has been called (McGee, 1985), is as follows. Consider (ii). In assessing this, one supposes that the antecedent, A, is true, and makes a judgment about the consequent under that supposition. As the consequent is also a conditional, one supposes that its antecedent, B, is also true. A judgment is then made about its consequent, C, under these suppositions. The thought-experiment is equivalent to that of making a judgment about C under the supposition that A & B.

For Hook, Import–Export holds. Gibbard (1981, pp. 234–5) has proved that for no conditional with truth conditions stronger than '⊃' does Import–Export hold. Here is the proof. Let → be any conditional connective for which Import–Export holds. Make two innocuous assumptions:

(a) $A \rightarrow B$ entails $A \supset B$;
(b)   if A entails B, $A \rightarrow B$ is a logical truth.

Now consider the formula

$$(A \supset B) \rightarrow (A \rightarrow B) \tag{17.1}$$

By Import–Export, it is equivalent to

$$((A \supset B) \mathbin{\&} A) \rightarrow B \tag{17.2}$$

The antecedent of (17.2) entails its consequent. So, by (b), (17.2) is a logical truth. So, by Import–Export, (17.1) is a logical truth. The damage is done, but to drive it home: by (a), (17.1) entails

$$(A \supset B) \supset (A \to B) \tag{17.3}$$

So (17.3) is a logical truth. A truth-functional conditional is a logical truth just in case its antecedent entails its consequent. So $(A \supset B)$ entails $(A \to B)$. So $\to$ is no stronger than $\supset$.

For instance, for Hook,

If it rains or snows, then if it doesn't rain, it will snow.

is trivially true, equivalent to

If it rains or snows, and doesn't rain, it will snow.

For Stalnaker, the former may well be false, and

If it rains or snows, then if it doesn't rain, it won't snow.

may be true, while also

If it doesn't rain, then if it rains or snows, it will rain.

may be true (see below).

The score is roughly even. Hook gets some things right, some things wrong. Similarly for Arrow. Can a perilous course be steered 'twixt Arrow and Hook?

17.2. Conditional Belief and Conditional Probability

Putting truth conditions aside for a while, consider what it is to believe, or to be more or less certain, that B if A – that John cooked the dinner if Mary didn't, that you will recover if you have the operation, and so forth. How do you make such a judgment? You suppose (assume, hypothesize) that A, and make a hypothetical judgment about B, under the supposition that A, in the light of your other beliefs. As Ramsey (1990a, p. 147) put it:

> If two people are arguing 'If p, will q?' and are both in doubt as to p, they are adding p hypothetically to their stock of knowledge, and arguing on that basis about q; . . . they are fixing their degrees of belief in q given p.

When one is neither certain that B nor certain that $\neg B$, there remains a range of different epistemic attitudes one may have to B: one may be nearly certain that B, think *B* more likely than not, etc. Similarly, one may be certain, nearly certain, think it more likely than not, etc., that *B*, given the supposition that *A*. Make the idealizing assumption that degrees of closeness to certainty can be quantified: 100 percent certain, 90 percent certain, etc.; and probability theory can be turned to for what Ramsey called the 'logic of partial belief.' There one finds a well-established, indispensable concept, 'the conditional probability of *B* given *A*.' It is this notion to which Ramsey refers by the phrase 'degrees of belief in *q* given *p*' [see chapter 16].

The earliest statement I know of the basic law concerning conditional probabilities is in an essay by Thomas Bayes published posthumously in 1763:

> The probability that two ... events will both happen is ... the probability of the first [multiplied by] the probability of the second *on the supposition that* the first happens [my emphasis].

A simple example: a ball is to be picked at random. Of the balls, 70 percent are red (so the probability that a red ball is picked is 70 percent). Of the red balls, 60 percent have a stripe (so the probability that a striped ball is picked, on the supposition that a red ball is picked, is 60 percent). The probability that a red striped ball is picked is 60 percent of 70 percent, i.e., 42 percent.

Ramsey, arguing that 'degrees of belief' should conform to probability theory,[2] stated the same 'fundamental law of probable belief' (1990c [1931], p. 77):

Degree of belief in (*p* and *q*) = degree of belief in *p* × degree of belief in *q* given *p*

For example, you are 50 percent certain that the test will be on conditionals, and 80 percent certain that you will pass on the supposition that it is on conditionals. So you are 40 percent certain that it will be on conditionals and you will pass.

Accepting Ramsey's suggestion that 'if', 'given that', 'on the supposition that' come to the same thing, writing '$p(-)$' for 'degree of belief in $(-)$', and '$p_A(-)$' for 'degree of belief in $(-)$ given *A*', and rearranging the basic law, gives:

$$p(B \text{ if } A) = p_A(B) = p(A \& B)/p(A) \qquad \text{provided } p(A) \neq 0$$

Figure 17.1 shows a partition (a set of mutually exclusive and jointly exhaustive propositions): One's degrees of belief in the members of a partition should sum to 100 percent: that is all there is to the requirement that degrees of belief have the structure of probabilities.

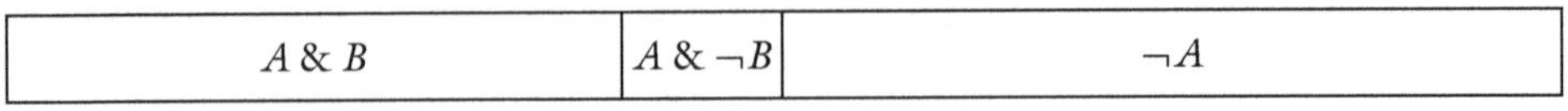

A & *B*	*A* & ¬*B*	¬*A*

Figure 17.1

Suppose a person *X* thinks it 50 percent likely that ¬*A* (hence 50 percent likely that *A*), 40 percent likely that *A* & *B*, and 10 percent likely that *A* & ¬*B*. (Note that as {*A*, ¬*A*} and {*A* & *B*, *A* & ¬*B*, ¬*A*} are both partitions, it follows that

$$p(A) = p(A \ \& \ B) + p(A \ \& \ \neg B)$$

How does X evaluate 'If A, B?' X assumes that A, that is, hypothetically eliminates $\neg A$. In the part of the partition that remains, in which A is true, B is four times as likely as $\neg B$; that is, under the assumption that A, it is four to one that B: $p(B \ \text{if} \ A)$ is 80 percent, $p(\neg B \ \text{if} \ A)$ is 20 percent. Equivalently, as $A \ \& \ B$ is four times as likely as $A \ \& \ \neg B$, $p(B \ \text{if} \ A) = \frac{4}{5}$, or 80 percent. Equivalently, $p(A \ \& \ B)$ is $\frac{4}{5}$ of $p(A)$. In non-numerical terms: you believe that if A, B to the extent that you think $A \ \& \ B$ is nearly as likely as A; or, to the extent that you think $A \ \& \ B$ is much more likely than $A \ \& \ \neg B$. If you think $A \ \& \ B$ is as likely as A, you are certain that if A, B. In this case, your $p(A \ \& \ \neg B) = 0$.

Note: this thought-experiment can only be performed when $p(A) \neq 0$. On this approach, indicative conditionals only have a role when the thinker takes A to be an epistemic possibility. If you take yourself to know for sure that Ann is in Paris, you don't go in for 'If Ann is not in Paris . . .' thoughts (though of course you can think 'If Ann had not been in Paris . . .'). In conversation, you may pretend to take something as an epistemic possibility, temporarily, to comply with the epistemic state of your hearer. When playing the skeptic, there are not many limits on what you *can*, at a pinch, take as an epistemic possibility – as not already ruled out. But there are some limits, as Descartes found. Is there a conditional thought that begins 'If I don't exist now . . .'?

On Hook's account, to be close to certain that if A, B is to give a high value to $p(A \supset B)$. How does $p(A \supset B)$ compare with $p_A(B)$? In two special cases, they are equal: first, when $p(A \ \& \ \neg B) = 0$ (and $p(A) \neq 0$), $p(A \supset B) = p_A(B) = 1$ (i.e., 100 percent). Second, if $p(A) = 100$ percent, $p(A \supset B) = p_A(B) = p(B)$. In all other cases, $p(A \supset B) > p_A(B)$. To prove the inequality, consider a picture of a partition, $\{A \ \& \ B, A \ \& \ \neg B, \neg A\}$, as in figure 17.1, drawn to scale. Focus on $p(A \ \& \ \neg B)$. Provided $p(A \ \& \ \neg B) \neq 0$ and $p(\neg A) \neq 0$, $p(A \ \& \ \neg B)$ must be a smaller proportion of the whole space than it is of the part of the space in which A is true. So, except in these two cases, $p(A \ \& \ \neg B) < p_A(\neg B)$. It follows that, except in these special cases,

$$p(A \supset B) > p_A(B)$$

for

$$p(A \ \& \ \neg B) = 1 - p(A \supset B)$$

and

$$p_A(\neg B) = 1 - p_A(B)$$

$p(A \supset B)$ and $p_A(B)$ come spectacularly apart when $p(\neg A)$ is high and $p(A \ \& \ B)$ is much smaller than $p(A \ \& \ \neg B)$. Let

$$p(\neg A) = 90 \text{ percent}$$

$$p(A \ \& \ B) = 1 \text{ percent}$$

$$p(A \& \neg B) = 9 \text{ percent}$$

$$p_A(B) = 10 \text{ percent}$$

$$p(A \supset B) = 91 \text{ percent}$$

For instance, I am 90 percent certain that Tom won't be offered the job, and think it only 10 percent likely that he will decline the offer if it is made.

$$p(\text{offer} \supset \text{decline}) = p(\text{not offer, or (offer and decline)}) = 91 \text{ percent}$$

(It is sometimes useful, as a heuristic device, to imagine a partition as carved into a large finite number of equally-probable chunks, such that the propositions with which we are concerned are true in an exact number of them. The probability of any non-conditional proposition is the proportion of chunks in which it is true. The probability of B on the supposition that A is the proportion *of the A-chunks* (those in which A is true) which are B-chunks. With some misgivings, I call these chunks 'worlds': they are equally-probable, mutually incompatible and jointly exhaustive, epistemic possibilities – enough of them for the propositions with which one is concerned to be true, or false, in each world. The heuristic value is that judgments of probability and conditional probability can then be stated as judgments about proportions.)

We can now compare Hook, Arrow, and our probability theorist whom we shall call Prob, with respect to two questions raised in section 17.1.

Question 1 You are certain that $\neg(A \& \neg B)$, but not certain that $\neg A$. Should you be certain that if A, B? (Equivalently: if you are certain that $\neg(A \& B)$, but not certain that $\neg A$, should you be certain that if A, $\neg B$? And: if you are certain that $A \vee B$, but not certain that A, should you be certain that if $\neg A$, B?)

Hook: Yes. Because $(A \supset B)$ is true whenever $A \& \neg B$ is false.

Prob: Yes. Here, $A \& B$ is just as likely as A. B is true in all my A-worlds. $p_A(B) = 1$.

Arrow: No, not necessarily. For $A \to B$ may be false when $A \& \neg B$ is false. With just the information that $A \& \neg B$ is false, I should not be certain that if A, B.

Question 2 If you think it likely that $\neg A$, might you still think it unlikely that if A, B?

Hook: No. $(A \supset B)$ is true in all the possible situations in which $\neg A$ is true. If I think it likely that $\neg A$, I think it likely that a sufficient condition for the truth of $(A \supset B)$ obtains. I must, therefore, think it likely that if A, B.

Prob: Yes. We had an example above. That most of my probability goes to $\neg A$ leaves open the question whether or not $A \& B$ is more probable than $A \& \neg B$. If $p(A \& \neg B)$ is greater than $p(A \& B)$, I think it's unlikely that if A, B. That's compatible with thinking it likely that $\neg A$.

Arrow: Yes. $(A \to B)$ may be false when A is false. And I might well think it likely that that possibility obtains.

Prob has squared the circle: He gets the right answer to both questions. In this, he differs from both Hook and Arrow. Prob's way of assessing conditionals is incompatible with the truth-functional way (they answer question 2 differently); and incompatible with stronger-than-truth-functional truth conditions (they answer question 1 differently). It follows that Prob's way of assessing conditionals is incompatible with the claim that conditionals have truth conditions at all. $p_A(B)$ does not measure the probability of the truth of any proposition. Suppose it did measure the probability of the truth of some proposition $A * B$. Either $A * B$ is entailed by $A \supset B$ or it is not. If it is, it is true whenever A is false, and hence cannot be improbable when $\neg A$ is probable. That is, it cannot agree with Prob in its answer to question 2. If $A * B$ is not entailed by $A \supset B$, it may be false when $\neg(A \& \neg B)$ is true, and hence certainty that $\neg(A \& \neg B)$ (in the absence of certainty that $\neg A$) is insufficient for certainty that $A * B$: it cannot agree with Prob in its answer to question 1. This remarkable result was first proved, in a different way, by Lewis (1986c [1976]).

Although Prob and Hook give the same answer to question 1, their reasons are different. Prob answers 'yes,' *not* because a proposition, $A * B$, is true whenever $A \& \neg B$ is false; but because B is true in all the worlds which matter for the assessment of 'If A, B': the A-worlds. Although Prob and Arrow give the same answer to question 2, their reasons are different. Prob answers 'yes,' not because a proposition, $A * B$, may be false when A is false, but because the fact that most worlds are $\neg A$-worlds is irrelevant to whether most *of the A-worlds* are B-worlds. To judge that B is true *on the supposition that A is true*, it turns out, is not to judge that something-or-other, $A * B$, is true, simpliciter.

17.2.1. *Validity*

Adams (1965, 1966, 1975) gave a theory of the validity of arguments involving conditionals as construed by Prob. He explained something important about classically valid arguments as well: that they are, in a special sense to be made precise, probability-preserving. This property can be generalized to apply to arguments with conditionals. The valid ones are those which, in the special sense, preserve probability or conditional probability. [See also chapter 16.]

First consider classically valid (that is, necessarily truth-preserving) arguments which do not involve conditionals. These are used in arguing from contingent premisses about which one is often less than completely certain. The question arises: how certain can one be of the conclusion of the argument, given that one thinks, but is not sure, that the premisses are true? Call the improbability of a statement one minus its probability. Adams showed this: if (and only if) an argument is valid, then in no probability distribution does the improbability of its conclusion exceed the sum of the improbabilities of its premisses. Call this the Probability Preservation Principle (PPP).

The proof of PPP rests on the Partition Principle – that the probabilities of the members of a partition sum to 100 percent – nothing else, beyond the fact that if A entails B, $p(A \& \neg B) = 0$.[3] Here are three consequences:[4]

(1) If A entails B, $p(A) \leq p(B)$
(2) $p(A \vee B) = p(A) + p(B) - p(A \& B) \leq p(A) + p(B)$
(3) For all n, $p(A_1 \vee \cdots \vee A_n) \leq p(A_1) + \cdots + p(A_n)$

Suppose $A_1, \ldots, A_n \vdash B$. Then

$$\neg B \vdash \neg A_1 \vee \cdots \vee \neg A_n$$

Therefore

$$p(\neg B) \le p(\neg A_1) + \cdots + p(\neg A_n)$$

The improbability of the conclusion of a valid argument cannot exceed the sum of the improbabilities of the premisses.

The result is useful to know: If you have two premisses of which you are at least 99 percent certain, they entitle you to be at least 98 percent certain of a conclusion validly drawn from them. Of course, if you have 100 premisses each at least 99 percent certain, your conclusion may have zero probability. That is the lesson of the 'Lottery Paradox.' Still, Adams's result vindicates deductive reasoning from uncertain premisses, provided that they are not too uncertain, and there are not too many of them.

So far, we have a very useful consequence of the classical notion of validity. Now Adams extends this consequence to arguments involving conditionals. Take a language with 'and', 'or', 'not' and 'if' – but with 'if' occurring only as the main connective in a sentence. (We put aside compounds of conditionals.) Take any argument formulated in this language. Consider any probability function over the sentences of this argument which assigns non-zero probability to the antecedents of all conditionals – that is, any assignment of numbers to the non-conditional sentences which conforms to the Partition Principle, and to the conditional sentences which conforms to Prob's thesis:

$$p(B \text{ if } A) = p_A(B) = p(A \& B)/p(A)$$

Call the improbability of a conditional 'If A, B,' one minus $p_A(B)$. *Define* a valid argument as one such that there is no probability function in which the improbability of the conclusion exceeds the sum of the improbabilities of the premisses. And a plausible logic emerges, with rules of proof, a decision procedure, and provable consistency and completeness (Adams, 1975, 1998).

Call a non-conditional sentence a factual sentence. If an argument has a factual conclusion, and is classically valid with 'if' interpreted as '⊃,' it is probabilistically valid. It was shown that in all distributions in which $p(A) \ne 0$, $p(A \supset B) \ge p_A(B)$. So if a factual conclusion follows from a premiss interpreted as the weaker $A \supset B$, it follows from the stronger $A \Rightarrow B$ (as I shall write Prob's conditional). But not all truth-functionally valid arguments with conditional conclusions remain valid on this interpretation of the conditional and this construal of validity. The premisses may entail the weaker $A \supset B$ without entailing the stronger $A \Rightarrow B$.

Conditional Proof fails. Indeed, all departures from truth-functional validity can be traced to the failure of Conditional Proof. In the following list, the inference on the left is valid, its partner on the right, derivable by a step of Conditional Proof, is not.

	Valid	Invalid
(1)	$A, B \vdash A$	$B \vdash A \Rightarrow B$
(2)	$A \vee B, \neg A \vdash B$	$A \vee B \vdash \neg A \Rightarrow B$
(3)	$\neg(A \,\&\, B), A \vdash \neg B$	$\neg(A \,\&\, B) \vdash A \Rightarrow \neg B$
(4)	$A \Rightarrow C, A \,\&\, B \vdash C$	$A \Rightarrow C \vdash A \,\&\, B \Rightarrow C$
(5)	$A \Rightarrow B, B \Rightarrow C, A \vdash C$	$A \Rightarrow B, B \Rightarrow C \vdash A \Rightarrow C$
(6)	$A \Rightarrow B, \neg B \vdash \neg A$	$A \Rightarrow B \vdash \neg B \Rightarrow \neg A$
(7)	$A \,\&\, B \Rightarrow C, A, B \vdash C$	$A \,\&\, B \Rightarrow C, A \vdash B \Rightarrow C$

At first sight it is puzzling that CP should fail on Prob's understanding of 'If'. He construes 'if'-clauses as suppositions – assumptions. What is the difference between the role of a premiss on the left of the turnstile, and the antecedent of a conditional on the right of the turnstile?

The antecedent of the conditional in the conclusion is indeed treated as an assumption. The premisses are not being treated as assumptions, but as beliefs; and moreover, as beliefs which need not be certainties. With arguments involving only factual statements, the difference does not matter. For these, a valid argument may be construed as

(a)   showing what follows necessarily from assumptions;
(b)   an argument which preserves certainty – certainty in the premisses entitles you to certainty in the conclusion;
(c)   an argument which preserves high probability, in line with PPP.

If an assumption is taken as a hypothetical certainty, (a) and (b) stay in line for arguments with conditionals also. However, with arguments involving conditionals, (b) can be satisfied while (c) is not. There are arguments which preserve certainty which do not preserve high probability, for example the 'invalid' argument forms on the right above. Their premisses can be arbitrarily close to 100 percent probable, their conclusion arbitrarily close to 0 percent probable.

The logico-mathematical fact behind this is the difference in the logical powers of 'All' and 'Almost all.' Consider (4) on the right: strengthening of the antecedent. If all A-worlds are C-worlds, then all $A \,\&\, B$-worlds are C-worlds. But we can have: almost all A-worlds are C-worlds, yet no $A \,\&\, B$-worlds are C-worlds. I can be almost certain that if you strike the match, it will light, yet give zero probability to its lighting if you dip it in water and strike it. Consider (5) on the right: transitivity. If all A-worlds are B-worlds, and all B-worlds are C-worlds, then all A-worlds are C-worlds. But we can have: all A-worlds are B-worlds, almost all B-worlds are C-worlds, yet no A-world is a C-world; just as we can have: all kiwis are birds, almost all birds fly, yet no kiwis fly. Take an example from Adams (1966):

If Jones is elected, Brown will resign (highly likely: almost all J-worlds are B-worlds).

If Brown dies before the election, Jones will be elected (all *D*-worlds are *J*-worlds).

but not

If Brown dies before the election, Brown will resign.

   Someone might react as follows: 'All I want of a valid argument is that it preserve certainty. I'm not bothered if an argument can have premisses close to certain and a conclusion far from certain, as long as the conclusion is certain when the premisses are certain.' Let us not argue about the word 'valid.' Use it in such a way that an argument is valid provided it preserves certainty, if you wish. If your interest in logic is confined to its application to mathematics or other *a priori* matters, that is fine. Further, when your arguments do not contain conditionals, if you have certainty-preservation, probability-preservation comes free. But if you use conditionals when arguing about contingent matters, then great caution will be required. Unless you are 100 percent certain of the premisses, the arguments on the right guarantee nothing about what you are entitled to think about the conclusion. The line between 100 percent certainty and something very close is hard to make out: it is not clear how you tell which side of it you are on. The epistemically cautious might admit that they are never, or only very rarely, 100 percent certain of contingent conditionals. So it would be useful to have another category of argument, the 'super-valid,' which preserves high probability as well as certainty. The arguments on the left are super-valid, those on the right are not.[5]

17.3.   Further Issues

17.3.1.   *Belief-relative propositions*

Adams's theory of validity emerged in the mid-1960s. 'Nearest possible worlds' theories were not yet in evidence. Nor was Lewis's result that conditional probabilities are not probabilities of the truth of a proposition. (Adams expressed scepticism about truth conditions for conditionals, but the question was still open.) Stalnaker's (1991b [1968]) (also 1981 [1970]) semantics for conditionals was an attempt to provide truth conditions which were compatible with Ramsey's and Adams's thesis about conditional belief. That is, he sought truth conditions for a proposition $A > B$ (his notation) such that $p(A > B)$ must equal $p_A(B)$ (Stalnaker, 1991b [1968], pp. 33–4):

   Now that we have found an answer to the question, 'How do we decide whether or not we believe a conditional statement?' [Ramsey's and Adams's answer to] the problem is to make the transition from belief conditions to truth conditions; . . . The concept of a *possible world* is just what we need to make the transition, since a possible world is the ontological analogue of a stock of hypothetical beliefs. The following . . . is a first approximation to the account I shall propose: Consider a possible world in which A is true and otherwise differs minimally from the actual world. *'If A, then B' is true (false) just in case B is true (false) in that possible world.*

If an argument is necessarily truth-preserving, the improbability of its conclusion cannot exceed the sum of the improbabilities of the premises. This was the criterion Adams used in constructing his logic. So Stalnaker's logic for conditionals must agree with Adams's over their common domain.[6] And it does. The argument forms on the right above are invalid on Stalnaker's semantics. Consider (4). The following is possible: in the nearest world in which you strike the match, it lights; in the nearest world in which you dip the match in water and strike it, it does not light. So Strengthening fails.[7]

Conditional Proof fails for Stalnaker's semantics.

$$A \lor B, \neg A \vdash B$$

is, of course, valid. But

$$(*) \ A \lor B \vdash \neg A > B$$

is not: it can be true that Ann or Mary cooked the dinner (for Ann cooked it); yet false that in the nearest world to the actual world in which Ann did not cook it, Mary cooked it.

Stalnaker (1991a [1975]) tried to show that although (*) is invalid, it is nevertheless a 'reasonable inference' when '$A \lor B$' is assertable, that is, when the speaker has ruled out $\neg A$ & $\neg B$, but $\neg A$ & B and A & $\neg B$ remain open possibilities. Indicative conditionals, he claims, are used only when their antecedents are epistemically possible for the speaker (here he agrees with Prob). Then comes the crucial claim: *worlds which are epistemically possible for the speaker count as closer to the actual world than those which are not.* All $\neg A$ & $\neg B$-worlds have been eliminated. Not all $\neg A$ & B-worlds have been eliminated. All the speaker's epistemically possible $\neg A$-worlds are B-worlds. So the closest $\neg A$-world is a B-world. '$A > B$' is true.

This makes the truth conditions of a conditional, e.g.,

If Ann didn't cook the dinner, Bob cooked it.

dependent on what the speaker believes. All that is common to different utterances of '$A > B$' is that they say that a certain A-world is a B-world. That is not news: provided that A and B are compatible, some A-world is a B-world. Which world is being said to be a B-world depends on the speaker's beliefs. With fixed meanings for A and B, there is no single proposition $A > B$, but a different one for each belief state: one might write $A >_p B$, where 'p' is itself indexed to a person and a time.

Earlier I argued as follows against non-truth-functionalist truth conditions: there are six incompatible logically possible combinations of truth values for A, B and $\neg A \to B$. You start off with no firm beliefs about which obtains. Now you eliminate $\neg A$ & $\neg B$, i.e., establish $A \lor B$. That leaves five remaining possibilities, including two in which '¬$A \rightarrow B$' is false. So you cannot be certain that ¬$A \rightarrow B$. Stalnaker replies: you cannot, indeed, be certain that the proposition you were wondering about earlier is true. But in your new epistemic state, you express a new proposition by '¬$A \rightarrow B$,' with different truth conditions, governed by a new nearness relation, and you know that that new proposition is true.

Disagreement and change of mind give way to equivocation. Suppose you and I start off knowing $A \vee B \vee C$. You then eliminate C. You accept 'If ¬A, B' and reject 'If ¬A, C'. I eliminate B. I accept 'If ¬A, C', and reject 'If ¬A, B'. I assent to a sentence from which you dissent, and vice versa. We do not disagree. We express different propositions, with different truth conditions, governed by our different epistemic states. Worlds which are near for me are far for you.

Are belief-relative truth conditions better than no truth conditions? They account for the validity of arguments; but Adams's logic has its own rationale without them. They account for sentences with conditional constituents. But we saw, and will see below, they sometimes give counterintuitive results. Do they escape Lewis's negative result? Although Lewis showed that there is no proposition $A * B$ such that $p(A * B) = p_A(B)$ in every belief state, he did not rule out that in every belief state there is some proposition or other, $A * B$, such that $p(A * B) = p_A(B)$. Nevertheless, in the wake of Lewis, Stalnaker himself proved this stronger result, for his conditional connective: the equation $p(A > B) = p_A(B)$ cannot hold for all propositions in a single belief state. If it holds for A and B, one can find two other propositions, C and D (truth-functional compounds of A and B) for which, demonstrably, it does not hold.[8] Gibbard (1981, pp. 231–4) showed just how belief-sensitive Stalnaker's truth conditions would be, and later, Stalnaker (1984) abandoned the claim that conditionals express belief-relative propositions, writing 'It follows that the conditional . . . expresses one proposition when it is asserted, and a different one when it is denied' (1984, p. 110).

17.3.2. Assertability

Jackson holds that 'If A, B' has the truth conditions of '$A \supset B$,' i.e., '¬$A \vee B$'; but it is part of its meaning that it is governed by a special rule of assertability. 'If' is assimilated to words like 'but', 'nevertheless' and 'even'. 'A but B' has the same truth conditions as 'A and B', yet they differ in meaning: 'but' is used to signal a contrast between A and B. When A and B are true but the contrast is lacking, 'A but B' is true but inappropriate. Likewise,

Even John can understand this proof.

is true when John can understand this proof, but inappropriate when John is a world-class logician.

In asserting 'If A, B' the speaker expresses his belief that $A \supset B$, and also indicates that this belief is 'robust' with respect to the A. In his early work Jackson (1979, 1981) explained 'robustness' thus: the speaker would not abandon his belief that $A \supset B$ if he were to learn that A. This, it was claimed, amounted to the speaker's having a high probability for $A \supset B$ given A, i.e., for $\neg A \vee B$ given A, which is just to have a high probability for B given A. Thus, assertability goes by conditional probability. Robustness was meant to ensure that an assertable conditional is fit for *modus ponens*. Robustness is not satisfied if you believe $A \supset B$ solely on the grounds that $\neg A$. Then, if you discover that A, you will abandon your belief in $A \supset B$ rather than conclude that B.

Jackson came to realize, however, that there are assertable conditionals which one would not continue to believe if one learned the antecedent. I say

If Reagan worked for the KGB, I'll never find out.

(Lewis's example 1986b, p. 155). My conditional probability for consequent given antecedent is high. But if I were to discover that the antecedent is true, I would abandon the conditional belief, rather than conclude that I will never find out that the antecedent is true. So, in his later work, Jackson (1987) defined robustness with respect to A simply as $p_A(A \supset B)$ being high, which is trivially equivalent to $p_A(B)$ being high. In most cases, though, the earlier explanation will hold good.

What are the truth-functional truth conditions needed for? Do they explain the meaning of compounds of conditionals? According to Jackson (1987, p. 129), they do not. We know what '$A \supset B$' means, as a constituent in complex sentences. But '$A \supset B$' does not mean the same as 'If A, B'. The latter has a special assertability condition. And his theory has no implications about what, if anything, 'if A, B' means when it occurs, unasserted, as a constituent in a longer sentence. Here his analogy with 'but' etc. fails. 'But' can occur in unasserted clauses:

Either he arrived on time but didn't wait for us, or he never arrived at all.

(Woods, 1997, p. 61). It also occurs in questions and commands:

Shut the door but leave the window open.

Does anyone want eggs but no ham?

'But' means 'in contrast.' Its meaning is not given by an 'assertability condition.'

Do the truth-functional truth conditions explain the validity of arguments involving conditionals? Not in a way that accords well with intuition, as has been seen, though Jackson (1987, pp. 50–1) claims that our intuitions are at fault here: we confuse preservation of truth and preservation of assertability. Nor is there any direct evidence for Jackson's theory. Nobody who thinks the Republicans won't win treats

If the Republicans win, they will double income tax.

as inappropriate but probably true, in the same category as

Even Gödel understood truth-functional logic.

Jackson is aware of this. He seems to advocate an error theory of conditionals: ordinary linguistic behavior fits the false theory that there is a proposition $A * B$ such that $p(A * B) = p_A(B)$ (Jackson, 1987, pp. 39–40). If this is his view, he cannot hold that his own theory is a psychologically accurate account of what people do when they use conditionals. Perhaps it is an account of how we *should* use conditionals, and would if we were free from error: we *should* accept that

If the Republicans win they will double income tax.

is probably true when it is probable that the Republicans will not win. Would we gain anything from following this prescription? On the contrary, we would deprive ourselves of the ability to discriminate between believable and unbelievable conditionals whose antecedents we think false.

17.3.3. Compounds

Lewis (1986c [1976], p. 134) wrote,

> Adams has convinced me. I shall take it as established that the assertability of an ordinary indicative conditional $A \to C$ does indeed go by the conditional subjective probability $[p_A(C)]$.[9]

Should we then deny that conditionals express propositions, with truth conditions? "I have no conclusive objection to [this] hypothesis," he writes. But he states an 'inconclusive objection' – that it 'requires too much of a fresh start' (p. 142):

> What about compound sentences which have such conditionals as constituents? We think we know how the truth conditions for compound sentences of various kinds are determined by the truth conditions of constituent subsentences, but this knowledge would be useless if any of those subsentences lacked truth conditions. Either we need new semantic rules for many familiar connectives and operators when applied to indicative conditionals . . . or else we need to explain away all seeming examples of compound sentences with conditional constituents.

Lewis argued that the truth conditions are truth-functional, but the assertability of a conditional, for Gricean reasons, goes by its conditional probability. In a postscript to a reprinting of this paper, Lewis (1986b, pp. 152–6) abandons Grice's in favor of Jackson's explanation of why assertability goes by conditional probability.

An account which requires a 'fresh start,' however, is preferable to one which already has unacceptable consequences for compounds of conditionals. Grice focuses on what is needed to justify the *assertion* of a conditional, beyond the belief that it is true. This is no help when it occurs, unasserted, as a constituent of a longer sentence. And as was seen above with negations of conditionals and conditionals in antecedents, the problem is reversed: sentences are asserted which would be believed false if the conditionals had been construed truth-functionally. Jackson (1987,

p. 129) explicitly denies that his theory implies that compounds of conditionals are meaningful.

Followers of Adams claim that when a sentence with a conditional subsentence is intelligible, it can be paraphrased by a sentence without a conditional subsentence. For some constructions this can be done in a general, uniform way. For others, it can be done only in the presence of contextual clues as to what is meant. They point out that some constructions are rarer, and harder to understand, than is to be expected if conditionals have truth conditions. Why do we never hear sentences of the form 'Either, if *A*, *B*, or, if *C*, *D* (I don't know which)'? Some are impossible to understand. Gibbard's example, said of a conference: 'If Kripke was there if Strawson was, then Anscombe was there.' 'Do you know what you have been told?' he asks (1981, p. 235.)[10]

'If *A*, then if *B*, *C*' is to be paraphrased as 'If *A* & *B*, then *C*.' For to suppose that *A*, then to suppose that *B* and make a judgment about *C* under those suppositions, is the same as to make a judgment about *C* under the supposition that *A* & *B*. Consider this as applied to a problem raised by McGee (1985) with the following example. Before Reagan's first election, Reagan was hot favorite, a second Republican, Anderson, was a complete outsider, and Carter was lagging well behind Reagan. Consider first

(1) If a Republican wins and Reagan does not win, then Anderson will win.

As these are the only two Republicans in the race, (1) is unassailable. Now consider

(2) If a Republican wins, then if Reagan does not win, Anderson will win.

We read (2) as equivalent to (1), hence also unassailable.

Suppose I am close to certain (say, 90 percent certain) that Reagan will win, and hence close to certain that

(3) A Republican will win.

But I don't believe

(4) If Reagan does not win, Anderson will win.

I am less than 1 percent certain that (4). On the contrary, I believe that if Reagan doesn't win, Carter will win. As these opinions seem sensible, we have a prima facie counterexample to *modus ponens*: I accept (2) and (3), but reject (4). Truth conditions or not, valid arguments obey the probability preservation principle. I am 100 percent certain that (2), 90 percent certain that (3), but less than 1 percent certain that (4).

Hook saves *modus ponens* by claiming that I must accept (4). For Hook, (4) is equivalent to

Either Reagan will win or Anderson will win.

As I'm 90 percent certain that Reagan will win, I must accept this disjunction, and hence accept (4). Hook's reading of (4) is, of course, implausible.

Arrow saves *modus ponens* by claiming that, although (1) is certain, (2) is not equivalent to (1), and (2) is almost certainly false. For Stalnaker,

(5) If a Republican wins, then if Reagan does not win, Carter will win.

is true. To assess (5), we need to consider the nearest world in which a Republican wins (call it *w*), and ask whether the conditional consequent is true at *w*. At *w*, almost certainly, it is Reagan who wins. We need now to consider the nearest world to *w* in which Reagan does not win. Call it *w'*. In *w'*, almost certainly, Carter wins. Stalnaker's reading of (2) is implausible; intuitively, we accept (2) as equivalent to (1), and do not accept (5). (On Stalnaker's semantics,

If Reagan doesn't win, then if a Republican wins Reagan will win.

is also true.)

Prob saves *modus ponens* by denying that the argument is really of that form. '$A \Rightarrow B$; A; so B' is demonstrably valid when A and B are propositions. For instance, if $p(A) = 90$ percent and $p_A(B) = 90$ percent, the lowest possible value for $p(B)$ is 81 percent. The 'consequent' of (2),

If Reagan doesn't win, Anderson will win.

is not a proposition. The argument is really of the form

If A & B, then C; A; so if B then C.

This argument form is invalid (Prob and Stalnaker agree). Take the case where $C = A$, and we have

If A & B then A; A; so if B then A.

The first premiss is a tautology and falls out as redundant; and we are left with 'A; so if B then A.' We have already seen that this is invalid: I can think it very likely that Fred is lecturing right now, without thinking that if he was injured on his way to work, he is lecturing right now. So Prob is not at a unilateral disadvantage when it comes to compounds of conditionals.

17.3.4. *Other conditionals*

As well as conditional beliefs, there are conditional desires, hopes, fears, etc. As well as conditional statements, there are conditional commands, questions, offers, promises, bets, etc. A conditional clause, 'If he phones,' plays the same role in

If he phones, what shall I say?

If he phones, hang up immediately.

and

If he phones, Mary will be pleased.

Which of our theories extends to these other kinds of conditional?

According to Prob, one believes that B to the extent that one thinks B more likely than not B; one believes that B if A to the extent that one thinks $A \& B$ more likely than $A \& \neg B$; and there is no proposition X such that one must believe X more likely than $\neg X$, just to the extent that one believes $A \& B$ more likely than $A \& \neg B$. Conditional desires appear to be similar: to desire that B is to prefer B to $\neg B$; to desire that B if A is to prefer $A \& B$ to $A \& \neg B$; there is no proposition X such that one prefers X to $\neg X$ just to the extent that one prefers $A \& B$ to $A \& \neg B$.

If Mary comes (M), I want her to meet Jane (J).

I prefer $M \& J$ to $M \& \neg J$. I do not necessarily prefer $M \supset J$, i.e., $\neg M \lor J$, to $M \& \neg J$. For I may also want Mary to come, and fear that the likeliest way of $\neg M \lor J$ being true is $\neg M$. Nor will my conditional desire be satisfied if in the nearest possible world in which Mary comes, she meets Jane. If the elusive Jane happened to be here when Mary had almost arrived, but then received an urgent call to return to work, which turned out to be a mistake, a wrong number, meant for someone else, I will not be pleased.

If I believe that B if A, i.e., think $A \& B$ much more likely than $A \& \neg B$, then this puts me in a position to make a conditional commitment to B: to assert that B, conditionally upon A. If A is true, my conditional assertion has the force of an assertion of B. If A is false, there is no proposition that I asserted. I did, however, express my conditional belief – it is not as though I said nothing.[11] I say

If you press that switch, there will be an explosion.

My hearer takes me to have made a conditional assertion of the consequent, one which will have the force of an assertion of the consequent if she presses the button. Provided she takes me to be trustworthy and reliable, she thinks that if she presses the switch, the consequent is likely to be true. That is, she acquires a reason to think that if she presses it, there will be an explosion; and hence a reason not to press it.

Conditional commands can, likewise, be construed as having the force of a command of the consequent, conditional upon the antecedent's being true. The doctor says to the nurse in the emergency ward,

If the patient is still alive in the morning, change the dressing.

Considered as a command to make Hook's conditional true, this is equivalent to

> Make it the case that either the patient is not alive in the morning, or you change the dressing.

The nurse puts a pillow over the patient's face and kills her. On the truth-functional interpretation, the nurse can claim that he was carrying out the doctor's order. Extending Jackson's account to conditional commands, the doctor said 'Make it the case that either the patient is not alive in the morning, or you change the dressing,' and indicated that she would still command this if she knew that the patient would be alive. This does not help. The nurse who kills the patient still carried out an order. Why should the nurse be concerned with what the doctor would command in a counterfactual situation? Extending Stalnaker's account to conditional commands,

> If it rains, take your umbrella.

becomes

> In the nearest possible world in which it rains, take your umbrella.

Suppose I have forgotten your command or alternatively am inclined to disregard it. However, it does not rain. In the nearest world in which it rains, I do not take my umbrella. On Stalnaker's account, I disobeyed you. Similarly for conditional promises: on this analysis, I could break my promise to go to the doctor if the pain gets worse, even if the pain gets better. This is wrong: conditional commands and promises are not requirements on my behavior in other possible worlds.

Among conditional questions one can distinguish those in which the addressee is presumed to know whether the antecedent is true, and those in which he is not. In the latter case, the addressee is being asked to suppose that the antecedent is true, and give his opinion about the consequent:

> If it rains, will the match be cancelled?

In the former case – 'If you have been to London, did you like it?' – he is expected to answer the consequent-question if the antecedent is true. If the antecedent is false, the question lapses: there is no conditional belief for him to express. 'Not applicable' as the childless might write on a form which asks

> If you have children, how many children do you have?

(Perverse childless undergraduates have been known to write '17' on the grounds that 'I have children ⊃ I have 17 children' is true.) You are not being asked how many children you have in the nearest possible world in which you have children. Nor are you being asked what you would believe about the consequent if you came to believe that you did have children.

Probability theory needs the notion of conditional probability, which is not the probability of the truth of a proposition (nor the probability of the occurrence of an event). It supplies us with an account of conditional belief, or better, degree of closeness to conditional certainty. Adams showed how to do logic for conditionals in these terms. Widening our perspective, this thesis fits a general pattern. Any propositional attitude can be held simpliciter, or under a supposition. Any speech act can be performed unconditionally, or conditionally upon something else. The phenomena are better explained without invoking conditional propositions.

Suggested further reading

First, here are some essays which aim to give an overview of work on conditionals, as well as presenting the authors' own conclusions. Mackie (1973, ch. 4), is of this type. Sanford (1989) includes the history, and pre-history, of the subject, and a thorough and thoughtful critique of contemporary work, as well as original proposals. Edgington (1995) is a 'State of the Art' survey commissioned by *Mind*. Woods (1997) is an insightful extended essay of this type, followed by a commentary by Edgington. Next, Jackson (1991) is a useful collection of articles, many of them classics. Harper et al. (1981) is also a valuable collection of articles, many of them concerned with the probabilistic approach and with reactions to Lewis's (1986c [1976]) proof that a conditional probability is not the probability of the truth of a proposition. Adams (1975) is the *locus classicus* for the logic Adams developed based on the probabilistic approach. This is further explained in Adams's (1998) textbook. Jackson (1987) is a sophisticated defence of the truth-functional account of the truth conditions of indicative conditionals, which argues that such conditionals are assertable to the extent that the conditional probability of consequent given antecedent is high. The classic writings on counterfactual conditionals are Goodman (1995, ch. 1), and Lewis (1973). Lewis (1986a [1979]) provides further elucidation of the notion of similarity between possible worlds, in response to critics of that notion. It is reprinted, with extensive postscripts, in Lewis (1986b). There is a huge number of articles on this still controversial subject. More complete bibliographies are found in Sanford (1989), Edgington (1995) and Woods (1997).

Notes

1 Dudman (1984a,b, 1988) has done most to promote this view. See also Gibbard (1981, pp. 222–6), Smiley (1984), Bennett (1988), Mellor (1993) and Woods (1997). Bennett (1995) recanted and returned to the traditional view. Jackson (1998a [1990]) also argues for the traditional view.

2 Probability theory is an abstract structure which can have more than one interpretation. Ramsey did not claim that the only interpretation of probability was degree of belief.

3 As we are here concerned only with simple entailments (and we are interpreting probability as degree of belief), we need only claim that if A is recognized to entail B, $p(A \& \neg B) = 0$, leaving aside the question what someone should believe about $A \& \neg B$ if A entails B but the entailment is so complex as to be beyond his ken.

4 (1) and (2) follow from the following facts:

- $p(A) = p(A \& B) + p(A \& \neg B)$
- $p(B) = p(A \& B) + p(\neg A \& B)$
- If A entails B, $p(A \& \neg B) = 0$
- $p(A \lor B) = p(A \& B) + p(A \& \neg B) + p(\neg A \& B)$

(3) is proved by mathematical induction. We have seen that (3) holds for $n = 2$. Assume that it holds for $n = m$. Then it holds for $n = m + 1$:

$$p((A_1 \vee \cdots \vee A_m) \vee A_{m+1}) \leq p(A_1 \vee \cdots \vee A_m) + p(A_{m+1}) \leq p(A_1) + \cdots + p(A_m) + p(A_{m+1})$$

5 The arguments on the right do preserve high probability in many normal applications. The counterexamples arise in clearly delimited circumstances. Sometimes we can state a restricted form which is valid. For example, restricted transitivity: $A \Rightarrow B$, $(A \& B) \Rightarrow C \vdash A \Rightarrow C$, is valid.

6 Adams does not treat of compounds of conditionals. As Stalnaker's conditionals have truth conditions, there is no problem in principle about their occurring as parts of longer sentences.

7 A semantics of this kind is justly famous for counterfactual conditionals. Stalnaker applied it to both indicatives and counterfactuals, while allowing that 'nearness' may be construed differently in the two cases. Lewis (1973) independently, developed a similar semantics for counterfactuals. (Lewis's logic also agrees with Adams's.) The idea has more intuitive plausibility for counterfactuals than for indicatives. The semantics agrees with the truth-functional semantics when A is true, and comes into its own when A is false. This is where the focus is for counterfactual thoughts, 'If Mary had been there . . .'; these are typically assertions about non-actual situations, and we try to decide what would be true in them. It is not where the focus is for indicative conditional thoughts – 'If Mary is there . . .'. Of course the antecedent of an indicative conditional may be false. But it is not part of the process of its evaluation to think: suppose Mary isn't there, then is 'If Mary is there, C' true? Is the nearest world in which she is there a C-world?

8 The proof is in Stalnaker's letter to van Fraassen published in van Fraassen (1976, pp. 303–4); also Gibbard (1981, pp. 219–20) and Edgington (1995, pp. 276–8).

9 In his earliest writing on the subject, Adams did state his thesis in terms of 'assertability'; but he abandoned the term as potentially misleading, and construes his thesis as about the acceptability, or believability, of a conditional.

10 See Appiah (1985, pp. 205–10), Gibbard (1981, pp. 234–8), Edgington (1995, pp. 280–4), Woods (1997, pp. 58–68 and pp. 120–4); also Jackson (1987, pp. 127–37), Dummett (1973, pp. 351–4); Dummett (1992, pp. 171–2), Mackie (1973, p. 73). There have also been sophisticated attempts at a general theory of compounds, compatible with Prob's thesis, involving quasi-propositional entities which take more than two values. One tradition makes the conditional true if $A \& B$, false if $A \& \neg B$, neither if $\neg A$, and the probability of a conditional the probability that it is true given that it has a truth value. A valuable survey of this work is found in Milne (1997). Another tradition uses belief-relative 'propositions' which are assigned 1 if $A \& B$, 0 if $A \& \neg B$, $p_A(B)$ if $\neg A$, and makes the probability of the conditional its expected value. See van Fraassen (1976), McGee (1989), Jeffrey (1991), and Stalnaker and Jeffery (1994). Unfortunately, these approaches still generate counterintuitive consequences for compounds. For some criticisms, see Edgington (1991, pp. 200–2), and Lance (1991).

11 Dummett (1992, p. 115) misrepresents the notion of a conditional assertion when he says it is "as if [someone] handed his hearers a sealed envelope marked 'Open only in the event that . . .'."

References

Adams, E. W. 1965: "A Logic of Conditionals," *Inquiry*, 8, 166–97.

Adams, E. W. 1966: "Probability and the Logic of Conditionals," in Hintikka and Suppes (1966, 256–316).

Adams, E. W. 1970: "Subjunctive and Indicative Conditionals," *Foundations of Language*, 6, 89–94.

Adams, E. W. 1975: *The Logic of Conditionals*, (D. Reidel, Dordrecht).

Adams, E. W. 1998: *A Primer of Probability Logic*, (CLSI Publications, Stanford).

Appiah, A. 1985: *Assertion and Conditionals*, (Cambridge University Press, Cambridge).

Bayes, T. 1763: "An Essay Towards Solving a Problem in the Doctrine of Chances," *Transactions of the Royal Society of London*, 53, 370–418.

Bennett, J. 1988: "Farewell to the Phlogiston Theory of Conditionals," *Mind*, 97, 509–27.

Bennett, J. 1995: "Classifying Conditionals: The Traditional Way is Right," *Mind*, 104, 331–44.

Dudman, V. H. 1984a: "Conditional Interpretations of 'If'-Sentences," *Australian Journal of Linguistics*, 4, 143–204.

Dudman, V. H. 1984b: "Parsing 'If'-Sentences," *Analysis*, 44, 145–53.

Dudman, V. H. 1988: "Indicative and Subjunctive," *Analysis*, 48, 113–22.

Dummett, M. 1973: *Frege: The Philosophy of Language*, (Duckworth, London).

Dummett, M. 1992: *The Logical Basis of Metaphysics*, (Duckworth, London).

Edgington, D. 1991: "The Mystery of the Missing Matter of Fact," *Proceedings of the Aristotelian Society Supplementary Volume*, 65, 185–209.

Edgington, D. 1995: "On Conditionals," *Mind*, 104, 235–329.

Eells, E. and Skyrms, B. (eds.) 1994: *Probability and Conditionals*, (Cambridge University Press, Cambridge).

Frege, G. 1960: "Begriffsschrift," in *Translations from the Philosophical Writings of Gottlob Frege*, P. Geach and M. Black. eds., (Basil Blackwell, Oxford), 1–20.

Gibbard, A. 1981: "Two Recent Theories of Conditionals," in Harper et al. (1981, 211–47).

Goodman, N. 1995: *Fact, Fiction and Forecast*, (Harvard University Press, Cambridge, MA).

Grice, H. P. 1989: *Studies in the Way of Words*, (Harvard University Press, Cambridge, MA).

Harper, W. L. and Hooker, C. A. (eds.) 1976: *Foundations of Probability Theory, Statistical Inference, and Statistical Theories of Science*, Vol. I, (D. Reidel, Dordrecht).

Harper, W. L., Stalnaker, R. and Pearce, C. T. (eds.) 1981: *Ifs*, (D. Reidel, Dordrecht).

Hintikka, J. and Suppes, P. (eds.) 1966: *Aspects of Inductive Logic*, (North-Holland, Amsterdam).

Jackson, F. 1979: "On Assertion and Indicative Conditionals," *Philosophical Review*, 88, 565–89.

Jackson, F. 1981: "Conditionals and Possibilia," *Proceedings of the Aristotelian Society*, 81, 125–37.

Jackson, F. 1987: *Conditionals*, (Basil Blackwell, Oxford).

Jackson, F. (ed.) 1991: *Conditionals*, (Clarendon Press, Oxford).

Jackson, F. 1998a: "Classifying Conditionals I," *Analysis*, 50 (1990), 134–47; reprinted in Jackson (1998b, pp. 27–42).

Jackson, F. 1998b: *Mind, Method and Conditionals*, (Routledge, London).

Jeffrey, R. 1991: "Matter of Fact Conditionals," *Proceedings of the Aristotelian Society Supplementary Volume*, 65, 161–83.

Lance, M. 1991: "Probabilistic Dependence among Conditionals," *Philosophical Review*, 100, 269–76.

Lewis, D. 1973: *Counterfactuals*, (Basil Blackwell, Oxford).

Lewis, D. 1986a: "Counterfactuals and Time's Arrow," *Noûs*, 13 (1979), 455–76; reprinted with postscripts in Lewis (1986b, 32–66).

Lewis, D. 1986b: *Philosophical Papers*, Vol. 2, (Oxford University Press, Oxford).

Lewis, D. 1986c: "Probabilities of Conditionals and Conditional Probabilities," *Philosophical Review*, 85 (1976), 297–315; reprinted, with postscript, in Lewis (1986b, 133–56).

Mackie, J. 1973: *Truth, Probability and Paradox*, (Clarendon Press, Oxford).

McGee, V. 1985: "A Counterexample to *Modus Ponens*," *Journal of Philosophy*, 82, 462–71.

McGee, V. 1989: "Conditional Probabilities and Compounds of Conditionals," *Philosophical Review*, 98, 485–542.

Mellor, D. H. 1993: "How to Believe a Conditional," *Journal of Philosophy*, 90, 233–48.

Milne, P. 1997: "Bruno de Finetti and the Logic of Conditional Events," *British Journal for the Philosophy of Science*, 48, 195–232.

Ramsey, F. P. 1990a: "General Propositions and Causality," in Ramsey (1990b, 145–63).

Ramsey, F. P. 1990b: *Philosophical Papers*, D. H. Mellor, ed., (Cambridge University Press, Cambridge).

Ramsey, F. P. 1990c: "Truth and Probability," in *Foundations of Mathematics and Other Logical Essays*, R. B. Braithwaite, ed., (Routledge and Kegan Paul, London), 1931 [reprinted 1965]; reprinted in Ramsey (1990b, 52–94).

Sanford, D. H. 1989: *If P, then Q: Conditionals and the Foundations of Reasoning*, (Routledge, London).

Smiley, T. 1984: "Hunter on Conditionals," *Proceedings of the Aristotelian Society*, 84, 113–22.

Stalnaker, R. 1981: "Probability and Conditionals," *Philosophy of Science*, 37 (1970), 64–80; reprinted in Harper et al. (1981, 107–28).

Stalnaker, R. 1984: *Inquiry*, (MIT Press, Cambridge, MA).

Stalnaker, R. 1991a: "Indicative Conditionals," *Philosophia*, 5 (1975), 269–86; reprinted in Jackson (1991, 136–54).

Stalnaker, R. 1991b: "A Theory of Conditionals," in *Studies in Logical Theory, American Philosophical Quarterly*, Monograph Series, 2, (Blackwell, Oxford), 1968; reprinted in Jackson (1991, 98–112).

Stalnaker, R. and Jeffrey, R. 1994: "Conditionals as Random Variables," in Eells and Skyrms (1994, 31–46).

Van Fraassen, B. 1976: "Probabilities of Conditionals," in Harper and Hooker (1976, 261–308).

Woods, M. 1997: *Conditionals*, (Clarendon Press, Oxford).

Chapter 18

Negation

Heinrich Wansing

18.1. Introduction

This chapter is concerned with logical aspects of negation, i.e. with the role of negation in valid inferences and hence with the contribution negation makes to the truth and falsity conditions of declarative expressions. Negation is an important philosophical and logical concept. Often differences between logical systems can – at least partially – be described as differences between the notions of negation used in these logics. In natural deduction, for example, classical logic can be obtained from intuitionistic logic on the addition of the double negation elimination rule:

$$\neg\neg A/A$$

Notwithstanding the importance of negation, the immense literature on negation[1] abounds with disagreement. According to Gabbay (1988), intuitionistic negation is a typical instance of negation as inconsistency, while according to Avron (1999), intuitionistic negation clearly fails to be a genuine negation. In the opinion of Tennant (1999), basing negation on the notion of disproof leads to negation in intuitionistic relevant logic, whereas by treating the notion of disproof on a par with the notion of proof, López-Escobar (1972) obtains the strong, constructive negation of Nelson (Almukdad and Nelson, 1984; Nelson, 1949; 1959), and independently investigated by von Kutschera (1969). Moreover, it can be shown that the latter negation fails to be a negation as inconsistency in the sense of Gabbay.

The question arises: What are at least necessary conditions under which a unary connective ought to be regarded as a negation operation? The disagreement about negation is, however, even more fundamental. According to Zwarts (1996), for instance, linguistic research has clearly revealed that negation in natural languages occurs in various syntactic categories, including sentence negation. However, Englebretsen (1981), for example, argues to the effect that whereas one ought to draw the Aristotelian distinction between predicate and predicate term negation, there is no such thing as external, sentential negation. Thus there is even disagreement concerning the syntactic types to which negation belongs.

Various strategies are available to obtain a single, uniform account of the multiplicity of syntactic types of negation or to reduce in the formal analysis the number of syntactic types in which negation occurs in natural languages:

Elimination: to explain away certain syntactic types

Generalization: to give an account such that various syntactic types of negation emerge as special cases of a general construction

Representation: to represent one type of negation in terms of another type

In section 18.2 instantiations of the first two strategies will be dealt with. Section 18.3 is then devoted to representing negation by means of unary connectives with a special emphasis on motivating strong, constructive negation. Moreover, various approaches toward defining and classifying notions of sentential negation will be surveyed. Some summarizing general ideas are assembled in section 18.4.

18.2. The Syntactic Categories of Negation

In the literature on syntactic categories in natural languages, it has sometimes been suggested to treat the Boolean particles 'not', 'and', and 'or' as variably polymorphic operations. In the case of 'not', this means that for *any* syntactic type (including sentences), 'not' may be combined with an expression of that type to form a compound expression of the same type; see, for example, van Benthem (1991, pp. 26f. and ch. 13). However, there is no general consensus on this variable polymorphism. The proponents of a neo-Aristotelian term logic, for example, have called into question the nowadays orthodox view that negation is a unary sentential connective. Most explicitly, Englebretsen (1981) has tried to explain away sentential negation, and the present section is, among other things, concerned with a critical examination of this eliminative view.

18.2.1. The neo-Aristotelian elimination of sentence negation

According to the Aristotelian term logic (as presented, for example, in Englebretsen (1981), Horn (1989, ch. 1), and Sommers (1982), every sentence consists of exactly one subject and exactly one predicate. Both the subject and the predicate are possibly complex terms. In the sentence

John is pleased.

the expression 'John' is the subject, the expression 'is pleased' is the predicate, and the expression 'pleased' is the predicate term. As Sommers (1982, p. 287) explains, "There is no reason to factor the predicate into a part that is the predicate term and a part that is the copula" 'is'. If "the terms are not explicit, the traditional logician will regiment the proposition to bring out its logical form. Thus 'Socrates runs' could be regimented as 'Socrates is a runner'." Every sentence affirms or denies what is denoted by its predicate of what is denoted by its subject. While

John is pleased.

affirms pleased of John,

John is not pleased.

denies pleased of John. This form of negation is called *predicate negation* (or predicate denial) and is to be distinguished from *predicate term negation*. In the case of predicate term negation, a predicate term is negated to obtain another predicate term. The predicate term negation of 'pleased' for instance is 'not-pleased', and the sentence

John is not-pleased.

affirms the predicate 'not-pleased' of John. If the predicate term of a sentence is negated, this results in a *contrary* of that sentence. A pair of contrary sentences cannot both be true. Whereas a predicate term 'P' may have many contraries, according to the neo-Aristotelian term logicians, it has exactly one logical contrary, namely 'not-P' (or 'non-P'). Among the non-logical contraries of the predicate term 'ancient', for example, are 'medieval' and 'modern'. If the predicate of a sentence is negated, one obtains a *contradictory* of that sentence. A pair of contradictory sentences can neither both be false nor both be true. Whereas the predicate term negation of a sentence implies the predicate negation of that sentence, the converse is not true. In this sense, predicate term negation is stronger than predicate denial.

Actually, the distinction between logical and non-logical contraries is quite subtle. There are passages in Aristotle's writings suggesting that contrariety is a polar notion (Horn, 1989, p. 37ff.) presupposing two extreme points of a scale:

> Since things which differ from one another may do so to a greater or a less degree, there exists also a greatest difference, and this I call 'contrariety'. (Aristotle, *Metaphysics* 1055a17–28)

Horn (1989, p. 39) distinguishes between

(i) contrariety simpliciter
(ii) immediate (alias strong or logical) contrariety, and
(iii) mediate (alias weak or non-logical) contrariety.

If by the span of a predicate term 'P' one means the class of entities that can be either P or not-P, two predicate terms are contraries simpliciter of each other iff (if and only if) both have the same span and what they denote cannot both be true of any element from their span. If two contrary predicate terms 'P' and 'Q' are such that for any a from their shared span, the sentences 'a is P' and 'a is Q' form a pair of contradictory sentences, the terms are said to be immediate contraries. This is the case if the scale associated with 'P' and 'Q' is binary. As Sommers (1982, p. 168) puts it, "[a] pair of logical contraries exhausts a range of predicability." When affirmed of numbers, 'even' and 'odd' form a pair of immediate contraries. Mediate contraries are contraries that are not immediate. If two mediate contraries denote the extremes of a (more than binary) scale, they are said to be *polar*, and otherwise they are called *simple*. While, for instance, 'black' and 'white' are lexicalized polar contraries, 'black' and 'red' are simple contraries. Any natural language predicate term has at most one polar contrary (with respect to a given scale). Also the immediate contrary of a given term is unique if it exists.[2] It would also make sense to classify immediate contraries as polar, if being polar is understood in the more general sense of forming the extremes of an at least binary scale. Both immediate and mediate non-simple contraries would then be polar in this more general sense.

The situation is more complicated if categorically mistaken sentences are also taken into account. Whereas 'John is well' and 'John is ill' are contradictories because 'well' and 'ill' are immediate contraries (at least according to Aristotle and Horn), '2 is well' and '2 is ill' fail to be contradictories, since neither of these categorially mistaken sentences is true. Likewise, if the name 'John' is non-denoting, then neither 'John is well' nor 'John is ill' are true.[3]

The term *logical contrary* suggests a correlation with some systematic syntactic device that – at the level of formalization – goes beyond merely pairing representations of lexical items like 'even' and 'odd.' Englebretsen (1981), Sommers (1982), and Horn (1989) use the predicate term negation 'not-P' ('non-P') to form the immediate (alias logical) contrary of a predicate term 'P'. The question arises how this is related to the morphology and the lexical repertoire of natural languages. Predicate term forming prefixes like 'dis-', 'un-', and 'im-' do not in general generate immediate contraries but often map a predicate term to its polar non-immediate contrary.[4] A person needs, for instance, neither to be pleased with a certain situation nor to be displeased with that situation. She might just not care. Nor need a person be either happy or unhappy. According to Englebretsen (1981, p. 50), category mistakes are the only sources of violations of the Law of Bivalence: "Every sentence which is sensible, category correct, is true or false." But as has just been seen, predicate term negation may also violate the Law of Bivalence in categorically correct sentences.

Since general polar contrariety is a more general concept than immediate contrariety insofar as polar contraries are immediate if the associated scale is binary, and since, moreover, the predicate term forming morphemes 'dis-', 'un-', and 'im-' often yield mediate non-simple contraries, it seems justified to use 'not-P' ('non-P') to form the unique polar contrary of a predicate term 'P' (in the sense of Horn) and not its immediate contrary. A further justification for this convention is that, in the case of categorically correct sentences, there is no need to distinguish between denying a predicate and affirming its immediate contrary, so that, for categorically correct declarative sentences, forming predicate term negation in a canonical way may be seen to yield unique polar contraries.

In an attempt to explain away sentence negation, as a first step, Englebretsen (1981, p. 36) attacks the view that every negation is sentential:

> Modern sentential logicians . . . fail to recognize anything but sentential negation. For such logicians any negated term must somehow be rendered part of a negated sentence. Nevertheless, notwithstanding what might look like notational economy, there are some sentences which cannot be analyzed in such a logic – sentences which are true and make use of term negation, but which become false or senseless when term negation is replaced by sentential negation. An example of such a sentence is 'Numbers are neither coloured nor noncoloured (uncoloured)'. Note that what is noncoloured is colourless, transparent, invisible, etc. Helium is noncoloured but not the number 2. The mathematical logician reparses the first as 'All things which are numbers are neither coloured nor noncoloured'; then as 'Everything is such that if it is a number then it is not coloured and not noncoloured', then as 'Everything is such that if it is a number then it is not the case that it is coloured and it is not the case that it is not the case that it is coloured', and finally as '$\forall x(Nx \supset (\neg Cx \wedge \neg\neg Cx))$'. But in the usual first order predicate calculus this entails that nothing is a number! [notation adjusted]

However, this argument clearly fails to show that there are sentences which cannot be represented using sentential negation. Instead, it demonstrates that using *a single* sentential negation operation to represent *both* predicate negation and predicate term negation may have undesirable consequences. Using the unary connective '$\neg$' to represent predicate negation and the unary connective '$\sim$' (strong negation) to represent predicate term negation, the translation of Englebretsen's example into predicate logic is:

$$\forall x(Nx \supset (\neg Cx \wedge \neg\sim Cx))$$

'Everything is such that if it is a number then it is not the case that it is coloured and it is not the case that it is non-coloured'.

In a second step, Englebretsen intends to show that "what is negated is never a sentence" (1981, p. 45):

> [W]hen 'p' is 'S is P', then 'It is not the case that p' ('$\neg p$') is 'S is not P'. Thus, 'It is not the case that 9 is even' is '9 is not even'. But sometimes 'it is not the case that' can be read as 'it is untrue that'. For example, 'It is not the case that I have stopped beating my wife' does not mean 'I have not stopped beating my wife', but rather 'It is untrue that I have stopped beating my wife'. In other words 'it is not the case that' is ambiguous. Usually it is the 'not' of predicate denial. Sometimes it is the predicate 'untrue'. The mathematical logician always takes it in the second way since he does not recognize predicate denial. (1981, p. 47f.) [notation adjusted]

He then continues to explain that "[i]f 'it is not the case that' is usually a sign of denial and sometimes a metalinguistic predicate (viz. 'untrue'), then it seems we are well on our way to the position that *no negation is sentential*" (1981, p. 49). First, one might object that

It is not the case that I have stopped beating my wife.

is itself ambiguous and may well mean that I have not stopped beating my wife. Second, if the external 'it is not the case that' may be read either as predicate negation or as a meta-linguistic predicate that can be affirmed or denied of propositions, one might also draw the conclusion that predicate denial and this meta-linguistic predicate are to be understood as external, sentential negation.

This is not the place for a general discussion of Aristotelian and neo-Aristotelian term logic. What the term logicians correctly point out is that a distinction must be drawn between predicate negation and predicate term negation. A natural idea is to represent these forms of negation by *distinct* unary connectives. Obviously, such a representation abstracts away from the innersentential syntactic realization of predicate negation and predicate term negation in natural languages. The representing connectives can be iterated and therefore, for instance, be interpreted as algebraic operations. To formally take into account the distinction between predicate negation and predicate term negation, it is therefore interesting to investigate algebraic structures comprising algebraic counterparts of at least two sentential negations.

18.2.2. Generalization on the basis of 2-negation algebras

Yet there must be a way to link the internal operators on predicates with the external operator (operators) on propositions, a bridge between the logic of terms and the logic of propositions. (La Palme Reyes et al., 1994, p. 50)

La Palme Reyes et al. (1994, 1999) develop a category-theoretic model for a pair of negations that can be applied to both predicates and sentences, "thereby incorporating in a single context both term logic and propositional logic" (1994, p. 51). This instance of the generalizing approach is based on the notion of a 2-negation algebra. A *2-negation algebra* is a bounded distributive lattice with two unary operations ($\neg$, negation, and $-$, supplement):

$$(\mathbf{B}, \leq, \vee, \wedge, 0, 1, \neg, -)$$

While negation is required to satisfy

$$y \leq \neg x \text{ iff } y \wedge x = 0 \tag{18.1}$$

supplement must satisfy

$$-x \leq y \text{ iff } x \vee y = 1 \tag{18.2}$$

La Palme Reyes et al. then use $\neg$ to represent predicate term negation and use $-$ to represent predicate negation.[5] This choice is surprising, because (18.1) defines the pseudocomplement of Heyting algebras. [See chapter 11.] The pseudo-complement is the algebraic counterpart of intuitionistic negation, which is a contradiction forming operation and not a contrary forming one.

The approach by La Palme Reyes et al. is not presented here in any detail, because it does not account for a certain important difference in terms of inference patterns

between predicate negation and predicate term negation. Whereas predicate negation satisfies contraposition as a rule, predicate term negation in general does not. If
the predicate term of a sentence is negated resulting in the polar contrary of that
sentence but not in its contradictory, then contraposition fails. If from

John is pleased (in his work).

it can be derived that

Jack is pleased (in his work).

it may nevertheless be the case that

John is displeased (in his work).

cannot be derived from

Jack is displeased (in his work).

because it may be that Jack is displeased and John is neither pleased nor displeased.
However, it is well-known that any pseudocomplement $\neg$ in a bounded lattice
satisfies[6]

$$x \leq y \text{ iff } \neg y \leq \neg x \qquad\qquad (18.3)$$

Contraposition for the supplement follows by duality. Therefore, although 2-
negation algebras are interesting, natural and simple algebras, they do not seem to
be the right kind of structures to represent predicate term negation.

18.3. Representing Negations as Sentential Operations

This section shows that predicate term negation can be represented as a sentential
negation that has an independent motivation, namely as strong, constructive negation.
Moreover, this section considers various suggestions for defining and classifying
notions of sentential negation that have been made in the literature.

18.3.1. Negation as falsity

There are several distinct justificatory roads to negation in the sense of definite
falsity; see, for instance, Pearce (1991). One of these roads is provided by Kripke
frames interpreted in terms of information states (or pieces) partially ordered by a
relation of 'possible expansion of information states.' The basic idea is that an
information state may not only support the truth of certain atomic formulas but also

support the *falsity* of certain atomic formulas; see Gurevich (1977), López-Escobar (1972), Routley (1974), and Thomason (1969). In other words, the idea is to treat verification and falsification on a par as equally important primitive semantic relations. These considerations give rise to the notion of a Nelson model. A *Nelson model* is a structure $\langle I, \sqsubseteq, v^+, v^- \rangle$, where $\langle I, \sqsubseteq \rangle$ is a partially ordered set and both v^+ and v^- are valuation functions assigning to every propositional variable p a subset of I. Intuitively, v^+ sends atoms to the information states at which they are verified, whereas v^- sends atoms to the information states at which they are falsified. Moreover, it is required that for every propositional variable p and every $t, u \in I$:

Persistence$^+$ if $t \sqsubseteq u$, then $t \in v^+(p)$ implies $u \in v^+(p)$

Persistence$^-$ if $t \sqsubseteq u$, then $t \in v^-(p)$ implies $u \in v^-(p)$

Let $M = \langle I, \sqsubseteq, v^+, v^- \rangle$ be a Nelson model, $t \in I$ and A a formula in the language with strong negation $\sim$, intuitionistic implication $\supset_h$, conjunction $\wedge$, and disjunction $\vee$ over the denumerable set *Atom* of propositional variables. The notions $M, t \models^+ A$ (A is verified at t in M) and $M, t \models^- A$ (A is falsified at t in M) are inductively defined as follows:

$M, t \models^+ p$	iff	$t \in v^+(p)$, $p \in Atom$
$M, t \models^- p$	iff	$t \in v^-(p)$, $p \in Atom$
$M, t \models^+ B \wedge C$	iff	$M, t \models^+ B$ and $M, t \models^+ C$
$M, t \models^- B \wedge C$	iff	$M, t \models^- B$ or $M, t \models^- C$
$M, t \models^+ B \vee C$	iff	$M, t \models^+ B$ or $M, t \models^+ C$
$M, t \models^- B \vee C$	iff	$M, t \models^- B$ and $M, t \models^- C$
$M, t \models^+ B \supset_h C$	iff	$(\forall u \in I)$ if $t \sqsubseteq u$, then $M, u \models^+ B$ implies $M, u \models^+ C$
$M, t \models^- B \supset_h C$	iff	$M, t \models^+ B$ and $M, t \models^- C$
$M, t \models^+ \sim B$	iff	$M, t \models^- B$
$M, t \models^- \sim B$	iff	$M, t \models^+ B$

With this definition, verification and falsification of arbitrary formulas are persistent with respect to $\sqsubseteq$. Semantic consequence is defined as follows: $\Gamma \models_{N4} A$ iff for every Nelson model $M = \langle I, \sqsubseteq, v^+, v^- \rangle$ and every $t \in I$, if $M, t \models^+ B$ for every $B \in \Gamma$, then $M, t \models^+ A$. Nelson's propositional logic **N4** is the theory of the class of all Nelson models in the given language. **N4** conservatively extends positive propositional logic, the positive part of intuitionistic logic. [See chapter 11.] **N4** can be axiomatized by adding to an axiomatization of positive logic the following axiom schemata:

A1 $\quad \sim\sim A \equiv A$

A2 $\quad \sim (A \wedge B) \equiv (\sim A \vee \sim B)$

A3 $\quad \sim (A \vee B) \equiv (\sim A \wedge \sim B)$

A4 $\quad \sim (A \supset_h B) \equiv (A \wedge \sim B)$

where $A \equiv B$ is defined as $(A \supset_h B) \wedge (B \supset_h A)$.

Contraposition as a rule does not hold in **N4**.[7] Moreover, provable equivalence fails to be a congruence relation on the set of formulas. If formulas A and B are defined as being *strongly equivalent* iff both A, B and their strong negations $\sim A$, $\sim B$ are provably interderivable, then it can be shown that strong equivalence is a congruence relation in **N4**, i.e., there is a replacement theorem for strongly equivalent formulas. **N4** is a system of paraconsistent logic, because not for every B, $\{A, \sim A\}$ $\vdash_{\mathbf{N4}} B$. Moreover, **N4** is a system of four-valued logic.[8] Every pair (v^+, v^-) of valuations induces a valuation $v: \mathbf{I} \times Atom \to \{1, 0, \varnothing, \{1, 0\}\}$ by defining:

$v(t, p) = 1 \quad$ iff $t \in v^+(p)$

$v(t, p) = 0 \quad$ iff $t \in v^-(p)$

$v(t, p) = \{1, 0\} \quad$ iff $(t \in v^+(p)$ and $t \in v^-(p))$

$v(t, p) = \varnothing \quad$ iff $(t \notin v^+(p)$ and $t \notin v^-(p))$

The model $\mathcal{M} = \langle \mathbf{I}, \sqsubseteq, v^+, v^- \rangle$ and the induced model $\mathcal{M}' = \langle \mathbf{I}, \sqsubseteq, v \rangle$ validate the same formulas of the language under consideration, if for every $p \in Atom$, we define

$\mathcal{M}', t \vDash^+ p \quad$ iff $v(t, p) = 1$

$\mathcal{M}', t \vDash^- p \quad$ iff $v(t, p) = 0$

The three-valued logic **N3** is the theory of the class of all Nelson models $\langle \mathbf{I}, \sqsubseteq, v^+, v^- \rangle$, where for every atom p, $v^+(p) \cap v^-(p)$ is empty. **N3** can be axiomatized by adding to an axiomatization of **N4** the *ex contradictione* schema $\sim A \supset_h (A \supset_h B)$. Strong negation in Nelson's logics **N3** and **N4** is also referred to as *constructive negation*, since in both systems negation satisfies

Constructible falsity $\quad \vdash \sim (A \wedge B)$ iff $(\vdash \sim A$ or $\vdash \sim B)$

In **N3** the contradictory forming intuitionistic negation $\neg_h$ can be defined using the primitive, contrary forming strong negation $\sim$ and intuitionistic implication $\supset_h$:

$\neg_h A$ iff $A \supset_h \sim A$

N3 provides a natural example of a logical system with two kinds of negation suitable for representing both predicate denial and predicate term negation.[9]

Considerations on the so-called Brouwer–Heyting–Kolmogorov (BHK) interpretation of the logical operations in terms of direct (or canonical) proofs (alias constructions) [see chapter 11] may also lead to Nelson's systems. According to this interpretation, a canonical proof of $(A \supset_h B)$, for instance, is a construction that applied to a proof of A results in a proof of B. López-Escobar (1972) suggested supplementing the BHK interpretation by the notion of (canonical) disproof. He gives the following disproof interpretation of the intuitionistic connectives $\wedge$, $\vee$, and $\supset_h$ and the strong negation $\sim$ (notation adjusted):

(i)   The construction c refutes $A \wedge B$ iff c is of the form $\langle i, d \rangle$ with i either 0 or 1 and if $i = 0$, then d refutes A and if $i = 1$ then d refutes B.

(ii)   The construction c refutes $A \vee B$ iff c is of the form $\langle d, e \rangle$ and d refutes A and e refutes B.

(iii)   The construction c refutes $A \supset_h B$ iff c is of the form $\langle d, e \rangle$ and d proves A and e refutes B.

(iv)   The construction c refutes $\sim A$ iff c proves A.

Under the proof *and* disproof interpretation, a proof of $\sim A$ is not conceived of as a proof of $A \supset_h \bot$ ('A implies absurdity'), but rather as a refutation of A. This is a completely natural and direct way of relating proofs and disproofs by means of negation. López-Escobar uses the following notion of provable sequent, with respect to which Nelson's logic **N4** emerges as sound:

$\{A_1, \ldots, A_n\} \rightarrow A$ is *valid* iff there exists a construction π such that $\pi(c_1, \ldots, c_n)$ proves A, whenever $c_1, \ldots, c_n$ are constructions proving $A_1, \ldots, A_n$ (if $1 \leq n$).

A sequent $\emptyset \rightarrow A$ is said to be valid iff a construction exists that proves A. Moreover, López-Escobar assumes that no construction both proves and disproves the same A. Note that $\{A, \sim A\} \rightarrow B$ is valid under the stronger assumption that no formula A is both provable and disprovable.[10]

Still another idea that naturally leads to Nelson's system **N4** is the idea of atomicity of strong negation. If the provability conditions of a compound formula depend on the provability conditions of its components, then also the refutability conditions of a compound formula ought to depend on the refutability conditions of its components. But then, if negation $\sim$ is to express falsity in the sense of refutability, one would need a negation normal form theorem to the effect that every negated formula $\sim A$ is provably equivalent to a formula $nf(A)$ in which every occurrence of $\sim$ stands immediately in front of an atomic formula. If, moreover, all literals (i.e. atoms and negated atoms) are to be treated on a par, because the refutability and the provability conditions of atomic formulas are independent of each other, then the result A^+ of replacing every occurrence of a negated atom $\sim p$ in $nf(A)$ by a fresh atom p' ought to leave the derivability relation unaffected. In Nelson's logics **N3** and **N4**, the wanted negation normal form theorem is obvious from the axiom schemata A1–A4. Moreover, by induction on proofs in **N4**, one can show that in fact atomicity of negation holds:

$$\Gamma \vdash_{\mathbf{N4}} A \quad \text{iff} \quad \Gamma^+ \vdash_{\mathbf{N4}} A^+$$

where $\Gamma^+ = \{B^+ \mid B \in \Gamma\}$.

This observation also leads to a simple derivation of the completeness of **N4** with respect to the class of all Nelson models from the completeness of positive logic with respect to the class of all intuitionistic Kripke models [see chapter 11]; cf. Gurevich (1977), Pearce (1991), or Rautenberg (1979).[11] Suppose that, in addition to the denumerable set *Atom* of propositional variables, the set $Atom' = \{p' \mid p \in Atom\}$ is also considered. An *intuitionistic Kripke model* for the language $L = \{\supset_h, \wedge, \vee\}$ based on $Atom \cup Atom'$ is a structure $\langle \mathbf{I}, \sqsubseteq, v \rangle$, where $\langle \mathbf{I}, \sqsubseteq \rangle$ is a partially ordered set and v is a valuation function mapping every propositional variable in $Atom \cup Atom'$ to a subset of $\mathbf{I}$. Moreover, persistence of atomic formulas is required: for every $p \in Atom \cup Atom'$ and every $t, u \in \mathbf{I}$ such that $t \sqsubseteq u$, $t \in v(p)$ implies $u \in v(p)$. The notion $M, t \vDash A$ (A is verified at t in M) is inductively defined as follows:

$M, t \vDash p$ iff $t \in v(p)$, $p \in Atom \cup Atom'$

$M, t \vDash B \wedge C$ iff $M, t \vDash B$ and $M, t \vDash C$

$M, t \vDash B \vee C$ iff $M, t \vDash B$ or $M, t \vDash C$

$M, t \vDash B \supset_h C$ iff $(\forall u \in \mathbf{I})$ if $t \sqsubseteq u$, then $M, u \vDash B$ implies $M, u \vDash C$

Given such a model $M = \langle \mathbf{I}, \sqsubseteq, v \rangle$, one can define a Nelson model $M' = \langle \mathbf{I}, \sqsubseteq, v^+, v^- \rangle$ by stipulating that for every $p \in Atom \cup Atom'$,

$$v^+(p) = v(p) \qquad \text{and} \qquad v^-(p) = v(p')$$

Lemma   For every L-formula A,

(i) $M', t \vDash^+ A$ iff $M, t \vDash A^+$, and
(ii) $M', t \vDash^- A$ iff $M, t \vDash (\sim A)^+$.

Proof   By simultaneous induction on the complexity of A. Consider only one case for the first claim, namely $A = \sim(B \supset_h C)$:

$M', t \vDash^+ \sim (B \supset_h C)$

iff $M', t \vDash^+ B$ and $M', t \vDash^- C$

iff   [$M, t \vDash B^+$ (by the induction hypothesis for (i))
     and $M, t \vDash (\sim C)^+$ (by the induction hypothesis for (ii))]

iff $M, t \vDash (B^+ \wedge (\sim C)^+)$ $[= (\sim(B \supset_h C))^+]$

Proposition   **N4** is strongly complete with respect to the class of all Nelson models.

Proof   Suppose $\Gamma \nvdash A$. Due to atomicity of negation in **N4**, $\Gamma^+ \nvdash A^+$. Since positive logic is strongly complete with respect to the class of all intuitionistic Kripke models, there is such a model $M = \langle \mathbf{I}, \sqsubseteq, v \rangle$ and $t \in \mathbf{I}$ such that for every $B \in \Gamma$, $M, t \vDash B^+$ and

$\mathcal{M}, t \nVdash A^+$. The first part of the previous lemma guarantees that there is a Nelson model $\mathcal{M}' = \langle \mathbf{I}, \sqsubseteq, v^+, v^- \rangle$ such that for every $B \in \Gamma$, $\mathcal{M}', t \Vdash^+ B$ and $\mathcal{M}', t \nVdash^+ A$. QED

A general definition of negation as falsity that is meant to encompass both intuitionistic negation and strong negation is suggested in Wansing (1999). Suppose that a single-conclusion consequence relation $\rightarrow$ over a formal language containing a unary connective $*$ is given. In other words, for all formulas A, B and all finite sets of formulas Δ, Γ:

Reflexivity $\vdash A \rightarrow A$

Monotonicity $\Gamma \rightarrow A \vdash \Gamma \cup \{B\} \rightarrow A$

Cut $\Gamma \cup \{A\} \rightarrow B, \Delta \rightarrow A \vdash \Gamma \cup \Delta \rightarrow B$

A binary relation $\leftarrow$ between finite sets of formulas and single formulas is called a *single-conclusion $*$-refutation relation* iff for all formulas A, B and finite sets Δ, Γ of formulas:

$*$-reflexivity $\vdash *A \leftarrow A, \vdash A \leftarrow *A$

$*$-cut $\Delta \leftarrow A, \Gamma \cup \{*A\} \leftarrow B \vdash \Delta \cup \Gamma \leftarrow B$

Assume that $\rightarrow$ and $\leftarrow$ are given as sequent calculi. If $\rightarrow$ is a single conclusion consequence relation, then $*$ is a *negation as falsity in* $\rightarrow$ iff

(α) the relation $\leftarrow$ defined by '$\Delta \leftarrow A$ iff $\Delta \rightarrow *A$' is a single-conclusion $*$-refutation relation

(β) for every formula A, not both $\vdash \emptyset \rightarrow A$ and $\vdash \emptyset \rightarrow *A$

(γ) there is a formula A such that not both $\vdash A \rightarrow *A, \vdash *A \rightarrow A$

If $\leftarrow$ is a single conclusion $*$-refutation relation, then $*$ is a *negation as falsity in* $\leftarrow$ iff

(α') the relation $\rightarrow$ defined by '$\Delta \rightarrow A$ iff $\Delta \leftarrow *A$' is a single-conclusion consequence relation

(β') for every formula A, not both $\vdash \emptyset \leftarrow A$ and $\vdash \emptyset \leftarrow *A$

(γ') there is a formula A such that not $\vdash A \leftarrow A$.

If $*$ satisfies both (α) and (α') for a single-conclusion consequence relation $\rightarrow$ and a single-conclusion $*$-refutation relation $\leftarrow$, then negation as falsity is a vehicle for either keeping $\rightarrow$ and dispensing with $\leftarrow$ or keeping $\leftarrow$ and dispensing with $\rightarrow$. Then both double negation introduction $A \rightarrow **A$ and double negation elimination $**A \rightarrow A$ are derivable. Clearly, the relation $\leftarrow$ defined by (α) is a single-conclusion $*$-refutation relation iff $*$ satisfies $\vdash A \rightarrow **A$, and double negation introduction and analogues of (β) and (γ) are satisfied by strong negation in **N3** and **N4**.

Tennant (1999) also motivates negation in his system of intuitionistic relevant logic by considerations on both proofs and disproofs. However, whereas in Tennant's natural deduction system there are direct proofs, there are no direct disproofs of compound formulas. In this system there are no derivations not merely revealing the inconsistency of a premise set, but rather leading to the conclusion that a certain compound formula is refutable. A discussion of Tennant's approach can be found in Wansing (1999).

18.3.2. *Negation as inconsistency*

Gabbay (1988) defines a syntactic notion of negation as inconsistency. Suppose again that a single-conclusion consequence relation $\rightarrow$ over a formal language containing a unary connective $*$ is given. The basic idea of Gabbay's definition is that the negation $*A$ of a formula A is derivable from a set of premises Γ iff some undesirable formula B from a set of unwanted formulas θ^* is derivable from Γ together with A. It is assumed that the logical object language either already contains or is conservatively extendible by a counterpart of the set-theoretical combination of premises. This counterpart is conjunction, $\wedge$, governed by the following introduction rules:

$(\rightarrow \wedge)$ $\Gamma \rightarrow A, \Gamma \rightarrow B \vdash \Gamma \rightarrow (A \wedge B)$

$(\wedge \rightarrow)$ $\Gamma \cup \{A, B\} \rightarrow C \vdash \Gamma \cup \{(A \wedge B)\} \rightarrow C$

The unary operation $*$ is then said to be a *negation (as inconsistency) in* $\rightarrow$ iff there is a non-empty set θ^* of formulas which is not the same as the set of all formulas such that for every finite set Γ of formulas and every formula A:

$\vdash \Gamma \rightarrow *A$ iff $(\exists B \in \theta^*) (\vdash \Gamma \cup \{A\} \rightarrow B)$

Moreover, θ^* must not contain any theorems. If such a collection of unwanted formulas exists, it can always be chosen as $\{C \mid \vdash \emptyset \rightarrow *C\}$, since by (reflexivity), the latter set is non-empty, if $*$ is a negation. The definition of negation as inconsistency can therefore be reformulated without appeal to θ^*. Namely, $*$ is a negation as inconsistency in $\rightarrow$ iff for every finite set Γ of formulas and every formula A:

$\vdash \Gamma \rightarrow *A$ iff $\exists C (\vdash \emptyset \rightarrow *C \,\&\, \vdash \Gamma \cup \{A\} \rightarrow C)$

Negation in quite a few familiar logical systems can be shown to be a negation as inconsistency. In minimal, intuitionistic, and classical logic, for example, θ^* can be identified with the set of all explicit contradictions $(A \wedge *A)$ in the respective language. In Gabbay and Wansing (1996) the notion of negation as inconsistency (alias inferential negation) is extended to a type of nonmonotonic inference relations between structured databases called *structured consequence relations*.

Every negation as inconsistency satisfies contraposition as a rule in the form:

$\Gamma \cup \{A\} \rightarrow B$ implies $\Gamma \cup \{*B\} \rightarrow *A$

Suppose $\Gamma \cup \{A\} \to B$. Since $*B \to *B$, by definition there is a $C \in \theta^*$ such that $\{*B, B\} \to C$. Applying (cut) one obtains $\Gamma \cup \{*B, A\} \to C$ and hence $\Gamma \cup \{*B\} \to *A$. Therefore, strong negation in Nelson's constructive logics fails to be a negation as inconsistency. Also, every negation as inconsistency validates the Law of Excluded Contradiction, $*(*A \wedge A)$. Since $*A \to *A$, we have $\{*A, A\} \to B$, for some $B \in \theta^*$. Hence, $*A \wedge A \to B$, for some $B \in \theta^*$, and therefore $\varnothing \to *(*A \wedge A)$. Also double negation introduction $\vdash A \to **A$ is provable:

$$\frac{\quad\quad\quad A, *A \to (A \wedge *A) \quad \text{contraposition}}{\dfrac{\varnothing \to *(A \wedge *A) \quad A, *(A \wedge *A) \to **A \quad \text{(cut)}}{A \to **A}}$$

Moreover, we have $\vdash ***A \to *A$:

$$\frac{\dfrac{\dfrac{\dfrac{*A \to *A \quad \text{(reflexivity)}}{\{*A, A\} \to B \quad \text{reformulated definition of negation}}}{\{*B, A\} \to **A \quad \text{contraposition}}}{\dfrac{\varnothing \to *B \quad \{*B, A\} \to **A \quad \text{(cut)}}{A \to **A \quad \text{contraposition}}}}{***A \to *A}$$

for some B such that $\vdash \varnothing \to *B$. In the inverse direction we have:

$$\frac{\dfrac{\dfrac{\dfrac{**A \to **A}{\{*A, **A\} \to B}}{\{*B, *A\} \to ***A}}{\dfrac{\varnothing \to *B \quad \{*B, *A\} \to ***A}{*A \to ***A}}}{}$$

for some B such that $\vdash \varnothing \to *B$.

Observation Suppose $\to$ is consistent in the sense that for no formula A of the underlying language, both $\varnothing \to A$ and $\varnothing \to *A$ are provable. Then $*$ is a negation as inconsistency iff $*$ satisfies contraposition as a rule, the Law of Excluded Contradiction, and double negation introduction.

Proof It has already been shown that the direction from right to left holds. For the direction from left to right suppose that $\vdash \Gamma \to *A$. Then $\vdash \wedge \Gamma \to *A$ and by contraposition, $\vdash **A \to *\wedge \Gamma$. By the structural rules and the rules for $\wedge$, $\vdash \Gamma$, $**A \to *\wedge \Gamma \wedge \wedge \Gamma$, and since $\vdash A \to **A$, one may apply (cut) to obtain $\vdash \Gamma$, $A \to *\wedge \Gamma \wedge \wedge \Gamma$. Thus one may choose as θ^* the set of all explicit contradictions $A \wedge *A$. This set θ^* does not contain any theorems, because otherwise $\vdash \varnothing \to C$ and $\vdash \varnothing \to *C$, for all formulas C. Suppose now that $\vdash \Gamma$, $A \to (C \wedge *C)$. Then, by contraposition, $\vdash \Gamma$, $*(C \wedge *C) \to *A$, and since $\vdash \varnothing \to *(C \wedge *C)$, an application of (cut) gives $\vdash \Gamma \to *A$. QED

Obviously, not every recognized negation is a negation as inconsistency. Strong negation in Kleene's three-valued logic [see chapter 14], for example, fails to be a negation as inconsistency, because due to the absence of any theorems, the Law of Excluded Contradiction fails. The notion of negation as falsity is also non-trivial. In normal modal logic, for instance, necessity $\Box$ fails to be a negation as falsity, because $\vdash (p \vee \neg p)$ and $\vdash \Box(p \vee \neg p)$ in contradiction of (β). In Wansing (1999), it is shown that every negation as inconsistency is a negation as falsity.

Observation Every negation as inconsistency is a negation as falsity.

Proof It must be shown that the defined relation $\leftarrow$ satisfies ($*$-reflexivity), ($*$-cut), (β), and (γ).
($*$-reflexivity): $*A \leftarrow A$ is immediate from $*A \rightarrow *A$ and the definition of $\leftarrow$. Since $\varnothing \rightarrow *(*A \wedge A)$ and $\{A, *A\} \rightarrow *A \wedge A$, there is a C such that $\varnothing \rightarrow *C$ and $\{A\} \cup \{*A\} \rightarrow C$, hence $A \rightarrow **A$ and thus, by the definition of $\leftarrow$, $A \leftarrow *A$.
($*$-cut): The ($*$-cut)-rule follows from the definition of $\leftarrow$ and (cut) for $\rightarrow$. Assume $\Delta \leftarrow *A$ and $\Gamma \cup \{A\} \leftarrow B$. This means $\Delta \rightarrow A$ and $\Gamma \cup \{A\} \rightarrow *B$. An application of (cut) gives $\Delta \cup \Gamma \rightarrow *B$, which means $\Delta \cup \Gamma \leftarrow B$, as required.
(β): Suppose that both $\varnothing \rightarrow A$ and $\varnothing \rightarrow *A$ for some A. Then there is a $B \in \theta^*$ such that $A \rightarrow B$. However, by (cut), $\rightarrow B$, that is, θ^* contains a theorem, *quod non*.
(γ): Suppose that for every formula A, $A \rightarrow *A$ and $*A \rightarrow A$. Then there is a $B \in \theta^*$ such that $A \rightarrow B$, that is $\varnothing \rightarrow *A$. Applying (cut) to the latter and $*A \rightarrow A$, gives $\varnothing \rightarrow A$. But then, since θ^* is non-empty, it must contain a theorem; a contradiction. QED

18.3.3. Negation as orthogonality

The interpretation of negation by means of the notion of orthogonality (or incompatibility) turns out to be very illuminating, because it enables a classification of different concepts of negation in terms of correlations between negation laws and algebraic as well as relational properties together with conditions on valuations. This semantic classification has been investigated in a series of papers by Dunn (1993, 1996, 1999).

Consider a partially ordered set $(\mathbf{A}, \leq, 0, 1)$ with bounds 0, 1. From an algebraic point of view, the elements of such a set may be seen as propositions. Intuitively, $x \leq y$ may be understood as 'x provably implies y.' In addition to $\leq$ one may consider another binary relation I on $\mathbf{A}$ and think of xIy as 'x is incompatible with y.' It is then natural to define two negations $\neg$ and $-$ as follows:

$x \leq \neg y$ iff xIy

$x \leq -y$ iff yIx

Obviously, both notions of negation coincide if the not implausible assumption is made that incompatibility is a symmetric relation. By imposing constraints on $\leq$, $\neg$, and $\neg$, various concepts of negation can be defined. Interestingly, the defining properties can be correlated with relational properties of an incompatibility relation in so-called perp models (together with conditions on valuations). A *perp frame* is a structure $(\mathbf{I}, \sqsubseteq, \perp)$, where the incompatibility relation $\perp$ satisfies

$(t \perp u$ and $t \sqsubseteq t')$ implies $t' \perp u$

$(t \perp u$ and $u \sqsubseteq u')$ implies $t \perp u'$

A *perp model* is a structure $\mathcal{M} = (\mathcal{F}, v)$, where $\mathcal{F}$ is a perp frame, and v is a valuation function persistent with respect to the relation $\sqsubseteq$. If X is a subset of $\mathbf{I}$, let

$t \perp X$ iff for every $u \in X$, $t \perp u$

$X \perp t$ iff for every $u \in X$, $u \perp t$

One may then define ${}^\perp X = \{t \mid t \perp X\}$ and $X^\perp = \{t \mid X \perp t\}$. Negated formulas are evaluated according to the following clauses:

$\mathcal{M}, t \vDash \neg A$ iff $t \in {}^\perp|A|$

$\mathcal{M}, t \vDash {-}A$ iff $t \in |A|^\perp$

where $|A| = \{t \in \mathbf{I} \mid \mathcal{M}, t \vDash A\}$. With these definitions, negated formulas are also persistent with respect to $\sqsubseteq$.

Dunn (1993, 1996) has shown that posets with bounds satisfying the properties listed below can be represented by perp frames satisfying the associated conditions:[12]

Negation	Posets	Perp models
Subminimal	$x \le y \Rightarrow \neg y \le \neg x$	$|\neg A| = |A|^\perp$
	$x \le y \Rightarrow {-}y \le {-}x$	$|{-}A| = {}^\perp|A|$
Galois	$x \le \neg y \Leftrightarrow y \le {-}x$	$|\neg A| = |A|^\perp, |{-}A| = {}^\perp|A|$
Minimal	$x \le \neg y \Leftrightarrow y \le \neg x$	$\perp$ symmetric
Intuitionistic	Minimal +	$\perp$ irreflexive, symmetric
	$(x \le y \ \& \ x \le \neg y) \Rightarrow x \le z$	
DeMorgan	Minimal + $\neg\neg x \le x$	$|A|^{\perp\perp} = |A|, \perp$ symmetric
Ortho	Intuitionistic + $\neg\neg x \le x$	$|A|^{\perp\perp} = |A|, \perp$ irrefl., symm.

The conditions on posets express inferential properties of negation. The negation logics defined by these properties are sound and, in view of Dunn's representation theorems, also complete with respect to the classes of perp models satisfying the associated conditions. Instead of considering partially ordered sets with bounds one may, of course, also study other algebraic structures, also for a logical object language richer than $\{\neg, {-}\}$; see, for example, Dunn (1996). Since every subminimal negation satisfies the contraposition rule, however, extensions of subminimal negation like the negations investigated by La Palme Reyes et al. are unsuitable for representing predicate term negation.

18.3.4. Perfect negation

According to Avron (1999), a unary connective of a logic Λ is a perfect negation if it enjoys a certain syntactic property and, in addition, Λ is *strongly normal* in a certain sense. To state the syntactic property, first, various definitions are needed.

Suppose Λ is presented as a single-conclusion sequent calculus (defined for premise multi-sets not necessarily satisfying monotonicity). Then its associated *internal consequence relation* $\rightarrow^i$ is defined by

$$A_1, \ldots, A_n \rightarrow^i A \quad \text{iff} \quad \vdash_\Lambda A_1, \ldots, A_n \rightarrow A$$

Λ's associated *external* consequence relation $\rightarrow^e$ is defined by:

$$A_1, \ldots, A_n \rightarrow^e A \quad \text{iff} \quad \rightarrow A_1, \ldots, \rightarrow A_n \vdash_\Lambda \rightarrow A$$

A unary connective $*$ is said to be an *internal negation* for a consequence relation $\rightarrow$ iff the relation $\rightarrow$ is closed under

$$A, \Gamma \rightarrow \Delta \vdash \Gamma \rightarrow \Delta, *A \quad \text{and} \quad \Gamma \rightarrow \Delta, A \vdash *A, \Gamma \rightarrow \Delta$$

The existence of an internal negation forces a consequence relation to be a multiple-conclusion relation. A single-conclusion consequence relation $\rightarrow$ over a language with a unary connective $*$ is said to be *strongly symmetric with respect to* $*$ iff there exists a multiple-conclusion consequence relation $\rightarrow'$ defined over the same language such that

$$\Gamma \rightarrow' A \quad \text{iff} \quad \Gamma \rightarrow A$$

and $*$ is an internal negation for $\rightarrow'$.

If Λ is presented as a single-conclusion sequent calculus over a logical language containing a unary operation $*$, then, according to Avron, $*$ is *a perfect negation from the syntactic point of view* if the internal consequence relation associated with Λ is strongly symmetric with respect to $*$. Intuitionistic negation and Nelson's strong negation fail to be perfect in this sense because every internal negation satisfies double-negation elimination and the contraposition rule. Indeed, Avron (1999, thm 4) shows that if $\rightarrow$ is any consequence relation, then it is strongly symmetric with respect to $*$ iff

(i) $A \rightarrow **A$
(ii) $**A \rightarrow A$, and
(iii) $\Gamma, A \rightarrow B$ implies $\Gamma, *B \rightarrow *A$.

If the requirement of strong symmetry is relaxed in a certain way, strong negation still emerges as perfect from the syntactic point of view in a sense. Suppose $\rightarrow$ is a consequence relation defined over a language containing the unary operation $*$.

Define the multiple-conclusion consequence relation $\to^s$ by requiring that $A_1, \ldots,$ $A_n \to^s B_1, \ldots, B_k$ iff for all $1 \le i \le n$ and $1 \le j \le k$:

$$A_1, \ldots, A_{i-1}, *B_1, \ldots, *B_k, A_{i+1}, \ldots, A_n \to *A_i$$

and

$$A_1, \ldots, A_n, *B_1, \ldots, *B_{j-1}, *B_{j+1}, \ldots, *B_k \to B_j$$

Then (Avron, 1999, propn 9)

(i) $\Gamma \to^s A$ implies $\Gamma \to A$
(ii) $\varnothing \to^s A$ iff $\varnothing \to A$, and
(iii) $\to^s$ is a conservative extension of $\to$ iff $\Gamma, A \to B$ implies $\Gamma, *B \to *A$.

If one tries to see $*$ as a negation in $\to$, then, in Avron's view, $\to^s$ is induced by $\to$ in a natural way. The operation $*$ in $\to$ is defined to be *weakly symmetric* iff it is an internal negation of $\to^s$. As Avron observes, $*$ is weakly symmetric in $\to$ if $A \to **A$ and $**A \to A$, and these conditions *are* satisfied by strong negation in Nelson's **N3** and **N4**.

A unary operation $*$ in a logical system Λ is *a perfect negation from the semantical point of view* if Λ is strongly normal. For Avron (1999, p. 15), "a semantics is, essentially, just a set S of theories," since "the essence of a 'model' is given by the set of sentences which are true in it." A unary connective $*$ is a (strong) semantic negation if in terms of validity in a model it reflects that every formula is either true or not true in a model and not both. Recall that a theory T is said to be *consistent* if there is no formula A such that both A and its negation are derivable from T. A theory T is *complete* if for every formula A, either A or its negation can be derived from T. If a theory is both consistent and complete, it is said to be *normal*. Assuming that Λ is given by a single conclusion consequence relation, that the underlying language contains a unary operation $*$ (considered to be a negation), and that for no formula A, both A and $*A$ are provable, Avron presents various characterizations of Λ (1999, propn 26):

- Λ is *strongly complete* iff whenever $T \nvdash A$ there is a complete extension T' of T such that $T' \nvdash A$.
- Λ is *weakly complete* iff whenever $\varnothing \nvdash A$ there is a complete theory T' such that $T' \nvdash A$.
- Λ is *strongly normal* iff whenever $T \nvdash A$ there is a complete and consistent extension T' of T such that $T' \nvdash A$.
- Λ is *weakly normal* iff whenever $\varnothing \nvdash A$ there is a complete and consistent theory T' such that $T' \nvdash A$.
- Λ is *c-normal* iff every consistent theory in Λ has a complete and consistent extension.
- Λ is *strongly c-normal* iff whenever T is consistent and $T \nvdash A$ there is a complete and consistent extension T' of T such that $T' \nvdash A$.

Avron (1999, propn 27) observes that if Λ is finitary, then it is strongly complete iff for every theory T and all formulas A, B:

$$T, A \vdash_\Lambda B \quad \text{and} \quad T, *A \vdash_\Lambda B \quad \text{implies} \quad T \vdash_\Lambda B$$

and that this condition is equivalent with the provability of $A \vee *A$, if the underlying language contains a disjunction operation $\vee$ such that $T, A \vee B \vdash_\Lambda C$ iff both $T, A \vdash_\Lambda C$ and $T, B \vdash_\Lambda C$. Therefore, intuitionistic negation and any representation of predicate term negation as a unary connective are bound to be imperfect in Avron's sense. Indeed, the only negation among the unary connectives considered by Avron that emerges as perfect from both the syntactic and the semantic point of view is the Boolean negation of classical logic. Whereas intuitionistic logic and Kleene's three-valued logic are still strongly consistent and c-normal, and **N3** is still strongly consistent, **N4** enjoys *none* of the listed properties.

18.4. Epilogue

Although there is no general agreement on what is negation, whether it is a unary connective or an innersentential operation, whether contraposition as a rule holds for it or not, etc., it is accepted knowledge that there is more than one kind of negation, be it in the same syntactic type or in different categories. This insight to a large extent rests on the Aristotelian distinction between predicate denial and predicate term negation. Moreover, whereas the contradictory forming predicate denial can be represented by a contradictory forming sentential negation, the contrary forming predicate term negation can be represented by the strong negation in many-valued logics such as Nelson's constructive systems **N3** or **N4**.

The classification of kinds of sentential negation may be approached from various points of departure. One idea is to define a general non-trivial notion of negation in a system, meant to cover all recognized negations. This is – quite explicitly – the intention behind Gabbay's (1988) definition of negation in a system. The notion of negation as falsity generalizes Gabbay's suggestion; other definitions or additional requirements may lead to more restricted notions of negation. A classification of negation may, however, also be seen primarily as a means for identifying non-negations. Avron (1999, p. 21), for example, puts his criteria to such a use when he concludes that "[t]he negation of intuitionistic logic is not really a negation." A third aspect of a classificatory scheme is that it may help to recognize the inter-relations between the items classified. In this respect, the semantic classifications of Dunn (1993, 1996, 1999) turn out to be particularly useful.

Suggested further reading

The classical reference as far as linguistic and philosophical aspects of negation are concerned is Horn's encyclopedic monograph (1989). This book also contains a careful introduction to

Aristotelian term logic. Another important reference to negation in Aristotelian term logic is Englebretsen (1981). More recent volumes devoted entirely to the study of negation are Wansing (1996) and Gabbay and Wansing (1999). The latter collection of research papers aims at providing a comprehensive account of negation from a logical, computational and philosophical point of view. A discussion of the notion of negation as finite failure to derive can be found in Fine (1989). The relation between monotonicity properties of natural language expressions and negative polarity items like 'anything' is dealt with, for example, in Zwarts (1996).

Notes

1 I shall not even try to survey this literature. Nor shall I deal with philosophically interesting negation related themes such as negative existentials, presupposition, or paraconsistency. Nothing at all will be said about the pragmatics or about psychological aspects of negation. Instead, the emphasis of this chapter will be on characterizing and classifying various notions of negation.
2 Horn (1989, p. 38) remarks that "[t]he unique polar contrary and the unique immediate contrary of a given term will not in general coincide."
3 Von Wright (1959, p. 5) criticizes Aristotle for his willingness to call both 'John is well' and 'John is ill' false, if the name 'John' does not denote anything:

> On this point Aristotle might be accused of obscuring a distinction which in other contexts he marks. I mean the distinction between the case when "x is P" is not true because x does not exist or because P cannot be "naturally predicated" of it, *and* the case when "x is P" is not true because not-P can be (truly) predicated of it. A convenient way of marking this distinction . . . would be to say that "x is P" is *false* only in the case when "x is not-P" is *true.*

4 There are exceptions such as 'undecidable' meaning 'not decidable'.
5 In the sequel I shall not always pay attention to the mention/use distinction and omit quotation marks if misunderstandings are unlikely to occur.
6 From $x \leq y$ one obtains $x \wedge \neg y \leq y \wedge \neg y$, and since $y \wedge \neg y = 0$, and 0 is the least element, (18.1) implies $\neg y \leq \neg x$.
7 Contraposible strong negation is studied in Nelson (1959).
8 A comprehensive study of four-valued logic, including Nelson's **N4**, can be found in Dunn (2000); see also Belnap (1977).
9 Other application areas in which the need for logics with more than one kind of negation arises include database theory, logic programming, and nonmonotonic reasoning; see, for instance, Wagner (1994), and Wansing (1995).
10 A more comprehensive discussion of the proof and disproof interpretation can be found in Wansing (1993).
11 An algebraic analysis of Nelson's logics can be found in Rasiowa (1974); axiomatic extensions of **N3** are investigated, for example, in Kracht (1998).
12 For DeMorgan and ortho negation we assume symmetry of $\perp$. Hence $\neg = -$ and we have $\mathcal{M}, t \vDash \neg A$ iff for every $u \in \mathbf{I}, t \not\perp u$ implies $\mathcal{M}, u \nvDash A$. Since an inference $A \vdash B$ is defined to be valid in a perp model $\mathcal{M} = (\mathbf{I}, \sqsubseteq, \perp, v)$ iff for every $t \in \mathbf{I}, \mathcal{M}, t \vDash A$ implies $\mathcal{M}, t \vDash B$, the validity of double negation elimination in $\mathcal{M}$ amounts to the validity of $\Box \Diamond A \supset A$ in the modal model $(\mathbf{I}, \not\perp, v)$. The latter formula is modally equivalent with the Sahlqvist formula $A \supset \Diamond \Box A$, and hence is first-order definable. It corresponds to

(DNE) $\forall t \exists u(t \not\perp u \land \forall s(u \not\perp s \supset t = s))$

From the modal point of view, double negation introduction expresses the axiom schema $A \supset \Box\Diamond A$, which is known to correspond with the symmetry of the accessibility relation. Note that in the case of (DNE) we have shown correspondence but not completeness.

References

Almukdad, A. and Nelson, D. 1984: "Constructible Falsity and Inexact Predicates," *Journal of Symbolic Logic*, 49, 231–3.

Avron, A., Jr. 1999: "Negation: Two Points of View," in Gabbay and Wansing (1999, pp. 3–22).

Belnap, N. D. 1977: "A Useful Four-Valued Logic," in *Modern Uses of Multiple-Valued Logic*, J. M. Dunn and G. Epstein, eds., (D. Reidel, Dordrecht), 8–37.

van Benthem, J. F. A. K. 1991: *Language in Action*, (North-Holland, Amsterdam).

Dunn, J. M. 1993: "Star and Perp: Two Treatments of Negation," in *Philosophical Perspectives (Philosophy of Language and Logic) 7*, J. Tomberlin, ed., (Ridgeview, Atascadero, CA), 331–57.

Dunn, J. M. 1996: "Generalized Ortho Negation," in Wansing (1996, pp. 3–26).

Dunn, J. M. 1999: "A Comparison of Various Model-Theoretic Treatments of Negation: A History of Formal Negation," in Gabbay and Wansing (1999, pp. 23–51).

Dunn, J. M. 2000: "Partiality and its Dual," *Studia Logica*, 66, 5–40.

Englebretsen, G. 1981: *Logical Negation*, (Van Gorcum, Assen).

Fine, K. 1989: "The Justification of Negation as Failure," in *Logic, Methodology and Philosophy of Science VIII*, J. E. Fenstad I. T. Frolov and R. Hilpinen, eds., (Elsevier, Amsterdam), 263–301.

Gabbay, D. M. 1988: "What is Negation in a System?," in *Logic Colloquium '86*, F. Drake and J. Truss, eds., (Elsevier, Amsterdam), 95–112.

Gabbay, D. M. and Wansing, H. 1996: "What is Negation in a System? Negation in Structured Consequence Relations," in *Logic, Action and Information*, A. Fuhrmann and H. Rott eds., (de Gruyter, Berlin), 328–50.

Gabbay, D. M. and Wansing, H. (eds.) 1999: *What is Negation?*, (Kluwer, Dordrecht).

Gurevich, Y. 1977: "Intuitionistic Logic with Strong Negation," *Studia Logica*, 36, 49–59.

Horn, L. 1989: *A Natural History of Negation*, (Chicago University Press, Chicago).

Kracht, M. 1998: "On Extensions of Intermediate Logics by Strong Negation," *Journal of Philosophical Logic*, 27, 49–73.

von Kutschera, F. 1969: "Ein verallgemeinerter Widerlegungsbegriff für Gentzenkalküle," *Archiv für Mathematische Logik und Grundlagenforschung*, 12, 104–18.

La Palme Reyes, M., Macnamara, J., Reyes, G. E. and Zolfaghari, H. 1994: "The Non-Boolean Logic of Natural Language Negation," *Philosophia Mathematica*, 2, 45–68.

La Palme Reyes, M., Macnamara, J., Reyes, G. E. and Zolfaghari, H. 1999: "Models for Non-Boolean Negations in Natural Languages Based on Aspect Analysis," in Gabbay and Wansing (1999, pp. 241–60).

López-Escobar, E. G. K. 1972: "Refutability and Elementary Number Theory," *Indagationes Mathematicae*, 34, 362–74.

Nelson, D. 1949: "Constructible Falsity," *Journal of Symbolic Logic*, 14, 16–26.

Nelson, D. 1959: "Negation and Separation of Concepts in Constructive Systems," in *Constructivity in Mathematics*, A. Heyting, ed., (North-Holland, Amsterdam), 208–25.

Pearce, D. 1991: "*n* Reasons for Choosing *N*," Technical report 14/91, Gruppe für Logik, Wissenstheorie und Information, Free University of Berlin.

Rasiowa, H. 1974: *An Algebraic Approach to Non-classical Logics*, (North-Holland, Amsterdam).

Rautenberg, W. 1979: *Klassische und Nichtklassische Aussagenlogik*, (Vieweg, Braunschweig).

Routley, R. 1974: "Semantical Analyses of Propositional Systems of Fitch and Nelson," *Studia Logica*, 33, 283–98.

Sommers, F. 1982: *The Logic of Natural Language*, (Clarendon Press, Oxford).

Tennant, N. 1999: "Negation, Absurdity and Contrariety," in Gabbay and Wansing (1999, pp. 199–222).

Thomason, R. 1969: "A Semantical Study of Constructive Falsity," *Zeitschrift für Mathematische Logik und Grundlagen der Mathematik*, 15, 247–57.

Wagner, G. 1994: "Vivid Logic. Knowledge-Based Reasoning with Two Kinds of Negation," *Lecture Notes in AI 764*, (Springer-Verlag, Berlin).

Wansing, H. 1993: "The Logic of Information Structures," *Lecture Notes in AI 681*, (Springer-Verlag, Berlin).

Wansing, H. 1995: "Semantics-Based Nonmonotonic Inference," *Notre Dame Journal of Formal Logic*, 36, 44–54.

Wansing, H. (ed.) 1996: *Negation. A Notion in Focus*, (de Gruyter, Berlin).

Wansing, H. 1999: "Negation as Falsity: A Reply to Tennant," in Gabbay and Wansing (1999, pp. 223–38).

von Wright, G. H. 1959: "On the Logic of Negation," *Commentationes Physico-Mathematicae*, 22 (Societas Scientarum Fennica, Helsinki), 2–30.

Zwarts, F. 1996: "Facets of Negation," in *Quantifiers, Logic and Language*, J. van der Does and J. van Eijck, eds., (CSLI Publications, Stanford), 385–421.

Chapter 19

Quantifiers

Dag Westerståhl

19.1. Routes to Quantifiers

There are two main routes to a concept of (generalized) quantifier. The first starts from first-order logic, FO, and generalizes from the familiar $\forall$ and $\exists$ occurring there. The second route begins with real languages, and notes that many so-called *noun phrases*, a kind of phrase which occurs abundantly in most languages, can be interpreted in a natural and uniform way using quantifiers.

This chapter takes the first route. One reason is that it leads most directly to a most general notion of a quantifier, subsuming those one finds in natural languages. Another reason is that FO is so familiar, and in any case is presented in chapter 1 of this book. Indeed, acquaintance with that chapter is assumed and (with few exceptions) the notation introduced there is used here. At the end of this chapter, I will indicate what quantifiers have to do with natural languages.

The actual historical development of the concept of a quantifier is slightly complicated. The expressions 'all', 'some', 'no', 'not all' from Aristotelian syllogistics are readily seen as (generalized) quantifiers of type $\langle 1, 1 \rangle$: they are *definable* from $\forall$ and $\exists$ but not the same as these; all of this will be explained shortly. Frege, who, if anyone, must be regarded as the inventor of FO, actually had in his possession essentially the concept of a generalized quantifier that will be encountered here (the main difference being that he quantified over a fixed universe of *all* objects, whereas, here, quantifiers are relativized to arbitrary (sub)universes). However, since he could express all the mathematics he needed with $\forall$ and $\exists$, he was content to have only these (in fact only $\forall$) in his *Begriffsschrift*. Much later, when first Mostowski (1957) and then Lindström (1966) introduced generalized quantifiers into mathematical logic, opening up the study of so-called model-theoretic logics, they were apparently unaware of Frege's notion. Later still, linguists noted the relevance of quantifiers to natural languages, for example, Barwise and Cooper (1981) and Keenan and Stavi (1986). They found, of course, that the four Aristotelian quantifiers were prime examples of 'natural language quantifiers', but also that there were many more, not definable from these.

I will not dwell further on history here; the interested reader can find more in Westerståhl (1989), which also presents the logical and linguistic properties of quantifiers in much more detail. Another survey, emphasizing the link to natural languages, is Keenan and Westerståhl (1997).

19.2. First-Order Logic Revisited

From chapter 1, first recall that a first-order language has a *signature* σ which is a set of non-logical symbols: relations symbols P, R, ... of various arities, function symbols F, G, ... of various arities, and individual constants c, d, ... A *structure* (or model) for σ, or simply a σ-structure, consists of a universe A and an appropriate interpretation $\cdot^A$ of the symbols in σ, so that if P is an n-ary relation symbol in σ then P^A is an n-ary relation over A; if F is an n-ary function symbol in σ then F^A is an n-ary operation on A; and if c is an individual constant in σ then c^A is an element of A. So one may write

$$A = (A, P^A, R^A, \ldots, F^A, G^A, \ldots, c^A, d^A, \ldots)$$

(Note that here A, B, ... are used for structures where chapter 1 uses I, J, ... instead, and moreover that here, to save notation, the very *same* letters are often used for the universes of those structures.)

The signature and its symbols can often be left implicit. For example, if one writes

$$\mathcal{N} = (N, <, +, \cdot, S, 0)$$

where $N = \{0, 1, 2, \ldots\}$, it is understood that this is a structure for a signature with one binary relation symbol denoting the usual order of the natural numbers, two binary function symbols denoting addition and multiplication respectively, one unary function symbol denoting the successor operation, and one individual constant denoting 0. In fact, one often uses '<', '+', etc. for both the symbols and their denotations in such a case. A structure is called *relational* if its signature contains only relation symbols.

Now, the fundamental relation

$$A \models \psi[a_1, \ldots, a_n] \tag{19.1}$$

means that ψ is true in A under a valuation v such that $v(x_i) = a_i$ for $1 \leq i \leq n$, where $\psi = \psi(x_1, \ldots, x_n)$ is a σ-formula with at most $x_1, \ldots, x_n$ free, A is a σ-structure, and $a_1, \ldots, a_n \in A$. When ψ is a *sentence*, i.e., a formula without free variables, $A \models \psi$ is often read 'ψ is true in A,' or 'A is a model of ψ.'

A sequence $\langle a_1, \ldots, a_n \rangle$ may be abbreviated as **a**. Then, with an obvious extension (or, if you will, abuse) of the above notation, one can write the standard explications of the universal and existential quantifiers as follows, where $\varphi = \varphi(x, x_1, \ldots, x_n)$:

$$A \vDash (\forall x)\varphi[x, \mathbf{a}] \quad \text{iff} \quad \text{for every } a \in A, \ A \vDash \varphi[a, \mathbf{a}] \tag{19.2}$$

$$A \vDash (\exists x)\varphi[x, \mathbf{a}] \quad \text{iff} \quad \text{for some } a \in A, \ A \vDash \varphi[a, \mathbf{a}] \tag{19.3}$$

19.3. What Do Quantifier Symbols Denote?

Equations (19.2) and (19.3) state what '$\forall$' and '$\exists$' mean, but they do so in an indirect way: they do not state what, if anything, they *denote*. On the other hand, the structure A does say what the symbols in σ denote: P denotes P^A, etc. With a medieval term, the σ-symbols are given *categorematically*, whereas $\forall$ and $\exists$ are defined *syncategorematically*. Can one give a categorematic definition of the quantifiers?

This has been a vexed question in the history of logic. Informally, one might try to think of something like 'a man' denoting some particular man. What then about 'every man' – it would seem to have to denote the set of all men. But matters worsen if one considers 'no men'; does this denote the empty set? If so, it has the same denotation as 'no dogs' – this seems wrong. Considerations like these may lead one to suppose that there is no coherent and uniform way of assigning denotations to quantified phrases. But in fact there is, and the theory of generalized quantifiers provides the solution.

Consider first the corresponding question for the propositional operators, say, conjunction. Everyone knows that '&' can be taken to denote a binary *truth function*. The corresponding clause in the usual truth definition does not mention this truth function explicitly, however; it is still syncategorematic:

$$A \vDash (\varphi \& \psi)[\mathbf{a}] \quad \text{iff} \quad A \vDash \varphi[\mathbf{a}] \quad \text{and} \quad A \vDash \psi[\mathbf{a}] \tag{19.4}$$

To reformulate this, begin by noting that in a structure A, a formula with k free variables denotes a k-ary relation over A: the set of k-tuples of elements of A satisfying the formula. Thus define, for any σ-formula $\varphi = \varphi(x_1, \ldots, x_n)$, any σ-structure A, and any n-tuple $\mathbf{a}$ of elements in A,

$$\varphi^{A,\mathbf{a}} = \begin{cases} T & \text{if } A \vDash \varphi[\mathbf{a}] \\ F & \text{otherwise} \end{cases} \tag{19.5}$$

Then (19.4) can be rewritten as

$$A \vDash (\varphi \& \psi)[\mathbf{a}] \quad \text{iff} \quad \& (\varphi^{A,\mathbf{a}}, \psi^{A,\mathbf{a}}) = T$$

(or even more compactly as $(\varphi \& \psi)^{A,\mathbf{a}} = \& (\varphi^{A,\mathbf{a}}, \psi^{A,\mathbf{a}})$), where the last '&' denotes the truth function given by the usual truth table for conjunction.

To do something similar for $\forall$ and $\exists$, extend the notation in (19.5) as follows. Let A be a σ-structure, $\varphi = \varphi(x, x_1, \ldots, x_n)$ a σ-formula with at most the free variables shown, and $\langle a_1, \ldots, a_n \rangle = \mathbf{a}$ an n-tuple of elements of A. Then

$$\varphi^{A,x,\mathbf{a}} = \{a \in A : A \vDash \varphi[a, \mathbf{a}]\}$$

In a structure A, a formula with one free variable denotes a set: the set of objects in A satisfying the formula. If φ has additional free variables $x_1, \ldots, x_n$, but these are interpreted as $a_1, \ldots, a_n$, respectively, then, relative to this interpretation, φ still denotes a set, and this set is $\varphi^{A,x,\mathbf{a}}$. Now (19.2) and (19.3) may be rewritten as

$$A \vDash (\forall x)\varphi[x, \mathbf{a}] \quad \text{iff} \quad \varphi^{A,x,\mathbf{a}} = A \tag{19.6}$$

$$A \vDash (\exists x)\varphi[x, \mathbf{a}] \quad \text{iff} \quad \varphi^{A,x,\mathbf{a}} \neq \varnothing \tag{19.7}$$

Just one small further step is needed. Let, on each universe A, $\exists_A$ be the set of non-empty subsets of A. And let $\forall_A$ be simply $\{A\}$. Then (19.6) and (19.7) become

$$A \vDash (\forall x)\varphi[x, \mathbf{a}] \quad \text{iff} \quad \varphi^{A,x,\mathbf{a}} \in \forall_A \tag{19.8}$$

$$A \vDash (\exists x)\varphi[x, \mathbf{a}] \quad \text{iff} \quad \varphi^{A,x,\mathbf{a}} \in \exists_A \tag{19.9}$$

That is, $\forall$ and $\exists$ may be thought of as denoting, on a universe A, a *set of subsets* of A. But then, *any* such set of subsets can be called a (generalized) quantifier on A.

For example, suppose one wants a quantifier that says "there exist at least n objects such that." Introduce a symbol '$\exists_{\geq n}$' and define, for each universe A,

$$(\exists_{\geq n})_A = \{X \subseteq A : |X| \geq n\}$$

($|X|$ is the cardinality of X). Then the clause

$$A \vDash (\exists_{\geq n}x)\varphi[x, \mathbf{a}] \quad \text{iff} \quad \varphi^{A,x,\mathbf{a}} \in (\exists_{\geq n})_A \quad \text{iff} \quad |\varphi^{A,x,\mathbf{a}}| \geq n \tag{19.10}$$

gives just what is wanted.

The pattern is clear, and completely general. That is, a *quantifier Q on A* is a set of subsets of A. 'Q' can also be thought of as a new symbol, such that whenever φ is a formula, so is

$$(Qx)\varphi$$

(Qx) binds free occurrences of x in φ just as usual, and its meaning is given by the clause

$$A \vDash (Qx)\varphi[x, \mathbf{a}] \quad \text{iff} \quad \varphi^{A,x,\mathbf{a}} \in Q_A$$

Here are some more examples:

$$\exists_{=n} = \{X \subseteq A : |X| = n\} \tag{19.11}$$
('there are exactly n objects such that')

$$Q_0 = \{X \subseteq A : X \text{ is infinite}\} \qquad (19.12)$$

('there are infinitely many objects such that'; the name 'Q_0' is standard and is due to the fact that the quantifier means 'at least $\aleph_0$')

$$Q_C = \{X \subseteq A : |X| = |A|\} \qquad (19.13)$$

(the 'Chang quantifier'; it means $\forall$ on finite sets but *not* on infinite sets)

$$Q_R = \{X \subseteq A : |X| > |A - X|\} \qquad (19.14)$$

(the 'Rescher quantifier'; on finite sets it means 'for more than half the elements of the universe').

To see the use of such quantifiers, here is a prime example of how one can express *new* things with them. Consider again the structure $\mathcal{N}$ from section 19.2. It is a fact about this structure that every element has a finite number of predecessors. There is no way to express this in FO – a proof of this will be given later. But using Q_0, the sentence

$$(\forall x) \sim (Q_0 y)(y < x)$$

says exactly this.

19.4. Monadic Quantifiers

Having considered quantifiers which are sets of subsets on a universe A, it is natural to go further and consider *relations* between subsets of A. It is here that one finds, to begin, the four Aristotelian quantifiers:

$all_A XY$ iff $X \subseteq Y$ (i.e. if all X are Y, where $X, Y \subseteq A$)

$some_A XY$ iff $X \cap Y \neq \emptyset$

$no_A XY$ iff $X \cap Y = \emptyset$

$not\ all_A XY$ iff $X \not\subseteq Y$

But there are many more binary relations between subsets of A, for example:

$I_A XY$ iff $|X| = |Y|$ \qquad (19.15)
(the Härtig quantifier)

$more_A XY$ iff $|X| > |Y|$ \qquad (19.16)

$most_A XY$ iff $|X \cap Y| > |X - Y|$ \qquad (19.17)
(on finite universes this means 'more than half of the X are Y')

at least $m/n_A XY$ iff $|X \cap Y| \geq m/n \cdot |X|$ (19.18)
$(0 < m < n$; the properly proportional quantifiers – they only make sense if X is finite).

These are just examples: if A has n elements, there are 2^n subsets of A, and 2^{4^n} binary relations between subsets of A. So over a universe with just two elements, there are $2^{16} = 65536$ such relations!

The quantifiers from section 19.3 are called of *type* $\langle 1 \rangle$, and those considered so far in this section are called of type $\langle 1, 1 \rangle$. One can go on to consider quantifiers of type $\langle 1, 1, 1 \rangle$, i.e., ternary relations between subsets of the universe, for example,

more than$_A XYZ$ iff $|X \cap Z| > |Y \cap Z|$ (19.19)
(more Xs than Ys are Z)

In general, a *monadic* quantifier of type $\langle 1, \ldots, 1 \rangle$ on A (with k 1s) is a k-ary relation between subsets of A, for some $k \geq 1$. This terminology indicates that there are also *polyadic* quantifiers, for example of type $\langle 2, 1, 3 \rangle$, but these are left until section 19.11.

Finally, note that the meaning of a quantifier like *some* or *most* is not dependent on a particular universe; rather it associates with each universe a corresponding quantifier on that universe. So the general definition is as follows:

A (monadic) quantifier of type $\langle 1, \ldots, 1 \rangle$ (with k 1s) is a function Q which associates with each universe A a quantifier Q_A of type $\langle 1, \ldots, 1 \rangle$ on A, in other words, a k-ary relation between subsets of A.

Such a quantifier Q can also be considered as a variable-binding operator, but now it operates on k formulas and binds one variable in each. That is;

(*Q*-syn) If $\varphi_1, \ldots, \varphi_k$ are formulas, then $(Qx)(\varphi_1, \ldots, \varphi_k)$ is a formula (where all free occurrences of x in each φ_i are bound by (Qx)).

whose meaning is given by the clause

(*Q*-sem) $A \vDash (Qx)(\varphi_1, \ldots, \varphi_k)[a]$ iff $(\varphi_1^{A,x,a}, \ldots, \varphi_k^{A,x,a}) \in Q_A$

19.5. Quantifiers and Quantities

The quantifiers considered so far have an important feature: they deal only with *quantities*. By contrast, here is an example of a type $\langle 1 \rangle$ quantifier that does *not* deal with quantities. Let John be an individual and define

$(Q_{John})_A X$ iff John $\in X$

That is, if John $\in A$ then $(Q_{\text{John}})_A$ consists of all those subsets of A containing John; otherwise $(Q_{\text{John}})_A$ is empty. This is not an unreasonable object (when John $\in A$). In mathematics, it is called the *principal filter* (over A) generated by John. In linguistics, it has been used to interpret the proper name *John*. But clearly, it says nothing about quantities.

To explain this, the concept of *isomorphism* between structures is needed. Intuitively, isomorphic structures 'have the same structure' and can for many purposes be identified. Let A and B be structures for the same signature σ, which, for simplicity, can be taken to be relational. An *isomorphism* between A and B is a bijection f from the universe A to the universe B (a one-one mapping from one onto the other) such that if P is an n-ary relation symbol in σ and $a_1, \ldots, a_n \in A$, then

$$\langle a_1, \ldots, a_n \rangle \in P^A \Leftrightarrow \langle f(a_1), \ldots, f(a_n) \rangle \in P^B$$

This is written as $f: A \cong B$, and $A \cong B$ says that A and B are isomorphic, i.e., that there is an isomorphism between A and B.

First-order logic cannot distinguish between isomorphic structures:

(*Isomorphism closure*)   If $A \cong B$ then every FO sentence which is true in A is true in B, and vice versa.

(The converse of this is far from true in general, though it does hold for finite structures.) In fact, isomorphism closure is usually a requirement on any logic, as shall be seen.

For the moment, however, I want to bring out the connection between isomorphism and quantity. First, note that if $A \cong B$ then $|A| = |B|$, since the latter means by definition that there is a bijection between A and B. But in the special case of *monadic* structures, i.e., structures with only unary relations, more can be said. Consider a signature with two unary relation symbols. A structure $A = (A, X, Y)$ for this signature partitions the universe into four parts as shown in figure 19.1.

Now if

$$f: (A, X, Y) \cong (A', X', Y')$$

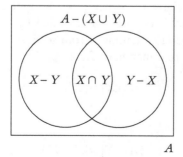

Figure 19.1

then the corresponding parts of the two structures must have the same cardinality. For the restriction of the bijection f to, say, $X - Y$ becomes a bijection between $X - Y$ and $X' - Y'$, and similarly for the other parts. But the converse holds too: if the corresponding parts have the same cardinality, then there are four bijections, whose union is an isomorphism between the two structures. That is,

Fact 19.1 $(A, X, Y) \cong (A', X', Y')$ iff

$$|X - Y| = |X' - Y'|$$
$$|X \cap Y| = |X' \cap Y'|$$
$$|Y - X| = |Y' - X'|$$

and

$$|A - (X \cup Y)| = |A' - (X' \cup Y')|$$

This generalizes to all monadic structures: if there are k unary relation symbols in the signature, the universe is partitioned into 2^k parts, and the number of elements in these is, up to isomorphism, all there is to say about the structure.

Now consider the following property of a type $\langle 1, 1 \rangle$ quantifier Q:

(ISOM)   If $(A, X, Y) \cong (A', X', Y')$ then $[Q_A XY \Leftrightarrow Q_{A'} X'Y']$.

This is what I mean by saying that Q deals only with quantities. If Q satisfies ISOM then, by fact 19.1, only the number of elements in $X - Y$, $X \cap Y$, $Y - X$, and $A - (X \cap Y)$ determines whether $Q_A XY$ holds or not. Now look at our examples of type $\langle 1, 1 \rangle$ quantifiers from section 19.4: each one is given by a condition on one or more of these quantities; hence they all satisfy ISOM. For example,

$all_A XY \Leftrightarrow |X - Y| = 0$

$some_A XY \Leftrightarrow |X \cap Y| > 0$

$most_A XY \Leftrightarrow |X \cap Y| > |X - Y|$

$more_A XY \Leftrightarrow |X - Y| + |X \cap Y| > |Y - X| + |X \cap Y|$

etc.

ISOM is expressed similarly for other monadic types. In the type $\langle 1 \rangle$ case, it says that whether $Q_A X$ holds or not is determined by the two quantities $|X|$ and $|A - X|$. Thus, all the type $\langle 1 \rangle$ quantifiers from section 19.3 satisfy ISOM, but the quantifier Q_{John} does not: one may have $X, X' \subseteq A$

$$|X| = |X'|$$

and

$$|A - X| = |A - X'|$$

but John $\in X - X'$.

It should come as no surprise that there is a tight connection between ISOM and isomorphism closure. To state it, we must sharpen our idea of what a *logic* is.

19.6. Logics with Generalized Quantifiers

In chapter 1, first-order logic FO is characterized as a collection of (artificial) languages: for each signature σ there is the set of σ-formulas, defined inductively, starting with the atomic formulas, and then one clause for each logical constant. Then, the relation $\vDash$ between a σ-structure, a σ-formula, and a valuation (of the variables in the universe of the structure) is defined with a corresponding induction, with (19.2) and (19.3) (or (19.8) and (19.9)) as the inductive clauses corresponding to $\forall$ and $\exists$.

Now let Q be any (for the time being monadic) quantifier. The logic FO(Q) is given, syntactically, by adding (Q-syn) (cf. section 19.4) as a defining clause of the σ-formulas, and, semantically, (Q-sem) as a defining clause for $\vDash$. Thus, FO(Q) has all the expressive machinery of first-order-logic, *plus* the quantifier Q.

Similarly, we can define FO($Q_1, \ldots, Q_n$), or even FO($\mathbf{Q}$) where $\mathbf{Q}$ is any set of quantifiers. By a *logic* I will mean a logic of this form (there are more general notions of a logic but they will not concern us here).

For example, FO(Q_0) is a logic, with atomic formulas, negations, conjunctions, existential and universal quantifications as usual, *and* formulas of the form

$$(Q_0 x)\varphi$$

whose meaning is given by

$$A \vDash (Q_0 x)\varphi[x, \mathbf{a}] \Leftrightarrow \varphi^{A,x,\mathbf{a}} \text{ is infinite}$$

FO($Q_0, \exists_{=17}$) is another logic, where in addition there are formulas of the form

$$(\exists_{=17} y)\varphi$$

where

$$A \vDash (\exists_{=17} y)\varphi[y, \mathbf{a}] \Leftrightarrow |\varphi^{A,y,\mathbf{a}}| = 17$$

The notion of isomorphism closure makes sense for any logic, and it is now easy to establish

Fact 19.2 If each quantifier in $\mathbf{Q}$ satsifies ISOM, then ismorphism closure holds for FO($\mathbf{Q}$).

(To show this, one proves by induction over formulas something a little more general, namely, that if $f: A \cong B$ and $a_1, \ldots, a_n \in A$ then

$$A \models \varphi[a_1, \ldots, a_n] \Leftrightarrow B \models \varphi[f(a_1), \ldots, f(a_n)]$$

for all φ in FO(Q) of the relevant signature. Fact 19.2 is the special case of this when φ is a sentence.)

One reason that ISOM is important is thus that Fact 19.2 needs to hold, or, put differently, quantifiers need to be *logical constants*. There has been some discussion as to just what logicality means, but it is generally agreed that isomorphism closure is at least a necessary condition: logic should be indifferent to which universe of objects one is talking about. It is 'topic-neutral,' it cares only about structure [see chapter 6]. In the case of monadic quantifiers, there is a further reason, as has been seen: these particular logical constants care only about quantities of things, not the things in themselves. Hence the adequacy of the term *quantifier*.

Are logics with generalized quantifiers *first-order* or not? There is a sense in which they are: they quantify only over individuals of the universe, not, as in second-order logic, over sets of such individuals [see chapter 2]. Thus, the notion of a signature, and the notion of a structure, are the same for these logics as for FO. However, the term *first-order logic* has become synonymous with FO, and, in this sense, many of the logics introduced here are not first-order, since their expressive power exceeds that of FO.

19.7. Expressive Power

Consider again the logic $FO(Q_0)$. Clearly this logic, and any logic of the form $FO(Q)$, *extends* FO: everything that can be said in FO can also be said in them. Moreover, it is also clear that $FO(Q_0)$ is *more expressive* than FO; for example, as mentioned in section 19.3 one can say in $FO(Q_0)$ that every element of $\mathcal{N}$ has a finite number of predecessors, but one cannot say the same thing in FO. Or, to take a simpler example, one can say in $FO(Q_0)$, but not in FO, that the universe is finite:

$$\sim (Q_0 x)(x = x)$$

To prove this, suppose there were an FO-sentence θ equivalent to $\sim (Q_0 x)(x = x)$. In FO one can write down, for every natural number n, a sentence φ_n saying that the universe has at least n elements. Consider the theory (set of sentences)

$$T = \{\theta\} \cup \{\varphi_n : n = 1, 2, \ldots\}$$

Now T has the property that every one of its finite subsets has a model (why?). By the *Compactness theorem* which holds for FO [see chapter 1, section 1.10], it then follows that T has a model. But that is impossible: the universe of that model would be finite, yet have at least n elements for every n. Hence, $\sim (Q_0 x)(x = x)$ is not equivalent to any FO-sentence. It also follows that the Compactness theorem does not hold for $FO(Q_0)$.

We take these intuitions as the way to compare the expressive power of logics. By definition, a logic L' *extends* a logic L, in symbols, $L \leq L'$, if each L-sentence is equivalent to – has the same models as – some L'-sentence (of the same signature). Thus, every logic of the kind considered here extends FO. Moreover, L' *properly* extends L, $L < L'$, if $L \leq L'$ and $L' \nleq L$. The latter condition means that there is some L'-sentence which is not equivalent to any L-sentence. For example,

$$FO < FO(Q_0) \tag{19.20}$$

as just seen. Finally, L and L' are said to be *equivalent*, $L \equiv L'$, if $L \leq L'$ and $L' \leq L$.

Note that equivalence between logics means same expressive power; it does not mean identity. Consider FO and $FO(\exists_{=17})$. These logics are equivalent: in FO it can be said, for example, that a set has exactly 18 elements:

$$(\exists x_1) \cdots (\exists x_{18})(\bigwedge_{1 \leq i \neq j \leq 18} (P(x_i) \mathbin{\&} (x_i \neq x_j)) \mathbin{\&} (\forall y)(P(y) \supset \bigvee_{1 \leq i \leq 18} (y = x_i)))$$

As can be seen, it takes 19 variables to say this. But in $FO(\exists_{=17})$ it is possible to say the same thing with just two variables:

$$(\exists y)(P(y) \mathbin{\&} (\exists_{=17}x)(P(x) \mathbin{\&} (x \neq y)))$$

Indeed, everything that can be said in $FO(\exists_{=17})$ can also be said in FO, only it sometimes takes more variables. The number of variables used is important for certain applications of logic, but not for expressive power as defined here.

19.8. Definability

Showing that $L \leq L'$ may seem like a substantial task: for each one of the infinitely many L-sentences, an equivalent L'-sentence must be found. But when L is of the form $FO(Q)$, the task is usually much simpler: it suffices to show that each quantifier in Q is *definable* in L'. For example, once it is seen that the quantifier $\exists_{=17}$ is definable in FO, it is rather clear that any $FO(\exists_{=17})$-sentence can be rewritten as an FO-sentence. And that $\exists_{=17}$ is definable in FO just means that the single sentence $(\exists_{=17}x)P(x)$ is equivalent to some FO-sentence, as of course it is.

To be precise: Suppose Q is a type $\langle 1, 1 \rangle$ quantifier. Q is said to be *definable* in a logic L if the sentence

$$(Qx)(P_1(x), P_2(x))$$

is equivalent to some L-sentence of the same signature (in this case the signature $\{P_1, P_2\}$ consisting of two unary relation symbols). Similarly for quantifiers of other types. Now it is not hard to show

Fact 19.3 $FO(Q) \leq L$ iff each quantifier in Q is definable in L.

Look at some examples. It has been seen that $FO \equiv FO(\exists_{=17})$; hence

$$FO(Q_0) \equiv FO(Q_0, \exists_{=17}) \tag{19.21}$$

since $\exists_{=17}$, being definable in FO, is *a fortiori* definable in $FO(Q_0)$.

$$FO(Q_0) \le FO(I) \le FO(more) \tag{19.22}$$

The first part holds since a set is infinite iff it has the same cardinality as some proper subset, so $(Q_0 x)P(x)$ is equivalent to

$$(\exists x)(P(x) \& (Iy)(P(y), P(y) \& (y \ne x)))$$

The second part holds because $(Ix)(P_1(x), P_2(x))$ is clearly equivalent to

$$\sim (more\ x)(P_1(x), P_2(x)) \& \sim (more\ x)(P_2(x), P_1(x))$$

One can show that both of the inequalities in (19.22) are in fact strict. (These are examples of *un*definability results; more about that in section 19.9.)

$$FO(most) \le FO(more) \tag{19.23}$$

since $(most\ x)(P_1(x), P_2(x))$ is equivalent to

$$(more\ x)(P_1(x) \& P_2(x), P_1(x) \& \sim P_2(x))$$

Again, this is a strict inequality in general. But note that if $X \cap Y$ is a *finite* set, then

$$|X| > |Y| \Leftrightarrow |X - Y| + |X \cap Y| > |Y - X| + |X \cap Y|$$
$$\Leftrightarrow |X - Y| > |Y - X|$$

So when (the interpretation of) $P_1 \cap P_2$ is finite, $(more\ x)(P_1(x), P_2(x))$ is equivalent to

$$(most\ x)((P_1(x) \& \sim P_2(x)) \vee (P_2(x) \& \sim P_1(x)), (P_1(x) \& \sim P_2(x)))$$

Let this last sentence be ψ_1. Next, when $X \cap Y$ is an *infinite* set, then $|X|$ is the maximum of $|X - Y|$ and $|X \cap Y|$, and likewise $|Y|$ is the maximum of $|Y - X|$ and $|X \cap Y|$. (These are facts of cardinal arithmetic.) It follows that, in this case,

$$|X| > |Y| \Leftrightarrow [|X - Y| > |Y - X| \text{ and } |X - Y| > |X \cap Y|]^1$$

That is, when $P_1 \cap P_2$ is infinite, $(more\ x)(P_1(x), P_2(x))$ is equivalent to

$$\psi_1 \& (most\ x)(P_1(x), \sim P_2(x))$$

Let the second conjunct above be ψ_2. It now follows that, on any universe, $(more\ x)$ $(P_1(x), P_2(x))$ is equivalent to

$$(\sim (Q_0 x)(P_1(x) \& P_2(x)) \& \psi_1) \vee ((Q_0 x)(P_1(x) \& P_2(x)) \& \psi_1 \& \psi_2)$$

Putting all of the above together, shows that

$$\mathrm{FO}(\textit{more}) \equiv \mathrm{FO}(Q_0, \textit{most}) \tag{19.24}$$

All type $\langle 1 \rangle$ quantifiers are definable in terms of type $\langle 1, 1 \rangle$ quantifiers (but not vice versa); in fact, there is a uniform way of strengthening a type $\langle 1 \rangle$ quantifier Q to its so-called *relativization*, which is the type $\langle 1, 1 \rangle$ quantifier Q^{rel} defined by

(Rel) $Q_A^{\text{rel}} XY \Leftrightarrow Q_X X \cap Y$

Roughly, Q^{rel} says (on any universe A) about X, Y what Q says on the universe X about $X \cap Y$. In other words, the quantification domain is restricted to the first argument of Q_A. We have $Q_A X \Leftrightarrow Q_A^{\text{rel}} AX$, that is, the following is logically valid:

$$(Qx)P(x) \leftrightarrow (Q^{\text{rel}}x)((x = x,\ P(x))$$

which means that

$$\mathrm{FO}(Q) \leq \mathrm{FO}(Q^{\text{rel}}) \tag{19.25}$$

Here are some examples of relativizations:

- $\forall^{\text{rel}} = \textit{all}$
- $\exists^{\text{rel}} = \textit{some}$
- $(\exists_{\geq n})^{\text{rel}} = \textit{at least } n$
- $(Q_R)^{\text{rel}} = \textit{most}$ (Q_R was defined in (19.14).)

So, note that the Aristotelian quantifiers are relativizations of familiar type $\langle 1 \rangle$ quantifiers. In the first three cases above, the relativizations are, in turn, definable from the unrelativized quantifiers, for example

$$(\textit{all } x)(P_1(x),\ P_2(x)) \leftrightarrow (\forall x)(P_1(x) \supset P_2(x))$$

$$(\textit{some } x)(P_1(x),\ P_2(x)) \leftrightarrow (\exists x)(P_1(x) \ \& \ P_2(x))$$

In other words,

$$\mathrm{FO} \equiv \mathrm{FO}(\textit{all}) \equiv \mathrm{FO}(\textit{some}) \equiv \mathrm{FO}(\exists_{\geq n}) \equiv \mathrm{FO}(\exists_{\geq n}^{\text{rel}}) \tag{19.26}$$

However, interestingly,

$$\mathrm{FO}(Q_R) < \mathrm{FO}(\textit{most}) \tag{19.27}$$

Even on finite universes, in fact, saying that $X \cap Y$ has more than half the elements of X is *not* expressible in first-order logic plus the quantifier saying that a set has more than half the elements of the whole universe.

19.9. Undefinability

To prove that a particular quantifier Q is definable in some logic L, a definition must be provided, i.e., a defining L-sentence. This can be more or less involved (as with the case with *more*, *most* and Q_0 in section 19.8), but is often straightforward. To prove that Q is *not* so definable, however, is harder. Here one really needs to verify that none of the infinitely many L-sentences works as a definition.

Sometimes one can manage by showing that L has some property that it would not have if Q were definable. This is how it was shown that Q_0 is not definable in FO, using the fact that FO has the compactness property. But this is more of an exception; most logics lack compactness, or other similarly useful properties. There are, however, more elementary and direct methods of showing undefinability, but a description of these falls outside the scope of this chapter. A thorough survey of (un)definability issues for logics with monadic quantifiers is given in Väänänen (1997).

Using these methods, it can be shown, for example, that the seemingly innocuous quantifier $most = (Q_R)^{rel}$ is essentially type $\langle 1, 1 \rangle$ in a very strong sense: not only is it not definable from Q_R, but:

> **Theorem 19.4** *most* is not definable in any logic of the form FO($Q_1, \ldots, Q_n$), where the Q_i are of type $\langle 1 \rangle$. (In fact, the same holds for all the properly proportional quantifiers.) Kolaitis and Väänänen (1995)

19.10. Monotonicity

Among the multitude of possible quantifiers, the ones that actually turn up in familiar logical or linguistic contexts often have characteristic properties. Logicians want to know if logics with generalized quantifiers are well-behaved in various ways, for example if the compactness property holds for them (see section 19.7), or if they are *complete*, i.e., if their sets of logically valid sentences are recursively enumerable (can be axiomatized by a formal system). Unfortunately, many logics fail to have either of these properties; examples are FO(Q_0) and FO(*most*); proofs of these facts can be found in Westerståhl (1989).

But one may more simply just look at the properties of the quantifiers themselves, and then the perhaps most conspicuous ones are the *monotonicity* properties:

- A type $\langle 1 \rangle$ quantifier Q is *upward monotone*, MON↑, if for all A,

$$Q_A X \quad \text{and} \quad X \subseteq Y \subseteq A \quad \text{implies} \quad Q_A Y$$

  Downward monotonicity, MON↓, is defined correspondingly.
- Similarly, for type $\langle 1, 1 \rangle$ quantifiers one can talk about upward or downward monotonicity in the first or second argument, and use MON with up- or down-arrows to the right and/or left to indicate this. For example, a type $\langle 1, 1 \rangle$ Q is ↓MON if, for all A,

$$Q_A XY \quad \text{and} \quad X' \subseteq X \quad \text{implies} \quad Q_A X' Y$$

And it is, say, $\uparrow$MON$\downarrow$ if it is upward monotone in the first argument and downward monotone in the second argument.

Now, looking at our examples notice that $\forall$, $\exists$, $\exists_{\geq n}$, Q_R, Q_0, Q_C are all MON$\uparrow$, whereas, say, $\exists_{\leq n}$ is $\downarrow$MON. A typical quantifier which is neither upward nor downward monotone is $\exists_{=n}$, but note that it is the conjunction of an upward and a downward one:

$$\exists_{=n} = \exists_{\geq n} \,\&\, \exists_{\leq n}$$

So monotonicity is ubiquitous. Here, however, is an example of a thoroughly non-monotone type $\langle 1 \rangle$ quantifier:

$$(Q_{\text{even}})_A X \Leftrightarrow |X| \text{ is even}$$

As to our type $\langle 1, 1 \rangle$ quantifiers, *some* and *at least n* are $\uparrow$MON$\uparrow$, *no* is $\downarrow$MON$\downarrow$, *every* is $\downarrow$MON$\uparrow$, *more* is $\uparrow$MON$\downarrow$, and *most* is MON$\uparrow$ but, as the reader can easily verify, not monotone (in either direction) in the first argument. *I* is non-monotone, but, as shown in section 19.8, it is definable with Boolean operations from the monotone *more*. And again, a thoroughly non-monotone type $\langle 1, 1 \rangle$ quantifier is *an even number of* $= (Q_{\text{even}})^{\text{rel}}$.

19.11. Lindström Quantifiers

Monadic quantifiers are, on a given universe, relations among subsets of that universe. But the business of mathematics is generalization, and it is then only natural to consider quantifiers that are relations between *relations* over the universe. This concept was introduced in Lindström (1966), and is the official notion of a generalized quantifier in logic. Our earlier definitions easily carry over to this *polyadic* case. This can be illustrated with an example.

A (generalized) quantifier of type $\langle 2, 1, 3 \rangle$ is a function Q which associates with each universe A a quantifier Q_A of type $\langle 2, 1, 3 \rangle$ on A, i.e., a ternary relation between a binary relation over A, a subset of A, and a ternary relation over A.

Such a Q can again be seen as a variable-binding operator, such that

(Q-syn) if φ, ψ, θ are formulas, then

$$(Qxy,\ z,\ uvw)(\varphi,\ \psi,\ \theta)$$

is a formula (where all free occurrences of x, y in φ are bound by the quantifier prefix, and similarly for the other variables).

The meaning of this formula is given by the clause

(Q-sem) $\quad A \vDash (Qxy,\ z,\ uvw)(\varphi,\ \psi,\ \theta)\ [\mathbf{a}]\quad$ iff $\quad (\varphi^{A,xy,\mathbf{a}},\ \psi^{A,z,\mathbf{a}},\ \theta^{A,uvw,\mathbf{a}}) \in Q_A$

Here

$$\varphi^{A,xy,\mathbf{a}} = \{(b,\ c) \in A^2 : A \vDash \varphi[b,\ c,\ \mathbf{a}]\}$$

etc. So the logic FO(Q) is defined as before by adding these new clauses to the definition of a formula and of satisfaction, respectively. The reader can easily formulate all of this for the general case of a quantifier of type $\langle k_1, \ldots, k_n \rangle$.

The property ISOM is defined for such a Q in the same way as before (below for the type $\langle 2,\ 1,\ 3 \rangle$ case, so $R \subseteq A^2$, $X \subseteq A$, $S \subseteq A^3$, etc.):

(ISOM) $\quad$ If $(A,\ R,\ X,\ S) \cong (A',\ R',\ X',\ S')$ then $[Q_A RXS \Leftrightarrow Q_{A'}R'X'S']$

Fact 19.2 generalizes too, so ISOM quantifiers earn the right to be called logical constants. However, they no longer say anything about quantities, so the name 'quantifier' should be taken with a grain of salt in the polyadic case. Consider some examples:

$D_A XR \Leftrightarrow R$ is a dense total ordering of X (type $\langle 1,\ 2 \rangle$) $\qquad\qquad$ (19.28)

$W_A R \Leftrightarrow R$ is a well-ordering of the universe (type $\langle 2 \rangle$) $\qquad\qquad$ (19.29)

To express that R is a dense total ordering of a set X is easy in FO, so FO $\equiv$ FO(D). But the notion of a well-ordering is not expressible (as can be seen by a simple application of the Compactness theorem): FO < FO(W).

Let Q, Q_1, Q_2 be type $\langle 1 \rangle$ quantifiers. The next few examples illustrate so-called *lifts* of monadic quantifiers to polyadic ones; in this version they lift type $\langle 1 \rangle$ quantifiers to type $\langle 2 \rangle$ quantifiers.

$Ram(Q)_A R \Leftrightarrow \exists X \subseteq A(Q_A X\ \&\ \forall a,\ b \in X(a \neq b \Rightarrow R(a,\ b)))$ $\qquad$ (19.30)

$Br(Q_1,\ Q_2)_A R \Leftrightarrow \exists X,\ Y \subseteq A((Q_1)_A X\ \&\ (Q_2)_A Y\ \&\ X \times Y \subseteq R)$ $\qquad$ (19.31)

$Res(Q)_A R \Leftrightarrow Q_{A^2} R$ $\qquad\qquad\qquad\qquad\qquad\qquad\qquad\qquad\qquad\qquad$ (19.32)

In all of these cases, it is assumed that the lifted type $\langle 1 \rangle$ quantifiers are MON↑. (Equation (19.30) is related to the so-called Ramsey Theorem; cf. any textbook of model theory.)

The lift *Br* is an example of *branching* quantification. This idea originally stems from Henkin (1961), who noted that the linear order of the quantifiers $\forall$ and $\exists$ in FO imposes certain restrictions that can be avoided if a *partial order* is allowed as well. This is, in fact, another way of generalizing FO quantification. Consider the formula

$$(\forall x)(\exists y) \atop (\forall z)(\exists u) \quad \varphi(x, y, z, u) \qquad (19.33)$$

This is read 'for all x there exists y *and* for all z there exists u such that $\varphi(x, y, z, u)$', where the y depends on x but not on z, and the u depends on z but not on x. Such dependencies cannot be expressed in FO. For example, in

$$(\forall x)(\exists y)(\forall z)(\exists u)\varphi(x, y, z, u) \qquad (19.34)$$

u depends on x and z, and in

$$(\forall x)(\forall z)(\exists y)(\exists u)\varphi(x, y, z, u) \qquad (19.35)$$

y and u both depend on x and z. These dependencies appear clearly if (19.34) and (19.35) are rewritten by means of so-called *Skolem functions*; then (19.34) becomes

$$(\exists F)(\exists G)(\forall x)(\forall z)\varphi(x, F(x), z, G(x, z))$$

and (19.35) is equivalent to

$$(\exists F)(\exists G)(\forall x)(\forall z)\varphi(x, F(x, z), z, G(x, z))$$

The formula (19.33), on the other hand, has the intended meaning

$$(\exists F)(\exists G)(\forall x)(\forall z)\varphi(x, F(x), z, G(z))$$

The quantifier prefix in (19.33) is called the *Henkin quantifier*. It can be subsumed under the notion of generalized quantifier: define the type $\langle 4 \rangle$ quantifier Q^H by

$Q_A^H R \Leftrightarrow$ there are functions f, g s.t. for all $a, b \in A$, $R(a, f(a), b, g(b))$

where $R \subseteq A^4$. Then (19.33) is equivalent to $(Q^H xyzu)\varphi(x, y, z, u)$. Other partially ordered quantifier prefixes with $\forall$ and $\exists$ can be defined similarly. Adding the Henkin quantifier already extends the expressive power of FO considerably. For example, one may show that Q_0 and even *more* are definable in FO(Q^H), so

$$FO < FO(\textit{more}) \leq FO(Q^H)$$

The proof of this observation (due to Ehrenfeucht) is too simple and too pretty to be left out here: we will express "there exists a one-one function F from P_1 to P_2"; this suffices since it means that $\sim (\textit{more } x)(P_2(x), P_1(x))$. Consider the sentence

$$(\forall x)(\exists y) \atop (\forall z)(\exists u) \quad (((x = z) \equiv (y = u)) \;\&\; (P_1(x) \supset P_2(y))) \qquad (19.36)$$

By definition, this means

$$(\exists F)(\exists G)(\forall x)(\forall z)(((x=z) \equiv (F(x)=G(z))) \,\&\, (P_1(x) \supset P_2(F(x))))$$

The (universally quantified) first conjunct gives, first (letting z be x) that $F(x)=G(x)$ for all x, so $F=G$, and second, that if $x \neq z$ then $F(x) \neq F(z)$, so F is one-one, and we are done!)   QED

Now Barwise (1979) suggested that one may also consider branching of (certain) other quantifiers than $\forall$ and $\exists$, and the polyadic $Br(Q_1, Q_2)$ is an example of this, which one could emphasize by writing the formula $(Br(Q_1, Q_2)xy)\varphi(x,y)$ as

$$\begin{matrix}(Q_1x) \\ \\ (Q_2y)\end{matrix} \quad \varphi(x,y)$$

It thus says that there is a set X satisfying Q_1 and a set Y satisfying Q_2 such that any pair (x,y) with $x \in X$ and $y \in Y$ satisfies $\varphi(x,y)$. The 'order-independence' of the lifted quantifiers here is witnessed by the fact that the formula is equivalent to

$$\begin{matrix}(Q_2y) \\ \\ (Q_1x)\end{matrix} \quad \varphi(x,y)$$

So, in fact, there are two ways of generalizing FO quantification: one is through the concept of a (Lindström) generalized quantifier (which, as noted, essentially occurs already with Frege), and the other is through relaxing the linear left-right order of FO logic. As seen, the latter can, for the case of $\forall$ and $\exists$, be subsumed under the former. But there also arises the question as to whether one can 'branch' arbitrary generalized quantifiers. Barwise considered some cases of branching of MON↑ quantifiers, but he explicitly stated that another definition is required for the branching of MON↓ quantifiers, and he also claimed that the branching of, say, a MON↑ and a MON↓ quantifier "makes no sense." In spite of this, others have tried to express the meaning of arbitrary partially ordered prefixes of arbitrary generalized quantifiers (Sher, 1997). It remains to be seen, in my opinion, whether these ideas yield a fruitful notion of (generalized) quantifier.

The lift $Res(Q)$, finally, is called the *resumption* (sometimes *vectorization*) of Q. Looking at a binary relation R as a set of ordered pairs, $Res(Q)_A R$ simply says about R what Q says about that set of pairs. For example,

$$Res(\exists_{\geq n})_A(R) \Leftrightarrow |R| \geq n$$

i.e., $Res(\exists_{\geq n})_A(R)$ says that R has at least n pairs. Likewise,

$$Res(Q_R)_A(R) \Leftrightarrow |R| > |A^2 - R|$$

As one would expect, polyadic quantifiers have in general more expressive power than monadic ones. As to the lifts, one can, for example, show that $(Br(Q_1, Q_2)xy)P(x,y)$

is usually stronger than the 'linear versions' $(Q_1x)(Q_2y)P(x, y)$ and $(Q_2y)(Q_1x)P(x, y)$. Indeed, Hella et al. (1997) prove that these lifts are *essentially* polyadic:

Theorem 19.5 $Br(Q_R, Q_R)$ is not definable in any logic of the form $FO(Q_1, \ldots, Q_n)$ where the Q_i are monadic, and the same holds for $Ram(Q_R)$.

Undefinability results for polyadic quantifiers can be very hard to prove. An example is the result in Luosto (2000) that $Res(Q_R)$ too is not definable from any finite number of monadic quantifiers added to FO; this proof requires quite advanced combinatorics.

19.12. Quantifiers and Natural Language

The most obvious connection between (generalized) quantifiers and natural languages is that many of these languages have a fundamental sentence construction of the form $[[[Q]_{Det}[X]_N]_{NP}[Y]_{VP}]_S$, or, in diagrammatic form,

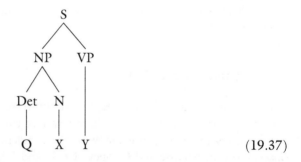

$$(19.37)$$

That is, (declarative) sentences are often formed by a noun phrase (NP) and a verb phrase (VP), where the noun phrase consists of a determiner (Det) and a noun (N).[2] Both nouns ('man', 'teacher', 'hungry dog', 'student who likes a teacher', ...) and verb phrases ('runs', 'smokes', 'likes Henry', 'gave a flower to some shop owner', ...) are naturally interpreted as sets, i.e., as subsets of the universe of discourse. Therefore, the determiner ('every', 'no', 'most', 'at least three', 'several of John's ten') can be taken as a relation between sets, i.e., as a type $\langle 1, 1 \rangle$ quantifier (on the universe, but the Det gives a quantifier on each universe, so it corresponds to a generalized quantifier in our sense). For example,

No student likes Henry. $\hspace{4cm}$ (19.38)

All but three teachers smoke. $\hspace{3.5cm}$ (19.39)

Most hungry dogs are friendly. $\hspace{3.3cm}$ (19.40)

Two thirds of John's friends are teachers. $\hspace{2cm}$ (19.41)

Other types as well turn up in connection with natural languages. The expressions 'everything' and 'something' naturally correspond to the type $\langle 1 \rangle$ $\forall$ and $\exists$. More generally, NPs may be interpreted as type $\langle 1 \rangle$ quantifiers, so that, for example, 'most students' denotes the set of subsets X of the universe whose intersection with the sets of students contains more than half of the students, and 'all but three dogs' denotes the set of those X such that the complement of X with respect to the set of dogs has exactly three elements, etc. Recall also that proper names like 'John' can be taken as type $\langle 1 \rangle$ quantifiers (note that this example as well as the last two do not satisfy ISOM).

One may see the type $\langle 1, 1, 1 \rangle$ *more than* ((19.4) from section 19.4) at work in the sentence

More students than teachers smoke. (19.42)

But also polyadic lifts appear in the context of natural language quantification; a survey of this can be found in Keenan and Westerståhl (1997). I will not go further into these matters here, but end with a few more words about the central type $\langle 1, 1 \rangle$ case, i.e., the determiner denotations.

Given the vast number of mathematically possible type $\langle 1, 1 \rangle$ quantifiers, a reasonable question is whether there are constraints as to which of these can be realized in natural languages. A prime observation is that the noun argument X in (19.37) plays a special role: it *restricts* the domain of quantification. This is borne out by looking at actual examples:

Exactly three dogs barked. (19.43)

can be seen as quantifying over the subuniverse of dogs; the non-dogs of the universe are irrelevant for the truth or falsity of this sentence. Also, a special role of the noun argument is consistent with the syntactic structure of (19.37). An early observation (in Barwise and Cooper (1981) and Keenan and Stavi (1986)) was that determiner denotations are *conservative*: they satisfy

(CONS) $Q_A XY \Leftrightarrow Q_A X \, X \cap Y$, for all A and all $X, Y \subseteq A$

This means, in effect, that the part $Y - X$ in figure 19.1 (page 443) plays no role in the truth conditions of $Q_A XY$. This seems to hold for determiner denotations, but it does *not* hold, for example, for the otherwise mathematically perfectly natural quantifiers I and *more* (section 19.4). And indeed, there do not seem to be any determiner expressions in natural languages which denote these quantifiers.

There is one more aspect of domain restriction, however: the part $A - (X \cup Y)$ should not matter to the truth conditions either. This can be expressed as the following condition of *extension*, first proposed by van Benthem (1986):

(EXT)   If $X, Y \subseteq A \subseteq A'$, then $Q_A XY \Leftrightarrow Q_{A'} XY$

That is, what a determiner denotes on a given universe does not 'change' if one goes to a larger universe. So, for example, there could not be a determiner *blik*, say, which meant *some* on universes with less than ten elements, but *most* on larger universes (note that this quantifier would still be conservative).

Now recall that the idea of domain or universe restriction was already defined in section 19.8 in terms of the notion of relativization. And indeed, conservativity and extension together capture exactly the same idea:

Fact 19.6 A type $\langle 1, 1 \rangle$ quantifier satisfies CONS and EXT iff it is the relativization of some type $\langle 1 \rangle$ quantifier.

To see this, check first that Q^{rel} always satisfies CONS and EXT. In the other direction, any CONS and EXT Q' has a type $\langle 1 \rangle$ 'counterpart' Q defined by

$$Q_A X \Leftrightarrow Q'_A AX$$

Then

$$Q_A^{\text{rel}} XY \Leftrightarrow Q_X X \cap Y \text{ (by (Rel) in section 19.8)}$$
$$\Leftrightarrow Q'_X X \, X \cap Y \text{ (by definition)}$$
$$\Leftrightarrow Q'_A X \, X \cap Y \text{ (by EXT)}$$
$$\Leftrightarrow Q'_A XY \text{ (by CONS)}$$

so $Q' = Q^{\text{rel}}$.

So quantifiers that are denoted by determiners in natural languages satisfy CONS and EXT. They also satisfy ISOM. The ISOM + CONS + EXT quantifiers form a natural class, but there have been several attempts to formulate further constraints or 'linguistic universals' that single out (important subclasses of) the 'natural language quantifiers.' Prime examples here are the various monotonicity properties discussed in section 19.10. It may seem – and it has been suggested – that all (monadic) quantifiers occurring in natural languages are Boolean combinations of monotone ones. However, an apparent exception to this would be *an even number of* $= (Q_{\text{even}})^{\text{rel}}$. And it is true that one can show (this follows from a result in Väänänen (1997)) that Q_{even} is not definable from MON↑ $\langle 1 \rangle$ type quantifiers. Perhaps surprisingly, however, it *is* definable from the relativization of such a quantifier, in fact from a CONS, EXT, ISOM, and MON↑ type $\langle 1, 1 \rangle$ quantifier. To see how, note that

an even number of $_A XY \Leftrightarrow |X \cap Y|$ is even

Now define Q by

$$Q_A XY \Leftrightarrow \begin{cases} |X \cap Y| \geq 1 & \text{if } |X| \text{ is even} \\ |X \cap Y| \geq 2 & \text{if } |X| \text{ is odd} \end{cases}$$

Q is clearly CONS, EXT, ISOM, and upward monotone in the *second* argument. Notice then that if $a \in X$,

$Q_A X\{a\} \Leftrightarrow |X|$ is even

But then

$|X \cap Y|$ is even $\Leftrightarrow X \cap Y = \emptyset$ or $\exists a \in X \cap Y \; Q_A X \cap Y\{a\}$

That is,

(*an even number of* x)$(P_1(x),\; P_2(x))$

is equivalent to

$\sim \exists x(P_1(x) \; \& \; P_2(x)) \vee \exists x(P_1(x) \; \& \; P_2(x) \; \& \; (Q\,y)((P_1(y) \; \& \; P_2(y)),\; (y = x)))$

Perhaps one could still argue that Q is 'unnatural' in some sense, but I will leave the matter here.

In early days of linguistic semantics, it was sometimes suggested that first-order logic, FO, suffices for the formalization of natural languages. This thesis can be refuted in many ways, I think, but perhaps the most convincing rebuttal comes from the theory of quantifiers. Certainly *most* is a natural language quantifier, but as has been seen, even if one restricts attention to finite universes, it is not FO definable, indeed it is not definable from any type $\langle 1 \rangle$ quantifiers (theorem 19.4). Essentially stronger logics than FO are needed to capture the intricacies of quantification in natural languages.

Suggested further reading

A detailed exposition of most of the aspects of quantification touched on in this chapter can be found in Westerståhl (1989). A more recent survey article, emphasizing the connection with natural languages, and in particular the occurrence of polyadic lifts, is Keenan and Westerståhl (1997). There are several technical papers on the expressive power of various quantifiers; I would suggest Kolaitis and Väänänen (1995), Väänänen (1997), and Hella et al. (1997), where the details are spelled out in an accessible way. The canonical collection of mathematical papers on logics with generalized quantifiers, and more generally on logics defined in a model-theoretic way, is Barwise and Feferman (1985). A more philosophical approach to the logic of quantifiers can be found in several of the papers in van Benthem's (1986) collection. All of the work cited so far approaches quantification from a logical point of view. For those interested in the various forms that quantification can take in the world's languages, Bach et al. (1995) is an invaluable source. The connection between this more empirical work and the logic of quantification still remains to be fully explored.

Notes

1 *Proof*: If

$$|X-Y| > |Y-X| \quad \text{and} \quad |X-Y| > |X \cap Y|$$

then

$$|X| \geq |X-Y| > \max(|X \cap Y|, |Y-X|) = |Y|$$

On the other hand, if

$$|X-Y| \leq |Y-X|$$

then

$$|X| = |X-Y| + |X \cap Y| \leq |Y-X| + |X \cap Y| = |Y|$$

And if

$$|X-Y| \leq |X \cap Y|$$

then

$$\begin{aligned} |X| &= |X-Y| + |X \cap Y| \\ &\leq |X \cap Y| + |X \cap Y| \\ &= |X \cap Y| \; \text{(since } X \cap Y \text{ is infinite)} \\ &\leq |Y| \end{aligned} \qquad \text{QED}$$

2 All of these phrases may in turn have internal structure; in particular, noun phrases can occur in many different positions in a sentence. Also, quantification can be effected by other means than determiners, for example using adverbs – I am just looking at the simplest case here.

References

Bach, E., Jelinek, E., Kratzer, A. and Partee, B. (eds.) 1995: *Quantification in Natural Languages (vols. I and II)*, (Kluwer, Dordrecht).

Barwise, J. 1979: "On Branching Quantifiers in English," *Journal of Philosophical Logic*, 8, 47–80.

Barwise, J. and Cooper, R. 1981: "Generalized Quantifiers and Natural Language," *Linguistics and Philosophy*, 4, 159–219.

Barwise, J. and Feferman, S. (eds.) 1985: *Model-theoretic Logics*, (Springer, New York).

van Benthem, J. F. A. K. 1986: *Essays in Logical Semantics*, (D. Reidel, Dordrecht).

Hella, L., Väänänen, J. and Westerståhl, D. 1997: "Definability of Polyadic Lifts of Generalized Quantifiers," *Journal of Logic, Language and Information*, 6, 305–35.

Henkin, L. 1961: "Some Remarks on Infinitely Long Formulas," in *Infinitistic Methods, (Proceedings of the Symposium on Foundations of Mathematics, Warsaw 2–9 September 1959),* (Pergamon Press, Oxford), 167–83.

Keenan, E. and Stavi, J. 1986: "A Semantic Characterization of Natural Language Determiners," *Linguistics and Philosophy,* 9, 253–326.

Keenan, E. and Westerståhl, D. 1997: "Generalized Quantifiers in Linguistics and Logic," in *Handbook of Logic and Language,* J. van Benthem and A. ter Meulen, eds., (Elsevier, Dordrecht), 837–93.

Kolaitis, P. and Väänänen, J. 1995: "Generalized Quantifiers and Pebble Games on Finite Structures," *Annals of Pure and Applied Logic,* 74, 23–75.

Lindström, P. 1966: "First-Order Predicate Logic with Generalized Quantifiers," *Theoria,* 32, 186–95.

Luosto, K. 2000: "Hierarchies of monadic generalized quantifiers," *Journal of Symbolic Logic,* 65, 1241–63.

Mostowski, A. 1957: "On a Generalization of Quantifiers," *Fund Math.,* 44, 12–36.

Sher, G. 1997: "Partially-Ordered (Branching) Generalized Quantifiers: A General Definition," *Journal of Philosophical Logic,* 26, 1–43.

Väänänen, J. 1997: "Unary Quantifiers on Finite Models," *Journal of Logic, Language and Information,* 6, 275–304.

Westerståhl, D. 1989: "Quantifiers in Formal and Natural Languages," in *Handbook of Philosophical Logic,* vol. IV, D. Gabbay and F. Guenthner, eds., (D. Reidel, Dordrecht), 1–131.

Chapter 20

Logic and Natural Language

Alice ter Meulen

Logicians have always found inspiration for new research in the ordinary language that is used on a daily basis and acquired naturally in childhood. Whereas the logical issues in the foundations of mathematics motivated the development of mathematical logic with its emphasis on notions of proof, validity, axiomatization, decidability, consistency, and completeness, the logical analysis of natural language motivated the development of philosophical logic with its emphasis on semantic notions of presupposition, entailment, modality, conditionals, and intensionality. The relation between research programs in both mathematical and philosophical logic and natural language syntax and semantics as branches of theoretical linguistics has increased in importance throughout the last fifty years. This chapter reviews the development of one particularly interesting and lively area of interaction between formal logic and linguistics – the semantics of natural language. Research in this emergent field has proved fruitful for the development of empirically, cognitively adequate models of reasoning with partial information, sharing or exchanging information, dynamic interpretation in context, belief revision and other cognitive processes.

20.1. Compositional Semantics

This section examines the principle of compositionality that Frege introduced, and how it leads to what is known as 'Montague grammar'.

20.1.1. Frege's puzzles

Gottlob Frege, the founder of modern logic, provided a core foundational principle for contemporary semantic theory by requiring that the meaning of an expression should be a function from the meaning of its parts and the way in which they are put together. This *Principle of Compositionality* serves as a major methodological constraint on the interface between the syntax, which generates a (fragment of a) natural language, and its semantics, which takes the form of either a recursive procedure to translate its expressions to formulas of a formal language or a set of rules that specify how its expressions are given meaning in a model. For a system of interpretation to be compositional, the syntax of the object language needs to be formulated in such a way that the semantic properties of each syntactic category are completely determined by it.

Given this methodological requirement of compositionality on a theory of meaning and interpretation, the two semantic puzzles which preoccupied Frege (1952) still constitute major foundational problems that direct much of contemporary linguistic and philosophical theories of meaning and interpretation. The first puzzle concerns the information expressed in identity statements with coreferential noun phrases (NP). The Fregean discussion is based on the question why

Hesperus is Phosphorus. (20.1)

once was an informative identity statement to the Babylonian astronomers, who learned from empirical observations of the stars that (20.1) was true, whereas

Hesperus is Hesperus. (20.2)

was never informative, even though (20.1) and (20.2) are both true statements and the NPs, all proper names, corefer to the one and the same object, the planet Venus. If coreferential expressions have the same semantic value, they must be substitutable for each other in any context without affecting its semantic value. But how can (20.1) then be informative, while (20.2), in which a coreferential expression is substituted, is completely uninformative? If a semantic theory is to account for such facts, it must allow for coreferential expressions to differ in semantic value. For this purpose, Frege (1952) introduced the fundamental distinction between the *reference* (*Bedeutung*) of an expression and its *sense* (*Sinn*). Different proper names and other referential NPs may refer to the same object, but they could still differ in their sense, as sense determines reference and not vice versa. Identity statements are informative when they contain expressions with different senses, and they are true when their NPs are coreferential. Conditions of 'informativeness' hence cannot be identified with or reduced to truth-conditions. Perhaps there is more to the semantic value of an expression beyond its sense and reference, like its psychological associations, connotation or 'color,' but that part of its meaning is, according to Frege, considered subjective and should be disregarded in semantics, for it cannot be the source of public, communicable information.

The sense of an expression determines its reference in different situations, but even when the reference of an expression in every situation is determined, this does not fix its sense uniquely. If one assumes that the reference of a sentence is its truth value, two sentences that necessarily have the same truth value in all situations, e.g.

Robin won the race. (20.3)

Everyone who did not compete or lost in the race has done something Robin did not do. (20.4) still differ in their Fregean sense. Similarly two distinct logical tautologies which are both necessarily true may have different senses, and convey different information depending on the situation in which they are used. The way in which the sense is expressed also determines its meaning, which Frege called its *way of being given* (*Art des Gegebenseins*), or *mode of presentation*, a notion still requiring clarification. If the semantics of natural language is to account for coreference, inference, efficient information sharing and reasoning, it should give a satisfactory analysis of the Fregean notions of sense, mode of presentation, and reference in compositional semantics.

The second problem Frege presented as a central question to a theory of meaning is related to the first one about informative identity statements. If such statements or any other two statements with the same truth value are embedded as sentential complements of verbs, the resulting statements may differ in truth value. For instance,

Robin believes that Hesperus is Phosphorus. (20.5)

Robin believes that Hesperus is Hesperus. (20.6)

(20.5) may be false, whereas (20.6) must be true, even if Robin knows nothing of Babylonian astronomy, or if he is not even aware of what the name 'Hesperus' refers to. For Frege, this meant that sentences embedded in *that*-clauses do not refer, as they ordinarily do, to their truth value, but refer *indirectly*, i.e., they refer to their customary senses and constitute opaque contexts. Substitution of coreferential or extensionally equivalent expressions in such opaque clauses does not necessarily preserve the truth value of the entire sentence.

Ordinary predicate logic cannot account adequately for these puzzles, as two of its basic laws fail in such opaque contexts:

(i)   Substitution of logical equivalents may not preserve truth value
(ii) Existential generalization may not be valid

The first problem was explained above, and the second one means that one cannot infer from a referential expression used in an opaque context that it actually has a referent. If John believes that the spy is watching him, even if someone is indeed watching him, he need not be a spy. It may even be that no one is watching him, but John erroneously believes someone, whom he believes to be a spy, is watching him. If two sentences differ in their sense, they express different thoughts, as Frege would say. But to provide a full fledged compositional semantic analysis of these sense differences in terms of their information content still constitutes a major driving force of current research. It requires a satisfactory account of equivalence of 'information content,' sufficiently fine-grained to explain when a statement expresses new information to someone in a particular context, which depends in part on the information that is already available to him.

As a first attempt at formalization of Fregean senses, Carnap defined the *intension* of an expression as a function from a set of indices to the extension of the expression

(Carnap, 1947). The indices could be given various kinds of interpretations; while Carnap thought of them as indexing a set of states of affairs, more recent conceptions have been based on Kripke's semantics of modal logic, i.e., as possible worlds; see Kripke (1980 [1972]) or van Benthem (1988). [See also chapter 7.] As a solution to the Fregean informative identity puzzle, Carnap introduced the notion of an *individual concept* for the intension of proper names and referring expressions. Coreferring NPs would differ in their meaning, if they are interpreted as individual concepts by different functions from indices to individuals. Different occurrences of the same referring expression would, however, have to be interpreted as having the same, constant reference. The problem is now transferred to the problem of telling functions apart, but this has a clear set-theoretic criterion: functions are identical just in case they assign the same values to each argument. One consequence of this set-theoretic criterion of function identity, however, is that all mathematical and logical truths together with all analytical ones are interpreted on a par by the same constant function, and, as a result, they have the same intension and are still substitutable in all contexts, even opaque ones. This leads to the *problem of logical omniscience* for accounts of belief reports that rely on possible worlds: Assuming you are rational, if you believe any contingent truth, you must believe any of its logical consequences, including all tautologies or necessary truths [see chapter 9]; (Stalnaker, 1984).

20.1.2. *Montague grammar*

Montague grammar, developed in the late 1960s by the logician Richard Montague, extended Carnapian ideas dramatically, and provided a major step towards a compositional theory of interpretation of ordinary language, since it specified in all required detail how the semantic value of a sentence could be computed from its syntactic derivation (Dowty et al., 1981; Partee, 1997). In the approach described here – called PTQ after the title of Montague (1974c) – compositionality takes the form sometimes referred to as *rule-by-rule compositionality*: each syntactic rule is mirrored by a semantic one that specifies how the meaning of the input to the syntactic operation determines the meaning of its output. A central issue for the compositional theory of interpretation was to provide a uniform function/argument structure to both sentences with quantified NPs and sentences with simple referential ones. Montague's insight was to interpret every NP, regardless of syntactic form, as denoting a set of properties of individuals, doing justice to compositionality, and reducing them if possible to the familiar Fregean interpretation using standard first-order representations of existential and universal quantifiers. Predicates deriving from the interpretation of verb-phrases (VPs) are then simply interpreted as properties of individuals which either are or are not in the set of properties interpreting the NP in subject position. Forms of quantification in natural language which are known not to be expressible or definable in terms of the first-order logical quantifiers can similarly be interpreted by this higher-order notion of generalized quantifiers. For example, *most students* is not first-order definable, since its interpretation requires a one-to-one mapping between two sets dependent on a well-ordering by cardinality [see chapter 19] (Barwise and Cooper, 1981).

In PTQ, Montague defined the interpretation procedure for any expression of the natural language fragment in two steps: first, the translation of the syntactically disambiguated natural language expression to an expression of the formal language of the intensional logic, in particular a typed higher-order lambda calculus, and, second, the interpretation of that formal expression in the model-theoretic semantics. Hence, in this framework, the formal language intervenes between the natural language and the specification of meaning in terms of truth conditions in a possible worlds model. Montague himself, however, emphasized that there is no real need for such an intermediate level of 'logical form' representing the meaning of an expression of natural language, and in another article (Montague, 1974a), he defined the semantic interpretation directly as a mapping from the syntactic structure of the English expressions to appropriate model-theoretic objects and functions. The reason why the PTQ approach with indirect interpretation via a formal language has prevailed over this direct approach is largely practical. It is easier to see, for instance, the quantifier scope dependencies as differences in the linear order of quantifiers in a formula than to follow the notation of complex model-theoretic functions assigning values to variables and all of the alternatives of such assignments. It should, however, not be forgotten that formulas merely encode their semantic interpretation in model-theoretic terms. One can, in principle, characterize any number of languages which can be used to intervene between the natural language and the model-theory, as if there were really a daisy chain of such interlocking levels of representation.

It is well-known that the intensional logic originally used in PTQ as the language of 'logical form' could be replaced without loss of expressive power by a language in which quantifiers could range over reference-points (worlds at a certain time) (Gallin, 1975). This seems to have initiated a research trend of fleshing out the formal language with different parameters which initially belonged to the model-theoretic realm. In the newest dynamic theories of interpretation elements of the non-linguistic context, as well as variable-assignment functions themselves may be quantified over; see section 20.3.

A general theoretical question remains at this point whether a many-sorted first-order logic would ultimately suffice for the semantics of natural language or whether it still needs to be enriched with tools or techniques of a higher-order logic, as in PTQ. The desiderata of axiomatizability, decidability and completeness for the logic of natural language still play an important background role in such new developments.

20.1.3. The nature of meaning-postulates

In PTQ, meaning-postulates are formulas of the intensional logic which are true, not only in all possible worlds, but in all possible models. In other words, by defining a set of meaning-postulates one characterizes which among all logically possible models provide a plausible interpretation for the natural language interpreted. They were, for instance, required to capture the necessary truth of analytic statements, i.e., statements which are always true due to the meaning of their descriptive vocabulary, such as

Bachelors are unmarried.

But meaning-postulates were designed to do a quite diverse number of jobs, e.g., the reduction of intensional formulas to extensional ones in contexts where existential generalization and truth-preserving substitutivity of coreferential expressions held. They also guaranteed that proper names are Kripkean rigid designators, i.e., referred to the same individual even in opaque contexts. As meaning-postulates were only required to be well-formed formulas of the intensional logic, there was no constraint on the kinds of tasks they could be designed for. The Montegovian strategy was to hardwire all semantic structure one might ever wish to use into the model-theoretic rules and then weed it out by meaning-postulates whenever appropriate. For instance, even a simple extensional sentence like

Mary walks. (20.7)

required higher-order and intensional types of logical expressions, computing its truth value at each possible world by determining of all properties which ones applied to a function from all worlds to Mary at each world. By making all functions total (i.e., defined for every argument of the appropriate type), PTQ requires one to determine of anyone who could walk, whether he did walk at each possible world, before one could determine whether (20.7) was true. The inefficiency and computational intractability of admitting only total functions made this strategy rather unattractive for any computational implementation of the inferences that PTQ could otherwise account for so beautifully.

20.2. Towards a New Theory of Meaning and Interpretation

This section looks at some problems that arise in Montague grammar, most notably problems with anaphora, and some other questions that lead to different theories of meaning and interpretation.

20.2.1. Anaphora in Montague grammar

Anaphora is the common phenomenon in which the interpretation of an expression, such as a pronoun, is determined by its relation to another expression, its antecedent. It has commonly been thought that such pronouns function either like individual constants coreferring with their antecedents or else as variables bound by their antecedents. Neither approach, however, seems to apply to all cases, and anaphora has often proved a stumbling block to formal semantic theories. In PTQ, since all NPs are interpreted as generalized quantifiers, pronouns are bound by using rules which syntactically replace the first occurrence of an indexed pronoun in a sentence, whether in a common-noun phrase with a relative clause or in a VP, by the antecedent NP which then semantically binds any subsequent pronoun bearing the same index in that sentence. These 'quantifying in' rules apply to any kind of NP – proper name, existential or universal – and any complex sentence, nested relative clause or complex VP. If the NP introduced by such a rule is quantificational, its translation has scope over any scope-bearing expression already present in the sentence, common-noun phrase (CN) or VP quantified into. This technique provides a universal compositional method of accounting for scope-ambiguity in natural language by syntactic disambiguation. The traditional ambiguities of universal and existential NPs are thus treated on a par with the ambiguities in intensional contexts – the *de re* and *de dicto* readings of NPs [see chapter 7]. The example discussed in section 20.1.1

John believes that a spy is watching him.

would be generated by quantifying in both NPs 'John' and 'a spy' in order to say there actually was a spy watching John. But if the sentence allows that the spy was a mere figment of John's imagination, the interpretation would proceed directly, composing 'a spy' with 'watch him', and not allow for existential generalization, which would imply the existence of an actual spy.

From a linguistic point of view, these rules of quantifying in overgenerate spurious ambiguities and fail to account for some essential differences in anaphoric potential of the three different kinds of NPs. Since the rules apply to any NP, for each NP in a sentence there are always at least two syntactic derivations of that sentence, one direct and one indirect derivation using a quantifying in rule. Even for the extremely simple extensional (20.7), PTQ would generate at least two non-trivially different interpretations, one directly composing the subject with the VP and the other quantifying in the subject into a proposition with a free variable. Semantically these distinct derivations would be logically equivalent, so these syntactically driven differences have no semantic effect. If this is the price one has to pay for the compositionality of the semantic interpretation, it would be relatively harmless. But despite its universality, there are very natural interpretations of NPs in intensional contexts which cannot be accounted for by quantifying in rules. Examples of such sentences started emerging in the philosophy of language as early as 1962 (Geach, 1962) and are based on the fact that it is not possible to evaluate an NP at a possible, non-actual world, retain its value while accessing another world. For instance, in (20.8)

John tries to catch a fish and wants to eat it.   (20.8)

one would like to interpret 'a fish' *de dicto*, with the fish John is trying to catch and then use that fish as referent of the subsequent pronoun. For such a coreferential *de dicto* reading the quantifying in rule would have to be applied after the two intensional VPs are conjoined, which would produce only a *de re* reading, which is counterintuitive. Further examples which demonstrate essential limitations on the technique of quantifying in are called *e-type pronouns*.

If Mary dates a guy her parents disapprove of, they will make his visit miserable.
                                                                                    (20.9)

Every woman who loves a man kisses him.   (20.10)

In (20.9), the pronoun 'his' refers to any guy Mary dates and her parents disapprove of. In (20.10) 'him' refers to any man loved by a woman. The readings PTQ will generate with such bound pronouns necessarily give widest scope to the existential antecedent NPs, contrary to our intuitions which tell us that neither (20.9) nor (20.10) must be interpreted as being about a specific existing individual.

Another objection already mentioned to the uniform treatment of NPs by the quantifying in rules is based in the fact that universal NPs in relative clauses cannot bind pronouns in the VP, but existential ones and proper names do; see (20.11)–(20.14).

* A woman who kissed every man left him.	(20.11)
A woman who kissed a man left him.	(20.12)
A woman who kissed Jim, left him.	(20.13)
No woman who kissed a man left him.	(20.14)

Quantifying in universal NPs hence needs to be restricted in a principled way to prevent such bindings as in (20.11) to arise, but the PTQ rules are entirely unrestricted. In the generative linguistic literature a host of facts concerning the difference in anaphoric potential of the three kinds of NPs has been reported, which any proper semantic theory of anaphora should take into account. Just to mention a few of the most interesting facts, consider the anaphoric dependencies in (20.15)–(20.17).

His mother loves John.	(20.15)
His mother loves a/every man.	(20.16)
A woman loves her.	(20.17)

Proper names allow for backwards anaphora, whereas existential or universal NPs generally do not, as is seen in (20.15) and (20.16), although the pronoun can still be bound by another antecedent or be interpreted deictically. In (20.17), PTQ would allow for a coreferential interpretation of the subject and the pronoun, if the subject were quantified in, contrary to our intuitions. In (20.18), inverse scope

A flag was hanging from every window.	(20.18)

of the NPs shows that the syntactic linear order of the NPs may be inverse to their preferred semantic interpretation. Such clear linguistic facts concerning the different anaphoric potential between NPs should be explained in a satisfactory and universal account of anaphora, which departs more radically from some of the fundamental assumptions of variable binding in formal languages which PTQ inherited from its logical tradition. What must be revised is the intrinsic connection between scope and variable binding.

The problem of spurious ambiguities was tackled first by Cooper (1983) by weakening compositionality in a precise and constrained way. His grammar was allowed to generate ambiguous sentences, and it did not include any quantifying in rules. Hence meaning was not completely determined by syntactic form and the grammar did not embody the rule-by-rule compositionality of PTQ. Instead, the semantic interpretation must choose for any NP it evaluates whether to determine its semantic value immediately or to put it 'in storage,' placing it on hold in a stack of NPs whose interpretation is deferred to a later point. When a stored NP is retrieved for evaluation, it receives scope over everything that is already interpreted at that stage of the semantic interpretation. This NP-storage technique circumvented one linguistic objection to quantifying in rules, but it still required overgenerating in the syntax, where gaps or empty NPs are generated to be bound by *wh*-quantifiers (formed, e.g., by words like 'who' and 'which'), but may be filtered out in the semantics, if the quantificational structure is deviant. No appeal is made in Cooper's framework to any syntactic notion of ill-formedness in such semantically uninterpretable strings. The problems with cross-world quantification and the e-type pronouns remain, however, since this framework has no means to keep track of information already obtained about the referent of a pronoun, lacking any notion of context and dynamic binding.

The problem of logical omniscience mentioned in section 20.1.1 – which also applies to PTQ – demonstrated that the logical mechanics in predicate logic would require substantial revision if they were to simulate how context, prior information and external situation of use might be used to draw inferences from given information. The characteristic topic-neutrality of logic is seen as one of the sources of the problem of logical omniscience in possible worlds semantics. A beginner in logic often experiences how difficult it is to rid oneself of the natural topicality and context dependent aspects of reasoning. For instance, learning the disjunctive law, disjoining a proven formula with any arbitrary formula, one must learn to consider formulas that may be completely irrelevant to the first one. To make more precise what it means for two sentences to be about the same topic, or to be relevant to each other, a more sensitive notion of the informative content of a sentence in a context is required. Also the requirement of PTQ that all semantic functions be total should be relinquished, for definite referential NPs could fail to pick out a referent at some worlds or presuppositions of other expressions could fail, and sentences with uninterpreted constituents should be neither true nor false (*pace* Russell and *vivat* Strawson).

Yet another problem of a more metaphysical nature faced possible world semantics. What are possible worlds, if not mere formal entities that serve to distinguish contingent from necessary truths? If an individual at two different worlds may have no properties in common, in what sense is it still one and the same individual? Kripke (1980 [1972]), along with other possible world semanticists reviving an Aristotelian essentialism, argued that some properties were essential to an individual, most notably the properties concerning its origin. Personal identity would only break down when such essential properties would be lost. Other possible world semanticists, especially David Lewis (1983), took the extreme opposite view and argued that individuals can never be the same across possible worlds, but are rather related by a much weaker counterpart relation and need not have any common properties. The philosophical debate continues to be lively and provides a plethora of philosophical options on choices of primitives, views on identity of individuals, properties and propositions (Almog et al., 1989; Stalnaker, 1984). But the need for possible worlds in the semantics of natural language is now also disputed by the theories of dynamic interpretation. Although intensional contexts and opacity phenomena obviously require tools beyond mere extensional first-order logic, one might reinterpret possible worlds in terms of possible states of information an interpreter can be in. Modality should accordingly range over possible updates of the given information, not over metaphysically possible states of the world. This epistemic turn of natural language semantics opens the way for dynamic interpretation, where the core concept is updating a given information state, by using a sentence in discourse to be interpreted as an instruction to add new information or constrain the given information in a particular way. By shifting away from the Fregean focus on truth functional meaning to a theory of informative content of sentences in discourse, but still characterizing various inferences as truth preserving operations on given information, the semantics of natural language is now merging the traditional issues of truth functional meaning with pragmatic issues of context-dependent interpretation, interpretation as action between people and sharing of information.

20.2.2. Discourse

The PTQ technique of quantifying in to obtain wide scope readings with bound pronouns was shown above to have some inherent shortcomings from a natural language point of view. Considering anaphoric dependencies that arise between sentences, one sees that no simple generalization of the quantifying in rules can ever account for such forms of binding in discourse. Binding of pronouns is not postponed until one reaches the end of a sequence of sentences. It is rather a more dynamic process, where the interpretation of a sentence in a sequence is constrained by what information is gained from preceding sentences and whatever common background is supposed, and in turn constrains the ways in which the information exchange may be continued. In discourse, universal NPs are again more limited in their anaphoric potential than either existential ones or proper names, as in (20.19)–(20.21).

> *Every woman kissed a man. She left. (20.19)

In (20.19), the pronoun 'she' cannot be referentially dependent upon the universal NP 'every woman' in the preceding sentence. Existential NPs, definite descriptions or proper names may, however, corefer with pronouns across sentences, as in (20.20) and (20.21).

> A/The woman kissed a man. She left. (20.20)

> Jane kissed a man. She left. (20.21)

Since the PTQ quantifying in rules do not apply to sequences of sentences, this characteristic difference in anaphoric potential of universal versus referential NPs cannot really constitute a principled objection to quantifying in. But if these rules were generalized to apply to sequences of sentences, quantifying in would not always give the desired result. For instance, to generate a bound reading of

Only one student is reading. He is sitting at the table. (20.22)

the NP 'only one student' should be quantified into the sequence 'he$_1$ is reading. he$_1$ is sitting at the table'. But then the interpretation is weaker than intuitively needed, requiring only that there be precisely one student who has both properties of reading and sitting at the table. It does not rule out other reading students, as (20.22) seems to require. Hence a generalization of the quantifying in rules will not make the correct predictions for bound pronouns in discourse (Gamut, 1991, ch. 8). But the similarity between binding pronouns across sentences as in (20.19)–(20.22) and within sentences as in (20.11)–(20.14) is striking. Any semantic theory of binding should not only account for the difference in anaphoric potential of the three kinds of NPs, but also admit generalization to the interpretation of pronouns in discourse. This insight has been a driving force behind the development of the theories of dynamic interpretation discussed in section 20.3.

20.2.3. The fallacy of misplaced information

The information one may derive from interpreting an expression depends on a host of different parameters. Consider an utterance of a simple sentence in (20.23).

My husband and I invited her for dinner today. (20.23)

The direct situation of use determines for instance the reference of indexical expressions like 'I' and 'today', but common sense knowledge may be necessary to understand what a dinner invitation is, and linguistic knowledge will help determine who 'her' could refer to. Informative content arises as a relation between these parameters, the syntactic form of the expression used, its meaning, and the external world. Barwise and Perry (1983) consider meaning as such a dependency of many parameters. They stress that a sentence may be used in different situations to convey different information, which is why communication in natural language is so efficient. The sentence used in (20.23) could be used in a different situation to express completely different information. Sentences may be used to describe parts of the world, situations, and the reference of a sentence should be the set of such described situations, and not merely a truth value as Frege would have it. The meaning of the sentence partially determines which situations it can be used to describe. But other contextual parameters come into play when interpreting the use of the sentence in a particular situation as giving information about a particular topic. To assume that the entire informative content of the use of an expression is determined solely by its interpretation is what Barwise and Perry call *the fallacy of misplaced information*.

The performative hypothesis, popularized in pragmatic theories of meaning, such as Searle's (1970), proposed to analyze any sentence as subordinate to a performative first person verb, e.g.,

It is raining. (20.24)

I inform you that it is raining. (20.25)

This is a clear example of the fallacy of misplaced information, as it attempts to put information about the situation of use overtly into the described situation. Similarly, the Russellian analysis of definite descriptions, which analyzes any definite description as referring to any unique individual who satisfies the describing properties, is prone to the fallacy of misplaced information, since definite descriptions can be used to give information about the situation of use, which is distinct from the described situation. Denying that proper names can be used in a context to contribute to its interpretation, as many direct reference theorists like Kripke have claimed, is another instance of the fallacy. If I introduce myself, this is a meaningful communicative act, because the addressee receives the information how to call me, and knows henceforth how to refer to me. If names had no meaning beyond referring directly to their bearers, it would not be possible to explain how one does extract useful information from such an introduction. Informative identities are informative because the two coreferring expressions each contribute a different property of being so named. If I use (20.26) to report to you Jane's belief that her husband is happy

Jane believes Jim is happy. (20.26)

I invite you to infer, by an implicature, revocable upon further information, that Jane herself would report this belief using the proper name *Jim*. If I had used instead of (20.26),

Jane believes her husband is happy. (20.27)

a different implicature would be invited. But both (20.26) and (20.27) may be true even when Jane denies that Jim is her husband. A Fregean theory of reference could never account this, as it avoids context-dependent parameters of language use. In a dynamic theory of interpretation the shifting reference of indexicals and demonstratives should be accounted for in constructing a context from which conclusions may be drawn which could also contain indexical expressions. The central assumption of classical logic, that context dependence should be avoided or eliminated, is no longer viable, once reasoning of human interpreters in natural language has become the target of investigation.

20.3. Theories of Dynamic Interpretation

This section presents some alternatives to Montague grammar. These are theories of a more dynamic interpretation.

20.3.1. Discourse representation theory (DRT)

DRT was developed by Kamp (Kamp, 1984; Van Eijck and Kamp, 1997) partly in response to the anaphora problems Montague grammar was facing. But it was also motivated by a more philosophical concern with the nature of reference, meaning, inference and interpretation. Independently, Heim (1982, 1983) developed a closely related theory of dynamic interpretation, File Change Semantics. The main ideas and concepts of DRT are presented here in the context of the presentation of natural language semantics. (See the Suggested Readings for more comprehensive expositions of the theory.)

The core claim of DRT is that interpretation should be considered a dynamic process, in which discourse representation structures (DRSs) are constructed representing the information and the anaphoric dependencies expressed in a sequence of sentences. Such information is true in a model just in case there is a structure-preserving embedding of the reference markers verifying the descriptive conditions relating them, which constitute the representation, into that model. The conditions in the representation arise incrementally from the interpretation of the sequence of sentences by application of the construction rules for DRSs. A condition is a property or relation with an appropriate number of reference-markers as arguments; these function in certain respects like context dependent referring variables. DRSs consist of different levels of conditions, where a reference marker is accessible from a lower level only if it is declared at a higher level. Negation, modality, conditionals and quantifiers create deeper levels of embedded structure in the DRS.

The DRS-construction rules require that a proper name introduces a reference marker in the top level of the representation, which remains accessible to any lower level, thus capturing the semantic property of names that they always take widest scope or refer rigidly to one and the same referent no matter what context they occur in. An indefinite NP introduces a new reference marker into the given level, which may be a lower one, and the predicate in its CN is attached as a property of the reference-marker. Definite NPs are treated differently; they must be identified with an accessible reference-marker present in the given or any higher level of the representation. Since pronouns are definite NPs too, their reference-marker is unified with the accessible reference-marker of their antecedent NP. Clauses with universal NPs force a split of the DRS into two levels, where the information in the universal NP is represented as a property of a new reference-marker in the first deeper level, and the information expressed in the remainder of the sentence by conditions in a new, deeper, subordinate level. The embedding conditions of such a split of levels requires that every verifying embedding of the conditions in the first deeper level can be extended to a verifying embedding of the conditions in the next deeper level. Some illustrations of these DRS-construction rules are given below, along with an analysis of (20.10), which constituted a problem for PTQ's account of anaphora.

A man came in. He sat down.   (20.28)

An indefinite NP is represented by introducing a new reference marker x and attaching the CN as a property of x, and representing the remainder of the sentence as a property of x too. The pronoun which is anaphoric to the indefinite NP is represented by its own reference marker y and identified with x, the marker for its antecedent.

$$\begin{array}{|l|}\hline x \quad y \\\hline \text{man } (x) \\ \text{come in } (x) \\ \text{sit down } (y) \\ y = x \\\hline\end{array}$$

(20.29)

The DRS in (20.29) is true in a model $\mathbf{M} = \langle D, I \rangle$ (where D is a domain of individuals and I the usual set-theoretic interpretation-function assigning sets of n-tuples to n-place predicates) iff (if and only if) there is a verifying embedding f mapping x and y into the same individual in D, and $f(x) \in I(\text{man})$, $f(x) \in I(\text{come in})$, $f(y) \in I(\text{sit down})$.

If the antecedent in (20.28) were a singular definite determiner, as in (20.30),

The man came in. He sat down. (20.30)

the construction of the DRS would essentially be the same, with the sole difference that the reference marker for the definite description should already be available either in the DRS representing preceding sentences, or as part of the assumed common ground of the discourse.

A universal NP gives rise to a split of the DRS into a top level containing reference markers for proper names and all referential NPs, if any were so far represented, a first deeper level which represents the CN in the universal NP, and a second deeper level which represents the VP of the sentence. Sentences to be represented after the split are processed at the top level above the split structure.

Every man came in. * He sat down. (20.31)

The first sentence in (20.31) is represented as:

$$\begin{array}{|ll|}\hline \\\hline x \\\hline \text{man } (x) \mid \text{come in } (x) \\\hline\end{array}$$

The second sentence should be represented as a condition of x, but due to the structure of the levels x is inaccessible from the top level, where the second sentence is to be processed. So the bound variable reading of the pronoun in (20.31) is excluded, although a deictic reading is still available.

Indefinite NPs in the restrictor of universal NPs which bind pronouns in the VP formed a major problem for a PTQ style quantifying in account of binding. In DRT, such anaphora are accounted for by the accessibility conditions between levels of the DRS. Sentence (20.10) is represented according to the construction rules for the DRS as in (20.10a).

Every woman who loves a man kisses him. (20.10)

$x\ y$	
woman (x)	kiss (x, y)
love (x, y)	
man (y)	

(20.10a)

With the embedding conditions for a subordinating construction (20.10a) is interpreted as true in any model where any man loved by any woman is kissed by her, no matter how many men each woman loves.

Deictically used referential NPs are directly referential to an individual in the immediate situation of use. In DRT, such a directly referential link is represented by an external anchor, which is an ordered pair consisting of the reference marker for that NP and some object in the immediate situation of use. Such external anchors are themselves not parts of the DRS but rather constrain the set of verifying embeddings of the DRS into the model. The semantic content of a deictically used referential NP is completely determined by the associated external anchor, but the information someone may obtain from the use of such an expression is partly dependent on the form of the NP itself.

20.3.2. Situation semantics (SS)

SS (Barwise, 1988; Barwise and Perry, 1983; Seligman and Moss, 1997) is a theory of dynamic interpretation which does not rely on a syntactic level of representation for anaphoric dependencies. Instead, information structure is constructed from semantic objects, which may or may not be parts of the actual world. Meaning arises as a relation between linguistic expressions, the context of use (including time of utterance, speaker, audience, location), linguistic and logical constraints, and the external world. Despite this important difference with DRT, the two theories are significantly similar in the insights and logical tools they offer to linguistic analyses. The primitive objects in SS are n-place relations, individuals, locations and polarities. They constitute events or situations, e.g. $\langle l, \langle\langle walk, Mary\rangle, 1\rangle\rangle$ represents a situation of Mary walking at l and, $\langle l, \langle\langle kiss, Mary, John\rangle, 0\rangle\rangle$ a situation at l in which Mary does not kiss John. Indeterminates or parameters act like reference-markers for locations, relations, individuals and polarities, and are equally constituents of situations. They are assigned appropriate values by partial assignment functions, or by context-dependent speaker connections to parts of the external world.

For example, a definite description can be interpreted as referring to an individual, determined by the speaker-connection, which is customarily called a *referentially* used definite description. A definite description which is so used to refer to an individual does not require its descriptive properties to be true of the referent. This is commonly recognized to be possible, when speaker reference is at stake. In SS, this usage is called the *value-laden* use of definite descriptions. But a definite description can also constrain a situation, picking up an individual to contribute to another situation. This is called the *value-free*, or *attributive* use of a definite description.

Thus, one can use the NP in (20.32)

The woman in the red skirt is tall. (20.32)

to refer to Mary wearing a red skirt in situation s. For such a value-laden interpretation one fixes the resource situation s, the speaker connections c and represent it as

$$_{d,\,c}|[\text{the woman in the red skirt}]\,|(s) = \text{Mary}$$

Third party reports of what was said may, of course, use other NPs to continue the reference to Mary, e.g. if Mary is also reading in s coreference is established with (20.33).

She said that this reader is tall. (20.33)

In the attributive use of this definite description, the interpretation is a relation between situations and individuals, whoever fits the descriptive properties. The condition of being tall is still a constituent of the interpretation of (20.33), but none of the individuals is. To achieve the attributive use, the describing properties are not constituents of the interpretation, and it picks out an individual, if the resource situation contains an individual who satisfies the properties.

Other uses of definite descriptions are still possible, like in appositive clauses, where their reference is already determined by the context, as in

John, the neighbor I play tennis with, is a nice guy.

and the description contributes new properties to it, or functional uses, where reference is made to the role itself, not to whoever plays the role in any given situation, as in

The next president must be elected.

In evaluating any sentence containing a descriptive referential NP, one has to be particularly careful in determining which situation is described, and cannot, in general, conclude that its truth value remains the same, if considering a larger situation of which the situation described is part or another situation which does not contain the individual referred to as constituent.

In SS, anaphora and other dependent NPs are interpreted dynamically by incrementally extending partial assignment functions. The core idea here is that the interpretation of an NP in a given context is an action which may affect the context in a systematic way. Current research is focusing on the details of an inductive definition of such dynamic interpretations of expressions of all categories as context-changing actions and its relation to the standard static satisfaction conditions of ordinary predicate logic. SS relies on indexing rules which operate on parsed sentences before their interpretation, such that every NP bears a unique referential index and every dependent NP is coindexed in subscript with its antecedent superscript. The interpretation of these indices form a crucial part in the dynamics of the procedural interpretations.

An important SS construction of semantic objects needed to interpret universal NPs are parameterized sets. They are semantic objects in which certain constituents are still undetermined, i.e., the parameters which need to be determined by extensions of a given assignment function. Thus, to interpret our old example of e-type anaphora

$$[\text{Every woman who loves [a man}]^j]^i \text{ kisses [him}]^k_j \qquad (20.10)$$

a parameterized set X needs to be formed which contains all pairs consisting of an individual a and an assignment function g such that kissing holds between a and the object $g(j)$. All such g are supposed to be defined on the same indices. Then, (20.10) is verified on this parameterized set, given an initial assignment function f, if for each g every a in its set X_g is a woman who, loving the man $g(j)$, kisses him; see Barwise (1987) for more discussion and details.

20.3.3. Quantification and anaphora

Further discussion of anaphoric binding for theories of dynamic interpretation leads to the most recent developments and open research problems.

One central issue is the interpretation of plural anaphora. They can be bound by singular universal antecedents, as in (20.34).

Every woman kissed John. They left him. (20.34)

The semantic operations with which the group consisting of all the women who kissed John is constructed as an appropriate referent for the plural pronoun in (20.34) is a central question of research. The converse of this issue is illustrated in (20.35), where the plural pronoun has a numerically appropriate plural antecedent.

All women gathered in the room. They were wearing a badge. (20.35)

The antecedent is an argument of a collective verbal predicate, denoting a property which can only be attributed to groups, not to the individuals constituting the group. The pronoun is, however, an argument of a distributive predicate denoting a property true of each member in the group of women. Some semantic operation is required to divide the group of all women as a single unit into the set of individual women (Lønning, 1997).

Binding of plural anaphora by an antecedent in the scope of a universal NP cannot cross sentential boundaries, as (20.36) shows.

Every father of two children sends them to Montessori school. * They love it. (20.36)

Furthermore, two occurrences of plural anaphora bound by the same antecedent can be interpreted as referring collectively and distributively within one sentence as

Mary and John invited their parents to their place. (20.37)

illustrates. The interpretation of (20.37) which is intended here makes the first anaphoric reference to the parents of each of Mary and John, but the second anaphoric reference to the place where they live together. Such issues of collective and distributive reference and predication provide a wealth of new puzzles for natural language semantics, which seem to lend themselves very well for analysis in these dynamic theories of interpretation that allow for a specific part-whole structure on their domains of reference-markers; see especially Kadmon (1987), Landman (1996), and Roberts (1987, 1989).

A third important problem for theories of anaphoric reference is called the 'proportion problem,' illustrated by (20.38).

Most women who love a man kiss him. (20.38)

The DRT analysis seems to predict (20.38) is true in a situation in which Jane, who loves Jim, does not kiss him, Paula, who loves Peter, does not kiss him, but Edith, who loves Eric, Eduard and Evert, kisses the three of them. The quantification merely counts the cases of a woman and a man loved by her, and counts Edith three times in verifying instances, whereas Jane and Paula are counted each only once in two falsifying instances. Solutions to this proportion problem have been proposed using the SS notion of parameterized sets, which suggest clearly that the dynamic interpretation should be constructed from the interpretation of expressions and constituents in all syntactic categories.

20.3.4. Dynamic Montague grammar (DMG)

The question remains whether the determinism of the syntax-semantics interface, as was required by the Fregean Principle of Compositionality, should be adhered to. It is clear that Montague's rule-by-rule compositionality is not adhered to in DRT, for there is only one syntactic rule putting determiners and common nouns together into noun phrases, but there are at least four different rules of DRS construction for NPs, depending on whether it is a proper name, a pronoun, an indefinite, existential or a universal NP.

Critical of DRT for abandoning the Compositionality Principle, but overall motivated by much the same evidence, Groenendijk and Stokhof (1991) developed DMG as a compositional theory of interpretation of discourse. An update of a given information state relates partial assignments to variables, constituting the current information state, to their continuations, preserving the prior assignments and adding values to new variables. Besides the customary context-independent variables, the formal language is enriched with discourse variables, comparable to the reference markers of DRT, functioning like context dependent names that create dynamic bindings across sentential boundaries. Logical constants may be interpreted either dynamically or statically, depending on their desired degree of stability across updates of the information states. Dynamic conjunction, for instance, is sensitive to the order of presentation, and hence not commutative, as the ordinary static conjunction is in first-order predicate logic.

A major bone of contention is the need for a pre-semantic representational level at which anaphoric dependencies are captured. DRT claims that such a syntactic representational level is essential, whereas SS and DMG claim they do better without. Compositional reformalizations of DRT have been presented, and alternative dynamic systems are being explored (Muskens, 1995; Muskens et al., 1997). The arguments are far from conclusive and an ultimate assessment of these issues must depend on the development of much more substantive and detailed semantic analyses of various linguistic phenomena.

20.4.   The State of the Art

This concluding section looks at some of the areas of research in logic and natural language today. First, some of the open problems that command attention are discussed, and then there is a brief glance at how developments in natural language semantics apply to cognitive science.

20.4.1.   Open problems

The great deal of attention devoted to anaphora in natural language semantics has spurred generalizations of such informational dependencies in other categories than NPs. Partee (1973) pointed out that tenses function very much like pronouns, in that their temporal reference can be determined deictically by the non-linguistic context, or depend on a referential, existential or universal antecedent. Sometimes these antecedents are adverbial, but they can also be verbs themselves.

A second analogy between NPs and VPs is commonly recognized. Mass NPs as 'some gold,' 'more peace,' 'all furniture' are seen to be analogous to certain kinds of descriptions of events, since both may contain parts of the same kind, e.g. part of some gold is gold and part of an event of John walking is also an event of his walking. Count NPs are on par then with event descriptions which include some inherent endpoint, like the NP, whose denotation does not contain the same man as part, and

John walking a mile.

whose denoted event does not contain another walking of a mile by John. These two analogies play a very important role in developing a compositional semantic theory of tense and aspect, of temporal reference and quantification. Such a theory has obvious consequences for philosophical views on the nature of events and their identity- and individuation-conditions. Hinrichs (1986) and Partee (1984) provide accounts of nominal and temporal anaphora using tools of DRT theory, but the topic has grown into a fruitful field for interdisciplinary research in logic and linguistics.

Another important area of current research is the semantics of generic expressions. There is an important distinction between generic statements which refer to a kind as an abstract object and statements which are essentially of quantificational form binding cases by a default operator. The two kinds of generic statements are illustrated in (20.39) and (20.40).

Elephants are rare. (20.39)

Elephants have valuable teeth. (20.40)

The main semantic difference between reference to kinds and default quantification is that only the default quantification allows for exceptions, e.g., for (20.40) an elephant whose teeth have been cut off. Much linguistic evidence supports the distinction, and it is especially interesting to study the interaction with anaphora. Generic statements with universal NPs seem to allow binding of pronouns across sentential boundaries more easily, as in

Every player chooses a pawn. He puts it on square one. (20.41)

Further observations that form explananda for natural language semantics are bindings which change the referential type as in (20.42).

There is a beaver in the creek. They build dams. (20.42)

In (20.42) there is first reference to an individual beaver, but this serves as antecedent of a pronoun which refers to the entire species. The converse dependency is possible too, although it appears to be more restricted as in (20.43).

Beavers build dams. I saw one/*him in the creek. (20.43)

A systematic account of such type-changing bindings is a topic of much current research (Carlson and Pelletier, 1994).

20.4.2. Cognitive science

To conclude this assessment of developments in natural language semantics, some questions about the entire research program should be addressed from a more general perspective. The renewed contact between logical theory and linguistic analysis prompts the question what kind of theory of inference semantics is after. Should it be a theory about the inferential abilities of idealized, competent users of a natural language, or should it be a theory of actual inferences exhibited in human linguistic behavior? Frege's abhorrence of psychological interpretations of logical laws had promoted a stark separation of logical and psychological research on inferential processes. Most psychologists nowadays are still apt to point out that abstract mathematical laws do not explain their actual data, because 'people are not rational,' 'human beings are no machines' or 'error is only human.' Yet the program of modeling inferential processes in natural language understanding by abstract logical representations has certain explanatory claims in cognitive science as a substantial contribution to a general theory of human cognitive capacities.

Here the classical Chomskyan distinction between a theory of competence and a theory of performance can clarify this apparent conflict. As a theory of inference, natural language semantics disregards the parameters of individual variation, cases of inferential failure, and normalizes its concepts by abstracting from actual practice and performance. Its empirical base is essentially the intuitive judgments of its users, not measured in a quantitative manner. Psychological theories of cognitive capacities, however, are rooted in experimentally gained evidence from actual, quantitatively measurable inferential behavior. As in any science, they too make fundamental assumptions about their subject matter, excluding certain parameters in the experimentation as irrelevant to their explanatory goals, and stabilizing the context of their experimentation by a host of *ceteris paribus* clauses, which rarely receive any independent justification. Both forms of theorizing are empirical in nature, essentially falsifiable, and have genuine predictive power. But they contribute to our understanding of human cognition at quite distinct levels. A theory of error in linguistic processing is immediately relevant and perhaps even part of a psychological theory of inferential processes, but it would not be of immediate interest to natural language semantics. But just as aphasia studies can provide us with arguments concerning the modularity of the brain and its cognitive functions, so too a theory of inferential failure may be able to provide evidence concerning the modularity of the brain for inferential processing and the interference with other cognitive functions.

If the two kinds of cognitive theory are seen contributing explanatory insights at different levels, they can be considered respectively as characterizing the algorithms of inferential processes and characterizing the actual implementations of such algorithms in the human wetware. Nevertheless, it is important to emphasize again that both areas of research regard inferential processes as a central theme in a theory of human cognitive capacities.

Suggested further reading

The Handbook of Logic and Language, edited by J. van Benthem and the author (1997), is an excellent resource for research in the interface of logic and linguistics; this hefty volume offers a comprehensive review of the state of the art as of 1996 in the logical aspects of syntax and semantics of natural language. *The Handbook of Contemporary Semantic Theory*, edited by S. Lappin (1996), is also an authoritative survey of selected topics in natural language semantics. *Language: An Invitation to Cognitive Science, Volume I*, edited by L. Gleitman and M. Liberman (1995), is the first volume of a set that offers a comprehensive and well-balanced introduction to the emergent interdisciplinary field of cognitive science. *Meaning and Grammar: An Introduction to Semantics*, by G. Chierchia and S. McConnell-Ginet (1990), is an elementary textbook of linguistics, teaching basic concepts, tools and results of semantic theory in the tradition of model theoretic semantics derived from Monatague grammar; it provides plenty of good exercises for hands-on practice in semantic analysis. L. F. T. Gamut's (1991) *Logic, Language and Meaning* (two volumes) is a basic textbook of first-order logic written for an audience of philosophy students; it also includes modal logic and higher-order intensional logics with application to natural language in Montague semantics. *English Grammar: A Generative Perspective* by L. Haegeman and J. Gueron (1999), is a comprehensive textbook of English syntax, with some relations to semantics and phonology; from the point of view of generative theory.

References

Almog, J. Perry, J. and Wettstein, H. (eds.) 1989: *Themes from Kaplan*, (Oxford University Press, Oxford and NY).

Barwise, J. 1987: "Noun Phrases, Generalized Quantifiers and Anaphora," in *Generalized Quantifiers, Linguistic and Logical Approaches*, P. Gärdenfors, ed., (D. Reidel, Dordrecht), 1–29.

Barwise, J. 1988: "The Situation in Logic," *CSLI Lecture Notes*, (University of Chicago Press, Stanford/Chicago).

Barwise, J. and Cooper, R. 1981: "Generalized Quantifiers and Natural Language," *Linguistics and Philosophy*, 4, 159–219.

Barwise, J. and Perry, J. 1983: *Situations and Attitudes*, (MIT Press, Cambridge, MA).

van Benthem, J. 1988: "A Manual of Intensional Logic," 2nd edn, *CSLI Lecture Notes*, (University of Chicago Press, Stanford/Chicago).

van Benthem, J. and ter Meulen, A. (eds.) 1997: *Handbook of Logic and Language*, (Elsevier Science Publishers, Amsterdam, and MIT Press, Cambridge, MA).

Carlson, J. and Pelletier, F. (eds.) 1994: *The Generic Book*, (University of Chicago Press, Chicago).

Carnap, R. 1947: *Meaning and Necessity*, (University of Chicago Press, Chicago).

Chierchia, G. and McConnell-Ginet, S. 1990: *Meaning and Grammar: An Introduction to Semantics*, (MIT Press, Cambridge, MA).

Cooper, R. 1983: *Quantification and Syntactic Theory*, (D. Reidel, Dordrecht).

Dowty, D., Wall, R. and Peters, S. 1981: *Introduction to Montague Semantics*, 2nd edn, (D. Reidel, Dordrecht).

van Eijck, J. and Kamp, H. 1997: "Representing Discourse in Context," in van Benthem and ter Meulen (1997, pp. 179–237).

Frege, G. 1952: "On Sense and Reference," in *Translations from the Philosophical Writings of Gottlob Frege*, P. T. Geach and M. Black, eds., (Basil Blackwell, Oxford), 56–78.

Gallin, D. 1975: *Intensional and Higher-Order Modal Logic, With Applications to Montague Semantics*, (North-Holland/American Elsevier, Amsterdam/New York).

Gamut, L. F. T. 1991: *Logic, Language and Meaning*. Vol. I and II, (University of Chicago Press, Chicago), translated from Dutch edition.

Geach, P. 1962: *Reference and Generality*, (Cornell University Press, Ithaca, NY).

Gleitman, L. and Liberman, M. 1995: *Language: An Invitation to Cognitive Science, Volume I*, (The MIT Press, Cambridge, MA).

Groenendijk, J. and Stokhof, M. 1991: "Dynamic Predicate Logic," *Linguistics and Philosophy*, 14, 39–100.

Haegeman, L. and Gueron, J. 1999: *English Grammar: A Generative Perspective*, Blackwell Textbooks in Linguistics, (Blackwell, Oxford).

Heim, I. 1982: "The Semantics of Definite and Indefinite Noun-Phrases," PhD dissertation, Linguistics, University of Massachusetts, Amherst.

Heim, I. 1983: "File Change Semantics and the Familiarity Theory of Definiteness," in *Meaning, Use and Interpretation of Language*, R. Bauerle, Ch. Schwarze and A. von Stechow, eds., (De Gruyter, Berlin), 164–89.

Hinrichs, E. 1986: "Temporal Anaphora in Discourses of English," *Linguistics and Philosophy*, 9, 63–82.

Kadmon, N. 1987: "On Unique and Non-unique Reference and Asymmetric Quantification," dissertation, University of Massachusetts, Amherst.

Kamp, H. 1984: "A Theory of Truth and Semantic Representation," in *Truth, Interpretation and Information*, GRASS 2, J. Groenendijk, T. Janssen and M. Stokhof, eds., (Foris Publications, Dordrecht), 1–41 [orig. 1981].

Kripke, S. 1980: *Naming and Necessity*, (Harvard University Press, Cambridge, MA), 1972; reprinted in 1980.

Landman, F. 1996: "Plurality," in Lappin (1996, pp. 425–57).

Lappin, S. 1996: *The Handbook of Contemporary Semantic Theory*, (Blackwell Publishers, Oxford).

Lewis, D. K. 1983: *Philosophical Papers, Vol 1*, (Oxford University Press, Oxford and New York).

Lønning, J.-T. 1997: "Plurals and Collectivity," in van Benthem and ter Meulen (1997, pp. 1009–53).

Montague, R. 1974a: "English as a Formal Language," in Montague (1974b, pp. 188–221).

Montague, R. 1974b: *Formal Philosophy*, R. Thomason, ed., (Yale University Press, New Haven).

Montague, R. 1974c: "The Proper Treatment of Quantification in Ordinary English," in Montague (1974b, pp. 247–70).

Muskens, R. 1995: "Combining Montague Semantics and Discourse Representation," *Linguistics and Philosophy*, 19, 143–86.

Muskens, R., van Benthem, J. and Visser, A. 1997: "Dynamics," in van Benthem and ter Meulen (1997, pp. 587–648).

Partee, B. 1973: "Some Structural Analogies between Tenses and Pronouns in English," *Journal of Philosophy*, 70, 601–9.

Partee, B. 1984: "Nominal and Temporal Anaphora," *Linguistics and Philosophy*, 7, 243–86.

Partee, B. 1997: "Montague Grammar," in van Benthem and ter Meulen (1997, pp. 5–92).

Roberts, C. 1987: "Modal Subordination, Anaphora, and Distributivity," PhD dissertation, University of Massachusetts, Amherst.

Roberts, C. 1989: "Modal Subordination and Pronominal Anaphora in Discourse," *Linguistics and Philosophy*, 12, 683–721.

Searle, J. 1970: *Speech Acts. An Essay in the Philosophy of Language*, (Oxford University Press, Oxford).

Seligman, J. and Moss, L. 1997: "Situation Theory," in van Benthem and ter Meulen (1997, pp. 239–309).

Stalnaker, R. 1984: *Inquiry*, (MIT Press, Cambridge, MA).

Index

Lightning Source UK Ltd.
Milton Keynes UK
UKHW05f0649060218
317403UK00005BA/575/P

9 780631 206934